Writing and Reading Arguments

Writing and Reading Arguments

A RHETORIC AND READER

RICHARD P. BATTEIGER

Oklahoma State University

ALLYN AND BACON

Boston London Toronto Sydney Tokyo Singapore

Editor in Chief, Humanities: Joseph Opiela
Editorial Assistant: Brenda Conaway
Production Administrator: Marjorie Payne
Editorial-Production Service: Chestnut Hill Enterprises, Inc.
Cover Administrator: Linda Dickinson
Composition Buyer: Linda Cox
Manufacturing Buyer: Louise Richardson

Copyright © 1994 by Allyn & Bacon
A Division of Simon & Schuster, Inc.
160 Gould Street
Needham Heights, MA 02194

Library of Congress Cataloging-in-Publication Data

Batteiger, Richard P.
   Writing and reading arguments :   a rhetoric and reader
Richard P. Batteiger.
    p.   cm.
   Includes bibliographical references.
   ISBN 0-205-14025-4
   1. English language—Rhetoric. 2. Persuasion (Rhetoric)
3. Critical thinking.   I. Title.
PE1431.B38 1994
808'.042—dc20   93-1714
                                         CIP

Credits

Chapter 1
Page 13. From *USA TODAY,* December 4, 1991. Copyright 1991, USA TODAY.
   Reprinted with permission.

*The credits continue on the pages following the index. They should be considered an
extension of the copyright page.*

Printed in the United States of America

10 9 8 7 6 5 4 3 2 1   99 98 97 96 95 94

for
Claudia

CONTENTS

CHAPTER THREE: **Writing an Argument 31**

CHAPTER FOUR: **Pro and Con:
Understanding Differences 47**

CHAPTER FIVE: **Beyond Pro and Con: Multisided Arguments 63**

CHAPTER SIX: **Supporting an Argument 81**

CHAPTER SEVEN: **Doing Research 103**

CHAPTER EIGHT: **Using and Citing Information from Sources 127**

PRO/CON ARGUMENTS 151

MULTISIDED ARGUMENTS 217

CLASSIC ARGUMENTS 359

STUDENT ARGUMENTS 595

PREFACE

A great many things pass for argument in American culture. If the media were our only example, argument would be a mixture of the quick-hit salesmanship of the television commercial, the shouting of political pundits on television, the elevated but often empty speechmaking of political conventions, and interscholastic debate. In contrast, *Writing and Reading Arguments* presents argument as a way of writing about, discussing, and debating questions and issues that have no single correct answer. Seen in this way, argument becomes a way of making difficult choices when faced with alternatives that seem equally plausible or compelling. Given this purpose, argument requires not power or a loud voice, but information and an open mind. Argument addresses questions that can be resolved, if at all, only through careful and thorough inquiry, discussion, and debate.

The single most important feature that distinguishes *Writing and Reading Arguments* from other argument texts currently available is that it connects the teaching of argument with the practices that have recently become known as critical thinking. These include

- defining issues and questions carefully and completely
- listening to and investigating all sides of an issue
- seeking alternate solutions and divergent views in an attempt to choose the best solution
- remaining open to others' views and being willing to change one's position when reason and evidence indicate that another position is more convincing or plausible
- realizing that the best solution is not the same for everyone
- questioning and comparing conflicting interpretations of data
- assessing the strength of reasoning and support
- evaluating conclusions
- applying values when having to choose among competing positions

The most common approaches to teaching argument are for-malist. That is, they concentrate on the components of an argu-ment, and they often focus almost exclusively on finished products rather than on the processes by which arguments are developed and composed. One of the most well-known, formal approaches to ar-gument and a popular pedagogical model is Stephen Toulmin's *The Uses of Argument* (Cambridge, 1958). Formalist analyses are valu-able for understanding how arguments work, but they can be less valuable as pedagogical tools. When formalist approaches to argu-ment are turned into formulaic prescriptions, inexperienced stu-dent writers can be forgiven for assuming that writing an argument consists of little more than filling in a pre-established pattern. In contrast to this approach, *Writing and Reading Arguments* focuses on the processes of critical thinking and analysis that bring an argument into existence by encouraging students to engage in effec-tive critical thinking practices.

The text presents argument and critical thinking in the follow-ing sequence:

1. It begins by asking students to state their own opinions about subjects that interest and concern them.

2. The text explains the concept of *arguability* and shows stu-dents how to transform their opinions into positions that can be argued. Beliefs and opinions are statements about oneself; they make no demands on other people or on what other people should believe or on how they should act. Arguments, in contrast (arguable statements/positions), are statements about what others should believe or do, or what the world is or should be like. *Writing and Reading Arguments* illustrates the differences between opinions and arguable statements; then it asks students to demonstrate their ability to change their opinions into positions and to provide sup-port.

3. *Writing and Reading Arguments* next introduces the two-sided or pro/con argument. Initially, pro/con arguments allow stu-dents to continue in their assumption that one side must be right and the other wrong. But this does not last long, as students are asked to consider that different or opposing positions need not be wrong or false but can be equally plausible. Students soon learn that choosing one position over the other is seldom a matter of deciding which one is right or wrong, but of choosing the one that presents the most complete or reasonable solution to the issue or question at hand.

4. *Writing and Reading Arguments* next introduces multisided arguments, in which participants have taken a variety of different positions and which are rarely divided neatly into sides. Individual arguments may not answer or respond to each other directly, and some may appear tangential to each other and to the central issue. In these cases, the central issue—what the argument is about—can often be defined only by carefully considering the various positions and attempting to determine where they focus.

The multisided arguments in *Writing and Reading Arguments* reflect the complex nature of arguments as they exist in the so-called *real world.* Thus, the reading selections that make up the multi-sided arguments in *Writing and Reading Arguments* do not present issues that have been tied neatly into packages. They do not necessarily all address the issue in the same way, they may not agree about what constitutes the central issue, and they will probably not reach a consensus or resolution. This situation leaves much for students to do: identify and define focal issues, understand what others have said, summarize the extended argument, find their own position and support, and find a way to join the argument.

5. The text also includes numerous classic arguments from a variety of sources. Some were originally speeches; others were written. While most are historical arguments, almost all of them address what students will regard as contemporary issues such as womens' rights, animal rights, freedom of speech, and the shape of society. Students will sometimes think that these authors wrote with uncanny foresight into the twentieth century, because many of the issues addressed in the classic arguments remain the subjects of active debate today. Reading these classic arguments should help students achieve some perspective not only on the complex, difficult issues that they address, but also on argument itself as a rhetorical form.

How the Text Is Organized

Writing and Reading Arguments is divided into two main sections. The first consists of eight chapters that provide instruction in the rhetorical principles and skills of argument. Following these eight chapters, there are four sections of readings: Pro/Con Arguments, Multisided Arguments, Classic Arguments, and Student Arguments.

Chapter One shows students how to identify and express their own beliefs and opinions.

Chapter Two illustrates how to make personal opinions into arguable statements that make some assertion about what others should believe or how they should act.

Chapter Three shows how to write the beginning, middle, and end of an argument.

Chapter Four uses pro/con arguments to introduce ways of understanding and responding to opposing positions.

Chapter Five presents complex arguments that involve a number of positions and perspectives.

Chapter Six presents an extended discussion and illustration of how to use information, reasons, and reasoning to support a position in an argument.

Chapter Seven illustrates and explains a variety of ways to do research.

Chapter Eight shows how to incorporate the results of research into an argument and how to document information taken from sources.

Each of the first eight chapters contains applications of the procedures it discusses, as well as questions, activities, and suggested writing assignments that will help students learn to write effective arguments.

Writing and Reading Arguments also includes more than 90 contemporary, classic, and student arguments. These are not intended as models for students to imitate, nor are they all meant as examples of excellent arguments. Their purpose here is to provide real arguments for students to read, analyze, and respond to. Each section of readings is accompanied by an apparatus consisting of questions and exercises, suggestions for research, and suggested writing assignments. Of course, these questions and activities are intended as guides and suggestions, not as the last word about argument.

Acknowledgments

A number of people helped me with this book. Guy Bailey, former Head of the English department at Oklahoma State University, provided important assistance and resources. Joye Alberts of the OSU Writing Project and Patricia Cheves, now of Appalachian State University, have read and used parts of the manuscript and offered important comments. Jeff Kersh, Betty Ann Sisson, Donna Choate, Michael Pratt, Gerald Cumbus, and Brooke Patrick have listened patiently while I clarified many of my ideas about argument. I appreciate their patience. Elizabeth Beal prepared the permissions file. Duncan Carter of Portland State University was an early reviewer who stayed with the project to the end. His comments have been invaluable. Joe Opiela has been a more patient and helpful editor than any author could want. His assistant, Brenda Conaway, has always been ready with assistance and information. Cynthia Newby at Chestnut Hill Enterprises has made production a model of cordiality and competence. I also want to thank the reviewers, who took time from their busy professional lives to read and write thoughtfully in response to my drafts and revisions. These reviewers included Sally Barr Reagan, University of Missouri; Robert Dees, Orange Coast College; Stephen Hahn, William Paterson College; David A. Jolliffe, University of Illinois—Chicago; Nevin Laib, Franklin and Marshall College; Barry Maid, University of Arkansas; Walter S. Minot, Gannon University; Richard Ramsey, Indiana University-Purdue University at Fort Wayne; Irwin Weiser, Purdue University; Richard Zbaracki, Iowa State University.

CHAPTER ONE

Taking Positions and Making Choices— An Overview of Argument

This chapter is about the various ways people resolve their differences and disagreements and make decisions about what they will think or do. Before you read the chapter, take a few minutes to think about how you resolve the differences and disagreements that arise in your life. Write a brief response to the following:

1. You have found a briefcase on a bus. When you open it to find out who owns it, you discover that, along with other personal papers, it contains $5000 in cash. What formal and informal rules guide your decision about what to do with the briefcase? (Note that the question does not ask you what you would do; it asks what rules would guide your decision.)
2. Describe an important decision you have made and how you made it. Focus on the formal and informal rules and the authorities you considered or consulted. List those rules and authorities and explain how two or three of them guided your decision.

The Contexts of Argument

Making decisions about what to believe and how to act may be the most important work that people do. It is certainly the most challenging, and possibly the most difficult and interesting. People must constantly make decisions about their actions and beliefs. As they make these decisions they must answer questions, solve problems, resolve disagreements with other people, and frequently choose among competing points of view that may seem equally reasonable and valid. The questions and issues may be large or small, but reaching a decision about them involves the same process of inquiry, argument, and choice. Sometimes it is possible to rely on established rules and authorities in making these decisions, but frequently the help they provide is partial or inconclusive.

Much of what people do and believe is prescribed for them. Authorities and rules prescribe how people should act or what they should believe in a wide variety of situations. When people have questions about what they should think or do, they consult the authorities and rules that guide their lives. Authorities can include religious and political rulers, parents, teachers, peers, the Bible, the Supreme Court, and hosts of other people, documents, or institutions that occupy positions of authority. Rules can be formal and written, like the Ten Commandments and the Constitution, or informal and unwritten, like the unspoken rules that guide how people are polite to each other. Though some people regard it as too restrictive to have authorities and rules control their lives, the advantages may outweigh the disadvantages. Rules and authorities actually save people the trouble of making separate decisions about many of the situations that they encounter. Without them, nearly every decision or choice, from the most trivial to the most important, would be possible only after extensive investigation, problem solving, and debate. This would complicate life almost intolerably. Accepted ways of thinking and acting allow people to answer routine questions and make routine decisions without having to perform extensive analysis. They can simply rely on what the rules and authorities tell them to do. Another advantage is that people who share the same rules and authorities can count on being able to predict accurately how others will act. In these ways, rules and authorities generally make life smoother, simpler, and easier by eliminating the need to struggle with decisions in each situation.

For example, it's not necessary to decide to stop at a red light, because the rule that requires a stop is explicit and widely known. Having the rule allows people to regulate their own behavior and predict what others will do. In fact, much of life is regulated in this way by rules and authorities, and people can make routine decisions about their beliefs and conduct without extensive inquiry or argument, because those decisions have already been made for them by the society at large. Adult members of society know that murder and robbery are crimes, that they should arrive at work on time, and that they should practice good personal hygiene. Thus, it is not necessary to debate whether it would be acceptable to shoot a rival for a job, or whether to do what the boss says.

Rules and authorities not only make life easier, they also make it possible. The alternative would be chaos, a situation in which people made individual decisions based on their beliefs and feelings at the time. Social life and relationships would be virtually impossible, because people could not predict how others would act in any given situation. And much activity would come to a stop as people spent their time investigating and debating questions for which the answers are already widely available and accepted.

Rules and authorities cement the social fabric of a community or society. They assure that, in similar situations, most people will make the same kind of decision most of the time and thus prevent anarchy and chaos. When people enter situations that are new to them, they can consult the rules and the relevant authorities to find out what behaviors are required or expected. Thus, though you may never have attended a formal dinner, you can consult an etiquette book, a set of rules compiled and interpreted by an authority, to find out about appropriate table manners and protocol. If you had a question about a matter of constitutional law, you would consult an expert or a textbook, or perhaps a Supreme Court decision, to find out how the Constitution has been interpreted in a specific situation.

Some rules and authorities have the force of law. They concern issues of belief and conduct that are so important to a community of society that they receive formal recognition. Societies and communities frequently enforce their important rules by establishing penalties, sometimes severe, for violating the rules or disregarding authorities. People who violate civil laws or ignore court orders can be put in jail. Communities and groups that are not necessarily subject to governmental laws usually have their own rules and penalties. Organized churches, for example, usually specify what a person must believe and how a person must behave in order to be a member. People who depart from the prescribed beliefs and behaviors can be disciplined, and even formally excluded from membership in the group.

Some rules and authorities do not have any sort of official status, but derive their force from custom, tradition, or widespread recognition. For example, long-standing custom specifies when brides should or should not wear white at their weddings. No one will be arrested for disregarding these rules, but people who believe the rules are important have the right to disapprove of a bride's decision to wear a white dress, just as brides have the right to disregard this custom. People use a variety of social sanctions to express their disapproval and encourage or force compliance with the rules.

But existing rules and authorities do not address some questions adequately, or at all, or people question or challenge them because they believe them to be unfair, incomplete, or simply wrong. For example, the following questions are typical of those that seem to have no easy answers:

Should society permit capital punishment or abortion?
What should be the penalties for drunk driving?
Should racist language be protected as free speech under the First Amendment?
What is pornography, and what (if anything) should be done about it?
Should sex and AIDS be discussed in public schools?
Should teenagers be given free condoms?
Should homosexuals be allowed to marry (each other)?
Should Roger Maris really hold the record for home runs? (His season was longer than Babe Ruth's.)
Should smoking be banned in restaurants?
Should there be a tax increase to support some worthy cause, such as education or the homeless?

People who are certain about what to believe and do will have few problems with questions of this sort. They live in a predictable, stable world in which everything is known and all important questions have been asked and answered. When they need guidance, they simply consult decisions that have been made for them by others—usually by tradition or by people in positions of authority. Authorities and rules present a restricted view of the world, one in which diversity and disagreements are generally deemphasized or even eliminated, and some people find such a world comfortable and secure.

But many people do not live in such a world. Instead, they experience doubt, and they find that knowledge is not finite and fixed, but indeterminate and changing. In order to chart a path through a frequently confusing maze of questions about ethics, values, beliefs, and actions, they ask difficult questions and attempt to answer them. They deliberately seek as much information and as many different points of view propose as possible, and then attempt to choose intelligently among them. They live in a lively, interesting world that constantly challenges them to make intelligent, sometimes difficult choices.

Where Inquiry and Argument Begin

Rules, procedures, and authorities do not regulate all aspects of life, and they do not always work well in those areas that they do attempt to regulate. Consider:

> Situations may arise that existing rules and authorities do not address, or do not cover adequately.

For example, advances in medical procedures have led to surrogate pregnancies. Couples who cannot have biological children can pay women to bear their babies. This practice was so new that for some time it was regulated only by contracts between the parties involved, and thus only by contract law. Consequently, when a surrogate mother insisted that she should be able to keep the child she had carried, there were no rules to consult. As the case was being resolved in court, legislators and others began to ask whether surrogate pregnancies are right or wrong and to what extent they should be regulated. Some people simply want to regulate them, while others believe they should be banned. The issue has not been settled, and the inquiry and discussion will probably continue for some time as people gather information and discuss what should be done.

> People may acknowledge that rules exist, but insist that the rules do not apply to their specific circumstances.

For example, a school dress code may prohibit shorts, but a female student might insist that she is not wearing shorts, but a garment that is more like a skirt, and thus that the rules do not apply. On a much larger scale, many Native American tribes make money by establishing gambling businesses on their lands and by selling untaxed cigarettes and alcohol. They acknowledge state laws that regulate these activities, but they contend that state laws do not apply on tribal lands, which are sovereign and not subject to state laws.

> People challenge existing rules and authorities as wrong, or unfair, and perhaps question whether their beliefs and acts should be regulated at all.

In recent years, for example, there have been increasingly vigorous discussions and debates about whether, when, and under what circumstances people have the right to die by their own choice, or under what conditions family members have the right to make decisions that might lead to death. Some say that existing laws are inadequate, while others say they should be abolished.

When established procedures and recognized authorities have nothing to say about an issue, or when too many people challenge existing rules and procedures, then critical inquiry and argument provide a means of answering questions and reaching agreements. Inquiry and argument are not sources of rules, but methods of resolving differences and answering difficult questions. Rules and authorities simplify problem solving and decision making by providing answers; they tell people what to think, believe, or do in specific situations. Critical inquiry and argument do not provide answers—at least not ready-made answers, and they often make things more complicated rather than simpler. *Critical inquiry* and *argument* require people to gather information, to identify alternative and varying perspectives, and to develop criteria for choosing the best answer or solution from numerous possibilities.

The goal of most inquiry and argument is to achieve the best possible decision about actions or beliefs under existing circumstances, given the information available at the time. And, of course, agreeing on what is the "best" is itself open to discussion. The best decision may not always be the ideal decision, or the most rational, practical, or the most emotionally satisfying decision. For example, it is possible to measure radiation, chemical toxicity, and other hazards and to estimate the effects that these substances might have on people's health. But no rule or authority can specify an acceptable level of risk. The ideal might be to permit no risk at all, but that may not be possible. Only after weighing all possibilities can an informed society decide what is acceptable. Will society accept a rate of 5, 25, or 100 cancers, birth defects, stillbirths, or diseases per 100,000 people exposed to a risk? What are the costs of having no risk at all? Is that possible? These kinds of questions have no ready-made answers. Answers and decisions come through a process of inquiry and argument in which participants attempt to gather as much information as possible and all points of view have the right to be heard.

Taking a Position

At the heart of this process of inquiry and argument is the act of stating and supporting a *position:* When people believe they know the answer to a question or the solution to a problem, they state their answer or solution publicly and then support it with facts, illustrations, examples, and reasons. As they subject their positions to public scrutiny in this way, they are explaining why they have reached their conclusion, and they are also explaining why others should agree with them. If others do not agree, they will state their own positions and support them, placing them in opposition or competition with other positions. On important questions, it's not unusual for there to be multiple positions, some of which are modifications and combinations of others. In addition to stating and supporting their own positions, participants are obligated to listen carefully to others and to be willing to change their minds and alter their own positions in response to positions that are convincingly supported. Ideally, this exchange of positions, support, and reasoning will result in a new solution or answer to which most participants can agree, at least for the time being.

APPLICATIONS

1. Describe a situation in which you have questioned an established authority, rule, or custom and explain why you challenged it. How did you make your decision?
2. Choose an established rule, custom, or authority that you believe should be changed. Explain the rule or custom, describe the changes you would make, and give your reasons for those changes.
3. Recall a situation in which you and someone else disagreed with each other about an important issue. Describe the issue or question and explain the reason for your disagreement and why the issue was important to you. How did you and the other person resolve the disagreement? What was the result?

The Components of Argument

Argument asks questions that do not have ready answers, questions that fall outside the normal range of widely accepted authorities and rules. These questions are often about values, policies, and facts. That is, they concern whether something is good or bad, whether something ought to be done, and whether something is true or false. Once a question has been posed, the next step is a careful, systematic inquiry into the question in which you look at as many answers as possible. Inquiry should help you identify your own position—a statement that reflects your decision about how to answer the question. Once you know your own position, all that remains is to state it convincingly for others.

The Questions and Issues of Argument

Argument and critical inquiry usually focus on questions that cannot be answered easily by referring to authorities or established
procedures. These questions frequently concern matters of quality
or value, of action, and of fact.

Questions of quality and value deal with whether something is
good or bad, or how good or bad, whether it is better or worse, or
preferable to something else. For example, discussions about the
best place to live, the best car to buy, and the best restaurant in
town are all questions of quality or value, because they all ask
whether one thing is better than others. The key to successful
argument about questions of quality and value is developing the
criteria for making a decision or choice. For example, discussions
about the best place to live make sense only in relation to what
specific people need. One place can't be best for everyone, because
people have different needs and preferences. The starting point is to
develop the criteria for deciding what makes a good place to live.
Once the criteria have been developed, it's possible to measure
places against them and rank those places according to how well
they meet the criteria. The criteria are what make questions about
quality and value more than matters of opinion. Without criteria
(what are the features a good car or a good place to live must have),
there is nothing to say except to express one's likes and dislikes. For
example, to express a dislike of broccoli is to state an opinion.
There is no room here for inquiry ("Why don't you like broccoli?"
"I just don't like it; it tastes bad.") or debate, because there is
nothing to debate. Likes, preferences, inclinations, and similar sensations or feelings are not suitable subjects for argument because
they are matters of purely personal tastes or preferences. For example, a wine taster may declare a wine to be an excellent Savignon
Blanc, but an individual customer may not like it. The taster's
judgment is subject to inquiry and argument, primarily among
those who have been trained as tasters, because there are established standards for excellence for each variety of wine. But the
second judgment is not subject to inquiry and argument, because it
is a matter of personal preference, for which there are no available
criteria.

Questions about facts concern whether something is true or
false, or actually exists. It's not possible to argue about facts themselves. For example, people don't argue about the temperature, or
about whether it's raining outside, or about whether a lake can no
longer support aquatic life. But it is possible to argue about whether
something is actually a fact. For example, while people don't argue

about whether a lake or pond is dead, they do argue about what killed it. People talked about acid rain for years before it was shown to exist and achieved status as a fact. People still argue about whether acid rain or some other phenomenon is responsible for the condition of the pond or lake. In the debate about abortion, no one denies that conception takes place, or when it takes place. But many people debate whether life actually begins at conception rather than at some later time. That is generally a decision reserved for argument and politics, not science.

Arguments also raise questions about actions: What should be done in a specific situation when there are no ready-made guidelines or rules? For example, recent public debates have focused on questions such as these:

Should surrogate mothers have parental rights over the children they carry?

Should people who have terminal illnesses or who are in relentless, permanent pain be able to end their own lives with the assistance of a physician?

Should animals be used in scientific research?

What should be done to protect U.S. businesses and industries?

These questions all involve policies, questions about what should be done or what rules should govern what people do. Some rules and authorities may apply to each of these questions, but not everyone involved will accept those rules and authorities, or agree that they apply. So the questions can be answered only through the inquiry and give-and-take of argument.

Inquiry

The first step in any argument is critical *inquiry.* The goal of inquiry is information and understanding. Without information and understanding, nothing else can take place, because discussions, decisions, and choices are impossible without knowledge of the subject.

One source of knowledge is personal experience and direct observation. For example, AIDS patients, victims of crime, women who have had abortions, and people who have been fired from their jobs can all speak directly about their experiences and how those experiences have affected their lives. What was it like? How did it feel? What happened? What do they think of it now? But personal experience has its limits. AIDS patients, and those who have worked with them, may be able to testify about the terrible pain of that illness, about the psychological and financial toll it takes, and about the agony of dying. Some might be able to discuss the methods and motivations to prevent the disease. These observations and conclusions can all be based on personal experience. But direct experience has limits. For example, persons who have AIDS are not automatically qualified to comment on the effectiveness of all methods of prevention, the quality of AIDS research, or whether the government or private agencies should devote more resources to research. These questions must be left to those who have studied them systematically.

Systematic study is a second source of information and knowledge. Perhaps the best known form of systematic study is the experiment, in which researchers attempt to create natural conditions in a laboratory and then control events very carefully in order to determine exact causes and effects. For example, if you wanted to determine the best shelf position for a product in a grocery store, you would put the product in different positions (keeping everything else the same) and keep track of sales to see if one position resulted in increased product sales. In one recent experiment, a sociologist wanted to discover what would get people to pay a highway toll at an unattended toll booth. For a time he simply watched (from out of sight) to see what people did. When he stood where people could see him, they were more likely to pay the toll. Later, he mounted a dummy TV camera at the booth to see how people would react. The camera resulted in the highest rate of payment. We can conclude from this that people are more likely to pay a toll if they are being watched, or think they are being watched. Is that true of everyone? It may be too early to tell. We need other experiments, more data, before reaching a conclusion.

A third source of information is *other people*. While it is impossible for one person to be an expert about everything, it is always possible to find out what other people know by reading what they have written or by talking with them. When you do this, it is important to select as sources people who have an established expertise and authority in the subject. It is also important to remember that very little of the information available in the world is neutral or objective. Thus, the information you gather from other people will usually (always?) be influenced by that person's experiences, beliefs, and values. For example, you might get different information about the social and economic status of women depending on what your source believes is the proper role of women in society, or whether your source is a woman or a man.

Stating a Position

To state a *position* is to make a statement that expresses a decision or choice about actions or beliefs. A position (sometimes called a claim or a proposition) addresses a question of value, belief, fact, or action. A position is more than an expression of an opinion or a feeling or a personal preference. Positions can be supported by evidence and criteria that are public and available to everyone. Feelings and personal preferences, in contrast, are private and cannot be supported or evaluated with criteria or evidence outside the person who expresses them. And positions are not statements about the obvious. That is, the questions and issues they address do not have answers that anyone could determine simply by checking. For example, people generally do not argue about whether a balanced diet is important to health, or whether alcohol consumption affects reaction time. The importance of a balanced diet, and the effects of alcohol on the human nervous system, are well-established in science. But people may argue about what foods contribute to a balanced diet, or just how much alcohol is required to produce impaired reactions. Vegetarians, for example, would argue that meat products are not necessary to a balanced diet. While state laws usually define a person whose blood alcohol level is .10 as intoxicated, many people assert that they are perfectly capable of driving and performing other tasks with that much alcohol in their blood. In fact, in many states juries must debate whether drivers with blood alcohol levels of .10 were in fact intoxicated.

Formulating a Position

After seeing a film, someone might say, "I didn't like it" or "I thought it was boring." These statements sound like positions, but they are not. They are not a basis for argument because there is no way to establish criteria for "like" or "boring." Both are personal responses. Someone who hears these statements might ask: "Why didn't you like it?" or "Why did you think it was boring?" These are invitations to turn the statements about preferences and feelings into positions by saying something substantive about the film. In reply, the person who was bored might say: "I thought there were too many long, slow shots of landscapes and the sky, and the director spent more time on the subplot than it deserved." Are these positions? Not quite, but they're coming along. They are not positions because they contain terms and statements that cannot be measured by criteria separate from the person expressing them. Statements about the number of shots of landscape and the sky, whether they were in fact slow, and whether the subplot received too much attention, are probably matters of individual perception and preference. It may not be possible to agree on how many is too many, how slow is too slow, or how much is too much. Of course, it would be possible to watch the film again and time the various shots and segments. This information might later serve as evidence or support in an argument, but it will not prove either of the statements given so far.

Pressed to explain further, the speaker might say that the subplot, which is about teenagers, is not believable because it does not portray what teenagers actually say and do. This is a position that can be argued. In fact, it may be several positions:

> It asserts that realism is a criterion for believability, and that the details in the film are not real, and thus not believable.

Both of these statements can be argued because both rely on criteria that are available to everyone rather than to a single person. It's possible to compare the events in the film with the behavior of actual people and determine how well the two match. It's also possible to determine whether audiences prefer realistic action. The popularity of science fiction and fantasy literature might suggest that audiences do not always demand realism, but it would not settle the question of whether only realistic plots can be believable.

Supporting a Position

A person who has stated a position should be able to explain his or her reasons for taking that position and provide evidence and reasons to show why the position is reasonable, correct, or preferable to other possible positions. In order to arrive at the positions they state, writers must go through a process of inquiry and analysis in which they examine their own beliefs, gather information, discover and evaluate a variety of possible choices, and choose the best one. Having made that choice, the writer shows others why they should agree or make the same choice. Writers support their arguments by giving reasons for their positions, by showing that their positions are the result of a careful process of reasoning and decision making, by stating facts and observations, by citing the testimony of witnesses and experts, and by convincing their readers that they are reliable sources of accurate information. For example, the following editorial supports its position in all of the ways listed here. Read it carefully and then answer (or discuss) the questions that follow it.

Don't Let Hate-Crime Laws Undermine Free Speech

THE EDITORS OF *USA TODAY*

One of the toughest instincts to resist is the urge to clamp your hand over the mouth of someone saying something loathsome. You just want it to stop.

In just the past few years, that instinct has led almost every state—and many communities—to pass laws banning offensive words or actions, like burning crosses or drawing racist graffiti.

Those laws make people feel good. But they pose a vivid threat, and not just to racists, vandals or loudmouths. They threaten everyone's right to free speech.

Today, the Supreme Court hears arguments challenging a well-intentioned St. Paul, Minn., ordinance that shows how hate-crime laws go wrong.

The ordinance outlaws words and acts that "one . . . has reasonable grounds to know [arouse] anger, alarm or resentment in others on the basis of race, color, religion or gender." Two teens were charged under the ordinance after burning a cross on the lawn of their neighborhood's first black family.

Neither of them defends the cross burning—an indisputably vile act. But one appealed his conviction under the city's hate-crime ordinance, arguing that it goes too far.

He's right.

The statute—like many others—is easily abused. Who's to say what causes "anger, alarm or resentment"?

The definition is broad enough to include a Washington Redskins T-shirt, since "Redskins" is considered a racial epithet by many Native Americans.

It even could be used to ban a sign inveighing against white racism.

Free speech can be protected without giving haters free reign to paint swastikas on synagogues or harass minorities with racial slurs. Other laws—against harassment, threats, vandalism and trespass—forbid such activities.

The St. Paul defendant, for instance, will face an assault charge even if the Supreme Court strikes down the city's hate-crime ordinance—as it should.

Abhorrent speech is hard to swallow. But silencing it with hate-crime laws could strangle precious freedoms.

APPLICATIONS

1. Identify this editorial's position, and restate it in your own words.
2. What reasons does the writer give for the position?
3. Describe the reasoning process this editorial takes its readers through.
4. What testimony does the editorial provide?
5. What information does the editorial include as support?

A well-stated position contains instructions for its support; that is, it tells you exactly what you must do next. For example, if your position is that all high-school students should take a course about computers, you are obligating yourself to say certain things and not to say others. Your support should focus on explaining *why* you believe all high-school students need to know about computers, and you will also have to explain just what such a course should cover. The type of course you describe will specify the knowledge you believe students need, and will help you explain why the course is needed. For example, if you want to require a course in computer programming, then you will need to show that most of the careers students might pursue will require a knowledge of programming. It might be more practical, or more in line with students' career goals to argue that they should learn to use word processing and database programs. In either case, you would be asserting that the course you propose fulfills a widespread need.

On the other hand, your position that a computer course should be required does *not* permit you to do any of the following:

Discuss why you like or dislike computers or why others should like or dislike them.

Tell a story about how you learned to use a computer, or discuss the computer class you took last year.

Explain what computers are and how they work.

None of these responds to the task set up in the statement of position itself, and so none is relevant to explaining or supporting that position. It's important that support be directly relevant to the position that has been stated. Support for a required computer course might include some or all of the following:

- A brief description of the course itself; for example, one that includes keyboarding, word processing, and databases.
- A statement about the prevalence of computers in the contemporary workplace, along with examples of the kinds of tasks that require a knowledge of computers.
- A statement of why such a course would be valuable to those who take it—that is, why is the information they will gain important, and will any advantage come from taking the course?
- Examples of how you or people you know have found knowledge of computers valuable.
- Testimony from experts (employers, your uncle the banker, former students who are now working or in college) about why they think knowledge of computers is important for high-school graduates.

Conclusion

When you encounter a question that you can't answer by consulting rules or authorities, or a situation in which you find people in genuine disagreement about what to believe or do, then you have a situation that is appropriate for argument and critical inquiry. A commitment to argument is a commitment to inquiry, discussion, and debate as methods of helping you decide what to do or what to believe. Once you discover what you believe is the right answer, you will need to state your position so that others can join you in the debate. As part of your argument you will provide support in the form of reasons, reasoning, and information to justify the position you have taken and encourage others to take it too.

Questions and Activities

1. Collect copies of four or five editorials, letters to the editor, or other brief forms of argument from newspapers and magazines. In a small group with classmates do the following: Read each editorial aloud

and identify the position the writer has stated and describe the support the writer provides. Discuss what would make the support more complete or more effective.

2. Make a list of five or six subjects you have strong beliefs about— things that make you angry or get your attention, or that you have had extended discussions about with family members or friends. For each item, write at least five statements in which you express an opinion or belief.

3. Choose at least five of the statements you made in question 2 and revise them so they state positions you can support. For two of these, explain how you came to believe what the position says you believe, and why others should agree with you.

Suggestions for Writing

1. Choose a well-known or widely observed rule or authority. Describe it and explain the purpose that it serves. Argue that this rule or authority is essential because of the stability it provides to individuals or society at large.

2. For one of the positions you stated in response to the Questions and Activities above, write the complete argument.

3. Select one of the editorials you reviewed in the exercises above and do one of the following: Write a response in which you take a position different from the one in the editorial or rewrite the editorial, improving it by restating its position and adding support.

CHAPTER TWO

Getting from Opinion to Argument

This chapter explains how arguments arise, distinguishes between opinions and positions, and explains how to state a position so that it is arguable. Before you read the chapter, write brief responses to the following:

1. How are the following statements different?
   a. I enjoy doing crossword puzzles.
   b. Everyone should do crossword puzzles; they're good for you.
2. Select an issue that is the focus of an argument (it can be a widely discussed public issue, or a private one) and explain why it is the subject of disagreement or controversy.

Opinions vs. Arguments

Everyone has an opinion about almost everything. All you have to do is ask, and people will tell you what they think. *Opinions* express personal tastes and preferences, but they make no assertions about what is or ought to be, and no demands on what other people should think. Thus, they do not necessarily state positions and so they are not arguable. You will argue more effectively if you learn to distinguish opinions from positions and to state your own positions in arguable form. This chapter will explain how to do that, as well as how everyday subjects become the focus of arguments, and how to state your position in an arguable form. Consider these two situations:

1. In 1990, President George Bush created a stir by announcing that he doesn't like broccoli and that, now that he's grown

up, he's not going to eat it. Broccoli growers were unhappy that such a prominent person would say that he doesn't like their product, and they feared that such an anti-endorsement would affect their sales.

2. A group that says it represents animal rights advocates vegetarianism and says that people should not eat animals, use animal products (milk, meat, fur, leather, etc.), or use animals in scientific research, because doing so violates the animals' basic right to live in peace without being harmed or exploited.

Both of these situations appear to be starting points for arguments, but they are actually quite different: Only one of these statements is arguable. Understanding how these situations are different will help you understand the difference between arguments and opinions.

In the first situation, President Bush was expressing a personal taste or preference based solely on his own experience of eating broccoli: the taste, texture, smell, and other qualities that he associates with it. Almost everyone has feelings like this about something, such as a food, a color, or a sound, ranging from an intense attraction to a strong aversion. But note that President Bush's statement makes no demands on other people. He is not saying that no one should eat broccoli, or that everyone should dislike it. He is simply expressing his personal taste, a highly individual response based on feelings and perceptions that other people do not necessarily share. Because his standards are personal and not available to anyone else, his statements about broccoli cannot be the start of an argument. An *argument* makes a statement about what other people should think or do, and then supports that statement by referring to standards that are available to everyone.

The animal rights group, for example, is opening an argument because it takes a position about what other people should believe and do, and supports that position by invoking generally held views about what is right and wrong. That is, the assertion that eating or using animal products is wrong is an attempt to invoke some sort of general standard that is available to all people, not just the person making the statement. So, this statement attempts to extend principles of right and wrong to a new area, animals, where it has not applied before, and asks people to change their behavior based on this new application of the principle. These assertions about the proper treatment of animals provide the foundation for several possible arguments—about right and wrong, about the standards of treatment that apply to animals, about vegetarianism, and other subjects.

George Bush's statements about broccoli led to a certain amount of discussion about the effects he might have on the broccoli industry, and in the process someone probably said that he should eat his broccoli because it's good for him. That begins to look like a place to begin an argument, although it's well established by now that vegetables are good for people's health, so this possible argument will probably fail on its own obviousness. Of course, it is remotely possible that a nutritionist could justify the President's opinion by finding something harmful about broccoli itself. Or a scientist could discover pesticide residues on the plants. But none of these possible arguments responds to the original statement, because they say nothing about *liking* broccoli. That is, though these statements appear to be for or against the president's statements about broccoli, in fact they are not, because they do not respond to his statement that he does not *like* broccoli. You can respond directly to his statement only if you have access to what broccoli tastes like to him, and that, of course, is not possible. In short, we have no argument here because:

The president made no statement about how other people should react to broccoli.

His tastes are entirely private and personal; others have no access to them and there are no public criteria for judging them.

The animal rights activists present a quite different situation. To say that everyone should become a vegetarian because animals have rights and should not be used in ways that cause death, pain, injury, or indignity is quite different from George Bush's statement about his dislike of broccoli. It will serve as the foundation of several arguments because:

It takes a position about what other (all) people should believe and do; it is not a private statement about a single person's preferences.

It asserts general standards of ethics, values, and conduct to which everyone has access and to which everyone is subject; it is not a statement of purely personal tastes.

It asserts that animals can suffer pain and indignity, and so raises questions that can be explored and answered.

It calls into question long-standing and widely accepted social practices and attitudes about animals and their position in relation to humans. Thus, it identifies as arguable something that had previously been unquestioned and widely accepted.

It permits a direct response based on information and criteria that are available to everyone, not just the people taking the position. For example, arguments could explore what the standards actually are, whether they should apply to animals, whether they might also apply to vegetables, and whether humans have the right to use other species for their own benefit, among other questions.

It creates a situation that requires or invites people to choose among a variety of positions that seem equally reasonable, plausible, and right.

Finally, and perhaps most importantly, something must be at stake for an argument to exist. The ideas or actions in question must have some consequence for the people involved. For example, animal rights advocates maintain that continuing to eat or use animals will violate animals' rights, cause pain, death, and indignity, and violate an ethical code that binds all people.

Scientists who believe the earth's atmosphere is getting warmer have claimed that significant warming could result in the end of life on earth as we know, resulting in dramatic storms, rising oceans, and the devastation of agriculture. Of course, the person who claims a consequence has the burden of convincing others that it is a real one. The more serious the consequences that can be claimed, the more likely that people will pay attention to it.

Summary

Arguments begin when someone takes a position that questions received knowledge or accepted ways of doing things, or suggests a discrepancy between what is and what ought to be, and asserts that something is at stake. The result is that a subject becomes an issue, a question to be answered or a discrepancy to be resolved. The purpose of argument is to encourage people to choose among two or more positions that are equally reasonable and plausible. The process of choosing will result in new agreements or understandings about what to believe or how to act.

APPLICATIONS

1. Choose a film you have seen recently or a book you have read. Divide a sheet of paper into two columns. In the first column, write

five or six opinions about the film or book. In the second column, write five or six arguable statements. Then, working in a small group, have each person present two statements from each column, and discuss these with the group in terms of the criteria set out in this chapter.
2. Everyone has opinions, usually about a variety of subjects. Make a list of at least six subjects you feel strongly about. For each subject, write two or three opinions. Choose two or three opinions about each subject and revise them into arguable positions.

How Subjects Become Issues

Arguments never arise all by themselves, out of thin air. They are not sitting around, fully formed, waiting for someone to notice them. Arguments and the issues they focus on always arise out of a social and political context, and they must be resolved within those same contexts. Subjects, events, and ideas are neutral in themselves, neither bad nor good, better nor worse, right nor wrong. Arguments arise as people interact with each other and the world around them. Their beliefs, values, and attitudes may lead them to question ideas, actions, policies, and procedures that have been widely accepted. This questioning of established policies and procedures, or widely held beliefs frequently results in:

Disagreement or doubt about what to believe and how to act
Assertions of discrepancies between what is and what ought to be
Questions for which there are competing and perhaps equally plausible answers

Argument—a presentation of multiple positions and solutions in order to choose the best—is one way of resolving the discrepancies and answering the questions.

For example, animals' rights and vegetarianism are related issues that arose when someone (or some group) questioned the ancient and customary practice (in Western culture, at least) of animals being subservient to humans and thus being used as food, clothing, and for other purposes. Other grounds for this argument are possible. One might argue for vegetarianism by asserting that it is healthier than eating meat, or because it does not involve the same ecological impact of raising, feeding, and slaughtering animals in great numbers. The point here is not whether one side is right and the other wrong, but that the argument exists only because someone questioned a practice that had been thought neutral, and natural.

Other subjects have become issues in much the same way. For example, when television became widely available in the 1940s, most people regarded it as a wonderful technological achievement that promised to revolutionize entertainment and education. By the early 1960s, some people had begun to question whether television was quite so wonderful. They said that people watched too much television, that the programming wasn't of a high enough quality, and that watching television might actually be harmful. That debate, of course, continues today. In addition, many people are concerned about the effects of violence and commercialism in children's programming.

Likewise, sexual harassment, wife abuse, and date rape have not always been subjects for argument. For a long time the social situation was such that men could do and say to women virtually anything they wanted. Many women simply had to accept what happened because they did not have the physical, political, or economic power to do otherwise. Women who complained about harassment at work were often fired, and the law would not protect them. But eventually many people challenged the prevailing social attitudes and insisted that women should be protected. As a result of the ensuing debate, many people have become more aware of the difficulties women face, and new laws provide civil and criminal penalties for people who commit acts of harassment or abuse, or other acts of emotional or physical violence against women.

Subjects like the effects of television and the appropriate treatment of women become the focus of arguments because someone questions existing attitudes and actions by taking a position that begins an extended argument. The argument encourages participants to generate a great deal of information and a variety of positions, so that decisions about actions and beliefs can be based on the greatest possible number of choices. This process may only rarely lead to a quick solution. For example, despite years of debate, questions about the effects of television or the treatment of women have not been completely resolved. No one has been able to determine definitively whether television is actually harmful. Debates continue about certain kinds of programming and advertising, and about how much television a person should watch in a day or a week. Nor have sexual harassment, wife abuse, and date rape ended. Argument, by itself, will not make them go away. A number of men and women continue to insist that sexual harassment is simply not an issue, that it doesn't exist, or that it can't be regulated. In the short term, it is possible that more people are sensitive to the possible effects of violence on television and sexual harassment. Over an extended period of time, the arguments about these issues may create new rules that define what is right and wrong, what is permitted and what is not, in relationships between men and women.

Thus, in the long run, an argument about a particular issue may produce changes in the social context that gave rise to it initially. For example, at one time it was common for children to work long days in dangerous situations, just as adults did. This practice was widely accepted in society until, for a variety of reasons, people began to question child labor and insist that children should go to school instead of work. Over a period of time, as a result of argument and discussion, child labor was increasingly regulated, and it remains so today.

Summary: From Subject to Issue

Arguments arise when people question accepted knowledge and practices and, by calling attention to them, make them the subject of debate and discussion. The following conditions contribute to making a subject arguable:

1. *Questioning* creates a discrepancy or identifies a disagreement. For example, there may be a discrepancy between what people say they believe and what they do, or between what exists and what people say ought to exist. Often, the first step is to convince others (get them to agree) that the discrepancy exists or the question is important. For example, one struggle for scientists in recent years has been to convince politicians and the public that the earth's temperature is rising. The first step in an argument is often convincing others that there is an issue that must be addressed.

2. *Something is at stake.* There must be some consequence of acting or not acting on the questions that have been asked. For example, someone concerned about violence on television might assert that the consequence of not studying this issue and acting on it will be an increased level of violence in society at large. To support this position they might point to the similarities between the behaviors portrayed on television and those observed in society.

3. *Change* of some kind is the preferred outcome. Issues must be resolved in some way, by clarifying or redefining terms, by reaching agreements, by setting the terms of a continuing argument, or in some other way. The preferred outcome for all sides is to change

what people think or what they do, and thus to change the social context that gave rise to the argument. For example, redefining certain actions as sexual harassment or date rape, rather than as flirting or consensual sex, constitutes an agreement to change beliefs, and is thus a change in the social context of relationships between men and women. Thus, all issues involve the need to choose among alternative actions and beliefs. The resulting change can take the form of informal social understandings or formal rules.

4. *A commitment to inquiry and discussion* as the means of seeking resolution and change. Issues can be resolved by means other than argument. For example, animal rights advocates have destroyed laboratories and freed animals that were being used in research. Civil rights activists in the 1950s marched in the streets, sat in at lunch counters, and boycotted businesses. Terrorists take hostages and plant bombs. But argument relies on a commitment to inquiry and discussion as the preferred means of resolving issues: stating positions that identify alternatives, subjecting each position to careful scrutiny, and developing criteria for deciding which one represents the best possible course of thought or action.

APPLICATIONS

1. Identify three or four established customs or beliefs and explain how you would call them into question and make them the focus of an argument. For two of these, explain how this argument would satisfy the four criteria listed in the summary to the preceding section.
2. Working in a small group, identify up to three debates or controversies that are presently under way. For each issue, identify the main positions and desired outcomes. Then discuss the various methods of reaching a solution or consensus, and the advantages and disadvantages of each. Be prepared to present the results of your discussion to the entire class.
3. Select a controversy or situation that is now being resolved by some means other than argument and inquiry (e.g., violence or some other form of direct action, legal action, legislation, etc.) and explain the advantages of argument rather than the method being employed.

Stating an Arguable Position

The foundation of all arguments is a statement of a position, a statement that establishes the subject as arguable. Arguable statements do the following:

1. Present the issue to an audience as something to be investigated, discussed, and debated, because an argument requires cooperative action. More than one person must be involved.
2. Assert that something is at stake, that action and inaction have consequences.
3. Assert that people should believe or act in a certain way; an arguable statement makes demands on the beliefs and actions of others and implies that evidence is available to support your assertion.
4. Invoke criteria that are available to everyone as a basis for choosing between competing positions. These criteria most often involve widely accepted standards of behavior or conduct.

Separating Argument from Opinion

Recall from the beginning of this chapter that opinions cannot be the basis of arguments. Statements like "I don't like broccoli," or "Miss Henley is my favorite teacher," are not arguable because they do not meet any of the criteria stated above. They do not question accepted knowledge, nothing is claimed to be at stake, no claim is being made about what others should think or do, and no criteria for choice are offered or implied. There is simply nothing to argue, because these statements express a personal preference. Someone might disagree with these statements, saying "I do like broccoli," or "I don't like Miss Henley," but these responses are simply statements of different opinions, not the beginnings of an argument. These statements do not state positions or articulate issues. They do not connect with any criteria or standards that are separate from the speakers, and they do not ask anyone to agree or disagree. To say that "Miss Henley is my favorite teacher" is not to suggest that she should be anyone else's favorite teacher.

It is possible to make an arguable statement about Miss Henley. Suppose someone says "Miss Henley should be chosen teacher of the year." This statement is arguable because it does what we expect of arguments:

- It identifies an issue in which something is at stake (the honor of being teacher of the year).
- It makes a claim about what others should believe and do (they should elect/choose Miss Henley rather than someone else to be teacher of the year).

- It implies that evidence is available to show that Miss Henley is qualified for or deserves this honor, and that this evidence is available to everyone.
- It suggests that the speaker will present acceptable criteria for choosing the teacher of the year.

Thus, the difference between an opinion and a position, between a statement that is arguable and one that is not, is that the opinion remains a statement about private preferences, while the position invites public scrutiny and the application of shared standards.

Arguments Are Not Permanent

Because they arise from specific social contexts, few arguments endure over long periods of time. When the social situation changes, arguments will change with it. What is arguable today may not be arguable next year, or ten years from now. What is not arguable today may become arguable tomorrow if someone successfully calls it into question. At any given time, a society needs a certain number of beliefs, attitudes, rules, and practices that are generally regarded as obvious or accepted practices and not arguable. Compliance with these allows a society to function. People wait their turns, observe traffic laws, and expect others to do the same. Obvious, noncontroversial actions and beliefs allow them to anticipate what will happen in certain situations and to respond appropriately.

As times and values change, what was considered obvious or noncontroversial at one time can become arguable if enough people begin to question it. For example, many people wait in line for long periods of time, sometimes several days, to get seats or tickets for very popular concerts or athletic events. In fact, waiting in line and the principle of "first come, first served" are widely accepted. People often justify their entitlement to something by saying "I was here first." But there are other ways of allocating goods and services, and it is possible to question standing in line and turn it into an issue. You could argue, for example, that it is unfair because it favors only those people who have the time to wait. And you might add that many of those people are probably supposed to be somewhere else, such as work or school, so the system actually favors those who are being irresponsible.

Similarly, in the past thirty or forty years seemingly established practices such as saying prayers at school functions, reciting the

Pledge of Allegiance, wearing furs, or raising farm animals can all become arguable given the proper circumstances. Forty years ago, prayers in public schools and at other public functions were commonplace and went unchallenged, even if they made some people uncomfortable. Eventually, school prayer was questioned with a position that goes something like this:

> Prayers should not be allowed in public schools because, since the schools are controlled by the government, prayers violate the constitutional principle of the separation of church and state.

This statement creates the issue by calling school prayer into question, and begins the argument by making a claim about what people should believe or do. By citing the Constitution, it also establishes the criterion that must be used to resolve the argument: Does school prayer violate the principles of the First Amendment? Despite a court decision in favor of those who opposed school prayer, this issue is far from being resolved. It has been argued vigorously for years as legislators and school boards have attempted to reinstate school prayer, while opponents continue to file suits and argue against it.

On the other hand, some arguments simply disappear, often without being resolved, in response to a social context that no longer regards them as important or as appropriate issues for argument. For example, except for a few holdouts, no one persists in arguing that African Americans are intellectually inferior to caucasians or that they should not be allowed to vote or participate fully in society. Nor does anyone seriously argue that adding fluoride to water supplies to prevent dental cavities is a communist plot to undermine the United States (though there now may be medical reasons for not using fluoride in water). During the past fifty years, both of these subjects have been argued loudly and often. But the social context has changed, and it might be difficult to start a serious argument about either one. What has changed, in both cases, is that they are no longer regarded as issues.

APPLICATIONS

1. Based on your own experience, identify at least three subjects that at one time were considered to be issues requiring argument, but that now are not arguable. These subjects may be from national or international events, or from your own life. Once you have identified them, explain why they are no longer the focus of arguments.

2. Working in a small group with classmates, try to identify five subjects that are not yet (and have not been) issues and thus have not been argued, but that you think could *become* arguable at some time in the future. Describe the circumstances that will have to exist for these subjects to become arguable. That is, if they are not arguable now, what changes will have to occur for them to become arguable. Be prepared to report your group's discussion to the class.

Conclusion

- Opinions and arguments are different. Opinions make no reference to criteria outside the person who expresses them. For this reason, opinions cannot be argued. Arguments make statements about what people should believe or do, and they invoke criteria to which everyone has access.

- Subjects become issues, and thus the focus of arguments, when someone questions accepted knowledge or behavior and thus begins a process of inquiry, analysis, and discussion.

- Positions must be stated in arguable form if they are to be the basis of arguments.

Questions and Activities

1. Review the responses you made to the exercises at the beginning of this chapter, and the Applications in the middle. Select several opinions or positions you stated there and revise them so they are arguable. Then, working in a group, present your arguable statements to classmates and discuss whether you have actually made them arguable.

2. The following practices are governed by generally accepted rules or beliefs, and are not generally considered to be arguable. Work in a group to explain how calling the rules or beliefs into question for each subject can lead to redefining the practice as arguable.
   Starting school at age five
   "Ladies first"
   Compulsory, free public education
   An adversarial legal system
   Required courses in school
   Getting a driver's license at age sixteen

3. Describe a situation in which you thought you were basing your actions or beliefs on accepted beliefs or practices (i.e., you thought you were following the rules), but someone challenged you. Explain:
   What were the rules you thought you were following?
   How and why were you challenged or questioned?
   What alternative was presented?
   How was the situation resolved?

Suggestions for Writing

1. Select a subject that is widely regarded as not arguable. State a position in arguable form about this subject, and write a brief paper in which you support your position.

2. Select a subject that people argue about frequently. Take the position that the issue should not be argued (i.e., that it can be resolved in other ways), or that it is not really arguable. Write a paper in which you support this position.

CHAPTER THREE

Writing an Argument

Once you have identified an issue as the focus of argument and determined, at least provisionally, your own position, actually writing the argument, complete with support, may seem anticlimactic. After all, you will have worked hard to gather information and understand the issue in order to make a decision about what you will believe or how you will act. But, if you want to join the ongoing discussion about the issue and influence what other people believe or do, you will need to present your position and provide reasons for agreeing with it. This chapter illustrates how to build an argument that presents and supports your position to an audience. To do this, the chapter will address:

- Getting started: writing effective beginnings
- Developing the middle: showing your readers appropriate support
- Ending: writing effective conclusions

Before you read the chapter, respond to the following:

1. What do you believe is the strongest or most effective way for an argument to begin?
2. Imagine that you are speaking about some controversial issue to a room filled with people who disagree with you. How does their reaction affect what you say or how you say it?

Before You Begin

Many people who have taken the time and effort to be informed and to evaluate and make decisions about issue are still confused or intimidated when it comes to presenting their views to others in writing or speaking. Perhaps they are inexperienced as arguers, or they may believe there is a single correct way to organize and write an argument. Of course, nothing could be further from the truth.

There is no single correct way to write an argument. Different situations and audiences require different approaches. And, just as there is no right way, there are no easy formulas, no all-purpose plans that always work. Virtually every decision you make about how to present an argument will depend on your subject, your audience, your relationship with your audience, and the goal you hope to accomplish. For example, it makes a difference whether your audience will agree or disagree with you. Will they be hostile, friendly, or indifferent? Will they believe what you say? Will they believe your definition of the situation?

What follows in this chapter is not meant to provide easy solutions or formulas for writing arguments. Rather, this chapter provides you with a variety of ways of *thinking about* how you will organize and present an argument in support of your position.

What Is Not an Argument?

Remember that an argument states and supports a position. Without those two elements, a position and support, no argument exists. It is important to remember this, because people often present their ideas in formats that are not arguments. Specifically, many people write summaries or pro/con presentations and present them as arguments. But they are not arguments. They may explain issues and positions, or give a balanced treatment to several positions. These approaches do not work as arguments because they do not take and support a position. Perhaps those who present them as arguments believe that information by itself is sufficient. But that is almost never true.

Information by itself is rarely adequate when it comes to asking people to change what they believe and how they act. The same information is available to people on all sides of an issue and, thus, will serve a variety of positions and purposes. The information does not change. What does change is what people do with the information available to them and how they interpret it and apply it to the question at hand. Politicians sometimes call this "spin." This, of course, is at the heart of argument, because argument is less concerned with facts than with how those facts should be taken.

For example, no one disputes that nuclear power plants produce radioactive waste that remains dangerous for possibly thousands of years. Disagreement arises over whether, and where, radioactive waste can be stored safely until it is no longer dangerous.

Summaries Are Not Arguments

Summaries are brief, concentrated surveys that attempt to convey as much information as possible in a relatively short space. Most summaries avoid small details and instead provide essential principles and information to help readers understand an idea or event. For example, if someone asks you "What was the film about?", one possible response is to give them a summary: "It was a comedy about a little boy whose family went to Paris for Christmas and left him behind, at home, by mistake. The movie showed how he survived and protected his home from burglars." Of course, a summary can be quite detailed, if necessary. The more complex and detailed the subject, the longer and more complex the summary will be, depending on what your audience needs.

The important distinction between summaries and arguments is that summaries do not take positions. Instead, the central task of a summary is to present and explain a position without actually advocating it. For example, note how the following summary identifies and explains a position, but avoids endorsing that position (or any other); it simply reports.

> Members of the Parents' Association met last night in the high school gymnasium to plan a campaign to oppose the school board's plan to distribute condoms and information about AIDS to students without their parents' consent. The group does not oppose distributing condoms and believes that it is important for everyone to be informed about AIDS. But it also believes that parents should be involved in these activities.

Summaries are important tools in argument; they are a means of presenting a variety of different positions or issues so that readers can understand the dimensions of the argument and the views of those who are participating in it. It is important to orient your readers in this way by summarizing the various positions that have been taken about an issue, and the support that has been offered for those positions. But summaries will not substitute for arguments because summaries do not take and support positions. They report the positions that others have taken.

Pro/Con Treatments Are Not Arguments

Many people substitute what are sometimes called pro/con papers for arguments. Perhaps they want to avoid the conflict and controversy that often accompany taking an unpopular or unusual position. Although pro/con treatments resemble summaries, they are a bit more complex. *Pro/con* treatments assume that an issue has two opposing sides and that fairness requires that each receive equal time and treatment. Thus, they divide the issue, sometimes artificially, into two sides and then summarize each one. This may take the form of a fairly complex compare-and-contrast essay that discusses each side in relation to the other, point-by-point. Rarely, if ever, do these pro/con treatments evaluate the positions and attempt to decide which one makes more sense or has better support. Thus, a pro/con approach never chooses. It is more likely to conclude that there is merit on both sides, or that the truth probably lies somewhere between the two positions.

Pro/con treatments are not arguments for two basic reasons. The first is that they do not state and support a position. Instead, they rely on summary. The second, and perhaps more important reason, is that they do not choose between the opposing positions that they summarize and discuss. Choosing between equally plausible, reasonable positions is the central purpose of argument. It is true that arguments often propose a compromise position that is, indeed, somewhere between the original positions (which may be more than two). But this choice emerges from a rigorous inquiry and debate that includes a careful evaluation of all positions being offered. Pro/con approaches seldom debate or evaluate; they simply present, and then often claim without support that both sides have merit, or that the truth lies in the middle. So these presentations avoid the very task that is central to argument: devising criteria and methods for making difficult choices. Pro/con presentations avoid taking positions, and thus avoid making those choices.

As with summaries, pro/con presentations are important tools for argument. Most arguments require that you be able to summarize, compare, and contrast the various positions that have been taken on an issue, and that you show that you are aware of the support that has been offered for those positions. But pro/con treatments will not substitute for arguments, which require that you take a position yourself rather than simply report what others have said.

How Arguments Begin

There is no fixed way for an argument to begin, and you will probably be better off if you do not think of a beginning or introduction as a brief paragraph with a thesis statement as its last sentence. Instead of thinking about what beginnings should include, think about what they need to do, and how you can best make them effective in view of your audience, your subject, and your purpose. Perhaps it is most important in an introduction to orient your readers by introducing them to the subject and to the argument you are asking them to join.

Orient and Motivate Your Readers

The most effective beginnings will always emerge from your knowledge of your audience and your subject and it will accomplish two tasks:

1. Orient your readers to the argument by providing them with enough information to enable them to understand the issue being argued.
2. Motivate them to read the argument by showing how it is important to them.

You can accomplish these tasks in a variety of ways, including (but not necessarily limited to) the following:

- Establish context.
- State your position.
- Provide a background summary of the issue.
- Develop a scenario that presents a variety of solutions, including your own.
- Show how your argument is related to an ongoing argument, or why you are starting a new argument.

Because the purpose of an argument is to state and support a position, many people may think they should begin an argument by stating their position and then immediately provide evidence. It's possible to do this effectively if you know that the issue is rather immediate and that most of your readers are familiar with it. For example, if your whole town has been discussing a recent series of accidents at a railroad crossing, you might begin by stating your position: "The railroad crossing at Third Street should be closed." This won't surprise anyone, because the issue has been receiving public attention, and everyone will know that you are joining an argument that is already under way.

But stating your position at the beginning is only one way to begin an argument, and it may not be the most effective if it surprises your readers or catches them off guard by introducing an issue that is new to them. To ask readers to commit to or support something before they understand the issue or what is at stake is to risk being rejected before you have actually begun.

Identify the Issue

Identify the issue and provide a brief summary/explanation of how it came to be an issue and why it is important. For example, since date rape became an issue, women on some campuses have used various means to publicize the names of men they believe are guilty of date rape. In most cases, they post lists in women's dorms or in rest rooms. They assert that, since the rapes often go unreported, and the men unpunished, this is a legitimate means of helping other women protect themselves from men they might otherwise date.

Provide Context

Provide context and background information that your readers might not have. That is, where does this issue fit in the context of other, perhaps larger issues? The contexts for this subject include the complex spoken and unspoken rules that govern male-female sexual relationships, men's attitudes toward women, the men's rights to due process and protection from slander, and the women's rights not to be assaulted.

Show Where You Fit

Show why you are beginning a new argument, or where you fit into one that is already in progress. You can join an argument like this in a variety of ways. You might urge that women on other campuses should publicize the names of date rapists, because you believe it will deter the offense. Or you might want to argue that the practice should stop because it can result in an innocent man being harmed. A third approach might be to argue for institutions to take a stronger hand, so that women will not believe they have to take matters into their own hands.

Establish Your Authority

Establish your own authority to write about the issue you have chosen. Readers must perceive you as a reliable and trustworthy source of information and positions; otherwise, they will either discount or ignore what you say. If you do a good job of introducing your subject and orienting your readers to it, you will be well on your way to establishing your authority. Authority is difficult to establish in a short space, and is really something that you confirm throughout your argument. At the outset, you can best establish your authority by showing your knowledge of the issue and the positions and information pertinent to it.

You undermine your authority if you take a position that has already been dismissed (arguing that date rape is always the woman's fault, for example), by pressing issues that others believe have been resolved or are obvious (that date rape never happens), or by providing information that is incomplete or wrong.

Effective and Ineffective Beginnings

It might be tempting to begin an argument about date rape this way, by stating a position simply and to the point:

> Men who commit date rape should have their names published so other women will know who they are and not date them.

While this might be an effective opening if everyone in your audience were completely familiar with the issue, it oversimplifies the subject and neglects information that other readers might need. The less your readers know about a subject, the more you will have to say to orient them adequately. A brief beginning like this one may indicate that a writer has done only a superficial audience analysis.

As you plan your introduction, spend some time considering your readers and what they might need. Who will be your readers? Are you writing for school officials, because you want them to take disciplinary action; for legislators who might write a law; or for the public in general, because you want them to realize that a problem exists? Your readers might legitimately ask "What is date rape?" "Why is it important?", and a host of other questions. The one-sentence beginning is inadequate because although it addresses the problem, it does not address an audience.

A revised opening that attempts to avoid the previous problems might be:

> Date rape occurs when a woman is raped during a date by a man she knows. It is a crime, the same as any other type of rape, but the police and others don't often take it seriously. So women should take matters into their own hands and let others know who the rapists are, so they won't date them.

This version is an improvement, because it defines date rape. But it does little else. In fact, it may provoke more questions, such as "How do you know it's rape?" and "Aren't the offenders punished? What happens to them?" Nor does this beginning provide much context for the subject of date rape or the rejection of police action. The writer assumes that readers will understand the issue and agree or sympathize with his or her position. An effective introduction to an argument needs to address these questions as well as the complexity of the issue itself. It might go something like this:

> Date rape recently received some much needed attention when women on one university campus began writing the names of accused rapists on the walls of campus restrooms. They justified their actions by saying that neither the university nor the local police were taking the problem of date rape seriously enough, and that accused rapists were not being punished for their acts. So the women took matters into their own hands, arguing that the only way to protect other women from these men was to identify them publicly. There are several problems with this approach. Posting names in public without filing charges violates several basic principles of the U.S. Constitution, including the presumption of innocence, the right to be confronted by one's accusers, and the right to due process. These protections are important because it is possible that a woman may consent to sex but later have second thoughts and accuse her partner of rape. It is also possible that a man who has done nothing could be accused because someone doesn't like him. The problem needs a solution that recognizes its complexity, that protects women from rape, and at the same time guarantees men their right to due process. As with fires, prevention may be easier than cleaning up the mess afterward. Preventing date rape will require changing the attitudes and the dating behaviors of both men and women.

This proposed introduction addresses the kinds of questions that earlier attempts ignored. It introduces the subject adequately because it attempts to explain a complex issue as fully as possible. This introduction assumes that its readers know what date rape is, and thus shows that the writer has some sense of who the readers will be: the men and women involved in date rape. Only they, the writer says, have enough control over the situation to make the necessary changes.

The third beginning offers a much more complex and interesting position than the first two. The first two simply assert that date rape is wrong and that women are right to take matters into their own hands. The third beginning turns the issue into an interesting, complex question that requires inquiry, analysis, and argument. It raises questions about protection for both parties, places the women's actions in the context of constitutional principles, and ends by clearly placing responsibility for change not on institutions or the law, but on the people involved. It introduces the issue, suggests what is at stake, takes a position, and indicates the kinds of reasoning and support that will be used to develop the argument.

APPLICATIONS

1. Choose three or four subjects that you know a lot about. For each one, state an arguable position and then expand that position into an introduction for an argument.
2. Read the beginnings of several arguments printed in this book and evaluate how well they actually introduce their subjects. Select one that you believe is especially ineffective and another that you believe is especially good, and present them, along with the reasons for your evaluation, to a group of your classmates. After you have discussed these introductions in your group, revise one of them to improve it.
3. Read the beginnings of at least four arguments printed elsewhere in this book and, for each one, make a list of the assumptions that the writer makes about readers. When you have finished these lists, share them with a group of classmates and discuss how each could speak more directly to its readers.

Developing Your Argument: Writing the Middle

Once your argument is under way, your next job is to develop the major points of the argument and provide support for your position. In order to do this, you will need to:

- Provide evidence, reasons, and reasoning to support your position.
- Show that you understand the other positions that exist (there must be at least *one* other position; otherwise there is no issue to argue).
- Be able to anticipate and respond (in advance) to objections your readers might raise to your position.
- Show the consequences of accepting the various positions, and explain why your position or solution is preferable to the others. This explains your choice and shows your readers why they should make the same choice you have made.

To support your position you will rely on what you already know as well as information that you gather through research. If you know enough to take a position, then you should already know a great deal about your subject. Try to resist the impulse to run to the library and begin looking for information about the subject you want to write about. Instead, let your own ideas take shape before you start reading what others have to say. Reading others' arguments first can be confusing and may cause you to lose sight of your own position and why you hold it. After you have clarified your own thinking, and perhaps even written a draft of your argument, then consult other sources.

Delaying your research will have two advantages. The first is that you will know where your own views fit when you encounter other arguments; the second is that your search for information can be focused and precise. In the process of thinking through your position and doing a provisional draft, you will discover what information you need. Thus, instead of looking for all available information about your subject, you can focus on what you need to know.

This is not to say that you cannot, or will not, change your mind in light of the information you discover. The basis of all argument and critical thinking is that it is possible to change a mind, including one's own, with information and reasoning. But, when you are initially entering an argument you are often attempting to set the foundation of your own position and articulate it as fully and carefully as possible. That's frequently difficult enough to do by itself, let alone at the same time that you are attempting to understand and evaluate the positions that others have taken. So first concentrate on discovering your own position, and then investigate what others have said.

For example, much has been written in recent years about date rape. Just locating and reading the information available in the library about this subject might take a week or more (assuming that you have other things to do as well). At the end of that week you will probably have a collection of photocopies and quotations from the sources you have read. You may even be tempted to look through those sources for quotable passages that can be stitched together into a paper. Of course, the resulting paper will not be your own; its ideas and many of its words will belong to your sources. And you may still not have formulated your own position.

Instead, tackle the subject directly, without the help of sources. The example beginning in the previous section established the following points that need to be developed and supported as the argument about date rape progresses:

> Simply writing the names of offenders on restroom walls (or publicizing them in other ways) will not solve the problem of date rape, for any number of reasons.
>
> Simply publicizing names of supposed offenders goes against a number of legal principles that are fundamental to public life in the United States.
>
> Preventing date rape (if that is the goal) is really a matter of changing the attitudes and actions of the men and women who are dating.

By developing these three points it will be possible to see whether they can contribute to the argument and discover the additional information that will be necessary to complete the argument. It's possible, of course, that some of these points may not lead anywhere and so will not appear in the final version. It's also possible that, in the process of developing these points, other ideas will arise and need to be included. The purpose of doing a draft is to discover what the subject has to offer and whether it will actually turn into an argument.

The first point, that writing date rapists' names on restroom walls is ineffective, might be developed by suggesting that women may not see the names and may date them anyway, that the men may move away, and that the men may be innocent. This method will work only for the women who are on campus, see the names, and believe the accusation. So, writing names on walls of women's rooms will not necessarily prevent date-rape nor see that the rapists are punished. To the extent that the women involved are interested in protecting women in general, they will have to go beyond writing names on walls.

The second point is that simply publishing the names of alleged rapists goes against well-established legal principles. Developing this point will require the writer to address the constitutional principles that people have the right to be considered innocent until proven guilty, the right to due process, the right to a fair trial by a jury of peers, and the right to confront their accusers. There may also be applicable civil laws about slander, libel, defamation of character, and other offenses. In addition, there is always the possibility that someone could be falsely accused. To say this in no way minimizes the seriousness of date rape. The conclusion here is that simply writing names on walls sidesteps the legal processes and safeguards that society has put in place for the protection of all. It may be that the women involved believe they are justified in stepping outside a legal system that they regard as unresponsive. Any argument about this subject may need to anticipate and respond to this attitude.

Finally, the third point, that attitudes and behaviors must change, can be developed by showing that men's attitudes toward women are partly responsible for date rape, and these attitudes need to be explored, along with ways of changing them. Where do those attitudes come from? Do men expect sex as part of a date? If so, why? And why do some of them get violent? Is their behavior part of a general attitude that it's alright to mistreat women? Also, it's possible that men and women do not know how to communicate effectively with each other about their intentions. Many men may believe that women really mean *yes*, no matter what they say, and women may feel intimidated into cooperating, even though they would prefer not to.

These three points are not yet a draft; much remains to be done. But even at this stage they point to the information you will need to collect to support your position. That is, each one points directly to the information that will be required to support it. Your search for this information will be easier because you have stated your own position: You know that you will argue that the people involved must change their attitudes and actions in order to prevent date rape.

Support for an argument usually fits into one of the following categories:

1. *Facts, data, and information.* For example, in order to convince your readers that date/acquaintance rape is a serious problem, you need to show them how often it happens, who is most likely to be involved. You will also need to examine the contention that date rape goes unpunished by conventional means, and provide available information about prosecutions, convictions, acquittals, and disciplinary actions at schools. As part of your discussion of prosecution, you will need to explain how the law regards date rape and what

penalties it provides. Because you argue against vigilantism, you will need to explain the protections that are available to any person accused of a crime.

2. *Examples and illustrations.* Sometimes an example or illustration is more effective than facts and figures. For example, to illustrate men's attitudes toward women and sex, you might talk with people you know, or even use a story you remember. Perhaps you have known someone who believes that women want sex with every man they date. Describe that person and his attitudes. Let him speak for you. It might also be effective to use a narrative to illustrate the situational factors that influence date rape, even though these could also be listed as facts or data. A story about a specific event could have a powerful effect on your readers, showing them how they put themselves in situations that result in date rape.

3. *Expert testimony.* Experts are people who have authority over a subject because they have studied it or experienced it first hand. Experts bring different perspectives to a subject or situation. A person who has experienced date rape, as either victim or rapist, brings the unique authority of personal experience to the situation. Victims can explain what happened, how it felt, and the after-effects. Offenders can explain how and why they did what they did, how they felt. But personal experience can be limiting, because it is confined to a single person's experiences. A sociologist who has studied a great many instances of date rape will be able to provide a profile of the typical situation, victim, or rapist. A counselor who has worked with victims or offenders will be able to discuss the consequences of date rape for both parties.

The information that you need should be relatively easy to find. For example, a quick review of a copy of the U.S. Constitution will provide all of the necessary information about the legal rights of the accused. You will not need to discuss these in detail, and it will be sufficient to mention them in passing. A quick search in a standard periodical index such as the *Readers' Guide* or in a computerized database should yield several relatively recent articles that will provide other needed information. Look under "date rape," or "acquaintance rape," or "rape—date" in these resources. The general heading of "rape," might reveal a great deal of information about rape, but not much of it will contribute directly to your argument. For information about local or state laws, you can contact your local police department or district attorney's office. For a complete discussion of this type of research, see Chapters 7 and 8.

In most cases, no single type of support is more important than any other type. Support that consists of all facts and data may be accurate but dull and difficult to understand. Using all examples might be unconvincing because they are individual rather than representative. Experts are important, but using them too much may result in your argument being a long string of quotations. So it's important to balance the types of support you use instead of relying exclusively on one type or another.

APPLICATIONS

1. Select one of the beginnings you wrote earlier in this chapter. Identify four or five points you can develop to support this beginning, and explain how you will develop each point. List the information you will use to support each point (or describe the kind of information you will need to use).
2. Read three or four of the arguments printed in this book. Look especially at how writers provide support. Identify main points, facts and information, examples and illustrations, expert testimony, and other types of support that may be present. How would you improve the support that the authors provide? When you have finished your analysis, present your results to a group of your classmates.

Endings: Wrapping Things Up

Arguments should not just stop. Readers will expect you to provide some type of ending, to wrap things up for them and remind them of where they began and how far they have come with you. Conclusions are also a good place to state your case, in brief, one last time, or emphasize something you want your readers to remember. The end of your presentation, regardless of its format, will receive special emphasis simply because of its position. It is important to take advantage of that emphasis.

- Conclusions signal that you have said all that you have to say, at least for now. Sometimes they do this quite obviously, with phrases such as "In conclusion," or "The evidence leads us to the following conclusions."
- Conclusions let readers know where they have arrived. Your readers may have just been through a complex discussion with you, and they may need to review where they began and

where you have brought them. This is the place to offer them the single idea or point you would like to leave them with. For example, the argument about date rape might conclude by reemphasizing the initial position that individuals, not police departments, prosecutors, and universities, must take responsibility for preventing date rape.

- Conclusions provide readers with a brief recap of the reasons and the reasoning process that led to the position you want your readers to adopt or consider. This can provide the connective thread that ties the various parts of your argument together. This is not a section-by-section summary, but a highlighting of what is important. For example, the conclusion to the argument about date rape might remind readers of the original goal, protecting women by preventing date rape, and show how the various actions that people have taken do not accomplish that goal.

- Conclusions can ask that readers do something, that they modify their beliefs or their actions. At the end of an argument about date rape, you might ask your readers (in this case, the people who are at risk) to examine their own dating behavior and make decisions about how to change it to protect themselves.

- Conclusions can look to the future, outlining the next step or showing the consequences (and advantages) of adopting your position. For example, you might suggest that date rape is easier to prevent than to prosecute, and point to a future in which it has been virtually eliminated because people have changed their dating behaviors and their attitudes and have learned to communicate their intentions to each other.

Few conclusions will do all of these tasks, but an effective conclusion will accomplish most of them in one form or another.

APPLICATIONS

1. Look closely at four or five arguments printed in this book, paying special attention to the conclusions. How many different kinds of endings do you find? Are they effective? Choose several that you believe are effective and ineffective and present them to a group of your classmates. Explain your evaluations.
2. Write at least three conclusions for one of the arguments you have been developing through this chapter.

Conclusion

Writing an argument is in many ways like writing anything else. You need to concentrate on providing an identifiable structure that will allow your readers to follow your reasoning from beginning to end.

- Effective beginnings introduce subjects thoroughly, orient readers to the situation, identify the central issues and questions, and suggest the main points that the argument will cover.

- Effective middles develop the points introduced at the beginning. They do this by providing reasons, information, and reasoning to serve as support.

- Effective conclusions may review the argument, restate a main point or position, or ask readers for a specific action.

Questions and Activities

1. Work with a small group of your classmates to identify a local or campus issue that you believe needs to be addressed. After you discuss the issue, each member of the group should write a brief (one or two page) individual argument. Read these arguments aloud to the group and discuss how they could be consolidated into a single argument.

2. Select an editorial or OP-Ed column from a national newspaper such as the *New York Times* or the *Washington Post*. Look closely at its structure. How does it begin? How is its middle related to its beginnings? How does the writer connect the conclusion with the beginning and middle? What changes would you make to improve the way this argument is structured?

Suggestions for Writing

1. Write a complete draft of an argument that you have been working on throughout this chapter.

2. Identify a local or campus issue that you believe should be receiving more (or less) attention from the public, the media, or both. Write an argument in which you support the position that this issue should receive more attention.

CHAPTER FOUR

Pro and Con: Understanding Differences

This chapter focuses on pro/con arguments as a place to begin learning about argument as a sustained interaction between you and your readers. All arguments have more than one position; if they did not, they would not be arguments. Pro/con arguments offer a convenient place to begin looking at argument as more than stating one's own position. Pro/con arguments reduce an issue to two sides that are sometimes mutually exclusive, and they ask readers to choose between these positions as though other alternatives did not exist.

Pro/con arguments also show that the different positions may be equally plausible and have an equal chance of being right. So the purpose of argument is not so much to decide which position is right and which is wrong, but to provide a way of choosing between two positions that may seem equally attractive. That is why choosing a position is sometimes so difficult. Remember, argument thrives in situations where there are no obvious answers or decisions.

Finally, this chapter shows you how to summarize other arguments as a way of understanding them and planning your own response.

Before you read this chapter, write brief responses to the following:

1. Identify an issue on which you have taken a relatively strong position. Summarize your own position as well as one that might oppose yours in a pro/con argument.
2. Identify an argument that you believe has two clear-cut sides. Summarize each side briefly and then state a third position that seems as plausible or attractive as the first two.

47

Motorcycle Helmet Laws: Pro and Con in Action

For at least the past twenty years there has been a vigorous debate about whether motorcyclists should be required to wear helmets. On one side of this debate, state legislators, some police and emergency workers, the insurance industry, safety advocates, and others have been pressing for laws that would require motorcyclists to wear helmets when they ride. Their primary reason for taking this position is safety. They believe statistics show that motorcyclists who wear helmets do not receive as many fatal or permanently disabling injuries when they are involved in accidents. They also believe that society at large has an interest in protecting the lives of its citizens, including motorcyclists, and thus has the right to make laws that require people to protect themselves.

Wearing a protective helmet might appear at first glance to be an obvious bit of common sense to which everyone would agree, and thus it should not be arguable. But large numbers of motorcyclists have refused to wear helmets voluntarily and have opposed laws requiring helmets. They argue that the states have no business requiring them to wear helmets, that it is their right to decide whether to risk fatal or disabling injuries. In addition, they say that helmets restrict their vision and thus are unsafe, and that helmets interfere with the very sense of freedom that led them to ride motorcycles to begin with.

Of course, the cliche is that there are two sides to everything. Differences make argument possible. But it's not necessarily true that just because the positions are different, one must be right and the other wrong, although the immediate temptation might be to see them that way. Wearing a motorcycle helmet may seem so eminently sensible that those who advocate mandatory helmet laws might appear to be right, and the motorcyclists wrong. But the motorcyclists deserve a chance to make their case, even though it may not seem at first that much of a case can be made for their position.

People reach different conclusions about an issue because they have different experiences, values, and beliefs. It's not that one person understands the situation better than the others, or that one is better informed. In fact, different positions are usually based on the same information. The differences arise from different interpretations of the information. In fact, the absence of a clear-cut wrong or right side is the dilemma that creates an argument. Most often, people must choose not between positions that are right or wrong, but between positions that are equally plausible or reasonable.

Right and wrong are absolute judgments. They apply most easily in closed, rule-governed systems. Math is such a system: If you follow the prescribed rules, you will get the correct answer. Right and wrong also apply when there is widespread agreement among the members of a community or group. When there are no rules, or little agreement, and different positions appear to be equally plausible or reasonable, given the evidence that is available, then people must attempt to make the best decision possible given the choices available and the situation that exists. Thus, any attempt to resolve the question of compulsory helmet laws will not have the luxury of deciding what is right or wrong. Instead, any attempt to enter the argument and resolve the questions depends on a careful, thorough analysis of the issue and the positions that have been offered.

Values in Conflict

This argument about motorcycle helmet laws shows that people on opposite sides of an argument do not necessarily argue the same examples or data, and they may often appear to be arguing completely different issues. Those who say that helmets should be required are arguing that society has a right, and perhaps even an obligation, to protect life. They cite what they believe to be common-sense statistics to show how easily a person who is not wearing a helmet can be injured, disabled, or killed. They believe they are offering a common-sense argument that virtually proves itself. They may find it difficult to understand why anyone would disagree with them.

Those who oppose helmet laws do not dispute the safety factor or the statistics about injuries and deaths. Those who oppose the law may need to begin by attempting to show that their position is at least as plausible and makes as much sense as requiring helmets. They will probably not get very far with the assertion that helmets don't save lives or prevent injuries. The data here are clearly against them. At best, they may come up with examples of cyclists being hurt because they were wearing helmets that restricted their vision. Instead, in order to show that their position deserves equal consideration, they will have to redefine the issue and focus on some point other than injury. They might shift the argument from safety to personal freedom. This would allow them to argue that helmet laws are an unwarranted, unjustified, possibly illegal restriction of their freedom to make decisions for themselves.

This shift in direction will force those who favor helmet laws to argue in favor of restricting personal freedom, rather than specifically for helmet laws. As a result, the argument will focus on whether people should be required to take precautions to save their own lives, or society should force them to do so. Evidence of increased safety will still have a place in the argument, but it will not be the central issue.

Thus, the choice between helmet laws and no helmet laws is not a choice between right and wrong. Rather, the choice becomes a matter of deciding which set of values will be more important. The choice is one of setting priorities, choosing which set of values will govern our beliefs and actions.

APPLICATIONS

1. Working in a group of three or four, select a film, book, music group, concert, record or other performance. Each person in the group should find a review of the performance you choose and provide a copy to each member of the group. Read each review and pay special attention to the values it evokes to make its points. Then discuss the reviews in your group. Which values do the reviews share? Which do they not share? Do the reviews address the same issues, or does each review seem to have its own agenda?
2. Based on your own experience, identify an argument or controversy in which people using the same data have reached different positions. Summarize the situation, the information available to both sides, and the positions. Then explain how each side reached its position.

Stating Opposing Positions Accurately

Once you have identified the other position in an argument, you will need to state it as thoroughly and accurately as you can. Giving complete and accurate summaries of positions that are not your own, and that you may disagree with, can actually help your own argument. Remember that you are attempting to influence your readers to agree with you as you present your own reasons for choosing between available positions. Because of this, your readers will expect you to give them an accurate and complete account of the positions that are available. If you do not do this, your readers will have incomplete information and may also come to distrust you if they discover that you are presenting incomplete or inaccurate information. On the other hand, they will respect you for accuracy and thoroughness when they see that you represent other positions accurately and completely. This should encourage them to listen sympathetically to your own position and the support you offer for it.

For example, an accurate summary of the antihelmet law position among motorcyclists might go something like this:

> Many motorcyclists oppose laws that would force them to wear helmets. They do not dispute the statistics that show helmets preventing or significantly reducing fatal and disabling injuries in motorcycle accidents, though some believe helmets restrict their vision. While granting the safety factor, they argue that laws making helmets mandatory are an unwarranted, perhaps illegal intrusion into their privacy and their right to make decisions for themselves.

An accurate statement of the prohelmet law position might be like this:

> Society has the right and the obligation to protect people who will not protect themselves from obvious dangers. Available statistics show that motorcycle helmets significantly reduce the possibility that a rider will be killed or seriously injured. Advocates of helmet laws argue that the safety factor alone makes requiring helmets the only responsible course of action for society at large. In addition, they argue that society has the right to protect itself and its assets (medical and emergency care, insurance, productivity) against the acts of people who will not protect themselves.

Note that both statements are straightforward, serious, and thorough. The summaries make every attempt to state each position accurately and give it the seriousness it would claim for itself.

Summarize Arguments

In addition to stating the positions in an argument, it will also be helpful to summarize the support for those positions. By forcing you to summarize both sides of an argument, these summaries will help you understand the issue as a whole rather than just one side of it. The summaries can later become part of your own argument as you establish your credibility with your readers by showing that you understand both sides of the argument. Summaries need not be elaborate or complex. They simply need to state briefly and accurately the main points of the other argument. For example, the

following summaries address the arguments for and against motorcycle helmet laws.

In Favor of Mandatory Helmet Laws: People who argue in
favor of mandatory motorcycle helmet laws have seen research
that shows helmets drastically reduce the risk of fatal or disabling injuries in accidents. They believe that these results
make it obvious that anyone who rides a motorcycle should
wear a helmet. They understand that some riders do not want
to wear helmets. They do not dispute the safety statistics, but
argue that helmet laws are an unfair, and perhaps illegal restriction of their personal freedoms. In response, supporters of laws
argue that governments have an inherent interest in preserving
life. They cite the numerous other ways in which governments
interfere with their citizens, freedoms, including health laws,
highway design, nutrition, speed limits, auto safety features, to
mention only a few. They also cite the costs of treating and
rehabilitating people who have been injured in serious accidents, the loss of productivity as a result of those injuries,
families left without support, increased costs of insurance and
medical care, and other factors, to support their position that
government has a responsibility to protect all of its citizens
from the consequences of the behavior of a few.

Opposing Mandatory Helmet Laws: People who oppose
mandatory helmet laws do not deny that they reduce the risk
of fatal or disabling injuries, though some riders insist that
helmets interfere with their vision. Instead, they oppose these
laws as an unwarranted and possibly illegal intrusion into their
privacy and a restriction of their freedom. They believe it is
their business if they want to risk being killed or permanently
injured, and that government has no business attempting to
protect them from themselves. If they are hurt or killed, they
are prepared for the consequences. Motorcyclists don't ride
their bikes to be safe. They are aware that cycles are dangerous,
and that riding without helmets makes them even more dangerous. If they were concerned with safety they would not ride at
all. They ride because of the feeling of freedom it gives them.
They are free spirits, and helmets diminish their sense of freedom. Some of them are prepared to die before giving up that
freedom. Living on the edge between life and death brings sat-

isfactions they can't find anywhere else. They are also rebels of
a sort. They like being unconventional and doing things that
other people do not do. Being forced to wear a helmet offends
their rebellious nature. They would rather be free and different
than safe.

Effective summaries are a valuable part of your argument:

- They help you understand your subject more thoroughly, and
  may show you how to write a more effective argument of
  your own.
- They help you situate your own argument in a rich context
  of other positions, evidence, and reasoning.
- They show your readers that you are in command of the
  subject of your argument.
- They show your readers, the people whose actions and beliefs
  you are trying to influence, that you are well informed about
  your subject, and that you understand the alternatives to
  your own position.
- They show people who hold different positions that you
  understand their point of view. This might make them more
  likely to attempt to understand your position.

Writing summaries can give you new insights. Summarizing
the two positions about helmet laws may have called attention to
a subject or a line of reasoning that you were not aware of before.
For example, the summaries presented here show that the issue of
safety is really secondary, and that effective arguments on both
sides will have to address the question of whether the government,
or society at large, has an interest in protecting life and preventing
people from engaging in unsafe behavior. Also, you might discover
that those who favor mandatory helmet laws are not really interested in motorcyclists, but are trying to protect themselves and
society from having to bear the costs of lost productivity, increased
medical and insurance expenses, emergency services, long-term
care, and other expenses that arise as a result of fatal and disabling
injuries. The summary should also show clearly that the argument
will need to address motorcyclists' concern that the laws restrict
their freedom. These few examples show how effective summaries
can show you how to address other positions and how to construct
your own argument.

Always Use Positive Statements

Always take care that your summaries do not insult, belittle, or reject the other positions or the arguments that support them. Don't simply dismiss a position by saying it's wrong, or silly, or stupid. Like this:

> The misguided opponents of motorcycle helmet laws apparently can't read, or they would know that wearing a helmet increases the possibility that they will survive a serious crash. They want to be free, with wind in their hair and bugs in their teeth. They are not only stupid, they are selfish. They don't seem to care that they have cost responsible riders (who wear helmets) thousands of dollars in increased medical and vehicle insurance premiums.

This statement is an insult. Summarizing a position or an argument in this way can damage your own argument in several ways:

- It invites readers to suspect that the information you present will be slanted and possibly inaccurate.
- It invites readers to give your position the same negative treatment.
- It invites readers to question the accuracy of other statements that you make.
- It shifts the level of the argument from inquiry and discussion to insult and sarcasm.

In contrast, a fair, complete summary of the positions and arguments that differ from yours can help your argument in a variety of ways:

- Readers will see you as informed and fair.
- Readers will see that you have nothing to fear from disclosing a complete and accurate account of other positions—that is, your own success does not depend on hiding or distorting what others believe.
- Readers may be more inclined to pay attention to your position and give it a fair hearing when they see that you are fair to others.
- They help you understand your subject more thoroughly and may show you how to write a more effective argument of your own.
- They give your own argument a rich context of other positions, evidence, and reasoning.

- They show your readers, the people whose actions and beliefs you are trying to influence, that you are well informed about your subject and that you understand the alternatives to your own position.

APPLICATIONS

1. Select one set of pro/con arguments printed in this textbook. Write summaries of the position and support provided in each one. Then, based on your summaries, explain where the two sides share common ground and where they disagree.
2. Choose an issue about which you have strong feelings or a well-defined position. Summarize your own position and your reasons for holding it, and then summarize a position that disagrees with yours.

From Summary to Plan

SUMMARIES SHOW HOW TO ENTER AN ARGUMENT

A thorough, accurate summary of the issue, the positions that have been taken, and the arguments that support each one can result in a plan for your argument. Many writers have difficulty deciding just where to begin, perhaps because they do not know how to enter the ongoing argument. Sometimes they do not know why to begin. After all, what would be the point of entering an argument simply to say "I agree with X." It is considerably more satisfying to make a new contribution to an argument, to take it somewhere it has not been before. A thorough, accurate summary can help you identify that entry point. Summaries show where different positions agree and disagree, and these are often effective starting points.

For example, both sides of the motorcycle helmet controversy will probably agree that helmets can save lives. Neither side will offer a significant argument on this point, so taking the position that helmets save lives may not be a good place to start. If no one will challenge a position, that is a sign that most people regard it as obvious and not really arguable. But the two sides do not agree about whether government should attempt to protect people by saying what they can or cannot do. Those who favor helmet laws obviously believe that government has a right, perhaps a responsibility, to protect its citizens, even from themselves. Those who oppose helmet laws obviously disagree with this position and assert their own right to do whatever they please. Because this is an important issue to both sides, it may also be the place to begin.

SUMMARIES POINT TO SUPPORT

Effective summaries also point to the information and evidence that will be necessary to support an argument. Those who believe that helmet laws are an intrusion into personal freedoms will need to find examples of other personal freedoms that society at large protects from regulation. The most obvious possibilities are those rights guaranteed in the Bill of Rights, such as freedom of speech and religion. Is it possible to maintain that refusing to wear a helmet is a type of political expression protected by the First Amendment? Or is that a bit far-fetched. It will also be important to give examples of other aspects of private life that are not regulated in some way.

Those who favor mandatory helmet laws will need to show, among other things, that government intrudes into and regulates private life in a variety of ways, and that such intrusions have been widely accepted and regarded as legal. For example, laws regulate a wide variety of behaviors related to safety, including auto safety standards, seatbelt use, medications, suicides and living wills, to mention only a few. So it might be argued that requiring motorcycle helmets is another example of the well-established principle that governments may act to protect their citizens, even from themselves.

Also, because it has raised the question of costs to society in general, this argument will have to provide information about how much it actually costs when someone is injured, killed, or disabled in a motorcycle accident. Effective support might give statistics that show the costs to individuals and to the economy of lost productivity, of supporting a family whose wage-earner is dead or unable to work, of medical care and increased insurance premiums. For example, evidence might include an estimate of the costs of caring for a head trauma victim over a period of twenty to thirty years. It might even be possible to estimate the intangible costs of the emotional stress of injury and recovery. All of this information, and more, will be necessary to show that requiring helmets is not an unusual or illegal intrusion into private life but an attempt by society to protect itself by regulating those who would endanger it by risky behavior.

These brief examples show clearly that entering an argument directly, by choosing and supporting one side or the other, is not the only course open. Frequently, an indirect entry is both more interesting and more fruitful, especially if it can uncover perspectives that have not been introduced. A direct entry into the continuing argument about motorcycle helmet laws would require that we pick a side for or against helmet laws. The subsequent argument might in most cases be a rehash of reasons and facts already presented and thus familiar to all.

But careful analysis and summary have shown that it is possible to enter the argument from a completely different direction by focusing on something that both sides regard as an issue. This new perspective is valuable in two ways: It makes the argument itself more interesting and, by increasing the number of positions and possible solutions, it may lead to a better solution.

Getting Beyond Pro and Con

Pro/con arguments provide a convenient way to simplify large, complex questions into a manageable format of two positions. But only rarely does a dualistic format adequately represent most issues or questions. But almost all arguments have more than two sides or two positions, and to reduce them to a two-sided format usually results in oversimplifying the issue and omitting important information. It is rarely, if ever, possible to be on one side or the other of a question, or simply for or against something.

Experience suggests that the best resolutions result from exploring the complexity of a situation rather than simplifying it. Attempting to see an issue as a complex question with many sides, and many possible positions, leads to a more thorough understanding of the issue itself. This deeper understanding leads to a better solution than would be possible if you were choosing between two positions. Examining multiple positions forces you to raise more questions, examine more information, and look at a greater variety of reasoning than would be available in a two-sided argument. For these reasons, people who want to write effective arguments will avoid the apparent simplicity of dualistic pro/con arguments and actively seek the complexity that comes with multiple positions and perspectives.

For example, the following editorials about the U.S. Bill of Rights take opposing positions. One side insists that the protections guaranteed in the Bill of Rights are being attacked and eroded by groups that do not want to tolerate dissent. The other side insists that the rights guaranteed in the Bill of Rights are intact and safe from erosion, despite a few reasonable limitations for the common good. Read the editorials before you move on to the discussion that follows.

Bill of Rights under Siege

USA TODAY

Forget the flag.

Forget the Capitol, the White House, all the armies Congress ever funded, all the laws it ever made. If you truly want to honor the USA, celebrate instead the document that turns 200 Sunday: the Bill of Rights.

Those first 10 amendments to the Constitution are the very essence of this country—and they need your help.

They're unique. Almost all governments begin by defining their own powers. The Bill of Rights defines government's limits, giving people rights to speak, worship and live as they choose.

For those lacking such assurances, history is a long procession of war and pain—all because societies couldn't tolerate dissent. The Bill of Rights has been America's saving grace simply because it ensures that Americans can tell their government to go to hell.

Yet this citadel is under heavy siege—from within. Mothers outraged over rock lyrics find the First Amendment's free-speech guarantee nettlesome—as do college radicals who'd bar ultraconservatives from speaking on campus.

In the name of doing God's work through the public schools, parents seek to strip away protections that make religion a matter of individual choice.

People trying to wring out a drug-soaked society decry Fourth Amendment curbs on police searches—the same curbs that keep government agents from walking into your house uninvited.

The Supreme Court, convinced that criminal suspects get too many advantages, has bled the "middle amendments" that regulate the police and mandate fair treatment for the accused.

"We love the Bill of Rights," say too many. "Just read it our way."

That's dangerous thinking. These 10 amendments are the ligaments that hold this contentious nation together and let it stride forward. Letting them atrophy—any of them—would cripple us all.

Bill of Rights in Fine Shape

BRUCE FEIN

As Mark Twain would have remonstrated, reports of the death of the Bill of Rights are vastly exaggerated.

Free-speech protections are thriving. Flag burning, publication of rape victims' names and Cecil B. DeMille-like televised trials are *au courant;* disclosures of classified intelligence-agency covert operations abound, fabrication of small defamatory lies by the press are beyond legal redress.

Last Tuesday, the Supreme Court unanimously overturned New York's "Son of Sam" law that offered crime victims a reasonable opportunity to claim earnings derived by criminals writing about their criminality. Only an understudy to Rip Van Winkle could believe the First Amendment is faltering.

Criminal-justice safeguards of the Fourth, Fifth and Sixth amendments stand unimpaired. Random drug testing is permitted only for significant health, safety or law enforcement reasons, akin to searching passengers and luggage to assure air transportation safety. Evidence intentionally seized in violation of the Constitution is excludable at trial. Suspects must be provided a battery of legal warnings prior to interrogation, and any psychologically or physically coerced confession is inadmissible.

The accused enjoys the right to confront and cross-examine accusers, with narrow exceptions for the testimony of allegedly abused children. The opportunity to challenge conviction is virtually endless if there is a non-frivolous claim of innocence. Should the Bill of Rights be criticized for making criminal trials a determination of guilt or innocence instead of social engineering of utopia?

By contriving concern over imaginary weakenings of the Bill of Rights, USA TODAY undermines the credibility that may be needed to reprove a genuine impairment if one should occur.

This two-sided argument reduces the complex history of the Bill of Rights, and the political and legal philosophy that it embod-

"Bill of Rights in Fine Shape" reprinted by permission of Bruce Fein.

ies, to such relatively simple dimensions that it is difficult to disagree with either side. It is true that the Bill of Rights has always been a focus of debate in the political and legal life of the United States. Some people believe that it goes too far in protecting actions that they find objectionable or believe are actually harmful to the society at large. Consider, for example, recent debates about prayer at public school functions and burning the U.S. flag as a form of political protest. Some people believe that the Bill of Rights should not prohibit prayer while it permits flag burning. They would refuse protection to actions that they consider unpatriotic or detrimental to society at large. They believe, for example, that it should be easier to convict drug dealers and other criminals. Those who take the other side argue that the personal rights guaranteed in the Bill of Rights, and the dissent they protect, are essential to the political life of the United States.

This type of pro/con arrangement simplifies a complex document with a rich history into a dualistic, yes/no question that encourages people to choose one side or the other within a rather narrowly defined range of possibilities. Whether people believe the Bill of Rights is under assault or perfectly safe will depend on their perspective, political philosophy, and other factors. Each time the Supreme Court decides a case involving the Bill of Rights, each side will see itself as gaining or losing ground in some abstract battle about individual rights vs. the common good.

But nothing is quite as simple as a two-sided argument might suggest. Each provision of the Bill of Rights has its own complex history, both in popular culture and in court. Pro/con arguments reduce this richness and complexity to a simple choice between two quite abstract positions that ask people to agree or disagree with them. You will make a stronger argument if you try to uncover the complexity and richness that the pro/con format obscures. The result will be interesting questions that permit and encourage complexity and depth, rather than the simplistic oppositions of a two-sided argument. This will permit a wider range of choices for a possible solution, which frequently results in a higher-quality decision.

For example, you might do a historical analysis of a single provision of the Bill of Rights, such as the prohibition against "unreasonable search and seizure" or the rights of someone accused of a crime. A historical approach would allow you to chart the differing interpretations of these provisions over time. This, in turn, might show whether there is a clear-cut historical trend toward expanding or restricting a particular provision of the Bill of Rights. It is also possible to argue that simplistic, pro/con arguments obscure more important issues, such as the sometimes profound disagreements in society about some of the provisions of the Bill of Rights.

Conclusion

It is important to understand that people disagree and take different positions on the same issue for reasons that they regard as legitimate and important. Arguing effectively about any issue requires that you understand others' positions and that you be able to present those positions and the arguments for them accurately and completely.

Questions and Activities

1. Identify a widely discussed public issue and summarize at least two positions that oppose or disagree with each other. Then work in a group with other students. Present your summaries and ask members of the group to add to them or contribute additional positions or "sides" to the argument. Revise your summaries to reflect these additional points of view.

2. Using the summaries you wrote in question 1, explain how you would present each position to someone who disagrees with it.

Suggestions for Writing

1. Select an issue that is important to you, one for which you have a well-articulated position. State your position and at least one that opposes it, and summarize the support for each side. Be sure to summarize them accurately, so they will be equally attractive and plausible. Then write the argument that supports your position.

2. Rewrite the argument you just wrote for question 1, but from the opposite side. Show your readers why they should adopt the position that disagrees with yours.

CHAPTER FIVE

Beyond Pro and Con: Multisided Arguments

Pro/con arguments often oversimplify issues by suggesting that it is possible to make a relatively easy, straightforward choice between two opposing sides. But most arguments have more than two sides, and choosing the best among a variety of positions can be difficult and often controversial. The difficulty has its rewards, though, because careful analysis of an issue from a variety of perspectives usually results in better solutions than pro/con arguments can provide. This chapter shows how to analyze multisided arguments that have multiple positions, and explains the role of values in choosing a position and presenting it to others. Effective arguments connect choices with values and urge readers to accept some values as more important than others. In order to argue convincingly you will need to:

- Show that you are aware of the complexity of the argument and the various positions that have been taken.
- Understand the values that support each position.
- Make your own position as attractive as possible by presenting it in the context of the values your audience holds.
- Make other positions less attractive to readers by showing that they do not support the values your readers hold.

Before you read the chapter, respond in writing to the following:

1. Choose an issue or question that is important to you, one that is frequently the subject of discussion and debate and obviously has more than two positions. Summarize the issue itself, and then summarize the various positions that have been taken during the argument. Explain how having a

variety of positions, rather than two opposing positions, can result in a better resolution.

2. How do your values influence the decisions you make? Select an important decision you have made and describe how your value system helped you make that decision.

Developing Multisided Arguments

As you saw in Chapter 4, pro/con arguments oversimplify issues in order to present two clear-cut positions. Since most issues have more than two sides, it is important to learn to analyze multisided arguments with multiple positions. Most pro/con arguments can be developed into multisided arguments by using the following guidelines. In almost all cases you can begin to develop a multisided argument by using what you already know; you do not need to do any research until you have expanded and analyzed the argument as thoroughly as possible on your own.

Read the following brief editorials about gun control and crime; then observe how the questions and approaches that follow can expand this pro/con situation into a multisided argument.

Curb Guns to Curb Slayings

USA TODAY

Around the world, the sounds of gunfire and screams of anguish have become a way of life.

In 1991, in war-torn Yugoslavia, as many as 10,000 died. In Northern Ireland, 36 civilians were killed. In South Africa, 2,000 died.

Here at home, we are at peace. Yet, the body count surpasses that of these bloody war zones.

1991 may have been the deadliest year ever, with an expected 23,700 homicides, up 300 from 1990.

Increasingly, life is too cheap and guns are too prevalent. Child abuse, drug abuse, poverty and neglect are excellent recruiters for this war on our streets.

Drug-related shootings bloody the landscape. Drive-by shootings mow down combatants and bystanders alike. Family feuds are settled with gunfire. Homicide, mostly by guns, is the major killer of black males aged 15 to 24.

This carnage has been considered a big-city plague. But a USA TODAY survey this week shows murder is becoming commonplace on small-town streets and in mid-sized cities.

We can fight back.

Columbus, Ohio, is pushing more values-centered programs in the schools. In Rochester, N.Y., community leaders are calling on people to stop protecting criminals, including relatives. More cops walk beats in New Haven, Conn.

Such efforts are needed; but without stronger efforts to get guns off the streets, these anti-crime measures will misfire.

Cities should expand use of cash-for-guns programs, massive seizures of illegal weapons, and tougher sentencing for gun-toting criminals.

Citizen lobbies must take on the gun lobbies. We need laws requiring waiting periods to allow background checks on gun purchasers. We need laws banning military-style weapons.

Enough is enough. Control the guns. Stop the killing.

Gun Curbs Are No Answer

LARRY PRATT

We are told by those opposed to private gun ownership that the solution to the nation's murder rate is to greatly restrict or ban guns. The assumption, of course, is that we no longer need to rely on privately owned firearms because the police will protect us.

The facts are quite different. Consider that there are only 150,000 police officers on duty at any one time to protect a quarter of a billion Americans. The "thin blue line" is stretched way too thin to be able to provide personal security for individual citizens.

Legally, the police are not required to protect anybody. If they had any such responsibility at all, they could be sued for those few occasions when they behave in a negligent fashion. But one cannot sue and win. Victims of crime have tried to sue the police for negligence during the 120 years or so that we have

---

"Gun curbs are no answer" reprinted by permission of Larry Pratt.

had professional police forces in the USA. The courts consistently rule that the police are not responsible for providing personal protection. Their job is to act as a cleanup crew after the criminal has left.

We could help ourselves and help the police by insisting that the politicians stop designing a criminal justice system friendly to criminals. Specifically, capital punishment should be swift and sure. Other criminals should be forced to compensate their victims.

Another measure that would help would be to restore our three-time-loser laws. This would result in the execution of those convicted of three serious crimes. A Willie Horton should not live to become a campaign issue.

Banning criminals, not guns, is the solution to our crime problem.

The following questions will guide you as you analyze a pro/con argument and expand it into a multisided argument. In this example the questions are applied specifically to arguments about gun control, but they will work equally well with any subject.

What Are Your Reservations about Each Position?

Explain what keeps you from agreeing with one side or the other. In this case, there may be little reason to disagree with either side. Both seem to take reasonable positions. However, the argument for controlling guns does not really show that fewer guns will result in fewer murders. It assumes that people will not adopt other weapons as eagerly as they have adopted guns. Also, this solution treats a symptom, not the cause of the problem. And the proposed solution has not been politically feasible so far. Only a few state and local governments have placed restrictions on guns of the kind advocated here. If a solution is not politically possible, then it's not a solution.

At the same time, it's not entirely convincing to say that a swift and certain death penalty will deter criminals. And the number of people on death row is relatively small compared to 23,700 murders in a single year. Information about the value of the death penalty as a deterrent would be helpful here. Nor does the author indicate what he means when he says the justice system is friendly to criminals. Specific examples here might make his position more attractive. Finally, this author does not speak directly to the other position, because he does not address the role of firearms in murders. Instead, he introduces subjects (such as the role of the police) that may not be pertinent.

What Changes Would You Make in Either Position?

The argument for banning or controlling weapons probably needs to show homicide statistics for countries (preferably democracies) that control weapons, to show that controlling guns reduces the murder rate. This writer also needs to state just how many murders are committed with guns. Most importantly, this writer needs to address how controlling guns could actually be done and how it could be made politically feasible.

The argument against controlling guns might be more effective if it addressed the issue directly by explaining in some detail how controlling guns would *not* reduce the homicide rate. The discussion of the police seems like a digression, except that the author is arguing that people must do for themselves when police cannot do so. This line of reasoning appears to assume that most homicide victims are killed by intruders and criminals with guns. The argument does not discuss the number of people who are killed with the guns they bought for protection.

How Do These Arguments Agree and/or Disagree?

These two arguments obviously disagree about whether controlling guns will reduce the homicide rate. They also disagree about what other policies will affect the homicide rate. The argument favoring gun control mentions a variety of programs including education, increased police patrols, and tougher jail sentences for criminals who use guns, among other measures. The opponent of gun control mentions no programs other than a get-tough policy that focuses on capital punishment as a response to homicide. The argument implies that "swift and sure" executions will deter others who might be considering homicide. The two arguments also disagree about the role of the police. The argument favoring gun control mentions increased police patrols, but the other argument states that protection is not the responsibility of the police. The question of whether it is really a police responsibility to protect citizens might actually be part of another argument.

The arguments agree that the homicide rate is a problem and that criminals who use guns should receive severe sentences. If these arguments share common ground, it is this.

What Common Ground Do the Positions Share?

The central issue of whether guns should be controlled is so central, so important to each side that they will probably never completely agree with each other—unless it could be shown that controlling guns is the definitive way of controlling crime, and perhaps not even then. They might be brought together with the position that criminals who use guns should receive tough, consistent sentences as punishment and as a deterrent to others.

How Can the Issue Be Made More Complex and Interesting?

What other positions or approaches are possible? The two arguments printed here provide a variety of entry points, each of which will improve the possibility of reaching a workable solution— among them:

1. Investigate to determine the number of deaths caused by guns, and the circumstances (accidental, during robberies, domestic disputes, etc.). Based on these statistics, you should be able to argue the effect that gun control would have on the homicide rate.
2. Both arguments call for tougher sentences for criminals who use guns. But neither argument actually gives any information to show that tougher sentences would be effective. It would be useful to approach the issue from this direction and investigate the role of sentencing as a deterrent. For example, some states have passed laws requiring stiff sentences for using guns in crimes. Have these laws had any noticeable effect on crime?
3. Most gun control efforts focus on assault weapons and handguns. Most opponents of gun control envision laws that take guns away from law-abiding citizens. The standard myth is that criminals will always be able to get guns. Does anyone know what kinds of guns are used in crimes and where they come from? Investigating this question might lead to an argument to control certain types of weapons but not others, or it might conclude that there is no real pattern.
4. Is it possible that guns and homicides are distributed differently in society? For example, people who own guns and oppose gun control might have some sort of political power

that would give them influence with lawmakers. Homicide victims could come from groups that have relatively little access to political power. If it were true, this might explain why gun control has been so difficult to enact and enforce. Investigating who the owners, victims, and criminals are might lead to a number of different positions.

5. Opponents of gun control argue that, without their guns, they will be unable to protect themselves from criminals. It would be useful to know whether this is a realistic claim. How often do gun owners actually prevent crimes or protect themselves with their guns? If they do this often, then it will lend weight to the opponents of control. But, if this does not happen often, then it will work against those arguments.

6. Opponents of gun control frequently cite the Second Amendment of the Bill of Rights, which mentions the "right of the people to keep and bear arms." Another way to approach this argument would be to explore the judicial and political history of the Second Amendment. What does it say? Why was it included? What have the courts said about it?

7. Some people are concerned that films and television encourage violence with guns by portraying too much violence and minimizing the damage that guns can do and paying little attention to safety. It would be possible to argue that guns are not really the problem at all, but that we need to change the way they are portrayed in the media.

Certainly other positions exist, and you will sometimes have to do some research to find them. You will find information about doing research in Chapter 8. But, as you can see from this brief list, it's possible to come up with a variety of ideas to generate a more complicated argument based on nothing more than a general awareness of the public issue involved. By generating multiple positions, you make the issue larger and more interesting. It raises more questions, provides more information, and extends the discussion into new areas that the dualistic, pro/con framework did not address. This variety and complexity, of course, make finding a solution or choosing a position more difficult than simply choosing between two positions. But the greater variety of choices may result in making a better choice or decision, because evaluating those choices carefully results in a deeper knowledge of the subject.

APPLICATIONS

1. Select a pro/con argument from those printed in this book (or find your own, if you wish). Summarize the argument and the two positions that have been taken. Then use the analytic schemes shown in this chapter to develop at least two additional positions. When you have done that, explain how the additional positions improve the chances of reaching a workable resolution or agreement.
2. Using a set of arguments from this book (or the argument you analyzed in question 1 above), identify several ways of entering the argument without simply agreeing or disagreeing with, or repeating, an argument that has already been made.

Analyzing Multisided Arguments

Once you have identified the positions in a multisided argument, a careful analysis will prepare you to enter the argument and contribute to it. Your readers will expect you to show that you have examined the widest possible range of positions if they are to accept your assertion that your position represents the best possible choice.

The following questions will help you do that analysis:

1. What is the central issue or question?
2. What is at stake in this argument? What are the consequences of choosing one position rather than another? What will be lost or gained?
3. What are the main positions that have been offered?
4. How do the existing positions agree and/or disagree?

Let's look at each of these questions separately and see how they provide a framework for analyzing the argument about the murder rate and gun control.

What Is the Central Issue or Question?

As presented in the pro/con arguments, the central issue is whether controlling or banning guns will reduce the murder rate in the United States. There are other, subsidiary issues, such as capital punishment, sentencing criminals, and the role of the police, but these are not the central issue.

What Is at Stake? What Are the Consequences of Acting or Not Acting?

This is sometimes difficult to figure out. Sometimes, as in the argument favoring gun control, an argument makes explicit what is at stake: in this case, reducing the number of people murdered in the United States each year by controlling the weapons used to murder them. According to this argument, unless something is done about guns, people will continue to die, perhaps in record numbers. In fact, that appears to be the only justification for controlling guns. The author of the opposing argument says that if guns are controlled, innocent, law-abiding people will be unable to protect themselves from criminals.

Of course, that may not be all that is at stake on either side. In many arguments what is at stake may not be explicit or immediately apparent. You may have to probe to discover the real reason that a person holds a position. For example, some people may want to ban guns because they believe they are evil or tools of violence. Those who oppose any controls on guns may believe that no benefit could outweigh giving up what they see as a constitutional right. Others may believe that controlling guns is contrary to the spirit of individualism and adventure that made the United States a great nation. These are only a few examples of what could be at stake in the argument about gun control.

The point here is that unless you know what is at stake, or what other participants in an argument believe is at stake, it will be difficult to build a convincing argument. You may be addressing important issues, such as the murder rate in the United States, but if your reader is less interested in the murder rate than in the threat to constitutional rights or freedom, you will make very little progress.

What Positions Have Been Taken on This Issue?

Unless you know the positions that have been (or could be) taken in an argument, you will not know how the argument has progressed. Nor will you be able to find a place to enter it with your own ideas. Without knowing how an argument has progressed, a new participant might take a position that other participants have considered and rejected. For example, a newcomer to the gun control debate might focus on the Second Amendment's guarantee of the right to "keep and bear arms." But the U.S. Supreme Court has never interpreted that amendment to apply to personal or private weapons, and this position has never made headway with people who did not accept it to begin with. At the same time, no one has successfully argued that the Second Amendment does not apply to private arms, or that it should be repealed.

Knowing the positions that have been taken in the history of an argument requires research, time in the library finding and reading individual contributions to a debate that has taken place over a period of time. Chapter 7 will cover this process in detail. Only by knowing the various positions and their relationships to each other can you identify the most productive way of entering the argument. For example, you will discover that some positions have been accepted or agreed to, that others have been dropped, and that some are still being actively contended. In the debate about gun control virtually everyone has conceded that some control is both necessary and inevitable. Most states do not allow people to carry firearms, especially concealed firearms, or to shoot them in certain areas.

Joining the Argument

Ongoing arguments are like discussions, and they can extend over a long period of time. Everyone can take a turn, but first it's necessary to know how to get in. In the gun control discussion, several positions remain active. Opponents of gun control argue that gun owners are law-abiding citizens who use their guns safely and do not harm others. They use their weapons, they say, for recreation and personal protection. On the other side, supporters of gun control often contend that gun control would now be a matter of law if it were not for the actions of a powerful "gun lobby" that prevents lawmakers at all levels from acting responsibly. Both of these positions seem to provide points of entry into the debate. For example, you could begin by observing that, since so many crimes are committed with guns, those people who commit the crimes must not actually own the guns they use. In other words, one possible direction for your argument would be to point out that opponents of gun control have created two categories of people: gun owners and criminals (who use guns). You could challenge this as an artificial division and argue that the criminals are gun owners too, and that they need to be controlled.

On the other hand, you could join the debate by investigating the assertion that gun control would be a reality except for the efforts of a powerful lobby. Persons who support gun control need someone to blame for their lack of success, and the gun lobby is both available and vocal. At the same time, the gun lobby may have good reasons to let everyone (opponents and members alike) assume it is as powerful as its opponents say it is. That is, there is some political advantage in having others believe you are tough and powerful.

The more you know about a debate and the positions that have been taken in it, the more likely you are to find a place to enter that debate with an informed, intelligent argument of your own.

How Do Existing Positions Agree and/or Disagree?

You can discover where to enter an argument by establishing how the various positions in the argument are related to each other: where they agree or disagree, where they overlap, and where they are totally opposed. Only rarely does an argument have only two sides. As you saw earlier, pro/con arguments usually oversimplify issues. For example, the debate about gun control consists of more than two absolute and mutually exclusive opposing positions. Some people favor a complete ban of all types of firearms. Some would ban only certain types of weapons. Some would not ban guns, but would require them to be registered. Some oppose any type of control. Some will accept certain controls in order to avoid others. Some opponents of gun control insist on a literal reading of the Second Amendment. Others argue that the problem is not guns, but bad people who use guns, and that almost anything will serve as a weapon.

Analyzing the relationships among the various positions will help you discover where your own views fit into the overall debate, and this should help you enter the debate yourself. Points on which the debate is still active, and areas of partial agreement may provide especially fruitful ways of entering the argument. For example, both sides of the gun control debate share some common ground, despite what they might say to the contrary. For example, both sides appear to have accepted some controls involving some kinds of guns. Machine guns must be licensed, concealed weapons are generally illegal or licensed, and it is generally not possible for minors to buy firearms.

Both sides seem to accept that people who use guns in crimes should receive stiff penalties. This might be a good entry point into the debate. Some states do specify special penalties for using a firearm to commit a crime, and you could investigate whether those laws have had any measurable effect. Depending on the results of your research, you might take one of at least two possible positions. On the one hand, you can argue that these laws are successful in reducing the number of crimes committed with guns and that they should be strengthened. On the other hand, if you find that the laws have had no effect, you can argue that stiffer penalties do not deter people from using guns to commit crimes. In the first case, the result would be to shift the focus away from the issue of controlling guns and toward the way the justice system deals with people who use guns. In the second case, a successful argument would remove the question of jail sentences and penalties from the debate and refocus it on attempting to control guns rather than people.

Obviously, no single argument is likely to resolve or settle an issue as large and complex as gun control. Most arguments extend over long periods of time, especially when they concern issues that people regard as important. Along the way, individual arguments address not only the central issue itself, but also how the debate will be conducted, what will count as evidence, and whether certain beliefs and positions will be considered acceptable in the argument. Individual arguments clarify, define, and explore different parts of the larger issue. Over time, individual arguments can accumulate into a comprehensive position based on extensive information, and this could lead to action. For example, during the 1940s, 1950s and 1960s, there was considerable debate in the United States about segregation, civil rights, and the role of African Americans in our society. Eventually this debate led to the end of legalized racial segregation in education, housing, professional sports, and other aspects of public life. Civil rights laws were passed. African Americans began to appear in the media in new roles. The process was long, slow, and often painful. It is certainly far from over. But the ongoing public debate has had a role in creating change.

APPLICATIONS

1. Select a set of arguments printed elsewhere in this book and analyze it using the following questions from earlier in the chapter:
   a. What is the central issue or question?
   b. What is at stake in this argument? What are the consequences of choosing one position rather than another? What will be lost or gained?
   c. What are the main positions that have been offered?
   d. How do the existing positions agree and/or disagree?

2. Working in a group, select a cluster of arguments printed elsewhere in this book (or use one you or your instructor chooses), and do the following:
   a. Identify the major areas of agreement and disagreement.
   b. Discuss how the areas of agreement point to a specific resolution or consensus.
   c. Discuss how the disagreements lead away from a resolution or consensus.
   d. Identify several ways you can enter the argument.

Using Values to Choose a Position

People usually call on their values to help them establish criteria when they must choose among multiple positions, many of which seem equally correct or plausible. Different values will lead to different choices. Thus, arguments about specific subjects are also arguments about which values will prevail.

For example, elsewhere in this book a cluster of arguments addresses whether sexually explicit language, including courtroom testimony, ought to be permitted on television. Some people may believe the subject is not an issue for argument, but is straightforward and obvious: Some will believe sexually explicit language never belongs on television. others may believe that anything goes. The authors in this section present a variety of positions that show the complexity of the issue and the difficulty of choosing. One major reason for the difficulty is that the argument is not simply about sexually explicit language on television; it is also about values, and values are never simple and straightforward.

One person might argue that sexually explicit language should not be allowed on television, and justify this position by saying that sex is not a subject for public discussion, but is appropriate in private settings only. This position rests on a value system that regards sex as a private matter that should not be talked about publicly, for whatever reason. Others may find sexually explicit language offensive or embarrassing to members of the audience, or fear that children might hear it and either repeat it, or learn things that are not considered appropriate for them. To offer these reasons is to assert values that, in this case, require that we not offend others and that some subjects are not appropriate for children to hear or talk about.

Those who oppose controlling sexually explicit language on television might cite the U.S. Constitution's guarantee of freedom of speech. Others might say that sexually explicit talk on television, including televised trials, can reduce ignorance and raise public awareness of such subjects as rape, AIDS, sexually transmitted diseases, and sexual harassment. These reasons assert the values that ignorance is bad and that people need to be informed about these subjects, even though some may find the language or the subjects themselves offensive.

Thus, an argument about sexually explicit language on television is only partly an argument about sex and television. The various positions taken on this subject suggest differing views of society at large and the values that should govern individual conduct and public affairs. As you choose one position or another, you are also choosing the values you believe provide the best guidance in the situation, or that best express your views about what society should be like.

Values at Work: An Example

The process of choosing a car illustrates the role of values in establishing criteria for making a choice or decision. As you shop and compare cars, you will probably consider a variety of factors, including price, handling, ease and cost of maintenance, economy of operation, safety, status, and any of a number of other features. These features will be the basis of the criteria you establish for your choice, and the criteria you select will usually be based on your values. For example, if money is not a problem, and status is important to you, you might choose a car that carries high status, regardless of its price or its other features. If your values dictate that safety is the most important feature in a car, then you will probably sacrifice other features such as style and economy in order to get the safest car you can afford.

It is usually not possible to find a car, or anything else, that satisfies all possible criteria or that is best for everyone in all situations for all time. Jeeps aren't really appropriate for the prom, and a sports car won't accommodate a family of four. Similarly, it is usually not possible to identify a position in an argument that will satisfy everyone who is concerned with it. The criteria for choosing may often be in conflict—for example, low price and safety may be incompatible criteria when choosing a car, because safety features are expensive. Similarly, the value system that would ban certain kinds of language or certain subjects from television conflicts with the value systems that include freedom of the press and what is sometimes called "the people's right to know." It is seldom possible to completely reconcile these values with each other and reach an agreement that satisfies everyone. Instead, some values will be given precedence over others. One of the purposes of argument is to show how a position and the values it represents are preferable to others.

Presenting Values to Your Audience

When you present your own position and the values associated with it as the best possible choice, you will have to argue in the context of the values that your readers already hold. Only rarely will people abandon their own values in order to adopt new values presented by someone else. Values often are deeply held and can express a person's most important beliefs. Rather than challenging a person's values or attempting to get them to adopt new values, it usually makes more sense to try to show how your position is compatible with the values they already hold.

Argue That Some Values Are More Important Than Others

Most people arrange their values in a hierarchy because they believe that some things are more important than others. For example, safety is often an effective selling point for cars because many people value safety over almost everything else. For this reason, a modest record for safety will often outweigh negative performances in other areas, such as economy, cost, and style. A car that has front seat air bags might outsell other cars that actually perform better in a variety of ways but do not have air bags. In view of this, selling a car without air bags might involve arguing that its other features make it equally safe, or that its other features outweigh its marginal safety performance.

Arguments about other subjects can work in much the same way because all arguments are ultimately about values. Arguments about gun control are in some sense also arguments about the relative importance of human life and gun ownership. Arguments about sexually explicit language on television are also about whether freedom of speech is more important than protecting people from talk they may regard as unpleasant or obscene. The most effective strategy might be to argue for a position that satisfies both sets of values and thus presents something that everyone can agree to. This is often difficult, especially if your readers are likely to see the values as incompatible or even in conflict with each other. For example, you might argue that protecting murder victims by controlling guns is completely consistent with the desire of law-abiding gun owners to protect themselves from burglars. The issue in both situations is human life. An argument to allow the broadcast of sexually explicit language that some people regard as offensive or obscene looks like an argument that individual rights are not important. But it is possible to argue that protecting free speech actually protects the individual, because it guarantees that no one can be censored. Thus, the traditional position has been that a few offensive words are a small price to pay for everyone's freedom of speech.

Choose a Position Based on a Combination of Values

Arguments based on a combination of values are almost always stronger and more convincing than those based on a single value. A reader or opponent can easily reject an argument based on a single value. For example, gun control advocates have never accepted the Second Amendment as the sole justification for private ownership of firearms. The strongest arguments for or against gun ownership will be based on a variety of reasons and values that many readers can accept. Those who favor gun control might cite not only the murder rate, but also:

> The number of convicted felons who have easily bought guns and used them in crimes
> The number of accidents resulting from irresponsible ownership
> Statistics about how often people actually protect themselves with guns

It might also be important to show how the proposed restrictions will not interfere in any way with the ideal, law-abiding gun owner that opponents of gun control mention so often. An argument that addresses this variety of criteria will be much stronger than one that simply asserts that controlling guns will automatically reduce crime or the murder rate.

APPLICATIONS

1. Select a single argument (something printed in this book or elsewhere, or an argument you used in Applications earlier in this chapter). Analyze this argument to determine:
   What criteria does the writer present for reaching a decision or making a choice?

What values support the writer's criteria?

How have values been arranged into a hierarchy?

2. Working in a group, choose an issue that is currently being debated in the news or on campus. Analyze the issue and the argument(s) that have developed around it so that you can answer the following questions. Then discuss your analysis in a group.

What are the major positions?

What values are associated or claimed by each position?

Based on your analysis, develop a position that rests on several of the criteria that participants in the argument believe to be crucial.

Conclusion

The strongest, most convincing arguments are based on a thorough knowledge of the issue involved. They acknowledge the variety of positions that others have taken, and they present the choices to be made in terms of the values that have been raised in the argument. If you want to argue effectively and convincingly you will:

- Show that you are aware of the complexity of the argument and the various positions that have been taken.

- Attempt to make your position attractive to as many people as possible by basing it on multiple criteria and values.

- Present your position in the context of values that your readers already hold.

Complex issues that involve multiple positions seldom get resolved by a single written argument, no matter how compelling or convincing that single argument might seem. Likewise, they are seldom resolved on the basis of a single criterion or value. For example, any argument in favor of gun control that rests solely on the death rate from guns is likely to fail. It will fail because those who disagree can simply point out that the number of deaths caused by guns is nowhere near the number of deaths caused by cars, and no one wants to ban cars. As you write, keep in mind all of the arguments that have been written about your issue and the different values that those arguments have invoked. Always remember that your argument will be stronger if you base it on a number of different values rather than relying on a single value or criterion. When you are involved in an ongoing, multisided argument, your role is not to provide the definitive solution. Instead, your efforts will be more productive if you attempt to define a critical term, examine a central assumption, or perhaps offer some new way of looking at the issue or the solutions that have been offered so far.

Questions and Activities

1. Select an issue that you believe is important. You can use a subject you have developed from earlier exercises in this book. Summarize the issue and the various positions that have been taken. Then explain the values that will be involved in choosing the best available position.

2. Read a set of arguments printed in this book and identify the values that the various writers invoke as they present and support their positions. Then, working in a group, discuss your analysis and devise a strategy for working with those values in your own entry into that argument.

Suggestions for Writing

1. Select an issue that is usually regarded as having only two sides. (You can use one of the pro/con sets of readings in this book if you like.) Instead of choosing a side, write an argument in which your position is that the issue is too complex for only two sides. Your goal is to show your readers the additional positions or sides that you believe they should consider.

2. Select a multisided issue (from this book or elsewhere) and write an argument in which you identify and analyze the values that the writers invoke. Your goal is to shift the argument's focus from the stated positions to the values that those positions rest on, so that your readers will be forced to deal with the issue explicitly in terms of those values.

CHAPTER SIX

Supporting an Argument

Support is the heart of any argument. Without adequate support, even the most reasonable argument will fail. When you support an argument effectively, you show your readers what you want them to believe or do, you explain why, and you show how your request is consistent with what they already believe and do. When you support an argument adequately you provide accurate, relevant information, good reasons, and clear reasoning. Your readers will expect you to support your argument by:

- *Providing information,* including facts, observations, expert testimony, examples, and illustrations, that supports your position
- *Giving good reasons* for holding the position you have taken
- *Showing a reasoning process* that leads to your position and shows it to be the result of careful thought and analysis
- *Demonstrating your reliability* and credibility as a source of information

Before you read this chapter, write brief responses to the following:

1. Recall a time when you asked someone (for example, your parents or a friend) to do something that you thought they would not do. What information and reasons did you provide to convince them to cooperate with you?
2. Recall the last time you discussed a controversial issue such as capital punishment or legalizing certain drugs with your friends, family, or classmates. Identify at least two positions

from that argument and describe how participants supported those positions.

The purpose of support is to show or explain why you have taken your position and to convince your readers to agree with you. As you do this, you will not only state your own case,, but you will also anticipate your readers' questions, objections, doubts, and challenges, and attempt to respond to them in advance. Presenting positions that do not agree with your own will actually strengthen your argument by helping your readers see you as a reliable source of accurate information. It will also show that you are capable of seeing the issue from a variety of perspectives and that you are not afraid that the other positions will undermine your own. This may help convince your readers that the position you have taken, and that you want them to adopt, is a reasonable one that is based on solid information. When you present other positions and the information and reasoning that support them, you provide a context for your own position and the support you offer for it. Thus, you give your readers an opportunity to see your position against a background of a variety of different positions. The more you include in that background, the more comfortable your readers will be that you have provided enough information for them to make a good decision.

For example, any time you are faced with a choice you will want to have several possibilities available to you. If you were buying a car, you would want to look at several different kinds before making your choice. If only one were available, then you would have to choose it or walk. But if you have several cars available to you, you can test drive them and compare them in a variety of other ways before making your choice. Having a variety available to you should result in a better choice or, in this case, a car that is of the highest quality you can afford or suits your needs as closely as possible.

Provide Information

It is impossible to write or argue effectively about any subject without an adequate amount of valid, reliable, relevant information at your command. No matter how solid or obvious you believe your position is, your readers will want information if they are to agree with you. The information you provide can come from a variety of places. You can rely on your own knowledge and experience, and you can use information that you and others have gathered.

Use Your Own Experience

It is perfectly acceptable to use your own knowledge and experience in an argument. Information based on your personal knowledge, observations, and experience is valuable because not only does it support your point, but it also establishes your personal authority over the subject. Personal experience gives you information you cannot acquire in any other way, and that many of your readers do not have. For example, if you have had any of the following experiences, you can write about them in ways that would not be possible for people who have not experienced them.

> Being a patient in a hospital
> Being in an auto accident
> Sailing to Europe on the Queen Elizabeth II
> Visiting the Grand Canyon
> Acting in a play
> Playing in a marching band

For example, in an argument about changing the way patients are treated in hospitals, your experience as a patient will be invaluable. It will help you recall the sounds, smells, and rhythms of life in a hospital. Did someone really wake you up to take a sleeping pill? Did you ever have any real privacy? What did it feel like to wear a hospital gown, or be totally dependent on someone else for almost everything you needed? How did the physicians and nurses talk to you? This information simply is not available to anyone who has not had the experience. Your first-hand knowledge adds authenticity to your descriptions and arguments and thus establishes your personal authority.

Limitations on Personal Experience

The very thing that makes personal experience valuable also limits it. Because it is the experience of only one person, it can have no general application. You can report your own experience, but you need to be aware that not everyone has had the same experiences. Even if others share your experiences, they may remember them differently and disagree with you about what happened or what the experience meant. Others may have had experiences completely different from yours in any given situation. And when you are relying on personal knowledge and experience, your authority extends only to those matters that your experience covers. A trip to the Grand Canyon during the peak of the tourist season entitles you to write about what you saw and heard. It does not make you an expert on National Park Service policies or the Colorado River ecosystem. You can learn about these subjects and become an authority, but to do so you will have to go beyond your personal authority to what others have learned.

For example, you may know of several people who were injured or killed in auto accidents because their seat belts kept them from escaping from the car. This knowledge might lead you to believe that seat belts are dangerous. But data based on studies of a great many accidents show that seat belts increase the probability of surviving a crash and reduce the possibility of serious injury. Similarly, you may know a number of people who have smoked cigarettes for a number of years without suffering any obvious ill effects such as coughing, emphysema, or lung cancer. Your personal experience may make smoking look safe, or at least not as dangerous as it is said to be. But studies of the whole population show a quite different picture. Once again, personal experience has given a mistaken impression of the general reality, which is that smoking causes cancer and other respiratory diseases.

Studies of groups, of course, cannot predict what will happen to specific individuals. Relying exclusively on personal experience or observation can lead to conclusions that more thorough data will not support.

Going beyond personal knowledge and experience will give you a broader view of your subject by providing information that applies to the population as a whole, not just the part of it that you have experienced directly. These limitations do not make personal experience and observations useless in arguments, but they do restrict the ways in which you can use them. For example, you can use your personal knowledge of seat belts and smokers to point out that there are exceptions to general trends, that statistics express probabilities, not certainties.

Personal experience supplements and dramatizes the other information you present. For example, if you want to argue that the number of tourist flights over and through the Grand Canyon should be reduced, you will want to present information about the number of flights per day, the noise they produce, and the number of accidents and crashes that have occurred. And, because you have first-hand experience (perhaps you took one of these flights yourself) you can describe the noise the helicopters and airplanes make, and explain how that affected your attempt to experience a natural scene. Such a description can bring statistics to life and help your readers visualize the subject you are writing about.

The following argument by Mary Arguelles, "Money for Morality," depends almost exclusively on the writer's own experience.
Using events she has read about, and that have occurred in her own
life, she addresses the question of whether honesty, achievement,
and other events require rewards beyond the satisfaction they
provide.

Money for Morality

MARY ARGUELLES

I recently read a newspaper article about an 8-year-old boy
who found an envelope containing more than $600 and returned
it to the bank whose name appeared on the envelope. The bank
traced the money to its rightful owner and returned it to him.
God's in his heaven and all's right with the world. Right?
Wrong.

As a reward, the man who lost the money gave the boy $3.
Not a lot, but a token of his appreciation nonetheless and not
mandatory. After all, returning money should not be considered
extraordinary. A simple "thank you" is adequate. But some of
the teachers at the boy's school felt a reward was not only
appropriate, but required. Outraged at the apparent stinginess of
the person who lost the cash, these teachers took up a collection for the boy. About a week or so later, they presented the
good Samaritan with a $150 savings bond, explaining they felt
his honesty should be recognized. Evidently the virtues of honesty and kindness have become commodities that, like everything else, have succumbed to inflation. I can't help but wonder
what dollar amount these teachers would have deemed a sufficient reward. Certainly they didn't expect the individual who
lost the money to give the child $150. Would $25 have been
respectable? How about $10? Suppose that lost money had to
cover mortgage, utilities and food for the week. In light of that,
perhaps $3 was generous. A reward is a gift; any gift should at
least be met with the presumption of genuine gratitude on the
part of the giver.

What does this episode say about our society? It seems the
role models our children look up to these days—in this case,

---

teachers—are more confused and misguided about values than their young charges. A young boy, obviously well guided by his parents, finds money that does not belong to him and he returns it. He did the right thing. Yet doing the right thing seems to be insufficient motivation for action in our materialistic world. The legacy of the '80s has left us with the ubiquitous question: what's in it for me? The promise of the golden rule—that someone might do a good turn for you—has become worthless collateral for the social interactions of the mercenary and fast-paced '90s. It is in fact this fast pace that is, in part, a source of the problem. Modern communication has catapulted us into an instant world. Television makes history of events before any of us has even had a chance to absorb them in the first place. An ad for major-league baseball entices viewers with the reassurance that "the memories are waiting"; an event that has yet to occur has already been packaged as the past. With the world racing by us, we have no patience for a rain check on good deeds.

Misplaced virtues are running rampant through our culture. I don't know how many times my 13-year-old son has told me about classmates who received $10 for each A they receive on their report cards—hinting that I should do the same for him should he ever receive an A (or maybe he was working on $5 for a B). Whenever he approaches me on this subject, I give him the same reply: "Doing well is its own reward. The A just confirms that." In other words, forget it! This is not to say that I would never praise my son for doing well in school. But my praise is not meant to reward or elicit future achievements, but rather to express my genuine delight in the satisfaction he feels at having done his best. Throwing $10 at that sends out the message that the feeling alone isn't good enough.

Kowtowing to ice cream.   As a society, we seem to be losing a grip on our internal control—the ethical thermostat that guides our actions and feelings toward ourselves, others, and the world around us. Instead, we rely on external "stuff" as a measure of our worth. We pass this message to our children. We offer them money for honesty and good grades. Pizza is given as a reward for reading. If fact, in one national reading program, a pizza party awaits the entire class if each child reads a certain amount of books within a four-month period. We call these things incentives, telling ourselves that if we can just reel them in and get them hooked, then the built-in rewards will follow. I recently saw a television program where unmarried, teenaged mothers were featured as the participants in a parenting program that offers a $10 a week "incentive" if these young women don't get pregnant again. Isn't the daily struggle of being a single, teenaged mother enough of a deterrent? No, it isn't, because we as a society won't allow it to be. Nothing is permitted to succeed or fail on its own merits anymore.

I remember when I was pregnant with my son I read countless child-care books that offered the same advice: don't bribe your child with ice cream to get him to eat spinach; it makes the spinach look bad. While some may say spinach doesn't need any help looking bad, I submit it's from years of kowtowing to ice cream. Similarly, our moral taste buds have been dulled by an endless onslaught of artificial sweeteners. A steady diet of candy bars and banana splits makes an ordinary apple or orange seem sour. So too does an endless parade of incentives make us incapable of feeling a genuine sense of inner peace (or inner turmoil).

The simple virtues of honesty, kindness and integrity suffer from an image problem and are in desperate need of a makeover. One way to do this is by example. If my son sees me feeling happy after I've helped out a friend, then he may do likewise. If my daughter sees me spending a rainy afternoon curled up with a book instead of spending money at the mall, she may get the message that there are some simple pleasures that don't require a purchase. I fear that in our so-called upwardly mobile world we are on a downward spiral toward moral bankruptcy. Like pre-World War II Germany, where the basket holding the money was more valuable than the money itself, we too may render ourselves internally worthless while desperately clinging to a shell of appearances.

APPLICATIONS

1. Re-read Mary Arguelles' argument, "Money for Morality." Work with a group of your classmates to identify the personal experiences she relies on to support her position. How would it affect her argument if she did not have these experiences to use as support?

2. Identify an issue you can argue using only (or mainly) your personal experience and the knowledge you already possess. Write a brief description of your experience and then explain how it will help you support your position. What additional information would you need that you do not already have?

3. Discuss the following question with a group of your classmates: Attorneys have known for years that eyewitness testimony can be very unreliable. Several witnesses to the same event can give different, conflicting versions of that event. In view of this, why do we usually attach so much importance and authenticity to personal experience? Wouldn't we be wiser to ignore personal experience altogether?

Using Information from Other Sources

In addition to your personal experience and knowledge, you will almost always need to provide information that others have gathered or compiled. For example, if you were writing an argument about underage drinking as a national issue, your own experiences with underage drinkers will certainly give vividness and immediacy to your discussion. But you would also need to provide information that does not come from your own experience. For instance, your readers might want you to provide information about the number of underage drinkers nationwide, the number who are alcoholics, and the other types of problems that alcohol causes in this population. This information will help you demonstrate that there is a nationwide problem that extends beyond your personal observations, and it will help convince your readers that the issue is one that affects a large portion of the population. Chapters 7 and 8 will explain in detail various kinds of research.

Putting Information to Work

It's always tempting to simply gather information and more or less throw it at your reader, assuming that it will speak for itself. But often that is exactly the wrong way to enter an argument because it often leads you to argue a position that is obvious or that your readers probably already agree with.

For example, if your purpose were to argue that people should stop smoking or wear seat belts when they drive or ride in cars, you might be tempted to gather statistics about the dangers of smoking or the advantages of wearing seat belts. At some point, though, it will occur to you that your readers probably already know what you are about to tell them. It has become so obvious that people should wear seat belts and not smoke that these positions are probably no longer arguable. Few people outside the tobacco industry will argue that smoking is safe. Even fewer would argue that seat belts don't save lives or reduce injuries. These positions were certainly arguable at one time, but no they are no longer arguable because almost everyone agrees with them. There is no point in arguing about something everyone agrees with.

However, the information you gather about these subjects will help you begin to ask different and more interesting questions, and these will give you new ways to enter old arguments. For example, if smoking is so dangerous, why is it permitted at all? Why not outlaw it completely, or at least ban it in public places and protect those who do not smoke? Seat belts obviously save lives, and many states require drivers and passengers to wear them. But many seat belt laws are either unenforceable or carry only token penalties. You could argue that these laws should be strengthened. For example, you could take the position that insurance companies should be released from their obligations if people are injured and are not wearing seat belts.

The argument that people should wear seat belts because they save lives and reduce injuries requires only some relatively simple and easy-to-find comparative statistics. You would need to show the frequency of deaths and injuries among those who do not wear seat belts and those who do. Using these statistics you can give your readers a lesson in probabilities to show them that their risk of death or injury is greater than they think it is. Arguments that people should quit smoking can proceed in the same way: Give the statistics for disease and death, and then show your readers the probability that they will develop lung cancer, emphysema, or some other disorder.

If you argue that smoking should be banned completely in public places, then you will need to provide a different kind of information. You will of course need to show the effects of what has been called secondary smoke. But your position has changed. You are no longer arguing that people should quit voluntarily. Instead, you are arguing that their behavior should be regulated because it injures others, and you may have to show that there is precedent for doing that. For example, a number of cities have banned smoking in public places, such as restaurants and airports. In addition to citing these laws you could give examples of other kinds of behavior that are regulated because they are harmful to others. For example, it is illegal to drive while intoxicated or to drink alcohol and drive at the same time. Many states and cities regulate who can carry a firearm and where it can be discharged. Many local governments regulate the private use of fireworks. In all of these cases, the point is to regulate behavior that might be dangerous to others and ignore, for the time being, the fact that they might be dangerous to those who are committing them as well.

Using Information: A Summary

Complete, accurate information is essential to any argument. When you present complete and accurate information you accomplish these important tasks in support of your argument:

> You establish that you are well-informed and that you have taken the time to review the subject thoroughly.
>
> You establish the information as part of your argument. Anyone who opposes you must deal with the information that you present.
>
> You place your argument in the context of concrete fact and event.

APPLICATIONS

1. Select an argument printed elsewhere in this book—for example, "Why Transplants Don't Happen" in the chapter about rationing health care. Analyze the information in the article. On a paper divided into two columns, list all the information that comes from the writer's direct experience or personal knowledge in one column. In the other, list the information that the writer has acquired from another source.
2. Select a local or campus issue or subject that is presently the focus of some debate or controversy. For example, perhaps the campus police have begun to ticket bicycles that are parked anywhere except in designated bicycle racks. Using only your personal experience and knowledge, construct an argument stating your position and support for it.

Reasons and Reasoning

While information is essential to any argument, it will not make your case by itself. In fact, even arguments that take positions completely opposed to each other rest on the same body of information, because facts tend to be constant and available to everyone. For example, the number of people who are not wearing seat belts who die each year in traffic accidents remains the same, no matter what position you are arguing. Of course, some people may attempt to withhold or alter information that seems to undermine their positions. But doing that is an act of bad faith with your readers. It has no place in argument or any other discussion. People who alter or withhold information eventually get caught, and thus compromise their ability to argue effectively because they can no longer claim to be a reliable source of information.

Some people believe that information by itself is enough to support an argument. They say things like "if you just knew the facts you would agree. . . ." And they spend their time explaining rather than arguing. But information by itself is *not* enough. If it were, there would be no need for argument. Instead of writing arguments, we would simply gather and exchange all of the information we could find about a subject.

But information never speaks for itself. It is always subject to interpretation. If you want your readers to understand the facts of a situation the way you do, you must show how those facts support your position rather than someone else's. For example, the number of people who die each year of lung cancer is the same for everyone, regardless of their position. But not everyone will agree that smoking causes all of those cases of lung cancer. Tobacco companies, for example, often argue that a direct, causal relationship between smoking and cancer cannot be proven. Thus, to support a position requires more than information by itself. Explaining and interpreting the information you provide will involve:

- Giving reasons for holding the position you have taken
- Showing a reasoning or thinking process that leads to your position

Giving Reasons

People usually like to believe that their actions and beliefs are reasonable, the result of a careful decision-making process. They do not want to believe that they are subject to whim or act on impulse. Many effective arguments appeal directly to this need by showing that the belief or action being argued for is something a reasonable person can easily agree to.

For example, when television commercials show groups of happy people dancing, singing, smiling, and talking with each other in a restaurant or while drinking beer, part of the appeal is to people's desire for affiliation with others (affiliation includes love, friendship, membership, and other types of relationship). The obvious message is that people who use the product will have friends as well as a good time. Everyone experiences this desire for affiliation, so it seems reasonable and natural to want to fulfill it. When AIDS activists argue that the government should allocate more money to AIDS research, or that successful experimental drugs should be approved quickly for public use, they are appealing to ethics, fair play, and government officials' sense of responsibility, as well as to what they hope are widely shared beliefs about the value of human life. Remember this:

> Reasons are usually based on what you believe will be likely to appeal to your readers. Thus, the reasons you choose will be determined to a large extent by the audience you are writing for.

Some reasons that appeal to almost everyone, and that can thus be useful to you in supporting an argument, include such things as:

self-esteem	self-interest	greed
affiliation	love	safety
fame	ethics	morality
fair play	responsibility	status

These reasons, also known as *appeals*, are directly related to values and to the ways people establish their own priorities about what is important to them. You can use reasons like these in your own arguments. The appeals you choose will depend on what you believe to be your readers' values.

Suppose you want to argue that parents should be charged with negligent homicide if their children are killed in auto accidents while not in approved safety restraints. Your audience in this argument would probably not be the negligent parents. You are more likely to be successful if you prepare your argument for the public at large, or for legislators who have the power to enact the law. Thus, you will give reasons that will appeal to these readers. You might appeal to their sense of responsibility, to what you believe are widely shared beliefs about the special status of children, to their self-image as protectors of society, and to their sense of ethics. Your argument might point out that small children are usually entirely dependent on their parents for their safety. You could also suggest that it is the responsibility of lawmakers to protect people who cannot protect themselves and to take the role of parents when parents neglect their responsibilities.

For a further illustration of presenting reasons, return to Mary Arguelles' essay, "Money for Morality." Her general position is that "The simple virtues of honesty, kindness and integrity suffer from an image problem and are in desperate need of a makeover" because "doing the right thing seems to be insufficient motivation in our materialistic world." She gives a number of reasons to support her position, most of them connected in some way to values that she believes will appeal to her readers. Among them:

> A reward is a gift; any gift should at least be met with the presumption of genuine gratitude on the part of the giver.

This reason asks readers to agree that fair play and a sense of responsibility require us to accept all rewards, no matter how small, as genuine expressions of gratitude.

> But my praise is not meant to reward or elicit future achievements, but rather to express my genuine delight in the satisfaction he feels at having done his best.

This passage insists that self-esteem should come from within, with a sense of satisfaction, rather than from material rewards. As she says elsewhere in the argument, "we rely on external 'stuff' as a measure of our worth."

> She implies that the difficulties of being a single, teenaged parent should be an adequate incentive to avoid future pregnancies.

Here Arguelles appeals to common sense and fair play: almost everyone has some idea of how difficult it is to be a single parent. She insists that we should not reward people for complicating their lives a second time. Such a reward would be unfair to those who play by the rules.

> So too does an endless parade of incentives make us incapable of feeling a genuine sense of inner peace or inner turmoil.

This statement appeals to ethics and social responsibility by saying that by having too many rewards and incentives society has deprived people of feeling and valuing simple satisfaction.

Reasons explain why your readers should agree with you or accept the position you are arguing. They frequently appeal to values because most people base their actions and beliefs on values. If you simply tell your readers that they should do something, such as not pay cash rewards for their children's grades, they may disagree with you at once. You are more likely to receive their cooperation if you connect your request to values that you know your readers believe are important. If they still want to disagree with you, they will have to do so in terms of their values, not your request, by showing how those values do not apply to the case at hand.

Showing Reasoning

Your readers might eventually accept your position if you give them information, reasons, and plenty of time. Most people need to go through a reasoning process before they accept positions, especially if those positions are new to them or ask them to depart in some way from their established beliefs or behaviors. And remember that most people like things the way they are, because change is often difficult. So they need some sort of incentive, some sense that they have something to gain, if they are to go through that process on their own. Effective arguments take readers through just such a process in order to show them how to reach a specific position or conclusion.

You went through a thinking process yourself in order to reach the position that you are arguing. That process probably had little to do with logic, and you should not confuse critical thinking with logic. Instead, your reasoning process probably involved analyzing, testing, inferring, and other activities that are usually lumped together as thinking or reasoning. As you went through that process, you collected and evaluated data, explored and tested alternative solutions, and chose a position for yourself. Along the way you probably experienced a number of false starts and blind alleys, and you probably reached a number of tentative or provisional conclusions before you reached your final position. In fact, the position you are arguing may itself be provisional, the best you can do for now, given the situation and the information available.

Since you reached your position as the result of a process of analysis and exploration, you can expect that your readers will want to see some sort of reasoning process before they accept your position. They could, of course, do this on their own, but your job is to motivate them to want to consider an issue and then to provide them with a reasoning process that leads to your position or conclusion. Readers won't want to go through the same reasoning process you went through. The blind alleys and false starts would make it too messy and indirect, and it would appear too tentative. Readers will want you to show them a more direct path to your conclusion.

Taking Readers Through a Reasoning Process

The information you provide is the foundation of your argument. The reasons you give show your readers why they should agree with you. When you show them a reasoning process you are showing them how they can get from where they are to where you are.

We'll illustrate this reasoning process by looking closely at Jessica Bram's "Beauty Calls." Read the essay carefully, and then the analysis that follows it.

Beauty Calls

JESSICA BRAM

We had a new baby sitter living with us last summer, a 19-year-old college student who could only be called beautiful. She had classic Scandinavian looks: wavy blond hair, gray-green eyes beneath an ivory brow and flawless white teeth. Tall and slender, her body was the *Sports Illustrated* swimsuit ideal: long legs, slim thighs, tanned young skin that wouldn't know the meaning of cellulite for years to come.

When we first spied her as she rounded the luggage carousel after her flight from Wisconsin, I couldn't help thinking: "Oh, no, now look what I've done. Did I have to hire someone this gorgeous?" But the thought dissipated when Julie got down on her knees, introduced herself to my two rapt young sons and, while we waited for her luggage, described to them the animals at her farm back home.

I was, however, frequently reminded of my initial reaction as my friends caught sight of Julie and registered their opinions. "Who needs such a beautiful girl in your house?" they asked, half in jest, watching her crouch on her long, tan legs alongside my children, sunlight gleaming off her gold curls. "You're not going to leave your husband alone with that, are you?" A neighbor, eyeing Julie's lithe young body in her swimsuit at the pool, took me aside: "I think you should pay her her whole salary in advance, and tell her you hope she has a very nice summer . . . back where she came from."

Fairy-tale maidens were rescued from drudgery simply by virtue of their innocent beauty, so potent it was feared by stepmothers and evil queens. Not only an end in itself, beauty possessed a magical, inexplicable power: for achievement, for success, for salvation.

The promise of beauty was that with it came the prince and the shimmering castle and all the other rewards that one could imagine in "happily ever after." It was the essential key without which doors to happiness would remain locked. (Perhaps the beast, being male, could get around this requirement, but no such luck for a homely princess.)

Years later, I found this same hope of redemption in the glossy, headily ink-scented pages of *Seventeen* magazine, whose fresh-faced models—Cheryl and Lucy and Colleen—could, like me, be transformed by the magic of make-overs.

Although my mother's promise to me has always dangled somewhat tantalizingly beyond the horizon, I have, over the years, made peace with my looks. That I do not receive the kind of stares and double takes that Julie did, I assure myself, has only made it easier to focus on other things, like grades and friends and life's decisions, large and small. And I remind myself that my marriage has survived threats for worse than Christie Brinkley. But to see it as an issue of appearance or even sexual rivalry is, for me, to miss a larger point.

For when I looked at Julie, I remembered that old promise of beauty. Her crown of gold curls, bestowed by God Himself, seemed to me the very embodiment of limitless potential—a sign that Julie, unlike the rest of us, had some kind of guarantee of happiness. This told me that my old fantasies about beauty's magic are still very much alive. Yet I realized that it is these very imaginings, fabricated out of fairy tales and magazines and thin air, that are the key to beauty's true power. By believing our own storybook assumptions, we somehow make them, for the beautiful, come true.

I began to understand the accusatory stares leveled at Julie, as though she has committed some grave offense or insult. Perhaps the insult was this: that she had painfully reminded us of the promise of beauty once made, as it was to me by fairy tale and fantasy and a well-meaning mother. A promise that, like so many other promises, would never materialize. Perhaps she reminded us that the kingdom is a nice community in the suburbs with good schools and a pool club. That the prince, for better or worse, does not exactly relish an endless waltz at the ball—if he'll go near a dance floor at all. That even achievement ends not with a heraldic trumpet blare but with a satisfied stretch of the muscles at the end of a day of hard work. That so many of childhood's sparkling dreams for the future, while we were busy elsewhere, became dreams laid to rest.

In the weeks that Julie was with us, I somehow came to stop noticing her beauty. What I mostly saw was how kind she was to my children, how helpful and cheerful to have around the house. And I discovered that there was, after all, really nothing terribly powerful about this girl who liked to draw Magic Marker pictures with my sons and eat big bowls of ice cream every evening with her long legs sprawled in front of the TV.

In other words, as my neighbor said to me about Julie, "You know, she's really so nice, you can't even hate her for her looks."

Getting Started

Bram begins with the premise that beautiful women, especially young beautiful women, are home wreckers, dangerous people to have around. She uses this attitude to establish an initial relationship with her readers by showing first her own reaction, "Oh, no, now look what I've done. Did I have to hire someone this gorgeous?" She then attributes this same attitude to her friends and neighbors: "my friends caught sight of Julie and registered their opinions. 'Who needs such a beautiful girl in your house?' they asked, half in jest. . . ." She senses the "cutting, almost sinister undertone to my friends' comments," and then asks the question she wants her readers to ask when she wonders "what unnamed feelings they [her neighbors' comments] masked." She acknowledges that the reaction seems extreme: "why should a kind, good-natured girl deserve such calumny?"

Having brought her readers to this point, Bram shifts the subject to beauty and asks the central question that she will go on to explore: She wonders "why beauty is so intimidating and, in the case of a young summer visitor, so feared and resented." To attempt an answer to this question, she first examines herself. Is she resentful because she is not beautiful? No, she thinks not, and she offers some evidence by describing her husband's reactions to her (an admittedly biased point of view). But as she examines her own appearance and her attitudes toward beauty she acknowledges that she never questioned the importance of being beautiful. Beauty was, she says, "a simple fact of life," that "possessed a magical, inexplicable power: for achievement, for success, for salvation." Beauty is also important, Bram says, because of the things it brings with it: "the prince, the shimmering castle, and all the other rewards that one could imagine in 'happily ever after.'" Beauty, she says, "was the essential key without which doors to happiness would remain locked."

Next Bram comes to terms with her own appearance and admits that not being beautiful has had its advantages, allowing her to focus on friends and academic success. And she acknowledges that a beautiful woman is not the worst threat to a stable marriage. And, by coming to terms with herself she realizes that there is a larger issue that has nothing to do with "appearance or sexual rivalry." This point is that beauty has only that power over us that we allow it to have. "By believing our own storybook assumptions, we somehow make them, for the beautiful, come true." It is this insight that allows her to "understand the accusatory stares leveled at Julie, as though she had committed some grave offense or insult."

Julie's offense is not that she will steal a husband or wreck a marriage, but that her beauty

> had painfully reminded us of the promise of beauty once made, as it was to me by fairy tale and fantasy and a well-meaning mother. A promise that, like to many other promises, would never materialize.

Having brought her readers through a carefully constructed process of thinking about beauty, Bram delivers her conclusion, confident that her readers will be right with her, nodding their heads in agreement:

> I discovered that there was, after all, nothing terribly powerful about this girl who liked to draw Magic Marker pictures with my sons and eat big bowls of chocolate ice cream every evening with her long legs sprawled in front of the TV.

In the space of this sentence, the "classic Scandinavian" beauty whose "body was the *Sports Illustrated* swimsuit ideal," has become a young girl who draws pictures and eats ice cream. But this can happen only because Bram has taken her readers step-by-step through a complex process of thinking about her subject. And she is so reasonable about it that she leaves the impression that only a true grump would disagree with her.

APPLICATIONS
---

1. Select an argument reprinted in this book—for example, one of the arguments about the Canadian health care system—and describe the reasoning process the author takes readers through. Note any improvements you would make in that reasoning process.
2. Select a completed argument that you have written for this course and explain the reasoning process you constructed for your readers. What changes would you make in that reasoning process?

Creating Belief and Trust

Your readers must believe you and trust you if your arguments are to succeed. You are, after all, asking your readers to make significant changes in what they believe or what they do on the basis of what you say. They will do so only if they sense you can be believed and trusted. And it's not enough to simply *be* trustworthy and believable; you must also *appear* to be trustworthy and believable. The two are not the same. People who want their arguments to be effective are careful to present accurate information and reasoning. They also learn how to present themselves as reliable and honest.

Some people establish their reliability and believability by reputation. After a period of time that can range from hours to years, depending on the situation, it is possible to acquire a favorable reputation as a person who is informed, honest, or believable. This reputation enters an argument with you and encourages people to believe you. For example, many scholars, writers, politicians, and business figures have established their reputations for honesty and integrity over many years. If you wanted to know something about ancient Greece, you would look to someone who has been studying it for a long time and has established a reputation for careful scholarship. If you need information about health care ethics, you would attempt to consult someone who has been working in that field for some time and who has acquired a reputation as an expert.

Of course, building a reputation takes time. It is also especially difficult for students to establish reputations as experts, because students do most of their writing for teachers. And teachers frequently, but not always, know more than their students. That does not mean that you cannot establish yourself as reliable and believable. You can communicate trustworthiness and reliability directly to your readers through what you say and how you say it. Of course, it is not helpful simply to say that you are reliable and trustworthy.

As soon as you openly claim to have these qualities, your readers will immediately begin to doubt you. If you really had them, they reason, you wouldn't need to say so.

You can create trust and belief in a variety of ways, all of them important.

- Present accurate, complete information, and always identify your sources. When you name a source you are also announcing that you are not afraid to have your statements verified. When readers check and find that your information is accurate and complete, this will work to your advantage. If readers discover that you have misrepresented or omitted important information, this will severely damage your credibility, and it will call into question almost everything else you say.
- Never hide or attempt to disguise information that works against your position. Acknowledge it fully and meet it head on. If it is so damaging that it will destroy your case, then perhaps you should reexamine why you still hold your position. Otherwise, explain why it has not caused you to abandon your position. That should be a powerful and convincing part of your argument.
- Present clear, accurate, complete summaries of positions and arguments that oppose your own. This shows that you are aware of but not afraid of opposing positions.
- Always be positive. Write about what works rather than what does not work. Instead of writing about your opponent's faults, write about your advantages. Avoid accusations, especially if you can't prove them. Stress the common ground you share with others rather than the differences that separate you.
- Do your best to be and appear to be a reasonable person. If you suggest extreme solutions to problems, such as banning tobacco altogether, people will dismiss you quickly. They have the historical example of Prohibition, which did not work, and they will be unlikely to believe that banning smoking will work either.

APPLICATIONS

1. Re-read the two arguments printed in this chapter. This time pay special attention to the ways the writers establish themselves as

believable and trustworthy. Then discuss these methods with a small group of classmates and try to determine if everyone in the group finds these methods equally effective.

2. Select an argument you wrote earlier in this course and review it carefully, paying special attention to how you can improve your presentation of yourself as a believable, trustworthy person. Describe the changes you will make in this argument to present yourself as someone who can be believed and trusted.

Conclusion

To successfully support an argument you must:

- Provide complete, accurate information.

- Give your readers reasons for accepting your position.

- Show a reasoning process that leads to your position.

- Present yourself as a trustworthy and believable source of information.

Questions and Activities

1. Select an editorial or column from your local or campus newspaper about some issue that interests you. Evaluate the support offered in this editorial and explain what you would do to improve that support. Rewrite the editorial to make its case more convincing.

2. Re-read the *Harper's* forum about rights and responsibilities printed in this book. Identify a position that you find unconvincing because it is inadequately supported. Explain how you would strengthen the support for this position, and then revise that section of the forum by presenting the support you believe is necessary.

Suggestions for Writing

1. Select an argument you wrote in response to an earlier assignment in this text. Review that argument carefully, paying special attention to the support you provided. Write a detailed description of the information, reasons, and reasoning you provided, and explain how

you will improve each. Revise the argument to improve the support. Be sure that you make significant changes.

2. Read the two arguments in this book about the differences between male and female athletes. Look specifically at the support the authors offer for their positions. Then write a response to one of these arguments. In your response do not take a position on the central issue of women's vs. men's athletic abilities. Instead, focus on the support, either adding to it or attacking it.

CHAPTER SEVEN

Doing Research

This chapter explains and illustrates how to do several kinds of research. After reading it, you should be able to locate the information you need to support your positions in arguments. Before you read the chapter, write brief responses to at least two of the following activities:

1. What do you do when you are given a writing assignment that requires research? Give a brief summary description of the steps you take to prepare for and do the required research.
2. When was the last time you did research on your own, without a class assignment? Describe the question you wanted to answer and how you conducted the research. (If you have not done research on your own, describe a question you would like to answer and how you would go about doing the research.)
3. Describe your most successful or your most frustrating research project. Explain why it was frustrating or successful.

Successful arguments depend on support, and finding effective support often depends on your ability to do research. No single chapter in a book of this sort can tell you everything you need to know about doing research. What you will find here is a general overview to get you started. Your investment will be time and hands-on experience. The more research you do, the more confident and successful you will become at it. The secret to initial success is not to allow the research methods or your library or any other factor to intimidate you. Just plunge ahead and see what you can find; you won't hurt anything.

Try to work systematically when you do research. Your best tools will be curiosity, persistence, and method. When you run out of ideas or resources, ask questions of librarians or experienced researchers. Friendly, helpful librarians are a researcher's treasure. Cultivate them and treat them with care and respect. They will love to help, especially if they see that you have already made an effort and done some work on your own. That way, you can approach them with specific questions about the information you need, rather than general questions about where you should look to find information about your subject.

Preparation: The Place to Start

When you receive a research assignment, don't just rush off to the library. Productive research begins with careful, thorough preparation. Unless you prepare, your research will be frustrating and difficult. Preparation helps you to discover what you know, to identify what you need to know, and to conduct an efficient search. Your goal is to collect the maximum amount of usable information as efficiently as possible. To do this you actually need to know a good bit about your subject before you begin doing research. This may seem strange to you, because you may be thinking of research as a way of learning things that you don't know. It is that, but before you can look for answers, you need to know what the questions are. Your knowledge of the subject will determine where you begin your research.

Background Reading

If you are working with a subject that you know little or nothing about, your most productive first step will be to go to a library and do some background reading. Depending on the subject area, you may be able to consult encyclopedias, almanacs, and general reference works. The card catalog may contain a book or two (or more) about your subject. General news magazines and newspapers are also useful sources of background information. *Time, Newsweek, U.S. News and World Report,* and *The New York Times* usually print feature articles that explain important current subjects in considerable detail. They often explain the main issues and questions, tell who has taken which side, and sometimes give information that can lead to further sources of information. (Later in this chapter you will see how to get access to the information in these magazines and newspapers.) If you need background information about your subject, your first step should be to find several general accounts and read them to find out what's going on. If you find several books about your subject, look them all over carefully before you choose one. Read the introduction or preface to each one, because authors will often tell you their intended audience. Read the first few pages of a chapter to see if it is too elementary or too complex for your present state of knowledge.

Background reading is not research. Its purpose is to help you acquire the information you need in order to do research. Background reading allows you to identify the major issues and questions related to your subject, the key positions that have been taken, and the people or groups that are involved. After you finish your background reading you should know where you stand (tentatively) on the issue and how your own position relates to the positions that other people have taken. You should also have enough information to allow you to ask intelligent questions about your subject and begin doing real research.

Four Places to Do Research

All research projects involve two kinds of information: (1) information that is already known and (2) information that is new. Researchers usually begin by determining what is already known and then use that knowledge as the basis for discovering new information. You will find information in four different locations. If the information already exists, you will either know it yourself or find that someone else has discovered it. Thus, you will look to your own knowledge or go to the library to find out what other researchers have discovered. New information will come either from field research or experimentation. The rest of this chapter will discuss each of these in turn.

1. *Yourself.* You possess knowledge about subjects, and it's legitimate and necessary that you use that knowledge to support your argument. While millions of people have been to the Grand Canyon, your own direct experience of that place will both establish your authority and provide information that you could get in no other way.
2. *The Library.* Libraries collect and store information that people discover, and you can use that information to expand your knowledge and experience. Though you have not studied AIDS directly yourself, others have, and you can benefit from what they have learned.

3. *In the Field.* Field observations involve going out into the world itself and observing events, objects, animals, and people directly. If you were writing about how people behave in grocery stores, field work would involve going to a grocery store and doing direct observation.
4. *In the Lab.* Sometimes observations need to be done under carefully controlled conditions in order to give precise answers to questions about causes and effects. For example, if you want to know which of two suntan lotions is more effective you could conduct a simple experiment. Use both brands at the same time, on different parts of your body, and expose them both to the sun for equal amounts of time. You will quickly find out which one gives you the most protection.

Researching Yourself: What Do You Already Know?

The first step in tackling any kind of research project is to establish what you know about the subject, and one of the best ways to do this is to write it down. For example, suppose someone has proposed that gambling on college and professional sports be legalized, and you want to participate in the discussion about that subject. Begin by taking a written inventory of what you know about sports and gambling, your own attitudes and beliefs, the values those beliefs are based on, the experiences you have had, and the things you remember reading or hearing about the effects of gambling on sports. It is important to recognize here whether you have personal attitudes, such as long-standing religious attitudes against gambling in any form, that will affect your argument.

Once you have finished recording your own knowledge, try to take a broader view of the subject. Ask why it should be an issue? What is at stake? Who will gain or lose by legalizing sports gambling? You may not be able to give specific names here, and they may not be important yet, but you can think about general groups. How would legalized gambling affect players, owners, fans, the betting public, gambling organizers, and government? Each group probably has something to gain and/or lose if sports gambling is legal or illegal, and you don't need to go to the library to come up with general ideas about what would happen to each group.

For example, you might decide that the public at large would have more fun with sports if they could place a bet and make (or lose) some money. The government might be able to tax gambling profits in several ways, and so increase its revenue. Players might be put in difficult situations by people who bet large amounts of money. As a result, some fans might wonder whether the games are fixed. With a little effort you should be able to come up with a description of the possible effects on each group listed above. These descriptions will be part of an inventory of what you already know about the subject.

SPECULATE ABOUT YOUR SUBJECT

Sometimes you can discover what you know about a subject (and what you don't know) by constructing scenarios in which you speculate about what might (or might not) happen in various circumstances. For example, you might construct a scenario in which you speculate that legalizing sports gambling will:

> *Generate a great deal of money,* but not necessarily for owners or players. This might be a positive result, since fans and others could share in some of the big money of professional sports. But increased money could also encourage criminal activity involving sports, including extortion, organized crime, robberies, money laundering, and embezzlement.
>
> *Generate increased interest in sports,* though that might not always be the kind of interest that players and owners prefer. For example, winning might be important because of the payoff, rather than because of team pride or loyalty.
>
> *Tempt people to spend their money* on betting instead of on essentials, such as food and clothing for their families.
>
> *Expose players and officials* to situations in which they may be tempted to control the outcomes of games by point shaving and other tactics.

This scenario that visualizes the consequences of legalized sports gambling produces more negative than positive results. It visualizes a situation in which all sorts of things could go wrong and many people would be worse off than before. The only people better off would be those who manage to manipulate the system to their own advantage.

Of course, other scenarios are possible, and you should always try to create more than one just to see if you can generate additional ideas and information. For example, a positive scenario for legalized sports gambling might speculate that it will:

> *Produce new jobs* because of the people who will be needed to work in the betting industry itself and also to regulate it, tax it, and write about it.

Generate more tax revenue, so all levels of government should be able to reduce other kinds of taxes or provide improved services.
Be less difficult and dangerous to regulate than illegal gambling.
Put organized crime out of business in gambling.
Produce economic benefits for teams and their cities by drawing larger audiences.
Give fans a share in the money that they help generate, resulting in fewer complaints about high player salaries.
Reduce the price of tickets and produce money for new facilities, taking these burdens off taxpayers and fans.

These scenarios are of course not facts. They are speculations based on educated guesses about what you think could happen. Their chief value is that they can point to the kinds of questions you might ask about a subject, and thus help you begin active research in the library, the field, or the lab. For example, these two scenarios should generate at least the following questions:

What has happened in places where gambling has been legalized, such as Nevada, New Jersey, and other countries? Have the results been positive or negative? Has it helped or hurt the local economy? Has it increased crime?
Is there any illegal sports gambling going on now? If so, what can be learned from it?
How much does it cost a city and its taxpayers to have a major professional sports team? Is it worth it?
What do fans, players, owners, league officials, and governments think about legalizing sports gambling? Have any of these groups taken positions? What are they?

Questions are the foundation of effective research. Carefully stated questions will result in productive research because they will give you specific information to look for. Sloppy, vague questions will result in frustrating and unproductive research. Your questions should allow you to conduct a planned search for specific information, rather than a random or general search for anything you can find. Research is a waste of time and effort unless you are carefully prepared in this way.

APPLICATIONS

1. Select two or three issues for argument. For each one selected, spend at least five to ten minutes writing about what you already know

about the subject. It may not be possible to write everything you know in this short period of time, but do as much as you can. You can write paragraphs or make lists. For each issue, explain what is arguable.

2. For one of the issues you wrote about in question 1, write at least two different brief scenarios. Share these scenarios with other students in a small group of three or four. Discuss each person's subject and attempt to make suggestions and ask questions about each one.

3. Using your scenarios as a basis, make a list of at least ten to twelve questions about your subject that you need to answer through research.

Using the Library

Many information searches will begin in a library. Those trips to the library will be more pleasant and productive if you:

Know what you are looking for. This may be the most important rule of library use. Unless you have planned carefully, you will end up doing a random search, and libraries are frustrating to people who conduct random, disorganized searches.

Take time to learn to use the library. Be patient. It takes time to find out where things are, and all libraries are different. Ask questions often and schedule plenty of time while you are learning. As you gain experience and knowledge, your library work will take less time.

The best way to learn how to use a library is to practice in the library. Just walk in (with questions) and begin looking around. Tours are sometimes helpful, but even they are no substitute for finding your own way around. With the information in this section, you should be able to enter a library and begin working.

Libraries contain three broad categories of publications: books, periodicals, and documents. In each category, some items will be published (or stored) on paper and some electronically or on microfilm or microfiche.

Books may seem to be the most numerous items in libraries, but in many libraries books are less than half of the collection. Books take a long time to write and publish—the whole process may take from two to five years—so they don't always contain the most up-to-date information. But they often give comprehensive overviews and specialized treatments of subjects. Libraries store books on shelves, which are generally called *stacks.*

Periodicals include popular magazines, newspapers, and scholarly journals. They may be published daily, weekly, monthly, quarterly, annually, or on some other schedule. The information and debates they contain are likely to be more current than what you will find in books.

Documents include single sheets, pamphlets, maps, and government publications. Locating government documents will usually require assistance from a librarian.

USING BOOKS

Books are easy to locate in the library because each one is listed in a card catalog or electronic (on-line) catalog (computer database) by title, subject, and author. The catalog lists only those books that your library owns. It won't tell you about books that have been published but that your library does not own. To find out whether the library has a book about sports gambling, you could look under the general subject heading of "Gambling." Depending on the size of the library, there may be a subheading for sports, so you would find "Gambling—sports." Reverse these headings and see if there are any entries under "Sports—gambling." Both the card catalog and the electronic catalog should tell you whether the library contains any books about sports gambling.

Tailoring Your Search. If your library's catalog is computerized, you can simply type in "gambling" as your subject, and you will receive a list of the books in the library about that subject. A quick look at that list might show that most of the books are about how to gamble, or the history of gambling, or betting on horses, or casino gambling. An advantage of computer searching is that you can focus your search on the exact subject you are investigating. To tailor your search to sports gambling, you would type in "gambling and sports." In most library computer database systems the "and" is a command that tells the computer to select only those entries that mention both subjects. You can do other specialized searches for other combinations, such as "gambling and law." If you ask the computer to search for "legalized gambling," it will give you only those entries in which these two words appear right next to each other. Not every library will have the same computer system; you will need to find out how yours works by consulting instruction books or on-line instructions.

The advantage of combining terms in a computer search is that you reduce the number of books on the list the computer provides. A list of books about "gambling" may yield several dozen or several hundred books, depending on your library size. An effective computer search in which you combine terms may yield a list of the six or seven titles that are significantly related to your subject, and it will do that in a matter of a few seconds.

Once you get a book from the shelf, look it over before you check it out and carry it home. You will save time if you collect a number of books about your subject and look through them systematically to see whether they contain the information you need.

> Using your notes and the scenarios and the questions you wrote, list the key words that relate to your subject. A word list about legalized gambling might include taxes, laws or legal aspects, sports, football, basketball, baseball, organized crime, and others.

> Using your list of key words, examine the table of contents and the index of each book to see if it contains information about the subjects you are interested in. This will help to eliminate books that do not suit your needs. You can also look at the introduction, if there is one. Skim it quickly to see if the author mentions the parts of the subject that interest you.

Using Periodicals

There are thousands of periodicals. They include newspapers, popular magazines such as *Sports Illustrated, Time, Newsweek,* and *Harper's.* Some periodicals are trade publications, such as *Personnel,* and others are scholarly publications such as *The American Sociological Review* and the *Journal of Accountancy.* Each periodical serves a distinct audience, or focuses on a specialized subject. Newspapers, faced with the task of getting the news out each day, will treat subjects less thoroughly than popular magazines, which have a week or a month to select stories, do research, and write. Specialized and scholarly publications have an even longer time to do their work and usually serve a highly specialized, knowledgeable audience. You can expect an article about U.S. foreign policy in *Foreign Affairs* to be much more thorough and specialized than a similar article in *U.S. News and World Report,* which is written for the intelligent, informed, general reader.

Getting Access to Periodicals

Using periodicals may seem to be more complicated than using books, but it really isn't. It's just different, and that difference will require some adjustment on your part. The tools that give you access to information published in periodicals are not limited (like the card catalog) to the library you are working in. They will lead you to any article in any periodical, and that can cause a brief problem. Your library may not own the periodical you need, and you may need to request a copy of an individual article through interlibrary loan. Ask a librarian how to do this.

You get access to periodicals by using references sources called periodical indexes, such as the *Readers' Guide to Periodical Literature* (Fig. 7-1) or the *Business Periodicals Index* or by using computerized databases (Fig. 7-2). No single index or database will list all periodicals, so you will have to use one that includes the periodicals you want to scan, or that focuses on the subjects you are writing about. For example, the *Readers' Guide* indexes general magazines. You might find something in it about sports gambling. But if you were looking for specialized information about the stock market or the economy you would need to consult the *Business Periodicals Index* or a specialized index in economics or finance.

Many libraries, especially university and research libraries, are making computerized databases available. These are just like the hard-copy indexes, except that you can search them quickly by using key words and combinations of key words, and you can print the resulting lists or load them onto your own disk so you can sort and print them later with your own computer. Computer databases can make your searches faster and, in many cases, more thorough, because they can include entries that would be contained in several different hard-copy indexes. Some indexes also provide abstracts of the articles they index, and others are able to print entire articles for you.

Searching. You can search most periodical indexes and databases by using key words and subject headings, just as you did when searching the card catalog and on-line catalog. Printed indexes may be slower to search, because you have to look at subject headings that are widely separated, and check through the list of "See Also" subject headings given at the end of each category. Depending on the index, the information you want could be listed under "Sports—gambling," or "Gambling—sports," or in a variety of other ways. A thorough search will require you to check them all.

COMPUTER SEARCHES

Searching by computer is faster, but it's also easier to overwhelm yourself with entries. For example, if you ask the computer for all entries about "sports gambling" or "sports and gambling," you

SPORTS ARENAS *See* Arenas
SPORTS BETTING
    See also
    Baseball betting
    Football betting
    Tennis betting
A losing bet [expansion of legalized gambling] W. F. Reed.
  por *Sports Illustrated* 75:124 Ag 26 '91
Not with our games you don't [pro leagues fighting against state-run
  sports lotteries] P. Y. Hong. il *Business Week* p24 Jl 22 '91

History
The spread's the point [point spread pioneers C. K. McNeil, B. Hecht,
  and E. Curd] D. Sheridan. il *Sport (New York, N.Y.)* 82:75-6 Jl '91

Taxation
A sure bet to lower debt. W. O. Johnson. por *Sports Illustrated*
  75:144 S 2 '91
SPORTS BROADCASTERS *See* Cable television—Sports;
  Radio broadcasting—Sports; Television broadcasting— Sports

Figure 7-1 Sample Entry from *Readers' Guide to Periodical Literature.*

---

could get several hundred, and it's likely that looking at them all
will not be worth your time. Only a few of these are likely to be
related to your subject. The goal is to retrieve a limited number of
items, perhaps no more than twenty, and to have most of them be
directly pertinent to your subject.

An efficient search will require that you combine key words,
just as you did for searching the on-line card catalog. For example,
you could search for "sports gambling and crime," or "sports gambling and taxes." These searches should yield short lists of articles
that are directly related to your subject. Several computerized indexes are available; you will need to spend some time becoming
familiar with the ones available to you. They are all essentially
similar; once you learn to use one, you should have no trouble
learning new ones that you encounter. All of these systems come
with instruction manuals, and it's always a good idea to ask a
librarian for help if you have trouble finding what you need.

Always try a variety of subject headings, key words, and combinations when you search. Different combinations should yield
different references. When you seem to be getting the same items
with each search, you have probably exhausted the entries in that
particular database. Neither indexes nor databases will give you

91118983
Title: A Sure Bet to Lower Debt
Authors: Johnson, William Oscar
Journal: Sports Illustrated Vol: 75 Iss: 10 Date: Sep 2, 1991 pp: 144
             Jrnl Code: GSPI ISSN: 0038-822X Jrnl Group: Lifestyles
Abstract: It is argued that the US could make billions of dollars by
             legalizing and taxing sports gambling. This lucrative and
             popular segment of sport has been relegated to organized
             crime and the office pool for too long. Photograph
Subjects: Gambling; Sports; Laws & legislation; Taxation
Type: Commentary
Length: Medium (10–30 col inches)

91116451
Title: A Losing Bet
Authors: Reed, William F
Journal: Sports Illustrated Vol: 75 Iss: 9 Date: Aug 26, 1991 pp: 124
             Jrnl Code: GSPI ISSN: 0038-822X Jrnl Group: Lifestyles
Abstract: Sports gambling should not be legalized. Doing so would
             result in more fan hostility toward athletes and would
             have a serious negative impact on horse racing and dog
             racing. The moral ramifications of legalized gambling are
             discussed. Photograph
Subjects: Sports; Gambling
Type: Commentary
Length: Medium (10–30 col inches)

91079517
Title: Gambling: Do Leagues Want Piece of the Pie?
Authors: Zani, Andrea
Journal: Sporting News Vol: 212 Iss: 2 Date: Jul 8, 1991 pp: 6
             Jrnl Code: GSPN ISSN: 0038-805X Jrnl Group: Lifestyles
Abstract: Given all the internal problems that plague sports leagues,
             to worry that being associated with gambling would
             tarnish their images is absurd. Suddenly the
             commissioners of the NBA, NFL and Major League
             Baseball are speaking out about how more legalized
             gambling would hurt their sports. Photograph
Subjects: Sports; Gambling; National Basketball Association;
             National Football League—NFL; Major League Baseball
Type: Commentary
Length: Medium (10–30 col inches)

Figure 7-2 Sample Entry from Computerized Database: Pro-Quest.

recent or current information, because it takes approximately six months for these resources to be updated. Thus, if you want to research a breaking news story—something you saw in the paper this morning—you will have a much more difficult time of it. You will have to look at dozens or hundreds of current periodicals, and check indexes, tables of contents, and even looking page by page, because truly current subjects are too recent to be in indexes.

Your search should result in a list of articles in periodicals and newspapers, much like the one in the accompanying example.

Scan the titles using the same guidelines you used when you looked at books. Use titles and any other available information (some computer databases provide additional information, such as brief abstracts and indicate whether an item is a feature or an editorial), to help you decide whether an item will be useful to you. Often the type of periodical will give you a clue about the type of article and whether it will be useful to you. An article about sports gambling in *Newsweek* or *Time* is likely to give you general background information, and perhaps a summary of the subject and the current issues. An article in *Sports Illustrated* or *The Sporting News* will probably provide greater depth and detail because of the special emphasis on sports in these periodicals. With practice, you will learn which sources are likely to be the most productive of information that you want.

Once you identify the items you want to look at, you find out which volumes your library owns and how to find them. Each library should have a list of the periodicals it owns, along with directions for finding them. No library can afford to own all periodicals, but most libraries can obtain copies of almost anything you need through an Interlibrary Loan service. This can take time—two to six weeks—so you'll need to plan ahead or do without. Most libraries display current issues (often the current year) for all to see. Back issues may be bound and stored in the stacks, like books. Some libraries buy periodicals in microfilm for ease of storage. If you can't figure out how to find what you need rather quickly, ask for help.

Once you have located the sources you want to use, try to work quickly. Don't stop to read each article thoroughly as though you were going to be tested over it. Instead, skim articles rapidly and decide whether they actually contain the information you need. If so, record that information in your notes, and always be sure to note where you got the information. In Chapter 8 you will learn how to document the sources of your information. You will need the following information, at a minimum:

- Title of article
- Author
- Title of periodical
- Date of publication
- Volume (and number) such as volume 143, number 6
- Pages where the information you use appears

If you don't record this information when you take notes, you'll have to go back and find it again later, so it's more efficient to simply do it now.

APPLICATIONS

1. Using one of the subjects you worked on earlier in this chapter, make a list of subject headings and key words you can use to search for information in periodical indexes and databases. Using this list, select an index or database and do a search. How many items do you find under the headings you have selected? What subject headings or key words do you find in the index that you had not thought of? How many items do you find under these new headings?
2. Using the searches you did in question 1, select at least two sources you have identified and locate them in your library. Once you have done that, write a brief set of instructions that another student could use to locate periodicals in your library.
3. Write a brief summary of one article that you located, and include the information you will need to document your use of that source.

Finding New Information

Once you have mastered the information that is already known about your subject, it is time to move on to information that no one has yet discovered. While the idea of discovering new information may at first seem intimidating or difficult, it is really easier than you might think. All that's required is a bit of thought and effort. The information in the rest of this chapter will help you get started. Discovering new information usually relies on direct observation of research subjects in their normal or natural settings, which is sometimes called *field research*, and through experiments, which are observations made under controlled conditions. Experiments are usually conducted in laboratories, but they may be conducted in natural settings as well. Much of what you read about your subject will consist of the results of others' observations and experiments. Reviewing what is already known will prepare you for conducting direct observations of your own. You can learn to conduct field work and experiments and incorporate the results into your own arguments. Neither type of research needs to be complicated or difficult in order to be effective.

Field Research

Field research involves collecting information by observing your subject directly in its natural setting. For example, if you were writing an argument urging that products not be overpackaged, your library research might consist partly of collecting data about how many tons of plastic, cardboard, and other materials are used to package products for sale. You could also probably find information about how much of that material is considered wasteful. You could also do some field work of your own by going to stores and looking at examples of product packaging. You can take notes about what you find, and you can even buy several items and then examine the packaging at home—perhaps weighing it and measuring it.

You will need a method of recording your observations. Some researchers take detailed notes and attempt to record everything they see (or hear, smell, taste, and touch). Others develop checklists or charts to help them make consistent, systematic observations. They want to pay attention to the same phenomena with each observation, or observe it in the same way each time. Some researchers use audio or video recordings or other technological means of preserving their observations. Over a period of time, carefully collected, consistent data will form a database that can then be interpreted. Consistency is important in field observations. The more consistent the information you collect, the more you will be able to compare it, or produce a composite picture. For example, if you examine the packaging of a dozen products, you will want to look at each product in the same way so that you can produce a composite analysis, instead of twelve separate analyses.

Once you have collected data, you will need to interpret it, because data never speaks for itself. You will need to tell your readers what it means and how it supports your position. For example, once you have collected information about product packaging, you can calculate its impact on the economy and the environment in a variety of ways. You could, for example, show the effect on your local landfill if everyone in town buys a specific product. Or, you could calculate the effect on the economy of eliminating the extra plastic and cardboard. For example, how many jobs would be lost if certain types of packaging were eliminated? Making your point

would thus rely on a combination of the information you have
gathered from other sources and in your own field observations.

APPLICATIONS

1. Using a subject you have worked with earlier in this chapter (you
   know something about it and you have done some library research)
   devise a means of doing direct observation that is related to your
   subject. Write a brief description of how you will do that observation, what you will look for, how you will make notes or records,
   and what you hope to learn.
2. Present your plan to a group of classmates and revise it according to
   their suggestions.
3. Do a brief observation, using your plan, and write a short explanation of your procedures and results. Explain the conclusions you can
   draw from this observation and how that conclusion relates to the
   subject you are writing about.
4. Present your results to a group of classmates.

Polls and Surveys

Polls and *surveys* attempt to discover what groups of people are
thinking or doing. Polls and surveys do not involve direct observation, but instead ask people to report their own beliefs or actions.
Polls and surveys present two problems. The first is that people
may not always tell the truth about themselves, for various reasons.
They may be embarrassed, or shy, or simply want to present themselves in the best possible light. Given the opportunity, almost
everyone will give you the answer they think you want to hear
rather than the truth. Experienced researchers attempt to protect
themselves against inaccurate answers by asking important questions several times, in several different ways, to see if respondents
answer consistently.

The second problem with polls and surveys is that they do not
report the responses of everyone in a given population. Instead, they
use the responses of a small group to predict the responses or
behavior of a larger group. Of course, this is also their chief advantage, because they do not require the effort and expense of questioning everyone in a population. This means that the small group (or
sample) that responds to the survey must be chosen carefully or its
responses will not reflect the views of the population as a whole.
The more closely this group resembles the larger population to

which it belongs, the more accurately the survey will reflect the views of that larger group.

For example, you may have been approached on the street or in shopping malls by pollsters who have asked your opinion about something—perhaps a store in that mall. But the person doing the poll has no idea whether you are typical of shoppers, and thus has no way of knowing whether your responses will actually reflect the views of people who regularly shop in the store in question. Thus, the survey could be completely worthless. On the other hand, television networks use polls to predict the outcomes of elections, and their predictions are usually quite accurate. This accuracy is possible because the pollsters have taken great pains to choose a sample of people (and locations, in the case of national elections) that exactly reflects the composition of the voters as a whole.

Samples are most accurate in predicting the views or behaviors of a larger group when the sample resembles that group in important ways. Thus, demographic factors such as age, sex, income, education, race, and religion, among others, will be useful in constructing a sample. If you want to know what women college students think of a particular question, you will need to construct a sample that reflects the general population of women college students in age, socioeconomic status, income, major, and other factors that might be important. The more closely your sample reflects the group it represents, the more accurate will be the conclusions you can draw from what that sample tells you.

DESIGNING THE SURVEY

Survey design is an art and science to itself, and if you are seriously interested in it you should consult the specialized literature that has accumulated about this subject. The results of a survey can be affected by the sequence of questions, the wording of questions, and even the race, age, and sex of the questioner. The object here is to consider a few basic principles of survey design so you can experience constructing your own survey and tabulating its results.

Most surveys avoid open-ended questions because the answers are difficult to tabulate and evaluate. Open-ended questions invite respondents to give unique responses, and there is seldom any way of analyzing those responses for trends or consensus. For these reasons, most surveys consist of multiple-choice questions that offer respondents predetermined answers, or questions or statements that ask for a response along a scale of intensity. For example, a person doing a survey about a campus meal plan might construct a question like this one:

Which of the following selections should meals consist of?
a. A single entree with no choice
b. Two entrees, choose one
c. An à la carte menu with limited choice
d. An à la carte menu with free choice of all items
e. An "all you can eat menu"

Respondents must choose one of these answers, and cannot make up their own. For this reason, it is important to design questions so that the answers provide the information you actually want.

The following example shows a question that asks for a response along a scale of intensity:

When I eat in the cafeteria, I want a second serving:
Always _____
Frequently _____
Sometimes _____
Rarely _____
Never _____

Scales like this one that have an odd number of possible responses sometimes draw a high number of responses in the middle, for example, at "Sometimes _____." Respondents may choose the center term for a variety of reasons (indecision, inability to recall, misunderstanding what the terms mean) and thus produce false results. To prevent this, many researchers devise scales that present an even number of responses using descriptive terms or a numbered scale. Of course, respondents need to be told what these numbers mean. Usually, they form a scale that uses descriptive terms such as Excellent or Always and Terrible or Never at its ends, as in the following examples:

The cafeteria presents a balanced meal.

1	2	3	4	5	6
(Never)					(Always)

Cafeteria food is always appetizing.

1	2	3	4	5	6
(Strongly disagree)					(Strongly Agree)

Once you have devised the questions you want to ask and know how you want people to respond to them, you can compile your questionnaire and decide how you want to gather the answers. Some researchers like to get answers right on the questionnaire, while others use separate answer sheets. Separate sheets will be especially helpful if your responses will be tallied by a machine or if your questionnaire has several pages, because handling multiple pages will take extra time.

DOING A PILOT STUDY

Before you spend time, effort, and money doing a full-scale survey, test your survey by doing a pilot study. Give the survey to a few people to see how it works. The size of the pilot study will depend on your situation. If you plan a small survey of no more than one hundred people, then a pilot of five or ten might be plenty. If you plan a large survey of thousands, then your pilot probably should survey at least one hundred. The purpose of a pilot study is to discover whether your survey will provide the information you are looking for. At the same time, you can see whether respondents are able to understand and answer your questions and how easy or difficult it is to tabulate the results. At this point you can add, delete, or revise questions, and change the way respondents record their answers, if necessary. The result of a pilot study should be a survey that runs smoothly without problems.

SURVEYS HAVE LIMITS

Remember that surveys have limits. They do not give you direct access to reality. Rather, they tell you what people believe, or sometimes what they want you to believe they believe. If people respond honestly and completely, then the results may be accurate and useful—that is, they may reflect what people actually think or what they actually did. Polls of voters on election day can predict who will win an election only if the voters report their votes accurately. But respondents do not always give accurate or truthful responses. For example, if two-thirds of the respondents to a survey say that they would choose fruit over potato chips for a snack, that information may bear little relation to reality. Respondents may believe the survey wants them to choose fruit, or they may be embarrassed to say that they would prefer a snack that is generally considered unhealthy.

Television networks have proven the accuracy of their polls. Year after year they are able to predict the winners of even close elections within a very small margin of error. The actual vote counts confirm the accuracy of the polls. Similarly, it would be possible (though perhaps more difficult) to test whether people would choose fruit or potato chips as a snack. You might look at the comparative sales figures for fruit and potato chips, especially in vending machines and snack bars. The information you find would help you judge the reliability of your survey. if what people say is different from what they do, then your survey may have proved that two-thirds of your respondents say they would choose fruit. That doesn't mean that they do so when given the chance. So the survey might be evidence more of what people think they should do rather than of what they actually do. Or it might be evidence that people don't tell the truth about their eating habits, especially if they believe others would disapprove.

The message here? Use surveys carefully, always in conjunction with other kinds of support if possible. Analyze the results thoroughly and, when possible, check those results using some other method.

APPLICATIONS

1. Locate a poll or survey in a newspaper or magazine. Read the results of the survey carefully, and then summarize those results. After you have written the summary, point out what the survey does not tell you and explain how that information would be helpful.
2. Design a brief survey you can use to investigate the opinions of members of a group about some question that is important to that group. For example, construct a survey that asks your fellow students their opinions about some campus issue. Once you have written the survey, give it to a group of students (at least ten) and then tabulate and summarize the results. Explain what those results mean.

Experiments

Experiments are a form of direct observation in which the observer attempts to control the situation very carefully in order to reach reasonably certain conclusions about causes and effects. Experiments need not be expensive or elaborate, and they need not involve complicated, high-tech equipment. For example, you could do a simple experiment to discover if it is possible to hold a seat in a busy library or cafeteria by simply leaving a book, a jacket, or a backpack to signal that the seat is taken. You could use all three methods of attempting to hold a seat and then observe how long people honor each different place holder. Your results would show you how strong an indicator of personal presence is required to keep people from taking a seat that is marked as being occupied.

The rules of experimental inquiry require that you make your methods and results public, so other researchers can repeat your experiment, using the same procedures you used, to determine whether it is possible to get the same results. In experimental science this type of repetition is called *replication,* and it is an important feature of all experimental knowledge. The more a specific result is replicated—i.e., the more times experimenters using the same materials and methods get the same results, the stronger the conclusions that can be drawn from the experiment.

USING EXPERIMENTAL RESULTS TO SUPPORT ARGUMENTS

Use experimental results carefully to support your arguments. Experiments never present absolute proof of anything. Rather, they proceed inductively from facts to conclusions, and their conclusions are always stated in terms of probability, never absolute certainty. But absolute certainty is rarely possible using any method of investigation. The value of knowledge based on experiments is that each replication adds weight and credibility. No single experiment can be conclusive by itself, but the collective weight of numerous replications can be highly effective as support in an argument. A single experiment is always open to challenge on the basis that it was not conducted carefully, or that the results have not been confirmed by other experiments. Despite their limits, experiments can still support your arguments. You simply need to recognize that they present probability rather than absolute truth.

For example, consider the following possible scenario: Backpacks have been disappearing from cafeterias on campus at the rate of one or two a day. A group of students has been advocating increased security—a campus police officer or cadet to stand guard during meal times. The administration has dismissed this as too expensive and proposes, instead, banning backpacks from cafeterias. You believe there is a simpler, less expensive solution, and you propose an experiment to see if your solution will work. Your experiment consists of announcing that randomly selected backpacks have been rigged with alarms that will go off when the backpack is picked up. But you don't want to wait for a thief to pick up the right backpack. What you don't announce is that you are going to stage a theft. You will arrange for someone to pick up the rigged backpack at the peak of a busy lunch hour. The alarm will go off; the "thief" will drop the pack and run, closely pursued by your accomplices, who make a big show of catching him and turning him in to the campus police. After your experiment, backpack thefts drop to one a week.

What has your experiment proved, and how can you use it in an argument? Your experiment suggests that thieves are deterred by the likelihood of being caught in the act. You can't claim that your method is more effective than a security guard or banning backpacks because you haven't tried those methods. You can say that your method is less expensive than a guard and not as inconvenient as one that requires students to take their backpacks to their rooms or cars while they eat lunch.

APPLICATIONS

1. Using a subject you researched earlier in this chapter, design an experiment you can conduct in order to gather more information. Write a description of the experiment.
2. Working in a group, explain your experiment to other students and solicit their comments and questions. After your discussion, revise your experiment.
3. Conduct the experiment you have designed and write a description of the procedures you followed and the results you obtained. Explain how these results will support your argument.

Conclusion

The purpose of research is to discover information about a subject you already know relatively well, so that you can use that information to illustrate and support your own positions. Your research will be most effective and productive if you have developed your ideas and positions and explored your own knowledge of your subject as thoroughly as possible before you turn to other sources.

Remember the four sources of information: your own knowledge, the library, the field, and the laboratory. Each of these has something important to contribute to your authority over your subject. Plan your research thoroughly, test it when possible, and then conduct it with care.

Questions and Activities

1. Review the subjects you have been researching in this chapter. What information do you need in addition to what you have already gathered? Make a list of questions and then write a brief explanation of how you will go about answering each one.

2. Locate an editorial or other brief argument (some suitable ones are reprinted in this book) that you believe would be stronger if it were supported with additional information. Identify the types of information you would add, and then conduct the necessary research to locate it. Then revise the argument by including the information you have found.

3. Working in a team with one other student, identify a research question related to a subject that one of you has been working on in this chapter. Tackle that question independently, without communicating with each other about what you will do to gather information. When you are finished, meet again and present your research to each other. Then write a brief description of how your methods were similar or different, and explain how your results fit together.

Suggestions for Writing

1. Using the issue or subject you have been working on in this chapter, write an argument in which you state your position and use the results of your research to support that position.

2. As you do research for writing an argument, keep a journal of your research steps. Record everything you do, list each source you use, each observation you make, and each experiment you conduct. Then write a description of your own research process. (You could write this for a real reader—a high-school student—and use your description to explain how your research tools and methods in college are different from the ones you used in high school).

CHAPTER EIGHT

Using and Citing Information from Sources

In Chapter 7 you saw how to use a variety of research methods to locate information to support your arguments. Chapter 8 will explain and illustrate how to:

Take notes and keep good research records
Incorporate information from sources into your own writing
Document your sources accurately and completely

Before you read the chapter, respond to the following in writing:

1. In your own words, explain why it is necessary to give credit to the authors of information that you borrow or adapt for your own writing.
2. Explain plagiarism.
3. Describe the system that you use for taking notes and keeping track of information during a research project.

Taking Notes: Keeping Good Research Records

Before you begin any research project, you should think about devising a system for keeping track of the information your research generates so you can get the maximum return from your efforts. The information you gather from sources or discover in original research will do you no good unless you record it accurately and organize it so you can find it later, when you are writing your paper. The system you adopt will depend on your equipment and preferences. Taking notes by hand may be the most common method, but copying machines and lap-top computers have made some tasks easier. Copying machines allow you to make copies quickly rather than spend time taking notes by hand. The chief disadvantage of making copies indiscriminately is that it can be expensive. Also, unless you read the material first, you will not know whether it will be useful to you. Lap-top computers allow you to enter your notes directly onto a computer disk and eventually incorporate them right into a paper. If you have already written a draft you may be able to enter some information directly into your argument and avoid taking separate notes. The main disadvantage of doing this is that it is easy to confuse your text with the source and unintentionally commit plagiarism. If you use a computer, *always* make a backup of each file.

When taking notes by hand you should devise a system and then use it consistently. For example, some people take notes in notebooks; others use note cards (5 × 8 cards work better than 3 × 5's, which are too small for effective note taking). Some people keep a separate folder for each project. The object is to record information accurately and have it available when you need it. If you have notes in several different places and formats, you are likely to lose something important.

Whatever system you establish, you will record information in three main forms: summary, paraphrase, and quotation. Each time you take notes about your subject, be sure you identify the source right on the note itself. This will allow you to include a complete citation for that source when you write your argument. It will also help you avoid the inadvertent plagiarism that can occur when sources are not clearly identified. Remember that you are looking for specific information, not general information, so you will not need to take notes about everything. Concentrate on information that appears to be useful in the argument you have already sketched out in some detail.

Taking Notes: An Example

This section will illustrate taking notes from sources. It assumes that you are writing an argument in which your position is that schools and society at large should treat males and females equally, at all ages and in all situations. As part of your research, you have found the following article, "Our Schools Still Are Shortchanging Girls" by Myrne Roe.

Our Schools Still Are Shortchanging Girls

MYRNE ROE

When I was about 6, I said or did something to make my cousin cry. I don't remember what. I do, however, remember my grandmother giving me one of her stern looks and telling me in her stern voice: "Remember, young lady, it's easier to iron a wrinkle in than it is to iron a wrinkle out."

I didn't have the slightest notion what she was talking about. And for years—every time I've plugged in the iron because someone in my family hasn't checked a clothing label and thus has purchased a hard-to-iron 100 percent cotton shirt—I've recalled the ironing wrinkles in and out wisdom. Now, nearly 50 years later, the lesson has taken on new meaning.

My insight came when I read the results of American Association of University Women's national survey on "How Schools Shortchange Girls." To put it in my grandmother's words: Little girls have a lot of negative self-images ironed into them by textbooks, teachers and curriculum from kindergarten through high school. And, my, how hard they can inflict injury that many never heal. Tell a little girl to give her math workbook to one of the boys in class, because girls won't need to know about numbers when they grow up, and she won't grow up to be very good at numbers. Tell her she has three choices—teacher, secretary or nurse—if she insists on going to college and getting a job, and then tell her that course-work choices will be limited according to which of the three she chooses. She'll get the message about her own future.

Make sure she won't be very good at athletics by limiting her physical education options to ballroom dancing and tumbling. When the basketballs, kickballs and baseballs are handed out at recess, give them to the boys. Give the girls jump ropes.

There'll be a lot of wrinkles ironed in if wanting to join in the classroom discussion is curtailed so the boys get to make their points first. If the first-string debate team is male because, she's told, females simply are too emotional to make good debaters. If she's laughed at when she asks a teacher what she has to do to go to law school. If she wants to write an essay on

"Our Schools Still Are Shortchanging Girls" reprinted by permission of Myrne Roe.

Eleanor Roosevelt, and she's told that Mrs. Roosevelt's husband, Franklin D., is a better choice for a topic.

All that happened in the '40s and '50s to me. All those wrinkles got ironed in, and I'm still dealing with them. So it makes me very angry, indeed, to find that many of the same things are still happening. For heaven's sake, in the mid-'70s I taught a Wichita State University college of education seminar on sexism in the schools. I told the teachers who took the course how to avoid ironing wrinkles of low self-esteem into the souls and minds and lives of young women. In the '70s, teachers were supposed to be learning about sexism and how to keep it out of their classrooms.

But in 1992, the AAUW reports that girls receive significantly less attention than boys from classroom teachers and that African American girls receive even less. It notes that sexual harassment of girls by boys is increasing. It talks about how the contributions of women are pretty much ignored in the schools.

The report also notes that women who are featured in textbooks are generally sex-role stereotyped—mothers, nurses, cheerleaders—but seldom seen as scientists or political leaders. Furthermore, too many schools fail to teach sex and health education. Since girls are more likely to be depressed, have eating disorders and attempt suicide, and since girls are the ones who get pregnant, evading these subjects hurts them more than it hurts boys. The report says SAT scores underpredict college grades of girls and overpredict college grades of boys.

There's more. Much of the report looks as if it could have been written in 1952 or 1972. It's outrageous that sexism is still so prevalent in the public schools in 1992.

March, by the way, is Women's History Month, so if you check with your neighborhood school, you many find that students at this time are actually learning about the contributions women have made. By the end of the month, however, girls will no doubt go right back to believing that women haven't contributed much, and probably shouldn't try to.

Sex discrimination has its roots in the same ugliness that fosters any other kind of prejudice. It grows out of belief based in ignorance. There's absolutely no earthly reason why little boys get more attention from teachers than do little girls except that teachers value—for all those prejudiced reasons—little boys more.

It's particularly disheartening that so many of the ironers of sexist wrinkles are female teachers. (Women still dominate elementary and secondary teaching.) But then, it is not unusual for victims of prejudice to pass on that prejudice. And that's very sad indeed. Until there's some breakthrough in awareness, some change of attitudes, 20 years from now this same column can be written again. No, make that eight years from now, in the year 2000, to match up with the president's goal of achieving educational excellence in America.

Because I submit that it's not possible to have national public school excellence without equality. And I also submit that ironing out those wrinkles that bigotry has ironed in continues to cost this country too much in terms of human dignity and potential. When little girls are shortchanged, so's everyone else.

WRITING A SUMMARY

A general summary of a source can provide the basis of a summary of your own position and those who support it, or of complete, accurate statements of positions different from your own. Summaries can have much or little detail, so long as you present the source accurately. For example, a brief summary of Roe's argument might go like this:

> Myrne Roe reports about a 1992 AAUW (American Association of University Women) survey, "How Schools Shortchange Girls," which asserts that schools give girls a negative self-image by neglecting them, portraying them most often in traditional roles such as wife, mother, and teacher, and implying that they have not contributed much to society. Roe asserts that the report could have been written twenty or forty years ago, and that she experienced some of the same discrimination in her own life. She says nothing will change for women until there is a significant change in society's attitude.

A more detailed summary would include some of the specific information that Roe provides from the survey, such as the observation that teachers pay less attention to girls or that sexual harassment is increasing. A detailed summary might also mention some of Roe's personal experiences, such as being told to write about Franklin Roosevelt instead of Eleanor Roosevelt. A much briefer summary might simply say that Roe is outraged that sexism is as prevalent in the schools now as it was forty years ago when she was in school.

PARAPHRASE

To *paraphrase* something someone else has said or written is to restate it in words that do not duplicate the original. Many times you will not want or need to summarize an entire article. As you read you will often find passages that contain facts or observations that support your own argument. At the same time, your source's exact words may not be distinctive enough to justify word-for-word quotation. You can paraphrase these passages: restate them in your own words. For example, in the original Roe says:

> Furthermore, too many schools fail to teach sex and health education. Since girls are more likely to be depressed, have eating disorders, and attempt suicide, and since girls are the ones who get pregnant, evading these subjects hurts them more than it hurts boys.

In paraphrasing that passage you might say:

> Using the information in the AAUW survey, Roe argues that schools need to provide better sex and health education to girls because they are more vulnerable than boys to depression, eating disorders, suicide, and pregnancy.

Most of the information you want to convey from sources can be paraphrased rather than quoted directly. And note, in the paraphrase above, how both the original AAUW survey and Roe receive credit for this observation. Always remember the following rules about paraphrasing:

> Restate the original in your own words. You must change more than a word here and there.
> Accurately represent the meaning of the original.
> Clearly indicate that the information is not original with you, but comes from a source.

QUOTATIONS

When you find a passage you want to quote, copy it into your notes exactly as it appears in the original, word-for-word, and be sure you note its exact source. Use quotations sparingly. Most of the information you use from sources can be summarized or paraphrased. Reserve quotations for situations in which you want to call attention both to what was said and to how it was said. It's not enough simply to think that someone else has said something better than you could say it. Quote something when only the exact words will create the effect you want. While most of Roe's argument may seem quotable, actually very little of it will convey information or produce an effect that cannot be achieved equally well with a paraphrase. Still, you could quote the following passage as part of a discussion of the similarities between sexism and other forms of prejudice, or as part of a discussion of the origins of sexism.

> According to Myrne Roe, "sex discrimination has its roots in the same ugliness that fosters any other kind of prejudice" (15).

This quotation will serve you as a lead-in or conclusion for a discussion of the similarities between sex discrimination and other forms of prejudice. But the quotation by itself is not really support for your argument. That is, just because someone has said something does not make it true. The quotation is simply a way of introducing a point you want to make. You still need to provide the information that will support this statement by giving facts and examples of the similarities Roe is claiming.

IDENTIFY YOUR SOURCES

Each time you take notes from a source, be sure you record complete publication information: author, title, place and date of publication, and page numbers. Some researchers use 3 × 5 cards (or 5 × 8) for this purpose. Cards are easy to carry, and they can eventually be the basis of the list of works cited or references that you will have to prepare. Recording this information now will keep you from having to relocate the source again in order to complete your documentation. For the Roe argument you will want the following:

> Roe, Myrne
> Our Schools Still Are Shortchanging Girls
> *Tulsa World*
> March 7, 1992, Section A, p. 15

Some researchers set up their reference cards using the standard format for a list of references or works cited. (These formats are explained and illustrated later in this chapter. Your teacher may require that you do this before you write a paper to demonstrate that you can use the formats correctly.)

APPLICATIONS

Working in a group, select a set of arguments printed in this book as the basis for the following exercises.

1. Without consulting with each other, members of the group should:
   Summarize the entire argument
   Summarize an important portion of the argument
   Paraphrase a specific passage
   Select a passage for quotation and copy it accurately
2. Reassemble your group and compare your summaries of the entire argument. Then, each person should present the other summary, the paraphrase, and the quotation to the group and explain why these passages were selected. In response, the group should check these carefully against the original and suggest changes that will make them more accurate and complete.

Incorporating Information into Your Own Writing

It is important to incorporate quotations, paraphrases, and summaries into your own writing as smoothly as possible. This is most effective if you take care to work the information into your own sentences, paraphrasing and summarizing as much as possible, rather than using extensive quotations. Incorporating information into your own writing involves three separate tasks:

1. *Leading into* the information by providing a context and an introductory phrase that announces the information and incorporates it into your own sentences
2. *Formatting* the information so it is easy to identify and read
3. *Identifying* the source of the information you are using

Leading-In

Your readers need to know immediately when the information they are reading is not yours—that is, when someone else is speaking. But they also need to be able to read that information without breaking their concentration. Thus, when you use information from sources you need to incorporate it smoothly into your own sentences and paragraphs. At the same time, you need to signal that it is not yours. You can do this in a variety of ways. Note that in each of the following examples the source is identified in some way.

> *A brief summary.* According to Myrne Roe, a 1992 survey by the American Association of University Women discloses that public schools are short-changing female students by not providing adequate career or health education and by

using textbooks that stereotype or ignore womens' contributions to society.

A paraphrase. Myrne Roe tells of being laughed at when she asked a teacher about attending law school.

A quotation. According to Myrne Roe, "sex discrimination has its roots in the same ugliness that fosters any other kind of prejudice" (15).

Making Quotations Fit Your Own Writing

You can make minor changes in quotations so that they will fit into your sentences and paragraphs, so long as you do not change the sense of the original. For example, the following kinds of changes are allowed:

You can change a capital letter at the beginning of a quotation to a lower-case letter (or do the opposite) to make the quotation part of your sentence. For example, the following quotation begins with a capital letter:

Sex discrimination has its roots in the same ugliness that fosters any other kind of prejudice (Roe).

That capital letter can be changed to accommodate a lead-in phrase:

According to Myrne Roe, "sex discrimination has its roots in the same ugliness that fosters any other kind of prejudice" (15).

You can change ending punctuation in a quotation so that it fits into your own sentence. For example, if the passage you are quoting ends with a comma or semicolon, you can change that to a period if it occurs at the end of your own sentence. Or, you can change a period at the end of a quotation to a comma or semicolon if your sentence requires it. Like this:

"Sex discrimination has its roots in the same ugliness that fosters any other kind of prejudice," according to Myrne Roe (15).

You can omit part of a quotation by using three dots, called an *ellipsis*, like this:

> bigotry . . . continues to cost this country too much in terms of human dignity and potential (Roe).

You can insert words, change the tense of verbs, or change nouns from singular to plural (or the reverse), to achieve clarity. These changes cannot change the sense of the original, and anything you insert into a quotation must be enclosed in square brackets (not parentheses). For example:

> According to Myrne Roe, "bigotry . . . cost[s] this country too much in terms of human dignity and potential" (15).

Remember, the goal is to incorporate information smoothly into your own sentences and paragraphs. Your readers should recognize that you are presenting information from sources, but they should not experience disruptions in their reading.

Formatting Quotations

Summaries and paraphrases will merge with your own writing and literally become part of your own text. But quotations require special formats that identify them as quotations. These special formats include quotation marks and special arrangements on the page.

Quotation marks enclose all quotations. Any time you use someone else's words, you *must* enclose them in quotation marks to indicate that you are reproducing exactly what someone else said. A quotation may be as long as a paragraph or more, or as short as one word if that word represents something distinctive about the person who used it. For example, in World War II the Germans demanded that the U.S. commander at the Battle of the Bulge surrender his command. He is said to have replied with one word: "Nuts." If you use that word in a way that implies you are quoting General McAuliffe, you will need to enclose it in quotation marks. In almost all cases you should put punctuation marks at the ends of quotations *inside* quotation marks.

Identify long quotations by indenting them ten spaces and setting them off from the rest of your text. The *Publication Manual of the American Psychological Association* (Third Edition, 1984) defines a long quotation as one longer than forty words. *The MLA Style Manual* specifies that a quotation longer than four lines should be set off from the rest of the text. Quotations set off in this way usually are not enclosed in quotation marks.

Quotations that are not set off from the text should be run into your text and punctuated as though they were part of your own sentences. For example: According to Myrne Roe, "it's not possible to have national public school excellence without equality" (Roe).

APPLICATIONS

1. In the previous Applications section you wrote summaries and paraphrases and selected passages for quotation. Now write brief passages in which you incorporate those summaries, paraphrases, and quotations into your own writing. Concentrate on using appropriate lead-in phrases and make the information from sources blend into your own sentences and paragraphs.
2. Read Roe's argument again. How does she use summary, paraphrase, and quotation? Identify her methods of incorporating these into her writing.
3. Read several of the arguments printed in this book, paying special attention to the way writers incorporate information from sources into their own writing. Identify examples of when the writers could identify sources more clearly or incorporate information into their own writing. Are their quotations appropriate, or should they be changed to summaries or paraphrases?

Documenting Your Sources

You *always* need to identify the source of information that is not your own, information that someone else has discovered, developed, or assembled. In part, identifying your sources is just a matter of intellectual honesty, of giving credit to the person who did the work. You expect people to give you credit for what you do; your teachers expect you to extend the same courtesy to others. There are other reasons for citing your sources accurately:

> Complete and accurate citations of your sources will enhance your own authority in your readers' eyes, because you will be showing your ability to find and use informed sources.
>
> Complete, accurate citations allow your readers to locate and evaluate your sources on their own if they wish to. And many will.

What Should You Cite?

As a general rule, you should cite the source of any information that does not originate with you. Now, it is true that almost everything we know comes from somewhere else, so it's important to use common sense and not try to give a source for every bit of information in your argument. For example, you do not need to cite a source for common knowledge, but sometimes it is difficult to tell what is common knowledge and what is not.

What Is Common Knowledge?

Common knowledge is information that is generally available and cannot be connected with a specific or identifiable source (a person, organization, etc.). For example, everyone knows that the cost of living increases every year, so it's common knowledge to say so. But if you say that the cost of living has increased by 6 percent in a year, you need to cite a source for that figure—unless you calculated it yourself. Similarly, it is now common knowledge that Abraham Lincoln was assassinated in April of 1865 in Ford's Theatre in Washington, D.C. But if you give many more details than this, such as what kind of day it was, or how the crowd reacted to the shot and Booth's escape, you will have to identify your source for that information.

Sometimes information looks like common knowledge, but isn't. You may have been following a news story for some months or even years, and you may believe that it has become common knowledge. For example, it is well known that AIDS is a fatal disease that can be transmitted through sexual contact with an infected partner, through use of an unsterile hypodermic needle, or through blood transfusions. But exact statistics about the number of people who have the disease and who have died from it are not common knowledge except in the most general sense. If you use those numbers, you will need to cite a source, because the person who did the calculations should receive credit for them. Similarly, if you discuss the exact means of transmission, or discuss specific probabilities of contracting the disease through various means, you will need to cite a source. It is common knowledge that the AIDS epidemic will probably get much worse before someone discovers a cure, but for accurate predictions about just how many people will die you will need to rely on and cite a source.

Of course, what is common knowledge varies from group to group. Experts usually share a great deal of information with other experts, and when they talk with each other or write for each other they have no need to give the source of information that everyone in the group already knows. For example, physicians regard it as common knowledge that common colds are caused by viruses. But, if someone who is not a physician wanted to say that, it might be necessary to cite a source.

Any time you use or adapt words, ideas, insights, descriptions, interpretations, statistics, or other information that someone else developed, you have to identify the source.

How to Cite Your Sources

Effective citation (also called *documentation*) has three components:

1. Attributive words or phrases that introduce and identify information from a source
2. Accurate citations in parentheses in your own text that identify the source of the information you are using
3. A complete, accurate list of your sources at the end of your paper

ATTRIBUTIONS

As you lead into information from a source, incorporating it into your own sentences and paragraphs, you can identify the source this way:

> Myrne Roe reports that schools discriminate against girls even though most teachers are women, and she observes that "it is not unusual for victims of prejudice to pass on that prejudice" (15).

In this example, the sentence identifies the source, but your reader will have to consult the list of references at the end to locate Roe's article and read it. You could, of course, provide complete information in the text, as in the following example.

> Myrne Roe, writing in the *Tulsa World* for March 7, 1992 (p. A 15) reports that schools discriminate against girls even though most teachers are women, and she observes that "it is not unusual for victims of prejudice to pass on that prejudice."

Some people believe that including this much information in the text interferes with readability, but the method is useful if you are writing in a situation that does not permit you to attach lists of references or works cited, such as business reports and newspaper and magazine articles.

PARENTHETICAL CITATIONS IN YOUR TEXT

In your reading you may have encountered books and articles that use footnotes and endnotes to document sources. You may even have been taught to do this at some time. Most academic disciplines no longer use footnotes and endnotes because most publishers have decided that they are too expensive to print. When scholarly publications make changes in their formats, academic writing in school changes as well. Footnotes and endnotes are now used almost exclusively for explanations that authors believe are necessary but that do not really belong in the text itself, perhaps because they are peripheral to the main thrust of the argument. And even then they are used only sparingly.

Instead of footnotes and endnotes, most academic disciplines now require writers to provide information about their sources in parenthetical citations in their texts. You have seen some citations of this type in earlier examples in this chapter. The information you include in parenthetical citations depends on the information you provide in your lead-in. For example, if you include the author's name in your lead-in, then you will not need to repeat that name in parentheses. If you do not give the author's name in your lead-in, then you will need to include it in the parenthetical citation. Like this:

> According to a 1992 survey by the American Association of University Women, SAT scores predict that boys will get higher grades than they actually receive, and that girls will get lower grades than they receive (Roe, 15).

The two citation systems presented here are those of the Modern Language Association (MLA) and the American Psychological Association (APA). Each of these organizations has published a manual explaining its system of documentation and manuscript preparation. Consult these manuals when you have questions you cannot answer based on the information available in this book. The MLA system appears in *The MLA Style Manual* (Modern Language Association, 1985, Walter S. Achtert and Joseph Gibaldi, eds.). It is broadly similar to the documentation systems used in the humanities. The most widely used documentation system in the social sciences is explained in the *Publication Manual of the American Psychological Association* (American Psychological Association, 3rd edition, 1984). Other academic disciplines have their own systems of documentation, and as you progress through school you should always ask your teachers which system they want you to use.

The information you include in the parenthetical citation will depend on the documentation system used. The general rule is that you must provide enough information so readers can identify the source in the list of references at the end of your paper.

APA style uses a combination of the author's name and the date of publication; both must appear in your text at a point that identifies the information you are attributing to the source you name. For example, in citing the Roe article printed in this chapter you would say:

> Roe (1992) alleges that discrimination against girls in school has not improved in the past fifty years.

If the author's name does not appear in your text, it should be in the parentheses.

> Discrimination against girls in school has not improved in the past fifty years (Roe, 1992).

If a source has two authors, use both names every time you refer to it. If it has more than two authors, mention all names the first time and in subsequent citations use the name of the first author and the abbreviation *et al.* (Latin for *and others*), like this:

> *For two authors*
> Cooper and Jones (1990) found that . . .
> *For more than two authors*
> Cooper, Jones, and Smith (1988) found that . . .
> *Second and subsequent citations of the same source*
> Cooper et al. (1988) found that . . .

You can provide these references in parenthetical citations rather than in your own sentence, like this:

> *Two authors*
> Recent research (Cooper & Jones, 1990) shows that . . .
> *More than two authors*
> Recent sociological research (Cooper, Jones, & Smith, 1988) suggests that . . .
> *Subsequent citations*
> Recent sociological research (Cooper et al., 1988)

If you use two works by the same author (or authors), published in the same year, then designate each date with a separate suffix, as in:

(Brown, 1990a, 1990b)

To cite a specific part of a source, simply include a page or chapter number, or some other specific information, in your parenthetical citation. Like this:

(Brown, 1990a, p. 14)

MLA style for parenthetical citations is slightly different from the APA style. Instead of using author and date, it uses author and page number(s). Someday, scholars and editors may get together and agree to a common system for documentation, but it hasn't happened yet. The MLA citation system works as follows:

> *If the author's name is in your text*
>   According to Alexander (113)
> *If the author's name is not in your text*
>   At least one researcher (Alexander, 113) has discovered

To cite two or more works by the same author, use a title, or a shortened version of the title of each in your citation, so readers will know which one you are referring to. For example, assume that J. Q. Andrews has written two books that you want to cite. One is titled *Race Relations in the United States;* the other is *Discrimination.* In your citations you can distinguish these books by using all or part of the title of each one. Like this:

> According to Andrews . . . (*Race,* 115).
> or
> As Andrews has pointed out . . . (*Discrimination,* 118)

Summary

Regardless of the system you use to document your sources, try to observe the following guidelines:

> Keep your text readable by using as few citations as possible and keep them brief.
> Provide enough information to enable your readers to identify the source in the list of references at the end of your paper.
> Use the guidelines provided here to help you decide how to present a complete citation each time you use information from a source. If you have questions, consult the MLA or APA handbook.

Be absolutely consistent in your citation format throughout your paper.

APPLICATIONS

1. Return to the summaries, quotations, and paraphrases that you prepared for earlier Applications in this chapter and provide appropriate lead-in statements, attributions, and parenthetical citations for each.
2. Look again at Roe's argument, this time focusing on her lead-in statements and attributions. Identify those places where you can improve Roe's lead-in's and attributions, and then make any necessary changes.
3. Select a subject you know reasonably well and make two lists, each containing a different kind of information about that subject:
   a. *Common knowledge*—information you do not have to give credit for, and explain why it is common knowledge.
   b. *Borrowed information* that you already know (without looking it up—perhaps you have read it somewhere), but that is *not* common knowledge and thus requires documentation.

Creating a List of References or Works Cited

To complete your documentation system you will make a complete list of the sources you have used in supporting your argument. This list will appear at the end of your paper and it will include all of the sources you have cited in the text of your paper. Conversely, all of the sources that appear in your list of references or works cited should also be cited in the text of your argument. That is, your list and your citations should match. Use the following guidelines in setting up this list:

Arrange the list alphabetically, using the authors' last names. If a source has more than one author, use the first-named author to put it in alphabetical order.

If you list more than one work by the same author, APA style requires that you arrange these in order by date, with the earliest first and list the author's name with each entry. MLA style arranges the items in alphabetical order by title and allows you to replace the author's name with three dashes after the first entry.

Give your list of sources a title. If you are using APA style you will call your list *References*. If you are using MLA style, your title will be *Works Cited.* In both systems, center the title at the top of the first page of your list of sources.

Listing Sources

Each entry in your list of References or Works Cited should include complete and accurate publication information for the source it identifies. Your readers should be able to use the information you provide to identify and locate any source listed. To accomplish this, you will need to provide the author, title, and complete publication information. The following examples show how to use APA or MLA guidelines to make entries for different kinds of sources. Using these examples as your starting point, you should be able to create an entry for virtually any type of source material, even if a direct example isn't given here. If you are uncertain about how to do that, you should consult the style manual you are using (APA or MLA) for a detailed example. In the following examples, the punctuation, capitalization, and spacing are done quite deliberately and carefully. Many teachers are particular about doing these entries correctly, so be sure you follow the examples closely.

Sample Entries for Sources

BOOKS

Single Author.
APA
   Gleick, James. (1987). *Chaos.* New York: Viking.
MLA
   Gleick, James. *Chaos.* New York: Viking, 1987.

Two Authors.
APA
   Schank, Roger, & Abelson, Robert. (1977). *Scripts plans goals and understanding: An inquiry into human knowledge structures.* Hillsdale, NJ: Lawrence Erlbaum Associates.
MLA
   Schank, Roger, and Robert Abelson. *Scripts Plans Goals and Understanding: An Inquiry Into Human Knowledge Structures.* Hillsdale, NJ: Lawrence Erlbaum Associates, 1977.

An Edited Book.
APA
> Simons, Herbert R. (Ed.). (1989). *Rhetoric in the human sciences*. London: Sage Publications.

MLA
> Simons, Herbert R. ed. *Rhetoric in the Human Sciences*. London: Sage Publications, 1989.

A Book by a Corporate Author.
APA
> American Psychological Association. (1983, Revisions, 1984). *Publication Manual of the american psychological association*. Washington, D.C.: Author.

(In this case, the author is also the publisher.)
MLA
> American Psychological Association. *Publication Manual of the American Psychological Association*. Washington, D.C.: American Psychological Association, 1983 (Revisions, 1984).

FILM

APA
> Eastwood, Clint. (Producer and Director). (1992). *Unforgiven* [Film]. Malpaso.

MLA
> *Unforgiven*. Dir. Clint Eastwood. With Clint Eastwood, Gene Hackman, and Morgan Freeman. Malpaso, 1992.

ARTICLES IN PERIODICALS, JOURNALS, BOOKS, OR NEWSPAPERS

APA
> Elbow, Peter. (1991). Reflections on academic discourse: How it relates to freshmen and colleagues. *College English*, *53*, 135–55.

MLA
> Elbow, Peter. "Reflections On Academic Discourse: How It Relates to Freshmen and Colleagues." *College English*. 53 (1991): 135–55.

A Chapter in a Collection or Anthology.
APA
> Prelli, Lawrence J. (1989). The rhetorical construction of scientific ethos. In Herbert W. Simons (Ed.), *Rhetoric in the human sciences*. (pp. 48–78). London: Sage Publications.

MLA

> Prelli, Lawrence J. "The Rhetorical Construction of Scientific Ethos." *Rhetoric in the Human Sciences.* Ed. Herbert W. Simons. London: Sage Publications, 1989. 48–78.

Magazine Article: Author Given.

APA

> Franklin, H. Bruce. (1991, December). The POW/MIA Myth. The Atlantic, pp. 45–81.

MLA

> Franklin, H. Bruce. "The POW/MIA Myth." *The Atlantic,* Dec. 1991: 45–81.

Magazine Article: No Author Given.

APA

> More death in the mailroom. (1991, November 25). *Time.* p. 51

MLA

> "More Death in the Mailroom." *Time* November 25, 1991: 51.

Newspaper Article.

APA

> Blumenthal, Ralph. (1992, February 27). Gambinos quit truck business in plea bargain. *The New York Times,* p. Al.

MLA

> Blumenthal, Ralph. "Gambinos Quit Truck Business in Plea Bargain." *The New York Times* February 27, 1992, Al.

Newspaper Editorial.

APA

> Staff. (1992, April 18). Why Johnny can't write. *The Tulsa World,* p. A12.

MLA

> "Why Johnny Can't Write." Editorial. *The Tulsa World* 18 April 1992, sec. A: 12.

PERSONAL INTERVIEW

APA

> Smith, John. (1992). Personal interview.

MLA

> Smith, John. Personal Interview. April 1, 1992.

Summary: Some General Guidelines

Using the examples presented here you should be able to make an entry for any source that you consult. Remember that the primary goal is to provide enough information that your readers can locate and consult your sources for themselves. The following general guidelines should help.

1. The logic of all entries is similar. For APA, provide author, date, title, and publication data, in that order. For MLA, provide author, title, and publication data, including the date, in that order.
2. When you encounter an unfamiliar type of source—one for which you have no example—look for an example that shows a similar type of source. Use the example to build your entry. If you can't figure out how to do the entry, consult the appropriate style manual directly.
3. The most likely information to be missing is the author. When that happens, place the title first and then proceed as usual with the rest of the entry.
4. If information other than the author is missing, indicate that in some way. For example, you will find some publications without dates. In place of the date, type the abbreviation *n.d.* so your readers will not think you forgot to include it.

Avoiding Plagiarism

Plagiarism is the presentation of someone else's ideas, words, statistics, or other information as though it were your own, or it involves taking credit for something that is not yours. Some people may distinguish between intentional and unintentional acts of plagiarism, but it's often very difficult to tell them apart, and many of your teachers will treat all instances of plagiarism as though they were intentional. Most schools impose severe penalties for plagiarism; you could receive a failing grade for the paper or for the entire course. Some schools expel students for honor code violations. Because the penalties are so severe, and avoiding plagiarism is so easy, spend some time now learning how to avoid difficulty.

As an example, consider various ways of using the following passage from Frank Deford's essay about Pearl Harbor, "We Should Forget It," which is printed elsewhere in this book. First, read Deford's own words:

In "Pearl Harbor Ghosts," a fascinating new study by Thurston Clarke, the author argues persuasively that we never would have nuked the Japanese cities if we hadn't been so determined not to forget to remember Pearl Harbor.

The most blatant and cynical form of plagiarism would be simply to use Deford's words without acknowledging him as the source, like this:

In August 1945, the United States dropped atom bombs on two Japanese cities, something that would never have happened if we hadn't been so determined not to forget Pearl Harbor.

This passage gives the impression that its words and ideas do not rely on Deford's sentence. This is plagiarism of the worst kind.

In the following modification of this passage the writer acknowledges Deford's article as a source:

In August 1945, the United States dropped atom bombs on two Japanese cities, something that would never have happened, according to Frank Deford, if we hadn't been so determined not to forget Pearl Harbor. (40)

But, even though this version acknowledges Deford, the writer is still using words lifted directly from Deford's sentence without using quotation marks, and completely misses Deford's attribution of this opinion to Thurston Clarke. Thus, this version also constitutes plagiarism, despite the attribution to Deford and the parenthetical citation.

A more appropriate use of this passage would be as follows:

In August 1945, the United States dropped atom bombs on two Japanese cities. According to Thurston Clarke, this bombing would not have occurred if Americans hadn't been so obsessed with remembering Pearl Harbor. (cited in Deford)

In this version, Thurston Clarke gets credit for his idea, and Frank Deford gets credit for referring to Clarke. The writer also avoids plagiarism by paraphrasing Deford rather than using his words. The following version is equally acceptable:

In August 1945, the United States dropped atom bombs on two Japanese cities. According to Frank Deford, author Thurston Clarke "argues persuasively that we never would have nuked the Japanese cities if we hadn't been so determined not to forget to remember Pearl Harbor." (40)

(Because Deford's name appears in the text, only the page number needs to be given in the parenthetical reference.) In this version, readers get an accurate picture of Deford referring to Clarke, and the writer uses quotation marks to indicate the words that are being quoted from Deford's essay. The decision to use a direct quotation rather than a paraphrase is yours to make, and it depends on your purpose and the context in which you are using the information.

APPLICATIONS

1. Read Roe's article again. Select three instances in which she uses information from the AAUW report. In each case, explain how she distinguishes her own statements from those in the report she is writing about.
2. Is there any instance in which Roe should be *clearer* about what is hers and what comes from a source? If so, describe the problem and make the necessary revisions to correct it.
3. Select a passage from one of the arguments printed in this text. Write a brief passage in which you quote, paraphrase, or summarize that passage accurately, using attributive phrases and in-text citations as necessary.
4. What are your school's policies about plagiarism? How does your school (or your teacher) define plagiarism, and what are the penalties? After you have gathered this information, write a brief explanation of plagiarism that you could present to new students.

Conclusion

Avoiding plagiarism will be easy if you follow the procedures outlined in this chapter and in Chapter 7:

- Use information from sources to support your own ideas, not as substitutes for your own ideas.
- Take notes and keep records carefully, so you always know the source of the information you use.
- Use attributive phrases and parenthetical citations to identify the words, phrases, ideas, statistics, and other information you have taken from sources.

- Provide complete parenthetical citations in your text.
- Construct a complete, accurate list of References or Works Cited in which you include every work you have cited in your paper.

Questions and Activities

1. Create APA and MLA References and Works Cited entries for the following items (which you locate):

   A book
   An article with one author published in a periodical
   An article with two authors published in a periodical
   An article published in a book

   Once you have created these entries, show them to a classmate for critique and, if necessary, correction.

2. From one of the sources you identified in question 1, select a passage that you believe is particularly important or informative and do the following:

   Summarize the passage
   Paraphrase part of the passage
   Quote a portion of the passage

   For each of these, use both APA and MLA guidelines to write an appropriate lead-in, provide a parenthetical citation, and construct an entry for a list of References and Works Cited.

PRO/CON ARGUMENTS

Female Athletes:
Can They Catch Up with Men?

Will women ever run as fast as men? It's true that many women can already outrun many men, but so far the fastest female runners in major marathons have not posted better times than the fastest male. Are there physical reasons for that? Will better nutrition and training enable women to run faster? As one of the writers here argues, it's possible that the limitations are not completely physical. Before you read the arguments in this section, respond in writing to the following:

Preparing to Read

1. *What do you believe are the major reasons that women have not posted better times than men in major track events?*
2. *Do you believe that men and women should compete directly with each other, in the same sports? Why or why not?*

Sexism Limits True Gauge . . . Pro

BROOKS JOHNSON

After assessing rapid improvements in track and field by women, a recent study at UCLA projects the day when women will outperform men.

Women have narrowed the gap between their performances and those of men, but because of sexism we might never know whether they can match the marks of men.

There is plenty of evidence of how women have been held back in track and field. They still don't have a women's triple jump or pole vault in the Olympics, the first women's marathon wasn't run in the Games until 1984, and women weren't allowed to run any event longer than 800 meters until 1972.

Sexism in track hasn't been limited to just the Olympics. The Boston Marathon, long the world's most prestigious distance race—didn't allow women until 1972.

Sexism has held women back from being involved in certain areas. In most cases where they are allowed to compete, sexism still clouds the expectations and demands put on them. We just do not expect women to excel at certain things, establishing a prophecy that we all work to fulfill.

There are events where the weight-to-strength ratio can be such that gender is not the most critical element. For example, in the marathon the needs are such that a woman can be expected to compete on equal terms with men.

Given the proper relationship between her strength and weight, a woman can endure the other rigors involved in a marathon as well as a man.

Ultimately, the winner in the marathon will be determined by biomechanics, not gender. The reason: biomechanics, or the efficient use of physics, is infinitely more important then gender once the optimum weight-to-strength ratio has been achieved.

The bottom line is simply this: In some events, physics are more important than physique. This changes somewhat when physical criteria is inherent in the event itself. The male shot put, discus, hurdles and hammer have built-in bias that favor men. But simple running events can be successfully contested by anyone with a favorable weight-to-strength ratio, good mechanics and a winning spirit. Given this, gender becomes incidental as far as performance is concerned.

The greatest step forward we have to make is in the eradication of sexism itself. From there, women will take it the rest of the way.

Men's 'Physical Advantages' Give Them Edge . . . Con

LOREN SEAGRAVE

Recent rekindling of the "Battle of the Sexes" controversy in sport has been prompted by a statistical analysis of the rate of improvement in men's and women's world records for the marathon.

Armed solely with the fact that the rate of improvement for women is twice as great as for men, the authors theorized women would be covering the 26-plus miles faster than men before the end of the century.

This vision of the athletic superwoman of the future has been inspired solely by mathematical data, while conveniently ignoring scientific fact.

In the past decade, similar research showed the rate of improvement in the marathon record exceeded the 100-meter dash. With a little mathematical blue smoke and mirrors, we could conclude tomorrow's athletes will run the marathon in less time than it takes to run the 100 meters. I don't think so.

It is fact that when analyzing all running events for both men and women, improvement shows no signs of leveling off. Historically, every scholarly attempt to define the limits of human achievements has been met with broken records before the proverbial ink has dried on the page.

Is it really surprising that women are improving at a greater rate? In spite of the increased opportunities made available during the past 30 years, athletics for women are still in the developing stages. Even today, women are routinely denied the opportunities and advantages that the male athletic community takes for granted. Women are actually racing to catch up.

When funding, facilities, quality of instruction and professional opportunities for women are equal to men, performance standards for women will enjoy another quantum leap. But unless men take an evolutionary U-turn, it is highly unlikely those marks will exceed those posted by comparably trained males.

Mother Nature has dealt men a better hand when it comes to physical performance measured by the stopwatch. We know the body's control system, the central nervous system, can be developed to equally high levels in both men and women. However, when the rubber meets the road, men have a larger engine. Physical advantages, such as strength and power on a pound-for-pound basis, along with myriad other physiological pluses have given the edge to the men.

Sociologically, women have only recently been given tacit approval to excel in some sporting events. The 1968 Olympics was the first time women were allowed to run 800 meters in the Games since their inaugural appearance in 1928.

Researchers hope the controversy around this latest prognostication will spurn interest in researching the supranormal human being, the elite athlete of today.

It certainly has not decreased feelings that exist on the elementary school playground, high school, collegiate and high performance sport or in the world of business. "I am never going to let a girl beat me." Women are not the "weaker sex," but it is highly unlikely that top women will out perform the top men in running contests.

Questions

1. Johnson contends that sports have evolved with a bias toward the male physique. How could sports be changed so that women are not at a disadvantage?

2. Working in a group, discuss the relationships between the restrictions placed on women in sports and the restrictions placed on women by society at large.

Suggestions for Further Research

1. Investigate the physical limits on men's and women's athletic performances and write a summary in which you compare the two.

2. Select a specific sport that is open to both men and women (skiing, golf, tennis, etc.) and compare the way they are treated. For exam-

ple, look at similarities and differences in men's and women's rules, prizes, etc. Write a summary of the information you discover.

Suggestions for Writing

1. Choose a sport in which women do not usually participate. Write a paper in which you argue that the sport should be modified, if necessary, and that women should be encouraged to participate in it equally with men.

2. Should women play on the same teams as men in basketball, baseball, and other sports? Some girls now play Little League baseball, and at least one is on a high school wrestling team. Argue for or against coed sports.

Buying American-Made Products:

Patriotism vs. Free Trade?

In recent years, concerns about the health of the U.S. economy have given new life to a long-standing effort to encourage people to buy products made in America by American workers. The "Buy American" campaign has become especially strident in response to fears that the Japanese are wrecking the U.S. economy by exporting large numbers of their products to the United States without allowing U.S. companies to sell their products in Japan. Somehow, in the midst of international trade negotiations, it has become the responsibility of U.S. consumers to save the economy by purchasing only those products made in the United States. The arguments in this section respond to the "Buy American" campaign. Before you read them, respond in writing to the following:

Preparing to Read

1. *Take a quick inventory of major items in your personal belongings. Make a list of those made in the United States, and a parallel list of those made elsewhere. Identify the country of origin for each.*
2. *When you buy something, do you pay any attention to where it was made? How does the product's origin affect your decision?*

Build the Green Machine

JESSICA MATTHEWS

Robert Stempel
CEO, General Motors
Detroit, Mich.
Dear Mr. Stempel:

Welcome home. I hope you had a nice trip and are now ready to tackle the real issues. Japanese imports of more auto parts and a few cars will be nice, but it won't change your bottom line or win back those 74,000 jobs.

Every American knows that your problems are here at home. You're losing market share right here. If you can't compete with Japanese cars in the United States, how are you going to compete with them in Japan, even if every last trade barrier were removed? (By the way, next time you go asking for marketing rights in an island country, at least be ready to sell right-hand-drive cars—you'll be taken more seriously.)

So what can you do? You've been hearing nothing but bad news lately, but in fact you have a terrific opportunity. You are in command of a company with technical brains second to none in the world–use them!

Call your top people together, and tell them you're tired of trying to catch up with the Japanese and then finding that when you do, they've moved on to the next generation of improvements. Starting now, for one product line at least, GM's goal will be to leapfrog the Japanese.

The way to do that is to figure out what consumers will want five and 10 years hence. What they'll want, and what GM will give them, is a world-class green car.

Pick your smartest, boldest and best engineers and give them this task: Design a mass-production car from the ground up that beats every government mileage, emission and safety standard two-, three-, or tenfold and that is fully recyclable. Make it stylish, comfortable, adequately peppy and capable of freeway speeds.

157

You know that technically your people can do it. Your battery-powered Impact car and the four-passenger, 100-mpg "Ultralite" demonstration model are proof of the first steps. Then, round up all the naysayers. Tell the lawyers and lobbyists who warn you that this will make it impossible to fight new regulations in Washington that you don't care; from now on GM will be way ahead of government standards, playing offense not defense. Tell them you know that gasoline is likely to remain cheap for the next few years, but you're looking at the long term. Tell your advertising and PR people to drop the "only big cars are safe" campaign.

Tell your financial wizards that running the company to maximize short-term profits has been tried long enough. Only a fool would continue to swim against the tide of red ink. Radical change is obviously necessary. Your plan is to make General Motors, once again, the world's automotive design leader—a car maker's car maker.

Tell your marketers who think Americans only want power and gadgets that they're missing something. Show them Honda's television ad of a Civic turning a desert into a tropical rain forest, and ask why the company that's now third in American car sales might be using that message.

Suggest they look at what cutting-edge companies in other sectors are doing and find out why. They'll discover what your own polls and focus groups probably already show: That since 1987 public concern about the environment has grown faster than concern for any other national problem.

They'll find companies such as Dow, Du Pont, AT&T, New England Electric, Monsanto, Northern Telecom, Southern California Edison and others setting company environmental goals vastly more ambitious than anything any regulator would dare propose. They'll learn that such companies are doing it because they think they know what their customers want and because when they looked, they found undreamt of efficiencies, technological opportunities and profit.

Tell your planning teams to forget about what's going on in Washington. Public policy is stalled way behind the public's desire for change. If they want guidance about where the world is headed, tell them to read the Japanese Ministry of International Trade and Industry's 100-year plan for planetary recovery to see what they think your markets will look like. Have your planners examine the proposals being debated by the European Community, which stress the need for urgent improvements in energy efficiency and reductions in greenhouse gas emissions.

If the experience of other companies that have adopted their own ambitious environmental goals is any guide, you'll find that setting and meeting your own targets is more rewarding (psychically as well as financially) than having the government tell you what to do. Yours is a corporate culture more resistant to change than any other, but once you get all the can't-do folks out of the way, you'll find more than enough employees excited, even inspired, by the challenge you have set for them.

Once you get things moving inside the company, get the message out. Start by putting the Ultralite in your showrooms. People will come in just to see it, and once they're there, they may buy. Get them thinking about what it would be like to own a car that fills up on five gallons of gas. Boast about the mean, green machine you've got planned.

One of your biggest assets right now is that most of your countrymen are looking for a reason to buy American. For some of them, this change in direction would be enough. Others will wait to see the product. But if you produce the car I've described, don't doubt that there'll be plenty of Americans, Europeans and, yes, even some Japanese, lined up to buy it.

Why I Voted for a Used Car

ANDREW TOBIAS

The biggest vote you make is not on Election Day but when you buy a car, as I just did. A new Mercedes? For the West German economy, 60,000 votes. A new Infiniti? For Japan, 40,000 votes. A new Chevy Beretta? For Detroit, 13,000.

Now don't get your yuppie BMW back up. I know you're every bit as patriotic as I am. And like you, I believe in free trade: you should buy whatever damn car you please. (And, yes, I know your Japanese car may have been built here, and that your Miata, built over there, is part American because Ford owns 25% of Mazda.)

What's all this nationalism, anyway? This is increasingly one world, and the goal for the whole globe to prosper, not to have the Japanese shun our rice, or we their cars, out of tribal paranoia. So what if Detroit just laid off more than 24,000 workers, with predictions of more to come?

Still, we're paying for a mountain of foreign goods that will be junk in ten years with land, buildings and the rights to *The Three*

Stooges—things that are eternal (well, maybe not buildings). We're like the Manhattan Indians, who had little immediate need for the island and couldn't resist the trinkets.

It's become a cliché that the Indians would have made out like bandits if they had merely invested the $24 they got at 8% (let alone in Fidelity's Magellan mutual fund). They'd have had $32 trillion by now. But the point is, they didn't take cash and invest it, they took trinkets. Today we're taking Nintendo games and Honda Preludes.

When it comes to productive tools, we should buy the best, regardless of origin, because it's in our long-term self-interest to do so. The best tools make for the most competitive products. But when it comes to trinkets, we should think twice. Of course, with a lot of today's trinkets–VCRs and camcorders, to name just two—there's no way to buy American. The only choice is whether to buy at all, or whether, perhaps, to invest that money instead.

But with a car, it's different. We still make some here, and while my friends assure me their foreign ones are a lot better, they all go at about the same speed.

So this is one area in which those who lament America's low savings rate and high trade deficit could—I'm not saying should, that's their business—vote differently:

> They could buy a less expensive car than they otherwise might, investing the difference, as the Indians should have, to grow richer. (Actually, many of us are not buying the trinkets with money we have. We're borrowing to buy the trinkets, which is really insane.)
> They could buy an American car, even if it began to shimmy at 90 or 100 m.p.h. on the autobahn.

Call me un-American for likening cars to trinkets—it's un-American not to take cars very seriously. But consider the irony as you call me un-American from behind the wheel of your $45,000 Porsche.

With these thoughts in mind, more or less, I bought a 1986 burgundy Chrysler LeBaron convertible.

I was sorely tempted to buy a new one—they look great, and I was hardly keeping Detroit ahum by buying this used one. But it seemed an awful waste of money for someone who drives as little as I do, and no small temptation to the car thieves who've come to think of my neighborhood as their own. Instead, I decided to spend part of the $14,000 or so I saved on one of Compaq's amazing new

6-lb. computers—in my line, a productive tool—and to invest the rest at 8% for 363 years, as the Indians should have.

Questions

1. Why should it matter where something is made, so long as it performs as it is supposed to? Write your own answer to this question, and then share your response with a small group of classmates. In the group, attempt to reach a consensus.

2. What would you have to give up if you bought only those products made in the United States? Would this require any sacrifices or changes in your lifestyle? After you have answered this question for yourself, share your answer with classmates in a group and attempt to find an answer that applies to all of you.

Suggestions for Further Research

1. Use recent issues of *Consumer Reports* or other consumer-oriented magazines to evaluate a specific type of product, such as automobiles, and attempt to determine whether U.S. made cars perform as well as those made elsewhere.

2. Many "Buy American" advocates often speak of "free trade," but they don't define their term. Investigate the meaning of "free trade" and summarize the information you find.

Suggestions for Writing

1. Write an argument in which you take the position that consumers should be free to purchase any product they want, without regard to where it was made. Be sure you provide adequate support and anticipate the objections of those who disagree with you.

2. Write an argument in which you take the position that consumers in the United States should buy only products made in the United States by American workers. Be sure you provide adequate support and anticipate the objections of those who disagree with you.

International Athletes:

Should They Be Allowed to Compete in U.S. Colleges?

Most discussions of intercollegiate athletes focus on how they are recruited and whether they are good students. Few people concern themselves with where athletes come from, though someone might occasionally observe that this or that state university seems to recruit almost exclusively out of state. The essays printed here call attention to the seldom-debated issue of international athletes competing on collegiate teams in the United States. Before you read the essays in this section, respond in writing to the following:

Preparing to Read

1. *Do you believe that athletes from other countries should be allowed to compete on teams at U.S. colleges? Why or why not?*
2. *What do you believe would be the consequences of allowing athletes from other countries to compete on teams at U.S. colleges?*

Diversity Benefits All Sides

JOHN COOK

Fairfax, Va.—I came over on the boat. In 1955, as a 14-year-old, I left Munich, Germany, with my mother, who had married a U.S. serviceman after my father was killed in War World II. Our new home was Columbus, Ga.

I know how it feels to be an outsider. I changed my name, from Hans Schaller, after the pronunciation was butchered. I was called a Nazi.

Because of my background, I'm an international type of guy. I don't like the term "foreign" athlete, which connotes strange. I prefer "international"; it's more positive.

I don't understand this assailing of internationals. Why don't we look at it positively? I think we have something to learn from them athletically. They can learn from us politically and economically. It's a cheap and valuable cultural exchange, preparing students for the future by dealing with people of different countries, cultures and languages.

I like that our locker room contains the flags of eight countries. I treasure the photo from last summer's World Championships in Tokyo that shows 11 George Mason athletes from six countries.

I remember coaching Abdi Bile of Somalia, later the '87 world champ at 1,500 meters, at the 1985 NCAA Championships. I discovered, because of the Islamic observance of Ramadan, he couldn't consume food or drink until after dark. He even refused to swallow saliva. I was appalled initially, but it was a good lesson.

I cast no aspersions on any culture or race. To me, it's diversity that makes this country great. Isn't that why so many came here anyway?

Americans are magnanimous for the most part. I think it's the small minds who are concerned that a kid from Hungary wins the NCAA pole vault. I'd like for people to see the big picture is bigger than what happens at the NCAA or IC4A championships.

163

A suggestion: Throw the NCAA team score out. Track's an individual sport, not a team contest like basketball. Put medals around the necks of the top three in each event. I'm into big performances. I'd rather see the NCAA pole vault won by an international at 19 feet than an American at 16.

If there's such a thing as the demise of U.S. track, it's not because colleges use internationals. It's because we don't build elementary, junior high and high school programs. In Virginia, coaches had to go to the wall to prevent the pole vault from being outlawed. I literally can't give away $20,000 worth of used poles because of litigation worries.

Meanwhile, the NCAA is cutting scholarships, coaches and practice time—all bigger problems than internationals.

Some of this anti-international feeling is prejudice. These are just kids competing. What difference does it make where they're from?

You get to know the athletes, and they're just like Americans. Most are good kids. You root for good kids, not countries. Nationalism and intercollegiate athletics should not have anything to do with one another.

Sport is a great common denominator that dismantles racial and cultural barriers. The only way most of us get involved with the rest of the world is through sports. It doesn't hurt for us to see how other people live.

Influx Must Be Regulated

BILLY PACKER

Advance, N.C.—There were cries of the ugly American in 1982 when I first brought attention to the influx of foreign athletes to our colleges.

It was my feeling then, and still is today, that colleges and the NCAA have not made the efforts to establish a policy to handle this problem.

This problem exists in a number of sports but appears most prevalent in track and field. The results of the NCAA's recent men's and women's cross country national championships support my contention.

The women's champion was Ireland's Sonia O'Sullivan of Villanova. Arkansas won the men's team division, led by Niall Bruton of Ireland. The individual champion was Sean Dollmon of Western

Kentucky, a South African. Four of the top five were foreign athletes. Iowa State, a school located in the heartland of America, finished second with all seven of its runners foreign athletes.

How can the taxpayers of a state university provide support for a program whose entire team has been recruited from overseas? Wouldn't the time and money be more wisely spent in trying to develop high school track in Iowa?

Even though Tennessee won last year's NCAA track championship with an all-American team, the individual titles are dominated by foreign athletes.

These athletes are recruited and trained on our campuses, only to return to their homeland to participate against the USA during Olympic and other major international events. They take time, scholarships and developmental funds away from our athletes.

The influx is not limited to track. Last year's NCAA men's golf champion is Warren Scutte, a South African who attends Nevada-Las Vegas.

Golf, soccer, tennis, swimming and basketball are among the sports where coaches are establishing international contacts for the sole purpose of a quick-fix towards NCAA national championships.

The problems are multifaceted. American student-athletes are not judged on the same basis as foreign athletes in regard to amateur standing, age, and academic record. In most foreign countries, amateur athletes do not perform or train in an academic environment but for club teams, athletic unions or, in some cases, corporate sponsored teams.

Recent NCAA cases involving basketball players Marco Baldi of St. Johns, Andrew Gaze of Seton Hall and Nadav Henefeld of Connecticut are examples of how difficult it is to discern athletic eligibility.

What can be done? Three suggestions to the NCAA:

Set aside funds to investigate the issue and establish new ground rules. Currently, the NCAA does not even know how many foreign athletes are competing at U.S. colleges.

Consider all foreign athletes as transfer students, thus requiring one full year of attendance before becoming eligible for participation.

Make foreign athletes ineligible for NCAA national titles.

These proposals would eliminate the quick-fix philosophy, which many coaches are presently employing, without eliminating the opportunity for a foreign athlete to compete in sports.

Questions

1. Based on the information printed here, and anything else you can learn, how does the presence of international athletes work to the disadvantage of U.S. athletes?

2. Why do the writers think this issue is important? What is at stake here?

Suggestions for Further Research

1. Use a standard newspaper or periodical index, or the *New York Times Index* to find more information about the individual athletes Packer mentions. Why was their eligibility a problem?

2. What proportion of championships in the United States do international athletes win each year? (Several publications, including *The New York Times*, print lists of championships annually. Check the index.)

Suggestions for Writing

1. Write an argument in which you agree or disagree with Cook's statement: "These are just kids competing. What difference does it make where they're from?"

2. Many U.S. athletes play for professional and amateur teams in other countries. Research the subject to find adequate information, and then write a paper in which you take a position for or against this practice. Should U.S. athletes stay home?

Active Euthanasia:
Should Assisted Suicide Be Legal?

In 1991, the state of Washington held a vote about a proposed law that would allow physicians to help certain terminally ill patients to end their lives. The essays printed in this section were published on the New York Times Op-Ed page the day before that election. Most citizens of Washington probably did not see the essays. The law was defeated by a narrow margin, but the issue itself has not gone away. Dr. Jack Kevorkian, a Michigan physician, continues to assist suicides, and numerous states are debating laws that would permit or prohibit assisted suicides. Before you read the essays in this section, respond in writing to the following:

Preparing to Read

1. *Do you believe people have or should have the right to decide when and how they will die? Explain your position.*
2. *In what circumstances should assisted suicide be legal or illegal?*

The Limits of Mercy: Going Gently, with Dignity

JAMES VORENBERG

Cambridge, Mass.—If I lived in Washington State, today I wold vote for Initiative 119, which permits doctors to assist terminally ill patients who wish to end their lives. But if I were the prosecutor in Oakland County, Mich., I would investigate Dr. Jack Kevorkian for helping two women kill themselves recently.

The initiative permits "aid in dying" only if two doctors examine the patient and give their written opinions that death will occur within six months. By contrast, it is not clear that either of Dr. Kevorkian's patients was terminally ill.

Until recently, most of the attention given to the "right to die" has been focused on patients who are unconscious, as doctors, hospitals and courts have struggled to decide when and on whose direction respirators and artificially administered nutrition and fluids may be turned off. The Washington initiative and Dr. Kevorkian make it clear that assisted suicide raises issues that are at least equally difficult.

In effect, existing law on assisted suicide places virtually unlimited discretionary power in the hands of doctors and prosecutors, and gives patients no assurance that they can decide when to end their lives if they are terminally ill. It is not a crime to attempt or commit suicide, but in many states assisting suicide is a crime and in others someone who caused death, say by such actions as injecting poison or placing pills in a patient's mouth, could be charged with murder or manslaughter.

It is well known among doctors and hospital staffs that some doctors will give a lethal dose of morphine or other medication to shorten the suffering of a terminally ill patient at the patient's request or when the patient is unable to make a request. But no doctor has ever been convicted of hastening death this way.

Prosecutors exercise their broad discretion and typically do not even investigate the cause of death, except in the very rare cases like those of Dr. Kevorkian or Dr. Timothy Quill, who confessed in The New England Journal of Medicine in March that he had assisted a patient's suicide.

Family members and friends who help patients die if the patients cannot persuade a doctor to help them die are much more likely to be detected and prosecuted because their unfamiliarity with the means of death and because they do not have the camouflage of medical treatment.

The Washington initiative offers protections to guarantee that the patient is competent and is acting voluntarily. Such protections cannot be assured if, as is generally true, the patient's ability to end a life that has become intolerable depends on the cooperation of a doctor who is obliged to act stealthily.

A strong argument is being made against decriminalizing assisted suicide by those who say it is dangerous for a society to take a step that might be an opening wedge for other kinds of allowed homicides. But assisted suicide is not the first wedge, or a bigger one, than capital punishment, the authority given to the police to shoot fleeing felons and the general authorization to kill in self-defense. It is not clear that deaths arising from a merciful motive are more likely to proliferate than these other kinds of permitted deaths.

For those terrified of ending their lives in pain and degradation that they lack the ability to end, and for those who worry about the Kevorkians who may be too willing and ready to provide assistance, the carefully limited and protective procedures of the Washington initiative offer promise.

That measure may help to preserve life if patients have confidence that they do not have to commit suicide at an early stage of an illness in order to avoid being physically unable to choose death later when their condition becomes intolerable.

Anyone who doubts that the issue of suicide is on people's minds should be sobered by the best-seller status of "Final Exit," a suicide manual.

An Unraveling of Mortality

YALE KAMISAR

If Washington State voters today approve what is euphemistically called the "death with dignity" or "aid in dying" referendum, their state will make tragic history—it will become the first jurisdiction in the Western world to legalize active euthanasia.

The people are being asked to approve direct and intentional killing by physicians, at least when patients have six months or less to live and make a written request to die.

One reason that there is so much support for the proposal is that everybody can conjure up a hypothetical situation or think of an actual case in which the argument for voluntary euthanasia seems strong. Nonetheless, if I could, I would vote against Initiative 119. A very moving case or hypothetical situation is one thing, but general legislation to cover a variety of situations is something else again.

Some people may favor legalizing active euthanasia because they trust their doctors completely or feel their doctors know them extraordinarily well. But not all doctors will be loving and caring. And in an era when patients change doctors frequently, few doctors are likely to know their patients especially well.

An eminent bioethicist, Tom Beauchamp, once expressed concern that if rules permitting active killing were introduced, as population increases occurred "the aged will be even more neglectable and neglected than they now are." Rules against killing, he pointed out, are not isolated moral principles but pieces of a web that form a moral code. "The more threads one removes," Mr. Beauchamp warned, "the weaker the fabric becomes."

The legalization of active euthanasia would have a much greater impact on the dynamics of the sick room than is generally realized.

The criminal law creates subconscious as well as conscious inhibitions against committing certain acts. The criminal law has a significant effect, perhaps its most important one, at basic stages in the pattern of conduct, eliminating from consideration alternatives that might otherwise present themselves. But if euthanasia were legalized, this alternative would not only be thinkable but speakable.

The physician might be the first to broach the subject, or a relative or close friend might be. It would hardly be surprising if the gravely ill person were to ask those close to her whether she should make use of the new alternative. Certainly, she is likely to wonder about her loved ones' attitudes. What should relatives and friends tell her? How will the patient react to the suggestion that she should avail herself of the new option?

How many patients will choose euthanasia because they feel obliged or pressured to do so in order to relieve their relatives of financial pressures or emotional strain? How many severely ill patients will feel that to reject euthanasia, once it is acceptable and others are "doing it," would be selfish or cowardly?

How many suicidal or potentially suicidal depressed people will avail themselves of too-easy release? How many patients, unaware of misdiagnoses, would choose death when they need not do so?

Two individuals with no family or financial ties to a patient would have to witness the patient's written request. Still, few physicians will assume the risks to their reputations, to say nothing of their pocketbooks, if a close relative objects to euthanasia. Members of the family may choose to do nothing and say nothing, but that too is a "choice."

Are these the kind of pressures we want to inflict on a very sick person? Or on a very sick person's family, which is probably emotionally shattered? And if so, why are they not also proper considerations for nonterminally ill people who are gravely ill or severely disabled?

We may be fairly sure of one thing. If Washington legalizes euthanasia, a distinctive feature of our civilization will eventually fade away—the distinction between "killing" and "letting die."

Questions

1. Working in a small group, identify the values that each writer invokes and then, using these values as your starting point, identify the values the two writers have in common, and describe their areas of agreement and conflict.

2. Has either essay caused you to change your initial position? Describe any change that has occurred and the reasons for it. If these essays have not changed your position, then explain briefly why these essays failed to move you.

Suggestions for Further Research

1. Investigate the activities of Dr. Jack Kevorkian and the authorities in Michigan (from 1990 to 1992) and write a summary of what you discover.

2. Locate statistics that show or estimate the frequency of euthanasia (active and passive), and describe public opinion on this subject. Summarize what you find.

Suggestions for Writing

1. Write an argument in which you argue for or against Vorenberg's assertion that legalizing assisted suicide will "be an opening wedge for other kinds of allowed homicides."

2. Write an argument in which you take and support a position for or against assisted suicide.

Canada's Health Care Insurance Plan:

Will It Work in the United States?

One of the most intense, complex, and confusing debates in the United States in recent years has focused on how to provide adequate, affordable health care to everyone, regardless of their ability to pay. Health care costs have risen dramatically in the past twenty years and, at the same time, fewer people have been covered by health care insurance. In the Congress, there has been much discussion of establishing a national health care plan. Some people have suggested that the United States adopt the Canadian health care plan. The essays in this section debate whether the Canadian plan would be appropriate for the United States. Before you read the arguments in this section, respond in writing to the following:

Preparing to Read

1. *Summarize briefly the problems you are aware of in the health care system in the United States, or in your own community.*
2. *What do you regard as essential health care services? That is, if a national health care plan were started, what should it do?*

No: We Won't Be Willing to Wait for Treatment

MALCOLM GLADWELL

If a Canadian-style national health-insurance system were adopted in the United States, the way residents in the Washington, D.C., region would receive care from hospitals and doctors would change almost beyond recognition.

This is the forgotten issue in the health-care reform debate, which has focused almost entirely on skyrocketing costs and the problem of insuring the 35 million Americans who are without medical coverage. In fact, Canadian-style health insurance would wreak major changes here. Hospitals and doctors would act differently; certain operations would be impossible to get and certain technologies would be unavailable. Some people would pay substantially more for health care and some would not receive the medical attention they once took for granted.

A simple way to look at the difference is to compare the delivery of medicine in Toronto and the Washington region, metropolitan areas of similar size.

Goodbye to K Street. A doctor here who sees a patient with Blue Cross insurance or other commercial coverage gets $60 for an office visit. Medicare pays $40 for the same visit and Medicaid $30. This is why there are so many more physicians in the downtown K Street corridor than in the poorer neighborhoods of Southeast Washington.

With the Canadian system, every patient pays the same amount. A physician is barred from taking money from a patient—even a tycoon—to supplement the government-approved fee. Instead of competing for the best-insured patients, in other words, doctors would compete for patients, period. This could bring an exodus from the region's K Streets. Clinics could sprout east of Rock Creek Park and throughout Prince George's County, Md.

The bad news: No more network of insurance companies looking over doctors' shoulders making sure they don't just see patients to line their own pockets. Canadian physicians perform about 20 percent more diagnostic and therapeutic procedures per patient

174

than Americans and have 56 percent more office visits. Such extra care is thought somewhat unnecessary and a major factor in pushing Ontario's health care costs up faster than U.S. costs.

The only mechanism holding down costs is a rule capping government payments at $450,000 per doctor yearly. This means a physician who reaches the cap early (for example, a high-charging specialist) has no incentive to continue working. Torontonians joke that the best place to find a dermatologist in the last quarter of the year is in Florida.

A smaller, leaner hospital industry. Ontario pays hospitals by means of a global budget, a single annual check that the hospitals split up among themselves. Costs are contained simply because the province never gives hospitals what they ask for. In 1992, the hospitals asked for an 8.6 percent increase in funding—and got 1 percent. In response, Toronto hospitals have closed 3,700 of the area's 12,500 acute-care beds over the past three years.

If Washington cut 30 percent of its hospital capacity, the current 11,379 beds would drop to 7,965—roughly equivalent to closing Capitol Hill Hospital, Sibley Memorial Hospital, Children's Hospital and Columbia Hospital for Women in the District; Montgomery General, Washington Adventist Hospital, Suburban and Doctor's hospitals of Prince George's County, Md.; and Arlington, Alexandria and Mount Vernon hospitals in Northern Virginia. The remaining hospitals would overflow, creating Toronto-style waiting lists of up to several months for elective surgery.

A different kind of hospital. With universal insurance, hospitals buy new equipment, build new facilities and renovate old ones with a special government capital-improvements fund. Since 1987, Ontario has limited this to $485 million for the 51 Toronto-area hospitals.

In the same period, the 14 hospitals in the District of Columbia alone spent $566 million. In other words, a Canadian-style system here would cut about $100 million from the building budget of D.C. hospitals—say the $50 million new wing at Washington Hospital Center and the $40 million medical complex and underground parking garage at Children's—and would have provided no money for building improvements for any other hospital in Northern Virginia or suburban Maryland over the past five years.

Put another way, a Canadian system means that no area hospital could afford to do anything but the most basic of improvements to the most basic, like roof repair or a better ventilation system.

But on the positive side, the gap between "rich" and "poor" hospitals would narrow. Last year, Sibley Hospital had a profit margin of 4.38 percent, largely because its patients were very affluent and it had to provide only $2.6 million in uncompensated care.

That means the hospital can afford to keep up with the latest technology. D.C. General can't. It had to provide $69 million worth of free care last year, which is why the hospital's revenue fell short of expenses by a whopping 22 percent. With a global budget, the financial gap between Sibley and D.C. General caused by differing charity care burdens would disappear.

No more bypass on demand. Instead of having 11 surgical teams that do cardiac bypass operations, Washington would have three. Because those programs would be booked solid, they would probably be more cost-efficient. Toronto Hospital can do a bypass for about $14,350. You would be hardpressed to get a bypass for twice that in Washington.

But three hospitals can do only a small fraction of the operations that 11 hospitals can. Toronto does about 2,200 bypasses a year, compared with this area's total of between 3,500 and 4,000. In Toronto, you may wait four months for your operation. In Washington, if you can't get a bypass within the week, you probably need a new cardiologist.

What are the consequences of waiting lists and eliminating 1,500 bypasses a year? Perhaps none at all: Canadian cardiac mortality rates are the same as America's. But some people wouldn't be able to live as full a life.

Quentin Macmanus, a cardiac surgeon at Fairfax Hospital in Northern Virginia, describes his typical patient as an active 79-year-old man who plays golf, lives alone, but whose medication is no longer controlling his chest pain. In today's system he gets the bypass and goes back to his golf. In a Canadian-style system he doesn't and has to slow down, quit playing golf and maybe live with his children.

"It's not mortality," says Macmanus. "It's quality of life."

Then there is the 52-year-old man with chest pain so bad he's afraid to work or travel and is in semi-retirement. Both systems give him a bypass. But with 11 hospitals to chose from, he gets it tomorrow. With three, he waits two months. The system saves money, but his employer loses money because he's in semi-retirement while he waits.

Less tech. Between Annapolis, Md., and Leesburg, Va., there are about 35 magnetic resonance imagers (MRIs). These $2 million diagnostic machines are the best—in some cases the only—way of looking at spines, brains and soft-tissue problems in joints, heart and abdomen. Toronto has five.

The arithmetic on this is easy. If each local machine sees 12 patients a day—about average—that's 420 patients a day. If each Toronto machine does 16 a day, that's 80 patients. So in a Canada-style system, 340 Washingtonians a day wouldn't get state-of-the-art radiological diagnosis.

Who are the 340? A patient with suspected ligament damage in the knee is a next-day patient in Washington but a nine-month wait or not at all in Toronto. Lower back pain with a suspected herniated disk is an automatic MRI here, but in Toronto it probably would be a myelogram—a cheaper, less advanced technology involving spinal injections that can cause splitting headaches, occasional seizures and an overnight hospital stay. An MRI is painless and takes 30 minutes. They rarely do myelograms anymore in Washington.

"I can point to about a dozen cases a year at my center where someone's health was directly jeopardized because they couldn't get an MRI," says Walter Kucharzyk, chairman of radiology at the University of Toronto. He says Toronto should have at least 14 MRIs to deliver a minimum standard of quality of care.

CAT scans, used predominantly to diagnose brain injuries, are the other big-ticket medical technology. In Washington there are between 75 and 100 of these machines. Toronto has 21.

"I think that is an absurdity beyond belief," says David Davis, chairman of radiology at George Washington University Hospital. "We do 4,000 scans a year, most of them head trauma. I suppose that with some of them, you could say well he got dinged but he's probably all right, and if he dies later of an epidural hematoma then you could say, well, I guess we had no way of knowing that."

No more perks. For the rich and famous, the Washington Hospital Center offers special executive suites, gourmet dinners on china and crystal and other frills.

It all goes. Supplemental private insurance, which is available in Ontario, may get you a private room instead of semi-private and a TV. Nothing else.

"It's not like going to a hospital in Russia," says Roger Hunt, president of St. Michael's Hospital in Toronto. "We have curtains in the windows and carpeting on the floor. But there's no fluff here. . . . The norm here is that you have the same services accessible to everyone."

A different payment method. Instead of paying health insurance, everyone would pay a payroll tax, probably of about 8 percent. The big losers here are small businesses, particularly restaurants and bars, about 75 percent of which currently don't buy any employee health insurance. To pay the tax, they would have to raise prices. The other losers are the upper-middle class. Assuming a family insurance policy now costs $5,000 a year, any family making more than $62,500 would pay more under a payroll tax. A lawyer making $100,000, for example, would pay $8,000.

The winners? Consider the Whitman-Walker Clinic in Washington, where several staff members ran up high medical bills because of AIDS. As a result, the clinic pays $533,912 in medical premiums out of a total payroll of $2.7 million. An 8 percent payroll tax cuts their health insurance costs to $216,000.

Doctors would behave differently. In a system with more sick people than beds, doctors make constant rationing decisions. And in a system where a hospital gets a flat fee at the beginning of the year instead of a payment for each patient, doctors have to think not only about what is good for the patient, but about what the hospital can afford. In other words, when you look at a doctor, your expectations of what will be done have to change.

"We doctors, when we sit across from you patients, have considered what is good for you first and looked at social policy secondarily," says Stuart Sides, a Washington cardiologist. "I look on myself as the patient's advocate in the system. To try to layer social policy on top of that will intrude in the relationship between doctor and patient. It will take a certain retooling in the mind of the American patient."

Yes: Then There Would Be Equality in Medical Care

UWE E. REINHARDT

"If you like the U.S. Postal Service, you will just love National Health Insurance!" goes an adage that has made millions of red-blooded Americans blanch at the mere mention of health-care reform. After all, who likes the neighborhood post office?

It is true that the U.S. Postal Service is not a lovable institution, though it probably *is* one of the cheapest mail services in the world. But think about the flip side of the adage. Imagine if our mail was in the hands of the friendly folks who run our private health-insurance system. Would that make you sleep better? If you think so, think again.

In a recent ABC News/Washington Post survey, 68 percent of respondents agreed that "I worry that health-care costs I may have in the future will not be taken care of." These folks are not crazy, nor are they unfair to a high-performance industry. They are merely perceptive.

If they are privately insured, they surely realize that their families' coverage would be lost with the particular job to which that coverage is tied. If the family's breadwinner loses that job—increasingly probably in our dynamic, recession-prone economy—and if a family member has a so-called "pre-existing medical condition," the family might not be able to get new coverage at all or might face a premium that could easily eat up much of the family's income.

The respondents probably also have read the increasingly frequent stories about entrepreneurial hit-and-run insurance carriers that raise the insured's premiums drastically after a major claim. Or perhaps the company's assets have vanished through the avarice or ineptness of management. On Jan. 4, the New York Times reported a number of such cases, among them a family that lost its home because its private insurer was insolvent and the family found itself being sued for medical bills.

Although the nation's largest private carriers—the Prudentials, the Aetnas and certainly many of the old-line Blue-Cross/Blue Shield plans—are likely to be much more trustworthy, would anyone really rate the overall performance of our private health-insurance industry as more *reliable* than that of our much-maligned Postal Service?

After all, the Postal Service does serve *all* Americans, rich and poor, near and far. In contrast, our private insurance carriers, particularly commercial carriers, carefully cherry-pick among different risk classes, selecting the low-risks and letting someone else worry about the high-risk (i.e., the sick) patients who cannot afford the high premiums the industry often imposes upon chronically ill people. In the process, the industry has turned its back on some 35 million uninsured Americans, most of whom are either full-time workers or their dependents.

But what about *efficiency?* Is it not axiomatic that private institutions, even if not always *equitable,* are at least more *efficient* than public ones? A fair answer would be: sometimes yes, sometimes no.

Consider, for example, how little of the premiums collected from the elderly for what are known as "Medigap" policies is actually paid out for health care. The elderly buy Medigap policies to cover expenses not covered by the federal Medicare program. As the General Accounting Office has reported several times, these policies have been so difficult to comprehend that many of the elderly have been induced to buy multiple, duplicate policies— probably an intended byproduct of an intended confusion. But the Medigap policies' efficiency record should also profoundly embarrass champions of commercial health insurance.

As reported by the bipartisan Pepper Commission in 1988, four commercial carriers selling individual policies to the elderly paid out fewer than 40 cents per premium dollar to doctors, hospitals and other providers of health care; the remaining 60 cents went to cover administration, commissions and profits. Only 11 companies managed to pay out 90 cents or more. The average payout ratio for all the commercial carriers analyzed in the study was only 66 percent. By contrast, the average for traditional Blue Cross/Blue Shield Plans was as high as 93.4 percent. The payout ratio for the federal Medicare program is even higher.

Lest we think that these low payout ratios are typical only of commercial Medigap policies sold to the elderly, it is instructive to examine the ratios for policies sold to small-business firms. According to material in the Bush administration's health-reform proposals unveiled in February, administrative expenses accounted for about 40 percent of claims for insurance policies sold to business establishments with fewer than five employees in 1987. The payout ratio was higher for bigger firms, although it was still as low as 77 percent for firms with fewer than 20 employees.

On what basis can anyone call such a market efficient? Surely the elderly and small business firms have the incentive to act as prudent purchasers. If even they cannot seem to discipline the health-insurance market, what makes us think that harried working mothers with children or other low-income families will be able to drive the market toward greater efficiency? Yet that is precisely the assumption underlying proposals, such as the administration's that would achieve universal health-insurance coverage simply by granting low-income families and small-business firms tax credits toward the purchase of individual policies.

Now, it is a fact that payout ratios in the Medigap market have been rising slightly over time and that policies sold to the elderly have become more standardized; but that is faint praise for the private insurance market. These improvements merely are a forced response to a 1980 law that sought to curb the many abuses in the Medigap market and, among other strictures, established a target payout ratio of 60 percent for individual policies. Congress raised this target to 65 percent in 1990. Think about this development for a moment: Here is an industry that must be forced by law to pay out in health benefits at least 65 cents of each premium dollar collected!

Similarly, President Bush has also proposed federal legislation to reform the insurance market for small-business firms. The intent would be to group small firms into aggregates so as to reap the economies of scale of larger group policies. Should that initiative succeed, however, it would not be the product of the free market but of government regulation that compensates for private-market failure.

And herein lies a lesson that should not be lost on the private insurance industry. If the industry is to be the successful cornerstone of our nation's health system, it will eventually come to resemble a model it has long decried as "socialism": the social-insurance systems of Western Europe whose semi-private insurance carriers are led towards socially desired ends through tight public regulation.

Indeed, even Bush's so-called market approach to health insurance calls for surprisingly stiff new regulations. But these rules are only a harbinger. In the end, nothing short of stiff and pervasive government regulation will make our private insurance industry a more trustworthy and accessible partner. Smart executives within the industry already know that; smart voters should know it too.

Questions

1. Summarize both essays and point out their major areas of agreement and disagreement.

2. What values do these arguments invoke (sometimes implicitly) in support of their positions? Compile a list of the values you encounter, and then discuss these with a small group of classmates.

Suggestions for Further Research

1. Gather statistics to show the growth of medical and health care costs in relation to the Consumer Price Index for the past twenty years. Graph or chart the information you find, and then write a summary.

2. Investigate a publicly sponsored health care plan such as Medicare or Medicaid. Summarize what you learn.

Suggestions for Writing

1. Gladwell points out a number of changes that will occur (he says) if the United States adopted a Canadian system for health care. His implicit (and sometimes explicit) attitude is that all of these changes are bad. Write an argument in which you take the position that some of these changes would be positive, or at least neutral.

2. Write an argument in which you urge your peers (traditional age college students who may have few health care problems or concerns) to pay attention to the health care debate.

Ice-T's "Cop Killer":

Is Music Dangerous?

It seems that parents have always been concerned about the music their children listen to, the films they watch, and the books they read, among other things. In recent years, that concern has grown in response to song lyrics, films, and even advertising that present increasingly graphic sex and violence. Music has received special attention, and some communities have responded to song lyrics with proposals for censorship and labeling, while others have attempted to prosecute artists for obscenity. The essays here focus on rapper Ice-T's "Cop Killer," which appears to advocate killing police officers. Should songs like this be protected as free speech and artistic freedom, or should they be censored because they advocate violent and illegal acts? Before you read the arguments in this section, respond in writing to the following:

Preparing to Read

1. *Do you believe that music lyrics, books, films, or other types of expression should be restricted or censored because their content might offend someone? Explain your reasons for the position you take on this question.*
2. *Summarize what you know about rap music and describe your attitude toward it.*

Ice-T: Is the Issue Social Responsibility . . .

MICHAEL KINSLEY

How did the company that publishes this magazine come to produce a record glorifying the murder of police?

> I got my 12-gauge sawed off
> I got my headlights turned off
> I'm 'bout to bust some shots off
> I'm 'bout to dust some cops off . . .
> Die, Die, Die Pig, Die!

So go the lyrics to *Cop Killer* by the rapper Ice-T on the album *Body Count*. The album is released by Warner Bros. Records, part of the Time Warner media and entertainment conglomerate.

In a *Wall Street Journal* op-ed piece laying out the company's position, Time Warner co-CEO Gerald Levin makes two defenses. First, Ice-T's *Cop Killer* is misunderstood. "It doesn't incite or glorify violence . . . It's his fictionalized attempt to get inside a character's head . . . *Cop Killer* is no more a call for gunning down the police than *Frankie and Johnny* is a summons for jilted lovers to shoot one another." Instead of "finding ways to silence the messenger," we should be "heeding the anguished cry contained in his message."

This defense is self-contradictory. *Frankie and Johnny* does not pretend to have a political "message" that must be "heeded." If *Cop Killer* has a message, it is that the murder of policemen is a justified response to police brutality. And not in self-defense, but in premeditated acts of revenge against random cops. ("I know your family's grievin'—f__ 'em.")

Killing policemen is a good thing—that is the plain meaning of the words, and no "larger understanding" of black culture, the rage of the streets or anything else can explain it away. This is not Ella Fitzgerald telling a story in song. As in much of today's popular music, the line between performer and performance is purposely blurred. These are political sermonettes clearly intended to endorse the sentiments being expressed. Tracy Marrow (Ice-T) himself has

183

said, "I scared the police, and they need to be scared." That seems clear.

The company's second defense of *Cop Killer* is the classic one of free expression: "We stand for creative freedom. We believe that the worth of what an artist or journalist has to say does not depend on preapproval from a government official or a corporate censor."

Of course Ice-T has the right to say whatever he wants. But that doesn't require any company to provide him an outlet. And it doesn't relieve a company of responsibility for the messages it chooses to promote. Judgment is not "censorship." Many an "anguished cry" goes unrecorded. This one was recorded, and promoted, because a successful artist under contract wanted to record it. Nothing wrong with making money, but a company cannot take the money and run from the responsibility.

The founder of Time, Henry Luce, would snort at the notion that his company should provide a value-free forum for the exchange of ideas. In Luce's system, editors were supposed to make value judgments and promote the truth as they saw it. Time has moved far from its old Lucean rigidity—far enough to allow for dissenting essays like this one. That evolution is a good thing, as long as it's not a handy excuse for abandoning all standards.

No commercial enterprise need agree with every word that appears under its corporate imprimatur. If Time Warner now intends to be "a global force for encouraging the confrontation of ideas," that's swell. But a policy of allowing diverse viewpoints is not a moral free pass. Pro and con on national health care is one thing; pro and con on killing policemen is another.

A bit of sympathy is in order for Time Warner. It is indeed a "global force" with media tentacles around the world. If it imposes rigorous standards and values from the top, it gets accused of corporate censorship. If it doesn't, it gets accused of moral irresponsibility. A dilemma. But someone should have thought of that before deciding to become a global force.

And another genuine dilemma. Whatever the actual merits of *Cop Killer*, if Time Warner withdraws the album now the company will be perceived as giving in to outside pressure. That is a disastrous precedent for a global conglomerate.

The Time-Warner merger of 1989 was supposed to produce corporate "synergy": the whole was supposed to be more than the sum of the parts. The *Cop Killer* controversy is an example of negative synergy. People get mad at *Cop Killer* and start boycotting the moving *Batman Returns*. A reviewer praises *Cop Killer* ("Tracy Marrow's poetry takes a switchblade and deftly slices life's jugular," etc.), and Time is accused of corruption instead of mere foolishness.

Senior Time Warner executives find themselves under attack for—and defending—products of their company they neither honestly care for nor really understand, and doubtless weren't even aware of before controversy hit.

Anyway, it's absurd to discuss *Cop Killer* as part of the "confrontation of ideas"—or even as an authentic anguished cry of rage from the ghetto. *Cop Killer* is a cynical commercial concoction, designed to titillate its audience with imagery of violence. It merely exploits the authentic anguish of the inner city for further titillation. Tracy Marrow is in business for a buck, just like Time Warner. *Cop Killer* is an excellent joke on the white establishment, of which the company's anguished apologia ("Why can't we hear what rap is trying to tell us?") is the punch line.

. . . Or Is It Creative Freedom?

BARBARA EHRENREICH

Ice-T's song *Cop Killer* is as bad as they come. This is black anger—raw, rude and cruel—and one reason the song's so shocking is that in postliberal America, black anger is virtually taboo. You won't find it on TV, not on the *McLaughlin Group* or *Crossfire*, and certainly not in the placid features of Arsenio Hall or Bernard Shaw. It's been beaten back into the outlaw subcultures of rap and rock, where, precisely because it is taboo, it sells. And the nastier it is, the faster it moves off the shelves. As Ice-T asks in another song on the same album, "Goddamn what a brotha gotta do/To get a message through/To the red, white and blue?"

But there's a gross overreaction going on, building to a veritable paroxysm of white denial. A national boycott has been called, not just of the song or Ice-T, but of all Time Warner products. The President himself has denounced Time Warner as "wrong" and Ice-T as "sick." Ollie North's Freedom Alliance has started a petition drive aimed at bringing Time Warner executives to trial for "sedition and anarchy."

Much of this is posturing and requires no more courage than it takes to stand up in a VFW hall and condemn communism or crack. Yes, *Cop Killer* is irresponsible and vile. But Ice-T is as right about some things as he is righteous about the rest. And ultimately, he's not even dangerous—least of all to the white power structure his songs condemn.

The "danger" implicit in all the uproar is of empty-headed, suggestible black kids, crouching by their boom boxes, waiting for the word. But what Ice-T's fans know and his detractors obviously don't is that *Cop Killer* is just one more entry in pop music's long history of macho hyperbole and violent boast. Flip the classic-rock station, and you might catch the Rolling Stones announcing "the time is right of violent revo-loo-shun!" from their 1968 hit "Street Fighting Man." And where were the defenders of our law-enforcement officers when a white British group, the Clash, taunted its fans with the lyrics: "When they kick open your front door/How you gonna come/With your hands on your head/Or on the trigger of your gun?"

"Die, Die, Die Pig" is strong speech, but the Constitution protects strong speech, and it's doing so this year more aggressively than ever. The Supreme Court has just downgraded cross burnings to the level of bonfires and ruled that it's no crime to throw around verbal grenades like "nigger" and "kike." Where are the defenders of decorum and social stability when prime-time demagogues like Howard Stern deride African Americans as "spear chuckers"?

More to the point, young African Americans are not so naive and suggestible that they have to depend on a compact disc for their sociology lessons. To paraphrase another song from another era, you don't need a rap song to tell which way the wind is blowing. Black youths know that the police are likely to see them through a filter of stereotypes as miscreants and potential "cop killers." They are aware that a black youth is seven times as likely to be charged with a felony as a white youth who has committed the same offense, and is much more likely to be imprisoned.

They know, too, that in a shameful number of cases, it is the police themselves who indulge in "anarchy" and violence. The U.S. Justice Department has received 47,000 complaints of police brutality in the past six years, and Amnesty International has just issued a report on police brutality in Los Angeles, documenting 40 cases of "torture or cruel, inhuman or degrading treatment."

Menacing as it sounds, the fantasy in *Cop Killer* is the fantasy of the powerless and beaten down—the black man who's been hassled once too often ("A pig stopped me for nothin'!"), spread-eagled against a police car, pushed around. It's not a "responsible" fantasy (fantasies seldom are). It's not even a very creative one. In fact, the sad thing about *Cop Killer* is that it falls for the cheapest, most conventional image of rebellion that our culture offers: the lone gunman spraying fire from his AK-47. This is not "sedition"; it's the familiar, all-American Hollywood-style pornography of violence.

Which is why Ice-T is right to say he's no more dangerous than George Bush's pal Arnold Schwarzenegger, who wasted an army of cops in *Terminator 2*. Images of extraordinary cruelty and violence are marketed every day, many of far less artistic merit than *Cop Killer*. This is our free market of ideas and images, and it shouldn't be any less free for a black man than for other purveyors of "irresponsible" sentiments, from David Duke to Andrew Dice Clay.

Just, please, don't dignify Ice-T's contribution with the word sedition. The past masters of sedition—men like George Washington, Toussaint-Louverture, Fidel Castro or Mao Zedong, all of whom led and won armed insurrections—would be unimpressed by *Cop Killer* and probably saddened. They would shake their heads and mutter words like "infantile" and "adventurism." They might point out that the cops are hardly a noble target, being, for the most part, honest working stiffs who've got stuck with the job of patrolling ghettos ravaged by economic decline and official neglect.

There is a difference, the true seditionist would argue, between a revolution and a gesture of macho defiance. Gestures are cheap. They feel good, they blow off some rage. But revolutions, violent or otherwise, are made by people who have learned how to count very slowly to 10.

Questions

1. Both essays imply very strongly that making money is incompatible with artistic expression and social responsibility. Working in a small group, discuss this notion and try to reach a consensus about whether you agree or disagree with it. Then be prepared to present and support your group's position to the rest of the class.

2. Review the essays carefully and identify the strongest points of agreement and disagreement. Then describe the common ground that the writers share and explain how they might use the ideas or values they share to resolve their disagreement.

Suggestions for Further Research

1. Both writers here use the word *sedition*. Define the term, using specific examples from American history as part of your definition. What are the penalties for sedition?

2. Use periodical indexes to locate published articles about the Ice-T controversy (June and July of 1992). Summarize what you find.

Suggestions for Writing

1. After reviewing both essays thoroughly, write a summary of the issue that gives full and fair treatment to both points of view expressed here. Write for an audience that knows nothing about the controversy.

2. Both writers seem to conclude that Ice-T is not really dangerous and that his lyrics should not be taken literally. Respond to that assertion in some way. (For example, if people ignore Ice-T, is that just a continuation of the attitude that made him angry in the first place?)

Gays in the Military:
Should They Be Allowed to Serve?

In many ways the United States has always been tolerant of alternate lifestyles. Some would say the country was founded to permit people to live as they choose. But homosexuals have always had a difficult time being tolerated or accepted in society at large, let alone in its more conservative corners. Recent attempts to change a long-standing rule that prohibits homosexuals from serving in the military have provoked spirited debates and intense resistance from within the military services. Before you read the arguments in this section, respond in writing to the following:

Preparing to Read

1. Why should the military want to prevent homosexuals from serving?
2. Homosexuals encounter considerable hostility from society at large. Why?

A Voice from the Trenches Says Keep Gays Out of the Military

DAVID HACKWORTH

Democratic Rep. Pat Schroeder of Colorado wanted to give women "equality and opportunity" by making them rucksack-toting grunts. Now she aims at putting homosexuals in the foxholes to "end the final bastion of discrimination."

I cannot think of a better way to destroy fighting spirit and gut U.S. combat effectiveness. My credentials for saying this are more than four decades' experience as a soldier or military reporter.

Despite the ban on service by homosexuals, gays have long served in the armed forces, some with distinction. Many perhaps felt no sexual inclination toward their heterosexual fellow soldiers. If they did, they had their buddies' attitudes and the Uniform Code of Military Justice hanging over their heads. Still, I have seen countless examples of inappropriate and morale-busting behavior.

In Italy, for example, in the postwar occupation, a gay soldier could not keep his hands off other soldiers in my squad. He disrupted discipline, mangled trust among squad members and zeroed out morale. In the same unit, the personnel major was gay. He had affairs with ambitious teenage soldiers in exchange for kicking up their test scores. This corrupted the command's promotion system and led to the commissioning of William Calley-like lieutenants not fit to lead combat soldiers.

During my second tour in the Korean War, a gay commanding officer gave combat awards to his lovers who had never been on the line. In Vietnam, a young captain in my unit was asked by the commander to go to bed with him. This almost destroyed the esprit of a fine parachute unit.

These are not isolated incidents: During my Army career I saw countless officers and NCOs who couldn't stop themselves from hitting on soldiers. The absoluteness of their authority, the lack of privacy, enforced intimacy and a 24-hour duty day made sexual urges difficult to control. The objects of their affection were impressionable lads who, searching for a caring role model, sometimes ended up in a gay relationship they might not have sought.

A majority of American citizens, according to polls, support Schroeder's bill. Many people look at the armed forces as they do the post office, the Bank of America or General Motors—an 8-to-5 institution where discrimination on the basis of sexual orientation is against basic freedom, human rights and the American way of life. If these polls are true, a lot of people don't understand what war is about.

Sure, banning gays from defending their country is discriminatory. But discrimination is necessary when a larger public purpose is served. Civilian standards of fairness and equality don't apply down where the body bags are filled.

On the battlefield, what allows men to survive is combat units made up of disciplined team players, who are realistically trained and led by caring skippers who set the example and know their trade. When all of these factors are in sync, a unit has the right stuff. It becomes tight, a family, and clicks like a professional football team. Spirited men who place their lives in their buddies' hands are the most essential element in warfare. The members of such combat teams trust one another totally.

One doesn't need to be a field marshal to understand that sex between service members undermines those critical factors that produce discipline, military orders, spirit and combat effectiveness. Mix boys and girls, gays and straights in close quarters such as the barracks or the battlefield, and both sexual contact and the consequent breakdown of morale are inevitable.

Many bright people are pushing for the ban to be lifted. I suspect that few if any have been down in the trenches, but I have no doubt their psychological/sociological/political clout will have considerable influence even if they don't have a clue what combat is about.

Unfortunately, most of the top brass won't sound off. They duck and weave and offer hollow and spurious Pentagonese doubletalk reasons for continuing the ban—reasons that only fuel the pro-gay argument. But they have told me in the "G" ring of the Pentagon that they're "against it, but sounding off would be the kiss of death, like opposing women in combat—a career killer, you know."

I hope that our lawmakers will visit Quantico and Fort Benning before they vote, and ask Marine gunnery sergeants and Army platoon sergeants what a few gays would do to the fighting spirit of units. These pros told me: Gays are not wanted by straight men or women in their showers, toilets, foxholes or fighting units. They say that in combat young men face death constantly, and what allows them to make it through the hell of it all is a feeling of toughness, invincibility and total trust in their buddies.

My experience with warriors in more than eight years of roaming the killing fields in seven wars confirms what these old salts are saying.

A serving lieutenant general recently wrote to me, "Ask Pat Schroeder if she'd like her kids under a gay first sergeant who might use his rank and authority to demand sexual favors from his subordinate 18-year-old kids. We just had that occur in my command."

No doubt advocates of gays in combat units will argue that they don't approve of demanding sexual favors and that the first sergeant deserved what he got—a court-martial. The problem is, all the court-martials and regulations in the world can't prevent the kind of morale problems that a change in the law is bound to create. Sure, the first sergeant is serving hard time at Fort Leavenworth, but Pat Schroeder and the two dozen lawmakers who support her bill must also ask themselves what happened to the morale and fighting spirit of his unit.

Debunking the Case against Gays in the Military

COLBERT I. KING

The military's racial exclusion policies of 50 years ago were based on nothing more than fear and raw prejudice. Finally with the bold and courageous action of President Truman in 1948, racial segregation in the military was brought to an end. The current Department of Defense ban on gays and lesbians in uniform hangs on similar phobias and narrow-mindedness. Unfortunately, there is no Harry Truman in the White House today.

Bill Clinton has already said that he will repeal the ban if he reaches the Oval Office. "I don't think it's right. People should have a right to serve their country. And if denied the right . . . it should be on the basis of behavior, not status," Clinton has said repeatedly since declaring his candidacy.

Ross Perot's position is a little harder to follow. Having first told Barbara Walters on May 29 on ABC News "20/20" that he didn't think allowing gays in the military was "realistic," Perot backed off only a few days later when asked by NBC "Today's" Katie Couric if he favored such a ban. Saying his earlier position had been misstated, Perot boasted about the homosexuals who had worked for him ("they are brilliant people, did outstanding work"), declaring that he never interfered with a person's private life. President Bush is keeping his hands off the ban.

But a president wanting to issue an executive order lifting the ban need look no farther for a strong justification than the just-released General Accounting Office study on the Department of Defense's Policy on Homosexuality. The GAO confirms what many critics of the Defense Department policy have maintained all along—that the ban on gays rests on the flimsiest of grounds.

All of the old chestnuts on which the military once relied—officially and unofficially—have been either blown out of the water by the GAO study or conceded by the Defense Department. There is agreement that the ban on gays can't be justified on psychological grounds—homosexuality is not a mental disorder. Neither can the Pentagon bar gays as security risks, especially since the secretary of Defense and the chairman of the Joint Chiefs of Staff have publicly said they are no longer concerned about that.

And the Defense Department's stance can't be buttressed by medical or sociological analysis because there is no credible scientific evidence to support the discrimination. Finally, the Defense Department can hardly draw comfort from the practice of other nations, since, as the GAO notes, some allies have more enlightened policies toward gays in their military, as do some fire and police departments in the United States—apparently without any significant decline in discipline, order or morale.

But perhaps worst of all, the military's bias has exacted a terrible price. The GAO reports that in 1990 alone, the military wasted $27 million replacing the men and women it hounded out of the services for being gays or lesbians. Pentagon officials strenuously dispute that estimate. But there is no disputing the fact that the military's witch hunts have caused untold pain and unnecessarily wasted thousands of lives.

Stripped of much of a rationale for the exclusion policy, the Defense Department has been left with its fall-back position, which comes down to a sort of: It's-a-military-thing, you-just-wouldn't-understand. "The policy is a matter of professional military judgment, not scientific or sociological analysis," wrote the Department of Defense in response to the GAO's report. Even if gay service members have exemplary performance records, their homosexuality seriously impairs overall combat effectiveness, the Pentagon said. And besides that, adds the military, gays and lesbians aren't generally accepted by the public—a questionable assertion—and especially in the military, where there are confined living and working conditions.

That argument is hard to follow, since strict enforcement of rules against uninvited sexual approaches, harassment or misconduct should more than adequately protect the rights of individuals to be left alone. In fact, the Pentagon ought to think about doing that anyway, given the nightmare and terror of Navy Lt. Paula Coughlin and 26 other Navy women who were sexually assaulted by at least 70 male Navy and Marine Corps officers—their presumably straight comrades in arms—at the infamous Tailhook convention last September. And to hear Army reserve specialist Jacqueline Ortiz tell her story about sexual abuse by her sergeant, Iraqi troops weren't the only soldiers to catch hell from U.S. forces during Desert Storm.

Ironically, the Navy of the 1940s was as unrepentant in its racism as today's Pentagon is in its prejudice against gays. The Navy then defended its discrimination on the grounds that whites would never accept blacks as equals, let alone in positions of authority. Said the Navy in a now-declassified 1942 defense of the anti-blacks policy, "These concepts may not be truly democratic, but it is doubted if the most ardent lovers of democracy will dispute them." Harry Truman did. But then again, that president had guts.

Questions

1. Hackworth admits that "banning gays from defending their country is discriminatory. But discrimination is necessary when a larger public purpose is served." Give an example of a type of discrimination you think would be justified, and then describe the larger good it would serve. Once you have finished this, discuss your example with classmates. Does the discussion change your opinion?

2. Which of these essays do you find the most convincing? Choose one and explain why. Discuss your choice with a small group of classmates, and then describe how the discussion has or has not altered your opinion.

Suggestions for Further Research

1. Many minorities have had difficulty gaining acceptance in the military. Women, African Americans, Japanese Americans, and other groups have struggled for full acceptance. Explore in depth the

relationship of a minority group to the military and then summarize the results of your search.

2. Homosexuals often assert that their struggle for acceptance is similar to the civil rights movement of the 1950s and 1960s. In what ways is this comparison true or false?

Suggestions for Writing

1. Write a brief summary of the controversy about gays in the military, and then explain the values that motivate each position.

2. Write an argument in which, rather than taking sides on this issue, you develop common ground and propose a compromise or solution that you believe both sides can accept.

Women in Combat:
How Equal Is Equal?

Women have had active roles in the U.S. military for many years. They have flown helicopters and transport planes, served as nurses in Vietnam, and commanded Military Police units in Panama. In both Vietnam and the 1991 war against Iraq, several women were killed as a result of hostile action. But women have never been permitted to serve in positions that might involve them in direct combat with an armed enemy. In recent years, there has been increasing pressure to allow or even require women to serve in combat positions, such as in the infantry, on warships, and in combat aircraft. Before you read the arguments in this section, respond in writing to the following:

Preparing to Read

1. *State your own views about whether women should participate in combat. Don't bother to frame or support a position; just write what you think.*
2. *Make a double-column list; in one column, give reasons for excluding women from combat. In the other column, give reasons for allowing them in combat.*

Women Warriors

ANNA QUINDLEN

The morning shows, the late-night shows, the radio call-in shows—all of them were out rounding up women, as though they were casting one of those distaff buddy movies Hollywood was fond of for a moment. Women officials. Women professors. Women soldiers. A woman had reportedly been taken prisoner in the Persian Gulf. Biology, if not destiny, was at least newsworthy.

Stop the presses: women really are at war. It's a little like the talking dog; no one seems to care how well she does it, only that she does it at all. There are 27,000 women just doing their jobs in the gulf; we should know this by now because they have been photographed and interviewed out of all proportion to their numbers. But the hard facts of women waging war seem to come home most keenly now, when one may be in the hands of the enemy. All these years the Pentagon has insulated us from that scenario with rules barring women in combat. What they didn't say was that in modern warfare, combat can be everywhere.

There's been an interesting side effect of war in the Persian Gulf. Just as it has distilled combat to its fast-forward essence—can it be only two weeks since we've been at this?—it has also writ large changes in society. We have talked for a decade about the extraordinary difficulties of the new American family, but they have been dramatized by couples going to Saudi Arabia and leaving children behind. We have discussed and discussed the revolution in the lives of American women, and in our attitudes toward what it means to be female. Women at war makes us think again, about how much we have changed, and how little.

One in ten soldiers today are women. They have turned to the service for some of the same reasons minorities have: for college money, technical training, a way out of a pink-collar ghetto filled with dead ends. Their decision has got mixed reviews. Some feminists believe it means that women have sunk to the level of men, that the role of women in wartime is to say, "That is wrong." Those men who long for the 19th century believe this shows that the armed forces have fallen on hard times, that women at the mercy of tides and lunar cycles will be unable to power a supply truck. Most people recognize the military for what it is. It's not an adventure; it's a job.

Until we get to the what ifs.

Well, we've got to the what ifs now: a 20-year-old Michigan woman, a former high school R.O.T.C. cadet, missing presumed captured. Her parents may well curse their imaginations at this moment, thinking of what the Iraqis might do to her. Saddam Hussein lives in a world in which women's liberation is a contradiction in terms, in which a woman with her sleeves rolled up is considered a rebuke to her creator. Perhaps this will inspire him to treat any female prisoners like pack animals. Or perhaps the paternalistic attitudes of the Muslim world will lead him to tread more carefully. In sexism will be salvation.

I've heard it said that the American public is not ready for this, as though we long ago made our peace with beaten and tortured men. But thinking about women prisoners is tough for some of us, and that is because the revelations of social change that have come with this war are revelations of changes not fully accepted. Any heightened horror at women warriors is tinged with a double standard. It assumes somehow that the travails of men are less heartbreaking than those of women. That is insulting to men, and to the people who love them. It assumes that some Americans, for whatever reason, are more tormented by the vision of a woman in a body bag than a man in one.

That happens to be true.

There are so many double standards in this binary society, and the military has taken full advantage of this one. Rules barring women from combat units were designed specifically to meet public comfort levels, the comfort level of the military, too. As Representative Pat Schroeder says, "By pretending they were protecting women from harm, all they were protecting them from was promotions." To become a Stormin' Norman, you have to have flown the bombing raids, led the troops through the jungles. Thousands of women who have chosen the service as their life's work face sanctioned job discrimination, a glass ceiling permitted by the statute.

But this war has already shown that the Pentagon policy is designed for the comfort level of a world that has ceased to exist, whether we all like it or not. Women will fight. Women may die. One woman may already be held prisoner. Sometimes the realities of life outstrip our perceptions. That is manifest when you consider this: A female P.O.W. could come home to a parade, a medal and the disclaimer that she is not fit for combat. In other words, insult as well as injury.

Women in Battle

THE NATIONAL REVIEW

The first reports had Captain Linda L. Bray leading her troops as they stormed a Panamanian Defense Forces outpost. At the end of the firefight the position was won, three of the enemy lay dead, none of the Americans were hurt, and a new era of opportunity for women was upon us. Representative Patricia Schroeder (D., Colo.) instantly, and sanctimoniously, declared that this showed that the distinction between combat and non-combat roles in the military was "a joke," and that the time had come to open the ranks of the infantry to women.

The unglamorous character of the target—the PDF K-9 corps kennels—was not given prominence in early reports, and it now appears that the gunfight lasted only ten minutes, that Captain Bray was half a mile away when the shooting started, and that no one on *either* side was killed. A legend in the making evaporated in embarrassment. The issue, however, is a real one. Should women go into combat? Are Representative Schroeder and the *New York Times* correct in their joint opinion that technological change and social evolution make restrictions on the military use of women unworthy atavisms, as unjust as they are outdated? Let's review the arguments.

Lots of other armies use women in combat roles: why shouldn't we? Actually very few serious armies have done so, save in the case of direst necessity where national survival was at stake. The Israelis make extensive use of women for all kinds of military work (including intelligence, education and training, and maintenance) but immediately pull them out of combat zones for three reasons, among others: if captured they will be raped, repeatedly; many men simply fall apart when they see young women they know well being disemboweled by shell splinters; Israeli society does not want girls to be killers. In the words of one Israeli general, "We don't do what you do in the United States, because unfortunately we have to take war seriously." Yes, men can be abused, and male casualties are horrifying, and no one likes the idea of his son being taught to shred another human being with machine-gun bullets or burn him with napalm. Nonetheless, there is an entirely different dimension to these matters when women are concerned. By brutal experience the Israelis (who draft most of their young women) have learned this.

Modern military technology no longer requires brute strength, so women can perform most combat tasks as well as men. In point of fact, combat still requires lots of brawn. It's easy to point a tank gun and shoot it—but what about loading the shells, or changing tank treads? Well, say the advocates of female grunts, why not have simple strength tests for the different combat specialties? When this has been tried there has been an enormous clamor because (surprise, surprise) it turns out that very few women meet the upper-body strength criteria. When *that* happened (surprise, surprise) feminist groups lobbied to have the tests revised. Moreover, the case for keeping combat units all male has a lot to do with "male bonding," a term that invariably evokes the sneers of (usually middle-aged, usually non-combat veteran) critics of the combat exclusion rules. But ask, or simply observe, a teenage boy on an athletic team and you will get a rather different answer.

Isn't this argument like the one that used to be made for keeping the military segregated by race? Most emphatically not. Black and white men are pretty much the same—men and women are different, with respect to physiognomy and, as many feminist authors now proclaim, with respect to psychology as well.

Representative Schroeder and those who agree with her see this issue as one of equal opportunities, much like disputes about private clubs, or differential pay scales. The reality is very different. This sort of decision is, ultimately, about suffering and death, and those shrillest in the clamor to have young women—even pregnant young women—kill and be killed for their country will not be the ones to pay for it. The Israelis are right, and we would be wise to learn from a nation that has learned these lessons in the hardest school. With all due respect for the undeniable coolness and professionalism of Captain Bray, neither she nor any other female soldier belongs in combat.

Questions

1. What values are involved in the discussion of whether women should participate in combat? Write a brief explanation of how values can affect responses to women in combat. Then share your own list with a small group of classmates and see if you can reach a consensus.

2. What other roles have women been excluded from, presumably for their own protection?

Suggestions for Further Research

1. Investigate the roles women played in the 1991 U.S. Operation Desert Storm in Kuwait. Write a summary of the information you discover.

2. What roles did women have in the military in World War II and Vietnam? Write a summary of what you find out.

Suggestions for Writing

1. Using reasoning similar to that used for excluding women from combat (or other roles), argue that men should be excluded from some role or activity.

2. Choose a single point or reason used on either side of this argument (for example, that women do not have sufficient upper body strength) and, after any necessary research, argue that this point or reason should or should not be part of the argument.

Defining Rape:

Is Rape about Sex, Violence, or Power?

Rape has traditionally been defined as an act of sexual intercourse to which one party—usually the woman—has not consented, and which involves the threat of force or physical violence. This definition seems straightforward and easy to understand. In recent years, rape has been the center of intense debate in which new attention has been focused on the concepts of date and acquaintance rape, and spousal rape—nonconsensual sex within a marriage. Others have argued that rape is really a hate crime against a minority. The essays printed here show a portion of that debate. Before you read the arguments in this section, respond in writing to the following:

Preparing to Read

1. *What would you tell a new freshman on your campus about date rape and how to avoid being a victim or a rapist?*
2. *What values does rape violate?*

A New Way of Looking at Violence against Women

LISA HEINZERLING

Last December, a man walked into the engineering school at the University of Montreal armed with a hunting rifle. He entered a classroom and divided the students he found there into two groups: women and men. Shouting at the women, "You're all a bunch of feminists," he picked them off as if they were ducks in a shooting gallery. By the time his deadly stalk was over, he had killed fourteen women and injured many others. A note found in his pocket after his suicide declared that women had ruined his life.

The man in Montreal killed these women because he hated them—not as individual persons, but as women. U.S. law, however, would not include these murders in the controversial new category known as "crimes of hate."

As now defined, "hate crime" refers to an act committed not out of animosity toward the victim as an individual, but out of hostility to a group to which the victim belongs. The 1986 attack on Howard Beach, New York, in which one black man was killed and two were beaten by white assailants, is a notorious recent example.

As recognition of this category of crime grows, some states have enacted laws to help them respond. California, for example, requires the collection and analysis of statistics on such crimes. In other states, if the "hate" criteria apply, a crime such as second-degree assault is automatically elevated to first-degree assault. Still other states have established a separate crime, such as "ethnic intimidation." The latest "hate crime" legislation is a federal law directing the government to gather statistics on such crimes.

Why are such statistics gathered? Legislators ask for numbers because, in deciding how laws should be fashioned, it's helpful to know the scope of the problem you're confronting. Statistics provide that sense of dimension, especially for a new category like hate crime. Unfortunately, many of the new laws share the same flaw: They do not include gender as one of the motivating factors that can

203

turn an ordinary crime into a crime of hate. The new federal law, for example, considers hate crimes to be those impelled by the victim's race, ethnicity, religion or sexual orientation. Other similar laws cite the victim's race, color, creed or national origin.

Thus, if a black man is beaten or killed *because* he is black, that counts as a hate crime. If a woman is beaten, raped or killed *because* she is a woman—as clearly happened to the victims in Montreal— that doesn't count. Women have to ask why.

"Race, color, religion, *sex* and national origin" has become a kind of refrain in our laws against discrimination. These characteristics invariably appear together as the criteria that must not be applied in allocating (or withdrawing) benefits such as education, employment and housing. And some states—like Connecticut, Minnesota, New Hampshire and California—*have* followed this model in the wording of their hate crime legislation. Thus, when other discrimination statutes—including the only existing federal law—do *not* include gender as one of the forbidden bases for conduct, we can only infer that the exclusion was deliberate.

Has sex been excluded here because women in the U.S. do not experience gender-motivated violence? Every woman reading this knows the answer, knows the special risk she faces *because* she is a woman. We've learned to order our lives according to our special danger, so much so that when we refuse to do so—say, by walking in a lonely section of town after dark—we are held as accountable as our aggressor for any injury that results.

Nor can the exclusion be based on the problem of differentiating between hate crimes against women and "ordinary" crimes. Not every mugging of a woman, for example, will fit the new category—but neither will every mugging of a Hassidic Jew. The resulting evidentiary difficulties haven't stopped us from creating the general category of hate crimes; indeed one of the purposes of the new federal statute is to establish a method for identifying which crimes are, in fact, motivated by hate.

The truth is, society does not think of crimes against women in the same way that it thinks of racial or ethnic violence. We tend, instead, to treat brutalizing acts against women as isolated cases or, more rarely, as manifestations of racial or ethnic hatred. Many observers have speculated that the young blacks who attacked the Central Park jogger—beating her so savagely that one doctor estimated she'd lost 80 percent of her blood by the time she'd reached the hospital—may have done so because she was white. *Almost none have suggested she was attacked because she was a woman.*

Certain acts against women *must* be recognized as hate crimes. The very act of excluding them may be a symptom of the same pathology that produces such a crime. For if studying such statistics tells our society that these crimes are important—more abhorrent, in fact, than other crimes—then excluding gender as a motivating factor sends an equally important message, one that's chilling indeed: These crimes are heinous, but *not* when they're committed against women; crimes like the murders in Montreal don't really trouble us much. That is a message welcome to none but the misogynist.

What Rape Is and Isn't

CATHY YOUNG

The vast majority of Americans, women or men, undoubtedly take a positive view of changes the women's movement has brought about in attitudes toward rape. It is now widely accepted that a woman does not have to be a paragon of chastity to prove she has been raped; that her sexual history should not be put on trial; that even if she has been having drinks with a man or invited him in, he has no right to force sex on her. These advances, however, may be undermined by the efforts of some feminists to so enlarge the concept of rape as to demonize men, patronize women and offend the common sense of the majority of both sexes.

A recent example of this extremism was provided by a panel discussion on an ABC News special, "Men, Sex and Rape." Men and women in the audience as well as the panel were seated separately, implicitly reinforcing the message that every man is a potential rapist.

Five of the six women panelists, among them legal scholar Catherine MacKinnon and "Backlash" author Susan Faludi, backed the view that rape, far from being a pathology, reflects the norm in male-female relations in our society. As proof, MacKinnon asserted that 47 percent of all American women have been sexually assaulted and 25 percent raped. When a male panelist questioned these numbers, she retorted, "That means you don't believe women. It's not cooked, it's interviews with women by people who believed them when they said it."

But not all researchers on the topic do believe the female respondents. University of Arizona psychologist Mary Koss, whose studies in the field are among the most frequently cited, wrote in a 1988 article that of those women whom the researchers classified as victims of rape by nonromantic acquaintances, only 27 percent considered themselves rape victims. In situations involving dating partners, only 18 percent of the researcher-classified victims thought they had been raped. (In surveys that directly ask women about forced intercourse, fewer than 10 percent report such experiences.)

Do these feminists believe women, or do they believe that women need expert guidance to know when they've been raped?

The reason for this startling "credibility gap" becomes clear when one looks at how the concept of rape has been broadened by the radical feminists. In their redefinition, physical force or threat of injury is no longer required.

In a recent volume of the *Journal of Social Issues,* for example, University of Kansas Professor Charlene Muehlenhard and three co-authors cite the finding that "the most common method men used to have sexual intercourse with unwilling women was ignoring their refusals without using physical force [emphasis mine]. . . . The prevalence of rape found in these studies would have been much lower if the definition required physical force."

A couple is necking, and at some point she says, "Please don't," and perhaps pulls back a little; he keeps trying and she eventually goes along rather than push him away or repeat her refusal more forcefully. Is this rape? Yes, say the hardliners: She does not resist because of fear. Even if the man does not threaten her, his size and muscle implicitly do.

But many people, myself included, will find it hard to believe that most women are afraid their dates will beat them up if they resist. Indeed, many who are attacked by strangers and have far stronger reasons to fear injury still fight back or scream.

Women have sex after initial reluctance for a number of reasons, and fear of being beaten up by their dates is rarely reported as one of them. Some may be ambivalent or confused; they may believe that they shouldn't want sex, and feel less guilty if they are "overpowered."

Sometimes both the man and the woman are drunk, which adds to the confusion and miscommunication. Some women may change their mind, perhaps because they get sexually excited by the man's attentions. Others may be genuinely unwilling but concerned about displeasing the man or hurting his feelings. As one student, prodded by a campus presentation on date rape to conclude that she was a victim, explained to a journalist, "I thought, 'Well, he's my friend . . . whatever happens, it's not going to be that bad' . . . no big deal."

Is it unfortunate that many women are brought up to be so anxious not to offend, to be liked? Yes. But the answer should be to encourage assertiveness, not make excuses for doormat behavior.

The redefinition of rape also includes "psychological coercion" such as "continual arguments." Muehlenhard and her co-authors suggest that if lack of resistance cannot be regarded as consent when a woman is threatened with being shot, it might be no different if she is threatened with being dumped. The old "If you loved me, you'd do it" line becomes a felony.

To the cutting-edge anti-date-rape activists, even a "no" is no longer necessary for a finding of coercion; the absence of an explicit "yes" will suffice. In the January/February issue of *Ms.*, a scene of clearly consensual (but wordless) rough sex from "Basic Instinct" is described as one in which "a woman experiences date rape and then kisses the perp."

All these definitional shenanigans might be funny if they didn't have serious practical consequences. Young men on college campuses are now being told in rape prevention workshops (mandatory for male freshmen at some schools) that they may have raped some of their seemingly willing sexual partners; and young women are being encouraged to abdicate responsibility for their sexual behavior by labeling unsatisfactory experiences as coercive. Harvard's Date Rape Task Force recently issued a report recommending that university police define rape as "any act of sexual intercourse that occurs without the expressed consent of the person," as well as sex with someone impaired by "intake of alcohol or drugs."

Of course, in the enterprise of redefining rape, there is no reason to stop at requiring verbal agreement. If a woman's failure to object to unwanted sex can be attributed to intimidation, so can explicit consent. Inevitably, on the outer limits, this patronizing line of thinking reaches the conclusion that in our oppressive society, there can be no consensual sex. Even if a woman thinks she wants it, that's only because her desire has been "constructed" by the patriarchy.

People have a right to the wackiest of ideas, but it is disturbing that some proponents of this theory are being treated as mainstream feminists. MacKinnon, who has emerged as a leading spokeswoman on sexual harassment and rape, has written such things as: "The similarity between the patterns, rhythms, roles and emotions, not to mention acts, which make up rape on one hand and intercourse on the other . . . makes it difficult to sustain the customary distinctions between violence and sex. . . . The issue is less whether there was force and more whether consent is a meaningful concept." When she appears on television or is quoted in the press, this (one would think) very relevant aspect of her beliefs is tactfully omitted.

So anxious are they to extend the concept of rape, these crusaders become almost annoyed when discussions focus too much on violent attacks by strangers or near-strangers. They want to hammer in the point that the greatest danger to women comes from male friends, lovers, husbands. (University of Washington professor Marilyn Frieman has compared Rhett Butler sweeping up Scarlett O'Hara and carrying her upstairs to mass murderer Richard Speck.) They insist that rape at knifepoint in a parking lot is not different from an ambiguous encounter in which a woman is pushed further sexually than she wanted to go, and further, that women have no responsibility whatsoever to avert situations of the latter sort.

On the ABC panel, Naomi Wolf (who is author of "The Beauty Myth") complained that "in this culture we tend to trivialize the harm that rape does to women." But if anything, much of the effort to broaden the definition of rape trivializes the horror of real sexual violence (by strangers or acquaintances).

The same program included footage of a treatment program for jailed sexual offenders, who were made to listen to a recording of a woman calling 911 just as a rapist breaks into her house. The terrified woman gasps, "He's here! He's here!" before her voice dissolves into screams and whimpers. One would have to be utterly removed from the real world to insist this is comparable to the experience of a woman who yields because she's tired of pushing away her date's roving hands.

A friend of mine, although acknowledging that some feminist rhetoric is excessive, believes that expanding the definition of rape to include noncoercive experiences is useful because it sensitizes the society to the pain that sexual pressure and manipulation often cause. But pressure and manipulation are not a one-way street; women can apply them too. Besides, the law is not there to ensure we have trauma-free relationships.

Trying to relabel insensitive behavior as illegal can only backfire: When a cad is accused of being a rapist, the unfairness of the charges may make him an object of sympathy, leading people to overlook his moral flaws.

Although I, personally, do not think that "no-maybe-yes" games are the stuff of romance, or that the vanishing of feminine coyness would be a great loss, to replace those rituals with new ones based on suspiciousness, calculation and consent forms in triplicate would hardly be a gain.

Questions

1. How does it change your understanding of rape to classify it as a political or hate crime? What is gained and/or lost by doing this?

2. In what ways do the authors of these essays challenge conventional ideas about rape?

Suggestions for Further Research

1. Gather statistics about rape to determine different kinds of rape (stranger, acquaintance, statutory, spousal, etc.) and then summarize what you find.

2. Investigate the concept of spousal rape. Is it recognized by the laws of any state (or the Federal government)? Has anyone been convicted?

Suggestions for Writing

1. Write an argument in which you explore the concept of consent (as it applies to rape) and attempt to reach a definition of it.

2. Write an argument in which you outline a campus policy for date rape, including prevention, treatment for victims, and consequences for perpetrators.

Gun Control:
Will It Stop the Violence?

Gun control has been the center of a heated, often angry debate for at least the past thirty years. The current debate began with the assassinations of John and Robert Kennedy and Martin Luther King, Jr. in the 1960s. The attempted assassinations of Presidents Ford and Reagan, and a number of widely publicized mass murders have fueled the debate. Advocates of gun control insist that it is the only way to contain a steadily increasing level of violence in the United States. Opponents say that gun control will not prevent violence, and that the U.S. Constitution guarantees the right to possess firearms. At this point, the debate seems to have reached an impasse, with few new ideas being brought in on either side. J. Warren Cassidy was Executive Vice-President of the National Rifle Association when he wrote this essay. Sarah Brady's husband was shot and permanently disabled by a man who was attempting to shoot President Ronald Reagan. Before you read the arguments here, respond in writing to the following:

Preparing to Read

1. *State your own position about firearms control, and give your reason for it.*
2. *Describe an experience you have had with firearms and explain how that experience contributes to your attitude toward them.*

The Case for Firearms . . .

J. WARREN CASSIDY

The American people have a right "to keep and bear arms." This right is protected by the Second Amendment to the Constitution, just as the right to publish editorial comment in this magazine is protected by the First Amendment. Americans remain committed to the constitutional right to free speech even when their most powerful oracles have, at times, abused the First Amendment's inherent powers. Obviously the American people believe no democracy can survive without a free voice.

In the same light, the authors of the Bill of Rights knew that a democratic republic has a right—indeed, a need—to keep and bear arms. Millions of American citizens just as adamantly believe the Second Amendment is crucial to the maintenance of the democratic process. Many express this belief through membership in the National Rifle Association of America.

Our cause is neither trendy nor fashionable, but a basic American belief that spans generations. The N.R.A's strength has never originated in Washington but instead has reached outward and upward from Biloxi, Albuquerque, Concord, Tampa, Topeka—from every point on the compass and from communities large and small. Those who fail to grasp this widespread commitment will never understand the depth of political and philosophical dedication symbolized by the letters N.R.A.

Scholars who have devoted careers to the study of the Second Amendment agree in principle that the right to keep and bear arms is fundamental to our concept of democracy. No high-court decision has yet found grounds to challenge this basic freedom. Yet some who oppose this freedom want to waive the constitutionality of the "gun control" question for the sake of their particular—and sometimes peculiar—brand of social reform.

In doing so they seem ready, even eager, to disregard a constitutional right exercised by at least 70 million Americans who own firearms. Contrary to current antigun evangelism, these gun owners are not bad people. They are hardworking, law abiding, tax paying. They are safe, sane and courteous in their use of guns. They have never been, nor will they ever be, a threat to law-and-order.

History repeatedly warns us that human character cannot be scrubbed free of its defects through vain attempts to regulate inanimate objects such as guns. What has worked in the past, and what we see working now, are tough, N.R.A.-supported measures that punish the incorrigible minority who place themselves outside the law.

As a result of such measures, violent crimes with firearms, like assault and robbery, have stabilized or are actually declining. We see proof that levels of firearm ownership cannot be associated with levels of criminal violence, except for their deterrent value. On the other hand, tough laws designed to incarcerate violent offenders offer something gun control cannot: swift, sure justice meted out with no accompanying erosion of individual liberty.

Violent crime continues to rise in cities like New York and Washington even after severe firearm-control statutes were rushed into place. Criminals, understandably, have illegal ways of obtaining guns. Anti-gun laws—the waiting periods, background checks, handgun bans, et al.—only harass those who obey them. Why should an honest citizen be deprived of a firearm for sport or self-defense when, for a gangster, obtaining a gun is just a matter of showing up on the right street corner with enough money?

Antigun opinion steadfastly ignores these realities known to rank-and-file police officers—men and women who face crime firsthand, not police administrators who face mayors and editors. These law-enforcement professionals tell us that expecting firearm restrictions to act as crime-prevention measures is wishful thinking. They point out that proposed gun laws would not have stopped heinous crimes committed by the likes of John Hinckley Jr., Patrick Purdy, Laurie Dann or mentally disturbed, usually addicted killers. How can such crimes be used as examples of what gun control could prevent?

There are better ways to advance our society than to excuse criminal behavior. The N.R.A. initiated the first hunter-safety program, which has trained millions of young hunters. We are the shooting sports' leading safety organization, with more than 26,000 certified instructors training 750,000 students and trainees last year alone. Through 1989 there were 9,818 N.R.A.-certified law-enforcement instructors teaching marksmanship to thousands of peace officers.

Frankly, we would rather keep investing N.R.A. resources in such worthwhile efforts instead of spending our time and members' money debunking the failed and flawed promises of gun prohibitionists.

If you agree, I invite you to join the N.R.A.

. . . And the Case against Them

SARAH BRADY

As America enters the next decade, it does so with an appalling legacy of gun violence. The 1980s were tragic years that saw nearly a quarter of a million Americans die from handguns—four times as many as were killed in the Viet Nam War. We began the decade by witnessing yet another President, Ronald Reagan, become a victim of a would-be assassin's bullet. That day my husband Jim, his press secretary, also became a statistic in America's handgun war.

Gun violence is an epidemic in this country. In too many cities, the news each night reports another death by a gun. As dealers push out in search of new addicts, Smalltown, U.S.A., is introduced to the mindless gun violence fostered by the drug trade.

And we are killing our future. Every day a child in this country loses his or her life to a handgun. Hundreds more are permanently injured, often because a careless adult left within easy reach a loaded handgun purchased for self-defense.

Despite the carnage, America stands poised to face an even greater escalation of bloodshed. The growing popularity of military-style assault weapons could turn our streets into combat zones. Assault weapons, designed solely to mow down human beings, are turning up at an alarming rate in the hands of those most prone to violence—drug dealers, gang members, hate groups and the mentally ill.

The Stockton, Calif., massacre of little children was a warning to our policymakers. But Congress lacked the courage to do anything. During the year of inaction on Capitol Hill, we have seen too many other tragedies brought about by assault weapons. In Louisville, an ex-employee of a printing plant went on a shooting spree with a Chinese-made semiautomatic version of the AK-47, gunning down 21 people, killing eight and himself. Two Colorado women were murdered and several others injured by a junkie using a stolen MAC-11 semiautomatic pistol. And Congress votes itself a pay raise.

The National Rifle Association, meanwhile, breathes a sigh of relief, gratified that your attention is now elsewhere. The only cooling-off period the N.R.A. favors is a postponement of legislative action. It counts on public anger to fade before such outrage can be directed at legislators. The N.R.A. runs feel-good ads saying guns are not the problem and there is nothing we can do to prevent criminals from getting guns. In fact, it has said that guns in the wrong hands are the "price we pay for freedom." I guess I'm just not willing to hand the next John Hinckley a deadly handgun. Neither is the nation's law-enforcement community, the men and women who put their lives on the line for the rest of us everyday.

Two pieces of federal legislation can make a difference right now. First, we must require a national waiting period before the purchase of a handgun, to allow for a criminal-records check. Police know that waiting periods work. In the 20 years that New Jersey has required a background check, authorities have stopped more than 10,000 convicted felons from purchasing handguns.

We must also stop the sale and domestic production of semi-automatic assault weapons. These killing machines clearly have no legitimate sporting purpose, as President Bush recognized when he permanently banned their importation.

These public-safety measures are supported by the vast majority of Americans—including gun owners. In fact, these measures are so sensible that I never realized the campaign to pass them into law would be such an uphill battle. But it can be done.

Jim Brady knows the importance of a waiting period. He knows the living hell of a gunshot wound. Jim and I are not afraid to take on the N.R.A. leaders, and we will fight them everywhere we can. As Jim said in his congressional testimony, "I don't question the rights of responsible gun owners. That's not the issue. The issue is whether the John Hinckleys of the world should be able to walk into gun stores and purchase handguns instantly. Are you willing and ready to cast a vote for a commonsense public-safety bill endorsed by experts—law enforcement?"

Are we as a nation going to accept America's bloodshed, or are we ready to stand up and do what is right? When are we going to say "Enough"? We can change the direction in which America is headed. We can prevent the 1990s from being bloodier than the past ten years. If each of you picks up a pen and writes to your Senators and Representative tonight, you would be surprised at how quickly we could collect the votes we need to win the war for a safer America.

Let us enter a new decade committed to finding solutions to the problem of gun violence. Let your legislators know that voting with the gun lobby—and against public safety—is no longer acceptable.

Let us send a signal to lawmakers that we demand action, not excuses.

Questions

1. What values are being invoked on each side of this debate? Do the two sides share values, or do they rely on completely different values? Can you use these values to identify common ground between the two positions?

2. What questions would you like to ask each writer? Make a list of three to five questions that you believe each writer should answer.

Suggestions for Further Research

1. Many gun control opponents argue that people need guns for self-defense and sport. Investigate this claim. How often do gun owners have to shoot in self-defense?

2. What does the public at large think about gun control? Consult public opinion polls to determine the public's attitude toward guns, gun control, hunting, the Brady Bill, and other issues. Summarize the information you find.

Suggestions for Writing

1. Write an argument in which you focus on *one* aspect of one side of this debate. For example, you could chose the claim that owning guns is constitutionally protected, or that guns are necessary and valuable for self-defense. Explore the issue in detail, do any necessary research, and then argue that it is or is not a valid part of the overall argument.

2. Write an argument for which your primary audience is people whose positions are opposed to yours (rather than people who have not yet committed to a position on this issue).

MULTISIDED ARGUMENTS

Remembering Pearl Harbor:
Who Really Won the War?

Since 1945, the United States and Japan have had an increasingly complex and difficult economic relationship with each other. Having lost the Second World War, Japan appears nevertheless to have achieved many of the economic goals it set for itself in the 1930s. Though the United States helped Japan recover from the war, the two countries seem unable to establish a positive political or economic relationship. For many Americans, the defining event in the relationship between the two countries is the Japanese surprise attack on Pearl Harbor in 1941. The arguments in this section approach U.S.–Japan relationships from a variety of perspectives. Before you read the selections printed here, respond in writing to the following:

Preparing to Read

1. *Summarize what you know about the existing political, social, and economic relationships between the United States and Japan.*
2. *Summarize what you know about the Japanese attack on Pearl Harbor in December 1941, and explain how that event could still be affecting relationships between the two countries.*

Maybe We Should Forget It:
What's Wrong with our Pearl Harbor Memories

FRANK DEFORD

The way it has turned out, the most significant thing about Pearl Harbor is not that it happened but that we are so determined to remember it. Much of this is because Dec. 7, 1941, was the first time in the American experience that the world stood still, the beginning of the Instant Age. Before then, before radio, we didn't hear news in the aggregate, immediately. News dribbled in by telegraph or word of mouth. In 1891, people didn't say they remembered exactly what they were doing when they heard about the Lincoln assassination.

Pearl Harbor was the first example of national cluster emotion. As that phenomenon, it lives not as a historic event but as personal recollection, not much different from a first kiss or a highschool graduation. Everyone sentient then remembers it; Americans born later have the family oral history thrust down their throats. By now, it's our own Kabuki theater. Remember in "Stalag 17" when the bad guy is trapped just because he remembered Pearl Harbor occurring at the wrong hour of the day? We make a to-do about remembering it each year. But we don't. Not really. What we actually do is: We Remember That We Remember Pearl Harbor.

In the American bumper-sticker mind, Pearl Harbor forever survives as the example of treachery, as if every other attack in every other war was fair by comparison. Hitler was never characterized as "treacherous," despite his blitzkriegs across the continent. (Of course, it's also true that Hitler wasn't Asian.) In fact, little that became A Day in Infamy originated with Adm. Isoroku Yamamoto, who conceived the plan. And even before the war was over, we virtually copied the essence of Yamamoto's design, thrusting hundreds of miles out of the way into Japanese territory, to surprise and shoot down the plane carrying Admiral Yamamoto himself in what is probably the closest we have ever come to a government-ordered assassination. And then came those two fateful mornings in August 1945: the surprise bombings of Hiroshima and Nagasaki, a slaughter of civilians that many consider more heinous—more infamous—than any attack on warships of a newly declared enemy. In "Pearl Harbor Ghosts," a fascinating new study by Thurston Clarke, the author argues persuasively that we never would have nuked the Japanese cities if we hadn't been so determined not to forget to remember Pearl Harbor.

Hollow victory: If we truly remembered—as opposed to Remembering That We Remember—we would, presumably, have learned something from that day. Demonstrably, we have not. The reason that the Japanese succeeded at Pearl beyond their wildest dreams is that Americans were (a) unprepared and (b) overconfident. The reason that we were overconfident is not only because we knew we were the smartest and best people in the world, but also because we saw the Japanese as little yellow people from the rice fields who couldn't do anything right. We have had two major wars since then. For Korea, we were (a) unprepared, and for Vietnam we were (b) overconfident. Neither have we been any more astute in that other war, the one now going on against Team Japan. We need only recall Lee Iacocca's words in 1971 when a close friend asked him if she should get in on a Toyota dealership, and Iacocca replied, certainly not: "We're going to kick their asses back into the Pacific Ocean."

Notwithstanding, it may well be that the Japanese remember Pearl Harbor even less wisely than we. It would be advisable for them to keep in mind, as they bestride the economic world now, that Pearl Harbor was only a brief, hollow victory for Japan. Yamamoto, a savvy guy educated at Harvard, then posted to Washington, had traveled across the United States. He so appreciated American economic power that, almost alone, he convinced Tokyo that Japan's only chance lay in a quick, demoralizing strike against Hawaii. But Yamamoto failed to comprehend American will. It never occurred to him that a raid on American soil would backfire and infuse Americans with determination for revenge. He had no conception of how obsessively we would make ourselves remember Pearl Harbor. As dreadful as this is to say flat out, as ugly as it is for the young sailors and soldiers who died that day, Pearl Harbor became, quickly, the ultimate photo op. It's fashionable to say that while Japan lost the war in 1945, it won the war that followed. That may be true. It's also true that, in the end, we won Pearl Harbor.

So, both of us go on remembering that we remember Pearl Harbor, and both of us learn nothing from it. Better, for example, that we remember the atrocities of Nanking and Bataan; then maybe there wouldn't have been a My Lai. Better to remember that for there to be a sinking of the Arizona, Japan had to build boats and planes and plot how to cross the Pacific unnoticed; then maybe there would still be a Detroit. Let it go now. Where were we that day when we heard the news? What exactly did Mom and Dad say? It doesn't matter anymore. We grew too close to it, and those memories of 1941 achieve nothing but distortion and poison. Let this 50th anniversary be the last Pearl Harbor Day. It's time to remember to forget.

Three Myths about Pearl Harbor

STANLEY WEINTRAUB

What didn't happen at Pearl Harbor?

What did not happen was a military catastrophe. Eighteen ships were indeed sunk, including eight battleships. At least 347 aircraft were destroyed or badly damaged. Nearly 4,000 men were killed or wounded. It looked very bad. Results even exceeded Japanese expectations.

Yet more than half the U.S. planes destroyed were obsolete, and battleships, the Navy's proud dinosaurs, played a minor role in the war. No aircraft carriers were lost at Pearl Harbor—none were there at the time of attack. This was crucial.

Addicted to card-playing as well as verse-making, Adm. Isoroku Yamamoto, the planner of Pearl Harbor, wrote ruefully in a verse from his flagship in Hiroshima Bay,

What I have achieved
Is less than a grand slam. . . .

The U.S. and Britain possessed no secret foreknowledge of the attack. Allegations have long rested on the "Winds" message decoded in Washington on Nov. 28, in which Tokyo had warned its officials abroad that an alert would be concealed in a radioed weather forecast. "East wind rain" would mean an imminent "crisis" with the U.S. and "the cutting off of our diplomatic relations."

Such a message may never have been sent before the shooting started. No "East wind rain" message survives anywhere. Revisionists and conspiracy die-hards have labeled the ghostly message a "Winds execute," claiming it warned of war, and even identified Pearl Harbor as a target, but there is no hard documentary evidence to support these charges.

An American general who asserted that he had seen a "Winds" warning of Pearl Harbor also described an event that never happened there. In a memoir, Brig. Gen. Elliot Thorpe, the Lend-Lease representative in Java, recalled that the "next morning" after the Japanese had struck, a Maj. Gen. Van Oyen of the Dutch Air Force "came to my office and told me the first-hand story of the disaster in Hawaii."

"Van Oyen," Thorpe wrote, "and a group of Dutch pilots were flying a dozen PBY flying boats from the U.S. to the Indies and had arrived at Ford Island in Pearl Harbor early in the evening of Dec. 6. The attack the next morning destroyed about half the Dutch planes. . . . Van Oyen took off with what was left . . . and made [the rest of] the trip without meeting any hostile aircraft."

In an oral history taken from General Thorpe on his retirement, the number of imaginary planes rose to 50 and the casualties to 35. But no Dutch PBYs were there and none destroyed. And no plane at that time could have overflown enemy territory across the Pacific at a height and speed to get to Java at all. Distortions like this have long dogged the "Winds" story, which warned neither of war nor of Pearl Harbor.

Although President Franklin D. Roosevelt and his staff did not need to conceal Japanese movements to draw the U.S. into war, other accounts charge that the Pearl Harbor strike force was traced but the information suppressed. Yet messages to the Japanese fleet from Tokyo were deciphered only after the attack, and the enemy fleet maintained absolute radio silence as it sailed. Meanwhile, radio signal noise from home ports deliberately confused American intelligence gathering.

All conspiracy theories related to Pearl Harbor lack credibility. As Edward R. Murrow said later, having been backstairs at a chaotic White House on the evening of Dec. 7, the leadership from the top down was shocked. Consummate actors, Murrow thought, could not have shammed surprise on that scale.

Besides, even the most Machiavellian conspiracy scenario would not have required a calamity. A raid repelled at great loss to the other side would have done just as much to push a reluctant U.S. into war.

Machiavellian designs have also been attributed to Winston Churchill, who was accused of learning of an impending attack from JN-25, the Japanese naval code the British had cracked, and then withholding the data from the U.S. The Murrow rule applies here as well. The evidence is persuasive that Churchill and his top planners were genuinely surprised; some of them had no idea where Pearl Harbor was.

Pearl Harbor did not push Germany into war with the U.S. Having resisted F.D.R.'s provocations in the Atlantic for months, Hitler greeted Pearl Harbor with glee. Yet the attack was only the final precipitant—Hitler had already concluded that a war with the U.S. was necessary sooner rather than later.

Paradoxically, Hitler's decision to declare war on the U.S. grew out of a secret Army study of American military unreadiness that isolationists had leaked to The Chicago Tribune. On Dec. 4, the Anglophobic paper featured the story on its front page. It reported that the U.S. was preparing contingency plans to counter Hitler before Japan. The report conceded that the U.S. would likely have to reclaim Europe alone and that it would need a 10 million-man Army to begin the job by July 1943. (The projection's pessimism turned out to be over-optimistic by a year.) While the article hardly mentioned Japan, it convinced Hitler to declare war while America was confessedly weak.

Ironically, then, the isolationists, whose case had been wrecked by the Japanese attack, impelled Hitler into doing what Congress might not have otherwise done. Shocked by what Hitler had wrought, his planning chief, Gen. Walter Warlimont, confided to Gen. Alfred Jodl, "So far we have never considered a war against the United States and have no data on which to base [it]."

Back in Oahu, what finally didn't happen was the golf game that Adm. Husband E. Kimmel and Gen. Walter C. Short, both of whom had received war warnings from Washington on Nov. 27, had scheduled for Sunday morning at 8. Unexpected visitors from out of town had dropped in at 7:53.

Faces of Japan

DAVID UNGER

After just a week in Japan, some familiar American stereotypes about this country and its people seem shockingly superficial and dangerously out-of-date. Japanese society differs from America's in important ways. But like American society, Japanese society is neither monolithic nor static.

Today's Japan is one of the world's most modern, most affluent societies, plugged into every trend in international pop culture and a powerful creator of new trends for others. Its young people are highly educated, fashion-conscious and remarkably well traveled. Its face is far more diverse, and youthful, then would ever be guessed from the cautious politicians and corporate tycoons who dominate the news.

Americans can usefully debate the nature of Japanese society and how America can best respond to Japan's competitive success. But for too many Americans, Japan's image is a crude caricature, drawn from half-digested sound bites and painted in racist hues.

The Japanese are portrayed as faceless and conformist, their real feelings impenetrable to non-Japanese. This supposedly monolithic society is explained in terms of Japan's militarist traditions, its consensus style of politics and a shared national anxiety over scarce resources. These are said to produce people committed to work unceasingly so that Japan can dominate the world economically, and perhaps militarily too.

There are Japanese who think like that, but fewer than there used to be. Meanwhile, a newer, youth-oriented leisure culture is emerging everywhere, from the nightclubs of Tokyo's Ginza and Roppongi districts to Kyoto's Kawaramachi Street.

Most of Japan's 123 million people have been born since 1960. Most adults have no personal memories of World War II or the U.S. occupation. Most Japanese today are children of affluence, not scarcity.

Older people still remember the hard times and hesitate to relax. The middle-aged worry more narrowly about astronomical housing costs and their children's increasingly expensive tastes. And for many school-aged children, the affluence achieved by past generations is there to be enjoyed now and the future can take care of itself. These younger Japanese pleasure-seekers are, their elders say, "nibbling on their parents' shins."

If the generational breakdown sounds familiar to Americans, there's good reason. An internationalized market and culture has homogenized experience to a remarkable extent, particularly in societies at comparable economic levels.

Japan *is* different from America, but also surprisingly familiar. There are unreconstructed militarists and nationalists who acknowledge no Japanese wrongdoing before or during World War II, but there are also potent pacifist and environmental movements. Traditional values are revered, but a growing feminist movement is challenging patriarchal traditions. Japanese culture values harmony and pleasing words, but some Japanese are bluntly outspoken, even to foreigners.

Why then do so many Americans see the Japanese as an army of ants? One reason may be unfamiliarity. Few Americans have spent much time in Japan. And the faces Japan turns to the outside world are usually those of its mumbling politicians and corporate samurai. It's also more comforting for Americans to explain embarrassing competitive setbacks by conspiracy theories rather than by poor American business practices.

The United States and Japan now have the world's two biggest economies. Their relationship is too important to fall victim to oversimplification and ignorance. Both societies have learned valuable and different lessons from history, lessons they might usefully share with each other. By better appreciating what we have in common with the Japanese, Americans might even discover how to benefit from Japanese successes.

Don't Blame Japanese for All Trade Problems

USA TODAY

Blaming Japan won't open doors to U.S. goods or create products people want to buy.

President Bush and 21 business leaders are off to Asia today. Their mission: open Asian markets to U.S. goods.

One goal is to get Japan to buy more U.S. cars and parts. That would help cut the USA's $41 billion trade deficit with Japan, 75% of which is automotive.

And Japan appears ready to listen.

This week, Japan's automakers pledged to double their use of U.S.-made parts by 1995. And the Japanese government said that some safety and environmental rules for imported cars might be cut.

More open markets would be good for the USA—each $1 billion in added exports means 20,000 jobs here.

But some in this country seem less focused on opening markets than on closing our own to Japan.

U.S. sensitivity about autos has risen with General Motors' recent announcement that it would cut 74,000 jobs and close 21 auto plants. And some politicians appear ready to exploit that sensitivity this election year by blaming Japan for the USA's economic woes.

Blaming the Japanese is easy, but it is dangerous if it increases protectionism that limits trade between nations.

Japan is the biggest importer of U.S. farm goods. It is the biggest customer for Boeing 747s. It is a major market for CAT scanners and nuclear reactors.

Trade barriers will cost both nations customers and make each poorer.

Japan isn't to blame if U.S. automakers don't produce the right-wheel-drive cars Japanese drive. Nor is it to blame if U.S. consumers prefer Japanese cars and VCRs. Nor is it to blame if its industrial processes are newer and more efficient than our own.

U.S. industry must work harder to meet consumer demand here and abroad. And government must cut its deficit so industry can borrow money to expand cheaply.

The success of the president's trip depends on opening doors for U.S. goods, not raising barriers to trade.

Make Japan Change the Rules

CLYDE PRESTOWITZ

As a fledgling U.S. diplomat in 1966, I was assigned to promote European exports to the USA. At the same time, the president was urging U.S. business to develop foreign sources of supply and to import more. These were small parts of a massive, postwar affirmative-action program to create prosperous, stable allies in Europe and Asia.

Over the past 45 years, it has become the accepted norm that the U.S. market will be more open than others and the U.S. leaders will subordinate economic issues to geopolitical imperatives while foreign leaders do the opposite. Naohiro Amaya, a former vice minister of Japan's Ministry of International Trade and Industry, has likened this situation to a game of golf in which players of lesser skill receive a handicap.

In 1950, says he, the United States gave the rest of the world a large handicap in the game of trade. The problem today is that, as a result of much practice, the other players have become quite proficient, but the handicap has not been fully adjusted.

Auto-import regulations are just one example. The USA accepts the certification of foreign producers that their products meet U.S. safety, emissions and other standards and does not require that cars be inspected as they enter the country. This saves exporters much time and money. In contrast, Japan, Korea and others will not accept the word of foreign producers but insist on time-consuming inspection procedures that effectively act as a tariff on imports.

It is past time for these non-reciprocal attitudes and practices to change. U.S. producers should, of course, be expected to meet reasonable safety and regulatory standards abroad; but such standards should not be thinly disguised barriers to imports. And it is not protectionism or special pleading for U.S. officials to request that the handicap be adjusted and that others make an effort to reciprocate the favors they have long been receiving.

Pearl Harbor's Unlearned Lessons

ROBERT J. SAMUELSON

The saddest thing about the 50th anniversary of Pearl Harbor is the enormous suspicion that still infects relations between the United States and Japan. The mistrust confounds a favorite American idea: that mutual prosperity breeds good feeling. Japan and the United States are increasingly interconnected economically, to the benefit of both. Yet, the growing interdependence has raised mutual ill will.

The subplot of much U.S. commentary on Pearl Harbor is: Who won the war, anyway? Japan is seen as a threat. The nature of the threat is usually left to the imagination. Will they bomb us? No. The idea seems to be that they'll take us over—make all our products, buy all our companies. This specter distorts. In 1990 our trade deficit with Japan ($41 billion) was three-quarters of 1 percent of U.S. gross national product. In 1990 Japan's direct investment in the United States ($84 billion) was about one percent of the net worth of all U.S. business.

What's also lost is that commerce with Japan involves large advantages for us. There are losers, of course, as always in competition. American companies have been bankrupted, American workers laid off. But the gains do not lie simply in high-quality Japanese products for U.S. consumers. Competitive pressures from Japanese firms—in technology and ways of doing business—force U.S. companies to improve. This raises our living standards. Although General Motors is no longer dominant, it produces better cars more efficiently.

Ill will, though, is not exclusively the result of overwrought American fears. Japan's paranoia is, if anything, greater. I call Japan the nation of Nixon. Like our former president, the Japanese are so automatically suspicious of everyone else (especially foreigners) that they risk making their worst fears come true by acting as if they're inevitable. The Japanese are eager to believe bad news. Every murmur of criticism or anti-Japanese rhetoric is amplified into a deafening roar.

Consider the recent experience of William Watts, a consultant who travels often to Japan. After talking with U.S. officials in

Washington, he concluded that relations were fairly calm. Then he flew to Tokyo, where Japanese officials and newspapers were abuzz with "daily reports from America of anti-Japanese speeches. . . . All this gives the impression that Americans spend their waking hours figuring out new ways to criticize Japan," he wrote in the Japan Digest, a newsletter. Little wonder that a recent poll by the Asahi newspaper found that 61 percent of Americans consider the relationship good compared with only 39 percent of Japanese.

What's worse is that distrust of America is concentrated among younger and better-educated Japanese, according to a new poll by Kyodo news service. Half of college graduates rated the United States as an untrustworthy ally. Both Japanese and Americans tend to ignore facts that contradict their preconceptions about each other. Almost reflexively, the Japanese dismiss criticism as "Japan-bashing" or racism. The intent is to stifle discussion by presuming that any criticism is inspired by a loathing of Japan.

Our selectivity is becoming almost as acute. We can picture our economic relationship with Japan only as one in which we are victims. Typical was a recent "Frontline" documentary—shown on public television—titled "Losing the War With Japan." It depicted Japanese companies systematically obliterating their U.S. rivals. Could it be that Americans sometimes exploit Japanese, or that Japan's own markets aren't hermetically sealed? The answer is yes, though you couldn't tell from the documentary.

Exploitation? Well, many U.S. office buildings were sold to Japanese investors in the 1980s at wildly inflated prices. As for Japan's markets, our exports are growing rapidly. Between 1985 and 1990, they jumped $26 billion, or 115 percent. Nor were the increases merely in raw materials (grain, logs): Manufactured exports rose faster. Between 1985 and 1990, they increased from 55 percent to 64 percent of U.S. exports to Japan, report analysts Peter Gold and Dick Nanto of the Congressional Research Service.

The sense of mutual grievance reflects mutual disappointments. When we promoted Japan's postwar recovery, we never expected that Japanese industries would challenge or dethrone our own. When the Japanese strove to boost exports, they never imagined that success would intensify foreign pressures to make Japan more open. Instead, they thought export surpluses would reduce their vulnerability to outside influences by ensuring they could easily buy essential imports (food, fuel and ores).

Neither Japanese nor Americans are adapting well to unanticipated roles. Americans are properly galled that the Japanese don't spontaneously support a world system—in trade and security—from which they hugely benefit. Why won't Japan allow rice imports? Japan insists on the right for its trade to disrupt other societies without accepting a similar obligation. Rice is supposed to be special. Tell that to a U.S. auto worker. Japan's $13 billion contribution for the Persian Gulf War was adequate, but the funds had to be cajoled.

The Japanese have lost respect for us, because we can't solve our own domestic problems. They also rightly object to being cast as a passive paymaster—that is, being asked to pay for decisions made by us. Why don't we propose Japan for a permanent seat on the United Nations Security Council? We can't expect the Japanese to act responsibly unless we treat them responsibly.

The danger is that all this bickering will hurt us both. We may demonize the Japanese and make them a scapegoat for our failings. Japan could gradually isolate itself. It cannot count on permanently leading an Asian bloc. Economic growth is slowing, while the population is aging. By 2010, its over-65 group will be 20 percent, up from 12 percent in 1990. Japan isn't liked by its neighbors, China and Korea. It needs to belong to a wider global system of trade and security. We provide that. Our efforts to make Japan more open do the Japanese a big favor.

For both countries, nationalism could clog the commerce on which we both depend. Our fates are linked, but our thinking isn't. We have come far from Pearl Harbor—and not far at all.

Remember Pearl Harbor How?

JAMES FALLOWS

It was almost three years ago, near the beginning of 1989, when I was living in Japan, that friends started to mention the "upcoming anniversary." I didn't know what they were talking about, but since I often didn't know what was happening around me in Japan, I decided to wait for enlightenment. I began to get the point when someone mentioned "the upcoming fiftieth anniversary," which he then nailed down with a date: December 8, 1991. By Japanese reckoning that is the fiftieth anniversary of the attack on Pearl Harbor. As Americans will be reminded this month, the Japanese planes came in on a Sunday morning, when U.S. sailors could be expected to be hung over and sleeping in. By that time it was already Monday, December 8, in Japan.

Americans old enough to remember that day certainly remember it vividly, but there are fewer and fewer of them around. For most of the American public this month's TV documentaries and commemorative ceremonies will be very much like the other documentaries and ceremonies we periodically see. Within the past two years the news media, ever alert to anniversaries, have invited the United States to take a look at Vietnam fifteen years after the fall of Saigon, at the space program twenty years after men first walked on the moon, and at Germany fifty years after Hitler rolled into Poland. This month we'll look back at Japan—with magazine features, a speech by President George Bush at Pearl Harbor, and a commemorative postage stamp—and then we'll move on to something else.

However the United Sates responds to the Pearl Harbor observances, it cannot possibly meet the expectations that have been building up in Japan. Indeed, by far the most interesting part of the fiftieth anniversary is the way Japan's opinion-making class—its popular press and foreign-policy specialists—has prepared the public to cringe in dread of U.S. outbursts this month.

Not every recent Japanese article about U.S.-Japanese relations has begun with a phrase like "As the clock ticks toward the anniversary of Pearl Harbor. . ." But a lot of them seem to start that way. Last summer a magazine called *Foresight* told readers about an ominous statistical indicator. In the previous forty-nine years a total of eighty-six books about Pearl Harbor had been published in the United States, but fifteen were scheduled for publication in 1991 alone. "A bipartisan bill has been submitted to Congress to set Dec. 7 aside as a national memorial day," *Foresight* said. "There is no doubt that the 50-year anniversary of Pearl Harbor is the big event for both Japanese and Americans." *Shukan Gendai,* a very popular weekly magazine, reminded readers that Bush was going to Pearl Harbor, and said,

> The United States is a most barbarous country. In Western movies, people always say, "If you have a complaint, come and fight me!" . . . Anti-Japanese feelings have reached the point that Americans are saying, "Now it's time for you to pay us what you owe us! If you don't surrender, the only solution is a war."

Shukan Themis, another weekly (*shukan* means "weekly"), carried an article saying that "fearful White Anglo Saxon Protestants, led by President Bush, have launched a retaliation against Japan. . . . The WASP is a white supremacist. He cannot tolerate nonwhites taking the initiative in a single area." *Shukan Shincho* reported on the success of a recent American book called *The Coming War With Japan,* which, like most books on U.S.-Japanese relations, is vastly more interesting to Japanese readers than to Americans. The magazine said that sales of the translated version of the book should reach 350,000 copies by Pearl Harbor Day.

It is a little misleading to quote at length from these magazines, collectively called *shukanshi*, because they occupy a particular niche in the Japanese press. Their look, heft, and nationwide following make them seem similar to *People* and *Sports Illustrated*, but they are known to be cavalier with the facts in a way much closer to the *Weekly World News*—"Latest Photos of Bigfoot" tradition. The same *Shukan Shincho* report on sales of *The Coming War* said that the book was also hugely popular in America, where in fact it has never appeared on any best-seller list. A somewhat higher toned magazine called *Sapio*, whose name is apparently derived from "sapience," said in all seriousness that with U.S.-Japanese tensions on the rise, a certain anti-Japanese joke was being "widely circulated" in the United States. Here is the joke, in its entirety as reported by *Sapio:* "Officers of the Ministry of Finance, Japan's elite, piss cold as ice. And an abacus is implanted in their brains." Forgive me if you've heard this one before.

For all their excesses, the magazines do shape public opinion, leaving the Japanese reader with the impression that Americans are waiting to run amok in December and meanwhile telling incomprehensible jokes. The Pearl Harbor mania in the weeklies seems to parallel more-respectable views. Every time I have interviewed a Japanese official in the past year, he has asked me how I thought Americans would react to the upcoming anniversary. A year ago in Tokyo a Japanese politician summoned me to his office. After we'd sipped tea for forty minutes, he said, "By the way"—the phrase that in practice means "Now let's get to the point." "What do you think about the reaction . . . ?" I've enjoyed looking for stories in the U.S. press about the countdown. They are almost always by correspondents in Tokyo who get the "by the way" treatment from nervous Japanese contacts every day.

The obvious question is why? Why should so many Japanese be counting the days until the anniversary, while so few Americans seem to have given it a thought?

There are a few time-honored and partly satisfactory explanations. The United States as a rule pays less attention to any given country than that country pays back. This is a source of strain in U.S. relations with Mexico, Canada, the Philippines, and many other countries, including Japan. In a way it would be more flattering to the Japanese if Americans really were telling "piss cold as ice" jokes: at least they'd be thinking about Japan. Also, Japan is famous for its edginess on the whole subject of the Second World War. Its experience with China and Korea, whose governments are always complaining about Japanese history textbooks and signs of nascent militarism in Japan, seems to have left it with the belief that old resentments can bubble up at any time.

But something more must be involved. Japan has less to be apologetic about this month than it did, say, four years ago, during the fiftieth anniversary of the "Rape of Nanking." (At least 100,000 Chinese were killed in Nanking, as compared with fewer than 3,500 Americans at Pearl Harbor, and the Chinese were nearly all civilians. This anniversary passed almost unnoticed in Japan.) The *way* the Japanese Imperial Army fought was sometimes atrocious, and Japan's relations with China, in particular, are still colored by both sides' awareness of this record. Americans tend to lump the attack on Pearl Harbor with Japan's war crimes in Asia, and to equate Japan's aggression with Hitler's. Few people in Japan see it that way.

The U.S. complaint about Pearl Harbor involves one very specific and one sweeping charge. The specific complaint is that the attack began while Japanese emissaries in Washington were still purporting to negotiate in good faith. For this the Japanese government has freely apologized. The broader complaint is that Japan brought America into the war by striking first. The Japanese response to this charge is a much more complicated matter.

For provoking the United States to fight, Japanese officials have often expressed "regret." The regret is understandable and sincere, since the consequence was a war that turned out, as Emperor Hirohito tactfully put it in his surrender message, "not necessarily to Japan's advantage." But there has been nothing like an outright "apology" for Pearl Harbor, and there is not likely to be one this month, because of the widespread Japanese view that the main thing to regret about the "Pacific War" is that the country unwisely took on a much more powerful foe.

Japan, of course, tried to occupy its neighbors by force in the 1930s, but it was hardly the first country to do so. As many Japanese writers emphasized at the time, the same countries the Japanese army was conquering had previously been conquered by armies from Britain, France, Holland, or, in the case of the Philippines, the United States. Japan's strategic ideal would have been to hold on to this empire without colliding head-on with the United States. Ben-Ami Shillony, an Israeli specialist in Japanese history, has said that if Japan had

> taken the side of the Western Allies in World War II, as she had done in World War I, or had she remained neutral, as she had been before Pearl Harbor, her prewar attempts at establishing a regional hegemony and her wartime violations of human rights might have

subsequently been condoned in the context of the Cold War, as was the case with many Asian countries.

Within the Japanese military government, the case for attacking Pearl Harbor was that America would sooner or later intervene to push Japan back in Asia. If war was inevitable, Japan's best chance lay with a first strike. Some Japanese strategists thought that even after Pearl Harbor the United States would lack the stomach for a long war, and would agree to a kind of demarcation line down the middle of the Pacific, separating Japanese and American zones of influence. For the Japanese, then, the tragedy of Pearl Harbor was that it indicated their inability to avoid a direct showdown with the United States, in addition to being a disastrous miscalculation of how America would respond to a sneak attack. Each of these was a failure for Japan; neither, in the general Japanese view, was an unpardonable sin. Even in the days of total humiliation immediately after the war, Emperor Hirohito expressed deep "regret" but declined to "apologize" to General Douglas MacArthur, saying, "It was not clear to me that our course was unjustified. Even now I am not sure how future historians will allocate the responsibility for war."

Shortly after the United States finished pummeling Saddam Hussein's army, a magazine called *Bungei Shunju,* Japan's counterpart to, well, *The Atlantic,* published an article with the charming title "Victor Nation America, Do Not Be Arrogant: Japanese People Should Discard Their Blind Trust in White Man's Society." After the Second World War, it observed, the United States "passed judgment on Japan, saying that 'Whatever reason there may have been, the side which started the war is in the wrong.' Japan . . . became stricken with shame."

A familiar chestnut holds that Japanese society is driven by shame more than by guilt—that people are more attuned to whether they are offending the sensitivities of others than to whether they are violating their inner "thou shalt not" rules. A sense that they are about to be subjected to a shaming ritual may account for the exaggerated countdown in Japan.

But perhaps the most powerful explanation lies in another Japanese instinct—the "victim consciousness," or *higaisha ishiki,* that governs many of Japan's relations with great powers from the outside world, which for the past century has meant the United States. Japanese leaders of the Tokugawa era felt victimized by Commodore Perry's arrival; the leaders of the 1930s felt victimized by American and British determination to deny Japan its place in the sun. Over the past twenty years the Japanese press has emphasized the country's victimization by American demands to open up the market. The preparation for Pearl Harbor is essentially a warning that Japan is about to be victimized again.

Questions

1. Based on the readings printed here, what is the nature of the relationship between the United States and Japan? What are the central issues in that relationship?

2. According to the writers represented here, what major misconceptions do Japanese and Americans have about each other?

Suggestions for Further Research

1. Consult a history of the 1930s and World War II to learn about the Japanese plan for a Greater East Asia Co-Prosperity Sphere. Summarize the information you find.

2. Consult newspapers for December 7th from at least five years since 1945 and read about anniversaries of the attack. Describe how attitudes toward the Japanese and the attack have changed or developed over time.

Suggestions for Writing

1. Write an argument for an audience of U.S. citizens in which you urge them to change their perceptions of the Japanese. Or, as an alternative, write for an audience of Japanese and argue that their perception of Americans is inaccurate.

2. Write an argument for an audience of U.S. citizens in which your position is that the United States either *should* or *should not* continue to celebrate the anniversary of Pearl Harbor as a "Day of Infamy."

The United States:
Land of Many Cultures—

Can It Achieve Peace with Itself?

In an essay reprinted in this section, Juan Williams says that "race remains the central domestic issue of the nation." Many people would agree that the future of the United States may depend on whether its citizens can learn to live together peacefully and productively in the midst of ethnic and racial diversity. Is it possible to accept differences, and even see them as positive, rather than insist that everyone be the same. Before you read the arguments in this section, respond in writing to the following:

Preparing to Read

1. Describe an experience you have had with a member of another race or culture, and explain how that experience made you feel.
2. Describe a situation in which you believe you were a victim of racism or discrimination because you were treated as a member of a group rather than as an individual. How did that experience make you feel?

The Case against Sensitivity

DAVID RIEFF

Well before Nelson Mandela arrived in New York this past summer to begin a triumphal passage through the great cities of the United States, his impending visit had inspired entrepreneurs to manufacture a line of T-shirts bearing the likeness of the ANC deputy president and ornamented with maps of Africa and slogans affirming black unity. The biggest sellers carried a simple message: *It's a black thing. You wouldn't understand.* Taken by itself, the sentiment expressed on the T-shirt, with its sad mixture of resignation and defiance, may not seem all that significant. Mandela, though he surely would have understood the message, would with equal certainty have repudiated such a slogan. But what the T-shirt says about blacks and America is not as important as what it says about Americans in general. For the phrase perfectly sums up the degree to which matters of ethics and allegiance—and even the most elementary questions of understanding—are now thought to be the exclusive intellectual and emotional property of those interest groups most affected by them. For "It's a black thing," substitute "It's a [blank] thing," and you're in business. Mandela's visit may have made the sentiments of many New York blacks legible to everyone who cared to look, but as a way of thinking about the world it is by no means restricted to certain rancorously politicized segments of black America. For more than a decade, and far longer in some circles, a spirit of particularism has been setting in on college campuses, in the ongoing debate on pornography and free speech, and most pronouncedly, in the gay and feminist movements. Not only do people seem persuaded by the proposition that, when all is said and done, nobody can understand anybody outside one's own group, but by its corollary: For a member of one group— be it ethnic, sexual, or racial—to criticize the activities, the views, or the culture of someone in some other group is to be guilty, according to the current terms of art, of disrespect ("dissing") or insensitivity.

235

At first glance, it seems more than a little peculiar to worry about sensitivity in a country whose shameful crime statistics, faltering economy, increasingly illiterate and innumerate population, and frivolous political leadership are not getting a fraction of the attention they deserve. Nevertheless, sensitivity is now as important an issue for the Left, and for the educational establishment, both in the public schools and on university campuses, as the repeal of abortion rights has been for the Right. Increasingly, in a United States that becomes more racially diversified each year, every group that views itself as oppressed or disenfranchised has chosen to construe its situation in the language of the Civil Rights movement. Like the Civil Rights movement, the battle has been partly legal and partly linguistic. Gays, the disabled, and women have all pressed for juridical redress, and that demand is self-evidently just. But more and more, the call has been for psychological and verbal redress as well, and that demand may not only be impossible to fulfill, but dangerous as well.

The United States remains a puritan country in which, despite everything that has happened during the past thirty years, the censor is never very far below the surface. It is also a country where people believe, as they always have, that there is little about themselves, whether it be their physiques or their beliefs, that they cannot alter if they change their behavior radically enough. So it should come as no surprise that Americans, finding themselves in a society in which the tensions of clashing interests, moralities, and ethnicities seem to grow each year, would imagine that if they could learn to think positively and respectfully about one another everything would be okay.

The idea is peculiarly American. Certainly, it is hard to imagine Europeans or Asians falling for the illusion that if only they could learn to be sufficiently sensitive to other cultures, then age-old conflicts would disappear. But then those cultures believe in tragedy, in the continuing authority of the past, whereas few Americans have ever really believed that the past is anything except a prelude to the future. The result has been that instead of wanting to see differences aired in public, many well-meaning Americans want to sweep them under the rug. It sometimes seems as if the only way you can get in trouble in the United States these days is by *saying* something offensive; think of the forced resignation of cabinet members Earl Butz and James Watt. They were not hounded out of office, as perhaps they should have been, for the policies they carried out, but rather for making offensive jokes.

The examples are legion. The racist remarks of a Jimmy Breslin or a Jimmy the Greek or an Al Campanis find their echoes in the attitudes of rap group Public Enemy, whose anti-Semitism, however indirectly phrased, is clear enough. Indeed, which of us had not felt the painful sting of hate speech? What is different about the current climate is that whereas in the past most Americans assumed that the best way to combat hate speech was with other speech, today many are looking for ways to suppress it. Many decent people apparently have come to believe in a sort of affirmative-action equivalent of the genteel old small-town say, "If you can't say something nice, don't say anything at all."

These well-intended thought police were neatly lampooned by Russell Baker, who recently wrote a column that imagined Wagner receiving advice from an American well-wisher about how he might reconceive *The Ring* to make it better conform to contemporary American values. "Rewrite the opening," Baker's socially conscious bowdlerizer suggests helpfully, "to eliminate the insensitive treatment of dwarfs embodied in the character of the dwarf Alberich. The Rhine Maidens' calling him ugly and toadlike is offensive to dwarfs, as is the suggestion that dwarf cannot be sexually interesting to mermaids. Having Alberich steal the Rhine Gold imputes criminal instincts to dwarfs and is an overt slur." Similar proposals to avoid offending the sensitivities of various oppressed groups are proffered concerning Wotan, Fricka, Siegmund, Brunhilde, and the rest. There is no Wagner left after this treatment, of course, but neither is there anything left in the opera that could remotely be interpreted as disrespectful toward anyone. Only the one group that the writer considers to be an oppressor, Episcopalians, is held up as suitable for scorn and slander. Wagner is invited to say anything he likes about them.

Baker's satire is actually a pretty faithful rendition of the views of an influential group of scholars, activists, and writers for whom free speech, when it offends those who can be called disempowered by society, is by no means an absolute right. Make fun of Episcopalians or real estate developers by all means, they argue, but don't say anything even passingly negative about members of oppressed groups, because such remarks are less expressions of opinion than harmful "speech acts" that have the effect of perpetuating this disempowerment. It was more or less on these grounds that Mari Matsuda, a law professor at Stanford, wrote an influential article in a 1989 issue of the *Michigan Law Review* calling for universities to forbid hate speech directed at minorities. Matsuda argued that freedom of speech, properly understood, was a guarantee really intended to protect the powerless. By this she did not mean powerless individuals, but members of outsider groups, like women or racial minorities. Thus, a rich woman would presumably be protected by the First Amendment but a poor white man (unless gay, or disabled, or otherwise "disenfranchised") would not.

Using logic similar to Matsuda's, 137 American universities (including Stanford and the University of Michigan) have in the last two years passed proscriptions on hate speech. The Michigan code was eventually struck down by the courts, but the extent to which the principle of restricting speech is gaining acceptance can be gauged by the divisiveness the issue has provoked even within the American Civil Liberties Union, which until recently was absolutist on all free-speech questions. True, the national organization has hewed to its traditional interpretation, but several of the largest affiliates, most notably in northern and southern California, have accepted the argument that speech is, at least in certain instances, less an expression of personal freedom than a form of power, and as such, is subject to curtailment. The catalogue of what is barred is broad. The University of Michigan policy prohibited "any behavior, verbal or physical, that stigmatizes or victimizes an individual on the basis of race, ethnicity, religion, sex, sexual orientation, creed, national origin, ancestry, age, marital status, handicap, or Vietnam-era-veteran status." Perhaps the "except Episcopalians" is implicit.

This kind of sensitivity used to be mainly the preserve of the Right. To cite an obvious example, the obscenity statutes have always been justified by the argument that most people in a given community are offended by pornography. The attacks that Senator Helms has been leading against the National Endowment for the Arts for underwriting exhibits of Robert Mapplethorpe's photos, and the decision by a federal judge in Florida to ban the sale of rap group 2 Live Crew's record *As Nasty As They Wanna Be*, are only the most recent examples of this orthodox censorship. "It's a question," said the judge in the 2 Live Crew case, "between two ancient enemies—'anything goes' versus 'enough already.'" Not for nothing was the first major New Left group at the University of California at Berkeley in the early 1960s called the Free Speech Movement. Indeed, as recently as 1984, the ACLU could issue a report in which the threat to constitutional rights was presented as coming entirely from the Right. Ah, the good old days.

As the ongoing debate over federal funding of the arts has amply demonstrated, the danger from the Rights has not receded. The neoconservatives have even joined the fray (with the Cold War over, they must have so much . . . . time). Samuel Lipman, the publisher of *New Criterion*, could be seen on a recent segment of the *Mac-Neil/Lehrer Newshour* arguing that the question of obscenity should really be decided by an ongoing process of popular referenda. Now, however, we are beginning to hear left-wing spins on the same argument, from what might be called the reform branch of the censorship movement. In place of "community standards," was "concern for the oppressed." A placard at a recent gay-rights march in Washington summed up this new mood nicely. BAN HOMOPHOBIA, it said, NOT HOMOSEXUALITY.

Among people on the Left, the conviction has taken root that disrespectful or offensive views can be blunted through the judicious application of what might be called linguistic martial law. Like all appeals for extreme measures, it has the force of righteous indignation and the limitations of both shortsightedness and wishful thinking. The demonstrator at the gay march probably never paused to wonder whether, if it came to *banning* anything, it might more likely be gays than gay bashing.

Of course, it makes little sense to argue that banning any kind of speech, no matter how odious, will undermine the whole basis of freedom of speech in America, if you believe that insensitive speech is not simply offensive, but harmful—an act, at the very least, of psychological violence. Some feminists go further, arguing that pornography actually incites men to rape and brutalize women. For Catherine MacKinnon, the ACLU's decision to defend pornographers in effect deprives women of *their* civil liberties. MacKinnon has drafted statutes (one became law in Indianapolis before it was struck down by the Supreme Court) that ban pornographic material of all kinds. Not surprisingly, her arguments have been warmly endorsed by Fundamentalist anti-pornography crusaders like the Reverend Donald Wildmon, with whom she cannot be imagined to have much else in common. For MacKinnon and Wildmon, as for so many utopian American reformers before them, symptom and cause have gotten mixed up. A copy of *Penthouse* found in the local 7-Eleven didn't cause the breakup of the family, although it may be a by-product of its onrushing dissolution. As for MacKinnon's notion that pornography caused violence against women, the truth is that violence against women is, alas, the bloody thread that unites almost all times and all cultures. What censors are offering is nothing more than the old American fantasy of prohibition. Ban alcohol and no one will drink; ban racist speech and no one will be a racist; ban pornography and no one will ever have a perverse thought again. Implicit in such thinking is the curious assumption—one that belies all the populist pretensions of both Right and Left—that Americans are so gullible and childish that they will follow the lead of anything they see or hear. Show Mapplethorpe in Cincinnati and everyone will turn gay; sanction hate speech and soon it will drown out every other sound in the land.

Not surprisingly, pornography aside, conservatives and radicals have disagreed about exactly what should be banned. In Texas, parents' groups have campaigned for the removal of books that teach what they call "secular humanism" and what in fact is liberalism. In California, equally committed groups of parents, most but not all black, have sought to remove *Huckleberry Finn* from school library shelves on the grounds that it is racist. Now, if only Jim could have been called "Episcopalian Jim." Reactions to all this tend to vary, depending on whose ox is being gored, although, if only because it originates on university campuses, the left-wing variant is usually described more respectfully in the media.

Still, what unites would-be censors of all political stripes is far greater, intellectually, than that which divides them, and what is abundantly clear is that in America today the idea of individual rights is steadily losing ground to the idea of group rights.

We have come a long way from the time when the ACLU decided to go to court to defend the American Nazi party's right to hold a demonstration in Skokie, a suburban Chicago town densely peopled with Holocaust survivors. The martial-law definition of free speech proceeds apace. Given the rise in racial attacks on nonwhite students on college campuses, the argument goes, and the seemingly intractable problems of rape and the sexual harassment of women, what practical solution is there except to carve out a series of legal exemptions to the doctrine of free speech? This is, of course, exactly the same argument that people worried about crime make regarding the rights of criminal defendants. And, indeed, it is a difficult one to rebut. Most criminal defendants, for all the nonsense we all speak, are guilty—and that probably included a certain Arizona criminal by the name of Miranda, he of the famous warning. Still, Aryeh Neier, the Jewish refugee from Nazi Germany who defended the Skokie fascists, had it right when he used in the introduction for his book on the affair an exchange from the play *A Man for All Seasons.* "What would you do? Cut a great road through the law to get after the devil?" Thomas More inquires of a pious disciple. And the man replies, "I'd cut down every law in England to do that." To which More retorts, "And when the last law was down, and the devil turned round on you—where would you hide, the laws all being flat?"

Not that the whole question can be defanged with a quotation, no matter how salient. If the MacKinnons of this world have never demonstrated to anyone's satisfaction but their own that pornography engenders violence against women, this does not make the problem of violence against women any less grave. And the Mari Matsudas of this world are right when they point out that hate crimes in universities *are* getting out of hand. Absolutist defenders of the First Amendment have to at least consider whether draconian legislation might have some positive effect, and not simply argue that the moral and political consequences are too severe. One has only to think back to Barry Goldwater's 1964 presidential campaign. "You can't legislate laws into the hearts of men," he intoned, denouncing the then-new Civil Rights law. But of course you can, up to a point anyway. When has force not ruled human affairs, whether in Little Rock or in Prague? At the very least, change often occurs only when force is imposed, as in the South in the 1950s and 1960s, or when it is withdrawn, as in Eastern Europe in 1989.

Today, the extent to which blacks and whites do work together (if not live together) in cities like Richmond, Atlanta, and Mobile, and in reasonable amity at that, is partly due to the laws that were rammed down people's throats a generation ago. But when the federal government superseded more than one hundred years of Jim Crow legislation, it was risking no major legal side effects. We risk everything when we tamper with the First Amendment. Legal ramifications aside, we should be doing everything in our power to avoid imposing yet one more layer of conformity and blandness on a country where conformity and blandness in politics and thought are more and more the rule. Americans need to take stock, to argue, ridicule, and defame without hurting one another's feelings. If the country were in better shape, people could pretend they were better than they are. But the country is in lousy shape, and attempting to paper over the antagonisms that divide us with a juridical smile button is not going to help.

For the arts, certainly, this new sensitivity, if it prevails, will be an unmitigated disaster. The Rushdie case provides the perfect example of what is at risk. Whatever can be said about the orchestration of the campaign against *The Satanic Verses*, there can be no doubt that Rushdie's book did offend the sensibilities of many Moslems. Moreover, in England, in India, and in South Africa, where much of the controversy originated, Moslems are an oppressed and beleaguered minority. A Moslem Mari Matsuda might well have argued, as a few leftist critics (notably the novelist John Berger) have done, that Rushdie's right to say what he wants is far less important than the rights of the immigrant Moslem "outsiders" to be free of what radical literary critics (who, along with lawyers, are the theorists of the new sensitivity) would doubtless call "narratives" that prevent their full empowerment. If the jeers of white students on a college campus cause black and other minority students to fail, as these critics assert, what is one to make of a book whose promulgation has, say its detractors, perpetuated unfair stereotypes about the entire Moslem universe? If the argument for barring disrespectful speech is justified legally, at least in America, on the grounds of the Supreme Court's "fighting words" exemption to the First Amendment, what is one to say about *The Satanic Verses?* Now *those* were fighting words.

The kind of sensitivity that is being pushed on university campuses these days would make all serious art nearly impossible, for only a genius could make anything worthwhile in a context where only positive images are acceptable. Certainly artists will be among the first casualties if the case for sensitivity, which can never be anything else but a case for censorship, prevails. Art will exist, of course, but as a species of folklore, the product not of individuals but of groups. Those who argue for this kind of art almost always say that it enhances self-esteem, particularly among those who have felt denigrated by the dominant society. The fact that such a conception of art precludes a Rushdie does not seem to trouble its advocates. A feminist wall poster in SoHo puts the argument succinctly: NO MORE MASTERPIECES, it reads.

This idea of self-esteem is even more central in American education. The examples are endless. In 1989 a New York State task force issued a report calling for a sweeping revision of the history curriculum taught in the public schools. Excessive emphasis on the Western (that is, the European) tradition, it was argued, had had a "terribly damaging effect on the psyches" of children of non-European origin. What was needed was a curriculum that would de-emphasize Europe and "validate"—a word most often used in educational theory and in parking lots—African, Latino, Native American, and Asian contributions to the United States. That way, minority-group students would feel better about themselves and white students would become less "arrogant." A similar case is commonplace in the literature departments of many American universities, where there is a strong push for more women writers, black writers, gay writers, et cetera, and for fewer DWEMs (Dead White European Males)—perhaps Proust will wind up being taught only in gay literature courses.

In the case of the New York history curriculum, the report was accepted by the education commissioner. The Board of Regents agreed to form a panel that would recommend revisions in the curriculum, stipulating further that the drafters of this new multicultural master plan were to be chosen in such a way as to ensure that "among the active participants will be scholars and teachers who represent the ethnic and cultural groups under consideration." The author of the task-force report was none other than Lionel Jeffries, a black anthropologist at the City University of New York, whose lifework it has been to argue that black people are *by nature* warm and generous, while whites are cold and greedy. (Inherited cultural traits! As the educator Diane Ravitch remarked at the time, there hasn't been anything so absurd since Lysenko.) But that was less interesting than the Regents' sober decision that each ethnic group should have, in effect, the right to decide now what their history had been then. Gore Vidal, hardly the most lenient narrator of the American pageant, has called this "good citizenship history," in which people will be taught that "the hispanics are warm and joyous and have brought such wonder into our lives, and before them the Jews, and before them the blacks. And the women."

Only in America could an educational reform be based more on its impact on the students' psyches than on its veracity. But the point isn't education (a piquant detail in New York is that the panel planning the revision of *history* curriculum may wind up seating only one historian); it's just what Vidal says it is, feeling good; and for that, one needs facts less than good intentions, and rigor less than sensitivity and respect. It has always been like this in America, where the academic content of the curriculum has taken a backseat to the moral effect the schools were supposed to produce. "Little children," ran a third-grade reading commonplace in American schools in the 1880s, "you must seek to be good rather than wise." At the time, American public education emphasized vocational achievement, but educators were already evincing contempt for academic learning, at least when compared with sports, or with what in the 1950s were referred to as "life values." In retrospect, there is only a short distance between this view and the current cult of self-esteem.

Of course, once you have set up a system in which the truth matters less than a sensitive or constructive narrative, all interactions, and for that matter, all institutions, are going to be judged on the basis of their contributions to people's sense of psychological well-being. The classroom radicals, however they may imagine themselves, are not so far removed from the aspirations of the larger, therapeutized culture that gave birth to them. Americans are obsessed with finding ways to think about themselves more positively. Whether it was Coué, with his slogan, "Every day, in every way, I'm getting better and better." or "I'm okay, you're okay" and beyond, Americans are suckers for the idea that if they could learn to love themselves enough they could do anything.

If positive thinking has been a constant in American thinking since the days of Benjamin Franklin, and I think it has, it has been most influential in times of crisis and among communities at risk.

Think if the widespread belief among cancer patients that they became sick because of negative self-image, or the conviction held by many gravely ill people—an attitude popularized by Norman Cousins—that if they reform their sense of self they may be able to induce remission. "Those of you who feel guilt because you believe you caused your own illnesses," instructs Dr. Bernie S. Siegel, author of the recent best seller *Peace, Love & Healing,* "or who feel like failures if you cannot cure them, are giving your healing system a destructive message. You must let go of feelings of guilt and failure so that, unencumbered by these negative messages, you can utilize to the fullest your innate healing capacities."

Black people, with their long and tragic history of enslavement and suffering, gay people in the midst of the AIDS pandemic, women, Native Americans—is it any surprise that these *Americans* have accepted the notion that positive thinking can relieve their oppression, and that negative thinking, whether its source is stereotypes imposed by outsiders, or self-hatred, will perpetuate that oppression? For that is the force behind the demand for sensitivity, the belief that attitude is the key to everything. Thus, high black crime rates are increasingly explained by many blacks not in the socioeconomic language of liberalism, let alone in the religious language of sin, but as a by-product of internalized self-hatred. What is necessary, then, is less material improvement than pride. As a result, more effort is given to demonstrating in front of a Korean fruit stand in Brooklyn, where a shopkeeper is said to have treated a black customer disrespectfully, than to demonstrating in front of the New York office of the Small Business Administration for more loans for blacks who want to start fruit stands of their own.

Similar attitudes are evident in the more materially privileged world of gay people, where the debate about outing has echoes of many of the same assumptions. Most gay people would probably still argue that they should be free to come out of the closet or to stay in as they choose. But others are saying that in fact the rights of the gay community must take precedence. If a famous gay, so the argument runs, were to come out, this would go a long way toward countering the negative self-images that many gays have, particularly if they live in small towns. If these gay role models were available, the suicide rate among gay teenagers might even drop. So the decision to come out, far from being a private matter, comes to be construed as a matter of life and death. Moreover, gayness is also viewed by many activists as an inherited cultural trait. A recent book called *Gay Men and Women Who Enriched the World,* on sale at my local bookstore, offers potted biographies of forty famous gay men and women, ranging rather improbably from Alexander the Great to Gertrude Stein. Though it would be hard to conjure up two human beings more different, the author insists they are bound by their "gay sensibilities."

In the end, it seems, Americans are so haunted by the division of the world according to special-interest groups that all other forms of differentiation have become unimportant. The gay activists who heaped scorn on Malcolm Forbes for concealing his alleged sexuality were, for the most part, fierce critics of the capitalist system. And yet they saw no inconsistency, so much had the racial or ethnic model of gayness won their allegiance, in demanding that this excoriated plutocrat come out so that he could serve as a model for other gays. Far from being an interesting or subtle way of understanding the world, this tribal conception robs the world of its complexity and its depth.

Though couched in the rhetoric of enlightenment, the politics of race and ethnicity are in fact a form of Know-Nothingism—the ultimate denial of politics. What matters is not what you think, or what you stand for, but the color of your skin, your gender, or your sexual tastes. This is cultural nationalism in the truest sense of the term, a romantic idea of identity in which there are no contradictions between groups. And since these groups, by definition, cannot understand one another, the only solution is difference, respect, sensitivity. "It's a [blank] thing. You wouldn't understand." There used to be name for that in America: It was called separate but equal. A lot of people died to get rid of it, but now, with a new wardrobe, it's back.

In the past, ambitious people had the idea that the role models could come from anywhere, not just from among members of their own ethnic group, or for that matter, from people they actually knew. The idea was to transcend the situation into which they were born. Today, many would agree with the admonition of the black playwright August Wilson, who told an interviewer: "Never transcend who you are." And, indeed, if one's identity is, by definition, both good and immutable, then to be anything other than sensitive is to perform a spiritual mugging. The problem is that identity is not fixed, it's fluid, and that a "pure" culture is as preposterous an idea as a "pure" race. Because cultures, like races, are hybrids, it makes no more sense to see nothing wrong in a culture, except the ways in which it has been deformed by oppression, than it does to see nothing wrong in a person. When the defenders of 2 Live Crew argue that the band is an expression of black culture, they are probably right, but they are begging the question. Cultures are mixtures of good and bad, and the greatest problem of the new sensitivity is that it makes condemning anything, or even thinking critically about anything, an impermissible act of bad faith.

Real respect comes not from restrictions on hate speech, or empty slogans promoting group pride, but from the acknowledgement of complexity. "What have I in common with the Jews?" Franz Kafka once wrote. "I have nothing in common with myself." Throughout history, all spiritual understanding has been based on the willingness to embrace these sorts of contradictions, and in doing so, to accept that human imperfection is not derived from the machinations of strangers but stems from the human condition itself. All the sensitivity training in the world, whether psychological or political, will not change this. For, despite what August Wilson says, the only hope for humanity *is* transcendence, not the polite fictions of sensitivity and respect, which are really invitations—"It's a [blank] thing. You wouldn't understand"—to mutual incomprehension. Far from being a time when we should be saying less, as the advocates of the new sensitivity keep insisting, we should be saying more. We need a hundred novels as offensive as *The Satanic Verses*. We need to let the tragedy in, not pretend we can legislate it away. In an age of slogans and mind-numbing hype, we do not need pabulum, no matter how well intended.

People often argue that the alternative to sensitivity is callousness. It isn't. The alternative is love, which is an emotion that does not come entailed with lies, or the reductive fictions of political activism and ethnic solidarity, or the exaggerated punctilio of a society that can no longer cope with the crisis of belief and community in which it finds itself becalmed. There is no point in pretending, as Americans so often try to do, that the world is not a tragic place. And there is no need to pretend that all cultures—or for that matter, all people—are good at the same things any more than sane parents would make such claims about their children. It is only necessary to love human beings—as individuals, not as groups or factions—in the same way that parents love their children, imperfections, weaknesses, and all. That, and, however insensitive the message may at first appear, to tell the truth.

Rethinking Race

EDITORS OF *THE NEW REPUBLIC*

Legally and institutionally, and in its collective image of itself, the United States is no longer a racist society. The civil rights movement smashed the apparatus of segregation and political exclusion, an irreversible achievement that brought America's civil structures into line with its civil religion of equality and tolerance. That social revolution has continued to score new gains ever since. Perhaps most significant among these is the emergence of a black middle class that has moved out of the ghetto and into mainstream American life. These achievements are worth celebrating. But not just now.

The moment is better suited to other kinds of reflection on the complicated condition of race relations in our society. Recently a black cadet was terrorized by whites dressed in Ku Klux Klan regalia at the Citadel in South Carolina. Black students were taunted and chased by whites at the University of Massachusetts-Amherst, a campus that has also been the scene of anti-Semitic incidents prompted by "Third World" students. At Christmastime, in the New York borough of Queens, three black men were chased and brutally beaten by a gang of white youths, simply because of the color of their skin. One was struck and killed by a passing car while he tried to escape. And on the eve of the national holiday honoring the birthday of Martin Luther King Jr., a mob of brick-throwing whites led by Ku Klux Klansmen assaulted an interracial march in all-white Forsyth County, Georgia.

Such repugnant incidents do not mean that racism and racist violence are once again rampant in America. Still, they are a discouraging reminder of the limited influence of law and policy on social life. Although formal institutions and rules now embody America's founding ideals, the informal rules that govern many streets, campuses, households, and individual consciences still do not. In many places there is a lag between society and law, between cultures and politics. In such places, particularly in our largest cities, blacks and whites continue to view each other across a gulf of physical and psychological separation. Public acceptance of the principle of equality has not been matched by the full integration of classrooms and voluntary associations. The key that would unlock all the doors would be integration of neighborhoods. But who wants to take a stand for this all-but-ignored issue from the old civil rights agenda? Black politicians aren't eager; residential integration, in dispersing blacks, would erode their power bases. Whites, for their part, often either resist the entry of black families—or leave once such families do move in—because they falsely associate all blacks with crime and welfare dependency.

Such impediments should not come as a surprise. It is, after all, only 32 years since Rosa Parks refused to give up her seat on an Alabama bus; only 19 years since the assassination of King. It takes longer than that for an entire nation to adapt its mores to its laws.

It takes longer than that for mutual suspicion and ingrained hostility to give way.

In the broadest sense, then, the challenges posed by the persistence of racial division and racial inequality today are no different from what they were at the height of the civil rights movement in the '60s. Racism and racial animosity are still shameful stains on American society that must be eliminated. In this sense, too, the task of national political leadership is no different now than it was in the '60s. It is to declare often and unequivocally the nation's collective commitment to its creed. Ronald Reagan has not measured up to the task. On many occasions, his administration has been insensitive to the concerns of blacks and succored the worst residual instincts among whites—most callously in the Justice Department's support for tax exemptions for segregated Bob Jones University.

As a result, civil rights professionals have been able to argue, against the evidence, that progress has been slight and remains precarious. In the area of voting rights, for example, they often wrongly assume that if a predominantly black voting district elects a white, the outcome is proof of racist intimidation. Even in our flawed democracy, this is nonsense. And to the extent that there has been some decline in the proportion of blacks in our elite colleges and universities, these activists would have us ascribe it to racism—rather than to the ongoing crisis in the ghetto that leaves more and more blacks less and less prepared to acquire the academic skills necessary to a gratifying and useful life.

All of which reflects the fact that in many ways the practical problem of achieving something that might be called radical justice has gotten more difficult. Politics is the arena in which we attempt to put morality into practice. And the morality of racial politics is more complicated now than it was in Martin Luther King's day.

One ugly factor on the scene is black racism. Take the Howard Beach case. First white racists attacked Cedric Sandiford, then black racists rushed to represent him. His testimony was vital to the prosecution of the white thugs who attacked him and two others, but his lawyers advised their client not to cooperate with the Queens district attorney, on the trumped-up grounds of a cover-up by the police, the DA, and "the white power structure" in general—all of whom were clumsily and falsely accused of being somehow involved in the attack. (See "The Legal Circus" by Eric Breindel, page 20.) To this was added an absurd call for a boycott of all pizzerias in New York (the attack took place near a pizzeria), and then for a boycott of all white businesses. Such demagogues have no interest in racial justice and harmony.

These particular calls for confrontation have been shunned by the majority of blacks and black leaders. They were simply too preposterously irrelevant to the tragedy. But desperation is not always so amenable to reason. In many areas of the country, blacks and whites alike have turned their frustrations and resentments into racist acts against recent Asian immigrants and Asian Americans. Some of this has also been violent, and not unlike Howard Beach. In New York and Washington, it has taken the form of boycotting and harassing Asian-owned businesses. There are disturbing indications that talented Asian students are being turned away from some campuses—perhaps in part to disguise the numerically disheartening contrast between Asian "success" and the "failure" of other minorities.

Resorting to boycotts and other such protests may recall the movements of the 1960s, but in a purely exploitative and politically manipulative way. The rhetoric and rituals of black extremism are not relevant to the crises of the black community. Rather, they are dangerously counterproductive. Marching in the streets and punishing businesses will do nothing to surmount the remaining economic and social barriers to the full and equal participation of black people in American life.

Indeed, it is far easier for blacks to march and for whites to ignore them than for blacks and whites alike to address the most urgent problem of racial justice today: the plight of the black urban underclass. Blacks are socially split. Two-thirds of them are not poor; there is still a large income gap compared with whites, but the black middle class is closing it. Yet among the underclass population—reckoning conservatively, some four million people—the indices of poverty have never been higher. Social disorganization has led to social pathology. One of the most heartbreaking of these is rampant pregnancy among unwed teenagers: it condemns both mothers and children to the cycle of poverty, dependency, and underachievement that now defines the lives of more and more black people. Black-on-black crime deepens the misery. Homicide is now the leading cause of death for black men aged 25 to 34. These men are being killed in gang warfare, family quarrels, robberies— and simply at random. In Detroit, which is 70 percent black, over 300 children under the age of 17 were reportedly shot last year.

Undeniably, the historical experience of racial oppression is at the root of black poverty today. And the historical fact of blacks' victimization at the hands of whites entitles them to the ongoing special concern of society as a whole. Economic opportunity and the elimination of racial discrimination are still necessary conditions for solving that predicament. But they are not sufficient.

"Racism has been the worst, most tragic strain in American life, and it still is," writes Nicholas Lemann in his recent study of the urban underclass in the *Atlantic*. "[B]ut it and the fate of the black poor since the mid-'60s simply don't match up." The law became more nearly colorblind, government more generous, whites more enlightened—and the misery of the ghetto deepened. The culture of poverty has taken on a life of its own. It was there before and during Ronald Reagan's presidency, and it will persist after it, even if Reagan should be succeeded by the most liberal Democrat who might run in 1988. Now much of the responsibility for that culture's persistence, and for overcoming it, belongs to blacks themselves.

Moreover, the claim of victimization invites counter-claims. The politics of black race resentment has collided with the politics of white class resentment. Whites in big-city communities like Howard Beach see neither their immigrant ancestors nor themselves as implicated in, or helped by, America's historical wrongs against blacks. Rather, they feel like not-very-privileged taxpayers who shouldered the costs of the government's expanding efforts against black poverty in the '60s and '70s. And they see *themselves* as victims—of neighborhood decline that they associate with blacks and of street crime that is disproportionately perpetrated by blacks. They know, too, that Johnny "Rotten" Lester, alleged ring-leader of the Howard Beach mob, and his comrades are criminal punks, evidence of a terrible social pathology all but ignored. (See "Inside Howard Beach" by Jonathan Rieder, page 17.) When cast in terms of victimization, debate about racial issues can degenerate into a no-win quarrel with blacks and whites shouting, "It all started when he hit me back."

Blacks, the great majority of whom reject the demagoguery of would-be separatists and nationalists, recognize that there are more productive ways to advance their cause. They have not been well served by their leaders. At last some of them, notably John Jacob of the National Urban League, have declared an intention to take on ghetto culture—and to do so publicly in a way that enlists the help of whites. The fact is, however, that these problems will be especially resistant to change. There probably can be no real strategy for dealing with the phenomenon of unwed and teenage mothers other than a vivid morality, which, alas, seems alien to the drift of the popular culture at large. And there is the problem of two mutually reinforcing insecurities. Whites fear that to say the problems of the ghetto must be treated primarily as a black problem will invite charges of racism from blacks. Blacks fear that accepting responsibility for the crisis of the underclass, or speaking of it frankly as a crisis of values and behavior, will encourage the impulse of many whites to wash their hands of black problems altogether.

The persistence of poverty and dependence despite the War on Poverty does not mean that "government programs don't work." It proves only that the programs we have tried so far haven't worked. Government action will have to be part of the solution. The urgency of the underclass's predicament underscores the continuing necessity to experiment with new solutions. (For one such proposal, see "The Work Ethic State" by Mickey Kaus, TNR, July 7, 1986.)

But just as important, the role of government is to provide the kind of moral leadership on issues of racial and economic equality that will enable blacks and whites alike to move beyond their outdated fears. National leadership can make white Americans understand their stake in a solution—their stake in ending the enormous waste of human potential that the ghetto's misery represents. And with such a commitment, black leaders will be able to redirect their efforts without fearing that they might be inviting white backlash or white apathy. It is too late now for Ronald Reagan credibly to provide such leadership. A president who thinks that segregation has ended in South Africa should not be expected to grasp the more subtle racial problems of our society. On the subject of race relations in America, his administration has taught largely complacency, and a premature feeling of triumphalism. Which makes it all the more urgent for other leaders to begin.

Closed Doors

JUAN WILLIAMS

A friend of mine, a drummer, recently went to Norway with his band. He called the other day to say he isn't coming back. Charles Mana can't believe the life he lives there as a 30-year-old black man. When he walks down the street at night he doesn't have to cut a wide path around white people. He's not used to being asked by an elderly white woman on the train to help her carry her bag to a dark parking lot. His efforts to gain the attention of nightclubs do not run into the racial barriers of heavy metal (white) versus urban progressive (black) rock. He can play his sound and people listen to it for what it is. The in-crowd that runs the music industry is not averse to a black musician who isn't already a celebrity. In the United States he had to deal with the elite and nervous group of black executives at white record companies who were chary of taking a risk on an unproven talent. And in Norway, he said, doormen, store owners, and salesmen don't treat him like a potential thief, "like a nigger back home."

I'm pleased for Charlie. But his call left me raw, stripping away any pretense left in my day-to-day existence that it is possible to be more than a "black" in America. Every nation, including Norway, has its own benighted minority. But in the United States it is the current fashion to pretend that we've put all that behind us. I'm not part of that fashionable crowd. Although I've become callused to much of the indignity that goes with having dark skin in white America, racism is a constant reality for me. And when the calluses peel away, I feel anew how much of my identity is drained from me in trying not to scare whites while walking down the street; in standing on a street corner fruitlessly waving my hand for a cab; in dealing with bosses who see me as a symbol of racial progress for the company or as another disgruntled black employee; in going shopping in a store where my skin color makes me an automatic robbery suspect.

This last point was raised in a recent controversial column by *Washington Post* columnist Richard Cohen. He supported Washington store owners who often won't let young black men through the door on grounds that they are potential thieves. If they are admitted to the store, salespeople surround them until they leave. Cohen rationally argued that the store owners' actions are justified since the statistics show that young black men commit most of the District's robberies and muggings. I found the column an outrageous offering of well-dressed bigotry, and I was dismayed to hear white friends defend it as an opinion rooted in truth.

In fact, it is a lie. A convenient, racist lie. Nationally, 21 percent of all robberies and muggings are committed by black males between the ages of 18 and 29. White males between the same ages commit exactly the same percentage of the muggings and robberies. (In Washington, where 70 percent of the population is black, the police department reports that 41 percent of all robberies and attempted robberies are committed by black males age 18 to 24.) My only association with any black muggers and robbers is my skin color. Most young black men in this city can make the same prosaic claim. That truth escapes those who are quick to draw dubious links between crime and race, even those liberal, presumably fair-minded whites such as Cohen. They work with blacks; they claim they are not bigoted at all. Their adherence to the old stereotypes is thus all the more baffling and insidious.

Whites have far less to fear from a potential black mugger than a black person does. For example, according to the Department of

Justice's "National Crime Victim Survey," in robberies committed by blacks, 14 percent of victims are white and 83 percent are black. Of course, anyone seeing another person approaching on a deserted street has reason to be paranoid. In one way or another, crime periodically intrudes upon the lives of most Americans. And young black men do commit a disproportionate share of muggings in some cities. But if a black person has been beaten up or robbed by another black person, he or she doesn't leap to the conclusion that young men with black skin should be automatically suspect as muggers and/or robbers. Those victims know other black people as brothers, friends, and so on, and retain their ability to treat them as individuals.

Some whites seem not to want to bother to make this distinction between individual blacks. They may figure it costs them less to close their doors to some blacks or to make black shoppers feel uncomfortable than to be robbed by a black thief. The price paid by blacks—the loss of their individual identity and achieved self-worth—is not an issue for them. It is for me.

In truth, Cohen's column is an exposé of the first order. The revealed instinct to bigotry and the attempt to justify it in print as protecting one's self (or store) against crime offer a rare public glimpse of the subterranean pool of prejudices now judged acceptable among some whites for news columns, over the dinner table, among sophisticated friends and colleagues, and even to a black friend from whom they seek reassurance that they have good reason for their racism. The operative principle guiding most of this is not so much simple racial hate as it is indifference. I find that whites generally prefer not to think about blacks or racial issues. It is too burdensome to go through the deep waters of race relations. There are too many instances of clear-cut injustice, too much guilt. (My favorite evasion: "I've never discriminated against anyone. Why do I have to do anything for blacks?") Let's talk about arms control and the Evil Empire.

Much of the increasing ease with which some whites avoid thinking about race (not to mention some blacks who either feel weary of discussing the subject or believe they can score points with whites by not mentioning it) is due to a sense of comfort from the progress that has been made in race relations since the not-so-long-ago evil days of strict segregation. The sight of well-dressed blacks in the corridors of big corporations and lunching downtown with their American Express cards is reassurance enough that race relations in the United States aren't deteriorating after all.

But whether you are black or white, there is, finally no pretending, as President Reagan would have it, that race doesn't matter in the United States because we are a "color-blind" society. Race remains the central domestic issue in the nation. Even if some blacks are doing better (there are more black doctors and lawyers than ever, although they still amount to less than one percent of the nation's doctors and lawyers), consider that 70 percent of blacks still earn under $20,000 a year. Black college graduates are often earning about the same as their white counterparts, but blacks still earn, on average, about 56 cents for every dollar earned by whites— a drop of about five points in the last decade. Unemployment is currently three times higher among black Americans than among white Americans.

Increasingly, those who bother to respond at all to these unpleasant truths contend that blacks need to practice more "self-help" to end their dependence on the government, to lower illegitimate birth rates, to encourage excellence in school. In policymaking and intellectual circles these days, "self-help" is the equivalent of a "Get Out of Jail Free" card in Monopoly. These people insist that blacks can solve their own problems, competing and succeeding in the American mainstream as have Asians, West Indians, Hispanics, or any other minority that has made a place for itself in the land of opportunity.

Black intellectuals such as Thomas Sowell and Glenn Loury have been among those who contend that blacks need to direct more energy into straightening their own house. Well, the argument is not without truth. There is much the black community can do to start and support its own businesses, offer clear moral guidance to children on the problems of drugs and teenage pregnancy. People need to know that some patterns of behavior hurt them and their community. But this is not a new argument. Throughout the history of this nation, blacks have practiced self-help in churches, black schools, black fraternities, and tightly knit families; and more recently through groups like the NAACP and Urban League. A far more urgent reality is this country's history of legal, government enforced discrimination against black people.

One recent study showed that for young men graduating from high school, the best route to a job was through relatives. The absence or small number of older black workers—due to outright discrimination in the '40s, '50s, and '60s—means that young black men don't get into the job pipeline at the same rate as white youngsters. Another study found that a black person renting an apartment or house hunting in the Washington, D.C., area has about a 50 percent chance of being turned away solely on the basis of race. A black, middle-class Boston developer told the *Boston Globe* last year that he was shut out by white architects and builders when he tried to get contracts in white neighborhoods. He found the banks reluctant to deal with a new developer who was black, and the insurance companies adamant in their refusal to adjust bonding requirements for a developer who was not one of the boys among the established white developers in town.

In Washington that benign racism continues to prevail. It is not only jewelry stores that exclude black people. Blacks are not even allowed in the door for the serious business of politics unless there is a black faction to be placated with a token face. The Democratic National Committee recently held a high-powered dinner for its top fund-raisers and best known politicians and did not invite a single black politician—not Bill Gray, chairman of the House Budget Committee, and not Jesse Jackson, the presidential candidate in 1984. When Mickey Leland, chairman of the Congressional Black Caucus, protested about the all-white meeting, he was told that Jackson had not raised money for the party and Gray was not a presidential candidate. This is the black community's reward for voting overwhelmingly for Democratic candidates. And yet blacks who criticize the Democratic Party for this sort of insult are denounced as demagogues.

It has gone almost without notice that President Reagan has not met with black civil rights leaders or spoken to major black groups in over five years. He also refuses to meet with elected black politicians. The Defense Department, the State Department, and the security agencies don't have blacks (with their perspectives and ideas) in executive positions and are not interested in Americans of color unless they need the face to satisfy an affirmative action goal.

The effect of the Reagan approach has been to narrow the entire civil rights policy debate to a zero-sum game in which blacks are trying to take away jobs and opportunity from whites. In that atmosphere there is little room for a middle ground. Blacks and whites are polarized. Even conservative, middle-class blacks who favor more discipline and hard work in the black community, and who are raising questions about affirmative action goals and quotas, are uneasy about the administration's civil rights ideals. It is all too apparent that while Reagan's men speak in self-righteous tones about discrimination against hardworking whites and the need for blacks to do more to help themselves, these men have neglected violations of black voting rights to the point where Reagan resisted signing an extension of the Voting Rights Act; twisted the Civil Rights Commission into an advocacy group for the administration's position that helping blacks is reverse discrimination; and tried to restore tax breaks to segregationist schools.

But perhaps the most damaging of all the race-conscious trends in America is a presumption I find common among whites. The presumption is that if a black person were skilled he would perform just like a white person—play office politics as a white would, get the same encouragement and the same measure of respect from his peers as a white would, be invited to the right dinner parties—in other words, earn the right to be treated white. This is what whites are saying when they confide to friends, some black, that they can't find black professionals able to handle the job or able to meet the standards of the other workers. We'd love to have a black, they say, but we can't sacrifice standards.

A bright black person still needs added support in a white work environment simply because to be black in most white corporate settings is to be an outsider, and outsiders don't do well in any corporation. They are not in on the gossip, they don't have the mentors or the contacts. Blacks are not party to the support system of corporate networks and old school ties that provide the boosts necessary to even the brightest white people. I've been in a job where I've worked hard, displayed loyalty to the company, and yet management never displays the trust in me that they place in my white colleagues. Contrary to popular belief, even today this nation is far from a meritocracy. Morris Abram, a white man on Reagan's reconstituted Civil Rights Commission and a firm believer in America as a color-blind meritocracy, obtained a job at the commission for a friend of his son. Self-help indeed.

Why should whites be asked to disregard race when discussing crime, but urged to take it into account when dealing with blacks in the workplace? When is discrimination racist, and when is it both legitimate and necessary? It is no secret that distinctions between black and white behavior have been used throughout this country's history to exclude blacks from the fundamental rights to enter a jewelry store without being harassed because of one's age, sex, or skin color is one of them. The purpose of the civil rights movement was not to abolish the differences among races, but to ensure that blacks (and women and other minorities) are granted the rights they have been systematically denied. Affirmative action in the workplace has played a critical role in that process. When can whites legitimately say they've redressed the sins of a racist past? I don't know. I do know that there must be better proof than there is today that the practice of discrimination through exclusion has been relinquished.

To be born black in this country today still means that you will likely go to a second-rate big-city public school. Even if you get through high school and into college, you will find a declining number of black students in colleges, and those who are left are often bitterly alienated by the absence of any concession to the difficulty of being black in an overwhelmingly white environment. Ed Meese and Ronald Reagan seem to be joined by increasing numbers of Americans who object to special treatment. Their anthem is equality for all. For Charlie Mana, that anthem wasn't enough.

Bashed in the U.S.A.

DAVID MURA

I am a sansei, a third-generation Japanese American. A couple of years ago, I asked a white friend what he felt about me the first time we met. He insisted he had learned not to stereotype people, that he had gone past racist classifications. Fine, I said, but what stereotypes came up? Finally, after a half-hour of my questioning, he relented. "I guess I thought you'd be too powerful for me," he said.

"What does that mean?" I asked.

"Well, my father always said that the Japanese lost the war but they were going to win the war after the war."

My friend's remarks brought up a question that still plagues Japanese Americans: Are you Japanese or American? Behind this question lies certain troubling racist assumptions.

In 1942, in the months after Pearl Harbor, Congressional hearings were held concerning the Japanese Americans and Japanese aliens on the West Coast. Although Earl Warren, then the Governor of California, acknowledged that there appeared to be no fifth-column activity, he argued that this was merely proof that such activity was planned.

Taking a somewhat different tack, Senator Tom Stewart of Tennessee maintained, "A Jap is a Jap wherever you find him. They do not believe in God and have no respect for an oath of allegiance."

As the son of internment camp prisoners, even now I feel the need to point out that no Japanese American was ever convicted of espionage. A 1982 study commissioned by Congress concluded that the causes for the internment were wartime hysteria, racism and lack of political leadership. The Congress acknowledged this in 1988 when it awarded damage payments to Japanese Americans who had been detained.

And yet, I know that the circular logic of Earl Warren and Tom Stewart is still present. Witness last year's best seller, "The Coming

War with Japan." In defending their title, George Friedman and Meredith Lebard argued that they did not have to prove that Japan was preparing for war, they merely needed to prove that such an act would be in its interest.

Japan's economic success will "inevitably give way to a more natural, and more fierce, national sensibility," they wrote. "Pacifism is not native to Japan, nor is national modesty." Implicit in this is the idea that the Japanese cannot change or accept foreign beliefs. (One wonders where pacifism *is* native?) Yet in a recent poll, only 10 percent of Japanese said they would fight for their country.

There are those who argue that charges of Japan bashing are exaggerated or even completely off the mark. In Michael Crichton's best seller, "Rising Sun," such claims are used by the Japanese to their own advantage and serve mainly as a smoke screen for the "real" issues.

Obviously, I look at Japan bashing from a different perspective. When I see people taking a sledgehammer to a Japanese car on TV, I wonder what would happen if my daughter and I happened to walk by. Would they care if we were Japanese or Japanese American?

To someone like Michael Crichton, I would ask: If the whiff of racism is not in the air, how does one explain the anti-Japan slogans painted on the walls of the Japanese American community center in Norwalk, Calif., in November? Or the message, "all Japs must die," written on the door of a Wellesley College Chinese American student in February? Or the Thai American man in Torrance, Calif., who was beaten by a white man who asked him if he was Japanese?

A conclusion reached through racism is not necessarily incorrect. A case can be made that the U.S. has legitimate trade differences with Japan and that Japan's success has hurt our economy. Where racism comes in is in the force of emotions and in the inability to distinguish between Japanese and Japanese Americans. It gives people a scapegoat. Since the scapegoated group is considered less human and less worthy, it cannot possibly do better than one's own group. Unless the group has some unfair advantage. Unless it cheats.

In Senator Ernest Holling's remarks that anyone who doubts U.S. power and skill should remember that we dropped an atomic bomb on Japan, in Lee Iacocca's angrily protectionist commercials, the underlying premise is that Americans are always the best. They only lose when the playing field isn't level.

Asian Americans are the largest group at the University of California, Berkeley, and at U.C.L.A. Their success has engendered resentment. They are grinds; they work too hard. They have an unfair advantage. Sounds a little like the complaints against the Japanese, doesn't it?

Such feelings were behind the Asian Exclusion Act of 1882, the Alien Land Law of 1913 and the internment of my parents and other Japanese Americans. They also have a lot to do with the recent rise in hate crimes against Asian Americans documented by the U.S. Commission on Civil Rights in February.

Perhaps if Americans had a better knowledge of the Japanese and Japanese Americans, such resentment would not flourish so easily. Unfortunately, most Americans still base their image of Asians and Asian Americans on stereotypes.

The success of "Rising Sun," with its picture of the Japanese as duplicitous and cruel, as the most racist people on earth, is merely another example of Orientalism. (Yes, the Japanese are racist, but Mr. Crichton's picture of racism in the U.S. is much less troubled than mine or Toni Morrison's or Louise Erdrich's.) Did resentment and fear cause some Americans to see Kristi Yamaguchi, who won a gold medal in figure skating at the Winter Olympics, as less American than her teammates?

Often, when white Americans tell me they are not racist, I reply that I grew up thinking of myself as less than 100 percent American. In certain ways I hated the way I looked and felt ashamed of my heritage. If I took racist values from society, I ask them, how is it they did not?

To dig out the roots of racial resentment, Americans must come to terms with their subjective vision of race. If someone of another color gets a job you're applying for, is your resentment more than if a person of your own color won the job? When you hear the word American, whose face flashes before your mind?

Wounds of Race

HENDRIK HERTZBERG

I have yet to meet a well-informed, unbigoted black American who would not firmly endorse the following statement: If you're black, you have to be twice as good to travel the same socioeconomic distance as a white person in this country—twice as talented, twice as ambitious, twice as determined.

To this, the average well-informed, un-bigoted white American will reply: Nonsense. Sure, that was true years ago, but today if you're black and minimally qualified all you have to do is show up, and bang—you're in college, you're in law school, you've got the job.

The gap between these two honest perceptions is a measure of the passion and pain of race in America. Race is the wound that will not heal, and the Supreme Court has just rubbed fresh salt in that wound with a series of decisions truncating the equal employment provisions of the Civil Rights Act of 1964—which, as of July 2, will have been the law for exactly 25 years. What a dismal anniversary present.

To read these decisions is to become aware of the dizzying moral fall from the Warren Court, a product of Eisenhower Republicanism, to the Rehnquist Court, a product of Reagan Republicanism. When the Warren Court took up this most divisive of American perplexities, it was careful to seek unanimity among its own members: *Brown* v. *Board of Education* was a 9–0 decision. The Rehnquist Court hacks away at settled precedent by repeated votes of 5 to 4. The Warren Court looked to the grandeur of the Constitution for guidance. The Rehnquist Court draws its arguments from abstruse (and questionable) points of contract law. The Warren Court took history (not just "legislative history") into account, and considered the building of social justice to be part of its writ. The Rehnquist Court renders its decisions in highly technical, almost impenetrable language wholly free of any hint of the suffering, the bitterness, and all the other human realities that inform the cases it decides.

"The linchpin of the 'impermissible collateral attack' doctrine—the attribution of preclusive effect to a failure to intervene—is therefore quite inconsistent with Rule 19 and Rule 24," writes Chief Justice Rehnquist in a typical passage of *Martin* v. *Wilks*—and that's about as exalted as his language gets. In that particular case, the Court, by the usual 5–4 majority, opened the way for endless legal assaults on an affirmative action program, the product of seven years of painful negotiations and lawsuits, that since 1981 has peacefully and effectively brought a measure of racial integration to the previously all-white fire department of Birmingham, Alabama.

After reading the decisions, I ended up sharing the dismay of Justice Blackmun, who wrote in dissent, "One wonders whether the majority still believes that race discrimination—or, more accurately, race discrimination against nonwhites—is a problem in our society, or even remembers that it ever was." But the cases themselves are less important than the larger questions about race (and about affirmative action) they raise.

The affirmative action debate takes place in a context shaped by the success of civil rights and the failure of social policy. The triumphant destruction of institutionalized segregation broke apart the old black communities in which people of all classes and levels of accomplishment lived together in oppression. The most ambitious, lucky, and talented were—and are—boiled off into the larger society. As an unintended consequence, those left behind have been distilled into an increasingly isolated, increasingly pathological, increasingly self-destructive subculture, the urban black underclass. Social programs designed to alleviate its condition have either proved unworkable or been starved. Reaganism's upward redistribution of income has sharpened the pain. But the failure is general. "Conservatives have ignored the problem, left the solution to 'market forces' or, worse, to social Darwinism," writes Joe Klein in a brilliant essay in the May 29 *New York* magazine. "Liberals seem to have abandoned critical thought entirely, allowing militants to dictate their agenda, scorning most efforts to impose sanctions on anti-social behavior by underclass blacks."

Affirmative action is a kind of homeopathic medicine, an effort to correct an immense historic injustice with small doses of "injustice" in the present. It is an effort to lift some blacks by main force into the middle class. It should properly be seen not as a sacrifice by whites for the benefit of blacks, but rather as a sacrifice by the present generation for the benefit of the next. The cost is paid today—by the whites shunted aside, and, more subtly, by the blacks obliged to doubt that their advancement is personally deserved. ("Social victims may be collectively entitled, but they are all too often individually demoralized," writes the black essayist Shelby Steele, quoted by Klein.) The payoff will come tomorrow, when a new generation of black children is born into the middle class— there to share, presumably, the un-self-conscious advantages and complexes of a bourgeois upbringing.

The psychic cost of affirmative action to its purported "realtime" beneficiaries is very high. In the post-slavery century of segregated oppression, few members of what W. E. B. DuBois called "the talented tenth" were troubled by lack of self-esteem. They *knew* that whatever they had they had more than earned, because there was no other way to get it. Their affirmative action counterparts of today cannot be so sure. Yes, the jobs are easier to get—and in this sense the white perception is correct. But the *respect* that is supposed to come with the job—that comes with it more or less automatically for whites—does not come automatically for blacks. It cannot be "demanded," Jesse Jackson notwithstanding. It must be struggled for and earned. This applies to self-respect as well as to the respect of others. "You're not here because you're smart or because you worked hard, you're here because there's a program for hiring black people." That's a natural enough thought for whites to have, and they don't have to be "racist" in any classic way to have it. It's a thought, moreover, that on some level the black beneficiaries of affirmative action are obliged to share. That is a high hurdle to overcome—as high, psychologically, as segregation was. The fact that the hurdle is subjective and invisible, that it cannot be measured by outward signs, does not make it any the less real. That is why, when blacks insist they must be "twice as good," they are merely reporting the existential truth of their own experience.

In any event, affirmative action can work only at the margins. It can pull up only those who are ready to be pulled up. It can do little or nothing for the mind-numbingly dreadful problems of the underclass—the powerful, self-reinforcing nexus of crime, drugs, children bearing children, family atomization, despair, peer pressure to fail in school, and all the fearful rest.

Against those problems—the real problems—affirmative action is helpless; and, in isolation, it fosters a cycle of mutual racial resentment destructive to the political will that is needed. There is no sign of that political will. President Bush and the Republicans have absolutely nothing to say about it. Black nationalism is a dead end, as many observers, black and white, have noted. But so is what might be called white nationalism. And in this connection the tragic elements of American history hang heavy—not because they are acknowledged but because they are ignored. Many of our reigning national myths, important parts of America's civil religion, simply exclude black people. I have been trying to imagine what it's like for a black person to listen to a speech about how America is a "nation of immigrants" and the "land of opportunity." The truth is that this is *not* a nation of immigrants. It is a nation of immigrants and slaves. Our ancestors did *not* come here full of hope, seeking freedom and a better life. They came seeking freedom and they came in chains.

The speeches of politicians and other national leaders seldom take this into account. In their anxiety to draw happy, uncomplicated morals, they seldom tell the full American story. No wonder black people—whose roots in this country, on average, go back further than those of white people—are alienated.

Consider a couple of exceptions, drawn from the two greatest speeches ever delivered by Americans.

"Fondly do we hope—fervently do we pray—that this mighty scourge of war may speedily pass away. Yet, if God wills that it continue, until all the wealth poled by the bondman's two hundred and fifty years of unrequited toil shall be sunk, and until every drop of blood drawn with the lash, shall be paid by another drawn with the sword, as was said three thousand years ago, so still it must be said, 'the judgments of the Lord, are true and righteous altogether.'"

"I still have a dream. It is a dram deeply rooted in the American dream. I have a dream that one day on the red hills of Georgia the sons of former slaves and the sons of former slaveowners will be able to sit down together at the table of brotherhood."

Abraham Lincoln and Martin Luther King Jr. told the whole truth about America, and that is one reason they are deified in the American memory. Few of their contemporary successors emulate them. Yet what is needed, as the spiritual precondition to a material commitment, is a refurbished national mythology that takes account of the historical experience of all Americans. That is something politicians can begin to provide without spending a dime. The dilemma is not a black dilemma (or a white one) but an American dilemma. The answer is not "black history" but American history, not "black pride" (or white guilt) but American determination.

Absorbing the Outsiders

WILLIAM SAFIRE

Riga Still-Occupied but Independent Latvia Sarmite Elerte, 34, strikes me as the most fascinating woman in the former Soviet union.

In the dangerous early days of breakup, she was a key agitator for the Latvian Popular Front; in the recent period of new independence, she took time out to have a baby; in the sobering time of building a nation, she is becoming managing editor of Diena, the most adamantly independent major new daily among the nations of post-Soviet Europe.

Ms. Elerte's fascination lies neither in her Audrey Hepburn looks nor her Clare Luce style, but in her grasp of the central issue of the days to come: how to bring disparate ethnic groups together in nationhood after the centralizing fervor for independence dissolves in success.

The prevalent urge is just the opposite: to get even by getting "pure." For two generations, Moscow has been pouring Russians into conquered Latvia until they make up half the population. These immigrants-invaders had most of the privileges, disdaining to learn the local language, many treating the native Latvians as second-class Soviet citizens.

Even today, with Latvia independent, 100,000 Soviet troops are still stationed in this nation, with an additional 60,000 officers "retired" here—altogether an oppressive foreign presence, occupying much of the best property. Dainis Ivans, the intrepid Popular Front leader who is now Vice Chairman of the Council of Ministers, is unsympathetic to the excuse that Red Army soldiers have no homes to return to, and need years of delay: "It took a day for them to move in, it should take a day to move out."

This reasonable resentment at the presence of unwanted outsiders in uniform, or at Russian newcomers who reject the native language, culminates in the citizenship issue: Who is a Latvian, with the right to vote? The Russian-speaking "minority" is as numerous as the majority; native Latvians do not want to lose at the ballot box the national identity lost to Hitler's tanks and Stalin's deals.

Accordingly, a citizenship law is being debated, based on the notion that the takeover 50 years ago is invalid, and that only those who were Latvian before 1940, and their descendants, are automatic Latvians now. No Red Army soldiers, former K.G.B. men or dope addicts need apply; that's reasonable, as is no dual citizenship. But then it gets mean: Russians who have lived here more than 16 years can be naturalized, but only if they learn Latvian and renounce Soviet citizenship.

That turning-back of the clock may be satisfying to nationalists, and a desire to settle scores is surely understandable, but getting even is no way to build a country.

Ex-Communists who were opposed to independence, who rooted for the coup in Moscow and some who collaborated with K.G.B. goons in Red Army uniforms are now pleading for "human rights" to Russians in Latvia. Coming from them, the plea is the height of hypocrisy—but their cause happens to be right.

You should end the era of privilege, but you cannot kick near-newcomers out. You have to give full recognition to their human rights, a phrase that now embraces political rights. That goes for Russians in Latvia, Ukrainians in Russia, Hungarians in Romania, Croats in Serbia, Slovaks in Bohemia, Arabs in Judea-Samaria.

Just as the Baltic example was the key to Soviet disunion, the Baltic treatment of its "minority" will serve as a criterion in much bigger republics. It's toughest when the ethnic numbers are close and the danger is the tyranny of the plurality.

Enter mediating forces like the journalist Sarmite Elerte. Diena, "The Day," has a Russian-language edition. The former agitator and editor-to-be reminds her Latvian compatriots that "most Russians here supported independence, and we must reward them." This means a 5-year residency for citizenship, not 16, and a conversational language requirement for younger people. "We not only have to make them citizens, but make them feel like citizens."

What accounts for the sense of letdown in Riga? "Since 1988, politics was the center of all life. The enemy was outside, in Moscow, easy to mobilize against. We thought that independence would solve everything."

"Now we are free," says Ms. Elerte, "but that means we must solve our own problems, and the first is living together."

Demonizing Our Adversaries

GENE OISHI

I call myself an American of the Japanese race, a formulation that used to strike many mainstream Americans as a contradiction in terms. Because of the perceived paradox in our identity, Japanese-Americans tend to downplay, even deny, their Japanese half, insisting that we are as American as anyone else. I will not argue that point one way or another. What I do wish to assert, however, is that I am different from most Americans. I have always felt, and still feel today, a kinship with Japan, the country where both my parents were born.

Although I was born in America, my first language was Japanese. My Americanism contains remnants of Japanese cultural influences and values. I react to events as an American, but when the events involve Japan or anything Japanese, my reactions no doubt are different from those of most Americans. When I read of Japanese atrocities during World War II and the years leading up to it, I feel more pain than anger. When I witness or read of Japanese bigotry, I am ashamed. When I see Japanese tourists playing the role "ugly Americans" used to fill, I am embarrassed.

Now we are commemorating the 50th anniversary of the Japanese "sneak attack" on Pearl Harbor, and I am being asked how I feel about it. It is not an easy question, since it is not clear to me what it is we are trying to remember. What are the lessons, if any, we wish to learn, the conclusion we are trying to draw? For most Americans, I fear, the lessons of Pearl Harbor remain essentially the danger of letting down our guard, of being complacent and unprepared. If there are any moral lessons to be learned, they are solely for the Japanese.

The war with Japan is thought to have begun on Dec. 7, 1941, like a thunderclap out of the blue. A more sophisticated analysis might conclude it actually began in the 1930s with Japanese aggression in China; Japanese tend to see World War II in the context of the 19th-century Western imperialism in Asia, which informed Japan's view of the West and determined its political and economic development.

My purpose, however, is not to assess blame for the war, nor to discuss its history. I wish only to say I experienced World War II as a racial conflict. If one examines wartime posters, books, songs, movies, it is clear I was not alone in this. Most Americans, I believe, saw the war in the Pacific in racial rather than ideological terms. Americans were fighting "Japs," because they were cruel, vicious, cunning and had an overweening ambition to rule the world. Substitute "greedy" and "acquisitive" for "cruel" and "vicious" and Toyotas for rickshaws, and we come uncomfortably close to how some politicians and journalists are portraying the Japanese today.

In even the most respectable publications it is said Japan is trying to accomplish through economic means what it failed to do through force of arms in World War II. What does that mean precisely? Given how Japanese war aims were distorted and imprinted on the popular imagination, it is conceivable the American public would come to believe during these hard economic times that Japan is out to destroy us. Do we commemorate the 50th anniversary of Pearl Harbor to drive home the message that "the Japs" remain implacably our enemy?

Internment camps

I was 8 years old, living with my family in California, when Japan attacked Pearl Harbor. I and my family were called "Japs" and shipped with 110,000 other "Japs" to internment camps. I mention this only to note how racial attitudes can distort judgment and rob people of their humanity. To white Americans, Japanese-Americans became simply "Japs," with all the cunning and treachery attributed to the enemy in the Pacific. Surely, the Japanese have much to learn from World War II, and perhaps American observers are correct in saying they have not accepted their share of responsibility for the deaths, suffering and destruction caused by the war. I am troubled by that, as I am by any sign of moral obtuseness among Japanese.

But I am also an American, and I am just as concerned about American morality. Because of my personal history, perhaps I worry more than others about the state of mind of my fellow Americans. My nightmare is that the commemoration of Pearl Harbor Day turns into an orgy of American self-righteousness and a renewed demonization of Japanese and other perceived adversaries.

I am reminded of how quick President Bush was to characterize Saddam Hussein as another Hitler. It troubled me to see the inordinate joy and pride many found in our "precision" bombing of Iraq. It was supposed to be a war with limited objectives. Was the systematic destruction of Iraq's infrastructure really necessary? I do not know the answer. But the swiftness with which the bombing was conducted still troubles me.

The United States has a right, perhaps even a duty, to protect its own interests. As a Japanese-American, if I had to choose between the collapse of either the Japanese or the American economy, I would sacrifice the Japanese. But for me, it would be a Hobson's choice.

Our country continues to grow more diverse in its racial and ethnic makeup, and I would hope this diversity will enable us to question our own perceptions and values more closely than we have in the past. Never mind what our enemies are like; a more important question for us is what are *we* like? If we must dehumanize other peoples in the world to reassure ourselves of our own goodness and to justify our actions, what kind of people are *we?* And what is a democracy worth that must propagandize its own people to function effectively?

If the Pearl Harbor commemoration leads some to ask such questions, it will have been worthwhile. We would be judging ourselves by a higher standard than prevails in most other places in the world, but what of that? It should make us proud to be Americans.

Questions

1. What are the chief arguments and evidence offered in this section to support the position that the United States has made great strides and is no longer a racist society? Write a summary in response to this question.

2. To what extent does the United States remain a racist society, according to the writers represented in this section? Summarize the information presented here and use your summary as the basis of a

group discussion about this question. Summarize the various positions that emerge in this discussion.

Suggestions for Further Research

1. Choose a specific event, concept, law, or court decision mentioned in the selections in this section, and investigate it. Write a summary of the information you discover. For example, you might choose Brown vs. Board of Education, the Civil Rights Act of 1965, Affirmative Action, or segregation, among others.

2. Use U.S. Census data to help you identify the various racial and ethnic groups that compose the population of the United States. How has the population's racial and ethnic composition changed since 1950?

Suggestions for Writing

1. What changes do you believe would have the greatest impact on improving interracial or intercultural relationships on your campus or in your community? Propose a specific change in a policy or practice, describe how it will change the situation that exists now, and argue that this change will be an improvement.

2. How would you resolve the question of what to do about racially motivated language—racial and cultural epithets and slurs? Write an argument in which you identify and summarize the major questions involved in this issue and propose and support a solution.

Rights vs. Obligations:
Who Owes What to Whom?

Many U.S. citizens see their relationship with the government in terms of the rights spelled out in the Bill of Rights in the U.S. Constitution. But there are other ways of seeing that relationship. Living in a community requires cooperation, which often demands that the welfare of individuals be subordinated to the welfare of the larger group. In a relatively new development, many public officials and political theorists have begun to discuss the relationship between individuals and society in terms of obligations and responsibilities that individuals have to the larger groups within which they live. The arguments in this section consist of a transcript of a roundtable discussion of rights and obligations. Before you read the discussion, respond in writing to the following:

Preparing to Read

1. *You live within a variety of social units or communities (family, clubs, cities, universities, various governments, etc.). Choose one of these and explain the rights it grants you and the obligations you owe it in return.*
2. *In your experience, what holds a group (any group) together? What gives groups a sense of cohesiveness? What gives individuals a sense of belonging to a group?*

Who Owes What to Whom?

HARPER'S FORUM

This year brings with it another American bicentennial: that of the passage of the Bill of Rights. Expect nearly every politician to come forward to extol its perfection. Expect few of them, and few Americans, to recall that the bill was understood by its framers not as something to be displayed under glass but rather as lab notes for the American Experiment. The Ninth Amendment, with its protection of unenumerated rights, in effect charged us to carry on the founders' conversation.

And we did. We fought a civil war about the meaning of some rights, and, in this century, mass movements have taken our understanding of rights beyond any conception known to history. But recently, dissenters have questioned whether this expansive talk of individual rights has undermined our notions of obligation and community. What *do* we owe one another? Do we have a duty to our family? Our country? The environment? Can a country that holds rights to be self-evident even have a conversation about responsibilities? In order to prompt further discussion, *Harper's Magazine* invited five latter-day framers to Independence Hall to speculate on whether we need a Bill of Duties and to begin the task of drafting one.

The following forum is based on a discussion held at Independence Hall in Philadelphia in November of 1991. Gerald Marzorati served as moderator.

GERALD MARZORATI
is a senior editor of Harper's Magazine.

BENJAMIN BARBER
is the Whitman Professor of Political Science at Rutgers University and the director of the Walt Whitman Center at Rutgers. His books include Strong Democracy *and* The Conquest of Politics.

MARY ANN GLENDON
*is a professor of law at Harvard University Law School. Her
book* Rights Talk: The Impoverishment of Political Discourse
will be published this spring by The Free Press.

DAN KEMMIS
is the mayor of Missoula, Montana, and the author of
Community and the Politics of Place.

CHRISTOPHER LASCH
*is a professor of history at the University of Rochester. His most
recent book,* The True and Only Heaven: Progress and Its Critics,
was published in January by W. W. Norton.

CHRISTOPHER D. STONE
*is a professor of law at the University of Southern California
Law Center and is the author of the book* Earth and Other Ethics.

The Origins of Duty

GERALD MARZORATI: I recently came upon this quotation from
Alexis de Tocqueville: "When the world was under the control of a
few rich and powerful people, they liked to entertain the sublime
conception of the duties of man." It seems that the subject of duty
is being entertained once again in the ongoing conversation that is
our democracy. William F. Buckley Jr. has recently published a book
on the subject. In numerous articles, writers have argued that the
vocabulary of rights is nearly exhausted and that a vocabulary of
responsibilities has yet to emerge. Has our country experienced an
authentic decline in "civic virtue," the communitarian spirit? Is
this debate simply one of America's periodic spasms of self-criti-
cism about its essentially individualistic, self-interested soul? Or is
the whole notion of duty a kind of ruse: Tocqueville, for instance,
ended the passage I quoted by stating that those who speak of duty
are merely interested in its "utility."

DAN KEMMIS: Unfortunately, we have come to think of democracy as the ongoing answer to a question that might be phrased,
"What do you want?" Rousseau warned that this kind of democracy
wouldn't work. What we have to ask is not what do we want as
individuals but what do we will as a people, what do we will our
common world to be?

MARY ANN GLENDON: A useful analogy may be to the natural
environment. For most of our history we seemed to be endowed
with inexhaustible social and natural resources. Only recently,
with consumer capitalism well advanced, with our heterogeneous

population growing even more diverse, have we sensed that we've been consuming our social capital without replenishing it. While rights have been proliferating, we have paid little attention to the seedbeds of civic virtue from which rights derive their surest protection. Now we are beginning to sense this erosion, and it scares us. People for the American Way recently completed a survey of the political attitudes of young Americans. The students were asked, "What makes America special?" Overwhelmingly, the young people answered, "Our rights and freedoms," which they characterized in a way that classical philosophers would recognize not as liberty but as license. People for the American Way, a group not noted for worrying about excessive liberty, said it's time to sound the alarm that America's youth has learned only half of the democratic equation: They have almost no sense of civic participation and responsibility. By the way, 7 percent mentioned that America is a democracy.

BENJAMIN BARBER: At least 7 percent got it right—there's more to democracy than voting.

GLENDON: Well, actually some of them said, "Democracy and rock and roll."

CHRISTOPHER D. STONE: Remember when John Kennedy said, "Ask not what your country can do for you; ask what you can do for your country"? At the time, the remark backfired. The commentary that followed argued that government was our servant and that Washington ought to help us out, not demand anything *from* us.

KEMMIS: Precisely. The sentiments of responsibility can't be felt on a national level. But on the local level, in the daily lives of most people and in their associations—where the real work of society gets done—people recognize duties among themselves. For example, a PTA decides that it's going to build a new playground at the neighborhood school, and the organizers ask you to put in a day of work. If you say you're going to be there, then you'll be there. If you're not, then the whole thing falls apart. There's an understanding that you have a duty to do what you said you would do.

STONE: Those are called "voluntary duties," though. There are lots of duties that arise when we make a promise or a vow. But we've got to distinguish those from so-called natural duties, duties that would fall on every citizen irrespective of their signaling any willing commitment.

KEMMIS: What we've done in America consistently, Christopher, is make that distinction, and I think it's false. We call these obligations "voluntary duties" or "voluntary associations." Tocqueville didn't call them "voluntary associations"; he called them "public associations," because he recognized that in taking on such duties people were engaging in a public act. We no longer recognize that public arena. We now talk about such work taking place in the *private* sector. But a duty has to exist in the context of a community. One has to feel the heat of duty—to know that one has made a promise, that others are depending on one's virtue. Consider the last, overlooked lines of the Declaration of Independence. The signers outlined their intentions and then concluded, "We mutually pledge to each other our Lives, our Fortunes, and our sacred Honor." It's the capacity for this kind of mutual pledging and mutual understanding that we have largely lost.

MARZORATI: The founders did not draft a Bill of Duties. But there is evidence that they assumed a certain level of duty. I have another quotation, this one from James Madison. He said, "No theoretical checks, no form of government can render us secure. To suppose that any form of government will secure liberty or happiness without any virtue in the people, is a chimerical idea." In effect, the drafters didn't believe that the mechanics of a constitution were enough to secure our liberty. There had to be civic virtue. What has happened since then?

CHRISTOPHER LASCH: Much of what was considered a citizen's duty was built upon the Jeffersonian assumption of a broad distribution of property ownership, especially agrarian property. The management of property was believed to confer the habits of initiative, enterprise, and responsibility, which were essential to citizenship. But industrialism gave rise to a class of permanent, *propertyless* wage earners, estranged by their condition from the wellspring of civic virtue: proprietorship. How Jeffersonian virtue can be reconciled with the unforeseen development remains a problem no one has resolved.

The culture of consumption has made this problem even more complicated. The rise of consumerism in this century—in which the individual's self-interest is the *only* good—created a society in which you don't need any public consensus as long as the economy can satisfy people's needs and expand them into ever increasing levels of desire and expectation. Beguiled by the prospect of limitless abundance, Americans came to believe that it was no longer necessary to grapple with underlying issues of justice and equality as long as the goods kept coming.

KEMMIS: The reason the ideal broke down was because classical republican theory held that the civic virtue needed to sustain a government emerged from participation and face-to-face contact. By definition, the "republic" has to be a small-scale polity.

The breakdown, in fact, began with the events in this room in the summer of 1787. The drafters came here not to continue a republic but to create a nation. And that nation was, even then, bigger than anything any republican ever believed could sustain the necessary interaction of democracy.

GLENDON: In the founding documents and throughout the nineteenth century there is very little rhetoric about duty at the highest public level. In the legal system, duties and rights are just two sides of the same coin. But for most of our history, and even now, which is why we are here today, we have not had a well-developed public language of responsibility to match our language of rights.

BARBER: Mary Ann, the language of duty was part of the language of civic culture rather than of government administration and of the law. The founding mission statements for American colleges in the eighteenth and nineteenth centuries all speak of preparing young people for the duties of citizenship. Where we don't find such language is in the laws and the Constitution. The decline of civic duty begins not with the absence of rhetoric in our Constitution but with the erosion of our civic culture.

LASCH: Let me give you some duty talk from the Massachusetts Constitution of 1780. Article II: "It is the right as well as the duty of all men in society, publicly and at stated seasons, to worship the Supreme Being." Article III notes that the "happiness of a people and . . . preservation of civil government . . . depend upon piety, religion and morality." And it requires the several towns and parishes to "make suitable provision for public worship and for the support and maintenance of public Protestant teachers of piety, religion and morality in all cases where such provision shall not be made voluntarily."

STONE: Such sternly written duties are the exception, even in eighteenth-century constitutions. If you look at the Massachusetts Constitution, it enumerates a duty to pray, but it is clear from the context that the duty is used to justify the right of each citizen to worship according to his own conscience.

BARBER: Is this the doleful residue of Calvinism, or are some of you suggesting that it is the result of a new constitutional order?

STONE: I'm questioning how critical is it that duties be in the Constitution. The socialist constitutions typically include a duty to educate your children. We don't provide for a child's education in the Constitution, but we effectively enforce it in the law anyway.

GLENDON: The United States is something of a special case because of the increasing heterogeneity I mentioned. We have fewer common histories, traditions, religions to bind us together. We look more to the law as a carrier of certain common values and to the Constitution for the most visible expression of these common values.

KEMMIS: There are difficulties in trying to impose duties in a constitution and make them a matter of law. A constitution is something besides just the imposition of law. It is an act through which people *constitute* themselves as a society. But when you talk to Americans now about what the Constitution means, they say it means *rights*—period, nothing else. We are a people who hold rights. We do not conceive of ourselves as a *people* in any other sense whatsoever. The other day I was standing in line at a polling place, waiting to vote. One man, recognizing the mayor, waved his ballot at me and said, "I guess this is my ticket to bitch, right?" and I thought, "Ah, yes. This is our thin conception of citizenship. This is what we come to when we constitute ourselves around rights alone."

STONE: Using the law to enforce a duty has a tendency to erode the self-generation of duties. A citizen's character is not being nourished when a good civic act is made to be a duty. Take voting. In some countries, the government compels you to vote. But if liberty is to mean something, I think we should be free *not* to vote. The founders understood that liberty implied such a choice. By definition, duties are antithetical to liberty, because they oblige you to do something whether you want to or not.

BARBER: The case against compulsion is Edmund Burke's argument against the Jacobins: At the end of the groves of *their* academy, Burke said, stands only the gallows. If you try to enforce duty only by the sword of state, you never create a moral being who has any interest in compliance or who feels obligated to do anything other than simply avoid the penalties of law. Again, that is a pinched form of citizenship.

The fact is, historically, if we can't repair the infrastructure of the civic culture, then we find ourselves settling for compensatory strategies. One such strategy is compensatory altruism, favored by such deep political philosophers as John D. Rockefeller Sr. and Ronald Reagan. Rockefeller's premise was, We can all be selfish six days a week, but one day a week we perform a little community service. Rockefeller made a lot of money, and he gave a little away when he was older. The language of duty tripped easily off the tongues of Gilded Age capitalists, particularly toward the end of their lives. The Reason interpretation of this school of thought held that if you extend your greedy pursuits to the seventh day and we catch you, we may sentence you to so many weekends of community service. Civic virtue is now a punishment for a little too much greed. The trouble is that neither of those compensatory strategies really works very well. The real questions is, Can we reknit our civic culture? If we can't, I despair of a solution.

STONE: You see Rockefeller's notion as "compensatory," Ben. I see it as preemptive—preempting Congress from taking his money from him through a graduated income tax.

MARZORATI: I sense that some of the discontent, and even shame, about our lack of civic duty—at least as reflected in recent writings on creating a national service and the like—stems from the outpouring of democratic spirit in Eastern Europe. Across the oceans, the politics seem so animated, and ours seems bloodless and bogged down from inertia. I think of someone like Václav Havel, who recently addressed his own people to tell them that all Czechoslovaks bear a responsibility for what happened to them in the last forty-five years. None of those young people Mary Ann referred to ever had a president charge them to assume responsibility.

BARBER: Jimmy Carter tried to talk like that in his famous "malaise" speech in 1979. Havel received standing ovations for his remarks; Carter was banished from government.

STONE: Weren't those revolutions in Eastern Europe in fact fueled by a rejection of certain onerous duties? Wasn't our own revolution a war against a lot of duties—the duty to pay taxes, the duty to bear certain burdens, like quartering troops, without any choice of compensation?

BARBER: It is true that America's rights language was invented and deployed in a period of dissent. It's a language that does allow you to rebel against an illegitimate authority in order to create freedom and equality. Our problem today is that we continue to speak this eighteenth-century language when there is no longer an obviously *illegitimate* authority to oppose.

MARZORATI: Would a lesbian activist say that?

BARBER: To the extent that there are people who are not yet part of the system, rights language continues to be not only appropriate but also the most successful language, from the Civil War amendments down to the language used by gay and lesbian groups and other groups who want in. But to refute Christopher Stone's observation that the American Revolution was a rejection of duty, remember that the cry was not "no taxation"; it was "taxation *without representation* is tyranny." The colonists acknowledged their duties but felt that it was unfair to carry them out without corresponding rights. The linkage between duties and rights has been severed so completely that today the Colonial pamphleteer James Otis might be yelling "representation without taxation!" That is what most Americans want, and that is the only promise in the last decade that any politician has made.

A Duty to Family

MARZORATI: The Industrial Revolution transformed local economies into a national one. The Great Depression represented a devastating collapse of this new national economy, and any hope it had of recovery required the intervention of national government. At least since the New Deal, the federal government has been woven into the nation's economy, and few argue that it could now be extricated from the workings of the economy. Perhaps one can argue that the nation's civil society has suffered a similar depression, that the crisis demands intervention, that we need a codified set of civic obligations—something like a Bill of Duties. Let's try to imagine such a bill and the sectors of civil society it might pertain to. How about beginning with the family. How might we phrase a constitutional duty devoted to family?

GLENDON: One of the striking differences between the American Constitution and the constitutions of other modern democracies is that ours has no mention of the family. Our eighteenth-century statesmen probably thought they could take families for granted, whereas the constitutions of most other liberal democracies were written in the rubble of World War II, when families had been devastated.

I don't think we could copy what some Western European countries do and say, "Marriage and family are under the special protection of the state." But we could recognize a special collective responsibility toward child-raising families. Some of the European constitutions say "toward motherhood and children." My language for Article I of a constitutional amendment on family duty might be: "The nation has a special responsibility for the protection and welfare of children and their families." And Article II might read: "The nurture and education of children are duties primarily incumbent on the parents."

LASCH: That amendment is a thicket. My amendment would read: Article I: "Fathers have the responsibility to marry the mothers of their children—"

BARBER: That's outrageous!

GLENDON: What if the mother doesn't want the marriage?

LASCH: "—and to contribute a fair share to their children's support unless the mothers *release* them from these obligations."

Article II: "Marriage should be undertaken only by those who view it as a lifelong commitment and are prepared to accept the consequences, foreseeable and unforeseeable, of such a commitment. No state shall pass laws authorizing divorce for any but the weightiest reasons. In the case of couples with children under the age of twenty-one, divorce is hereby forbidden."

BARBER: Let me sidestep for a minute the *obviously* controversial. There are still two major problems. Both Mary Ann and Christopher address the erosion of the family. But the very erosion that troubles both of you began with the modern lack of agreement about what a family *is*. Even with the relatively uncontroversial language that Mary Ann introduces, I suspect a great many Americans are going to say, "That doesn't include me; that puts me in a second-class citizenship category; I'm in a family, even though I don't have children." The very forces that created the problem will resist the solutions set out in your amendments. The second line of criticism I have is Burkean. Legislating these things from above may actually contribute to weakening further the impulses of, say, husbands to take responsibility for their children.

MARZORATI: Wait a minute. Most states already coerce you to keep your kid in school up to a certain age. There's little hue and cry about this demand. People aren't saying that because they are made to send their children to school that they insist on a right not to educate them at all.

BARBER: There's an extensive conservative argument, for which I have some sympathy, that says it's precisely the state's assuming these paternalistic functions—telling people what families are, issuing instructions about how to run a family, taking the children away from the family when the state decrees that the children aren't being properly cared for—that has contributed to the erosion of a sense of family responsibility. There are other nongovernmental influences contributing to this erosion, but my question is: Does government intervention compensate for that erosion or contribute to it by punishing wayward fathers and mothers for failing to live up to their obligations?

GLENDON: Let's not discuss the function of the law as merely punishments and sanctions. Another function of the law, especially at the constitutional level, is educational and symbolic: to state prominently a society's central commitments. The Preamble to the Constitution and the entire Declaration of Independence are not self-executing law. They perform a hortatory function. They articulate the broader ideas around which we the people "constitute" ourselves as a political society. The main difference between Christopher Lasch's language and my own is that mine is more in the hortatory mode, deliberately general, and leaves such things as Christopher proposes to be worked out at the state or local level.

LASCH: Exhortation probably isn't enough in this case, unless it is backed up by a few sanctions. But I don't intend to dismiss the hortatory value of laws in expressing the underlying ethical norms on which people are able to agree—which is why such matters as the definition of the family shouldn't be left to the private decision of individuals.

STONE: Another problem is that your language, Mary Ann, is easily mirrored in rights language. Couldn't we also be discussing a bill of rights for children?

GLENDON: I prefer a language of duties, because when you say that "children have rights," you're really just saying the state or a parent is going to assert them. It is better to talk about the responsibilities of the community to children or the responsibilities of parents to children. But the main reason my language is so general is that at a constitutional level, what's important is to put the concept of "family" in play in the same way that "liberty" and "equality" are in play. If we can accomplish that through this Bill of Duties, then we might think about the goal of family protection not as windy political rhetoric that blows through every two or four years but as an ongoing fundamental value, guiding the formation of policy at all levels.

MARZORATI: I wonder why so much of this discussion has been about punishments and sanctions. Isn't there a long history in this country of trying to coax people into doing certain things and then rewarding them? If you sign up for the army or air force, you have access to a veterans' hospital and the GI Bill. Why not offer parents interest-free loans for their child's college education or perhaps insure the bank deposits of those who stick out their marriages and raise their kids?

LASCH: My reservations about using entitlements as inducements are similar to those expressed by Mary Ann regarding rights. Recipients of entitlements, like rights bearers, are regarded as autonomous individuals, and that is precisely the style of thinking we are trying to avoid.

BARBER: Exactly. The problem of resorting to the law, any kind of law, in a modern constitutional liberal democracy is that the central character becomes the "legal person" and is always the most powerful entity. The standing of the family in such an arena will always be compromised by the fact that those who make up the family—child, wife, husband—have stronger legal standing as individuals than as a family. How—in a system that atomizes us, privatizes us, and rewards us as legal persons—do we reinforce social entities that are based on kinship?

GLENDON: We don't know any more about how to revitalize social environments such as the family than we know about natural environments. But we do know a little bit about how to stop harming these environments. One thing that is missing from our family policy is any national, coherent commitment to it. In our federal system most family law is fashioned at the state level. Christopher Lasch mentions divorce law. In European countries divorce law is nationwide; divorce reform engenders a vigorous democratic discussion, on national television and in all the newspapers. Here, where it's state by state, the issues Christopher raises do not command national attention.

STONE: But state by state allows for more liberty too. Quickie divorces originated in Nevada at a time when it was very hard to get divorces in other states. So you get, as you do in corporate law, a certain competition among the states that produces different patterns and opportunities.

BARBER: Federalism enhances liberty only if everybody has equal mobility; that is, the wealth needed to move from state to state to obtain those benefits. If you don't have mobility, you have less liberty, not more.

GLENDON: That is why the federal government got active in child support and why we now have, finally, long after most other countries, vigorous enforcement of child-support obligations—thanks only to federal intervention.

LASCH: The assessment here of the state of our knowledge about families is too modest. We know more than you all are asserting. We know, for example, that divorce is bad for kids. There's no question about that.

GLENDON: Christopher, restricting divorce will not prevent parents from separating. The social phenomenon is family breakdown. The legal result is divorce. You can ban divorce, but you can't make people live in the same household and be good parents.

MARZORATI: That is the central question, the age-old question, isn't it? Can we create virtue? In the case of Mary Ann's duty language, can we improve American family life simply by giving voice to the idea that it is shameful to abandon one's children? Haven't we begun to accomplish something when we the people write that idea into our Constitution? I think of Dan's example of the man who forsook his obligation to help the PTA. He broke his promise. It seems to me that if this forum were actually a constitutional convention—if there were, in fact, people gathered here to create a constitutional language for the family—it would focus the country's attention, gain media coverage, and ignite a conversation, which is, in fact, democracy at work. If there were a sense that we the people really want parents to raise their children, maybe people would be a little more hesitant about walking out, maybe they would try a little harder to patch things up.

STONE: Shame is the link to virtue. But it's most effective in a small community. Relationships between people are increasingly impersonal. Shoppers now call in their credit card numbers rather than experience a face-to-face exchange with a storekeeper. The people who determine our environment are increasingly distant and digital. When you're not in a community that allows for that intimacy, there is little to be ashamed about and little sense of duty. Essentially, that is why we have the law. At a certain level our values have to be enforced. Today, shame is no longer operative.

KEMMIS: Well, shame is not the only operative force in such situations. Think of pride or habit.

GLENDON: Honor.

STONE: Guilt would do it. It would have in my day.

KEMMIS: If we believe that civic virtue is capable of making a difference in the way people behave, then we have to ask ourselves at what level it is possible or most effective to instill that civic virtue. Christopher Stone has just said what small "r" republicans always understood: that there is a scale beyond which civic virtue cannot operate. We have, as a nation, forcibly made ourselves forget that lesson. We have denied it over and over again, and we have made ourselves act as if it's possible to have a civil society, a polity, on a scale at which there is no evidence that it's possible. Now, that's injurious in a lot of different ways, but mainly it soaks up all of the resources—material and civil—that might be available at the level where such a polity *would* be possible. A necessary step toward putting such civic virtue to work is to begin to withdraw from the consensus that the nation is what we mean by a polity.

A Duty to Country

BARBER: The ideal democratic polity has been seen by every theorist, from the Greeks down to modern times, as a small rural republic or a town republic or a vibrant municipality. There's no question that at the local level democracy works naturally and works well. But it is also the case that we live in a world of institutions and problems that are not only national but also international and interdependent. Solutions that reemphasize the local level run up against the historical reality that we are a nation, as well as the facts that power is being deployed in international arenas and that reaction at the local level is ineffective. Besides, at this national level the rhetoric of duty *is* alive and well. Consider that the President has dispatched almost a half million American troops abroad, without congressional authorization and with considerable public discontent and a little of my own, but with an overwhelming majority agreeing that the young still have a duty to respond to the country's call.

MARZORATI: Sure, Ben. How many of those troops enlisted because they wanted to serve their nation? The come-on was, "Be all that *you* can be." And how has recruitment fared since last August 2? Enlistment rates, by all accounts, have plummeted.

BARBER: For whatever reasons they enlisted, almost all have shipped out without complaint.

KEMMIS: Ben, at the level of national service, people only sense a duty to bear arms and a duty to respect the flag. Nothing else.

BARBER: But, Dan, at least on the national level, we already have a residual language of duty that we can attempt to expand. I would prefer to see this idea of duty expressed in Preamble language to avoid the paternalism of enforcement from above. I'd really hate to see a Supreme Court that spent its time enforcing duties rather than defending rights. So a duty to country might read, "The right to life, liberty, and the pursuit of happiness obligates every citizen to participate in the democratic polity that alone secures these and other rights." In more popular language, we might say, "Liberty isn't free; it's paid for in the currency of obligation." "I'm trying to do what Mary Ann sought to do: not force a sense of duty through the law but create language in the law that is educational.

MARZORATI: How might this manifest itself in an actual duty?

BARBER: I've often thought that we ought to consider an anti-poll tax. In this case, the government would actually pay people to vote, just as we pay jurors a per diem.

GLENDON: They used to do that in Chicago!

BARBER: Yeah, but you had to be dead. Or perhaps we reverse the logic: Certain benefits of citizenship will be *withheld* if you don't participate in national service.

STONE: In international law such negative inducements are precisely what motivate sovereign states to comply. Nations that fail their obligations are forbidden from participating in scientific conventions or from receiving the benefits of other international arrangements.

MARZORATI: How would this work at home?

STONE: Perhaps you wouldn't be allowed to vote.

LASCH: I'm not sure the deprivation of the vote would be considered a punishment in this country anymore. Perhaps you ought to consider using it as a reward.

BARBER: Maybe there could be a pass that grants access to all state and federal parklands. Obtaining the pass would be contingent upon the exercise of certain duties and obligations. These parklands wouldn't exist without an organized democratic polity, and if you didn't want to take part in the polity, fine, then you couldn't ask for access to something that the polity alone has provided.

LASCH: Why not favor a provision that simply made voting an obligation?

BARBER: In voting, a liberal democracy needs a *deliberative* citizen, not simply somebody who pulls a lever. If you force everyone to vote, you may enhance private opinion and private prejudice at the polls, which is not what a democracy is looking for.

MARZORATI: What do the small "r" republicans think about a national service?

KEMMIS: The proposal for a national service is just one more way to soak up resources at a level where they won't do good and to remove them from a level where they might. The idea of service to a polity is a good idea. But it should be service to polities that allow people to connect in meaningful ways. I agree there are problems that transcend the local level. But why do we jump to the conclusion that such issues are, by their nature, national? In most cases they are, in fact, global. I would also like to suggest that we substitute for the word "duty" the word "responsibility." Duty suggests a one-way obligation, like a debt. We lack the sense of the connectedness of the rights bearers. In the word "responsibility" we do have that sense of connectedness, the idea that here is a claim and a response to that claim—a responsibility.

GLENDON: When I tried to draft my language, I called it a Declaration of Responsibilities. I prefer "declaration" over "bill" because I prefer the hortatory mode over the coercive. And I prefer "responsibility" over "duty" for precisely the reasons you did, Dan. Before coming here, I combed the founding documents in search of duties. The only duty I could find in these documents was the duty to overthrow an oppressive government in the Declaration of Independence! But the Preamble to the Constitution does contain language that is suggestive of obligation, the commitment "to secure the blessings of liberty" not only for ourselves but for *posterity.* Perhaps the only way to reconcile Ben's proposal with Dan's is to make the commitment to civic service at the national level and the organization and fulfillment at the local level.

MARZORATI: Why wouldn't we want this particular duty to be a national service, with citizens leaving their localities? Don't we want wealthy kids to leave their wealthy communities and to experience and understand that all communities are not wealthy? Don't we want black urban kids and white farm kids to mingle? Is all this talk—which you hear from many who support the idea of mandatory national service—just rhetoric?

STONE: Gerry, there is the possibility that human resources will be allocated to tasks for which they're not best suited. You may find yourself taking people who are better at being business executives or doctors and putting them into public service, building roads.

MARZORATI: But I thought we were talking about encouraging virtue. Isn't there a good in a doctor's understanding that some people in his society are making roads and for him to have this experience building roads himself so that he might better understand the road builder's life, the value of roads, the value of his country's maintaining roads?

STONE: Yes. But there will be a conflict between maximizing virtue and maximizing production as an economist would see it. And we are a nation that has put its predominant faith into allocating human resources according to what the market regards as the best use.

BARBER: Wait. Dan's not trying to conserve these human resources from being soaked up so that they can go back home and be executives or doctors. Christopher Stone's argument against national service is the same as Oscar Wilde's argument against socialism: It takes up too many free evenings.

STONE: But Dan is saying that the sense of duty you are trying to inspire, Ben, requires a prior sense of community. And where people know their neighbors, sense a connectedness, and feel their politicians are genuinely responsible to them, then building a park or organizing a public gathering will inculcate a sense of duty at that level. Duties are apt to be spare and rarefied at the national level, such as the duty to defend one's country and to bear arms. A finer sense of duty obtains at the local level—one that calls upon your body to serve on a jury, help out in civic productions, or sit on the board of an opera company.

GLENDON: If you made service a national obligation and let people choose whether to render it locally or to see the world, then you would have achieved both ends. There are many small-town people who would like to help out in the South Bronx, as the Vista program demonstrated.

STONE: But why not simply increase taxes and pay people to perform work in the South Bronx so that those who are most inclined to do this work can choose to do it? Why do you prefer fulfilling certain functions by imposing a blanket conscription of everyone?

LASCH: Well, how do you feel about hiring substitutes when called on to do military service? There's a classic case.

MARZORATI: That's what we're doing now. Isn't a volunteer army in some sense the hiring of one class by another?

BARBER: The point of national service is not solely to solve a set of problems. We're not arguing that because our most intractable problems were not solved by throwing money at them, we will now throw free labor at them. The target of community service and national service is the attitudes and virtues of the participants in the service. This is why the issue is legislation versus education, or coercion versus persuasion. When you legislate duties, you're using penalties and sanctions to compel people to act. True, education also is a form of compulsion; we call it "authority." But we assume with young people that as they grow and come to understand what it means to belong to a community, they must assume responsibilities and exercise their liberty in a way that is responsive to the liberty of others. To "educate" in a democracy doesn't mean giving the young license and then leaving them alone. Educational authority compels our children, in the name of growth and liberty, to assume certain responsibilities, whereas legislation makes demands on fully developed human beings who, whether they like it or not, must act in certain ways.

STONE: Am I the only one here who is uneasy about the state educating its young citizens in patriotism? In my mind I think of China, or Nazi Germany, of states having kids get together in the morning and sing hymns to IBM.

BARBER: Christopher, we are nowhere near that. In China I might want to read the young the Bill of Rights. In France today, I would not necessarily want to talk about compulsory service—they have enough compulsory bureaucracy as it is. But we're talking about the United States, with its language of rights and obsession with privatization. I think we can stand a fairly strong dose of . . . call it patriotic rhetoric, duties rhetoric, responsibility rhetoric, education-for-liberty rhetoric, without singing hymns to IBM. Somewhere down the line you might find me saying, "Enough talk of duty; let's have some more rights talk." But that's hardly our problem now.

LASCH: Will we have more than talk about duties, which is part of my uneasiness with all this Preamble-like writing? Does everything just continue with a veneer of talk about responsibilities, or is there some compulsion? Dan, I share your view that local government is best, but some issues can be resolved only by national action, coercive action at that. The civil rights movement—the most striking example of democratic politics in our time—was solidly based on local black communities in the South. Yet its success also depended, in the final analysis, on federal legislation.

KEMMIS: Yes, but let me give you an example of what I am talking about. If you survey people now about what they consider the nation's number one domestic social problem, drug abuse comes up the most often. We've addressed it as a national problem, and, by and large, our efforts have proved hopeless. On the local level, as mayor, I go to the kids in my town and say, "Like every other town in America, we've got a problem here. What should we do about it?" It's just good public policy to bring the kids into the discussion at this point, because they are going to know what's most likely to work with their peers. But such a conversation also says, in effect, "As a community we expect you to help us solve this problem." Now, it's at that level of interaction that one can impose and expect a sense of duty. You could never pull this off on the national level, because you lose the concept of peership and the people's sense that what is really at stake is the quality of their neighborhood, their town, their place.

A Duty to Place

STONE: Well, let's talk about place for a minute. A duty to place, or the environment, or the land, is distinguishable from the other duties we have discussed. My duty to keep off your property is simply the mirror of your right of ownership. When we talk about our obligations to the oceans, or to the whales, or to future generations, there is no rights holder on the other side with the freedom to waive or sell or trade that protection. I think we do have a duty to the environment, but at the same time we should recognize that if we put ourselves under a duty to, say, whales, there is no way to sit down with whales and adjust things if the situation gets too extreme.

KEMMIS: I came across one interesting assignment of rights in Montana law recently. The Montana Floodplain and Floodway Management Act holds that a river has a right to overwhelm its banks and inundate its floodplain. Well, that's interesting, because it's not a right that *we* assign to the river. The river has earned it through centuries of deluging and shaping the floodplain, and the floodplain has a right to its rampaging river. They've earned their rights through a kind of reciprocal action.

STONE: We must be careful with this kind of language. The concept of rights exists within a framework of law that supplies, for example, a right to counsel.

KEMMIS: There's some usefulness in the metaphor. Missoula is where it is because of a gathering of rivers. The Clark Fork River is the most outstanding feature of my town, which we have come to realize after years of turning our back on the river. I have sometimes spoken of the river as Missoula's "oldest and wisest citizen." Now, that is metaphorical language, and yet it brings to mind the concept of inhabitation, that what calls us to political activity is our living together in a shared space. Those spaces aren't arbitrary. We are there because of the shape of the surroundings. And our relationship to the surroundings, then, is not an accidental relationship but a reciprocal one—like the river to the floodplain.

MARZORATI: Somehow I feel that we all want to promote a sense of duty, but no one, except Christopher Lasch, wants to actually create a duty. I am surprised, because the history of our country is replete with examples of our doing so. I imagine that back at the turn of the century there might have been a guy who was furious that his state government was imposing on all car drivers the duty to obtain a license before hitting the road. Did he spend nights at home wrestling with the profound questions of philosophy and issues of loss of liberty? No. He grumbled, took a test, and got his license, and came to see it as something that, community-wise, was for the best. So I wonder: What if we created a new ecological duty for, say, Missoula? Someone buys a house in town, and Dan tells him or her that before the water gets turned on, before all the governmental amenities are provided, the owner has to take a test. He must understand the ecology of the neighborhood: where the watershed is, where the garbage goes, the vicissitudes of the river, the special features of the land. Since we have made it a duty to know a certain minimal amount about car driving before you get behind a wheel, why not insist upon a similar level of competence before you get to settle in a place?

BARBER: Gerry, you have to remember that in the twentieth century, duty has to accommodate liberty. Wordsworth called duty the "stern daughter of the voice of God." Remember that, theologically, duty was what God commanded you to do, and your *autonomy* was no part of it. The modern conception of duty has to balance itself with the individual's autonomy, with human choices. This is why I prefer the word "responsibility"; it entails this accommodation. Rousseau said freedom is obedience to a law we prescribe to ourselves. Democracy provides the link between autonomy and duty that's missing in other societies and that we require in the absence of a God who can simply mandate that His will *is* our duty.

KEMMIS: Ben, any sense of duty or any Bill of Duties has to draw upon the notion of connectedness that is implicit in the idea of responsibility. When I was thinking about family and how we might impose a duty within that structure, I tried to imagine the family longitudinally—that is, between members of different generations. A duty to family or a duty to place must enjoin people to *remember* and to live in a way that deserves to be remembered and nurtures the practice of remembrance. Meeting in this room is a wonderful way of doing that. This conversation reminds us of the traditions out of which this gathering was born. When we think about our relationship to the environment, we should know where we are, where we come from, and then agree to live intentionally in those places in a way that will allow people to remember us well. It is when we reaffirm that compact between ourselves and our progeny that duty is born.

Questions

1. What is the difference between liberty and license? What is at stake here? Write your own answer to this question, then work with classmates in a group to try to reach a consensus.

2. The concept of "civic virtue" is mentioned several times in this discussion. What do you take it to mean? How would you define it? Develop your own definition, then share that definition with a group of your classmates. Try to achieve a definition of civic virtue that everyone in the group can accept. Be sure that your definition includes examples of behavior.

Suggestions for Further Research

1. Consult recent periodical and newspaper indexes to investigate the concepts of community and communitarianism. Summarize the information that you find.

2. Survey a group of students on your campus to determine whether they feel a sense of obligation or responsibility to the groups or communities they belong to. Be sure to ask how they put that sense of obligation into action. Summarize the results of your survey.

Suggestions for Writing

1. Write a paper in which you propose a specific duty, obligation, or civic virtue and argue in favor of its importance to both individuals and the community.

2. Choose a specific point at which you can enter the discussion you have read here. Identify an issue you want to argue, or a point you want to make or respond to. Then write your argument as a part or extension of the discussion here. For example, you might want to write about the question of whether an obligation should be voluntary or required.

Sex on Television:
How Much Is Too Much?

Sexually explicit content seems to be increasing on television. Movies, talk shows, newscasts, and live broadcasts of trials and Senate hearings have presented sexually explicit language and descriptions that only a few years ago would not have been permitted on television. Some people have welcomed the opportunities for frank discussion of sex on the bases of both free speech and sex education—especially AIDS education. But others have questioned whether explicit sexual content on television, where anyone can see it, is appropriate or necessary. As the following arguments show, the debate has many dimensions. Before you read the arguments printed here, respond in writing to the following:

Preparing to Read

1. *What is your personal reaction to the question of whether television should present programming with explicit sexual content, even in the form of news and education?*
2. *Who should decide what kinds of sexually explicit content should be broadcast on television (or published in other media)?*

Women Pay High Price
for Sexual Revolution

JOAN BECK

Except for AIDS, the changes in sexual behavior and moral assumptions loosely known as the "sexual revolution" exact a much higher price from women than from men.

It's a revolution that men have clearly won and women are paying for—in the name of equality.

But there is nothing equal about how the medical and social costs of our changing behavior are falling due. This is not to argue for a return to the old double standard of sexual behavior, to sexual repression, to male domination of women in the name of sexual protection or any other curb on women's equality, sexual or otherwise.

It is to suggest a revisionist look at the current consequences of the sexual revolution and ask if there are ways to reduce what it is costing millions of women.

For example, it is women who pay with 1.6 million abortions every year when unintended and unwanted pregnancy occurs. However insistently women feel they must defend their right to terminate a life they are carrying, it's still a difficult, unpleasant, demeaning price men don't have to pay.

Men, in fact, have shrugged off most of the responsibility for contraception. Research to find better methods of birth control concentrate almost solely on women; men are generally skittish about risks and side effects and researchers apparently assume women provide a better potential market.

Sexually transmitted diseases—other than AIDS—harm both men and women. But only women suffer one of the most serious and common consequences: pelvic inflammatory disease, caused in particular by chlamydia and gonorrhea. So serious has PID become that the whole current issue of the Journal of the American Medical Association is devoted to the epidemic.

The damage report goes like this:

More than 1 million women suffer acute pain from PID each year. One in 10 American women will have pelvic inflammatory disease sometime during her reproductive years.

One fourth of these women will experience serious, long-term problems, including infertility, recurrent infections, chronic pelvic pain and ectopic pregnancy in which the fetus begins to grow outside the uterus and life-saving surgery is usually necessary.

About 200,000 women must be hospitalized for PID annually. Half of them need surgery.

Total health care costs for pelvic inflammatory disease came to about $4.2 billion last year. By 2000, assuming no decrease in the incidence of the disease, the bills are projected to be almost $10 billion.

The earlier a woman begins having sexual intercourse—and the more male partners she has over her lifetime—the greater her risk of pelvic inflammatory disease.

A JAMA article also recommends women ask potential sex partners about sexually transmitted diseases and, using more clinical language, tells them to inspect their partner's critical areas for signs of infection before allowing them to proceed.

Whatever happened to romance?

Sex wasn't supposed to turn into a game of Russian roulette played with nasty and deadly diseases instead of bullets.

Women are far more likely to get AIDS through heterosexual relations than are men, although their numbers are still small. The Centers for Disease Control is proposing to change the official definition of AIDS to include those with an immune system weakened by HIV. That will add about 160,000 people to the current toll of 195,718.

The social pressures generated by the sexual revolution have not only cost women the pleasures of courtship and the luxury of allowing a relationship to grow slowly into love but even social support when they really want to say no.

Many of the girls who are pressured into having sex at 15 or 16 because it seems to be a norm and an expected part of dating (even the schools are passing out condoms) get the message that sex really isn't very special. It's not, compared to sex that flowers from love and commitment. And that is another loss to women.

The weakening ties between sex and marriage, however violated in the past, also cost women far more than men. Teen-age girls bear the responsibilities for babies born out of wedlock, often never finish high school and may be stuck on welfare for a generation—not the boys who brag about the babies they beget but never intend to parent.

Changes in sexual and moral behavior have been linked too closely with the push for women's equality and women's rights. But what is supposed to be equality now often looks like exploitation. And it's time we all learn to tell the difference.

America Is Shocked. Shocked!

WALTER GOODMAN

The age of X-rated educational television has arrived, with flourishes. The William Kennedy Smith rape trial and the Senate committee hearings on Anita F. Hill's charges against Judge Clarence Thomas may have owed their popularity to the spicy nature of the encounters. But viewers who managed to keep their calm, while all around them were being titillated by uncommonly explicit discussions of common doings, could glimpse matters that are usually treated in drier fashion. There was much to be noted about the interplay of money, class, race and gender in America today.

Alert viewers could see how Kennedy money and power play to a nation of outsiders looking in, through the tube. They could see class differences being used to influence a society that often deludes itself into thinking it is classless. They could see expectations of black failure, based on long experience and ingrained assumptions, upset by displays of education and success. And they could be even more confused than usual by the mixed messages about sexual relations that have for some time been sent forth by television. And so unlike the packaged goods that fill television, most of these events came through unedited, unpolished, raw. They made "The MacNeil-Lehrer Newshour" seem like junior high school.

All right, millions did not tune in day after day for incidental insights into the confusions of race and class in America. They were drawn there, as George Bush would surely put it, by the woman-man thing and were rewarded with some curious disquisitions on sexual behavior.

In their vociferous championings of Judge Thomas, Senator Orrin G. Hatch and Senator Alan K. Simpson rested their case largely on the impossibility that a man like the judge would say the things that Ms. Hill said he said because such things could only be said to a women by a certified pervert, in Utah and Wyoming anyhow. And in her questioning of William K. ("Who's Michael?") Smith and her summation, the prosecutor, Moira K. Lasch, waxed sarcastic at the possibility that this young man and young woman (perhaps any man and woman) could meet in a bar one Friday night and have intercourse an hour or so later, even in Florida during Easter break.

When the stakes are high and protagonists are playing to a camera or a jury, it often becomes difficult to take them seriously or to know how seriously they take themselves, but you can tell what they think will work on the audience. The Hatch-Simpson line was more successful than Ms. Lasch's, but both were cast into a general unease, evident on television, about what the right relations are these days between men and women.

The tube is more awash than ever with sex in many forms; everybody is doing it with everybody. That's show biz. But under pressure to exhibit social responsibility along with the flesh, news and entertainment divisions have picked up fast on the evils of sexual harassment, date rape, AIDS, pornography and various pathologies celebrated on talk shows. Sex is dangerous.

Here is the piety of the panderer. Television is like a brothel with rooms set aside for lectures on why visitors should stay out of brothels. The virtuous voyeur can add the satisfaction of judgment to the kick of peeping; Shame on him! On her! On them! On television! (The criticism of CNN and Court Television for lowering the level of television by carrying the Smith trial wins the year's Emmy for high-minded mindlessness.)

Senator Hatch and Senator Simpson played into widespread disgust for the dirty stuff all over the tube and distaste for the urban sophisticates who create and defend it and probably practice it when the Senate is not watching. Imagine what the Senators would have made of the Palm Beach scene.

Ms. Hill's supporters and to some extent supporters of Mr. Smith's accuser, also known as Alleged Victim (but don't call her Cathy), resorted to a vision of sex promulgated by some feminists as an age-old imposition upon women: to accuse a man of rape is a tautology, to acquit him is in effect lynching his accuser. Meanwhile, Mr. Smith's supporters were swinging along with the sex-comes-naturally crowd who seem bent on emulating television's beautiful people. Palm Beachers will have to dance fast to keep up the reputation lately shed on them by the tube.

Watching the Smith defense team batter the prosecution was like taking a course in the power of cash. You knew that Roy E. Black and the two other men who took turns presenting their case and the lone woman at the defense table who never said a word but was probably mistressminding the whole campaign and the lesser lawyers off camera and the rent-by-hour experts who delivered the

objective conclusions that benefited the defendant and the anony-
mous researchers and investigators and all the travel and hotels and
who knows what else did not come cheap. Jurors heard it cost $1
million, and they might have been forgiven a chuckle when Mr.
Smith said he could not afford to fly first class from Washington to
Palm Beach.

And it was not just money, it was Kennedy money. Ms. Lasch
did not fail to draw attention to the defense's resources, the family's
history of sex and booze and its proven ability to manipulate press
and television, but it didn't take. The popularity of shows like
"Falcon Crest" and concoctions like "A Current Affair" indicate
that people like to watch the rich living it up and acting down.
Despite a strain of populism that seems to have reawakened in this
difficult period, most Americans do not spend much time hating
the very rich. The nobs seem to exist not to exploit the plebes but
for their vicarious enjoyment. Marx got it wrong again.

In his counterattack, Mr. Black touched on the affectionate
fascination with the Kennedys, kept alive by movies and television
since John F. Kennedy's assassination. The clan being the closest
this this country has ever had to a royal family, we can cluck over
a night of hopping from bar to Au Bar, but the royals are ours just
as the Windsors belong even to British Socialists.

Mr. Black made sure the jurors and viewers were reminded in
the testimony of Senator Edward M. Kennedy, Jean Kennedy Smith
and the defendant himself that the family's many sacrifices and its
record of public service and good works add up to more than Chap-
paquiddick, the albatross that immobilized Senator Kennedy during
the Thomas hearings. After the trial Mr. Black said he saw tears in
jurors' eyes during Ms. Lasch's direct examination of the Senator,
and there must have been a little mist in front of television sets too.

Mr. Black put on a class act. It may have been just fortuitous
that the main corroborating witness for the prosecution, Anne
Mercer, turned out to have sold her story to a junk television show
and that the friend whom the accuser did not at first remember
visiting on the big night turned out to be a bartender named Anthony Liott, whom Mr. Black made sure to display on the stand.
The lawyer knew as well as any soap opera director how to set such
types against the clean-cut young assistant district attorneys who
were Kennedy house guests that Easter weekend. Look at the people
the accuser associates with, Mr. Black was saying without saying
it, and then look at the nice young folks who sit around playing
parlor games at the compound.

Class differences showed up in the Thomas hearings too. Remember the woman, a character witness for judge Thomas, who

presented herself as just your ordinary middle American, by way of putting down the big-name women who were supporting Ms. Hill, not to mention Ms. Hill herself? What made the criticisms of Ms. Hill for not being one of the girls striking, of course, was that she is black. Is it possible, a viewer might fairly ask, that even people who are by no means racist may find a black woman as self-possessed as Ms. Hill was in her committee appearance a little off-putting? Is it possible that even some black women feel that way? You could imagine that Ms. Hill, the Yale Law School graduate, might find it easier to get along with, say, Jean Kennedy Smith than with some of her co-workers in the Washington lower bureaucracy.

The main revelation of the Thomas hearings was the appearance, like a line of sparkling cars of tomorrow being unshrouded for the cameras, of an array of successful black professionals. People who rely on local news must have been astonished: Where have these folks been hiding?

Not only were they not in show business or sports or jail, they were not all liberals. They actually disagreed but on matters like affirmative action that are articles of faith among black personages who are confirmed as leaders by their frequent appearances on talk shows. You might not care to spend a lot of time with the woman who seemed to be rigid with dislike of Ms. Hill or with the self-infatuated man who thrust his ego at the audience, but their peculiarities did not fit any racial stereotype.

It's all so complicated for the tube. But to get back to sex, which is where most viewers doubtless wanted to be in the first place, one thing is simple and sure: Television can be counted on to respond to whatever is in the wind. After the Thomas hearings, sexual harassment in the workplace was decried on all channels. The Smith trial brought new exhortations against date rape. Now, with the acquittal, watch for the the latest prescription for young men on the prowl: For really safe sex, wear a good lawyer.

Report from "Twin Peaks"—Incest for the Millions: Saying No to David Lynch

WARREN GOLDSTEIN

A couple of Saturday nights ago, as Leland Palmer (and his savage alter ego "Bob") were beating his (their?) niece to death, I turned off the television and said goodbye to "Twin Peaks" and David Lynch.

I know I wasn't alone. That scene, remarkable for its prolonged, calculated, almost loving gruesomeness, was the final straw.

I'm not about to claim the squeaky-clean virtue of ex-smokers or the recently converted. Since last spring "Twin Peaks" has had me edgy and a little defensive, titillated and a little guilty—but completely in its spell. I loved the music and the atmosphere, the lurking danger that kept me from relaxing, Agent Cooper's wacky combination of steel-trap rationality and Tibetan intuition, Nadine's eyepatch, and Dr. Jacoby's earplugs.

And it was sexy. There was bad sex and good sex, but sex was everywhere: from the discovery of Laura Palmer's naked body to Audrey's slinky come-ons to *Flesh* magazine to nearly everyone's secret love affairs.

It was like nothing I'd ever seen on TV before, and if Leo Johnson's wife-beating seemed a little overdone, if Donna Hayward seemed a little too good to be true, well, then, the ensemble, the gestalt, the Lynchian vision, at least, seemed to work, to shake me up, to create unpredictable postmodern atmospherics in the place of one-liners and laughtracks. I was seduced.

David Lynch will not be surprised that I cannot stop thinking about that final scene, which I turned off just as I guessed Leland/Bob was about to shove a small letter deep under Maddy's bloody fingernail. Leland and his beast-like twin, the deranged long-haired mystery man, were twirling in a deadly dance with the dark-haired stand-in for Leland's murdered daughter. The figure alternated between kissing the girl (as Leland) and screaming incoherently and making as if to bite her throat (as "Bob"). The camera stayed close through this bloody and terrifying *pas de deux*, delighting in its ability to show both men. The point for "Twin Peaks" (get it?) fans is that Leland killed his own daughter—that's who killed Laura Palmer.

Even this discovery is just part of the story. For the real secret to "Twin Peaks" and Laura's murder, the real message of that scene, is incest: father-daughter incest. I suppose I knew it, didn't want to think about it. Lynch had seduced me into his forbidden world. And now it's the morning after and I'm ashamed.

The poles of sexuality in last season's episodes were good girl Donna and bad girl Audrey. They're both high-school girls with the bodies of Playmates. Laura was sleeping with (at least) Ben Horne, Dr. Jacoby, Leo Johnson, James, Bobby, and patrons of One-Eyed Jacks. Audrey lusts for Agent Cooper, who can barely resist her, and in a scene which lasted quite a long time, nearly slept with her own father at the brothel. Nadine has survived her suicide attempt thinking she's sixteen while her husband is forty-ish. James and

Donna are sleeping with Laura through each other, while James nearly has a fling with Laura's look-alike cousin.

The patterns here are all incest: brother-sister, father-daughter, and mostly the latter. What's Lynch saying? That all sex is incest? That we all carry the marks of Oedipal struggle in our psyches? Maybe so. But I bet it's something a lot crasser; underneath all the fancy music it's fairly simple: forbidden sex sells. Why else have Donna tell a dreamy story about her and Laura skinny-dipping and partying with college boys when they were thirteen and fourteen.

If that was gratuitous what shall we call the week-by-week layering of details reconstructing Laura's murder: the number of men she slept with that night, the nature of her injuries, the kinds of drugs she'd consumed, how she'd been tied up, how she'd been pecked by the Myna bird named Waldo . . . I can hardly believe I'm writing this stuff down. It's as though Lynch tried to think of a series of cruelties that would boggle any imagination and add them on, week by week. That way we wouldn't notice all at once; we'd be gradually seduced, in the way that a diabolical wife might addict her husband to a drug by doctoring his food over a period of months.

Once you start this process, what you used to be able to chalk up to quirky weirdness looks much more malevolent. I mean, I thought the camera used to stay just a little too close to Leo as he beat Shelley with a bar of soap in a sock. But what about now, as Leo vegetates in the wheelchair, drooling and flopping? The genuine discomfort you feel is perfectly justified. Or how did you like the detail as Audrey, bound and helpless at the brothel, was frequently injected with drugs? This isn't offbeat—the goriness quotient is out of control.

If taboo sex and violence with classy background music add up to a vision, I'll pass. No doubt Lynch will figure out how to put a tragic-flaw kind of moral in the story: that Leland's rape of his daughter (like Macbeth's guilty ambition) led to all the rest. But it's taken too long, and he likes the story too much. He's still pandering. I think he's getting away with murder.

Safe Sex and Self-Respect

MARK SIMON

We are awash in sexuality. It turns up everywhere and with the kind of explicitness that would have kept a movie out of most theaters just 30 or 40 years ago.

Perfume commercials. Beer commercials. Television programs. Senate debates about Supreme Court justices.

We are overwhelmed by the constant presence of sex. Most of us understand it as a subject of political debate, or that it infiltrates most debates and discussions between people. Most consistently the message is that sex is something to pursue and to enjoy.

Magic Johnson isn't going to change that.

I heard someone say on the radio the other day that the sexual revolution is over, and we lost.

But things we set in motion seldom respond to our own schedule, and the sexual revolution is far from over.

Rather, it is out of control.

And its end product may be a generation buffeted by a constant barrage of sexy images, even as they become convinced that sex can equal death.

Most of us want to make something good out of something bad.

So, we have heard from people in the last several days that perhaps Magic Johnson was afflicted with the AIDS virus for a reason—to bring voice to the tragedy that has taken thousands quietly, ignominiously, anonymously, and without public recognition of the disease that threatens to be the next Black Death.

Perhaps it was a divine sign, as has been suggested, that Magic was chosen to be, as he put it, a spokesman for the HIV virus.

But if by this, Johnson intends to be a spokesman for what is commonly defined as safe sex, while it's an interesting and well-meaning start, it hardly competes with the constant barrage of images that run counter to this idea.

And it hardly fills the gaping need ignored by the Bush administration and the Reagan administration for a meaningful program to combat HIV and AIDS.

In both instances, this is a problem they preferred to treat as though it simply did not exist, in keeping with the attitude in both administrations towards gays and women.

We would be on our way toward true awareness and understanding of the problem of AIDS, a key to solution, if the Reagan administration had devoted as much attention to human health as it did to appearances, or that the Bush administration devoted to lip service in lieu of honesty.

Honesty is at the heart of the matter.

There were those who thought that drug use might decline—particularly among those most at risk—when burgeoning basketball star Len Bias died of a cocaine overdose.

But it didn't, anymore than it declined when Richard Pryor set himself on fire or when Elvis died, bloated and self-abused.

John Belushi's death caused no decline in drug use among the white middle and upper-middle class people who identified with him. Among those people, drug use declined only when it became apparent that they had something to lose by continuing.

Similarly, safe sex will become common when it is defined in such a way as to demonstrate to people that they have something to lose by acting in some other way.

What that involves is more than just condoms.

It involves the issues of promiscuity and responsibility, to which Magic Johnson can speak with some authority.

Underlying the issue of promiscuity are even more fundamental matters of self-respect and personal integrity.

No self-respecting parent would teach a child to be promiscuous.

Perhaps Magic Johnson can lead the way to teach us all about the promulgation of respect for the individual in body and spirit, the undermining of which can manifest itself in promiscuous behavior.

The sexual revolution was supposed to be a celebration of the body and sex without guilt.

What it neglected to teach us was that any true celebration of the body is a tribute to respect for others, founded on self-respect.

What we need to learn now, more than that sex might equal death, is that self-respect and personal integrity equal life.

The Television Question

MEG GREENFIELD

The William Kennedy Smith trial in Palm Beach has raised the Television Question again. Should television have been there at all? And, more broadly, what is this infernal, ever present invention doing to us, anyhow, to our consciousness, to our very way of life? The answer to the second set of questions is: everything. Our lives have already been irreversibly transformed in ways that make the pre-television America of less than 50 years ago seem like the dark ages—literally. My opinion is that this has been almost without exception for the good and that our fitful complaining about it rests on turning legitimate worries about the role of TV coverage in a few specific circumstances into a mindless condemnation of the whole.

Actually, the confined areas of legitimate worry have hardly changed in the years since television took off. These have mainly to do with privacy and political opportunism. The plaintiff in the Palm Beach trial had her face, that is her identity, blotted out electronically. Is it fair to people who may be victims of crimes or criminal defendants or objects of investigation to be televised on the stand? This issue has been with us since the beginning of the television age: in the 1951 televised congressional investigation of organized crime (the Kefauver hearings), some witnesses argued in court that they were justified in refusing to testify while TV cameras were present. And the king of witnesses, mobster Frank Costello, declined to have his face televised. So we all sat there for a prolonged stretch and watched his fidgeting hands, which the cameras held in focus. It was very dramatic and maybe the first of the unforgettable TV sequences that came to make up our new nationally shared TV memory bank.

My instinct is that most of these events—hearings and trials—should be open to live TV coverage. I think there are times when it is unwise, even destructive, though, as in the Thomas-Hill purported inquiry when those who are there to inquire and shed light on what happened (the legislators) are likely instead to perform for the TV audience, which in turn is flooding them with telegrams on what to conclude. I'd have kept that closed for an investigation and immediately after it was over released a full transcript. This—the political opportunism problem—is not nearly so troubling with a jury trial, since the jury is making the only choice that matters, and it gets no telegrams and loses or wins no job-sustaining voter constituencies by its behavior.

Still, there is the question of whether people who are victims of crimes, say, or unjustly accused criminal defendants should have to have their lives exposed in every living room of America. The hangup here is that print journalism can report fully and (if it wishes) outrageously on such proceedings, and logic argues that TV should be allowed into the courtroom too. I keep trying to work out some rules in my head by which (the Frank Costello rule?) those having to take the stand could be granted some say in the matter, but I will confess I have come up empty so far in contriving such a procedure.

For the rest, I say have at it. The Kefauver hearings in fact opened the new age of expanded consciousness that television has brought. They represent just about the first universally shared images from the then new medium. There weren't yet all that many television sets. There were more for the next images (political conventions, U.S. space shots coming to grief, Nikita Khrushchev banging his shoe on his table at the United Nations, the murder of JFK and its aftermath which, as with the subsequent tragedies right up to the Challenger explosion, was shown and shown and shown). A nephew of mine came home from a trip to Italy during which he had not seen the Tiananmen carnage. I told him he should contrive to see a tape because the image of the guy in the white shirt, as the whole world now knew him, standing down the tank was something that should be part of his understanding, of his own mental film library.

More coverage, not less: Time and space as we once knew them in my lifetime are obliterated. And so too are psychic distance and political solitude. Politicians, when they are not themselves seeking to manipulate their television personas, are forever worrying that the rest of us will be manipulated by seeing something we won't understand. The Vietnam War is exhibit A. I would concede that seeing the violence, the gore was not a seminar on the complicated sources of the war and that the press can weight coverage in some misleading direction. Maybe it does so by political disposition or because it is being used by officialdom or because it is only free to film one side of the dispute, the bad guys getting away with murder because they keep the cameras out. But to me, the answer to all this is more coverage, not less.

The danger is, of course, that by seeing so much more and knowing so much more we will believe we have seen and known everything and that we understand much more than we do. But that is surely no reason for trying to curtail what we do see. And I believe in any case that for all the supposed dangers of public misunderstanding that televising live events produces, television has had an overall benign effect, first, in embarrassing some misguided public officials around the world out of pursuing some hateful policy, next in creating your basic Sadat-to-Barbara Walters international public diplomacy that puts a premium on explanation and even, against the odds, occasional reasonableness on the part of the terminally unreasonable. Yes, you look around today and see national and ethnic violence of the most terrible kind that does not seem to be fazed by the public stare of people all over the world. But you see a lot too where the presence of that electronic vigilance compels better behavior. I wish CNN had been around for World War II and the awful run-up to it.

I know, I know: the totalitarians were very good at keeping their terrible secrets. But in a world in which so many more people know so much more about other places and expect and demand to know more yet, it would have been much harder for them. I can think of circumstances where individuals, as in criminal trials, may be hurt and circumstances in which a premium may be put on political misbehavior because the camera is rolling. But I can't think of any in which the viewing public has been one whit harmed by the presence of the force—TV—which has been the real revolution in our time.

No Sex, Please; We've Already Got Plenty Here

JULIAN SCHEER

I think it is safe to say that we have our share of sex out here in the country. We may not be Big City or Very Cosmopolitan, but we know sex when we see it. And, frankly, we think we're seeing (and hearing and watching) too much of it these days.

Don't be misled. I haven't polled all my neighbors, but I have talked to enough of my friends up and down Route 667 to know that I am not alone. We're simply fed up with Public Sex.

It has all come to a head over the past few weeks when almost every talk show on radio and television has been engrossed in discussions with ex-basketball great Wilt Chamberlain. The event is the publication of his book and the featured part seems to be not the night he scored an incredible 100 points, but the 20,000 times he scored with women. Here we have a tall, not-so-handsome, rather dissipated ex-jock trying to appear "modest" and "sensitive" about his prowess.

Gimme a break! Why would anyone care?

As if that much ridiculous conversation is not enough, we have been subjected to a major, major media event, the rape trial of William Kennedy Smith in Florida. I am proud to say that I did not watch a second of the trial on television and most of my pals went deer or bird hunting during its broadcast time.

What is even more insulting is the coverage. CNN, the folks we relied upon during Desert Storm, was purveyor of the trial, blow by blow, and it seemed so proud to be doing this public service. It was a peep show, and who really cares? Don't tell me that you wanted to see justice done. You may want to hear a word like ejaculation, which got big play on Day 1 of the trial, but justice? No way.

Even USA TODAY felt compelled to put quotations in a front-page headline, large type, which included, "She was forced onto her back. The defendant was on top of her, he held her down with his body weight and chest. . . . She told him to stop it. She told him no."

Compounding the voyeur in us are the Oprah Winfrey- and Phil Donohue-type shows: fathers having affairs with daughters, mothers loving sons, husbands promoting wives' prostitution. These programs slink across our screens all day. God help us if we have to stay home with a bad cold!

It's not just the daytime fare, either. The old-fashioned situation comedies with a Mary Tyler Moore or Dick Van Dyke have given way to Candice Bergen, who can't remember who got her pregnant, or Roseanne Barr, who wants to make certain her teen daughter is not going to have sex at her house when her daughter's boyfriend comes for Thanksgiving dinner.

I've thought a lot about this. Is it advancing age that taints me? Is it some deep-seated Victorianism I've long suppressed? Am I just a little jaded because I learned so much of all this generations ago from the older guys on the schoolyard?

I'm not sure we want to retreat to the days my father hid *Lady Chatterly's Lover* on the top shelf to keep it out of the hands of my brother and me. But I'm beginning to wonder where all of this so-called "openness" and our sex obsession is taking us. Between the talk shows, soap operas, kiss-and-tell books, TV commercials and comedy specials, I'm seeing more breasts than an attendant in a ladies' locker room.

Enough is enough. Some days, one wants to retreat to the other side of the barn, sit in the glow of a winter sun and think about the days when sex was private and the bedroom door was locked. Gimme a break.

Protect Us from TV Trials

BEVERLY LAHAYE

The live TV broadcasts of the Thomas-Hill hearings and the Smith rape trial were inappropriate and unnecessary.

Because networks have no control over their potential viewers, unsuspecting children and others were exposed to a barrage of vivid descriptions of sexual acts.

During the Thomas-Hill hearings, one anchorman wanly tried to warn young children—who had tuned in to watch their Saturday morning cartoons—of the adult material contained in the pre-empting program. So explicit were the Smith trial highlights that some parents were forced to turn off the evening news rather than expose their children to the networks' repeated reports of the proceedings.

Network broadcasts were unnecessary because the TV viewing audience was not Thomas's tribunal nor Smith's jury. We elect senators and select juries to deliberate and balance accusations against facts, and we trust them to dispense judgments on serious matters. Their task must not be reduced to titillating entertainment for tabloid television.

Who benefited by learning the sordid details of Smith's sexual encounters in Palm Beach? Certainly not the children and other viewers who weren't expecting to relive it in their living rooms.

The effect of more sensitivity to important issues like sexual harassment and date rape came at too high a cost. The names and reputations of those involved will never be fully recovered.

Both proceedings should have been conducted behind closed doors so the truth could come to light without victimizing or offending anyone.

The news media must continue to inform the public of important courtroom and Senate proceedings. But sensitive testimony such as this should not be broadcast as entertainment under the guise of "the public's right to know."

Public Doesn't Need to Be Protected from TV Trials

USA TODAY

When someone wants to protect you from yourself, be on guard. When your would-be protector comes from the government, double the guard.

President Bush wants you protected.

Like others, the president was bothered by graphic descriptions during the televised rape trial of William Kennedy Smith. In a TV interview this week, Bush said people have "a right to be protected against some of these excesses."

A right to be protected? How about the right to decide for yourself?

Protection is as close as the TV dial.

The Palm Beach trial was an eloquent argument for keeping cameras in court, not pushing them out. People watched or chose not to. They weighed evidence and reached a verdict, just like the jury.

Along the way, they learned a valuable lesson: The trial system works.

Only a few voiced complaints.

Some sounded Bush's concern about language. But the subject was no more racy—and far more useful—than soap operas appearing on other channels.

Some said the trial was televised for entertainment, not education. So what? Long before movies and TV, people attended trials for entertainment. Then, as now, they got educated along the way.

Some worried that TV will warp the legal process. But the judge and jurors in the Palm Beach trial said it did not.

Significantly, no one complained that the coverage offered a distorted view.

All states, except Indiana, Mississippi, Missouri, South Carolina, South Dakota and the District of Columbia, now let cameras in court after years of banning them. Federal courts are experimenting.

If you'd like to see the upcoming Los Angeles police brutality, you'll need that access.

If you'd like to follow major abortion cases that will change lives across the nation, you'll need more.

If you'd like to get a fundamental understanding of the law, you'll need TV access to the U.S. Supreme Court, which still closes its doors.

Mr. President, leash the taste police. People can make choices for themselves.

Questions

1. What is at stake here? What are the major issues involved in allowing or prohibiting sexually explicit content on television? Write your own answer to this question, then work with classmates in a group to try to reach a consensus.

2. Based on the arguments printed here, what appear to be the most compelling arguments for and against sexually explicit language and behavior on television?

Suggestions for Further Research

1. What laws regulate the content of broadcast and cable television?

2. Watch several films or television shows from the 1950s and 1960s. Pay special attention to the ways that these films and programs approach and manage the opportunities for sexually explicit language or conduct. Write a summary of what you discover.

Suggestions for Writing

1. Write an argument in which you respond to the assertion that demystifying sex by portraying it on television has made it less special and thus diminished an important dimension of human relationships.

2. Television affects contemporary life in many ways. Choose one effect that you are aware of (not necessarily the portrayal of sex) and write an argument in which you take the position that the effects of television have been either positive or negative. You can discuss these effects in relation to yourself or to society at large, or any social unit in between.

Rationing Medical Care

In recent years there has been considerable discussion of the need to control dramatically rising medical costs in the United States. Some have suggested that one way to contain costs would be to control access to expensive procedures so that only the most deserving or appropriate patients would receive them. Others have argued that such rationing is inherently unfair and antidemocratic. The arguments in this section explore the issue of health care rationing and advocate a variety of solutions. Before you read the arguments, respond in writing to the following:

Preparing to Read

1. *What are your personal feelings and beliefs about rationing health care? Do you believe all procedures should be available to everyone, or do you believe that some selection process is necessary? Why?*
2. *If you were to allocate some type of health care, such as organ transplants or expensive diagnostic tests, what criteria would you use to make your decision?*

Must We Ration Health Care?

WILLIAM B. SCHWARTZ AND
HENRY J. AARON

Continuous and rapid increases in health care costs over the last decade have caused rising concern in the business community and government. With expenditures on medical services now consuming more than 11% of gross national product, and no end of the cost spiral in sight, rationing is now surfacing as a major national policy issue. And one state—Oregon—already has enacted a law that involves rationing by specifying which types of illness can be covered by Medicaid.

Many observers argue that rationing has always been a feature of the American health care system. In one sense, they are right. Health care, like all other goods and services, has been readily available only to those with the means to pay for it. A disproportionate number of the poor are uninsured and depend on the willingness of taxpayers to foot the bill. However odious such rationing may be, it is certainly not new.

A second type of rationing that would be new to the United States is the denial of some care to even the affluent and well-insured. We believe, however, that only through such rationing can the problem of health care costs be brought under control and that American insurers consequently will soon face a new environment in the delivery of health services.

Why Are Costs Rising?

Three forces, all either difficult or impossible to control, are responsible for the rise in health care costs. The single most important force is the rapid and steady introduction of new diagnostic and therapeutic technologies. Dramatic advances in biomedical research have added enormously to the effectiveness of medical care, but have also driven costs up at a real rate of 5% to 6% per year. Among the major cost increasing advances of the 1970s and 1980s were such technologies as intensive care units, chronic dialysis, CT scanning, hip replacement, kidney and heart transplantation, coronary bypass grafts and immunosuppressive therapy.

Even new services that replace higher-priced predecessors typically add substantially to costs. Because many older diagnostic techniques were invasive, physicians usually weighed the risk of the procedure, and the pain and anxiety it caused, against the value of the information they could gain. Newer diagnostic methods, such as CT scanning and magnetic resonance imaging, have freed physicians from such concerns. As a result, even when now procedures are priced below their predecessors, they add substantially to costs because physicians use them more readily and more widely.

And a host of emerging technologies will add to the pressures on costs. Erythropoietin, a hormone critical to the production of red blood cells, will add at least $1 billion a year to expenditures. It is used to treat the severe anemia encountered in patients on chronic dialysis and in patients undergoing treatment for AIDS. The automatic implantable cardiac defibrillator, a remarkably effective method of preventing sudden death in certain cardiac patients, will add still another billion dollars.

Improved Effectiveness

And the list goes on. Positron emission tomography, proton beam accelerators, gene therapy, monoclonal antibodies, cochlear implants, the artificial heart and fetal surgery are a partial list of medical advances that will greatly improve the effectiveness of medical care, but at a steep price. Indeed, most observers of the medical scene believe that the rate of change in the 1990s will exceed that in any previous decade. Cost increases will also accelerate—unless the provision of new services is limited.

The second major force driving costs upward is a continued rise in the real wages of hospital personnel. The hands-on nature of hospital care sharply limits hospitals' ability to increase productivity. Nevertheless, hospitals must provide a steady increase in wages to attract and hold skilled personnel. In this respect, service sectors of the economy are at a considerable disadvantage compared to the manufacturing sector, where wages can grow without raising costs because productivity growth largely offsets higher pay.

The aging of the population is the final factor pushing costs upward. The importance of this demographic change will increase after the year 2000 as baby-boomers reach retirement age, an age at which per capita health outlays rise sharply.

These considerations lead us to the conclusion that there will be no easy way to control the spiraling costs of the health care system. But others disagree. They argue that a variety of strategies, with managed care as the centerpiece, can solve the cost problem painlessly.

Enhanced competition, second opinions, the closing of under-utilized hospitals, managed care and other techniques have all been touted at one time or another as potential saviors of the system. But none have achieved, or can be expected to achieve, this goal.

The major cost containment efforts of American insurers and businesses currently focus on managed care as a means of eliminating inappropriate services—in particular, unnecessary hospitalizations. Such efforts to cut back inappropriate services make medical and economic sense. They effected a dramatic reduction of some 20% of hospital days between 1981 and 1988, and in 1984 and 1985 were responsible for an annual cutback of 6% to 8%. For those two years the real rate of rise in costs slowed from more than 6% per year to 2% to 2.5%. Many observers concluded from this slowdown that the problem of rising medical costs were solved. Indeed, many employers and insurers assumed that the rapid rise in premiums was over.

Like calm in the eye of a hurricane, this respite was brief. Many who said the war on costs had been won failed to recognize that they had achieved only one-time reductions. Eventually, the underlying rise in costs driven by new technology, rising wages and the aging of the population reasserted itself. Thus, by 1988, when there was virtually no further cutback in days, real outlays rose by more than 7% despite the steady expansion of managed care.

What, then, are the prospects for managed care as a future cost containment strategy? The development and implementation of new practice guidelines could produce a further cutback in hospital days. If practice guidelines accomplish this goal (and how successful they will be remains quite uncertain), another brief respite from rising costs may occur. Forcing down the salaries of U.S. physicians, who are better paid relative to average earnings than are physicians in most other developed countries, may achieve additional savings. But the pressure on costs will remain.

Once the elimination of unnecessary care achieves further savings, we will again face the same cost spiral. Even under the optimistic assumption that another 20% of days can be saved between 1990 and 1995, we will soon run out of ways to painlessly offset the underlying rate of increase.

At that point the nation will have to decide between two alternatives. It can reap the full benefits available from the system and accept a continuous rise in the share of the gross national product devoted to health care. Or, if we wish to hold down the increase of health care costs, we will need to turn to non-price rationing as a control mechanism. If we do choose rationing as a solution, key questions will arise. Who decides which patient gets what kind of care? And what criteria will they use in making such decisions?

Implementing Rationing

The United States has had virtually no experience with non-price health care rationing. Great Britain, a country that spends only about two-fifths as much per person on medical care, has had much experience with health care rationing. Although the two countries differ in many ways, they also share important characteristics—in culture and social values, language, standards of medical education and medical competence. For this reason the British experience provides important insights into the problems we will face in dealing with denying beneficial services.

Perhaps the most striking feature of the British system is its seeming failure to allocate resources efficiently, that is, to apply them to their highest-valued uses. For example, many major teaching hospitals went for a decade or more without a single CT scanner while they spent much money on an expensive form of intravenous nutrition which commonly yields marginal benefits.

Our study indicated that social values override the concern for medical benefits per se. Age often determines who gets access to expensive care. If patients with kidney failure were 55 or older, they were rarely entered into chronic dialysis programs, even when they were otherwise highly suitable candidates. Only the recent advent of a less costly means of dialysis has given such patients readier access to treatment.

By contrast, diseases of the young, especially if the illness is readily visible, were treated aggressively. For example, treating hemophilia, a disease which costs about $25,000 per year per patient, continues despite severe budget constraints.

Other nonmedical factors also affect clinical decision-making. A dread disease such as cancer receives favored funding, whereas coronary artery disease is grossly underfunded. The distressing consequence is that many pain-ridden patients, for whom bypass surgery promises relief, receive surgery only after long delay, if at all. Similar social factors undoubtedly will play an important role in determining resource allocation in the United States.

Rationalizing Actions

In Great Britain, physicians bear the responsibility for determining who gets what care, as they almost certainly would for the entire U.S. population and as they already do for patients in HMOs. Meeting this responsibility runs counter to the fundamental ethic which demands that physicians press on, regardless of costs, until all possible medical benefits have been exhausted.

Physicians in Britain, caught between this commitment and the reality of resource limits, redefine criteria for treatment. Some patients are deemed "unsuitable" for a treatment that they would routinely receive in the United States and other more affluent countries. Pain must be more severe, the risk of death greater, before the British physician recommends an expensive treatment, such as hip replacement, coronary bypass graft or admission to an intensive care unit.

As one thoughtful doctor remarked, physicians in Britain spend much time finding reasons why they should not treat a patient and, as he put it, there are always some such reasons—medical, social or whatever. This process of rationing by rationalization allows physicians to strike a balance between standards of practice and available resources.

Lack of Public Outcry

The British public has accepted rationing with much less outcry than one would expect in the United States. They accept a badly underfunded system partly because the quality of care for most people in Britain was extremely low before the advent of the National Health Service. Thus, the improvement that has occurred over the last several decades, limited as it may be by U.S. standards, has been greeted with great enthusiasm by the bulk of the population. Indeed, pollsters report that the National Health Service stands second only to the monarchy as the most popular institution in Britain.

Part of the willingness of the average British citizen to put up with denial of many services stems from a continued acceptance of the physician as an authority figure. Told that chronic dialysis is not a suitable form of treatment for terminal kidney failure, the typical patient (and family) accepts the physician's judgment. Imposing rationing is much easier under these circumstances than it would be in a society where patients are often well-informed about medical options and not loathe to challenge the doctor or to seek other advice.

Paradoxically, the unwillingness of a small segment of British society to accept rationing also contributes to the system's viability. Affluent, aggressive and well-informed patients have developed effective ways to circumvent virtually all the constraints which most people face. Some 10% of the population has purchased private health insurance that provides prompt access to consultation with top-level specialists and to high-quality care in a private hospital.

However, private hospitals typically cannot handle problems other than elective surgery. Thus, for complex care even the affluent must turn to the National Health Service. But even in the NHS they usually manage to get the best the system has to offer by, for example, pressing their local practitioner, who acts as the gatekeeper for the system, to refer them for specialized care. Or, they may arrange for hospitalization in another region where there are few delays. By using these strategies, the professional and managerial classes are able to obtain from the NHS 40% more resources per episode of illness than do most other citizens.

A U.S. system of rationing would create barriers to such an uneven distribution of medical services. Because of close public scrutiny, the United States is likely to be far more egalitarian. But if an unregulated system is allowed to evolve, people with the resources undoubtedly will use them to free themselves from the constraints of rationing. If such regulation is imposed, the affluent will turn to facilities outside the United States. Almost certainly there will be much greater resistance to rationing than has arisen in Britain.

How It Will Happen

By the mid-1990s frustration with the present cost containment efforts will lead the president and Congress to modify health care financing. As indicated earlier, the savings achieved through elimination of useless care soon will disappear. At that point, continued efforts to control costs will yield little return unless beneficial care is curtailed. The key to effective limits, we suggest, will be hospital budget ceilings that allow annual increases only for inflation and a modest growth in real expenditures.

Under these circumstances, hospitals and their staffs must effectively use each scarce dollar. How to assure that they accomplish this end will be the major challenge to the health care system. To reach this goal it will be necessary , first, to develop a system for setting priorities that satisfies the demands of both equity and efficiency. A second difficult task will be to develop a system that effectively monitors performance but is, at the same time, relatively non-intrusive. Since we will need such a system soon, it is imperative that we begin its development now.

Health Care Rationing

MICHAEL REAGAN

What Does It Mean?

With health care expenditures in the United States running close to 12 percent of the gross national product, it is certainly not surprising that many are calling for strong cost-containment measures. One of the most frequently mentioned approaches is rationing, which is becoming almost identical in meaning with cost containment in general.

For example, a recent editorial in the *Los Angeles Times* stated that rationing "already is part of the American system for an increasing number of people"[1]; more generally, Berliner calls the word "rationing" "a generic term subsuming all measures for limiting utilization."[2]

Were this only a matter of terminology, it would not justify the space taken here, but it is not. The question of cost control in health care is high on the agendas of policy makers, and in policy-making disputes, words are powerful symbolic weapons.[3] As Stone writes, "The way in which we think about problems is extremely sensitive to the language used to describe them."[4]

Perspectives on Rationing

Philosophers, physicians, economists, and sociologists, as well as dictionaries, all provide pertinent definitions of rationing. The best starting point for discussion, however, is the book, published in 1984, that stimulated the application of concepts of rationing to health care: *The Painful Prescription: Rationing Hospital Care.*[5] In that book Aaron and Schwartz explicitly define rationing as meaning that "not all care expected to be beneficial is provided to all patients."

Hypothesizing a system of budgetary limits for hospitals similar to those in effect in Great Britain's National Health Service,

Aaron and Schwartz state that a consequence of accepting such limits would be that doctors would "persuade themselves that it is good medical practice to deny treatment to a patient who might benefit from it were it available." They go on to say that denying care that could produce some benefit means that "the value of care is being weighed against its costs, explicitly or implicitly." This statement, in turn, equates rationing with a currently fashionable decision rule[6] from economics: cost–benefit analysis. Under this rule, whether to provide care would be decided not simply by judging whether the care would be beneficial but whether its benefits would be greater than its costs—i.e., substituting economic for medical criteria.

Aaron and Schwartz's study is informative, insightful, and provocative. Their use of the term "rationing," however, is misleading, because it does not fit either of the word's two most commonly accepted senses—that reflected in dictionary definitions or, of greater importance for policy, that of the main American experience of rationing: rationing during World War II.

Common Meanings. Beginning with dictionary definitions, we find that an element of equity is often part of the usage of the term "rationing." Thus, *Webster's Third New International Dictionary*[7] says that to ration is "to distribute or divide (as commodities in short supply) in an equitable manner," and Baily[8] quotes the 1977 edition of *Webster's New Collegiate Dictionary* as stating that to ration "implies . . . , often, equal sharing . . . freely extended to scarce things made available either equally or equitably in accord with need."

Linking rationing with equity also conforms to the nation's experience with rationing during World War II. At the time, certain foods and industrial products were scarce. Rationing was what we did to distribute equitably such commodities as sugar, meat, and gasoline. In this context, rationing connotes "a national judgment that goods should be distributed according to collective standards of priority and fairness, rather than solely according to ability to pay."[9] By way of example, a C coupon on the windshield of one's automobile entitled one, as I recall, to a small amount of gasoline for personal use.

Two points are worth making explicit. First, rationing in this sense is not primarily a response to a money problem and, therefore, cannot be resolved by the price system. The shortages during the war were of real resources. Second, rationing in this model is a deliberate, conscious policy, chosen by representatives of the community at large for reasons of the public interest—not simply the financial strategy of an interested party.

The Perspective of Economics. In discussing rationing as a response to scarcity, the perspective of economics—sometimes defined as the study of allocating scarce resources—is clearly relevant. Sometimes economists use both "ration" and "allocate" to describe how scarce resources are distributed. More commonly, however, a distinction is made between the terms. In the ordinary workings of the market, "price allocation" describes how one person wants, can afford, and therefore "demands" a Mercedes or a BMW, for instance, whereas another is not "allocated" one of these vehicles because he or she lacks the money with which to register demand. "Rationing" is usually used to describe the administrative distribution of goods, outside the market, that have suddenly become physically scarce— or, in the case of products deemed essential for ordinary living, scarce at a socially acceptable price. Although such phrases as "rationing by price" or "rationing through the market"[10] are sometimes used, the meaning is clearer if we agree to use "price allocation" to describe the workings of the market system and reserve "rationing" for situations of deliberate sharing of a scarce commodity.

Health Care Perspectives. In the literature specifically addressed to problems of health care resources, there is a terminological parallel to the issue of rationing in a paper by Evans on the costs of technology, as a stimulant to the making of hard choices in health care.[11] Evans distinguishes allocation and rationing as "macro-level" and "micro-level" decisions about distribution, respectively. The proportions of the federal budget accounted for by Medicare, Medicaid, health care for veterans, health services for Indians, and public health programs represent allocations for health care, as opposed to the use of the same funds for defense, housing, or another program. A decision at this level does not involve which patient will get how much care (although it will probably have effects at that level). On the other hand, when two persons have end-stage renal disease, a decision that Patient A is to receive dialysis on the one machine available in a rural town, whereas Patient B will not receive dialysis, is rationing. It differentiates among individual patients. In Evans' conception, there is thus a distinction between allocation, which deals with patients in the aggregate, at the "macro" level, and rationing, which deals with patients as individuals, at the "micro" level. This argument can be compared with Mechanic's concepts of implicit and explicit rationing.[12,13]

The clearest illustration of allocation is a fixed budget for health care, as in Great Britain, where the budget for the National Health Service has come close to making up the nation's total expenditure for health care. An example of rationing—this time in the United States—is that of organs for transplantation. The shortage (reportedly 20 percent worse now than a couple of years ago[14]) of appropriate hearts, kidneys, and other organs from donors clearly necessitates choosing who among many eligible patients will receive transplants and who will not. That is rationing, both in the sense of sharing scarce resources and in the sense of attempting to apply criteria found equitable by consensus in making the choices among individual patients.

The notion of selecting some patients for treatment from a larger pool of eligible persons injects into the concept of rationing the element of comparison among persons. Thus, Strauss et al. describe the rationing of intensive care services as "apportioning their use equitably based on need . . . among individuals."[15] Stone provides another example in her discussion of illness certification in the workplace, a process in which physicians "weigh the relative merits of different patients' claims"[16] to help within financial limits set by governmental organizations.

Allocation and rationing come together in a way that may be superficially confusing. When the British restrict the number of dialysis machines or CAT scanners, that is an allocation—an earmarking of certain dollars for equipment to a particular medical use. Because the amount allocated pays for fewer such machines than would be needed to serve all the patients who might benefit from them, rationing is necessary—in the sense that physicians must make choices about which patients get the care or are assigned a high priority for receiving care. Although many discussions mix the two terms as elements of a single strategy, it is analytically useful to keep "allocation" and "rationing" distinct, because they involve distinguishable social processes with sharply differing effects on the ethical quandaries of individual doctors, and because they involve different decision makers.

The concept of rationing, then, can be summarized as a system of deliberate choices about the sharing of health care resources among persons (i.e., who gets what care, and in what order of priority) on grounds that go beyond an individual patient's clinically defined needs; the criteria specifically include both comparative medical need and social equity.

It is also important to define what rationing is not. First, it is not the same as simply reducing the volume of services,[17] either by "managed care" decisions or by denial of Medicare reimbursement for autologous bone marrow transplantation. Second, rationing is not a process of making choices by deduction from economic decision rules, such as cost–benefit analysis[18] or risk stratification.[19] Finally, it is not appropriate to apply the term "rationing," with its implications of community standards, to a situation—such as that encountered in the Medicaid program—in which a person's eligibility for medical care results from his or her fitting into a specific category, which is often a matter of chance.

Rationing and Cost Containment

It follows from this framework that rationing is not identical to cost containment. Rather, the relation between the two is one of means to an end, although the means is perhaps not necessary to reach the end in question, since many other approaches to cost containment that do not involve the restriction of useful care are actively being pursued.[20-33]

From a policy perspective, to accept a reduction in services for purely financial reasons, under the guise of rationing, would be to "blame the victim." To do so would place on the patient and his or her personal physician the entire burden of choice, for which all of us are collectively responsible through the political process. And to call what we are now doing rationing is to dignify what is really discrimination in access to health care services on the basis of income, and thereby to defuse criticism of this highly questionable practice.

References

1. Freudenheim M. Hospitals fault limit on heart drug funds. New York Times. March 31, 1988.
2. Berliner HS. Strategic factors in U.S. health care: human resources, capital, and technology. Boulder, Colo.: Westview Press, 1987.
3. Edelman M. The symbolic uses of politics. Urbana, Ill.: University of Illinois Press, 1964.
4. Stone DA. Policy paradox and political reason. Boston: Scott, Foresman, 1988:200.
5. Aaron HJ, Schwartz WB. The painful prescription: rationing hospital care. Washington, D.C.: Brookings Institution, 1984.
6. Lave LB. The strategy of social regulation: decision frameworks for policy. Washington, D.C.: Brookings Institution, 1981.
7. Webster's third new international dictionary. 3rd ed. Springfield, Mass.: Merriam-Webster, 1965.

8. Baily MA. "Rationing" and American health policy. J Health Polit Policy Law 1984; 9:489–501.
9. Rosenblatt RE. Rationing 'normal' health care: the hidden legal issues. Texas Law Rev 1981; 59:1401–20.
10. Fuchs VR. The "rationing" of medical care. N Engl J Med 1984; 311:1572–3.
11. Evans RW. Health care technology and the inevitability of resource allocation and rationing decisions. Part II. JAMA 1983; 249:2208–19.
12. Mechanic D. Future issues in health care: social policy and the rationing of medical services. New York: Free Press, 1979:95–6.
13. *Idem.* From advocacy to allocation: the evolving American health care system. New York: Free Press, 1986:64–6.
14. Kosterlitz J. Health focus. National Journal. February 27, 1988:563.
15. Strauss MJ, LoGerfo JP, Yeltatzie JA, Temkin N, Hudson LD. Rationing of intensive care unit services: an everyday occurrence. JAMA 1986; 255:1143–6.
16. Stone DA. Physicians as gatekeepers: illness certification as a rationing device. Public Policy 1979; 27:227–54.
17. Fuchs, VR. Has cost containment gone too far? Milbank Q 1986; 64:479–88.
18. Thurow LC. Learning to say "no." N Engl J Med 1984; 311:1569–72.
19. Knaus WA. Rationing, justice, and the American physician. JAMA 1986; 255:1176–7.
20. Eggers PW. Effect of transplantation on the Medicare end-stage renal disease program. N Engl J Med 1988; 318:223–9.
21. Kramon G. Bargaining on fee with a surgeon. New York Times. April 19, 1988.
22. Block JA, Regenstreif DI, Griner PF. A community hospital payment experiment outperforms national experience. JAMA 1987; 257:193–7.
23. Evans RG. Finding the levers, finding the courage: lessons from cost containment in North America. J Health Polit Policy Law 1986; 11:585–615.
24. Callahan D. Setting limits: medical goals in an aging society. New York: Simon & Schuster, 1987.
25. Scitovsky AA, Capron AM. Medical care at the end of life: the interaction of economics and ethics. Annu Rev Public Health 1986; 7:59–75.
26. Marmor TR, Klein R. Cost vs. care: America's health care dilemma wrongly considered. Health Matrix 1986; 4:19–24.
27. Mushlin AI. The analysis of clinical practices: shedding light on cost containment opportunities in medicine. QRB 1985; 11:378–84.
28. Schwarz JS. The role of professional medical societies in reducing practice variations. Health Aff (Millwood) 1984; 3(2):90–101.
29. Wennberg JE. Dealing with medical practice variations: a proposal for action. Health Aff (Millwood) 1984:3(2); 6–32.
30. Eddy DM. Variations in physician practice: the role of uncertainty. Health Aff (Millwood) 1984; 3(2):74–89.

31. Caper P. The physician's role. In: McCardle FB, ed. The changing health care market. Washington, D.C.: Employee Benefit Research Institute, 1987.
32. Ellwood PM. Outcomes management: a technology of patient experience. N Engl J Med 1988; 318:1549–56.
33. Reinhardt UE. Resource allocation in health care: the allocation of lifestyles to providers. Milbank Q 1987; 65:153–76.

Access to Comprehensive Healthcare Must Be Basic Right for All U.S. Citizens

REV. JESSE L. JACKSON

To be a good and great nation—not just a strong nation—we must provide basic healthcare coverage to all Americans. Of the industrialized nations of the world, only the United States and South Africa do not have some form of national healthcare for all of their citizens.

Access to healthcare—both acute care and long-term care—must become a basic right in the United States. It is immoral that 37 million people, more than one third of them children, have no form of health insurance. It is immoral that 3 million families were refused medical care in 1985 because they could not pay for it. It is immoral that a child from a low-income family is twice as likely to die in the first year of life as a child from a higher-income family.

It is time to end the patchwork system of healthcare in America. No other nation spends so much on healthcare, yet gets so little in return. We need a new healthcare delivery system that guarantees cradle-to-grave protection.

The American public overwhelmingly wants universal and comprehensive healthcare. But the right to universal healthcare has been blocked by powerful insurance companies and hospital and medical lobbies that fear universal coverage would bring with it control of the huge profits they make from our illnesses. During the past two elections, political action committees representing physicians and the health insurance, drug and hospital equipment industries gave 14 times as much money to candidates running for federal office as the consumer or trade associations that favor national health coverage.

The healthcare industry's desire for high salaries for certain jobs and corporate profits that dwarf those of the service industry as a whole must not prevent people who need healthcare from getting it. It is time the United States joined the community of civilized nations by guaranteeing healthcare coverage for all Americans.

National healthcare. We need a national healthcare program that will build upon our current Medicare program and incorporate some changes:

> The program should be universal, covering not only the elderly but all U.S. citizens and residents.
>
> The program should be comprehensive, so that people can get all of the care they need, no matter what their income. For example, Medicare now leaves more than 50% of senior citizens' health costs uncovered. Senior citizens would be spared that expense under a comprehensive program.
>
> The program should be federally administered to ensure equal protection for everyone. It should be subsidized by health taxes and general revenues.
>
> All Americans should enjoy the freedom to choose their health-care providers.

Costs and Funding

Under a national health program, the total cost of healthcare would decline. This would occur in spite of universal coverage. How is this possible? First, comprehensive care emphasizes prevention, which means fewer illnesses. Second, greater public oversight minimizes unnecessary operations and treatment. Finally, the excessive profits made by insurers, equipment suppliers and many providers can be brought under control, and the high cost of advertising and much administrative overhead can be eliminated. Administrative costs for Medicare average 2% per year. On the other hand, 25% to 40% of private health insurance premiums pay for overhead costs. A national healthcare program can be funded with a combination of revenues similar to those funding healthcare now and still save us money.

Public, Private Sectors

Under a national healthcare program, the majority of healthcare institutions would continue to be in the private sector. Providers would contract with the federal government, with fees being federally regulated to ensure a reasonable return.

National healthcare would be more accountable to the public. State and local authorities would develop plans for the delivery of healthcare in their region to ensure that all people are provided for. The public would be better represented on the boards of health institutions to ensure that all members of the community have a voice in decisions about healthcare priorities.

With a universal and comprehensive program, national healthcare finally will become a basic right in the United States.

Why Transplants Don't Happen

JOEL L. SWERDLOW AND FRED H. CATE

Last year organ transplants saved or dramatically improved the lives of more than 13,000 Americans. Heart transplants alone saved 1,673 lives. But 1,600 people continue to wait for new hearts; almost a third of them have waited longer than six months. A third will die before they receive a heart. The situation is similar for other organs (kidneys, lungs, livers, pancreases) and tissues (bone, skin, corneas, ligaments, tendons, blood vessels, heart valves). Surgeons performed 8,886 kidney transplants in the United States last year. But more than 17,000 people continue to wait for kidneys. Thousands of patients face near-certain death unless they receive bone-marrow transplants. All the while, there are people living in America who could donate small amounts of their marrow and save them. These potential donors are never contacted, because no one knows who they are. Every year tens of thousands of life- enhancing or life-giving operations cannot be performed for lack of organs and tissues, and shortages of organs and tissues stymie research projects to fight fatal diseases.

These shortages need not exist. Almost 2.2 million people die every year in the United States. As many as 25,000 of those people would qualify medically as organ donors; fewer than 4,000 actually donate. The same shortage applies to tissues, which are used increasingly to restore sight and hearing, save cancerous limbs from amputation, and treat burn victims. Many of those 2.2 million people could donate valuable tissues; fewer than 45,000 people do so. According to Raymond Pollak, a transplant surgeon at the University of Illinois in Chicago, transplantation confronts a "shortage in the face of plenty."

A number of factors lie behind this dramatic and deadly shortfall. Even many of those in favor of the donation of organs and tissues find discussing their own death or that of a loved one difficult; often people simply fail to act on their desire to help others. Present law exacerbates the tendency to procrastinate by assuming that any given person wishes *not* to donate organs or tissues upon death, unless that person has indicated otherwise. A person may, for example, sign a donor card. Doctors and hospitals, however, fear professional criticism and lawsuits if they procure organs against the wishes of the next of kin, even if the deceased has indicated a desire to be a donor. A donor card is therefore useless unless the next of kin approve the donation. Under laws enacted in every state and the District of Columbia, a spouse or parent or adult child can approve the donation of a decedent's organs and tissues. But too few people discuss donation with their relatives, and following the death of a loved one the grieving next of kin rarely have donation on their minds. Many health-care workers often fail even to raise the possibility of donation with the next of kin, despite laws and regulations requiring them to do so.

The law also poses an obstacle by not clarifying who "owns" a donated organ or tissue. The California Supreme Court further confused the issue last July, when it ruled, in *Moore* v. *Regents of the University of California,* that whatever property interests John Moore at one time possessed in his spleen, there were "several reasons to doubt" whether he retained any ownership interest following its removal during surgery. The court held that on the other hand, if Moore's physicians failed to inform Moore that they were likely to profit from the use of tissue taken from his spleen, then they may have violated their professional obligations to their patient. (Cells from the spleen were used to produce the drug interferon and other lucrative products.) The *Moore* decision is not binding outside California. Moreover, it is not clear that the case relates to the ownership of organs and tissues donated after death, and no other court has yet addressed this issue.

Some scholars suggest that if officials treated human organs and tissues with the same respect they accord to real property, such as a television or a house (which the legal system acts immediately and forcefully to protect upon the death of the owner), a far greater supply of transplantable body parts would result. The state and the next of kin would respect the decedent's wish to donate organs and tissues, just as they respect the decedent's wishes regarding the disposition of other property. If the decedent had not communicated any decision about donation, the next of kin would be forced to confront the issue—along with issues about the disposition of the rest of the estate—and might better appreciate the value of organs and tissues.

Because there is no automatic transferal of property interests in organs and tissues upon death to patients on the waiting list, no one watches out for the interests of would-be recipients. And the fact that people die every day because our health-care system discards lifesaving organs arouses no comment.

A legal determination by Congress or the courts as to who owns donated organs and tissues—the potential recipient, the procurement organization, or a national network linking transplant centers—would help assure that the law protected those it now largely ignores.

Obtaining consent is only the first of the problems facing transplantation. Once consent is obtained, the organ or tissue must be removed, a recipient must be identified, the body part must be transported to that recipient (or, in some cases, processed for storage, which may last several years), and then it must be transplanted.

But the systems needed to provide rapid and efficient coordination are lacking. For instance, a federally funded computerized national registry and a variety of private registries compete to identify bone-marrow donors, who, like blood donors, are living. Patients in need of a transplant must pay to search the national registry, yet they may still miss the name of a potentially lifesaving donor who happens to be listed on a different registry. A young women in Denver recently mangled her arm in an automobile accident. An elbow taken from a cadaver and stored in a local bone bank made her whole again. Her surgeon told reporters that she was "lucky" that a bone her size had been available in Denver. Why did she have to rely on luck? A resident of Denver can get airplane or hotel reservations anywhere in the world in a matter of minutes. Physicians should be able to order a bone by computer from any city in the country.

Today different coordination mechanisms exist for organs and for tissues; different coordination mechanisms also exist for transplants and for body parts for research. All these systems have their problems, and cooperation among them is almost nonexistent.

The most elaborate system for coordinating supply and demand for organs is the Organ Procurement and Transplantation Network, which connects fifty-two organ-procurement organizations and 250 transplant centers twenty-four hours a day. This network is the result of a 1984 compromise between proponents of government coordination and Reagan Administration opponents of any federal involvement at all. As a result of the compromise, the transplant network enjoys a monopoly on coordination—but with respect only to organs, not to tissues or body parts for research. Even for this limited task the network is significantly underfunded. Its total annual budget, by law, may not exceed $2 million: the largest annual appropriation it has ever received was $1.5 million. Compared with other federally funded data bases—not to mention private networks for airline reservations and autoparts—this money is insignificant.

Some critics charge that the operator of the Organ Procurement and Transplantation Network—the United Network for Organ Sharing (UNOS), in Richmond, Virginia—does not run the network efficiently. Despite its statutory monopoly on information relating to organs available for transplant and people waiting for organs, UNOS has yet to provide patients, the public, and the medical profession with important data that would show differences in age, sex, race, and severity of illness among patients at all of the transplant centers.

More significant, critics have charged that UNOS has greatly exceeded its original statutory mandate and made fundamental policy decisions about who should have access to organs. For instance, UNOS has promulgated guidelines on how to weigh various criteria—such as length of time on the waiting list, medical necessity, and the location of the donated organ relative to that of the potential recipient—in determining who on the waiting list will have a chance to live and who will almost certainly die. Until recently federal law required that all transplant centers and organ-procurement organizations abide by those rules, even though UNOS is a private organization. A decision by the Department of Health and Human Services, however, now subjects UNOS rules to the department's approval.

James F. Blumstein, a professor at Vanderbilt University Law School, has observed that UNOS's evolution from a voluntary network into a "comprehensive, top-down, coercive" system runs counter to the trend in favor of competition and decentralization in other facets of health-care policy. Congress must decide whether to condone this development or to permit competition in organ procurement and supply. If Congress chooses in favor of centralization, it must determine whether to permit UNOS to engage in activities other than operating the network and whether to expand its mandate to include tissues and body parts for research. Congress will also have to consider how to ensure that the network has the resources necessary to fulfill its responsibilities.

The area of greatest growth in transplantation is not organs but tissues. A healthy donor can provide at least thirty kinds of tissue, many of which can be taken from the body fifteen or more hours after death. But without an equivalent, for tissue, of the Organ Procurement and Transplantation Network, half a dozen overlapping private national networks have emerged. Many tissue banks specialize in recovering only a single kind of tissue; others handle combinations such as skin and bone or corneas and bone.

An already confused situation is growing steadily more confused, because every organ donor is automatically a potential tissue donor. The federal government requires only that organ-procurement organizations cooperate with tissue banks. Some of these organizations are beginning to procure and distribute tissues in competition with existing tissue banks; others play favorites among competing tissue banks by notifying only one that a body will be available for tissue recovery once the organs have been removed. People involved in organ and tissue transplantation talk openly about "warfare."

One of the biggest battles is between the American Red Cross, which has started a national tissue service, and other procurement agencies and tissue banks. The Washington, D.C., chapter of the Red Cross recently tried to increase the fee that it charges for blood to any hospital that had not agreed to give tissue to the Red Cross, but then pulled back after the proposed contracts aroused concern in Congress. A 1984 federal statute prohibits the sale of human body parts but leaves tissue recovery and distribution largely unregulated. This absence of government regulation could easily lead to scandals down the road that would lessen the already pitiful donation rate; such scandals could focus, for example, on the absence of mandated safety standards or on possible abuse of the no-sale policy.

What happens to blood is instructive. In the United States virtually all blood comes from altruistic donors. Yet, according to a series of articles in *The Philadelphia Inquirer* last fall, blood banks, even nonprofit blood banks, buy and sell from one another more than a million pints of blood a year. The ultimate recipient of the blood could pay as much as $120 for a pint that was donated free of charge. This payment greatly exceeds the cost of processing and transporting the blood. From 1980 to 1988, according to the *Inquirer*, the Red Cross blood program generated profits of more than $300 million. Current statutes do not regulate the potential for excessive earnings among organizations that procure, process, and distribute organs and tissues. A fully utilized body generates a substantial amount of medical business—the cost of transplanting the heart, kidneys, lungs, liver, and pancreas alone can reach $1 million—and the money cannot be ignored. The law prohibits donors or their heirs from receiving money for lifesaving body parts. But the surgeon, the hospital, even the chaplain who advises the grieving next of kin to make the donation, are all paid for their services. Although no one argues against fair payment, it's very likely that people will be less willing to donate parts of their bodies if they know that others will profit exorbitantly from the use of those parts.

Human organs and tissues are also increasingly necessary to biomedical research. The use of animals in experiments has clear limitations, and even a seemingly useless object like a cancerous human organ can be vital to scientists. Researchers now generally obtain organs and tissues on a personal, informal basis, from patients undergoing surgery, from unclaimed bodies at morgues, from women giving birth, and through back-door arrangements with coroners.

The absence of a steady supply of human organs and tissues has frustrated countless research projects, many of them vital to battles against major diseases. For instance, the absence of a sufficient and steady supply of colons has slowed research on colon cancer. A committee of outside consultants commissioned by the National Institutes of Health recommended in 1987 that the "NIH should take a leadership role in the development of a communications network and information distribution database for human-tissue research." The NIH has taken steps, including partially funding the National Disease Research Interchange, which facilitates the recovery and distribution of donated human cells, tissues, and organs. But so far the NIH's response has not met the needs its own committee identified.

If cooperation and coordination are so obviously needed, why haven't they happened?

"In a system dependent on altruism," says Emanuel Thorne, an economist at Brooklyn College who is writing a book on the regulation of human organs and tissues, "organizations must be nonprofit. Were they profit-making, competition and takeovers might result in a rational system. However, because they're nonprofit, mergers and acquisitions can't take place through market mechanisms, but must occur through politics and persuasion, which can take a long time. Moreover, the desired outcome is not at all assured."

Other difficult issues demand attention. Good medicine requires uniform data collection and the pooling of donor registries. Transplantation is a worldwide phenomenon. Organs and tissues increasingly cross national borders, although safety standards and reimbursement procedures vary from country to country. We need rules covering international trade and exchange.

We also need to establish national safety and quality standards that guarantee the adequate testing of body parts for AIDS, hepatitis, and other infectious diseases. The Food and Drug Administration checks apples and aspirin but sets standards for only a few of the tissues and none of the organs that are transplanted directly from one body to another.

The cost of transplantation is another significant issue. According to UNOS, the average kidney transplant costs $25,000 to $30,000, a heart transplant $57,000 to $110,000, a liver transplant $135,000 to $230,000. (Pre- and post-transplant treatment, which can increase the cost significantly, have not been included in these estimates.) Permanent maintenance on immunosuppressive drugs may cost from $4,000 to $10,000 annually, and there will inevitably be fees for other medical care associated with the transplant. Transplantation, however, is often less costly than alternative treatments. For example, it costs more to keep a kidney patient on dialysis for a year than it does to buy a year's worth of post-transplant drugs. The Health Care Financing Administration estimates that a kidney transplant pays for itself in three or four years. Even allowing for such problems as the possible need for retransplantation, doubling the supply of kidneys could cut down on health-care costs by hundreds of millions of dollars.

Many transplant centers won't put a person on a waiting list for an organ unless that person can demonstrate the ability to pay for the transplant. Indeed, one of the most intractable problems for all of medicine pervades transplantation: the "green screen." Should anyone be denied a transplant for lack of the money? Many times access is denied for financial reasons, but not straightforwardly. For instance, in the case of bone-marrow transplantation, once the computer has identified potential matches, a patient may have to pay $175 to $600 to have each of them tested. Fees for the search and for subsequent laboratory work on donors also vary dramatically, and frequently exceed actual costs. Since insurance usually does not pay for testing anyone but the patient, families have had to mortgage homes or borrow from friends. When the money runs out, most marrow registries stop working. This situation persists even though, for some forms of leukemia, marrow transplantation may be less expensive than treatment with chemotherapy and/or radiation.

Roger Evans, of the Battelle-Seattle Research Center, calculates that 67 million people in the United States lack the insurance to cover the cost of a major organ transplant, such as that for a heart or lungs. They can donate organs and tissues but may be ineligible to receive them. This includes many residents of states such as Oregon and Wyoming, where Medicaid funding for major organ transplants is not available. "I do not believe you should ask anyone to participate as a donor when he can't participate as a recipient," says Terry Strom, an immunologist and professor of medicine at Harvard Medical School. "It becomes the rich buying health at the expense of the poor."

Notwithstanding such hard issues, the ultimate reason reality lags so far behind medical possibility is the lack of federal effort. The government has for too long resisted establishing and funding a national policy to encourage an adequate supply—and the efficient and equitable use—of donated organs and tissues. And the public remains largely uninformed. Surgeons, still pioneering new types of transplantation, have pressed for action. Families unwilling to accept that no more can be done to save loved ones have formed marrow registries, mounted their own organ-procurement efforts, and tried to attract public attention. Most have come to the exasperated conclusion that something better must be possible. It is. In ways never before imagined, we can transform death and pain into life and hope.

Questions

1. According to the arguments printed here, what are the major advantages and disadvantages of rationing or allocating health care?

2. Choose two or three points on which the arguments here disagree. Describe the disagreement and explain how you would resolve it.

Suggestions for Further Research

1. In 1990, Oregon began a new system of state health care allocation. Read about that system and summarize it.

2. How does a person get on the "list" to receive an organ transplant? Summarize the procedure, including the criteria for accepting or rejecting an applicant for a transplant.

3. Investigate the procedures for become an organ donor.

Suggestions for Writing

1. Select a single criterion, such as age or income, and argue that it should or should not be used in allocating health care.

2. Based on your reading and research, and any additional information you need to gather, write an argument in which you state and support a position for or against becoming an organ donor.

Reforming Education:

How Can the Schools Become Better?

Education has often been controversial in the United States, usually because someone thinks the schools are not doing their job. In recent years surveys have shown that students in U.S. schools do not perform as well in math, science, geography, and other subjects as students from other countries. Nearly everyone agrees that the education at all levels needs to be reformed and improved, but there is little agreement about what needs to be done or how to do it. The arguments in this section approach educational reform from a variety of perspectives. They propose small and large changes. They do not necessarily reach a consensus, or even identify common issues. Before you read the arguments, respond in writing to the following:

Preparing to Read

1. *How well has your education prepared you up to this point in your life? If you could change one thing about your pre-college education, what would it be and why?*
2. *What is the purpose of education? What do you expect it to do for individuals and for society?*

Cut Off from the New Reality

DAVID GELERNTER

New Haven, Conn. When The New York Times uses the term "operating system," it usually feels obliged to define it. Other newspapers do the same. They're not patronizing the readership. They're just facing facts. But suppose they felt the same way about "election" or "touchdown"?

"Operating system" is that kind of term. An operating system is a fundamental item in the world of software. If you don't know what one is, you're not going to learn on the basis of a single phrase, no matter how artfully crafted. And how likely are you to grasp the point of the news story when you literally don't know the first thing about the topic?

Whenever this newspaper defines operating system for you, it's assuming that you don't give a damn about technology. The topic finds most people bored and disengaged. They are diners at a high-tech feast, wolfing down the latest goodies without wasting a thought on the mere science going on in the kitchen. This rift between the patrons and the help is growing worse and getting dangerous.

For one, we're not getting the people we need. In 1991, A Department of Commerce report concluded that the U.S. "is in danger of being surpassed by the Japanese in 11 major 'emerging' areas of technology." Meanwhile, the number of computer science majors at American universities continued to drop, down by almost 25 percent since 1986. In 1990, the proportion of U.S. computer science doctorates awarded to non-U.S. citizens was 45 percent, up from 36 percent a decade earlier. Students at Yale are five times more likely to pursue law, business or finance than graduate school in science or technology.

In the technology community, we need people. Even more, we need engagement. Your reactions to our new ideas, your own new ideas in turn. It used to work like that. Technology would play a theme; urban planners, industrial designers, architects, painters, writers and random visionaries would respond. The 1939 New York World's Fair perfectly captured that vanished music. Today, silence. Plans for the U.S. pavilion at the 1992 World's Fair in Seville call for a limp bunch of geodesic domes.

Telecommunications and multimedia are stymied: great technology, but what to *do* with it? The newspaper industry withers slowly, refusing to face the electronic future creatively. A few sponsor database services; almost none shows interest in electronic editions. In the humanities, computers are ubiquitous, doing tired, primitive chores: creating and printing documents, once in a blue moon handling electronic mail. In commercial settings, desktop computers are routinely idle 98 percent of the time. No engagement.

In a recent issue of The New Republic, Martin Peretz wrote feelingly about our "drastic shortage of young scientists." But he's part of the problem, part of the intellectual establishment that regards science and technology as unfit topics for a real intellectual's attention. The last 28 issues of The New Republic published, on average, one-quarter of an article each on technology or science. The competition is a lot worse.

The feelings are mutual. Scientists and technologists are getting comfortable behind their wall, too. They do not solicit meddling by outsiders, whom they have always considered—they weren't going to tell you this, but since you insist—just the tiniest bit dim. Explaining research clearly to the nontechnical community is widely placed, in the pantheon of scientific duties, right up there in urgency and appeal with emptying the pencil sharpeners.

A leading electronics engineering magazine, IEEE Spectrum, publishes wistful musings about the fading of the "heroic image of the scientist"; young people in the field don't even realize that the public once found technology downright inspiring. In the 1950's, popular culture was a fantasy on technology themes: jet planes and atomic power, miracle fibers and electronic brains, the rockets and robots of the future. Remember?

The need for engagement will grow steadily more acute. Today's technology crisis is a slow boil. Tomorrow's will be an explosion. However large it looms today, technology is guaranteed to grow radically more important. We will stop looking at computers and start gazing through them. They will be our windows on the world, purveyors of repackaged reality. The images we know and deal with—of our businesses, hospitals, governments, communities—will be computer-generated.

But this "mirror reality" of the future is a score for many voices. The lay public has charge of the crucial parts dealing with political, esthetic and ethical issues. The technical stuff merely fills in the harmonics. This performance will transform the social world—

whether or not we bother to do it right. Repackaging reality is a big responsibility. Are you content to wash your hands of it? To leave it all to the computer sciencearchy?

Recently, technology issues have been shooting off like fireworks. You will find them at the heart of public policy disputes, major industry realignments, entire regional economies, progress in science and the threats and promises of a software-powered future. Meanwhile, of Stanford, Berkeley, Princeton, Harvard and Yale, exactly one requires a technology course of every student. Top U.S. universities were far more interested in debating "multiculturalism"—a masterful response to modern times. It has all the cogency of smashing Japanese cars with pickaxes.

Out of College, Out of Work

STEPHEN SHERRILL

One of the things my classmates and I were not told at our college graduation four years ago was what papers we would need for a visit to the unemployment office. Luckily, however, in addition to being told that we were the future, etc., we were told to always be prepared. Thus, when I made my first visit a few months ago, all of my papers were in order. I had suspected that getting "processed" would be time consuming, and I was right. But that was OK; I wanted it that way. Like graduation ceremonies and funeral services, applying for unemployment insurance is one of those lengthy rituals whose duration almost seems designed to make one sit and think. It's a valuable time to take stock.

What I was not prepared for was the TV crew facing me as I walked in. The "MacNeil/Lehrer" news team was doing a story on white-collar unemployment, and they had come to the right place. I had expected the office to be like a great mixing pool, like the Department of Motor Vehicles. But the people in the endless line ahead of me—with their trenchcoats and folded newspapers—looked like the same ones I used to fight with for a seat on the Wall Street-bound subway train every morning when we all had jobs. Like them, I did my indicted-mobster-leaving-the-courthouse imitation, evading the cameras as I inched ahead in line. After finally reaching the front, and giving the clerk evidence of the life and impending death of Wigwag magazine, where I was a writer, I was told to sit down in the next room and wait.

The next room looked exactly like a college classroom (when I squeezed into a seat I realized I'd forgotten how uncomfortable school desks are). Looking around me, I was struck by the number of people in the room who were, like me, twentysomething—not the middle-aged crowd I'd expected. But after giving it some thought, it made more sense. I knew that, along with seemingly every other industry, Wall Street and the big law firms were trimming down after the fat years of the '80s: last hired, first fired, sit down in the next room and wait. So here we were, members of the generation accused by our older siblings of being mercenary and venal, back in the classroom again, only this time having to raise our hands with questions like, "I didn't get the little pink form in my information booklet." Who among us would have guessed it in the heady days of 1986?

In truth, I was never that proud of my generation. I too had been scornful of those who happily graduated to fast, easy money. And although I had rejected that route myself, that suddenly seemed irrelevant. At this perverse reunion I found myself a kinship with my new daylong classmates, squirming in their desks around me, who had embraced the '80s. Most of these wunderkinder were now counting themselves lucky to have found their little pink forms.

Like most of them, my notions of college and post-college life were formed by watching the '60s generation. To be young, energetic and full of conviction seemed important and exciting. The world had listened to them and we looked forward to our turn. There were many of us who would have liked to help stop a war, disrupt political conventions, take over deans' offices or volunteer in the South for civil rights. We would have welcomed the chance for a few years of world-changing before settling down to more responsible (i.e. lucrative) activities, as so many of the thirtysomething crowd, now with kids and mortgages, had done.

Bicycle Messenger

But we had graduated into a different world—one so harsh and competitive that a *Republican* president would soon declare the need for something "kinder and gentler." AIDS, skyrocketing tuition, disappearing federal grants, the lack of so easy a common cause as peace and love (or hating hatred) and a dazzling job market offering salaries that when offered to people so young with four years of loan indebtedness, left virtually no other choices. We weren't in the '60s anymore—we never had been. Those who hadn't realized this by graduation quickly found out that student-loan officials don't grant deferments for time spent "finding" oneself.

When comparing themselves to us, members of the '60s generation, while using their own college years to rationalize their recent,
less than idealistic choices, imply that we younger "careerists"
didn't pay our dues before joining them in their 20th-story offices.
Ironically, though, depending on the severity of the recession, my
generation may ultimately come to resemble our grandparents'
generation more than the one we always wanted to be a part of.
When I talk to my friends about job prospects and we compare our
experiences at various unemployment offices (one ex-co-worker
had *two* camera crews to dodge) I wonder if we, like our grandparents in the '30s, will be permanently shaped by these few years.
Will we one day say, "Son, when I was your age, in the Great
White-Collar Depression, we didn't fool around after college. We
took whatever office-temp or bicycle messenger work we could get
and we were *grateful.*"

My name was soon called and, along with several others, I filed
into another classroom for a 90-minute lecture on how unemployment insurance works—sort of a "Principles of Bureaucracy 101."
The last item on my day's agenda was figuring out how to leave
while avoiding the only people in the room with jobs: the camera
crew. (I began to wonder if their eagerness was due to spending the
day with a bunch of former job-holders). When we all finally left the
office, most of us had been there for about 3 hours. But we were not
the irritated, impatient New York crowd one would expect—we had
lots of time on our hands and we were learning how to deal with
having even more. We were at last getting the long-awaited "year
off," albeit a crueler and less gentler version. Although we can't be
quite as free and easy as our counterparts were 20 years ago—we
have to mail in our coupons every week, and we've promised to
look for work—this may be the only chance for a coming of age my
generation will get.

How Not to Get Into College

WILLIAM R. DILL

For those who hope to be enrolled next year in one of America's
most selective undergraduate or professional schools, these are the
days of taking tests, seeking campus interviews, writing essays and
soliciting glowing references. This is the time ambitious applicants
suffer sleepless nights—and not necessarily to be sure of acceptance, but simply to get a chance to be *considered* for admission.

For those who make it, the agony is worth the effort: to be accepted to one of our best schools these days is to be virtually assured of graduating. As many as 90 percent of the students admitted to the top colleges and universities can make it all the way through. Because initial acceptance has become an almost automatic ticket for a degree, admission committees have become more important than faculty in deciding who goes though life with a Harvard or Wellesley B.A. or a Stanford M.B.A.

I have run the game myself as a business-school dean and a college president. I now believe that it's wrong to put such a tight tourniquet on numbers that top schools let in and to assume that such large percentages should graduate. In the name of fairness and opportunity, we need a different approach.

Our best schools should admit 25 to 50 percent more people than they expect to graduate, then tighten grading for the first half of their programs. Increase the risk of flunking out. Make true again the warning once given new students on many campuses: "Look to your right. Look to your left. Work hard. One of the three of you is not likely to make it to graduation."

Such a change moves toward honesty about admissions. The idea that elite schools now pick the best from their pools of candidates is a myth. The more qualified the pool, the more likely it is that many who are turned down are as good as or "better" than others who get in.

Studies on how the admission lottery is working are not reassuring. They show only modest power to predict an applicant's grades for even the first year after entry and almost no ability to identify who will stand out as scholars or leaders or contributors to society later in life. Whether dominated "by the numbers" of grades and test scores or "sensitive review" and interviews, admissions choices are more chance than science.

The game is expensive. Candidates invest heavily in both time and money to maximize chances of getting on sometimes 10 or more different prospect lists. They or their parents pay for campus visits, aptitude-test cram courses and application fees. They all assume that the longer a list is relative to planned enrollment, the greater an institution's "quality." Perversely, competitive efforts to increase reputations by inflating applicant lists also inflate tuition charges. Schools today spend hundreds, sometimes thousands of dollars on promotion and admission for every student enrolled.

When acceptance or denial has such deep consequences, controversies about admissions practices are bound to turn ugly. Does Berkeley unfairly limit admission of Asians? Does Georgetown's

Law School give undeserved breaks to blacks? Was the Washington Monthly magazine right to charge that worse concessions are made in the Ivy League to underqualified children of wealthy alumni than to minorities in the name of affirmative action?

'Weeding Out':

I am not advocating open admissions. Today's most sought-after schools would still be, relatively speaking, the hardest to get into. But they would improve access and opportunity by letting more good applicants prove their potential and by insuring that earned degrees reflect performance on campus, not anointment at time of admission. If some special concessions do get made to blacks, alumni or candidates from Nepal, reactions ought to be less heated since more candidates will get in and because everyone faces tough screening for a degree.

The changes will not come easily. In exchange for greater access to the toughest programs, applicants must accept larger risks of flunking out and finishing on another campus. Yes, students will face greater competitive pressures from their peers; but coping will prepare them more realistically for the "weeding out" experience that jobs and life hold in store after graduation.

Faculty, will have to apportion more of their teaching time to first-year classes. But for the kind of schools which should lead this change, taking in more from good pools of applicants should not make classes any less fun to teach. Grading papers will take more time, but we might see an end to grade inflation.

Students who do not "make the cut" need help to take failure in stride. Reaching, trying and not succeeding ought not to carry a stigma. Schools should improve arrangements and networks which already exist to counsel and to facilitate transfers to others campuses. If schools grade and counsel responsibly, society should restrain temptations to make flunking out another occasion for legal challenges.

America is meant to be a place where one can scramble for chances to perform and make performance count. Yet today, the pursuit of reputations for "quality" puts too much weight on the credentials of students coming in, not educational accomplishments on campus. Our best colleges and universities risk being more gatekeepers than facilitators of social mobility. A move to give more candidates a chance to show their potential and to test all admitted students more rigorously on eligibility for degrees would be a step forward toward both quality and opportunity.

School Reform Fraud (Cont'd)

ROBERT J. SAMUELSON

Our "school reform" debate is a farce and, if you doubt it, you ought to follow Congress's current effort to renew the Higher Education Act. It provides roughly $20 billion annually in grants and government-guaranteed loans to 6 million college and other postsecondary students. It is the largest federal education program—and also the most wasteful.

There are virtually no educational standards. Students who meet the various income tests can get federal aid as long as they have a high-school degree. In practice, this standard is meaningless, because high-school graduation requirements are so low. Less than half of high-school seniors attain adequate reading skills for their grade. The obvious way to toughen college entrance requirements is (as I have argued before) to insist that students wanting federal aid pass a test showing they can do college work.

Why should this be controversial? It makes no sense for taxpayers to send unprepared students to college. It isn't even fair to many students, who become saddled with huge loans that they can't repay. The default rate now runs at about 20 percent. In fiscal 1991, defaults cost the government $3.6 billion. But political interest in tougher standards is zilch. The new law almost certainly won't include any. "We had 447 witnesses," said Thomas Wolanin, staff director of the subcommittee that rewrote the Higher Ed Act. "Nobody advocated new academic requirements."

Gulp. This truly captures the hypocrisy of the school-reform debate. The commitment to "excellence" exists in speeches, not in practice. President Bush and his secretary of education, Lamar Alexander, propose sweeping goals for the year 2000: for example, American students should be first in the world in science and math (in a comparison of 14-year-olds in 17 countries, U.S. students tied for third to last place). But a more mundane goal—setting standards for federal college aid—is beneath them.

Congress is of the same mind. It won't offend college-bound students or their parents. Going to college has become a mass-market entitlement. The idea that it should be earned by academic achievement has vanished. More than 90 percent of our 3,400 colleges and universities essentially have "open admissions": anyone with the money and a high-school diploma can go.

Colleges and universities don't want higher standards. Student enrollment might decline and, with it, tuition payments. Most colleges seek to maximize revenues, not education. If this judgment seems harsh, listen to Robert Atwell, head of the American Council on Education, the trade group of colleges and universities. A few years ago the ACE staff proposed a test colleges might give to their students. The idea was to set standards—not for admissions, but for a baccalaureate degree.

"We no longer know what a baccalaureate degree means," says Atwell. "Shouldn't there be some underlying level of achievement [for] all degree holders?" Swell idea. It bombed. "The constituency I serve—college and university presidents—simply wanted no part of it," he recalls.

You might think that, given the prominence of the school-reform issue, the press would pay a lot of attention to the Higher Education Act and its implications. Nope. Education reporters generally don't connect colleges to "the school problem." Their indifference, I suspect, reflects a belief in three pervasive myths.

Myth One: Higher education is the last bastion of U.S. 'excellence.' A delusion. Higher education consists of more than elite institutions and, as a whole, it's hugely wasteful. More than half of college students never get degrees. Put another way, dropout rates for colleges are much higher than for high schools. Graduate quality is also slipping. Since the 1960s, scores on more than half of 24 graduate-school admissions tests have dropped. One reason is that research-conscious professors pay less attention to teaching.

Myth Two: Colleges are the victims of lousy public schools. This is half backwards. Lax college admissions standards are a major cause of lax high-school standards. The two feed on each other. Many students work only as hard as they must to get into college—and that isn't hard. Typically, high-school seniors do less than an hour of daily homework.

Myth Three: The nation's 'school problem' is mainly the inadequate education of the poor and minorities. Again, half true. Not even elite students have escaped the effects of low standards and "dumbed down" courses. Since 1972, the share of students scoring above 600 on the verbal Scholastic Aptitude Test (on a scale of 200 to 800) has dropped from 11 to about 7 percent, reports historian Daniel J. Singal in the November issue of The Atlantic Monthly. He documents how students at top colleges are less well prepared than they were 20 years ago. He quotes one historian at Berkeley with students who can't distinguish between the American Revolution and the Civil War.

I *guarantee* that a meaningful test requirement for federal college aid—we could argue over details—would improve matters quickly. Nearly half of all college students now receive some sort of federal aid. A standard for them would become a standard for most incoming students. In high school, college-bound students would work harder. Average students would do better, putting more pressure on the best students. Public schools would face demands from parents—to strengthen courses, monitor teacher competence—to ensure that their children passed the test. Fewer students might go to college, but those who did would be better prepared. Graduation rates would rise. Waste would fall. We could use the savings to do a better job educating those who don't go to college.

In practical terms, college aid is the federal government's only weapon to force schools and students to change. The weapon has been sheathed, not because reform is undoable but because the problem is misunderstood and there's no political will. Congress will merely expand these programs. Grants and guaranteed loans will increase. Colleges and universities will approve. They want more money and less accountability.

The results are predictable. Greater aid will abet tuition increases and foster continued loan defaults. There will be no improvement in standards, no reduction in waste. This is not educational policy. It's educational pork barrel.

Children Need Calculators: It's Not Cheating

KENNETH M. HOFFMAN

Forget the upcoming presidential election or Madonna's new movie. The next time you want to pick an argument with someone, tell them our country's school children should be using pocket calculators more often to learn mathematics.

I've said so to people I've met on airplanes and at parties, and they often look at me like I'm crazy. "If children use calculators in class," they sputter, "how will they learn the multiplication tables?" Or, "Students will know how to push the buttons but won't understand the underlying mathematics." Then they tell me about the time they went to the store when the cash register wasn't working and the teenage cashier didn't know how to make change.

The very idea of using calculators in classrooms hits a vital nerve in many Americans. They view it as cheating and fear that our already dismal level of mathematics performance will worsen.

As one who has spent a lifetime teaching mathematics, I disagree profoundly with these criticisms. There is no evidence that the average young cashier today is any worse at arithmetic than teenagers were 50 years ago, although the growth of the service sector does make their inadequacies more obvious. Teenagers of the past depended on a pad and pencil instead of on a cash register. In practical terms, what's the difference?

The real problem with calculators, I think, is that many Americans view mathematics as something painful that youngsters must study because it's good for them. If Mom and Dad spent countless hours doing long division problems, then, by God, Jason and Kimberly can, too. Such attitudes explain why our students perform so miserably. They have been led to view math moralistically rather than as a liberating tool for understanding the world. Mathematics is seen as a test not only of brains but of character, of whether someone has the grit to calculate problems day after day, year after year. No wonder people hate it.

Calculators can change this equation. Students still must master the basic skills, but now they can escape the drudgery of endless repetition and do new and exciting things. Elementary school students, for instance, can use calculators and other tools to explore subjects reserved for higher grades, such as geometry.

Suppose youngsters spent as much time learning about volume and area, by pouring liquids from one container to another, as they now devote to long division. They could discover that a cylinder holds enough liquid to fill three cones with the same base and height as the cylinder. They'd find that three spheres hold just enough liquid to fill two cylinders that have the same radius as the spheres and a height equal to the spheres' diameter. Centuries ago, Archimedes said these relationships are among the most profound truths of nature. Why shouldn't our students have the chance to discover them as well?

Similarly, children should be using blocks and tiles to learn that doubling the sides of a square results in an area four times as great. For older children using calculators, it then is a short step to learn about fractals, chaos, and other topics that go far beyond the clerk-training curriculum now in place.

Young children can learn about statistics by measuring the heights of their classmates. A teacher then can guide them to consider ways of determining the center. Is it the average of the heights, the height in the middle, or the height that occurs most frequently? Calculators make it possible to assess these possibilities quickly, keeping student focused on the big picture.

Contrary to many people's assumptions, mathematics is not an unchanging body of facts and procedures. It is the language of science, and it evolves continually. When chalkboards were introduced in schools many years ago, some teachers feared children would lose the ability to write. Modern worries about calculators are likely to prove similarly groundless.

Technology is not a panacea, as many school systems have learned with computer-based learning materials and other reputed innovations. Dedicated teachers and sound pedagogy remain essential. Yet, used appropriately, calculators can make the job easier, and we should not fear them. They give students what their parents lacked: time and freedom to become better problem-solvers and to discover the beauty of mathematics.

Colleges Must Prepare the Next Generation of Public Intellectuals

HARVEY J. KAYE

Editorials and commentaries from the political left, right, and center seem to agree on at least one point—that a crisis exists in the way we determine the collective priorities and policies that make up our public culture. Commentators decry the fact that only 50 per cent of the American electorate vote in Presidential elections. They lament the low quality of public debate and the lack of new answers and formulas to address the social problems, economic difficulties, and moral dilemmas that we confront. They acknowledge that our foremost public institutions—from political parties, labor unions, and corporations to public-interest lobbying movements—are failing to produce the kinds of discussion that ought to characterize a great liberal-democratic nation.

There is little agreement, however, on how to revitalize public debate in the United States. Some observers call for teaching students about traditional values; others for teaching critical-thinking skills. Still others focus on reforming such parts of the political system as campaign finance and the primary-election caucuses.

I would argue that America's colleges and universities can be an important part of the solution—but not in the way many people think. Institutions of higher education cannot stand in for enfeebled social institutions and organizations, nor provide a specific program or ideology to rescue society. There is no more consensus on how to reform society within academe than without, nor should there be. Commentators such as Russell Jacoby, Christopher Lasch, and Norman Birnbaum have challenged scholars to become "public intellectuals," speaking on public issues to a wide audience outside academe, but that alone will not fill the void in public debate. I challenge my colleagues to teach our *students* to become the next generation of public intellectuals.

I would argue that along with transmitting the skills, knowledge, and commitment to critical thinking that, at least in principle, have long characterized our academic disciplines, we ought to be cultivating in our students the perspectives and practices that will enable them to practice social and political criticism in their daily lives.

This is no simple project. For a start, it means revising or expanding our conceptions of knowledge and its purposes. Our foremost intellectual traditions in the humanities and the natural and social sciences have long stressed "objectivity," usually defined as, at the least, a willingness to examine an issue from different perspectives and recognize that our personal assumptions do not always hold up to investigation. Although objectivity recently has been besieged within the academy by proponents of "relativism," who hold that "truth" is merely a matter of perspective, I believe it remains a most worthy and necessary ideal. But unfortunately, over time *objectivity* has become confused with *neutrality*, the assumption that we should not make value judgments and, most especially, not in a public and committed fashion. It is this stance that has strongly contributed to the withdrawal of intellectuals from public debate.

I would insist that even as we impress upon our students the value of objectivity *and* its limits, we must reject the spurious equation of objectivity with neutrality; we must encourage students to apply their scholarly skills, knowledge, and insights to analyzing public issues. We might call this the *democratic* conception of learning, the goal of which is developing citizens not only capable of choosing among the alternatives provided by civic and political leaders, but also themselves capable of formulating alternative choices. I have in mind that decidedly democratic vision of education in which the student is seen, in the words of the Italian political theorist Antonio Gramsci, "as a person capable of thinking, studying, and ruling—or controlling those who rule."

Stated in the most preliminary and practical terms, we ought to assign exercises that require students to think and write not for us alone but also for the wider campus and, even better, for audiences locally and nationally. These assignments might take the form of articles, essays, or op-ed pieces. Indeed, in these years in which so many of use are attempting to institute "writing-across-the-curriculum programs," why shouldn't we organize other courses specially intended to develop the art of writing social, cultural, and political criticism?

In these courses students might begin by exploring the careers and works of American public intellectuals such as Thomas Paine, Frederick Douglass, Charles and Mary Beard, Margaret Mead, and C. Wright Mills. Students would come to appreciate the personal and social costs of engaging in public debate, as well as alternative ways of meeting the challenge. Moreover, such biographical studies would acquaint students with the rich variety of intellectual and political traditions upon which they might draw in formulating their own social criticisms. They could go on to debate both issues already present in the public media and concerns they believe ought to be debated; then they could develop their own perspectives on these questions in papers submitted both to the instructor and to a newspaper or other popular periodical.

The classroom experience itself should be organized as much as possible in the manner of an editorial board or workshop, including open consideration and criticism of each student's writing—not to secure consensus on the ideas expressed but, rather, to sharpen the words and arguments. Admittedly, this type of pedagogy is already under way in various quarters—for example, in journalism and composition courses. However, it has not been widely applied in social-science courses, and particularly not to the teaching of social and cultural criticism explicitly directed to an audience outside academe. Indeed, asking students to take stands on issues of pressing social concern has generally been considered a violation of academic neutrality and hence illegitimate in the humanities and social sciences.

In 1989, I taught a course such as I am proposing as an experiment. Titled "History, Politics, and Criticism," it ranks among the most successful teaching experiences I have had, and beginning next semester I will offer it regularly. The class consists of lots of reading, writing, and talking—all in preparation for writing a 1,000-word opinion piece to be submitted to a popular newspaper. In the coming semester the syllabus will begin with works dealing with being a social critic: Michael Walzer's *Interpretation and Social Criticism* and *The Company of Critics* and selections from Russell Jacoby's *The Last Intellectuals*. We will then move on to works representing conservative criticism (for example, Robert Nisbet's *The Present Age*), neo-conservative criticism (Peter Berger's *The Capitalist Revolution*), liberal criticisms (Walter Russell Mead's *Mortal Splendor*), and social-democratic criticism (Barbara Ehrenreich's *The Fear of Falling*.) Along the way we will also consider articles from national and local magazines and newspapers. The last time I taught this course it was limited to 10 students; next time, I have negotiated a 20-student limit.

If the last time is any indication, the experience will be emotionally demanding of students *and* teacher alike, requiring persistent questions, negotiating, and thinking aloud. Nevertheless, it was thrilling to see our language, ideas, and arguments take finer and firmer shape after apparent demolitions and disasters. The issues and grievances that students addressed included educational vouchers, The Iran-contragate trials, the practices of temporary employment agencies, threatened changes in welfare programs, and the political potential of youth culture. Most of the students had articles on these topics published in campus, city, and regional newspapers.

It was fascinating and encouraging to see the degree to which students, in one semester, learned to harness knowledge and discipline intellect without giving up passion, thereby enhancing their capacities to capture the imaginations of others. For their part, students were pleased to see their thoughts published and to sense an active connection to public debate when they received responses to their articles. I am not suggesting that such teaching should inculcate a particular critical perspective. (Indeed, although I consider myself a socialist and radical democrat, I most enjoy the times when my students and I study the writings of conservative and neo-conservative thinkers, for they are, unfortunately, all too often better composed, however mistaken, than are ours on the left!)

Nor should such courses be conceived of as scarifying the pursuit of "knowledge" in favor of simply voicing one's opinion. It is important to stress to students that they must ground their arguments in history and evidence. Moreover, training in the practice of "criticism" should not be restricted to students in the humanities and social sciences. Surely, in the light of the technological possibilities and environmental challenges before us, it is imperative that such skills and orientations also be possessed by students majoring in the sciences.

The attempt to develop a new generation of public intellectuals is very much in the spirit of our best academic traditions. As Benjamin Barber, a political scientist at Rutgers University, recently observed about the links between the university upheavals of the 60's and classical pedagogical practice: "All education is and ought to be radical—a reminder of the past, a challenge to the present, and a prod to the future."

Harvey J. Kaye is Ben and Joyce Rosenberg. Professor of Social Change and Development at the University of Wisconsin at Green Bay.

Tune In, Turn Off, Drop Out

JOHN S. RIGDEN AND SHEILA TOBIAS

Every year at a typical large state university as many as 3,000 students enroll in introductory chemistry courses. Crowding into lecture halls and sometimes even into adjoining rooms outfitted with closed-circuit television are premedical students, agriculture majors and budding engineers, all there to fulfill a requirement for their specialties. But elbow to elbow with them are students who are in it for the chemistry. Attracted to the subject in high school or simply curious, they enroll as a possible first step to a chemistry major.

On the first day of class there is excitement in the air. And why not? Here is a chance for profound insight into the workings of the everyday world, for a grand, synthetic story of burning and decay; breathing and photosynthesis; the complexities of the atmosphere, the oceans and the soil; and, of course, the properties of millions of everyday and exotic materials; fuels and flame retardants, foods and poisons, bleaches and dyes, perfumes and deodorants and ultimately the stuff of life. Certainly there is also trepidation in the hall, for by reputation the subject will be hard. But for many students the anticipated intellectual mastery and the control of powerful laboratory tools will be rewards enough for their efforts.

The scene now shifts forward in time. Three years have passed, and the students are still at the university, as seniors. But most of them—even the ones who are intelligent and highly motivated—have left the crowded chemistry courses for other fields. Chemistry is so populous at the introductory level that some instructors are responsible for sections of 250 students each. In contrast, advanced chemistry classes are made up of merely a handful of students. Fewer than one out of fifty in beginning chemistry complete the major.

A similar pattern is repeated in other introductory science courses at the college level. Every year nearly half a million students leave high school planning to concentrate in science or engineering in college. And every year only 200,000 students, or 40 percent of the science-oriented high school graduates, complete one of those majors. Although it is true that many high school students are not being attracted to science in college, perhaps more ominous is that the majority of those who reach college hoping to do science end up changing their minds.

Some observers think such numbers presage a shortfall of scientists. The proportion of science majors who go on to earn doctorates has traditionally been small. The annual crop of 200,000 graduates yields about 10,000 PhD's—too few in some views to sustain the technological base of the U.S. economy. Foreign graduate students are filling the places vacated by American students, but there is no guarantee they will stay in the United States instead of taking their skills back home.

Whether a shortfall of scientists will develop, though, depends on several elusive factors: the vagaries of the economy, the rate at which scientists retire or otherwise leave the profession and the future level of spending for military research and development, which consumes much scientific talent. What is beyond doubt is that the drain of students from science drags down the country's level of scientific literacy, however that rather slippery term may be defined. Insofar as students quit science because of poor grades or boredom, their exodus also risks creating a voting public that will be uncomfortable with science or even hostile to it. Concern about diminishing enrollment takes many forms, but at bottom the message is this: too few Americans are studying too little science.

One set of solutions, much discussed these days, would encourage more youngsters to enter the science pipeline. Better science teaching in elementary and secondary schools might produce more students able and willing to begin college science majors. But finding common solutions for the multitude of school programs around the country is a daunting challenge. And high schools, for all their failings, deliver more than twice as many science-oriented students to college as complete a science major. A more direct approach is to focus on introductory college science, where the hemorrhaging of would-be science students is most severe. Indeed, given the nature of the great majority of introductory science courses for undergraduates, there is no guarantee that a more powerful pump at one end of the pipeline would have a proportional effect on the trickle emerging at the other end.

It is usually assumed that students who leave the study of science in college have simply been weeded out because they are not intelligent in science. Certainly many who abandon science are better off in other disciplines. But what about those who start off with both a taste for science and the necessary aptitude but choose, after a semester or two, not to go on? College science programs should struggle to keep those able students as well as to make converts of the ones who enroll because of curiosity or the requirements of another major. Doubtless, pre-college science education needs attention. So does the support of science graduates: it is critical that prospective students be able to look forward to employment and grants at the end of their formal scientific education. But the introductory college science course presents a clear and urgent target for reform.

What goes wrong in introductory science? How can one improve the chances of retaining able students who are not yet deeply committed to science? To answer these questions, one of us (Tobias) did a series of studies focusing on students' experiences in physics and chemistry courses. The studies sought testimony about the failings of the courses from learners themselves.

College students, concerned about grades and careers and being short on time for reflection, might not be ideal observers of their courses and classmates. Instead, surrogate learners—faculty and graduate students in fields other than science—were recruited and placed in college science courses. In preliminary studies, at Indiana University at Bloomington and the University of Chicago, nonscience faculty members observed course segments. In a later, more extensive study, supported by the Research Corporation in Tucson, Arizona, seven stand-ins, among them a professor of classics and graduate students in literature and philosophy, enrolled in basic physics and chemistry courses at the Universities of Arizona and of Nebraska at Lincoln.

The participants kept up with homework and took the quizzes and midterm examinations. Throughout each course they kept journals in which they recorded their observations about the lectures, the work and their fellow students. At the end of the study, instead of taking the final examination, they wrote reports reflecting on the course as a whole, the culture of the classroom and their own attitudes about studying science.

In many ways the surrogates were good representatives of the many potential scientists who slip through the sieve of introductory courses. All were confident in their abilities and eager for intellectual rewards. Most had strong grounding in science and mathematics from high school, and many had considered science before settling on other fields. All were eager to reacquaint themselves with science. Yet most of them came away with serious reservations about the atmosphere of the classes, the teaching methods and the course structure.

To judge by the comments in their journals and final reports, these learners would not have stayed with science even if they had not already been committed to other careers. Yet their difficulties represented not a failure of intellect (most of them did well on the tests) but a failure of fit. Science as it was presented in their courses did not yield the intellectual rewards they hoped for.

The classroom atmosphere, for one, tended to dampen any spirit of intellectual adventure. The rapid pace of the courses, the large class size and the machine-graded examinations fostered the erroneous impression that science is authoritarian. As one participant wrote, the effect is to discourage beginners from thinking they can "interact creatively with the material." Midway through his chemistry course the classics professor wrote:

> The instructor's approach, probably set by department policy, was to recapitulate the textbook and work sample problems. . . . It was difficult to sit there for an hour of this without participating. And participation was definitely not encouraged.

The result, witnessed by many of the observers, is that students become "incredibly passive" in science lectures.

Outside the lecture hall there was little community among the students, little discussion or collaboration. Grades were the major topic of conversation. Typically, students in introductory science courses are graded on a curve, which permits only a fixed proportion of the class to receive top grades. On the one hand, this grading scheme led to a sense of helplessness. One learner wrote, "The message . . . seems to be that no matter how hard you work—so long as everyone else works as hard or has more talent or experience—you *cannot* improve your grade." On the other hand, the limited number of high grades promotes intense competition, which the learners found destructive: "Suddenly your classmates are your enemies."

The lectures offered few intellectual rewards to compensate for these rigors. The surrogates reported that instructors were reluctant to present the intellectual or historical background of the material they taught. Students never got what one of them called the big picture. In physics courses the amazing idea that "sitting at rest on a front porch" can be equated with "flying through the troposphere at 600 miles an hour"—the basic concept of inertia, which eluded the best minds for more than 2,000 years—was routinely presented as a codified law, with little or no discussion.

"I found myself craving some theory," a graduate student in anthropology reported of introductory chemistry, "some discussion of how the laws of nature were developed, rather than just being presented with the finished product." The classicist studying chemistry experienced a similar frustration. After some weeks, he noted that the class had spent more time on Avogadro's number than on Avogadro's insight that equal volumes of different gases contain equal numbers of molecules. He wanted to know "more of the background of Dalton's laws in ancient atomic theory and of the work done on gas laws during the 18th century." Instead the professor kept "working problems hour after uncomfortable hour."

The relentless problem solving frustrated many of the participants. Many of them realized they were learning techniques that belong in any scientist's toolbox. But almost without exception they found basic physical science to be characterized by a "tyranny of technique." "Simply by intuition," wrote one learner, "I know physics, and more generally science, to involve creativity and finesse; but [this professor] makes it into a craft, like cooking, where if someone follows the recipe, he or she will do well."

Even when instructors tried to step outside this arid regimen, they often undermined their own efforts. Some of them, learners reported, did present and expand on the concepts underlying the problem-solving techniques. One course even took a historical approach to Newtonian mechanics, describing Newton's rivalry with Descartes and the theological background of his laws of motion. But because none of this material ever appeared in homework assignments or was tested in examinations, students ignored these excursions. The professor was disappointed, but one of the participants observed perceptively:

> The way an instructor operationalizes the goals for his course is not simply to speak them or put them in a handout, but to incorporate them into his exams. While [the professor] was talking concepts, his exams were testing numerical solutions. And he probably never realized what the students knew very well, namely that the "concepts" and the "history" didn't really count.

In addition to longing for intellectual content, the surrogate students complained of what one of them called the missing overview. After a group of nonscience professors sat in on a basic physics course on waves in elastic media, one of them wrote:

> It seemed to me during these lectures that I lacked any framework of prior knowledge, experience or intuition that could have helped me order the information. . . . I had no way of telling what was important and what was not. I had difficulty distinguishing between what I was supposed to be learning and what was being communicated merely for the purpose of illustration or analogy.

A graduate student in creative writing, taking part in a course on Newtonian mechanics, was even more explicit:

> I never really knew where we were heading or how much . . . we had already covered. Each topic the professor discusses feels like it's being pulled out of a hat. So the general feeling I was left with was that physics was endless, that there would always be one more complex way of describing motion. . . . Why, I wanted to

know, did we begin by studying only the idealized motion of particles in straight lines? What about the other kinds of motion?

The content of the course was presented piecemeal, class by class, according to a logic internal to the subject but never articulated by the instructor. A concept was developed one day because it would be needed two weeks later. The instructor knew this; the students, as our observers reported, did not. In a physics course, for example, the transition from Newtonian dynamics to the work-energy theorem is a natural one for the professor; for the students it is a trip from one conceptual galaxy to another, a trip devoid of motivation and understanding.

The surrogate students were mature, interested and capable—everything a science instructor could wish. Yet their experiences in science were uniformly negative. How could this happen in courses that should introduce students to the beauty and power of science?

In a mature science such as physics or chemistry the conversation between the scientist and nature is a grand dialogue, leading to surprises, new mysteries, insights and syntheses. The terms of the dialogue change continually, as discovery modified theory and theory suggests new routes for investigation. Science thrives on this dynamism, and for scientists it is a source of exhilaration. Contrast it with the rendition of science presented to students in introductory courses. There science appears static and dull. Analytical techniques that equip scientists to probe the universe are treated as ends in themselves—a hallowed body of knowledge that must be absorbed.

To some extent, of course, such an approach is implied by the nature of science. The knowledge that defines the content of basic courses is often centuries old, far removed from the dynamism that disturbs the sleep of contemporary scientists. And beginning students are not ready to take part in the dialogue of science. The freshman in introductory English and the graduate student in a literature seminar each can interpret a sonnet; they just do so at different levels of sophistication. Science, in contrast, is regarded as a vertical subject: finger exercises must come before music. As a professor of chemistry put it, the material "is dull to learn, and it is dull to teach. Unfortunately, it is the basic nuts and bolts stuff that must be mastered before anything useful can be accomplished." How are students to master this material? In quantitative sciences such as physics and chemistry the answer is clear: solve problems—lots of problems.

Even when instructors realize how uninviting the courses can be, many of them view their students' discouragement as a necessary evil. The true converts to science, they believe, will not be deterred, and introductory science is no place for making new ones. Many instructors view it as a training ground for those with a long-standing commitment to science. One professor wrote, "I assume that students in [my course] are preprofessionals who have already decided on a career in science and are in class to learn problem-solving techniques that will be required of them in their careers."

Some studies suggest that most scientists in the current generation discovered their calling very early, well before any college science course could influence them. But that finding can just as well be interpreted as showing that the colleges are losing many, if not most, of the students who might be attracted to science if college courses were more appealing. Undoubtedly there is a core of committed young people who are unshaken by classroom competition, relentless problem solving and the neglect of intellectual context. To capture the others, we need something better. Introductory science could—and should—become the best advertisement for the discipline.

Science instructors should begin by rooting out their own prejudices: Students who leave science, even the ones who leave with poor records, are not necessarily poor academic material. Understanding is not a function of cognition alone—of the "higher-order thinking" instructors value—and passivity is not merely an expression of poor motivation. A desire to understand is fueled by confidence that one *can* understand; apathy, as Che Guevara said in another context, is the "revolt of the powerless."

There are obvious ways of giving students a sense of greater power over their subject. Classes should be smaller, less competitive and more reliant on discussion. Science departments should conduct exit interviews of students leaving the major—in effect transforming the studies discussed here into an ongoing project. Professors should consider adding lessons on intellectual history, and examinations should test the additional material.

But improving the classroom climate and tinkering with course content will not be enough. Introductory physics or chemistry will always be time-consuming and sometimes counterintuitive and frustrating—the toughest course of the year for many students. "To some extent," one auditor wrote, "science is hard simply because it is hard." But the testimony of surrogate learners suggests it becomes still harder when the subject is atomized, presented one law or technique at a time with no sense of narrative. Course structure too needs attention.

Students who see their subject assembled one concept at a time cannot know where each piece fits into the larger whole. Instructors must find ways of giving students an early glimpse of where the class is going and why. Basic science must become a rigorous adventure instead of a catechism.

A Dismal Report Card

BARBARA KANTROWITZ AND PAT WINGERT

How bad are eighth graders' math skills? So bad that half are scoring just above the proficiency level expected of fifth-grade students. Even the best students did miserably; at the top-scoring schools, the average was well below grade level. Hardly any students have the background to go beyond simple computation; most of these kids can add but they have serious trouble thinking through simple problems. These grim statistics, released last week in the first large-scale state-by-state study of math achievement, prompted Education Secretary Lamar Alexander to declare a math emergency in the nation's schools. "None of the states are cutting it," he said. "This is an alarm bell that should ring all night throughout this country."

What's really frightening about these results is that the alarm has been ringing since the 1983 publication of "A Nation at Risk," the federally sponsored study that highlighted vast problems in the public schools. Yet despite years of talk about reform—and genuine efforts at change in a few places—American students are still not making the grade and remain behind their counterparts in other industrialized nations.

Many mainstream educators already agree that American math instruction needs a drastic overhaul, with more emphasis on group problem-solving and creative thinking rather than repetitive drills. But local schools continue to resist these prescriptions. "It's like we have a cure for polio, but we're not giving the inoculation," said Bill Honig, California's superintendent of schools. Fewer than a third of the students surveyed regularly spent time in small-group work and the vast majority had never done mathematics projects or written reports on math. And most math classes are still mired in the Victorian age, eschewing the use of calculators and computers. About a third of the students had never used a calculator in math class and two thirds had never used a computer. Educators say too many children are wasting time practicing adding, subtracting, multiplying and dividing when they could be moving on to more interesting and challenging math.

The math study, part of the National Assessment of Educational Progress (commonly called the Nation's Report Card), was administered last year to a representative sampling of 126,000 students in public and private schools. Students in three grades—4, 8, and 12—were tested. The eighth-grade results have attracted the most attention because the scores were broken down by state for the first time since the inception of the test in 1973. State politicians originally lobbied Congress to forbid the release of this kind of detail, because they feared a backlash from outraged voters. Thirty-seven states, along with the Virgin Islands, Guam and the District of Columbia, finally agreed to participate. The 13 states that refused cited various reasons, most often a lack of funds. Participation cost each state $100,000.

Most educators predicted a poor showing on the math test, but the final tally was worse than expected. "Don't let the fascination with 'which state did better than which state' blind you to the state of the forest," says Chester E. Finn Jr., author of "We Must Take Charge: Our Schools and Our Future" and a leading advocate of national testing. "The forest did dismally." Even in the top states— North Dakota, Montana and Iowa—only a tiny minority of eighth graders scored above their grade level. The lowest scoring eighth graders could only do second-grade work. Says Finn: "We are on various positions on the cellar stairs."

Analysts emphasized that the math problem is nationwide. Only 14 percent of eighth graders scores at the seventh-grade level or above—and that includes students in well-regarded, wealthy suburban systems. The study showed that only 1 percent of the eighth-grade students in one state, Virginia, were ready for calculus.

Money alone doesn't seem to be the answer. Finn notes that the highest-ranking state, North Dakota, is 32nd in terms of per-pupil spending, while the District of Columbia, which spends the most per student, is second to last. There is even compelling evidence that the longer kids stay in school, the farther they fall behind expected achievement. For example, the majority of fourth graders (72 percent) tested at or above the third-grade level, and 11 percent scored at or above the fifth-grade level. But by the time students reach the end of high school, many have fallen far, far behind. Only 46 percent of 12th graders can do seventh-grade work and only 5 percent can do precalculus work.

Instead of responding with defensive criticism, most educators seemed to welcome the test as a cleareyed look at the status quo— and an opportunity to start over. "We've all been led to believe that we were above average," said Francie Alexander, California's associate superintendent of schools. "These results should take care of that myth." Some potential criticism may have been defused by the structure of the test, which reflects the most current thinking on what an exam should contain. The questions were designed to evaluate problem-solving ability, not just mere computational skills; in fact, every student had a calculator at his side. The only other available state-by-state comparisons are college boards like the SAT and the ACT, but those are only for students going on to college—a self-selected group. The national math test is a random sampling of all kinds of students taking the same test at the same time.

Almost immediately after the results were announced, schools began announcing blueprints for change. In California (ranked in the bottom third), officials said they would revamp their junior-high-school curriculum by stressing real-life problem solving, use of calculators and computers, and writing about mathematics. Honig said the program will begin in 100 schools in the fall, and branch out from there as textbooks are ordered and teachers are retrained to use new techniques and curriculum.

While these changes may help, other data gleaned from the study indicates that curriculum reform by itself won't cure everything. A range of factors, from income level to television habits to parents' marital status, were linked with performance. Alexander called this the "91 percent factor," referring to the 91 percent of students' time that is spent outside school. "The only ones who can do something about these results are first, the students, then, their parents, the schools and the communities," he said.

Students with higher scores tended to have parents with some education beyond high school and were more likely to live with both their parents. These students also reported doing more homework, missing less school and watching fewer hours of television than students who had lower scores. Across the country, eighth graders watched at least three hours of television a day, but in the lowest-scoring schools, such as the District of Columbia, students said they watched six or more hours per day. Eighth graders in private and parochial schools had slightly higher scores than public-school students although the difference was reduced by grade 12.

Not surprisingly, Asian-Americans did best overall, with scores in all age groups significantly higher than any other racial or ethnic group. However, Hawaii, the state with the highest proportion of Asian-Americans (67 percent) was one of the poorest-scoring states. One possible explanation: Hawaii's Asian-Americans include many who have been in this country for generations. This may indicate that assimilated Asian-Americans perform just like other Americans. The results showed no difference between the performance levels of girls and boys in grades four and eight; however, in the 12th grade, boys did better than girls—suggesting that cultural pressures don't kick in until high school.

While the task of overhauling math instruction may seem monumental, educators say it is urgent—and essential—if the nation is to compete in a global economy. "Until recently, the public was perfectly happy with students who could do the basics of adding and subtracting," says Shirley Hill, chairman of the National Research Council's Mathematical Sciences Education Board. "Now we realize how much more students need to know, and people are going to be upset that they don't know it." In most of the rest of the world, adding and subtracting are considered merely steps in mathematical mastery, just as spelling and grammar are the building blocks of literacy. Many so-called reforms are standard procedure in other countries. Honig says that in Japan, students routinely talk and write about math, and work with real-life examples.

In this country, teachers say they're most optimistic about the performance of children in the early grades, where reforms are more widespread. Young kids are used to hands-on mathematical-learning tools, such as blocks, puzzles and games, that make numbers relevant and fun. Today's first and second graders are on the cutting edge, says Iris Carle, president of the National Council of Teachers of Mathematics. "Soon these young children will be coming into the middle schools," she says, "and they will force change because of their personal experience with critical thinking and application of real-life math skills."

Is that just wishful thinking? Since 1973, the results on the national math tests have shown a steady record of disgraceful performance. This time we know which states are the worst; before this we knew only that something was terribly wrong. The nation is still at risk and time is running out.

Questions

1. What are the admissions standards at the school you attend? In a small group, discuss whether (based on your own experience) those requirements should be changed to make them easier or more difficult. Try to reach a general agreement in your group about the standards you would use and why you believe they would be best for your school.

2. What is the most exciting or rewarding educational experience you have had (in or out of school)? Describe it, and then explain how that kind of excitement could be transferred to other parts of your education.

Suggestions for Further Research

1. Survey a group of students on your campus to determine whether they are satisfied with the education they are receiving, and what changes they would make in either the school or themselves. Summarize the results of your survey.

2. Much has been said about declining standardized test scores among high school and college students in the United States. Use standard periodical indexes and other sources (e.g., look for materials published by the companies that make the tests) to find out what the test scores indicate and whether the decline is something to be concerned about. Write a summary of the information you find.

Suggestions for Writing

1. Propose a single change that you would make in your education (past or present, high school or college). Describe the existing or original situation and your change, and argue that your proposal would result in an improvement.

2. Sometimes arguing for change is easier than arguing for the status quo. Choose some aspect of education that you are familiar with (or that is important to you) and argue that it should *not* be changed, that it is fine the way it is.

CLASSIC ARGUMENTS

The arguments that follow are classic in the sense that they have all been important in their own time and have also influenced what later generations thought about the same issues. But, in addition to being important historically, each is also an example of effective argument about a complicated and important issue.

The Seneca Falls Declaration

ELIZABETH CADY STANTON

Elizabeth Cady Stanton (1815–1902) was one of the earliest advocates of women's rights in the United States. In 1848, she helped organize the first women's rights convention in the United States, at Seneca Falls, New York. With her guidance, and using Jefferson's Declaration of Independence as a model, the convention produced the following declaration of women's rights.

When, in the course of human events, it becomes necessary for one portion of the family of man to assume among the people of the earth a position different from that which they have hitherto occupied, but one to which the laws of nature and of nature's God entitle them, a decent respect to the opinions of mankind requires that they should declare the causes that impel them to such a course.

We hold these truths to be self-evident: that all men and women are created equal; that they are endowed by their Creator with certain inalienable rights; that among these are life, liberty, and the pursuit of happiness; that to secure these rights governments are instituted, deriving their just powers from the consent of the governed. Whenever any form of government becomes destructive of these ends, it is the right of those who suffer from it to refuse allegiance to it, and to insist upon the institution of a new government, laying its foundation on such principles, and organizing its powers in such form, as to them shall seem most likely to effect their safety and happiness. Prudence, indeed, will dictate that governments long established should not be changed for light and transient causes; and accordingly all experience hath shown that mankind are more disposed to suffer, while evils are sufferable, than to right themselves by abolishing the forms to which they were accustomed. But when a long train of abuses and usurpations, pursuing invariably the same object evinces a design to reduce them under absolute despotism, it is their duty to throw off such government, and to provide new guards for their future security. Such has been the patient sufferance of the women under this government, and such is now the necessity which constrains them to demand the equal station to which they are entitled.

The history of mankind is a series of repeated injuries and usurpations on the part of man toward woman, having in direct object the establishment of an absolute tyranny over her. To prove this, let facts be submitted to a candid world.

He has never permitted her to exercise her inalienable right to the elective franchise.

He has compelled her to submit to laws, in the formation of which she had no voice.

He has withheld from her rights which are given to the most ignorant and degraded men—both natives and foreigners.

Having deprived her of this first right of a citizen, the elective franchise, thereby leaving her without representation in the halls of legislation, he has oppressed her on all sides.

He has made her, if married, in the eye of the law, civilly dead.

He has taken from her all right in property, even to the wages she earns.

He has made her, morally, an irresponsible being, as she can commit many crimes with impunity, provided they be done in the presence of her husband. In the covenant of marriage, she is compelled to promise obedience to her husband, he becoming, to all intents and purposes, her master—the law giving him power to deprive her of her liberty, and to administer chastisement.

He has so framed the laws of divorce, as to what shall be the proper causes, and in case of separation, to whom the guardianship of the children shall be given, as to be wholly regardless of the happiness of women—the law, in all cases, going upon a false supposition of the supremacy of man, and giving all power into his hands.

After depriving her of all rights as a married woman, if single, and the owner of property, he has taxed her to support a government which recognizes her only when her property can be made profitable to it.

He has monopolized nearly all the profitable employments, and from those she is permitted to follow, she receives but a scanty remuneration. He closes against her all the avenues to wealth and distinction which he considers most honorable to himself. As a teacher of theology, medicine, or law, she is not known.

He has denied her the facilities for obtaining a thorough education, all colleges being closed against her.

He allows her in Church, as well as State, but a subordinate position, claiming Apostolic authority for her exclusion from the ministry, and, with some exceptions, from any public participation in the affairs of the Church.

He has created a false public sentiment by giving to the world a different code of morals for men and women, by which moral delinquencies which exclude women from society, are not only tolerated, but deemed of little account in man.

He has usurped the prerogative of Jehovah himself, claiming it as his right to assign for her a sphere of action, when that belongs to her conscience and to her God.

He has endeavored, in every way that he could, to destroy her confidence in her own powers, to lessen her self-respect, and to make her willing to lead a dependent and abject life.

Now, in view of this entire disenfranchisement of one-half the people of this country, their social and religious degradation—in view of the unjust laws above mentioned, and because women do feel themselves aggrieved, oppressed, and fraudulently deprived of their most sacred rights, we insist that they have immediate admission to all the rights and privileges which belong to them as citizens of the United States.

In entering upon the great work before us, we anticipate no small amount of misconception, misrepresentation, and ridicule; but we shall use every instrumentality within our power to effect our object. We shall employ agents, circulate tracts, petition the State and National legislatures, and endeavor to enlist the pulpit and the press in our behalf. We hope this Convention will be followed by a series of Conventions embracing every part of the country.

Resolutions

Whereas, the great precept of nature is conceded to be, that "man shall pursue his own true and substantial happiness." Blackstone in his Commentaries remarks, that this law of Nature being coeval with mankind, and dictated by God himself, is of course superior in obligation to any other. It is binding over all the globe, in all countries and at all times; no human laws are of any validity if contrary to this, and such of them as are valid, derive all their force, and all their validity, and all their authority, mediately and immediately, from this original; therefore,

Resolved, That such laws as conflict, in any way, with the true and substantial happiness of woman, are contrary to the great precept of nature and of no validity, for this is "superior in obligation to any other."

Resolved, That all laws which prevent woman from occupying such a station in society as her conscience shall dictate, or which place her in a position inferior to that of man, are contrary to the great precept of nature, and therefore of no force or authority.

Resolved, That woman is man's equal—was intended to be so by the Creator, and the highest good of the race demands that she should be recognized as such.

Resolved, That the women of this country ought to be enlightened in regard to the laws under which they live, that they may no longer publish their degradation by declaring themselves satisfied with their present position, nor their ignorance, by asserting that they have all the rights they want.

Resolved, That inasmuch as man, while claiming for himself intellectual superiority, does accord to woman moral superiority, it is pre-eminently his duty to encourage her to speak and teach, as she has an opportunity, in all religious assemblies.

Resolved, That the same amount of virtue, delicacy, and refinement of behavior that is required of woman in the social state, should also be required of man, and the same transgressions should be visited with equal severity on both man and woman.

Resolved, That the objection of indelicacy and impropriety, which is so often brought against woman when she addresses a public audience, comes with a very ill-grace from those who encourage, by their attendance, her appearance on the stage, in the concert, or in feats of the circus.

Resolved, That woman has too long rested satisfied in the circumscribed limits that corrupt customs and a perverted application of the Scriptures have marked out for her, and that it is time she should move in the enlarged sphere which her great Creator has assigned her.

Resolved, That it is the duty of the women of this country to secure to themselves their sacred right to the elective franchise.

Resolved, That the equality of human rights results necessarily from the fact of the identity of the race in capabilities and responsibilities.

Resolved, therefore, That, being invested by the Creator with the same capabilities, and the same consciousness of responsibility for their exercise, it is demonstrably the right and duty of woman, equally with man, to promote every righteous cause by every righteous means; and especially in regard to the great subjects of morals and religion, it is self-evidently her right to participate with her brother in teaching them, both in private and in public, by writing and by speaking, by any instrumentalities proper to be used, and in any assemblies proper to be held; and this being a self-evident truth growing out of the divinely implanted principles of human nature, any custom or authority adverse to it, whether modern or wearing the hoary sanction of antiquity, is to be regarded as a self-evident falsehood, and at war with mankind.

[At the last session Lucretia Mott offered and spoke to the following resolution:]

Resolved, That the speedy success of our cause depends upon the zealous and untiring efforts of both men and women, for the overthrow of the monopoly of the pulpit, and for the securing to woman an equal participation with men in the various trades, professions, and commerce.

Questions and Activities

1. Summarize Stanton's argument, including her position and the support she provides. What values does she invoke to justify her statements about how women ought to be treated?

2. Choose one of the "repeated injuries and usurpations" that Stanton insists men have inflicted on women. Research the present situation of this injury. For example, what are the rights of married women, especially in relation to their husbands. Using your research as a foundation, write an argument in which you urge necessary changes in present-day practices.

A Vindication of the Rights of Women

MARY WOLLSTONECRAFT

Mary Wollstonecraft, an Englishwoman of Irish descent, lived from 1759 to 1797. She worked as a nanny in England, was an eyewitness to the French Revolution, and belonged to a group of radical writers that included Thomas Paine, who later became famous in the American colonies. She wrote "A Vindication of the Rights of Women" in 1792. Her daughter, Mary, wrote Frankenstein.

Men complain, and with reason, of the follies and caprices of our sex, when they do not keenly satirize our headstrong passions and groveling vices. Behold, I should answer, the natural effect of ignorance! The mind will ever be unstable that has only prejudices to rest on, and the current will run with destructive fury when there are no barriers to break its force. Women are told from their infancy, and taught by the example of their mothers, that a little knowledge of human weakness, justly termed cunning, softness of temper, *outward* obedience, and a scrupulous attention to a puerile kind of propriety, will obtain for them the protection of man; and should they be beautiful, everything else is needless, for, at least, twenty years of their lives. . . .

How grossly do they insult us who thus advise us only to render ourselves gentle, domestic brutes! For instance, the winning softness so warmly, and frequently, recommended, that governs by obeying. What childish expressions, and how insignificant is the being—can it be an immortal one? who will condescend to govern by such sinister methods! . . .

I may be accused of arrogance; still I must declare what I firmly believe, that all the writers who have written on the subject of female education and manners from Rousseau to Dr. Gregory, have contributed to render women more artificial, weak characters, than they would otherwise have been; and, consequently, more useless members of society. I might have expressed this conviction in a lower key; but I am afraid it would have been the whine of affectation, and not the faithful expression of my feelings, of the clear result, which experience and reflection have led me to draw. . . [I]n the works of the authors I have just alluded to . . . my objection extends to the whole purport of those books, which tend, in my opinion, to degrade one half of the human species, and render women pleasing at the expense of every solid virtue.

Though, to reason on Rousseau's ground, if man did attain a degree of perfection of mind when his body arrived at maturity, it might be proper, in order to make a man and his wife *one,* that she should rely entirely on his understanding; and the graceful ivy, clasping the oak that supported it, would form a whole in which strength and beauty would be equally conspicuous. But, alas! husbands, as well as their helpmates, are often only overgrown children; nay, thanks to early debauchery, scarcely men in their outward form—and if the blind lead the blind, one need not come from heaven to tell us the consequence. . . .

Rousseau declares that a woman should never, for a moment, feel herself independent, that she should be governed by fear to exercise her *natural* cunning, and made a coquettish slave in order to render her a more alluring object of desire, a *sweeter* companion to man, whenever he chooses to relax himself. He carries the arguments, which he pretends to draw from the indications of nature, still further, and insinuates that truth and fortitude, the corner stones of all human virtue, should be cultivated with certain restrictions, because, with respect to the female character, obedience is the grand lesson which ought to be impressed with unrelenting rigour.

What nonsense! when will a great man arise with sufficient strength of mind to puff away the fumes which pride and sensuality have spread over the subject! If women are by nature inferior to men, their virtues must be the same in quality, if not in degree, or virtue is a relative idea; consequently, their conduct should be founded on the same principles, and have the same aim.

Connected with man as daughters, wives, and mothers, their moral character may be estimated by their manner of fulfilling those simple duties; but the end, the grand end of their exertions should be to unfold their own faculties and acquire the dignity of conscious virtue. They may try to render their road pleasant; but ought never to forget, in common with man, that life yields not the felicity which can satisfy an immortal soul. I do not mean to insinuate that either sex should be so lost in abstract reflections or distant views, as to forget the affections and duties that lie before them, and are, in truth, the means appointed to produce the fruit of life; on the contrary, I would warmly recommend them, even while I assert, that they afford most satisfaction when they are considered in their true, sober light.

Probably the prevailing opinion, that woman was created for man, may have taken its rise from Moses's poetical story; yet, as very few, it is presumed, who have bestowed any serious thought on the subject, ever supposed that Eve was, literally speaking, one of Adam's ribs, the deduction must be allowed to fall to the ground; or, only be so far admitted as it proves that man, from the remotest antiquity, found it convenient to exert his strength to subjugate his companion, and his invention to show that she ought to have her neck bent under the yoke, because the whole creation was only created for his convenience or pleasure. . . .

To speak disrespectfully of love is, I know, high treason against sentiment and fine feelings; but I wish to speak the simple language of truth, and rather to address the head than the heart. To endeavor to reason love out of the world, would be to out Quixote Cervantes, and equally offend against common sense; but an endeavour to restrain this tumultuous passion, and to prove that it should not be allowed to dethrone superior powers, or to usurp the sceptre which the understanding should ever coolly wield, appears less wild.

Youth is the season for love in both sexes; but in those days of thoughtless enjoyment provision should be made for the more important years of life, when reflection takes place of sensation. But Rousseau, and most of the male writers who have followed his steps, have warmly inculcated that the whole tendency of female education ought to be directed to one point:—to render them pleasing.

Let me reason with the supporters of this opinion who have any knowledge of human nature, do they imagine that marriage can eradicate the habitude of life? The woman who has only been taught to please will soon find that her charms are oblique sun-beams, and that they cannot have much effect on her husband's heart when they are seen every day, when the summer is passed and gone. Will she then have sufficient native energy to look into herself for comfort, and cultivate her dormant faculties? or, is it not more rational to expect that she will try to please other men; and, in the emotions raised by the expectation of new conquests, en-deavor to forget the mortification her love or pride has received? When the husband ceases to be a lover—and the time will inevita-bly come, her desire of pleasing will then grow languid, or become a spring of bitterness; and love, perhaps the most evanescent of all passions, gives place to jealousy or vanity.

I now speak of women who are restrained by principle or prejudice; such women, though they would shrink from an in-trigue with real abhorrence, yet, nevertheless, wish to be con-vinced by the homage of gallantry that they are cruelly neglected by their husbands; or, days and weeks are spent in dreaming of the happiness enjoyed by congenial souls till their health is under-mined and their spirits broken by discontent. How then can the great art of pleasing be such a necessary study? it is only useful to a mistress; the chaste wife, and serious mother, should only con-sider her power to please as the polish of her virtues, and the affection of her husband as one of the comforts that render her task less difficult and her life happier. But, whether she be loved or neglected, her first wish should be to make herself respectable, and not to rely for all her happiness on a being subject to like infirmities with herself.

The worthy Dr. Gregory fell into a similar error. I respect his heart; but entirely disapprove of his celebrated Legacy to his Daughters. . . .

Dr. Gregory . . . actually recommends dissimulation, and ad-vises an innocent girl to give the lie to her feelings, and not dance with spirit, when gaiety of heart would make her feet eloquent without making her gestures immodest. In the name of truth and common sense, why should not one woman acknowledge that she can take more exercise than another? or, in other words, that she has a sound constitution; and why, to damp innocent vivacity, is she darkly to be told that men will draw conclusions which she little thinks of?—Let the libertine draw what inference he pleases; but, I hope, that no sensible mother will restrain the natural frank-ness of youth by instilling such indecent cautions. . . .

Of the same complexion is Dr. Gregory's advice respecting delicacy of sentiment, which he advises a woman not to acquire, if she have determined to marry. . . .

If all the faculties of woman's mind are only to be cultivated as they respect her dependence on man; if, when a husband be obtained, she have arrived at her goal, and meanly proud rests satisfied with such a paltry crown, let her grovel contentedly, scarcely raised by her employments above the animal kingdom; but, if, struggling for the prize of her high calling, she look beyond the present scene, let her cultivate her understanding without stopping to consider what character the husband may have whom she is destined to marry. Let her only determine, without being too anxious about present happiness, to acquire the qualities that ennoble a rational being, and a rough inelegant husband may shock her taste without destroying her peace of mind. She will not model her soul to suit the frailties of her companion, but to bear with them: his character may be a trial, but not an impediment to virtue. . . .

That a proper education; or, to speak with more precision, a well stored mind, would enable a woman to support a single life with dignity, I grant; but that she should avoid cultivating her taste, lest her husband should occasionally shock it, is quitting a substance for a shadow. To say the truth, I do not know of what use is an improved taste, if the individual be not rendered more independent of the casualties of life; if new sources of enjoyment, only dependent on the solitary operations of the mind, are not opened. . . .

The question is, whether it procures most pain or pleasure? The answer will decide the propriety of Dr. Gregory's advice, and show how absurd and tyrannic it is thus to lay down a system of slavery; or to attempt to educate moral beings by any other rules than those deduced from pure reason, which apply to the whole species.

Gentleness of manners, forbearance and long-suffering, are such amiable God-like qualities. . . . but what a different aspect it assumes when [gentleness] is the submissive demeanour of dependence, the support of weakness that loves, because it wants protection; and is forbearing, because it must silently endure injuries; smiling under the lash at which it dare not snarl. . . .

How women are to exist in that state where there is to be neither marrying or giving in marriage, we are not told. For though moralists have agreed that the tenor of life seems to prove that *man* is prepared by various circumstances for a future state, they constantly concur in advising *woman* only to provide for the present. Gentleness, docility, and a spaniel-like affection are, on this ground, consistently recommended as the cardinal virtues of the sex; and, disregarding the arbitrary economy of nature, one writer has declared that it is masculine for a woman to be melancholy. She was created to be the toy of man, his rattle, and it must jingle in his ears whenever, dismissing reason, he chooses to be amused. . . .

If . . . [women] be really capable of acting like rational creatures, let them not be treated like slaves; or, like the brutes who are dependent on the reason of man, when they associate with him; but cultivate their minds, give them the salutary, sublime curb of principle, and let them attain conscious dignity by feeling themselves only dependent on God. Teach them, in common with man, to submit to necessity, instead of giving, to render them more pleasing, a sex to morals. . . .

These may be termed Utopian dreams. Thanks to that Being who impressed them on my soul, and gave me sufficient strength of mind to dare to exert my own reason, till, becoming dependent only on him for the support of my virtue, I view, with indignation, the mistaken notions that enslave my sex.

I love man as my fellow; but his sceptre, real, or usurped, extends not to me, unless the reason of an individual demands my homage; and even then the submission is to reason, and not to man. In fact, the conduct of an accountable being must be regulated by the operations of its own reason; or on what foundation rests the throne of God?

It appears to me necessary to dwell on these obvious truths, because females have been insulated, as it were; and, while they have been stripped of the virtues that should clothe humanity, they have been decked with artificial graces that enable them to exercise a short-lived tyranny. Love, in their bosoms, taking place of every nobler passion, their sole ambition is to be fair, to raise emotion instead of inspiring respect; and this ignoble desire, like the servility in absolute monarchies, destroys all strength of character. Liberty is the mother of virtue, and if women be, by their very constitution, slaves, and not allowed to breathe the sharp invigorating air of freedom, they must ever languish like exotics, and be reckoned beautiful flaws in nature. . . .

[I]f strength of body be, with some show of reason, the boast of men, why are women so infatuated as to be proud of a defect? Rousseau has furnished them with a plausible excuse, which could only have occurred to a man, whose imagination had been allowed to run wild . . . that they might, forsooth, have a pretext for yielding to a natural appetite without violating a romantic species of modesty, which gratifies the pride and libertinism of man.

Women, deluded by these sentiments, sometimes boast of their weakness, cunningly obtaining power by playing on the *weakness* of men; and they may well glory in their illicit sway, for, like Turkish bashaws, they have more real power than their masters: but virtue is sacrificed to temporary gratifications, and the respectability of life to the triumph of an hour. . . .

And if it be granted that woman was not created merely to gratify the appetite of man, or to be the upper servant, who provides his meals and takes care of his linen, it must follow, that the first care of those mothers or fathers, who really attend to the education of females, should be, if not to strengthen the body, at least, not to destroy the constitution by mistaken notions of beauty and female excellence. . . .

To preserve personal beauty, woman's glory! the limbs and faculties are cramped with worse than Chinese bands, and the sedentary life which they are condemned to live, whilst boys frolic in the open air, weakens the muscles and relaxes the nerves. As for Rousseau's remarks . . . that they have naturally, that is from their birth, independent of education, a fondness for dolls, dressing, and talking— they are so puerile as not to merit a serious refutation. . . .

I have, probably, had an opportunity of observing more girls in their infancy than J. J. Rousseau—I can recollect my own feelings, and I have looked steadily around me; yet, so far from coinciding with him in opinion respecting the first dawn of the female character, I will venture to affirm, that a girl, whose spirits have not been damped by inactivity, or innocence tainted by false shame, will always be a romp, and the doll will never excite attention unless confinement allows her no alternative. Girls and boys, in short, would play harmlessly together, if the distinction of sex was not inculcated long before nature makes any difference. I will go further, and affirm, as an indisputable fact, that most of the women, in the circle of my observation, who have acted like rational creatures, or shown any vigour of intellect, have accidentally been allowed to run wild. . . .

Ah! why do women, I write with affectionate solicitude, condescend to receive a degree of attention and respect from strangers, different from that reciprocation of civility which the dictates of humanity and the politeness of civilization authorize between man and man? And, why do they not discover, when "in the noon of beauty's power," that they are treated like queens only to be deluded by hollow respect, till they are led to resign, or not assume, their natural prerogatives? Confined then in cages like the feathered race, they have nothing to do but to plume themselves, and stalk with mock majesty from perch to perch. It is true they are provided with food and raiment, for which they neither toil nor spin; but health, liberty, and virtue, are given in exchange. . . .

I lament that women are systematically degraded by receiving the trivial attentions, which men think it manly to pay to the sex, when, in fact, they are insultingly supporting their own superiority. It is not condescension to bow to an inferior. So ludicrous, in fact, do these ceremonies appear to me, that I scarcely am able to govern my muscles, when I see a man start with eager, and serious solicitude to lift a handkerchief, or shut a door, when the *lady* could have done it herself, had she only moved a pace or two.

A wild wish has just flown from my heart to my head, and I will not stifle it though it may excite a horse-laugh. I do earnestly wish to see the distinction of sex confounded in society, unless where love animates the behaviour. For this distinction is, I am firmly persuaded, the foundation of the weakness of character ascribed to woman; is the cause why the understanding is neglected, whilst accomplishments are acquired with sedulous care: and the same cause accounts for their preferring the graceful before the heroic virtues. . . .

Women have seldom sufficient serious employment to silence their feelings; a round of little cares, or vain pursuits frittering away all strength of mind and organs, they become naturally only objects of sense. In short, the whole tenor of female education (the education of society) tends to render the best disposed romantic and inconstant; and the remainder vain and mean. In the present state of society this evil can scarcely be remedied, I am afraid, in the slightest degree; should a more laudable ambition ever gain ground they may be brought nearer to nature and reason, and become more virtuous and useful as they grow more respectable. . . .

With respect to virtue, to use the word in a comprehensive sense, I have seen most in low life. Many poor women maintain their children by the sweat of their brow, and keep together families that the vices of the fathers would have scattered abroad; but gentlewomen are too indolent to be actively virtuous, and are softened rather than refined by civilization. Indeed, the good sense which I have met with, among the poor women who have had few advantages of education, and yet have acted heroically, strongly confirmed me in the opinion that trifling employments have rendered woman a trifler. Man, taking her body, the mind is left to rust; so that while physical love enervates man, as being his favourite recreation, he will endeavor to enslave woman:—and, who can tell, how many generations may be necessary to give vigour to the virtue and talents of the freed posterity of abject slaves?

Questions and Activities

1. Wollstonecraft says that people who write about women's education "render women pleasing at the expense of any solid virtue." Explain what she means, and then gather evidence from contemporary

images of women and write an argument in which you take the position that Wollstonecraft's observation is or is not true of contemporary women.

2. Wollstonecraft says that she wishes "to see the distinction of sex confounded [eliminated] in society." Explore the implications of this statement in some detail and then write an argument in which you take a position that agrees or disagrees with it.

A Modest Proposal

JONATHAN SWIFT

Jonathan Swift was an English clergyman, novelist, satirist, and poet. He was born in Ireland, and lived from 1667 to 1745. He is best known for Gulliver's Travels. *Swift wrote "A Modest Proposal" (1729) in response to the famine in Ireland. Swift was a satirist, and he wrote out of what he called his "savage indignation" at the follies and injustices he saw in the world.*

FOR PREVENTING THE CHILDREN OF POOR PEOPLE FROM BEING A BURTHEN TO THEIR PARENTS OR COUNTRY, AND FOR MAKING THEM BENEFICIAL TO THE PUBLIC.

It is a melancholy object to those who walk through this great town, or travel in the country, when they see the streets, the roads, and cabin-doors crowded with beggars of the female sex, followed by three, four, or six children, *all in rags,* and importuning every passenger for an alms. These mothers, instead of being able to work for their honest livelihood, are forced to employ all their time in strolling, to beg sustenance for their helpless infants, who, as they grow up, either turn thieves for want of work, or leave their dear Native Country to fight for the Pretender in Spain, or sell themselves to the Barbadoes.

I think it is agreed by all parties that this prodigious number of children, in the arms, or on the backs, or at the heels of their mothers, and frequently of their fathers, is in the present deplorable state of the kingdom a very great additional grievance; and therefore whoever could find out a fair, cheap, and easy method of making these children sound useful members of the commonwealth would deserve so well of the public as to have his statue set up for a preserver of the nation.

But my intention is very far from being confined to provide only for the children of professed beggars; it is of a much greater extent, and shall take in the whole number of infants at a certain age who are born of parents in effect as little able to support them as those who demand our charity in the streets.

As to my own part, having turned my thoughts, for many years, upon this important subject, and maturely weighed the several schemes of other projectors, I have always found them grossly mistaken in their computation. It is true a child, just dropped from its dam, may be supported by her milk for a solar year with little other nourishment, at most not above the value of two shillings, which the mother may certainly get, or the value in scraps, by her lawful occupation of begging, and it is exactly at one year old that I propose to provide for them, in such a manner as, instead of being a charge upon their parents, or the parish, or wanting food and raiment for the rest of their lives, they shall, on the contrary, contribute to the feeding and partly to the clothing of many thousands.

There is likewise another great advantage in my scheme, that it will prevent those voluntary abortions, and that horrid practice of women murdering their bastard children, alas, too frequent among us, sacrificing the poor innocent babes, I doubt, more to avoid the expense than the shame, which would move tears and pity in the most savage and inhuman breast. *[margin note: murder alternative to scheme]*

The number of souls in this kingdom being usually reckoned one million and a half, of these I calculate there may be about two hundred thousand couple whose wives are breeders, from which number I subtract thirty thousand couples who are able to maintain their own children, although I apprehend there cannot be so many under the present distresses of the kingdom, but this being granted, there will remain an hundred and seventy thousand breeders. I again subtract fifty thousand for those women who miscarry, or whose children die by accident or disease within the year. There only remain an hundred and twenty thousand children of poor parents annually born: The question therefore is, how this number shall be reared, and provided for, which, as I have already said, under the present situation of affairs, is utterly impossible by all the methods hitherto proposed, for we can neither employ them in handicraft, or agriculture; we neither build houses (I mean in the country), nor cultivate land: they can very seldom pick up a livelihood by stealing till they arrive at six years old, except where they are of towardly parts, although, I confess they learn the rudiments much earlier, during which time they can however be properly looked upon only as *probationers,* as I have been informed by a principal gentleman of the County of Cavan, who protested to me that he never knew above one or two instances under the age of six, even in a part of the kingdom so renowned for the quickest proficiency in that art.

I am assured by our merchants that a boy or a girl, before twelve years old, is no saleable commodity, and even when they come to this age, they will not yield above three pounds, or three pounds and half-a-crown at most on the Exchange, which cannot turn to account either to the parents or the kingdom, the charge of nutriment and rags having been at least four times that value.

I shall now therefore humbly propose my own thoughts, which I hope will not be liable to the least objection.

I have been assured by a very knowing American of my acquaintance in London, that a young healthy child well nursed is at a year old a most delicious, nourishing, and wholesome food, whether stewed, roasted, baked, or boiled, and I make no doubt that it will equally serve in a fricassee, or a ragout.

I do therefore humbly offer it to public consideration, that of the hundred and twenty thousand children already computed, twenty thousand may be reserved for breed, whereof only one fourth part to be males, which is more than we allow to sheep, black-cattle, or swine, and my reason is that these children are seldom the fruits of marriage, a circumstance not much regarded by our savages, therefore one male will be sufficient to serve four females. That the remaining hundred thousand may at a year old be offered in sale to the persons of quality, and fortune, through the kingdom, always advising the mother to let them suck plentifully in the last month, so as to render them plump, and fat for a good table. A child will make two dishes at an entertainment for friends, and when the family dines alone, the fore or hind quarter will make it a reasonable dish, and seasoned with a little pepper or salt will be very good boiled on the fourth day, especially in winter.

I have reckoned upon a medium, that a child just born will weigh 12 pounds, and in a solar year if tolerably nursed increaseth to 28 pounds.

I grant this food will be somewhat dear, and therefore very proper for landlords, who, as they have already devoured most of the parents, seem to have the best title to the children.

Infants' flesh will be in season throughout the year, but more plentiful in March, and a little before and after, for we are told by a grave author, an eminent French physician, that fish being a prolific diet, there are more children born in Roman Catholic countries about nine months after Lent than at any other season; therefore reckoning a year after Lent, the markets will be more glutted than usual, because the number of Popish infants is at least three to one in this kingdom, and therefore it will have one other collateral advantage by lessening the number of Papists among us.

I have already computed the charge of nursing a beggar's child (in which list I reckon all cottagers, labourers, and four-fifths of the farmers) to be about two shillings *per annum*, rags included, and I believe no gentleman would repine to give ten shillings for the carcass of a good fat child, which, as I have said, will make four dishes of excellent nutritive meat, when he hath only some particular friend or his own family to dine with him. Thus the Squire will learn to be a good landlord, and grow popular among his tenants, the mother will have eight shillings net profit, and be fit for work till she produces another child.

Those who are more thrifty (as I must confess the times require) may flay the carcass; the skin of which, artificially dressed, will make admirable gloves for ladies, and summer boots for fine gentlemen.

As to our City of Dublin, shambles may be appointed for this purpose, in the most convenient parts of it, and butchers we may be assured will not be wanting, although I rather recommend buying the children alive, and dressing them hot from the knife, as we do roasting pigs.

A very worthy person, a true lover of this country, and whose virtues I highly esteem, was lately pleased, in discoursing on this matter, to offer a refinement upon my scheme. He said that many gentlemen of this kingdom, having of late destroyed their deer, he conceived that the want of venison might be well supplied by the bodies of young lads and maidens, not exceeding fourteen years of age, nor under twelve, so great a number of both sexes in every country being now ready to starve, for want of work and service: and these to be disposed of by their parents if alive, or otherwise by their nearest relations. But with due deference to so excellent a friend, and so deserving a patriot, I cannot be altogether in his sentiments; for as to the males, my American acquaintance assured me from frequent experience that their flesh was generally tough and lean, like that of our schoolboys, by continual exercise, and their taste disagreeable, and to fatten them would not answer the charge. Then as to the females, it would, I think with humble submission, be a loss to the public, because they soon would become breeders themselves: And besides, it is not improbable that some scrupulous people might be apt to censure such a practice (although indeed very unjustly) as a little bordering upon cruelty, which, I confess, hath always been with me the strongest objection against any project, however so well intended.

But in order to justify my friend, he confessed that this expedient was put into his head by the famous Psalmanazar, a native of the island Formosa, who came from thence to London, above twenty years ago, and in conversation told my friend that in his country when any young person happened to be put to death, the executioner sold the carcass to persons of quality, as a prime dainty, and that, in his time, the body of a plump girl of fifteen, who was crucified for an attempt to poison the emperor, was sold to his Imperial Majesty's Prime Minister of State, and other great Mandarins of the Court, in joints from the gibbet, at four hundred crowns. Neither indeed can I deny that if the same use were made of several plump young girls in this town, who, without one single groat to their fortunes, cannot stir abroad without a chair, and appear at the playhouse, and assemblies in foreign fineries, which they never will pay for, the kingdom would not be the worse.

Some persons of a desponding spirit are in great concern about that vast number of poor people, who are aged, diseased, or maimed, and I have been desired to employ my thoughts what course may be taken to ease the nation of so grievous an encumbrance. But I am not in the least pain upon that matter, because it is very well known that they are every day dying, and rotting, by cold, and famine, and filth, and vermin, as fast as can be reasonably expected. And as to the younger labourers they are now in almost as hopeful a condition. They cannot get work, and consequently pine away for want of nourishment, to a degree, that if at any time they are accidentally hired to common labour, they have not strength to perform it; and thus the country and themselves are happily delivered from the evils to come.

I have too long digressed, and therefore shall return to my subject. I think the advantages by the proposal which I have made are obvious and many, as well as of the highest importance.

For first, as I have already observed it, it would greatly lessen the number of Papists, with whom we are yearly over-run, being the principal breeders of the nation, as well as our most dangerous enemies, and who stay at home on purpose with a design to deliver the kingdom to the Pretender, hoping to take their advantage by the absence of so many good Protestants, who have chosen rather to leave their country than stay at home, and pay tithes against their conscience to an Episcopal curate.

Secondly, The poorer tenants will have something valuable of their own, which by law be made liable to distress, and help to pay their landlord's rent, their corn and cattle being already seized, and *money a thing unknown.*

Thirdly, Whereas the maintenance of an hundred thousand children, from two years old, and upwards, cannot be computed at less than ten shillings a piece *per annum*, the nation's stock will be thereby increased fifty thousand pounds *per annum*, besides the profit of a new dish, introduced to the tables of all gentlemen of fortune in the kingdom, who have any refinement in taste, and the money will circulate among ourselves, the goods being entirely of our own growth and manufacture.

Fourthly, The constant breeders, besides the gain of eight shillings sterling *per annum*, by the sale of their children, will be rid of the charge of maintaining them after the first year.   *economic*

Fifthly, This food would likewise bring great custom to taverns, where the vintners will certainly be so prudent as to procure the best receipts for dressing it to perfection, and consequently have their houses frequented by all the fine gentlemen, who justly value themselves upon their knowledge in good eating; and a skillful cook, who understands how to oblige his guests, will contrive to make it as expensive as they please.   *economic*

Sixthly, This would be a great inducement to marriage, which all wise nations have either encouraged by rewards, or enforced by laws and penalties. It would increase the care and tenderness of mothers toward their children, when they were sure of a settlement for life, to the poor babes, provided in some sort by the public to their annual profit instead of expense. We should see an honest emulation among the married women, which of them could bring the fattest child to the market, men would become as fond of their wives, during the time of their pregnancy, as they are now of their mares in foal, their cows in calf, or sows when they are ready to farrow, nor offer to beat or kick them (as it is too frequent a practice) for fear of a miscarriage. *economic*

Many other advantages might be enumerated: For instance, the addition of some thousand carcasses in our exportation of barrelled beef; the propagation of swine's flesh, and improvement in the art of making good bacon, so much wanted among us by the great destruction of pigs, too frequent at our tables, which are no way comparable in taste or magnificence to a well-grown, fat yearling child, which roasted whole will make a considerable figure at a Lord Mayor's feast, or any other public entertainment. But this and many others I omit, being studious of brevity.

Supposing that one thousand families in this city would be constant customers for infants' flesh, besides others who might have it at merry-meetings, particularly weddings and christenings, I compute that Dublin would take off annually about twenty thousand carcasses, and the rest of the kingdom (where probably they will be sold somewhat cheaper) the remaining eighty thousand.

I can think of no one objection that will possibly be raised against this proposal, unless it should be urged that the number of people will be thereby much lessened in the kingdom. This I freely own, and was indeed one principal design in offering it to the world. I desire the reader will observe, that I calculate my remedy for this one individual *Kingdom of Ireland, and for no other that ever was, is, or, I think, ever can be upon earth.* Therefore let no man talk to me of other expedients: *Of taxing our absentees at five shillings a pound: Of using neither clothes nor household furniture, except what is of our own growth and manufacture: Of utterly rejecting the materials and instruments that promote foreign luxury: Of curing the expensiveness of pride, vanity, idleness, and gaming in our women: Of introducing a vein of parsimony, prudence, and temperance: Of learning to love our Country, wherein we differ even from* Laplanders, *and the inhabitants of* TOPINAMBOO: *Of quitting our animosities and factions, nor act any longer like the Jews, who were murdering one another at the very moment their city was taken: Of being a little cautious not to sell our country and consciences for nothing: Of teaching landlords to have at least one degree of mercy toward their tenants. Lastly, of putting a spirit of honesty, industry, and skill into our shopkeepers, who, if a resolution could now be taken to buy only our native goods, would immediately unite to cheat and exact upon us in the price, the measure, and the goodness, nor could ever yet be brought to make one fair proposal of just dealing, though often and earnestly invited to it.*

Therefore I repeat, let no man talk to me of these and the like expedients, till he hath at least some glimpse of hope that there will ever be some hearty and sincere attempt to put them into practice.

But as to myself, having been wearied out for many years with offering vain, idle, visionary thoughts, and at length utterly despairing of success, I fortunately fell upon this proposal, which as it is wholly new, so it hath something solid and real, of no expense, and little trouble, full in our own power, and whereby we can incur no danger in *disobliging* ENGLAND. For this kind of commodity will not bear exportation, the flesh being of too tender a consistence to admit a long continuance in salt, *although perhaps I could name a country which would be glad to eat up our whole nation without it.*

After all I am not so violently bent upon my own opinion as to reject any offer, proposed by wise men, which shall be found equally innocent, cheap, easy, and effectual. But before something of that kind shall be advanced in contradiction to my scheme, and offering a better, I desire the author, or authors, will be pleased maturely to consider two points. First, as things now stand, how they will be able to find food and raiment for an hundred thousand useless mouths and backs. And secondly, there being a round million of creatures in human figure, throughout this kingdom, whose whole subsistence put into a common stock would leave them in debt two millions of pounds sterling; adding those, who are beggars by profession, to the bulk of farmers, cottagers, and labourers with their wives and children, who are beggars in effect. I desire those politicians, who dislike my overture, and may perhaps be so bold to attempt an answer, that they will first ask the parents of these mortals whether they would not at this day think it a great happiness to have been sold for food at a year old, in the manner I prescribe, and thereby have avoided such a perpetual scene of misfortunes as they have since gone through, by the oppression of landlords, the impossibility of paying rent without money or trade, the want of common sustenance, with neither house nor clothes to cover them from the inclemencies of the weather, and the most inevitable prospect of entailing the like, or greater miseries upon their breed for ever.

I profess in the sincerity of my heart that I have not the least personal interest in endeavoring to promote this necessary work, having no other motive than the *public good of my country, by advancing our trade, providing for infants, relieving the poor, and giving some pleasure to the rich.* I have no children by which I can propose to get a single penny; the youngest being nine years old, and my wife past child-bearing.

Questions and Activities

1. Many of Swift's original readers took "A Modest Proposal" literally and were outraged at what they believed was a serious proposal. How is it possible to tell that Swift is writing satire rather than a literal proposal?

2. Choose a situation you are familiar with—one that deserves "savage indignation," and write an argument in which you make an outrageous proposal in order to call your readers' attention to needed action.

Civil Disobedience

HENRY DAVID THOREAU

Henry David Thoreau (1817–1862), is best known for Walden, which is based on the two years he spent living alone on Walden Pond. The twentieth century has recognized Thoreau as an important writer and thinker. "Civil Disobedience," which he wrote in 1848, has

become an important and influential document in political and le-
gal thought. It influenced Mahatma Gandhi and Martin Luther
King, Jr. Many people who violate laws that they disagree with cite
the concept of civil disobedience.

I heartily accept the motto, "That government is best which governs least;" and I should like to see it acted up to more rapidly and systematically. Carried out, it finally amounts to this, which also I believe—"That government is best which governs not at all;" and when men are prepared for it, that will be the kind of government which they will have. Government is at best but an expedient; but most governments are usually, and all governments are sometimes, inexpedient. The objections which have been brought against a standing army, and they are many and weighty, and deserve to prevail, may also at last be brought against a standing government. The standing army is only an arm of the standing government. The government itself, which is only the mode which the people have chosen to execute their will, is equally liable to be abused and perverted before the people can act through it. Witness the present Mexican war, the work of comparatively a few individuals using the standing government as their tool; for, in the outset, the people would not have consented to this measure.

This American government—what is it but a tradition, though a recent one, endeavoring to transmit itself unimpaired to posterity, but each instant losing some of its integrity? It has not the vitality and force of a single living man; for a single man can bend it to his will. It is a sort of wooden gun to the people themselves. But it is not the less necessary for this; for the people must have some complicated machinery or other, and hear its din, to satisfy that idea of government which they have. Governments show thus how successfully men can be imposed on, even impose on themselves, for their own advantage. It is excellent, we must all allow. Yet this government never of itself furthered any enterprise, but by the alacrity with which it got out of its way. *It* does not keep the country free. *It* does not settle the West. *It* does not educate. The character inherent in the American people has done all that has been accomplished; and it would have done somewhat more, if the government had not sometimes got in its way. For government is an expedient by which men would fain succeed in letting one another alone; and, as has been said, when it is most expedient, the governed are most let alone by it. Trade and commerce, if they were not made of india-rubber, would never manage to bounce over the obstacles which legislators are continually putting in their way; and, if one were to judge these men wholly by the effects of their actions and not partly by their intentions, they would deserve to be classed and punished with those mischievous persons who put obstructions on the railroads.

But, to speak practically and as a citizen, unlike those who call themselves no-government men, I ask for, not at once no government, but *at once* a better government. Let every man make known what kind of government would command his respect, and that will be one step toward obtaining it.

After all, the practical reason why, when the power is once in the hands of the people, a majority are permitted, and for a long period continue, to rule is not because they are most likely to be in the right, not because this seems fairest to the minority, but because they are physically the strongest. But a government in which the majority rule in all cases cannot be based on justice, even as far as men understand it. Can there not be a government in which majorities do not virtually decide right and wrong, but conscience?—in which majorities decide only those questions to which the rule of expediency is applicable? Must the citizen ever for a moment, or in the least degree, resign his conscience to the legislator? Why has every man a conscience, then? I think that we should be men first, and subjects afterwards. It is not desirable to cultivate a respect for the law, so much as for the right. The only obligation which I have a right to assume is to do at any time what I think right. It is truly enough said that a corporation has no conscience; but a corporation of conscientious men is a corporation *with* a conscience. Law never made men a whit more just; and, by means of their respect for it, even the well-disposed are daily made the agents of injustice. A common and natural result of an undue respect for law is, that you may see a file of soldiers, colonel, captain, corporal, privates, powder-monkeys, and all, marching in admirable order over hill and dale to the wars, against their wills, ay, against their common sense and consciences, which makes it very steep marching indeed, and produces a palpitation of the heart. They have no doubt that it is a damnable business in which they are concerned; they are all peaceably inclined. Now, what are they? Men at all? or small movable forts and magazines, at the service of some unscrupulous man in power? Visit the Navy-Yard, and behold a marine, such a man as an American government can make, or such as it can make a man with its black arts—a mere shadow and reminiscence of humanity, a man laid out alive and standing, and already, as one may say, buried under arms with funeral accompaniments, though it may be,—

Not a drum was heard, nor a funeral note,
  As his corse to the rampart we hurried;

Not a soldier discharged his farewell shot
O'er the grave where our hero was buried.

The mass of men serve the state thus, not as men mainly, but as machines, with their bodies. They are the standing army, and the militia, jailers, constables, *posse comitatus*, etc. In most cases there is no free exercise whatever of the judgment or of the moral sense; but they put themselves on a level with wood and earth and stones; and wooden men can perhaps be manufactured that will serve the purpose as well. Such command no more respect than men of straw or a lump of dirt. They have the same sort of worth only as horses or dogs. Yet such as these even are commonly esteemed good citizens. Others—as most legislators, politicians, lawyers, ministers, and office-holders—serve the state chiefly with their heads; and, as they rarely make any moral distinctions, they are as likely to serve the devil, without *intending* it, as God. A very few—as heroes, patriots, martyrs, reformers in the great sense, and *men*—serve the state with their consciences also, and so necessarily resist it for the most part; and they are commonly treated as enemies by it. A wise man will only be useful as a man, and will not submit to be "clay," and "stop a hole to keep the wind away," but leave that office to his dust at least:—

I am too high-born to be propertied,
To be a secondary at control,
Or useful serving-man and instrument
To any sovereign state throughout the world.

He who gives himself entirely to his fellow-men appears to them useless and selfish; but he who gives himself partially to them is pronounced a benefactor and philanthropist.

How does it become a man to behave toward this American government today? I answer, that he cannot without disgrace be associated with it. I cannot for an instant recognize that political organization as *my* government which is the *slave's* government also.

All men recognize the right of revolution; that is, the right to refuse allegiance to, and to resist, the government, when its tyranny or its inefficiency are great and unendurable. But almost all say that such is not the case now. But such was the case, they think, in the Revolution of '75. If one were to tell me that this was a bad government because it taxed certain foreign commodities brought to its ports, it is most probable that I should not make an ado about it, for I can do without them. All machines have their friction; and possibly this does enough good to counterbalance the evil. At any rate, it is a great evil to make a stir about it. But when the friction comes to have its machine, and oppression and robbery are organized, I say, let us not have such a machine any longer. In other words, when a sixth of the population of a nation which has undertaken to be the refuge of liberty are slaves, and a whole country is unjustly overrun and conquered by a foreign army, and subjected to military law, I think that it is not too soon for honest men to rebel and revolutionize. What makes this duty the more urgent is the fact that the country so overrun is not our own, but ours is the invading army.

Paley, a common authority with many on moral questions, in his chapter on the "Duty of Submission to Civil Government," resolves all civil obligation into expediency; and he proceeds to say that "so long as the interest of the whole society requires it, that is, so long as the established government cannot be resisted or changed without public inconveniency, it is the will of God . . . that the established government be obeyed—and no longer. This principle being admitted, the justice of every particular case of resistance is reduced to a computation of the quantity of the danger and grievance on one side, and of the probability and expense of redressing it on the other." Of this, he says, every man shall judge for himself. But Paley appears never to have contemplated those cases to which the rule of expediency does not apply, in which a people, as well as an individual, must do justice, cost what it may. If I have unjustly wrested a plank from a drowning man, I must restore it to him though I drown myself. This, according to Paley, would be inconvenient. But he that would save his life, in such a case, shall lose it. This people must cease to hold slaves, and to make war on Mexico, though it cost them their existence as a people.

In their practice, nations agree with Paley; but does any one think that Massachusetts does exactly what is right at the present crisis?

> A drab of state, a cloth-o'-silver slut,
> To have her train borne up, and her soul trail in the dirt.

Practically speaking, the opponents to a reform in Massachusetts are not a hundred thousand politicians at the South, but a hundred thousand merchants and farmers here, who are more interested in commerce and agriculture than they are in humanity, and are not prepared to do justice to the slave and to Mexico, *cost what it may.* I quarrel not with far-off foes, but with those who, near at home, coöperate with, and do the bidding of, those far away, and without whom the latter would be harmless. We are accustomed to say, that the mass of men are unprepared; but improvement is slow, because the few are not materially wiser or better than the many. It is not

so important that many should be as good as you, as that there be
some absolute goodness somewhere; for that will leaven the whole
lump. There are thousands who are *in opinion* opposed to slavery
and to the war, who yet in effect do nothing to put an end to them;
who, esteeming themselves children of Washington and Franklin,
sit down with their hands in their pockets, and say that they know
not what to do, and do nothing; who even postpone the question of
freedom to the question of free trade, and quietly read the prices-
current along with the latest advices from Mexico, after dinner,
and, it may be, fall asleep over them both. What is the price-current
of an honest man and patriot today? They hesitate, and they regret,
and sometimes they petition; but they do nothing in earnest and
with effect. They will wait, well disposed, for others to remedy the
evil, that they may no longer have it to regret. At most, they give
only a cheap vote, and a feeble countenance and God-speed, to the
right, as it goes by them. There are nine hundred and ninety-nine
patrons of virtue to one virtuous man. But it is easier to deal with
the real possessor of a thing than with the temporary guardian of it.

All voting is a sort of gaming, like checkers or backgammon,
with a slight moral tinge to it, a playing with right and wrong, with
moral questions; and betting naturally accompanies it. The character of the voters is not staked. I cast my vote, perchance, as I think
right; but I am not vitally concerned that that right should prevail.
I am willing to leave it to the majority. Its obligation, therefore,
never exceeds that of expediency. Even voting *for the right* is *doing*
nothing for it. It is only expressing to men feebly your desire that it
should prevail. A wise man will not leave the right to the mercy of
chance, nor wish it to prevail through the power of the majority.
There is but little virtue in the action of masses of men. When the
majority shall at length vote for the abolition of slavery, it will be
because they are indifferent to slavery, or because there is but little
slavery left to be abolished by their vote. *They* will then be the only
slaves. Only *his* vote can hasten the abolition of slavery who asserts
his own freedom by his vote.

I hear of a convention to be held at Baltimore, or elsewhere, for
the selection of a candidate for the Presidency, made up chiefly of
editors, and men who are politicians by profession; but I think,
what is it to any independent, intelligent, and respectable man
what decision they may come to? Shall we not have the advantage
of his wisdom and honesty, nevertheless? Can we not count upon
some independent votes? Are there not many individuals in the
country who do not attend conventions? But no: I find that the
respectable man, so called, has immediately drifted from his position, and despairs of his country, when his country has more reason

to despair of him. He forthwith adopts one of the candidates thus selected as the only *available* one, thus proving that he is himself *available* for any purposes of the demagogue. His vote is of no more worth than that of any unprincipled foreigner or hireling native, who may have been bought. O for a man who is a *man*, and, as my neighbor says, has a bone in his back which you cannot pass your hand through! Our statistics are at fault: the population has been returned too large. How many *men* are there to a square thousand miles in this country? Hardly one. Does not America offer any inducement for men to settle here? The American has dwindled into an Odd Fellow—one who may be known by the development of his organ of gregariousness, and a manifest lack of intellect and cheerful self-reliance; whose first and chief concern, on coming into the world, is to see that the almshouses are in good repair; and, before yet he has lawfully donned the virile garb, to collect a fund for the support of the widows and orphans that may be; who, in short, ventures to live only by the aid of the Mutual Insurance company, which has promised to bury him decently.

It is not a man's duty, as a matter of course, to devote himself to the eradication of any, even the most enormous, wrong; he may still properly have other concerns to engage him; but it is his duty, at least, to wash his hands of it, and, if he gives it no thought longer, not to give it practically his support. If I devote myself to other pursuits and contemplations, I must first see, at least, that I do not pursue them sitting upon another man's shoulders. I must get off him first, that he may pursue his contemplations too. See what gross inconsistency is tolerated. I have heard some of my townsmen say, "I should like to have them order me out to help put down an insurrection of the slaves, or to march to Mexico;—see if I would go"; and yet these very men have each, directly by their allegiance, and so indirectly, at least, by their money, furnished a substitute. The soldier is applauded who refuses to serve in an unjust war by those who do not refuse to sustain the unjust government which makes the war; is applauded by those whose own act and authority he disregards and sets at naught; as if the state were penitent to that degree that it hired one to scourge it while it sinned, but not to that degree that it left off sinning for a moment. Thus, under the name of Order and Civil Government, we are all made at last to pay homage to and support our own meanness. After the first blush of sin comes its indifference; and from immoral it becomes, as it were, *unmoral*, and not quite unnecessary to that life which we have made.

The broadest and most prevalent error requires the most disinterested virtue to sustain it. The slight reproach to which the virtue of patriotism is commonly liable, the noble are most likely to incur. Those who, while they disapprove of the character and measures of a government, yield to it their allegiance and support are undoubtedly its most conscientious supporters, and so frequently the most serious obstacles to reform. Some are petitioning the State to dissolve the Union, to disregard the requisitions of the President. Why do they not dissolve it themselves—the union between themselves and the State—and refuse to pay their quota into the treasury? Do not they stand in the same relation to the State that the State does to the Union? And have not the same reasons prevented the State from resisting the Union which have prevented them from resisting the State?

How can a man be satisfied to entertain an opinion merely, and enjoy *it?* Is there any enjoyment in it, if his opinion is that he is aggrieved? If you are cheated out of a single dollar by your neighbor, you do not rest satisfied with knowing that you are cheated, or with saying that you are cheated, or even with petitioning him to pay you your due; but you take effectual steps at once to obtain the full amount, and see that you are never cheated again. Action from principle, the perception and the performance of right, changes things and relations; it is essentially revolutionary, and does not consist wholly with anything which was. It not only divides States and churches, it divides families; ay, it divides the *individual*, separating the diabolical in him from the divine.

Unjust laws exist: shall we be content to obey them, or shall we endeavor to amend them, and obey them until we have succeeded, or shall we transgress them at once? Men generally, under such a government as this, think that they ought to wait until they have persuaded the majority to alter them. They think that, if they should resist, the remedy would be worse than the evil. But it is the fault of the government itself that the remedy *is* worse than the evil. *It* makes it worse. Why is it not more apt to anticipate and provide for reform? Why does it not cherish its wise minority? Why does it cry and resist before it is hurt? Why does it not encourage its citizens to be on the alert to point out its faults, and *do* better than it would have them? Why does it always crucify Christ, and excommunicate Copernicus and Luther, and pronounce Washington and Franklin rebels?

One would think, that a deliberate and practical denial of its authority was the only offence never contemplated by government; else, why has it not assigned its definite, its suitable and proportionate, penalty? If a man who has no property refuses but once to earn nine shillings for the State, he is put in prison for a period unlimited by any law that I know, and determined only by the discretion of those who placed him there; but if he should steal ninety times nine shillings from the State, he is soon permitted to go at large again.

If the injustice is part of the necessary friction of the machine of government, let it go, let it go: perchance it will wear smooth—certainly the machine will wear out. If the injustice has a spring, or a pulley, or a rope, or a crank, exclusively for itself, then perhaps you may consider whether the remedy will not be worse than the evil; but if it is of such a nature that it requires you to be the agent of injustice to another, then, I say, break the law. Let your life be a counter friction to stop the machine. What I have to do is to see, at any rate, that I do not lend myself to the wrong which I condemn.

As for adopting the ways which the State has provided for remedying the evil, I know not of such ways. They take too much time, and a man's life will be gone, I have other affairs to attend to. I came into this world, not chiefly to make this a good place to live in, but to live in it, be it good or bad. A man has not everything to do, but something; and because he cannot do *everything*, it is not necessary that he should do *something* wrong. It is not my business to be petitioning the Governor or the Legislature any more than it is theirs to petition me; and if they should not hear my petition, what should I do then? But in this case the State has provided no way: its very Constitution is the evil. This may seem to be harsh and stubborn and unconciliatory; but it is to treat with the utmost kindness and consideration the only spirit that can appreciate or deserves it. So is all change for the better, like birth and death, which convulse the body.

I do not hesitate to say, that those who call themselves Abolitionists should at once effectually withdraw their support, both in person and property, from the government of Massachusetts, and not wait till they constitute a majority of one, before they suffer the right to prevail through them. I think that it is enough if they have God on their side, without waiting for that other one. Moreover, any man more right than his neighbors constitutes a majority of one already.

I meet this American government, or its representative, the State government, directly, and face to face, once a year—no more—in the person of its tax-gatherer; this is the only mode in which a man situated as I am necessarily meets it; and it then says distinctly, Recognize me; and the simplest, the most effectual, and, in the present posture of affairs, the indispensablest mode of treating with it on this head, of expressing your little satisfaction with and love for it, is to deny it then. My civil neighbor, the tax-gatherer, is the very man I have to deal with—for it is, after all, with men and not with parchment that I quarrel—and he has voluntarily chosen to be an agent of the government. How shall he ever know well what he is and does as an officer of the government, or as a man, until he is obliged to consider whether he shall treat me, his neighbor, for whom he has respect, as a neighbor and well-disposed man, or as a maniac and disturber of the peace, and see if he can get over this obstruction to his neighborliness without a ruder and more impetuous thought or speech corresponding with his action. I know this well, that if one thousand, if one hundred, if ten men whom I could name—if ten *honest* men only—ay, if *one* HONEST man, in this State of Massachusetts, *ceasing to hold slaves,* were actually to withdraw from this copartnership, and be locked up in the county jail therefor, it would be the abolition of slavery in America. For it matters not how small the beginning may seem to be: what is once well done is done forever. But we love better to talk about it: that we say is our mission. Reform keeps many scores of newspapers in its service, but not one man. If my esteemed neighbor, the State's ambassador, who will devote his days to the settlement of the question of human rights in the Council Chamber, instead of being threatened with the prisons of Carolina, were to sit down the prisoner of Massachusetts, that State which is so anxious to foist the sin of slavery upon her sister—though at present she can discover only an act of inhospitality to be the ground of a quarrel with her—the Legislature would not wholly waive the subject the following winter.

Under a government which imprisons any unjustly, the true place for a just man is also a prison. The proper place to-day, the only place which Massachusetts has provided for her freer and less desponding spirits, is in her prisons, to be put out and locked out of the State by her own act, as they have already put themselves out by their principles. It is there that the fugitive slave, and the Mexican prisoner on parole, and the Indian come to plead the wrongs of his race should find them; on that separate, but more free and honorable, ground, where the State places those who are not *with* her, but *against* her—the only house in a slave State in which a free man can abide with honor. If any think that their influence would be lost there, and their voices no longer afflict the ear of the State, that they would not be as an enemy within its walls, they do not know by how much truth is stronger than error, nor how much more eloquently and effectively he can combat injustice who has experienced a little in his own person. Cast your whole vote, not a strip of paper merely, but your whole influence. A minority is powerless while it conforms to the majority; it is not even a minority then; but it is irresistible when it clogs by its whole weight. If the alternative is to keep all just men in prison, or give up war and slavery, the State will not hesitate which to choose. If a thousand men were not to pay their tax-bills this year, that would not be a violent and bloody measure, as it would be to pay them, and enable the State to commit violence and shed innocent blood. This is, in fact, the definition of a peaceable revolution, if any such is possible. If the tax-gatherer, or any other public officer, asks me, as one has done, "But what shall I do?" my answer is, "If you really wish to do anything, resign your office." When the subject has refused allegiance, and the officer has re-signed his office, then the revolution is accomplished. But even suppose blood should flow. Is there not a sort of blood shed when the conscience is wounded? Through this wound a man's real manhood and immortality flow out, and he bleeds to an everlast-ing death. I see this blood flowing now.

I have contemplated the imprisonment of the offender, rather than the seizure of his goods—though both will serve the same purpose—because they who assert the purest right, and conse-quently the most dangerous to a corrupt State, commonly have not spent much time in accumulating property. To such the State ren-ders comparatively small service, and a slight tax is wont to appear exorbitant, particularly if they are obliged to earn it by special labor with their hands. If there were one who lived wholly without the use of money, the State itself would hesitate to demand it of him. But the rich man—not to make any invidious comparison—is al-ways sold to the institution which makes him rich. Absolutely speaking, the more money, the less virtue; for money comes be-tween a man and his objects, and obtains them for him; and it was certainly no great virtue to obtain it. It puts to rest many questions which he would otherwise be taxed to answer; while the only new question which it puts is the hard but superfluous one, how to spend it. Thus his moral ground is taken from under his feet. The opportunities of living are diminished in proportion as what are called the "means" are increased. The best thing a man can do for his culture when he is rich is to endeavor to carry out those schemes which he entertained when he was poor. Christ answered the Herodians according to their condition. "Show me the tribute-money," said he;—and one took a penny out of his pocket;—if you use money which has the image of Cæsar on it, and which he has made current and valuable, that is, *if you are men of the State,* and gladly enjoy the advantages of Cæsar's government, then pay him back some of his own when he demands it. "Render therefore to Cæsar that which is Cæsar's, and to God those things which are God's"—leaving them no wiser than before as to which was which; for they did not wish to know.

When I converse with the freest of my neighbors, I perceive that, whatever they may say about the magnitude and seriousness of the question, and their regard for the public tranquillity, the long and the short of the matter is, that they cannot spare the protection of the existing government, and they dread the consequences to their property and families of disobedience to it. For my own part, I should not like to think that I ever rely on the protection of the State. But, if I deny the authority of the State when it presents its tax-bill, it will soon take and waste all my property, and so harass me and my children without end. This is hard. This makes it impossible for a man to live honestly, and at the same time comfortably, in outward respects. It will not be worth the while to accumulate property; that would be sure to go again. You must hire or squat somewhere, and raise but a small crop, and eat that soon. You must live within yourself, and depend upon yourself always tucked up and ready for a start, and not have many affairs. A man may grow rich in Turkey even, if he will be in all respects a good subject of the Turkish government. Confucius said: "If a man is governed by the principles of reason, poverty and misery are subjects of shame; if a state is not governed by the principles of reason, riches and honors are the subjects of shame." No: until I want the protection of Massachusetts to be extended to me in some distant Southern port, where my liberty is endangered, or until I am bent solely on building up an estate at home by peaceful enterprise, I can afford to refuse allegiance to Massachusetts, and her right to my property and life. It costs me less in every sense to incur the penalty of disobedience to the State than it would to obey. I should feel as if I were worth less in that case.

Some years ago, the State met me in behalf of the Church, and commanded me to pay a certain sum toward the support of a clergyman whose preaching my father attended, but never I myself. "Pay," it said, "or be locked up in the jail." I declined to pay. But, unfortunately, another man saw fit to pay it. I did not see why the schoolmaster should be taxed to support the priest, and not the priest the schoolmaster; for I was not the State's schoolmaster, but I supported myself by voluntary subscription. I did not see why the lyceum should not present its tax-bill, and have the State to back its demand, as well as the Church. However, at the request of the selectmen, I condescended to make some such statement as this in writing:— "Know all men by these presents, that I, Henry Thoreau, do not wish to be regarded as a member of any incorporated society which I have not joined." This I gave to the town clerk; and he has it. The State, having thus learned that I did not wish to be regarded as a member of that church, has never made a like demand on me since; though it said that it must adhere to its original presumption that time. If I had known how to name them, I should then have signed off in detail from all the societies which I never signed on to; but I did not know where to find a complete list.

I have paid no poll-tax for six years. I was put into a jail once on this account, for one night; and, as I stood considering the walls of solid stone, two or three feet thick, the door of wood and iron, a foot thick, and the iron grating which strained the light, I could not help being struck with the foolishness of that institution which treated me as if I were mere flesh and blood and bones to be locked up. I wondered that it should have concluded at length that this was the best use it could put me to, and had never thought to avail itself of my services in some way. I saw that, if there was a wall of stone between me and my townsmen, there was a still more difficult one to climb or break through before they could get to be as free as I was. I did not for a moment feel confined, and the walls seemed a great waste of stone and mortar. I felt as if I alone of all my townsmen had paid my tax. They plainly did not know how to treat me, but behaved like persons who are underbred. In every threat and in every compliment there was a blunder; for they thought that my chief desire was to stand the other side of that stone wall. I could not but smile to see how industriously they locked the door on my meditations, which followed them out again without let or hindrance, and *they* were really all that was dangerous. As they could not reach me, they had resolved to punish my body; just as boys, if they cannot come at some person against whom they have a spite, will abuse his dog. I saw that the State was half-witted, that it was as timid as a lone woman with her silver spoons, and that it did not know its friends from its foes, and I lost all my remaining respect for it, and pitied it.

Thus the State never intentionally confronts a man's sense, intellectual or moral, but only his body, his senses. It is not armed with superior wit or honesty, but with superior physical strength. I was not born to be forced. I will breathe after my own fashion. Let us see who is the strongest. What force has a multitude? They only can force me who obey a higher law than I. They force me to become like themselves. I do not hear of *men* being *forced* to live this way or that by masses of men. What sort of life were that to live? When I meet a government which says to me, "Your money or your life," why should I be in haste to give it my money? It may be in a great strait, and not know what to do: I cannot help that. It must help itself; do as I do. It is not worth the while to snivel about it. I am not responsible for the successful working of the machinery of society. I am not the son of the engineer. I perceive that, when

an acorn and a chestnut fall side by side, the one does not remain
inert to make way for the other, but both obey their own laws, and
spring and grow and flourish as best they can, till one, perchance,
overshadows and destroys the other. If a plant cannot live according
to its nature, it dies; and so a man.

The night in prison was novel and interesting enough. The
prisoners in their shirt-sleeves were enjoying a chat and the evening
air in the doorway, when I entered. But the jailer said, "Come, boys,
it is time to lock up"; and so they dispersed, and I heard the sound
of their steps returning into the hollow apartments. My room-mate
was introduced to me by the jailer as "a first-rate fellow and a clever
man." When the door was locked, he showed me where to hang my
hat, and how he managed matters there. The rooms were white-
washed once a month; and this one, at least, was the whitest, most
simply furnished, and probably the neatest apartment in the town.
He naturally wanted to know where I came from, and what brought
me there; and, when I had told him, I asked him in my turn how he
came there, presuming him to be an honest man, of course; and, as
the world goes, I believe he was. "Why," said he, "they accuse me
of burning a barn; but I never did it." As near as I could discover,
he had probably gone to bed in a barn when drunk, and smoked his
pipe there; and so a barn was burnt. He had the reputation of being
a clever man, had been there some three months waiting for his
trial to come on, and would have to wait as much longer; but he
was quite domesticated and contented, since he got his board for
nothing, and thought that he was well treated.

He occupied one window, and I the other; and I saw that if one
stayed there long, his principal business would be to look out the
window. I had soon read all the tracts that were left there, and
examined where former prisoners had broken out, and where a grate
had been sawed off, and heard the history of the various occupants
of that room; for I found that even here there was a history and a
gossip which never circulated beyond the walls of the jail. Probably
this is the only house in the town where verses are composed,
which are afterward printed in a circular form, but not published. I
was shown quite a long list of verses which were composed by some
young men who had been detected in an attempt to escape, who
avenged themselves by singing them.

I pumped my fellow-prisoner as dry as I could, for fear I should
never see him again; but at length he showed me which was my
bed, and left me to blow out the lamp.

It was like travelling into a far country, such as I had never
expected to behold, to lie there for one night. It seemed to me that
I never had heard the town clock strike before, nor the evening

sounds of the village; for we slept with the windows open, which were inside the grating. It was to see my native village in the light of the Middle Ages, and our Concord was turned into a Rhine stream, and visions of knights and castles passed before me. They were the voices of old burghers that I heard in the streets. I was an involuntary spectator and auditor of whatever was done and said in the kitchen of the adjacent village inn—a wholly new and rare experience to me. It was a closer view of my native town. I was fairly inside of it. I never had seen its institutions before. This is one of its peculiar institutions; for it is a shire town. I began to comprehend what its inhabitants were about.

In the morning, our breakfasts were put through the hole in the door, in small oblong-square tin pans, made to fit, and holding a pint of chocolate, with brown bread, and an iron spoon. When they called for the vessels again, I was green enough to return what bread I had left; but my comrade seized it, and said that I should lay that up for lunch or dinner. Soon after he was let out to work at haying in a neighboring field, whither he went every day, and would not be back till noon; so he bade me good-bye, saying that he doubted if he should see me again.

When I came out of prison—for some one interfered, and paid that tax—I did not perceive that great changes had taken place on the common, such as he observed who went in a youth and emerged a tottering and gray-headed man; and yet a change had to my eyes come over the scene—the town, and State, and country—greater than any that mere time could effect. I saw yet more distinctly the State in which I lived. I saw to what extent the people among whom I lived could be trusted as good neighbors and friends; that their friendship was for summer weather only; that they did not greatly propose to do right; that they were a distinct race from me by their prejudices and superstitions, as the Chinamen and Malays are; that in their sacrifices to humanity they ran no risks, not even to their property; that after all they were not so noble but they treated the thief as he had treated them, and hoped, by a certain outward observance and a few prayers, and by walking in a particular straight though useless path from time to time, to save their souls. This may be to judge my neighbors harshly; for I believe that many of them are not aware that they have such an institution as the jail in their village.

It was formerly the custom in our village, when a poor debtor came out of jail, for his acquaintances to salute him, looking through their fingers, which were crossed to represent the grating of a jail window, "How do ye do?" My neighbors did not thus salute me, but first looked at me, and then at one another, as if I had returned from a long journey. I was put into jail as I was going to the shoemaker's to get a shoe which was mended. When I was let out the next morning, I preceeded to finish my errand, and, having put on my mended shoe, joined a huckleberry party, who were impatient to put themselves under my conduct; and in half an hour—for the horse was soon tackled—was in the midst of a huckleberry field, on one of our highest hills, two miles off, and then the State was nowhere to be seen.

This is the whole history of "My Prisons."

I have never declined paying the highway tax, because I am as desirous of being a good neighbor as I am of being a bad subject; and as for supporting schools, I am doing my part to educate my fellow-countrymen now. It is for no particular item in the tax-bill that I refuse to pay it. I simply wish to refuse allegiance to the State, to withdraw and stand aloof from it effectually. I do not care to trace the course of my dollar, if I could, till it buys a man or a musket to shoot one with—the dollar is innocent—but I am concerned to trace the effects of my allegiance. In fact, I quietly declare war with the State, after my fashion, though I will still make what use and get what advantage of her I can, as is usual in such cases.

If others pay the tax which is demanded of me, from a sympathy with the State, they do but what they have already done in their own case, or rather they abet injustice to a greater extent than the State requires. If they pay the tax from a mistaken interest in the individual taxed, to save his property, or prevent his going to jail, it is because they have not considered wisely how far they let their private feelings interfere with the public good.

This, then, is my position at present. But one cannot be too much on guard in such a case, lest his action be biased by obstinacy or an undue regard for the opinions of men. Let him see that he does only what belongs to himself and to the hour.

I think sometimes, Why, this people mean well, they are only ignorant; they would do better if they knew how: why give your neighbors this pain to treat you as they are not inclined to? But I think again, This is no reason why I should do as they do, or permit others to suffer much greater pain of a different kind. Again, I sometimes say to myself, When many millions of men, without heat, without ill will, without personal feeling of any kind, demand of you a few shillings only, without the possibility, such is their constitution, of retracting or altering their present demand, and without the possibility, on your side, of appeal to any other millions, why expose yourself to this overwhelming brute force? You do not resist cold and hunger, the winds and the waves, thus obstinately; you quietly submit to a thousand similar necessities. You do not put your head into the fire. But just in proportion as I regard this as not wholly a brute force, but partly a human force, and consider that I have relations to those millions as to so many millions of men, and not of mere brute or inanimate things, I see that appeal is possible, first and instantaneously, from them to the Maker of them, and, secondly, from them to themselves. But if I put my head deliberately into the fire, there is no appeal to fire or to the Maker of fire, and I have only myself to blame. If I could convince myself that I have any right to be satisfied with men as they are, and to treat them accordingly, and not according, in some respects, to my requisitions and expectations of what they and I ought to be, then, like a good Mussulman and fatalist, I should endeavor to be satisfied with things as they are, and say it is the will of God. And, above all, there is this difference between resisting this and a purely brute or natural force, that I can resist this with some effect; but I cannot expect, like Orpheus, to change the nature of the rocks and trees and beasts.

I do not wish to quarrel with any man or nation. I do not wish to split hairs, to make fine distinctions, or set myself up as better than my neighbors. I seek rather, I may say, even an excuse for conforming to the laws of the land. I am but too ready to conform to them. Indeed, I have reason to suspect myself on this head; and each year, as the tax-gatherer comes round, I find myself disposed to review the acts and positions of the general and State governments, and the spirit of the people, to discover a pretext for conformity.

> We must affect our country as our parents,
> And if at any time we alienate
> Our love or industry from doing it honor,
> We must respect effects and teach the soul
> Matter of conscience and religion,
> And not desire of rule or benefit.

I believe that the State will soon be able to take all my work of this sort out of my hands, and then I shall be no better a patriot than my fellow-countrymen. Seen from a lower point of view, the Constitution, with all its faults, is very good; the law and the courts are very respectable; even this state and this American government are, in many respects, very admirable, and rare things, to be thankful for, such as a great many have described them; but seen from a point of view a little higher, they are what I have described them; seen from a higher still, and the highest, who shall say what they are, or that they are worth looking at or thinking of at all?

However, the government does not concern me much, and I
shall bestow the fewest possible thoughts on it. It is not many
moments that I live under a government, even in this world. If a
man is thought-free, fancy-free, imagination-free, that which is *not*
never for a long time appearing *to be* to him, unwise rulers or
reformers cannot fatally interrupt him.

I know that most men think differently from myself; but those
whose lives are by profession devoted to the study of these or
kindred subjects content me as little as any. Statesmen and legislators, standing so completely within the institution, never distinctly
and nakedly behold it. They speak of moving society, but have no
resting-place without it. They may be men of a certain experience
and discrimination, and have no doubt invented ingenious and even
useful systems, for which we sincerely thank them; but all their wit
and usefulness lie within certain not very wide limits. They are
wont to forget that the world is not governed by policy and expediency. Webster never goes behind government, and so cannot speak
with authority about it. His words are wisdom to those legislators
who contemplate no essential reform in the existing government;
but for thinkers, and those who legislate for all time, he never once
glances at the subject. I know of those whose serene and wise
speculations on this theme would soon reveal the limits of his
mind's range and hospitality. Yet, compared with the cheap professions of most reformers, and the still cheaper wisdom and eloquence of politicians in general, his are almost the only sensible and
valuable words, and we thank Heaven for him. Comparatively, he
is always strong, original, and, above all, practical. Still, his quality
is not wisdom, but prudence. The lawyer's truth is not Truth, but
consistency or a consistent expediency. Truth is always in harmony
with herself, and is not concerned chiefly to reveal the justice that
may consist with wrong-doing. He well deserves to be called, as he
has been called, the Defender of the Constitution. There are really
no blows to be given by him but defensive ones. He is not a leader,
but a follower. His leaders are the men of '87. "I have never made
an effort," he says, "and never propose to make an effort; I have
never countenanced an effort, and never mean to countenance an
effort, to disturb the arrangement as originally made, by which the
various States came into the Union." Still thinking of the sanction
which the Constitution gives to slavery, he says, "Because it was
part of the original compact—let it stand." Notwithstanding his
special acuteness and ability, he is unable to take a fact out of its
merely political relations, and behold it as it lies absolutely to be
disposed of by the intellect—what, for instance, it behooves a man

to do here in America today with regard to slavery—but ventures, or is driven, to make some such desperate answer as the following, while professing to speak absolutely, and as a private man—from which what new and similar code of social duties might be inferred? "The manner," says he, "in which the governments of those States where slavery exists are to regulate it is for their own consideration, under their responsibility to their constituents, to the general laws of propriety, humanity, and justice, and to God. Associations formed elsewhere, springing from a feeling of humanity, or any other cause, have nothing whatever to do with it. They have never received any encouragement from me, and they never will."

They who know of no purer sources of truth, who have traced up its steam no higher, stand, and wisely stand, by the Bible and the Constitution, and drink at it there with reverence and humility; but they who behold where it comes tricking into this lake or that pool, gird up their loins once more, and continue their pilgrimage toward its fountain-head.

No man with a genius for legislation has appeared in America. They are rare in the history of the world. There are orators, politicians, and eloquent men, by the thousand; but the speaker has not yet opened his mouth to speak who is capable of settling the much-vexed questions of the day. We love eloquence for its own sake, and not for any truth which it may utter, or any heroism it may inspire. Our legislators have not yet learned the comparative value of free trade and of freedom, of union, and of rectitude, to a nation. They have no genius or talent for comparatively humble questions of taxation and finance, commerce and manufactures and agriculture. If we were left solely to the wordy wit of legislators in Congress for our guidance, uncorrected by the seasonable experience and the effectual complaints of the people, America would not long retain her rank among the nations. For eighteen hundred years, though perchance I have no right to say it, the New Testament has been written; yet where is the legislator who has wisdom and practical talent enough to avail himself of the light which it sheds on the science of legislation?

The authority of government, even such as I am willing to submit to—for I will cheerfully obey those who know and can do better than I, and in many things even those who neither know nor can do so well—is still an impure one: to be strictly just, it must have the sanction and consent of the governed. It can have no pure right over my person and property but what I concede to it. The progress from an absolute to a limited monarchy, from a limited monarchy to a democracy, is a progress toward a true respect for the individual. Even the Chinese philosopher was wise enough to regard the individual as the basis of the empire. Is a democracy, such as we know it, the last improvement possible in government? Is it not possible to take a step further towards recognizing and organizing the rights of man? There will never be a really free and enlightened State until the State comes to recognize the individual as a higher and independent power, from which all its own power and authority are derived, and treats him accordingly. I please myself with imagining a State at least which can afford to be just to all men, and to treat the individual with respect as a neighbor; which even would not think it inconsistent with its own repose if a few were to live aloof from it, not meddling with it, nor embraced by it, who fulfilled all the duties of neighbors and fellow-men. A State which bore this kind of fruit, and suffered it to drop off as fast as it ripened, would prepare the way for a still more perfect and glorious State, which also I have imagined, but not yet anywhere seen.

Questions and Activities

1. Write an argument in which you take the position that civil disobedience is never justifiable, no matter how bad or unjust the law may be. In your argument, make specific reference to Thoreau's reasoning in favor of civil disobedience.

2. Summarize Thoreau's ideas about civil disobedience and then relate them directly to the arguments in the "Declaration of Independence," Stanton's "Seneca Falls Declaration," or Wollstonecraft's "Vindication."

Address Delivered at the Dedication of the Cemetery at Gettysburg, November 19, 1863

ABRAHAM LINCOLN

Lincoln's Gettysburg Address has become so familiar to most Americans that it has faded into the woodwork and become, for many, little more than an example of nineteenth century political oratory. But, as Gary Wills has pointed out in his recent book, *Lincoln at Gettysburg: The Words that Remade America* (New York: Simon and Shuster, 1992), the address is an important document in American history because its ideas about democracy and the purpose of the Civil War shaped the ideas and attitudes of subsequent generations.

Four score and seven years ago our father brought forth on this continent, a new nation, conceived in Liberty, and dedicated to the proposition that all men are created equal.

Now we are engaged in a great civil war, testing whether that nation, or any nation so conceived and so dedicated, can long endure. We are met on a great battle-field of that war. We have come to dedicate a portion of that field, as a final resting place for those who here gave their lives that that nation might live. It is altogether fitting and proper that we should do this.

But, in a larger sense, we can not dedicate—we can not consecrate—we can not hallow—this ground. The brave men, living and dead, who struggled here, have consecrated it, far above our poor power to add or detract. The world will little note, nor long remember what we say here, but it can never forget what they did here. It is for us the living, rather, to be dedicated here to the unfinished work which they who fought here have thus far so nobly advanced. It is rather for us to be here dedicated to the great task remaining before us—that from these honored dead we take increased devotion to that cause for which they gave the last full measure of devotion—that we here highly resolve that these dead shall not have died in vain—that this nation, under God, shall have a new birth of freedom—and that government of the people, by the people, for the people, shall not perish from the earth.

Questions and Activities

1. Summarize Lincoln's argument: include his position, the support he provides, and his reasoning. Once you have done this, paraphrase the address and discuss whether part of its effect is its language, rather than its ideas alone.

2. Compare Lincoln's address with the Declaration of Independence and then write a careful argument/analysis in which you take the position that the two documents are or are not consistent with each other.

The Declaration of Independence

THOMAS JEFFERSON

Thomas Jefferson, principal author of the Declaration of Independence and third president of the United States, lived from 1743 to 1826. He was a farmer, architect, writer, and politician. He also founded the University of Virginia. The Declaration was approved by Congress on July 4, 1776. Though it does not have the force of law, the Declaration of Independence continues to be an important influence on American political thought.

In Congress, July 4, 1776.

The Unanimous Declaration of the Thirteen
United States of America,

When in the Course of human events, it becomes necessary for one people to dissolve the political bands which have connected them with another, and to assume among the powers of the earth, the separate and equal station to which the Laws of Nature and of Nature's God entitle them, a decent respect to the opinions of mankind requires that they should declare the causes which impel them to the separation.—We hold these truths to be self-evident, that all men are created equal, that they are endowed by their Creator with certain unalienable Rights, that among these are Life, Liberty, and the pursuit of Happiness.—That to secure these rights, Governments are instituted among Men, deriving their just powers from the consent of the governed,—That whenever any Form of Government becomes destructive of these ends, it is the Right of the People to alter or to abolish it, and to institute new Government, laying its foundation on such principles and organizing its powers in such form, as to them shall seem most likely to effect their Safety and Happiness. Prudence, indeed, will dictate that Governments long established should not be changed for light and transient causes; and accordingly all experience hath shewn, that mankind are more disposed to suffer, while evils are sufferable, than to right themselves by abolishing the forms to which they are accustomed. But when a long train of abuses and usurpations, pursuing invariably the same Object evinces a design to reduce them under absolute Despotism, it is their right, it is their duty, to throw off such Government, and to provide new Guards for their future security.—Such has been the patient sufferance of these Colonies; and such is now the necessity which constrains them to alter their former Systems of Government. The history of the present King of Great Britain is a history of repeated injuries and usurpations, all having in direct object the establishment of an absolute Tyranny over these States. To prove this, let Facts be submitted to a candid world.—He has refused his Assent to Laws, the most wholesome and necessary for the public good.—He has forbidden his Governors to pass Laws of immediate and pressing importance, unless suspended in their operation till his Assent should be obtained; and when so suspended, he has utterly neglected to attend to them.—He has refused to pass other Laws for the accommodation of large districts of people, unless those people would relinquish the right of Representation in the Legislature, a right inestimable to them and formidable to tyrants only.—He has called together legislative bodies at places unusual, uncomfortable, and distant from the depository of their public Records, for the sole purpose of fatiguing them into compliance with his measures.—He has dissolved Representative Houses repeatedly, for opposing with manly firmness his invasions on the rights of the people.—He has refused for a long time, after such dissolutions, to cause others to be elected; whereby the Legislative powers, incapable of Annihilation, have returned to the People at large for their exercise; the State remaining in the mean time exposed to all the dangers of invasion from without, and convulsions within.—He has endeavoured to prevent the population of these States; for that purpose obstructing the Laws of Naturalization of Foreigners; refusing to pass others to encourage their migration hither, and raising the conditions of new Appropriations of Lands.—He has obstructed the Administration of Justice, by refusing his Assent to Laws for establishing Judiciary powers.—He has made Judges dependent on his Will alone, for the tenure of their offices, and the amount and payment of their salaries.—He has erected a multitude of New Offices, and sent hither swarms of Officers to harass our people, and eat out their substance.—He has kept among us, in times of peace, Standing Armies without the Consent of our legislatures.—He has affected to render the Military independent of and superior to the Civil power.—He has combined with others to subject us to a jurisdiction foreign to our constitution, and unacknowledged by our laws; giving his Assent to their Acts of pretended Legislation:—For quartering large bodies of armed troops among us:—For protecting them, by a mock Trial, from punishment for any Murders which they should commit on the Inhabitants of these States:—For cutting off our Trade with all parts of the world:—For imposing Taxes on us without our Consent:—For depriving us in many cases, of the benefits of Trial by jury:—For transporting us beyond Seas to be tried for pretended offences:—For abolishing the free System of English Laws in a neighboring Province, establishing therein an Arbitrary government, and enlarging its Boundaries so as to render it at once an example and fit instrument for introducing the same absolute rule into these Colonies:—For taking away our Charters, abolishing our most valuable Laws, and altering fundamentally the Forms of our Governments:—For suspending our own Legislatures, and declaring themselves invested with power to legislate for us in cases whatsoever.—He has abdicated Government here, by declaring us out of his Protection and waging War against us.—He has plundered our seas, ravaged our Coasts, burnt our towns, and destroyed the lives of our people.—He is at this time transporting large Armies of foreign Mercenaries to compleat the works of death, desolation and tyranny, already begun with circumstances of Cruelty & perfidy scarcely paralleled in the most barbarous ages, and totally unworthy the Head of a civilized nation.—He has constrained our fellow Citizens taken Captive on the high Seas to bear Arms against their Country, to become the executioners of their friends and Brethren, or to fall themselves by their Hands.—He has excited domestic insurrections amongst us, and has endeavoured to bring on the inhabitants of our frontiers, the merciless Indian Savages, whose known rule of warfare, is an undistinguished destruction of all ages, sexes and conditions. In every stage of these Oppressions We have Petitioned for Redress in the most humble terms: Our repeated Petitions have been answered only by repeated injury. A Prince, whose character is thus marked by every act which may define a Tyrant, is unfit to be the ruler of a free people. Nor have We been wanting in attentions to our Brittish brethren. We have warned them from time to time of attempts by their legislature to extend an unwarrantable jurisdiction over us. We have reminded them of the circumstances of our emigration and settlement here. We have appealed to their native justice and magnanimity, and we have conjured them by the ties of our common kindred to disavow these usurpations, which, would inevitably interrupt our connections and correspondence. They too have been deaf to the voice of justice and of consanguinity. We must, therefore, acquiesce in the necessity, which denounces our Separation, and hold them, as we hold the rest of mankind, Enemies in War, in Peace Friends.— WE, THEREFORE, THE REPRESENTATIVES OF THE UNITED STATES OF AMERICA, in General Congress, Assembled, appealing to the Supreme Judge of the world for the rectitude of our intentions, do, in the Name, and by authority of the good People of these Colonies, solemnly publish and declare, That these United Colonies are, and of Right ought to be FREE AND INDEPENDENT STATES; that they are Absolved from all Allegiance to the British Crown, and that all political connection between them and the State of Great Britain, is and ought to be totally dissolved; and that as Free and Independent States, they have full Power to levy War, conclude Peace, contract Alliances, establish Commerce, and to do all other Acts and Things which Independent States may of right do.—And for the support of this Declaration, with a firm reliance on the protection of divine Providence, we mutually pledge to each other our Lives, our Fortunes and our sacred Honor.

JOHN HANCOCK

BUTTON GWINNETT
LYMAN HALL
GEO WALTON.
W^M HOOPER
JOSEPH HEWES,
JOHN PENN
EDWARD RUTLEDGE.
THO^S HEYWARD JUN^R.
THOMAS LYNCH JUN^R.
ARTHUR MIDDLETON
SAMUEL CHASE
CARTER BRAXTON
ROB^T MORRIS
BENJAMIN RUSH
BENJ^A. FRANKLIN
JOHN MORTON
GEO CLYMER
JA^S. SMITH.
GEO. TAYLOR
JAMES WILSON
GEO. ROSS
CASAR RODNEY
GEO READ
THO M: KEAN
W^M FLOYD
PHIL. LIVINGSTON
FRAN^S. LEWIS
LEWIS MORRIS
RICH^D. STOCKTON

W^M PACA
THO^S. STONE
CHARLES CARROL OF
    CARROLLTON
GEORGE WYTHE
RICHARD HENRY LEE.
TH JEFFERSON
BENJ^A HARRISON
THO^S NELSON JR.
FRANCIS LIGHTFOOT
    LEE
JN^O WITHERSPOON
FRA.^S HOPKINSON
JOHN HART
ABRA CLARK
JOSIAH BARTLETT
W^M: WHIPPLE
SAM^L ADAMS
JOHN ADAMS
ROB^T TREAT PAYNE
ELBRIDGE GERRY
STEP HOPKINS
WILLIAM ELLERY
ROGER SHERMAN
SAM^{EL} HUNTINGTON
W^M. WILLIAMS
OLIVER WOLCOTT
MATTHEW THORNTON

Questions and Activities

1. Re-state Jefferson's central position and summarize the support—information and reasoning—he offers.

2. Choose one of Jefferson's statements and use it as the starting point of an argument in which you take the position that the United States as it exists today is or is not consistent with Jefferson's vision of it.

Animal Liberation

PETER SINGER

*Peter Singer teaches philosophy at Monash University in Australia and
directs the Center for Human Bioethics. The argument printed here
first appeared in the* New York Review of Books *on April 15, 1973.
It has since become recognized as an important statement in the
movement for animal rights. While Singer's argument is not as old
as the other classic arguments printed here, it may ultimately be as
important as they have become, because it marks the first effort to
extend to animals a body of rights that had previously been thought
to belong exclusively to humans.*

All Animals Are Equal . . .

or why the ethical principle on which human equality rests
requires us to extend equal consideration to animals too

"Animal Liberation" may sound more like a parody of other liberation movements than a serious objective. The idea of "The Rights
of Animals" actually was once used to parody the case for women's
rights. When Mary Wollstonecraft, a forerunner of today's feminists, published her *Vindication of the Rights of Woman* in 1792,
her views were widely regarded as absurd, and before long an anony-
mous publication appeared entitled *A Vindication of the Rights of
the Brutes.* The author of this satirical work (now known to have
been Thomas Taylor, a distinguished Cambridge philosopher) tried
to refute Mary Wollstonecraft's arguments by showing that they
could be carried one stage further. If the argument for equality was
sound when applied to women, why should it not be applied to
dogs, cats, and horses? The reasoning seemed to hold for these
"brutes" too; yet to hold that brutes had rights was manifestly
absurd. Therefore the reasoning by which this conclusion had been
reached must be unsound, and if unsound when applied to brutes,
it must also be unsound when applied to women, since the very
same arguments had been used in each case.

In order to explain the basis of the case for the equality of
animals, it will be helpful to start with an examination of the case
for the equality of women. Let us assume that we wish to defend
the case for women's rights against the attack by Thomas Taylor.
How should we reply?

One way in which we might reply is by saying that the case for equality between men and women cannot validly be extended to nonhuman animals. Women have a right to vote, for instance, because they are just as capable of making rational decisions about the future as men are; dogs, on the other hand, are incapable of understanding the significance of voting, so they cannot have the right to vote. There are many other obvious ways in which men and women resemble each other closely, while humans and animals differ greatly. So, it might be said, men and women are similar beings and should have similar rights, while humans and nonhumans are different and should not have equal rights.

The reasoning behind this reply to Taylor's analogy is correct up to a point, but it does not go far enough. There are obviously important differences between humans and other animals, and these differences must give rise to some differences in the rights that each have. Recognizing this evident fact, however, is no barrier to the case for extending the basic principle of equality to nonhuman animals. The differences that exist between men and women are equally undeniable, and the supporters of Women's Liberation are aware that these differences may give rise to different rights. Many feminists hold that women have the right to an abortion on request. It does not follow that since these same feminists are campaigning for equality between men and women they must support the right of men to have abortions too. Since a man cannot have an abortion, it is meaningless to talk of his right to have one. Since dogs can't vote, it is meaningless to talk of their right to vote. There is no reason why either Women's Liberation or Animal Liberation should get involved in such nonsense. The extension of the basic principle of equality from one group to another does not imply that we must treat both groups in exactly the same way, or grant exactly the same rights to both groups. Whether we should do so will depend on the nature of the members of the two groups. The basic principle of equality does not require equal or identical *treatment;* it requires equal consideration. Equal consideration for different beings may lead to different treatment and different rights.

So there is a different way of replying to Taylor's attempt to parody the case for women's rights, a way that does not deny the obvious differences between human beings and nonhumans but goes more deeply into the question of equality and concludes by finding nothing absurd in the idea that the basic principle of equality applies to so-called brutes. At this point such a conclusion may appear odd; but if we examine more deeply the basis on which our opposition to discrimination on grounds of race or sex ultimately rests, we will see that we would be on shaky ground if we were to demand equality for blacks, women, and other groups of oppressed humans while denying equal consideration to nonhumans. To make this clear we need to see, first, exactly why racism and sexism are wrong. When we say that all human beings, whatever their race, creed, or sex, are equal, what is it that we are asserting? Those who wish to defend hierarchical, inegalitarian societies have often pointed out that by whatever test we choose it simply is not true that all humans are equal. Like it or not we must face the fact that humans come in different shapes and sizes; they come with different moral capacities, different intellectual abilities, different amounts of benevolent feeling and sensitivity to the needs of others, different abilities to communicate effectively, and different capacities to experience pleasure and pain. In short, if the demand for equality were based on the actual equality of all human beings, we would have to stop demanding equality.

Still, one might cling to the view that the demand for equality among human beings is based on the actual equality of the different races and sexes. Although, it may be said, humans differ as individuals, there are no differences between the races and sexes as such. From the mere fact that a person is black or a woman we cannot infer anything about that person's intellectual or moral capacities. This, it may be said, is why racism and sexism are wrong. The white racist claims that whites are superior to blacks, but this is false; although there are differences among individuals, some blacks are superior to some whites in all of the capacities and abilities that could conceivably be relevant. The opponent of sexism would say the same: a person's sex is no guide to his or her abilities, and this is why it is unjustifiable to discriminate on the basis of sex.

The existence of individual variations that cut across the lines of race or sex, however, provides us with no defense at all against a more sophisticated opponent of equality, one who proposes that, say, the interests of all those with IQ scores below 100 be given less consideration that the interests of those with ratings over 100. Perhaps those scoring below the mark would, in this society, be made the slaves of those scoring higher. Would a hierarchical society of this sort really be so much better than one based on race or sex? I think not. But if we tie the moral principle of equality to the factual equality of the different races or sexes, taken as a whole, our opposition to racism and sexism does not provide us with any basis for objecting to this kind of inegalitarianism.

There is a second important reason why we ought not to base our opposition to racism and sexism on any kind of factual equality, even the limited kind that asserts that variations in capacities and abilities are spread evenly among the different races and between the sexes: we can have no absolute guarantee that these capacities and abilities really are distributed evenly, without regard to race or sex, among human beings. So far as actual abilities are concerned there do seem to be certain measurable differences both among races and between sexes. These differences do not, of course, appear in every case, but only when averages are taken. More important still, we do not yet know how many of these differences are really due to the different genetic endowments of the different races and sexes, and how many are due to poor schools, poor housing, and other factors that are the result of past and continuing discrimination. Perhaps all of the important differences will eventually prove to be environmental rather than genetic. Anyone opposed to racism and sexism will certainly hope that this will be so, for it will make the task of ending discrimination a lot easier; nevertheless, it would be dangerous to rest the case against racism and sexism on the belief that all significant differences are environmental in origin. The opponent of, say, racism who takes this line will be unable to avoid conceding that if differences in ability did after all prove to have some genetic connection with race, racism would in some way be defensible.

Fortunately there is no need to pin the case for equality to one particular outcome of a scientific investigation. The appropriate response to those who claim to have found evidence of genetically based differences in ability among the races or between the sexes is not to stick to the belief that the genetic explanation must be wrong, whatever evidence to the contrary may turn up; instead we should make it quite clear that the claim to equality does not depend on intelligence, moral capacity, physical strength, or similar matters of fact. Equality is a moral idea, not an assertion of fact. There is no logically compelling reason for assuming that a factual difference in ability between two people justifies any difference in the amount of consideration we give to their needs and interests. *The principle of the equality of human beings is not a description of an alleged actual equality among humans: it is a prescription of how we should treat human beings.*

Jeremy Bentham, the founder of the reforming utilitarian school of moral philosophy, incorporated the essential basis of moral equality into his system of ethics by means of the formula: "Each to count for one and none to count for more than one." In other words, the interests of every being affected by an action are to be taken into account and given the same weight as the like interests of any other being. A later utilitarian, Henry Sidgwick, put the point in this way: "The good of any one individual is of no more importance, from the point of view (if I may say so) of the Universe, than the good of any other." More recently the leading figures in contemporary moral philosophy have shown a great deal of agreement in specifying as a fundamental presupposition of their moral theories some similar requirement that works to give everyone's interests equal consideration—although these writers generally cannot agree on how this requirement is best formulated.[1]

It is an implication of this principle of equality that our concern for others and our readiness to consider their interests ought not to depend on what they are like or on what abilities they may possess. Precisely what our concern or consideration requires us to do may vary according to the characteristics of those affected by what we do: concern for the well-being of children growing up in America would require that we teach them to read; concern for the well-being of pigs may require no more than that we leave them with other pigs in a place where there is adequate food and room to run freely. But the basic element—the taking into account of the interests of the being, whatever those interests may be—must, according to the principle of equality, be extended to all beings, black or white, masculine or feminine, human or nonhuman.

Thomas Jefferson, who was responsible for writing the principle of the equality of men into the American Declaration of Independence, saw this point. It led him to oppose slavery even though he was unable to free himself fully from his slaveholding background. He wrote in a letter to the author of a book that emphasized the notable intellectual achievements of Negroes in order to refute the then common view that they had limited intellectual capacities:

> Be assured that no person living wishes more sincerely than I do, to see a complete refutation of the doubts I myself have entertained and expressed on the grade of understanding allotted to them by nature, and to find that they are on a par with ourselves ... but whatever be their degree of talent it is no measure of their rights. Because Sir Isaac Newton was superior to others in understanding, he was not therefore lord of the property or persons of others.[2]

Similarly, when in the 1850s the call for women's rights was raised in the United States, a remarkable black feminist named Sojourner Truth made the same point in more robust terms at a feminist convention:

> They talk about this thing in the head; what do they call it? ["Intellect," whispered someone nearby.] That's it. What's that got

to do with women's rights or Negroes' rights. If my cup won't hold
but a pint and yours holds a quart, wouldn't you be mean not to
let me have my little half-measure full?[3]

It is on this basis that the case against racism and the case
against sexism must both ultimately rest; and it is in accordance
with this principle that the attitude that we may call "speciesism,"
by analogy with racism, must also be condemned. Speciesism—the
word is not an attractive one, but I can think of no better term—is
a prejudice or attitude of bias in favor of the interests of members
of one's own species and against those of members of other species.
It should be obvious that the fundamental objections to racism and
sexism made by Thomas Jefferson and Sojourner Truth apply
equally to speciesism. If possessing a higher degree of intelligence
does not entitle one human to use another for his or her own ends,
how can it entitle humans to exploit nonhumans for the same
purpose?[4]

Many philosophers and other writers have proposed the principle of equal consideration of interests, in some form or other, as a
basic moral principle; but not many of them have recognized that
this principle applies to members of other species as well as to our
own. Jeremy Bentham was one of the few who did realize this. In a
forward-looking passage written at the time when black slaves had
been freed by the French but in the British dominions were still
being treated in the way we now treat animals, Bentham wrote:

> The day *may* come when the rest of the animal creation may
> acquire those rights which never could have been withholden
> from them but by the hand of tyranny. The French have already
> discovered that the blackness of the skin is no reason why a
> human being should be abandoned without redress to the caprice
> of a tormentor. It may one day come to be recognized that the
> number of the legs, the villosity of the skin, or the termination of
> the *os sacrum* are reasons equally insufficient for abandoning a
> sensitive being to the same fate. What else is it that should trace
> the insuperable line? Is it the faculty of reason, or perhaps the
> faculty of discourse? But a full-grown horse or dog is beyond
> comparison a more rational, as well as a more conversable animal,
> than an infant of a day or a week or even a month, old. But suppose
> they were otherwise, what would it avail? The question is not,
> Can they *reason?* nor Can they *talk?* but, Can they *suffer?*[5]

In this passage Bentham points to the capacity for suffering as
the vital characteristic that gives a being the right to equal consideration. The capacity for suffering—or more strictly, for suffering

and/or enjoyment or happiness—is not just another characteristic like the capacity for language or higher mathematics. Bentham is not saying that those who try to mark "the insuperable line" that determines whether the interests of a being should be considered happen to have chosen the wrong characteristic. By saying that we must consider the interests of all beings with the capacity for suffering or enjoyment Bentham does not arbitrarily exclude from consideration any interests at all—as those who draw the line with reference to the possession of reason or language do. The capacity for suffering and enjoyment is *a prerequisite for having interests at all*, a condition that must be satisfied before we can speak of interests in a meaningful way. It would be nonsense to say that it was not in the interests of a stone to be kicked along the road by a schoolboy. A stone does not have interests because it cannot suffer. Nothing that we can do to it could possibly make any difference to its welfare. The capacity for suffering and enjoyment is, however, not only necessary, but also sufficient for us to say that a being has interests—at an absolute minimum, an interest in not suffering. A mouse, for example, does have an interest in not being kicked along the road, because it will suffer if it is.

Although Bentham speaks of "rights" in the passage I have quoted, the argument is really about equality rather than about rights. Indeed, in a different passage, Bentham famously described "natural rights" as "nonsense" and "natural and imprescriptible rights" as "nonsense upon stilts." He talked of moral rights as a shorthand of referring to protections that people and animals morally ought to have; but the real weight of the moral argument does not rest on the assertion of the existence of the right, for this in turn has to be justified on the basis of the possibilities for suffering and happiness. In this way we can argue for equality for animals without getting embroiled in philosophical controversies about the ultimate nature of rights.

In misguided attempts to refute the arguments of this book, some philosophers have gone to much trouble developing arguments to show that animals do not have rights.[6] They have claimed that to have rights a being must be autonomous, or must be a member of a community, or must have the ability to respect the rights of others, or must possess a sense of justice. These claims are irrelevant to the case for Animal Liberation. The language of rights is a convenient political shorthand. It is even more valuable in the era of thirty-second TV news clips than it was in Bentham's day; but in the argument for radical change in our attitude to animals, it is in no way necessary.

If a being suffers there can be no moral justification for refusing to take that suffering into consideration. No matter what the nature of the being, the principle of equality requires that its suffering be counted equally with the like suffering—insofar as rough comparisons can be made—of any other being. If a being is not capable of suffering, or of experiencing enjoyment or happiness, there is nothing to be taken into account. So the limit of sentience (using the term as a convenient is not strictly accurate shorthand for the capacity to suffer and/or experience enjoyment) is the only defensible boundary of concern for the interests of others. To mark this boundary by some other characteristic like intelligence or rationality would be to mark it in an arbitrary manner. Why not choose some other characteristic, like skin color?

Racists violate the principle of equality by giving greater weight to the interests of members of their own race when there is a clash between their interests and the interests of those of another race. Sexists violate the principle of equality by favoring the interests of their own sex. Similarly, speciesists allow the interests of their own species to override the greater interests of members of other species. The pattern is identical in each case.

Most human beings are speciesists. The following chapters show that ordinary human beings—not a few exceptionally cruel or heartless humans, but the overwhelming majority of humans—take an active part in, acquiesce in, and allow their taxes to pay for practices that require the sacrifice of the most important interests of members of others species in order to promote the most trivial interests of our own species.

There is, however, one general defense of the practices to be described in the next two chapters that needs to be disposed of before we discuss the practices themselves. It is a defense which, if true, would allow us to do anything at all to nonhumans for the slightest reason, or for no reason at all, without incurring any justifiable reproach. This defense claims that we are never guilty of neglecting the interests of other animals for one breathtakingly simple reason: they have no interests. Nonhuman animals have no interests, according to this view, because they are not capable of suffering. By this is not meant merely that they are not capable of suffering in all the ways that human beings are—for instance, that a calf is not capable of suffering from the knowledge that it will be killed in six months time. That modest claim is, no doubt, true; but it does not clear humans of the charge of speciesism, since it allows that animals may suffer in other ways—for instance, by being given electric shocks, or being kept in small, cramped cages. The defense I am about to discuss is the much more sweeping, although correspondingly less plausible, claim that animals are incapable of suffering in any way at all; that they are, in fact, unconscious automata, possessing neither thoughts nor feelings nor a mental life of any kind.

Do animals other than humans feel pain? How do we know? Well, how do we know if anyone, human or nonhuman, feels pain? We know that we ourselves can feel pain. We know this from the direct experience of pain that we have when, for instance, somebody presses a lighted cigarette against the back of our hand. But how do we know that anyone else feels pain? We cannot directly experience anyone else's pain, whether that "anyone" is our best friend or a stray dog. Pain is a state of consciousness, a "mental event," and as such it can never be observed. Behavior like writhing, screaming, or drawing one's hand away from the lighted cigarette is not pain itself; nor are the recordings a neurologist might take of activity within the brain observations of pain itself. Pain is something that we feel, and we can only infer that others are feeling it from various external indications.

In theory, we *could* always be mistaken when we assume that other human beings feel pain. It is conceivable that one of our close friends is really a cleverly constructed robot, controlled by a brilliant scientist so as to give all the signs of feeling pain, but really no more sensitive than any other machine. We can never know, with absolute certainty, that this is not the case. But while this might present a puzzle for philosophers, none of us has the slightest real doubt that our close friends feel pain just as we do. This is an inference, but a perfectly reasonable one, based on observations of their behavior in situations in which we would feel pain, and on the fact that we have every reason to assume that our friends are beings like us, with nervous systems like ours that can be assumed to function as ours do and to produce similar feelings in similar circumstances.

If it is justifiable to assume that other human beings feel pain as we do, is there any reason why a similar inference should be unjustifiable in the case of other animals?

Nearly all the external signs that lead us to infer pain in other humans can be seen in other species, especially the species most closely related to us—the species of mammals and birds. The behavioral signs include writhing, facial contortions, moaning, yelping or other forms of calling, attempts to avoid the source of pain, appearance of fear at the prospect of its repetition, and so on. In addition, we know that these animals have nervous systems very like ours, which respond physiologically as ours do when the animal is in circumstances in which we would feel pain: an initial rise of blood pressure, dilated pupils, perspiration, an increased pulse rate, and, if the stimulus continues, a fall in blood pressure. Although human beings have a more developed cerebral cortex than other animals, this part of the brain is concerned with thinking functions rather than with basic impulses, emotions, and feelings. These impulses, emotions, and feelings are located in the diencephalon, which is well developed in many other species of animals, especially mammals and birds.[7]

We also know that the nervous systems of other animals were not artificially constructed—as a robot might be artificially constructed—to mimic the pain behavior of humans. The nervous systems of animals evolved as our own did, and in fact the evolutionary history of human beings and other animals, especially mammals, did not diverge until the central features of our nervous systems were already in existence. A capacity to feel pain obviously enhances a species' prospects of survival, since it causes members of the species to avoid sources of injury. It is surely unreasonable to suppose that nervous systems that are virtually identical physiologically, have a common origin and a common evolutionary function, and result in similar forms of behavior in similar circumstances should actually operate in an entirely different manner on the level of subjective feelings.

It has long been accepted as sound policy in science to search for the simplest possible explanation of whatever it is we are trying to explain. Occasionally it has been claimed that it is for this reason "unscientific" to explain the behavior of animals by theories that refer to the animal's conscious feelings, desires, and so on—the idea being that if the behavior in question can be explained without invoking consciousness or feelings, that will be the simpler theory. Yet we can now see that such explanations, when assessed with respect to the actual behavior of both human and nonhuman animals, are actually far more complex than rival explanations. For we know from our own experience that explanations of our own behavior that did not refer to consciousness and the felling of pain would be incomplete; and it is simpler to assume that the similar behavior of animals with similar nervous systems is to be explained the same way than to try to invent some other explanation for the behavior of nonhuman animals as well as an explanation for the divergence between humans and nonhumans in this respect.

The overwhelming majority of scientists who have addressed themselves to this question agree. Lord Brain, one of the most eminent neurologists of our time, has said:

I personally can see no reason for conceding mind to my fellow men and denying it to animals. . . . I at least cannot doubt that the interests and activities of animals are correlated with awareness and feeling in the same way as my own, and which may be, for aught I know, just as vivid.[8]

The author of a book on pain writes:

Every particle of factual evidence supports the contention that the higher mammalian vertebrates experience pain sensations at least as acute as our own. To say that they feel less because they are lower animals is an absurdity; it can easily be shown that many of their senses are far more acute than ours—visual acuity in certain birds, hearing in most wild animals, and touch in others; these animals depend more than we do today on the sharpest possible awareness of a hostile environment. Apart from the complexity of the cerebral cortex (which does not directly perceive pain) their nervous systems are almost identical to ours and their reactions to pain remarkably similar, though lacking (so far as we know) the philosophical and moral overtones. The emotional element is all too evident, mainly in the form of fear and anger.[9]

In Britain, three separate expert government committees on matters relating to animals have accepted the conclusion that animals feel pain. After noting the obvious behavior evidence for this view, the members of the Committee on Cruelty to Wild Animals, set up in 1951, said:

. . . we believe that the physiological, and more particularly the anatomical, evidence fully justifies and reinforces the common-sense belief that animals feel pain.

And after discussing the evolutionary value of pain the committee's report concluded that pain is "of clear-cut biological usefulness" and this is "a third type of evidence that animals feel pain." The committee members then went on to consider forms of suffering other than mere physical pain and added that they were "satisfied that animals do suffer from acute fear and terror." Subsequent reports by British government committees on experiments on animals and on the welfare of animals under intensive farming methods agreed with this view, concluding that animals are capable of suffering both from straightforward physical injuries and from fear, anxiety, stress, and so on.[10] Finally, within the last decade, the publication of scientific studies with titles such as *Animal Thought, Animal Thinking,* and *Animal Suffering: The*

Science of Animal Welfare have made it plain that conscious awareness in nonhuman animals is now generally accepted as a serious subject for investigation.[11]

That might well be thought enough to settle the matter; but one more objection needs to be considered. Human beings in pain, after all, have one behavioral sign that nonhuman animals do not have: a developed language. Other animals may communicate with each other, but not, it seems, in the complicated way we do. Some philosophers, including Descartes, have thought it important that while humans can tell each other about their experience of pain in great detail, other animals cannot. (Interestingly, this once neat dividing line between humans and other species has now been threatened by the discovery that chimpanzees can be taught a language.[12]) But as Bentham pointed out long ago, the ability to use language is not relevant to the question of how a being ought to be treated—unless that ability can be linked to the capacity to suffer, so that the absence of a language casts doubt on the existence of this capacity.

This link may be attempted in two ways. First, there is a hazy line of philosophical thought, deriving perhaps from some doctrines associated with the influential philosopher Ludwig Wittgenstein, which maintains that we cannot meaningfully attribute states of consciousness to beings without language. This position seems to me very implausible. Language may be necessary for abstract thought, at some level anyway; but states like pain are more primitive, and have nothing to do with language.

The second and more easily understood way of linking language and the existence of pain is to say that the best evidence we can have that other creatures are in pain is that they tell us that they are. This is a distinct line of argument, for it is denying not that non–language-users conceivably *could* suffer, but only that we could ever have sufficient reason to *believe* that they are suffering. Still, this line of argument fails too. As Jane Goodall has pointed out in her study of chimpanzees, *In the Shadow of Man*, when it comes to the expression of feelings and emotions language is less important than nonlinguistic modes of communication such as a cheering pat on the back, an exuberant embrace, a clasp of the hands, and so on. The basic signals we use to convey pain, fear, anger, love, joy, surprise, sexual arousal, and many other emotional states are not specific to our own species.[13] The statement "I am in pain" may be one piece of evidence for the conclusion that the speaker is in pain, but it is not the only possible evidence, and since people sometimes tell lies, not even the best possible evidence.

Even if there were stronger grounds for refusing to attribute pain to those who do not have a language, the consequences of this refusal might lead us to reject the conclusion. Human infants and young children are unable to use language. Are we to deny that a year-old child can suffer? If not, language cannot be crucial. Of course, most parents understand the responses of their children better than they understand the responses of other animals; but this is just a fact about the relatively greater knowledge that we have of our own species and the greater contact we have with infants as compared to animals. Those who have studied the behavior of other animals and those who have animals as companions soon learn to understand their responses as well as we understand those of an infant, and sometimes better.

So to conclude: there are no good reasons, scientific or philosophical, for denying that animals feel pain. If we do not doubt that other humans feel pain we should not doubt that other animals do so to.

Animals can feel pain. As we saw earlier, there can be no moral justification for regarding the pain (or pleasure) that animals feel as less important than the same amount of pain (or pleasure) felt by humans. But what practical consequences follow from this conclusion? To prevent misunderstanding I shall spell out what I mean a little more fully.

If I give a horse a hard slap across its rump with my open hand, the horse may start, but it presumably feels little pain. Its skin is thick enough to protect it against a mere slap. If I slap a baby in the same way, however, the baby will cry and presumably feel pain, for its skin is more sensitive. So it is worse to slap a baby than a horse, if both slaps are administered with equal force. But there must be some kind of blow—I don't know exactly what it would be, but perhaps a blow with a heavy stick—that would cause the horse as much pain as we cause a baby by slapping it with our hand. That is what I mean by "the same amount of pain," if we consider it wrong to inflict that much pain on a baby for no good reason then we must, unless we are speciesists, consider it equally wrong to inflict the same amount of pain on a horse for no good reason.

Other differences between humans and animals cause other complications. Normal adult human beings have mental capacities that will, in certain circumstances, lead them to suffer more than animals would in the same circumstances. If, for instance, we decided to perform extremely painful or lethal scientific experiments on normal adult humans, kidnapped at random from public parks for this purpose, adults who enjoy strolling in parks would become fearful that they would be kidnapped. The resultant terror would be a form of suffering additional to the pain of the experiment. The same experiments performed on nonhuman animals would cause less suffering since the animals would not have the anticipatory dread of being kidnapped and experimented upon. This does not mean, of course, that it would be *right* to perform the experiment on animals, but only that there is a reason, which is *not* speciesist, for preferring to use animals rather than normal adult human beings, if the experiment is to be done at all. It should be noted, however, that this same argument gives us a reason for preferring to use human infants—orphans perhaps—or severely retarded human beings for experiments, rather than adults, since infants and retarded humans would also have no idea of what was going to happen to them. So far as this argument is concerned nonhuman animals and infants and retarded humans are in the same category; and if we use this argument to justify experiments on nonhuman animals we have to ask ourselves whether we are also prepared to allow experiments on human infants and retarded adults; and if we make a distinction between animals and these humans, on what basis can we do it, other than a bare-faced—and morally indefensible—preference for members of our own species?

There are many matters in which the superior mental powers of normal adult humans make a difference: anticipation, more detailed memory, greater knowledge of what is happening, and so on. Yet these differences do not all point to greater suffering on the part of the normal human being. Sometimes animals may suffer more because of their more limited understanding. If, for instance, we are taking prisoners in wartime we can explain to them that although they must submit to capture, search, and confinement, they will not otherwise be harmed and will be set free at the conclusion of hostilities. If we capture wild animals, however, we cannot explain that we are not threatening their lives. A wild animal cannot distinguish an attempt to overpower and confine from an attempt to kill; the one causes as much terror as the other.

It may be objected that comparisons of the sufferings of different species are impossible to make and that for this reason when the interests of animals and humans clash the principle of equality gives no guidance. It is probably true that comparisons of suffering between members of different species cannot be made precisely, but precision is not essential. Even if we were to prevent the infliction of suffering on animals only when it is quite certain that the interests of humans will not be affected to anything like the extent that animals are affected, we would be forced to make radical changes in our treatment of animals that would involve our diet, the farming methods we use, experimental procedures in many fields of science, our approach to wildlife and to hunting, trapping and the wearing of furs, and areas of entertainment like circuses, rodeos, and zoos. As a result, a vast amount of suffering would be avoided.

So far I have said a lot about inflicting suffering on animals, but nothing about killing them. This omission has been deliberate. The application of the principle of equality to the infliction of suffering is, in theory at least, fairly straightforward. Pain and suffering are in themselves bad and should be prevented or minimized, irrespective of the race, sex, or species of the being that suffers. How bad a pain is depends on how intense it is and how long its lasts, but pains of the same intensity and duration are equally bad, whether felt by humans or animals.

The wrongness of killing a being is more complicated. I have kept, and shall continue to keep, the question of killing in the background because in the present state of human tyranny over other species the more simple, straightforward principle of equal consideration of pain or pleasure is a sufficient basis for identifying and protesting against all the major abuses of animals that human beings practice. Nevertheless, it is necessary to say something about killing.

Just as most human beings are speciesists in their readiness to cause pain to animals when they would not cause a similar pain to humans for the same reason, so most human beings are speciesists in their readiness to kill other animals when they would not kill human beings. We need to proceed more cautiously here, however, because people hold widely differing views about when it is legitimate to kill humans, as the continuing debates over abortion and euthanasia attest. Nor have moral philosophers been able to agree on exactly what it is that makes it wrong to kill human beings, and under what circumstances killing a human being may be justifiable.

Let us consider first the view that it is always wrong to take an innocent human life. We may call this the "sanctity of life" view. People who take this view oppose abortion and euthanasia. They do not usually, however, oppose the killing of nonhuman animals—so perhaps it would be more accurate to describe this view as the "sanctity of *human* life" view. The belief that human life, and only human life, is sacrosanct is a form of speciesism. To see this, consider the following example.

Assume that, as sometimes happens, an infant has been born with massive and irreparable brain damage. The damage is so severe that the infant can never be any more than a "human vegetable," unable to talk, recognize other people, act independently of others, or develop a sense of self-awareness. The parents of the infant, realizing that they cannot hope for any improvement in their child's condition and being in any case unwilling to spend, or ask the state to spend, the thousands of dollars that would be needed annually for proper care of the infant, ask the doctor to kill the infant painlessly.

Should the doctor do what the parents ask? Legally, the doctor should not, and in this respect the law reflects the sanctity of life view. The life of every human being is sacred. Yet people who would say this about the infant do not object to the killing of nonhuman animals. How can they justify their different judgments? Adult chimpanzees, dogs, pigs, and members of many other species far surpass the brain-damaged infant in their ability to relate to others, act independently, be self-aware, and any other capacity that could reasonably be said to give value to life. With the most intensive care possible, some severely retarded infants can never achieve the intelligence level of a dog. Nor can we appeal to the concern of the infant's parents, since they themselves, in this imaginary example (and in some actual cases) do not want the infant kept alive. The only thing that distinguished the infant from the animal, in the eyes of those who claim it has a "right to life," is that it is, biologically, a member of the species Homo sapiens, whereas chimpanzees, dogs, and pigs are not. But to use *this* difference as the basis for granting a right to life to the infant and not to the other animals is, of course, pure speciesism.[14] It is exactly the kind of arbitrary difference that the most crude and overt kind of racist uses in attempting to justify racial discrimination.

This does not mean that to avoid speciesism we must hold that it is as wrong to kill a dog as it is to kill a human being in full possession of his or her faculties. The only position that is irredeemably speciesist is the one that tries to make the boundary of the right to life run exactly parallel to the boundary of our own species. Those who hold the sanctity of life view do this, because while distinguishing sharply between human beings and other animals they allow no distinctions to be made within our own species, objecting to the killing of the severely retarded and the hopelessly senile as strongly as they object to the killing of normal adults.

To avoid speciesism we must allow that beings who are similar in all relevant respects have a similar right to life—and mere membership in our own biological species cannot be a morally relevant criterion for this right. Within these limits we could still hold, for instance, that it is worse to kill a normal adult human, with a capacity for self-awareness and the ability to plan for the future and have meaningful relations with others, than it is to kill a mouse, which presumably does not share all of these characteristics; or we might appeal to the close family and other personal ties that humans have but mice do not have to the same degree; or we might think that it is the consequences for other humans, who will be put in fear for their own lives, that makes the critical difference; or we might think it is some combination of these factors, or other factors altogether.

Whatever criteria we choose, however, we will have to admit that they do not follow precisely the boundary of our own species. We may legitimately hold that there are some features of certain beings that make their lives more valuable than those of other beings; but there will surely be some nonhuman animals whose lives, by any standards, are more valuable than the lives of some humans. A chimpanzee, dog, or pig, for instance, will have a higher degree of self-awareness and a greater capacity for meaningful relations with others than a severely retarded infant or someone in a state of advanced senility. So if we base the right to life on these characteristics we must grant these animals a right to life as good as, or better than, such retarded or senile humans.

This argument cuts both ways. It could be taken as showing that chimpanzees, dogs, and pigs, along with some other species, have a right to life and we commit a grave moral offense whenever we kill them, even when they are old and suffering and our intention is to put them out of their misery. Alternatively one could take the argument as showing that the severely retarded and hopelessly senile have no right to life and may be killed for quite trivial reasons, as we now kill animals.

Since the main concern of this book is with ethical questions having to do with animals and not with the morality of euthanasia I shall not attempt to settle this issue finally.[15] I think it is reasonably clear, though, that while both of the positions just described avoid speciesism, neither is satisfactory. What we need is some middle position that would avoid speciesism but would not make the lives of the retarded and senile as cheap as the lives of pigs and dogs now are, or make the lives of pigs and dogs so sacrosanct that we think it wrong to put them out of hopeless misery. What we must do is bring nonhuman animals within our sphere of moral concern and cease to treat their lives as expendable for whatever trivial purposes we may have. At the same time, once we realize that the fact that a being is a member of our own species is not in itself enough to make it always wrong to kill that being, we may come to reconsider our policy of preserving human lives at all costs, even when there is no prospect of a meaningful life or of existence without terrible pain.

I conclude, then, that a rejection of speciesism does not imply that all lives are of equal worth. While self-awareness, the capacity to think ahead and have hopes and aspirations for the future, the capacity for meaningful relations with others and so on are not relevant to the question of inflicting pain—since pain is pain, whatever other capacities, beyond the capacity to feel pain, the being may have—these capacities are relevant to the question of taking life. It is not arbitrary to hold that the life of a self-aware being, capable of abstract thought, of planning for the future, of complex acts of communication, and so on, is more valuable than the life of a being without these capacities. To see the difference between the issues of inflicting pain and taking life, consider how we would choose within our own species. If we had to choose to save the life of a normal human being or an intellectually disabled human being, we would probably choose to save the life of a normal human being; but if we had to choose between preventing pain in the normal human being or the intellectually disabled one—imagine that both have received painful but superficial injuries, and we only have enough painkiller for one of them—it is not nearly so clear how we ought to choose. The same is true when we consider other species. The evil of pain is, in itself, unaffected by the other characteristics of the being who feels the pain; the value of life is affected by these other characteristics. To give just one reason for this difference, to take the life of a being who has been hoping, planning, and working for some future goal is to deprive that being of the fulfillment of all those efforts; to take the life of a being with a mental capacity below the level needed to grasp that one is a being with a future— much less make plans for the future—cannot involve this particular kind of loss.[16]

Normally this will mean that if we have to choose between the life of a human being and the life of another animal we should choose to save the life of the human; but there may be special cases in which the reverse holds true, because the human being in question does not have the capacities of a normal human being. So this view is not speciesist, although it may appear to be at first glance. The preference, in normal cases, for saving a human life over the life of an animal when a choice *has* to be made is a preference based on the characteristics that normal humans have, and not on the mere fact that they are members of our own species. This is why when we consider members of our own species who lack the characteristics of normal humans we can no longer say that their lives are always to be preferred to those of other animals. This issue comes up in a practical way in the following chapter. In general, though, the question of when it is wrong to kill (painlessly) an animal is one to which we need give no precise answer. As long as we remember that we should give the same respect to the lives of animals as we give to the lives of those humans at a similar mental level, we shall not go far wrong.[17]

Notes

1. For Bentham's moral philosophy, see his *Introduction to the Principles of Morals and Legislation,* and for Sidgwick's see *The Methods of Ethics,* 1907 (the passage is quoted from the seventh edition; reprint, London: Macmillan, 1963), p. 382. As examples of leading contemporary moral philosophers who incorporate a requirement of equal consideration of interests, see R.M. Hare, *Freedom and Reason* (New York: Oxford University Press, 1963), and John Rawls, *A Theory of Justice* (Cambridge: Harvard University Press, Belknap Press, 1972). For a brief account of the essential agreement on this issue between these and other positions, see R.M. Hare, "Rules of War and Moral Reasoning," *Philosophy and Public Affairs* 1 (2) (1972).
2. Letter to Henry Gregoire, February 25, 1809.
3. Reminiscences by Francis D. Gage, from Susan B. Anthony, *The History of Woman Suffrage,* vol. 1; the passage is to be found in the extract in Leslie Tanner, ed., *Voices From Women's Liberation* (New York: Signet, 1970).
4. I own the term "speciesism" to Richard Ryder. It has become accepted in general use since the first edition of this book, and now appears in *The Oxford English Dictionary,* second edition (Oxford: Clarendon Press, 1989).
5. *Introduction to the Principles of Morals and Legislation,* chapter 17.
6. See M. Levin, "Animal Rights Evaluated," *Humanist* 37: 14–15 (July/August 1977); M.A. Fox, "Animal Liberation: A Critique," *Ethics* 88: 134–138 (1978); C. Perry and G.E. Jones, "On Animal Rights," *International Journal of Applied Philosophy* 1:39–57 (1982).
7. Lord Brain, "Presidential Address," in C.A. Keele and R. Smith, eds., *The Assessment of Pain in Men and Animals* (London: Universities Federation for Animal Welfare, 1962).
8. Lord Brain, "Presidential Address," p. 11.
9. Richard Serjeant, *The Spectrum of Pain* (London: Hart Davis, 1969), p. 72.
10. See the reports of the Committee on Cruelty to Wild Animals (Command Paper 8266, 1951), paragraphs 36–42; the Departmental Committee on Experiments on Animals (Command Paper 2641, 1965), paragraphs 179–182; and the Technical Committee to Enquire into the Welfare of Animals Kept under Intensive Livestock Husbandry Systems (Command Paper 2836, 1965), paragraphs 26–28 (London: Her Majesty's Stationery Office).

11. See Stephen Walker, *Animal Thoughts* (London: Routledge and Kegan Paul, 1983); Donald Griffin, *Animal Thinking* (Cambridge: Harvard University Press, 1984); and Marian Stamp Dawkins, *Animal Suffering: The Science of Animal Welfare* (London: Chapman and Hall, 1980).

12. See Eugene Linden, *Apes, Men and Language* (New York: Penguin, 1976); for popular accounts of some more recent work, see Erik Eckholm, "Pygmy Chimp Readily Learns Language Skill," *The New York Times*, June 24, 1985; and "The Wisdom of Animals," *Newsweek*, May 23, 1988.

13. *In the Shadow of Man* (Boston: Houghton Mifflin, 1971), p. 225. Michael Peters makes a similar point in "Nature and Culture," in Stanley and Roslind Godlovitch and John Harris, eds., *Animals, Men and Morals* (New York: Taplinger, 1972). For examples of some of the inconsistencies in denials that creatures without language can feel pain, see Bernard Rollin, *The Unheeded Cry: Animal Consciousness, Animal Pain, and Science* (Oxford: Oxford University Press, 1989).

14. I am here putting aside religious views, for example the doctrine that all and only human beings have immortal souls, or are made in the image of God. Historically these have been very important, and no doubt are partly responsible for the idea that human life has a special sanctity. (For further historical discussion see Chapter 5.) Logically, however, these religious views are unsatisfactory, since they do not offer a reasoned explanation of why it should be that all humans and no nonhumans have immortal souls. This belief too, therefore, comes under suspicion as a form of speciesism. In any case, defenders of the "sanctity of life" view are generally reluctant to base their position on purely religious doctrines, since these doctrines are no longer as widely accepted as they once were.

15. For a general discussion of these questions, see my *Practical Ethics* (Cambridge: Cambridge University Press, 1979), and for a more detailed discussion of the treatment of handicapped infants, see Helga Kuhse and Peter Singer, *Should the Baby Live?* (Oxford: Oxford University Press, 1985).

16. For a development of this theme, see my essay, "Life's Uncertain Voyage," in P. Pettit, R. Sylvan and J. Norman, eds., *Metaphysics and Morality* (Oxford: Blackwell, 1987), pp. 154–172.

17. The preceding discussion, which has been changed only slightly since the first edition, has often been overlooked by critics of the Animal Liberation movement. It is a common tactic to seek to ridicule the Animal Liberation position by maintaining that, as an animal experimenter put it recently, "Some of these people believe that every insect, every mouse, has as much right to life as a human." (Dr. Irving Weissman, as quoted in Katherine Bishop, "From Shop to Lab to Farm, Animal Rights Battle is Felt," *The New York Times*, January 14, 1989.) It would be interesting to see Dr. Weissman name some prominent Animal Liberationists who hold this view. Certainly (assuming only

that he was referring to the right to life of a human being with mental capacities very different from those of the insect and the mouse) the position described is not mine. I doubt that it is held by many—if any—in the Animal Liberation movement.

Questions and Activities

1. Write a summary of Singer's argument, including his position and support, for a group of people who are not familiar with the idea that animals should have rights.

2. Compare Singer's ideas with those expressed in the "Declaration of Independence," Stanton's "Seneca Falls Declaration," or Wollstone-craft's "Vindication of the Rights of Woman." In particular, identify those occasions when the writers call on similar values to support their positions. Then write an argument in which you support or oppose using identical values to support animal and human rights.

Declaration of the Rights of Man and Citizen

NATIONAL ASSEMBLY OF FRANCE

The first draft of the following document was prepared in the summer of 1789, at the beginning of the French Revolution. The version printed here became the preamble to the Constitution of France in 1791.

The representatives of the French people, organized in National Assembly, considering that ignorance, forgetfulness, or contempt of the rights of man are the sole causes of the public miseries and of the corruption of governments, have resolved to set forth in a solemn declaration the natural, inalienable, and sacred rights of man, in order that this declaration, being ever present to all the members of the social body, may unceasingly remind them of their rights and their duties: in order that the acts of the legislative power and those of the executive power may be each moment compared with the aim of every political institution and thereby may be more respected; and in order that the demands of the citizens, grounded henceforth upon simple and incontestable principles, may always take the direction of maintaining the constitution and the welfare of all.

In consequence, the National Assembly recognizes and declares, in the presence and under the auspices of the Supreme Being, the following rights of man and citizen.

1. Men are born and remain free and equal in rights. Social distinctions can be based only upon public utility.
2. The aim of every political association is the preservation of the natural and imprescriptible rights of man. These rights are liberty, property, security, and resistance to oppression.
3. The source of all sovereignty is essentially in the nation; no body, no individual can exercise authority that does not proceed from it in plain terms.
4. Liberty consists in the power to do anything that does not injure others; accordingly, the exercise of the natural rights of each man has for its limits those that secure to the other members of society the enjoyment of these same rights. These limits can be determined only by law.
5. The law has the right to forbid only such actions as are injurious to society. Nothing can be forbidden that is not interdicted by the law and no one can be constrained to do that which it does not order.
6. Law is the expression of the general will. All citizens have the right to take part personally or by their representatives in its formation. It must be the same for all, whether it protects or punishes. All citizens being equal in its eyes, are equally eligible to all public dignities, places, and employments, according to their capacities, and without other distinction than that of their virtues and their talents.
7. No man can be accused, arrested, or detained except in the cases determined by the law and according to the forms that it has prescribed. Those who procure, expedite, execute, or cause to be executed arbitrary orders ought to be punished: but every citizen summoned or seized in virtue of the law ought to render instant obedience; he makes himself guilty by resistance.
8. The law ought to establish only penalties that are strictly and obviously necessary and no one can be punished except in virtue of a law established and promulgated prior to the offence and legally applied.
9. Every man being presumed innocent until he has been pronounced guilty, if it is thought indispensable to arrest him, all severity that may not be necessary to secure his person ought to be strictly suppressed by law.

10. No one ought to be disturbed on account of his opinions, even religious, provided their manifestation does not derange the public order established by law.
11. The free communication of ideas and opinions is one of the most precious of the rights of man; every citizen then can freely speak, write, and print, subject to the responsibility for the abuse of this freedom in the cases determined by law.
12. The guarantee of the rights of man and citizen requires a public force; this force then is instituted for the advantage of all and not for the personal benefit of those to whom it is entrusted.
13. For the maintenance of the public force and for the expenses of administration a general tax is indispensable; it ought to be equally apportioned among all the citizens according to their means.
14. All the citizens have the right to ascertain, by themselves or by their representatives, the necessity of the public tax, to consent to it freely, to follow the employment of it, and to determine the quota, the assessment, the collection, and the duration of it.
15. Society has the right to call for an account from every public agent of its administration.
16. Any society in which the guarantee of the rights is not secured or the separation of powers not determined has no constitution at all.
17. Property being a sacred and inviolable right, no one can be deprived of it unless a legally established public necessity evidently demands it, under the condition of a just and prior indemnity.

Questions and Activities

1. Assume that this declaration is an argument—that it takes a position about the way the world *ought* to be. Choose one or more of the Articles of the declaration and write an argument in which your position is different from the one stated here.

2. The preamble and Article 2 state that the rights asserted here are inalienable. First, establish what "inalienable" means in this context. Then, write an argument in which your position is that these rights are not inalienable, but depend on society to allow them to exist. Give specific examples and reasoning to show that these rights depend on social consensus.

Universal Declaration of Human Rights

GENERAL ASSEMBLY OF
THE UNITED NATIONS

The following document was adopted in 1948 by the U.N. General Assembly.

Preamble

Whereas recognition of the inherent dignity and of the equal and inalienable rights of all members of the human family is the foundation of freedom, justice, and peace in the world,

Whereas disregard and contempt for human rights have resulted in barbarous acts which have outraged the conscience of mankind, and the advent of a world in which human beings shall enjoy freedom of speech and belief and freedom from fear and want has been proclaimed as the highest aspiration of the common people,

Whereas it is essential, if man is not to be compelled to have recourse, as a last resort, to rebellion against tyranny and oppression, that human rights should be protected by the rule of law,

Whereas it is essential to promote the development of friendly relations between nations,

Whereas the peoples of the United Nations have in the Charter reaffirmed their faith in fundamental human rights, in the dignity and worth of the human person and in the equal rights of men and women and have determined to promote social progress and better standards of life in larger freedom,

Whereas Member States have pledged themselves to achieve, in cooperation with the United Nations, the promotion of universal respect for and observance of human rights and fundamental freedoms,

Whereas a common understanding of these rights and freedoms is of the greatest importance for the full realization of this pledge.

Now, therefore, the General Assembly *proclaims*

This universal declaration of human rights as a common standard of achievement for all peoples and all nations, to the end that every individual and every organ of society, keeping this Declaration constantly in mind, shall strive by teaching and education to promote respect for these rights and freedoms and by progressive measures, national and international, to secure their universal and effective recognition and observance, both among the peoples of Member States themselves and among the peoples of territories under their jurisdiction.

Article 1

All human beings are born free and equal in dignity and rights. They are endowed with reason and conscience and should act toward one another in a spirit of brotherhood.

Article 2

Everyone is entitled to all the rights and freedoms set forth in this Declaration, without distinction of any kind, such as race, color, sex, language, religion, political or other opinion, national or social origin, property, birth, or other status.

Furthermore, no distinction shall be made on the basis of the political, jurisdictional, or international status of the country or territory to which a person belongs, whether it be independent, trust, non-self-governing or under any other limitation of sovereignty.

Article 3

Everyone has the right to life, liberty, and security of person.

Article 4

No one shall be held in slavery or servitude; slavery and the slave trade shall be prohibited in all their forms.

Article 5

No one shall be subjected to torture or to cruel, inhuman, or degrading treatment or punishment.

Article 6

Everyone has the right to recognition everywhere as a person before the law.

Article 7

All are equal before the law and are entitled without any discrimination to equal protection of the law. All are entitled to equal protection against any discrimination in violation of this Declaration and against any incitement to such discrimination.

Article 8

Everyone has the right to an effective remedy by the competent national tribunals for acts violating the fundamental rights granted him by the constitution or by law.

Article 9

No one shall be subjected to arbitrary arrest, detention, or exile.

Article 10

Everyone is entitled in full equality to a fair and public hearing by an independent and impartial tribunal, in the determination of his rights and obligations and of any criminal charge against him.

Article 11

1. Everyone charged with a penal offense has the right to be presumed innocent until proved guilty according to law in a public trial at which he has had all the guarantees necessary for his defense.
2. No one shall be held guilty of any penal offense on account of any act or omission which did not constitute a penal offense, under national or international law, at the time when it was committed. Nor shall a heavier penalty be imposed than the one that was applicable at the time the penal offense was committed.

Article 12

No one shall be subjected to arbitrary interference with his privacy, family, home, or correspondence, nor to attacks upon his honor and reputation. Everyone has the right to the protection of the law against such interference or attacks.

Article 13

1. Everyone has the right to freedom of movement and residence within the borders of each State.
2. Everyone has the right to leave any country, including his own, and to return to his country.

Article 14

1. Everyone has the right to seek and to enjoy in other countries asylum from persecution.
2. This right may not be invoked in the case of prosecutions genuinely arising from nonpolitical crimes or from acts contrary to the purposes and principles of the United Nations.

Article 15

1. Everyone has the right to a nationality.
2. No one shall be arbitrarily deprived of his nationality nor denied the right to change his nationality.

Article 16

1. Men and women of full age, without any limitation due to race, nationality, or religion, have the right to marry and to found a family. They are entitled to equal rights as to marriage, during marriage and at its dissolution.
2. Marriage shall be entered into only with the free and full consent of the intending spouses.
3. The family is the natural and fundamental group unit of society and is entitled to protection by society and the State.

Article 17

1. Everyone has the right to own property alone as well as in association with others.
2. No one shall be arbitrarily deprived of his property.

Article 18

Everyone has the right to freedom of thought, conscience, and religion; this right includes freedom to change his religion or belief, and freedom, either alone or in community with others and in public or private, to manifest his religion or belief in teaching, practice, worship, and observance.

Article 19

Everyone has the right to freedom of opinion and expression; this right includes freedom to hold opinions without interference and to seek, receive, and impart information and ideas through any media and regardless of frontiers.

Article 20

1. Everyone has the right to freedom of peaceful assembly and association.
2. No one may be compelled to belong to an association.

Article 21

1. Everyone has the right to take part in the government of his country, directly or through freely chosen representatives.
2. Everyone has the right of equal access to public service in his country.
3. The will of the people shall be the basis of the authority of government; this will shall be expressed in periodic and genuine elections which shall be by universal and equal suffrage and shall be held by secret vote or by equivalent free voting procedures.

Article 22

Everyone, as a member of society, has the right to social security and is entitled to realization, through national effort and international cooperation and in accordance with the organization and resources of each State, of the economic, social, and cultural rights indispensable for his dignity and the free development of his personality.

Article 23

1. Everyone has the right to work, to free choice of employment, to just and favorable conditions of work and to protection against unemployment.
2. Everyone, without any discrimination, has the right to equal pay for equal work.

3. Everyone who works has the right to just and favorable remuneration ensuring for himself and his family an existence worthy of human dignity, and supplemented, if necessary, by other means of social protection.
4. Everyone has the right to form and to join trade unions for the protection of his interests.

Article 24

Everyone has the right to rest and leisure, including reasonable limitation of working hours and periodic holidays with pay.

Article 25

1. Everyone has the right to a standard of living adequate for the health and well-being of himself and of his family, including food, clothing, housing, and medical care and necessary social services, and the right to security in the event of unemployment, sickness, disability, widowhood, old age, or other lack of livelihood in circumstances beyond his control.
2. Motherhood and childhood are entitled to special care and assistance. All children, whether born in or out of wedlock, shall enjoy the same social protection.

Article 26

1. Everyone has the right to education. Education shall be free, at least in the elementary and fundamental stages. Elementary education shall be compulsory. Technical and professional education shall be made generally available and higher education shall be equally accessible to all on the basis of merit.
2. Education shall be directed to the full development of human personality and to the strengthening of respect for human rights and fundamental freedoms. It shall promote understanding, tolerance, and friendship among all nations, racial or religious groups, and shall further the activities of the United Nations for the maintenance of peace.
3. Parents have a prior right to choose the kind of education that shall be given to their children.

Article 27

1. Everyone has the right freely to participate in the cultural life of the community, to enjoy the arts, and to share in scientific advancement and its benefits.
2. Everyone has the right to the protection of the moral and material interests resulting from any scientific, literary, or artistic production of which he is the author.

Article 28

Everyone is entitled to a social and international order in which the rights and freedoms set forth in this Declaration can be fully realized.

Article 29

1. Everyone has duties to the community in which alone the free and full development of his personality is possible.
2. In the exercise of his rights and freedoms, everyone shall be subject only to such limitations as are determined by law solely for the purpose of securing due recognition and respect for the rights and freedoms of others and of meeting the just requirements of morality, public order, and the general welfare in a democratic society.
3. These rights and freedoms may in no case be exercised contrary to the purposes and principles of the United Nations.

Article 30

Nothing in this Declaration may be interpreted as implying for any State, group, or person any right to engage in any activity or to perform any act aimed at the destruction of any of the rights and freedoms set forth herein.

Questions and Activities

1. Choose one of the articles in this Declaration and argue that under certain circumstances the common good may require that an individual's right be abridged or denied, at least temporarily. Be sure you

specify the circumstances fully and provide adequate support for your position.

2. Write an argument in which your position is that the provisions of the U.N. Declaration should have the force of law in all countries that belong to the United Nations—even if they supersede national laws.

From "An Oration, Delivered in Corinthian Hall, Rochester, July 5, 1852"

FREDERICK DOUGLASS

Frederick Douglass (1817–1895) was born as a slave in Maryland. In 1838, he escaped to Massachusetts, where he became a free man and a prominent abolitionist speaker and writer. He wrote Narrative of the Life of Frederick Douglass *in 1845; and from 1847 to 1860, he edited the abolitionist newspaper* North Star. *The speech printed here is an excellent example of nineteenth-century American oratory.*

My business, if I have any here to-day, is with the present. The accepted time with God and his cause is the ever-living now.

> Trust no future, however pleasant,
>   Let the dead past bury its dead;
> Act, act in the living present,
>   Heart within, and God overhead.

We have to do with the past only as we can make it useful to the present and to the future. To all inspiring motives, to noble needs which can be gained from the past, we are welcome. But now is the time, the important time. Your fathers have lived, died, and have done their work, and have done much of it well. You live and must die, and you must do your work. You have no right to enjoy a child's share in the labor of your fathers, unless your children are to be blest by your labors. You have no right to wear out and waste the hard-earned fame of your fathers to cover your indolence. Sydney Smith tells us that men seldom eulogize the wisdom and virtues of their fathers, but to excuse some folly or wickedness of their own. This truth is not a doubtful one. There are illustrations of it near and remote, ancient and modern. It was fashionable, hundreds of years ago, for the children of Jacob to boast, we have "Abraham to our father," when they had long lost Abraham's faith and spirit. That people contented themselves under the shadow of Abraham's great name, while they repudiated the deeds which made his name great. Need I remind you that a similar thing is being done all over this country to-day? Need I tell you that the Jews are not the only people who built the tombs of the prophets, and garnished the sepulchres of the righteous? Washington could not die till he had broken the chains of his slaves. Yet his monument is built up by the price of human blood, and the traders in the bodies and souls of men, shout— "We have Washington to *'our father.'* "—Alas! that it should be so; yet so it is.

> The evil that men do, lives after them,
> The good is oft' interred with their bones.

Fellow-citizens, pardon me, allow me to ask, why am I called upon to speak here to-day? What have I, or those I represent, to do with your national independence? Are the great principles of political freedom and of natural justice, embodied in that Declaration of Independence, extended to us? and am I, therefore, called upon to bring our humble offering to the national altar, and to confess the benefits and express devout gratitude for the blessings resulting from your independence to us?

Would to God, both for your sakes and ours, that an affirmative answer could be truthfully returned to these questions! Then would my task be light, and my burden easy and delightful. For *who* is there so cold, that a nation's sympathy could not warm him? Who so obdurate and dead to the claims of gratitude, that would not thankfully acknowledge such priceless benefits? Who so stolid and selfish, that would not give his voice to swell the hallelujahs of a nation's jubilee, when the chains of servitude had been torn from his limbs? I am not that man. In a case like that, the dumb might eloquently speak, and the "lame man leap as an hart."

But, such is not the state of the case. I say it with a sad sense of the disparity between us. I am not included within the pale of this glorious anniversary! Your high independence only reveals the immeasurable distance between us. The blessings in which you, this day, rejoice, are not enjoyed in common.—The rich inheritance of justice, liberty, prosperity and independence, bequeathed by your fathers, is shared by you, not by me. The sunlight that brought life and healing to you, has brought stripes and death to me. This Fourth of July is *yours*, not *mine. You* may rejoice, *I* must mourn. To drag a man in fetters into the grand illuminated temple of liberty, and call upon him to join you in joyous anthems, were inhuman mockery and sacrilegious irony. Do you mean, citizens, to mock me, by asking me to speak to-day? If so, there is a parallel to your conduct. And let me warn you that it is dangerous to copy the example of a nation whose crimes, towering up to heaven, were thrown down by the breath of the Almighty, burying that nation in irrecoverable ruin! I can to-day take up the plaintive lament of a peeled and woe-smitten people!

"By the rivers of Babylon, there we sat down. Yea! we wept when we remembered Zion. We hanged our harps upon the willows in the midst thereof. For there, they that carried us away captive, required of us a song; and they who wasted us required of us mirth, saying, Sing us one of the songs of Zion. How can we sing the Lord's song in a strange land? If I forget thee, O Jerusalem, let my right hand forget her cunning. If I do not remember thee, let my tongue cleave to the roof of my mouth."

Fellow-citizens; above your national, tumultuous joy. I hear the mournful wail of millions! whose chains, heavy and grievous yesterday, are, to-day, rendered more intolerable by the jubilee shouts that reach them. If I do forget, if I do not faithfully remember those bleeding children of sorrow this day, "may my right hand forget her cunning, and may my tongue cleave to the roof of my mouth!" To forget them, to pass lightly over their wrongs, and to chime in with the popular theme, would be treason most scandalous and shocking, and would make me a reproach before God and the world. My subject, then, fellow-citizens, is AMERICAN SLAVERY. I shall see, this day, and its popular characteristics, from the slave's point of view. Standing, there, identified with the American bondman, making his wrongs mine, I do not hesitate to declare, with all my soul, that the character and conduct of this nation never looked blacker to me than on this 4th of July! Whether we turn to the declarations of the past, or to the professions of the present, the conduct of the nation seems equally hideous and revolting. America is false to the past, false to the present, and solemnly binds herself to be false to the future. Standing with God and the crushed and bleeding slave on this occasion, I will, in the name of humanity which is outraged, in the name of liberty which is fettered, in the name of the constitution and the Bible, which are disregarded and trampled upon, dare to call in question and to denounce, with all the emphasis I can command, everything that serves to perpetuate slavery—the great sin and shame of America! "I will not equivocate; I will not excuse;" I will use the severest language I can command; and yet no one word shall escape me that any man, whose judgment is not blinded by prejudice, or who is not at heart a slaveholder, shall not confess to be right and just.

But I fancy I hear some one of my audience say, it is just in this circumstance that you and your brother abolitionists fail to make a favorable impression on the public mind. Would you argue more, and denounce less, would you persuade more, and rebuke less, your cause would be much more likely to succeed. But, I submit, where all is plain there is nothing to be argued. What point in the anti-slavery creed would you have me argue? On what branch of the subject do the people of this country need light? Must I undertake to prove that the slave is a man? That point is conceded already. Nobody doubts it. The slaveholders themselves acknowledge it in the enactment of laws for the government. They acknowledge it when they punish disobedience on the part of the slave. There are seventy-two crimes in the State of Virginia, which, if committed by a black man, (no matter how ignorant he be,) subject him to the punishment of death; while only two of the same crimes will subject a white man to the like punishment.—What is this but the acknowledgement that the slave is a moral, intellectual and responsible being. The manhood of the slave is conceded. It is admitted in the fact that Southern statute books are covered with enactments forbidding, under severe fines and penalties, the teaching of the slave to read or to write.—When you can point to any such laws, in reference to the beasts of the field, then I may consent to argue the manhood of the slave. When the dogs in your streets, when the fowls of the air, when the cattle on your hills, when the fish of the sea, and the reptiles that crawl, shall be unable to distinguish the slave from a brute, *then* will I argue with you that the slave is a man!

For the present, it is enough to affirm the equal manhood of the negro race. Is it not astonishing that, while we are ploughing, planting and reaping, using all kinds of mechanical tools, erecting houses, constructing bridges, building ships, working in metals of brass, iron, copper, silver and gold; that, while we are reading, writing and cyphering, acting as clerks, merchants and secretaries, having among us lawyers, doctors, ministers, poets, authors, editors, orators and teachers; that, while we are engaged in all manner of enterprises common to other men, digging gold in California, capturing the whale in the Pacific, feeding sheep and cattle on the hill-side, living, moving, acting, thinking, planning, living in families as husbands, wives and children, and, above all, confessing and worshipping the Christian's God, and looking hopefully for life and immortality beyond the grave, we are called upon to prove that we are men!

Would you have me argue that man is entitled to liberty? that he is the rightful owner of his own body? You have already declared it. Must I argue the wrongfulness of slavery? Is that a question for

Republicans? Is it to be settled by the rules of logic and argumenta-
tion, as a matter beset with great difficulty, involving a doubtful
application of the principle of justice, hard to be understood? How
should I look to-day, in the presence of Americans, dividing, and
subdividing a discourse, to show that men have a natural right to
freedom? speaking of it relatively, and positively, negatively, and
affirmatively. To do so, would be to make myself ridiculous, and to
offer an insult to your understanding.—There is not a man beneath
the canopy of heaven, that does not know that slavery is wrong *for
him.*

What, am I to argue that it is wrong to make men brutes, to rob
them of their liberty, to work them without wages, to keep them
ignorant of their relations to their fellow men, to beat them with
sticks, to flay their flesh with the lash, to load their limbs with
irons, to hunt them with dogs, to sell them at auction, to sunder
their families, to knock out their teeth, to burn their flesh, to starve
them into obedience and submission to their masters? Must I argue
that a system thus marked with blood, and stained with pollution,
is wrong? No! I will not. I have better employment for my time and
strength, than such arguments would imply.

What, then, remains to be argued? Is it that slavery is not
divine; that God did not establish it; that our doctors of divinity are
mistaken? There is blasphemy in the thought. That which is inhuman, cannot be divine! *Who* can reason on such a proposition? They
that can, may; I cannot. The time for such argument is past.

At a time like this, scorching irony, not convincing argument,
is needed. O! had I the ability, and could I reach the nation's ear, I
would, to-day, pour out a fiery stream of biting ridicule, blasting
reproach, withering sarcasm, and stern rebuke. For it is not light
that is needed, but fire; it is not the gentle shower, but thunder. We
need the storm, the whirlwind, and the earthquake. The feeling of
the nation must be quickened; the conscience of the nation must
be roused; the propriety of the nation must be startled; the hypocrisy of the nation must be exposed; and its crimes against God and
man must be proclaimed and denounced.

What, to the American slave, is your 4th of July? I answer; a day
that reveals to him, more than all other days in the year, the gross
injustice and cruelty to which he is the constant victim. To him,
your celebration is a sham; your boasted liberty, an unholy license;
your national greatness, swelling vanity; your sounds of rejoicing
are empty and heartless; your denunciations of tyrants, brass
fronted impudence; your shouts of liberty and equality, hollow
mockery; your prayers and hymns, your sermons and thanksgiv-
ings, with all your religious parade, and solemnity, are, to him,

mere bombast, fraud, deception, impiety, and hypocrisy—a thin veil to cover up crimes which would disgrace a nation of savages. There is not a nation on the earth guilty of practices, more shocking and bloody, than are the people of these United States, at this very hour.

Go where you may, search where you will, roam through all the monarchies and despotisms of the old world, travel through South America, search out every abuse, and when you have found the last, lay your facts by the side of the every day practices of this nation, and you will say with me, that, for revolting barbarity and shameless hypocrisy, America reigns without a rival.

Take the American slave-trade, which we are told by the papers, is especially prosperous just now. Ex-Senator Benton tells us that the price of men was never higher than now. He mentions the fact to show that slavery is in no danger. This trade is one of the peculiarities of American institutions. It is carried on in all the large towns and cities in one half of this confederacy; and millions are pocketed every year, by dealers in this horrid traffic. In several states, this trade is a chief source of wealth. It is called (in contradistinction to the foreign slave-trade) *"the internal slave-trade."* It is, probably, called so, too, in order to divert from it the horror with which the foreign slave-trade is contemplated. That trade has long since been denounced by this government, as piracy. It has been denounced with burning words, from the high places of the nation, as an execrable traffic. To arrest it, to put an end to it, this nation keeps a squadron, at immense cost, on the coast of Africa. Everywhere, in this country, it is safe to speak of this foreign slave-trade, as a most inhuman traffic, opposed alike to the laws of God and of man. The duty to extirpate and destroy it is admitted even by our DOCTORS OF DIVINITY. In order to put an end to it, some of these last have consented that their colored brethren (nominally free) should leave this country, and establish themselves on the western coast of Africa! It is, however, a notable fact, that, while so much execration is poured out by Americans, upon those engaged in the foreign slave-trade, the men engaged in the slave-trade between the states pass without condemnation, and their business is deemed honorable.

Behold the practical operation of this internal slave-trade, the American slave-trade, sustained by American politics and American religion. Here you will see men and women, reared like swine, for the market. You know what is a swine-drover? I will show you a man-drover. They inhabit all our Southern States. They perambulate the country, and crowd the highways of the nation, with droves of human stock. You will see one of these human flesh jobbers, armed with pistol, whip, and bowie-knife, driving a company of a hundred men, women, and children, from the Potomac to the slave market at New Orleans. These wretched people are to be sold singly, or in lots, to suit purchasers. They are food for the cotton-field, and the deadly sugar-mill. Mark the sad procession, as it moves wearily along, and the inhuman wretch who drives them. Hear his savage yells and his blood-chilling oaths, as he hurries on his affrighted captives! There, see the old man, with locks thinned and gray. Cast one glance, if you please, upon that young mother, whose shoulders are bare to the scorching sun, her briny tears falling on the brow of the babe in her arms. See, too, that girl of thirteen, weeping, *yes!* weeping, as she thinks of the mother from whom she has been torn! The drove moves tardily. Heat and sorrow have nearly consumed their strength; suddenly you hear a quick snap, like the discharge of a rifle; the fetters clank, and the chain rattles simultaneously; your ears are saluted with a scream, that seems to have torn its way to the centre of your soul! The crack you heard, was the sound of the slave-whip; the scream you heard, was from the woman you saw with the babe. Her speed had faltered under the weight of her child and her chains! that gash on her shoulder tells her to move on. Follow this drove to New Orleans. Attend the auction; see men examined like horses; see the forms of women rudely and brutally exposed to the shocking gaze of American slave-buyers. See this drove sold and separated for ever; and never forget the deep, sad sobs that arose from that scattered multitude. Tell me citizens, WHERE, under the sun, you can witness a spectacle more fiendish and shocking. Yet this is but a glance at the American slave-trade, as it exists, at this moment, in the ruling part of the United States.

I was born amid such sights and scenes. To me the American slave-trade is a terrible reality. When a child, my soul was often pierced with a sense of its horrors. I lived on Philpot Street, Fell's Point, Baltimore, and have watched from the wharves, the slave ships in the Basin, anchored from the shore, with their cargoes of human flesh, waiting for favorable winds to waft them down the Chesapeake. There was, at that time, a grand slave mart kept at the head of Pratt Street, by Austin Woldfolk. His agents were sent into every town and county in Maryland, announcing their arrival, through the papers, and on flaming *"hand-bills,"* headed CASH FOR NEGROES. These men were generally well dressed men, and very captivating in their manners. Ever ready to drink, to treat, and to gamble. The fate of many a slave has depended upon the turn of a single card; and many a child has been snatched from the arms of its mother, by bargains arranged in a state of brutal drunkenness.

The flesh-mongers gather up their victims by dozens, and drive them, chained, to the general depot at Baltimore. When a sufficient number have been collected here, a ship is chartered, for the purpose of conveying the forlorn crew to Mobile, or to New Orleans. From the slave prison to the ship, they are usually driven in the darkness of night; for since the anti-slavery agitation, a certain caution is observed.

In the deep still darkness of midnight, I have been often aroused by the dead heavy footsteps, and the pitious cries of the chained gangs that passed our door. The anguish of my boyish heart was intense; and I was often consoled, when speaking to my mistress in the morning, to hear her say that the custom was very wicked; that she hated to hear the rattle of the chains, and the heart-rending cries. I was glad to find one who sympathized with me in my horror.

Fellow-citizens, this murderous traffic is, to-day, in active operation in this boasted republic. In the solitude of my spirit, I see clouds of dust raised on the highways of the South; I see the bleeding footsteps; I hear the doleful wail of fettered humanity, on the way to the slave-markets, where the victims are to be sold like *horses, sheep,* and *swine,* knocked off to the highest bidder. There I see the tenderest ties ruthlessly broken, to gratify the lust, caprice and rapacity of the buyers and sellers of men. My soul sickens at the sight.

> Is this the land your Fathers loved,
>   The freedom which they toiled to win?
> Is this the earth whereon they moved?
>   Are these the graves they slumber in?

But a still more inhuman, disgraceful, and scandalous state of things remains to be presented.

By an act of the American Congress, not yet two years old, slavery has been nationalized in its most horrible and revolting form. By that act, Mason & Dixon's line has been obliterated; New York has become as Virginia; and the power to hold, hunt, and sell men, women and children, as slaves, remains no longer a mere state institution, but is now an institution of the whole United States. The power is co-extensive with the star-spangled banner, and American Christianity. Where these go, may also go the merciless slave-hunter. Where these are, man is not sacred. He is a bird for the sportsman's gun. By that most foul and fiendish of all human decrees, the liberty and person of every man are put in peril. Your broad republican domain is hunting ground for *men. Not* for thieves and robbers, enemies of society, merely, but for men guilty of no crime. Your law-makers have commanded all good citizens to engage in this hellish sport. Your President, your Secretary of State, your *lords, nobles,* and ecclesiastics, enforce, as a duty you owe to your free and glorious country, and to your God, that you do this accursed thing. Not fewer than forty Americans, have, within the past two years, been hunted down, and, without a moment's warning, hurried away in chains, and consigned to slavery, and excruciating torture. Some of these have had wives and children, dependent on them for bread; but of this, no account was made. The right of the hunter to his prey, stands superior to the right of marriage, and to *all* rights in this republic, the rights of God included! For black men there are neither law, justice, humanity, nor religion. The Fugitive Slave *Law* makes MERCY TO THEM, A CRIME: and bribes the judge who tries them. An American JUDGE GETS TEN DOLLARS FOR EVERY VICTIM HE CONSIGNS to slavery, and five, when he fails to do so. The oath of any two villains is sufficient, under this hell-black enactment, to send the most pious and exemplary black man into the remorseless jaws of slavery! His own testimony is nothing. He can bring no witnesses for himself. The minister of American justice is bound, by the law to hear but *one* side; and *that* side, is the side of the oppressor. Let this damning fact be perpetually told. Let it be thundered around the world, that, in tyrant-killing, king-hating, people-loving, democratic, Christian America, the seats of justice are filled with judges, who hold their offices under an open and palpable *bribe,* and are bound, in deciding in the case of a man's liberty, *to hear only his accusers!*

In glaring violation of justice, in shameless disregard of the forms of administering law, in cunning arrangement to entrap the defenceless, and in diabolical intent, this Fugitive Slave Law stands alone in the annals of tyrannical legislation. I doubt if there be another nation on the globe, having the brass and the baseness to put such a law on the statute-book. If any man in this assembly thinks differently from me in this matter, and feels able to disprove my statements, I will gladly confront him at any suitable time and place he may select.

I take this law to be one of the grossest infringements of Christian Liberty, and, if the churches and ministers of our country were not stupidly blind, or most wickedly indifferent, they, too, would so regard it.

At the very moment that they are thanking God for the enjoyment of civil and religious liberty, and for the right to worship God according to the dictates of their own consciences, they are utterly silent in respect to a law which robs religion of its chief significance, and makes it utterly worthless to a world lying in wickedness. Did this law concern the *"mint, anise* and *cummin"*—abridge the right to sing psalms, to partake of the sacrament, or to engage in any of the ceremonies of religion, it would be smitten by the thunder of a thousand pulpits. A general shout would go up from the church, demanding *repeal, repeal, instant repeal!*—And it would go hard with that politician who presumed to solicit the votes of the people without inscribing this motto on his banner. Further, if this demand were not complied with, another Scotland would be added to the history of religious liberty, and the stern old covenanters would be thrown into the shade. A John Knox would be seen at every church door, and heard from every pulpit, and Fillmore would have no more quarter than was shown by Knox, to the beautiful, but treacherous Queen Mary of Scotland.—The fact that the church of our country, (with fractional exceptions,) does not esteem "the Fugitive Slave Law" as a declaration of war against religious liberty, implies that that church regards religion simply as a form of worship, an empty ceremony, and *not* a vital principle, requiring active benevolence, justice, love and good will towards man. It esteems sacrifice above mercy; psalm-singing above right doing; solemn meetings above practical righteousness. A worship that can be conducted by persons who refuse to give shelter to the houseless, to give bread to the hungry, clothing to the naked, and who enjoin obedience to a law forbidding these acts of mercy, is a curse, not a blessing to mankind. The Bible addresses all such persons as "scribes, pharisees, hypocrites, who pay tithe of *mint, anise,* and *cummin,* and have omitted the weightier matters of the law, judgment, mercy and faith."

But the church of this country is not only indifferent to the wrongs of the slave, it actually takes sides with the oppressors. It has made itself the bulwark of American slavery, and the shield of American slave-hunters. Many of its most eloquent Divines, who stand as the very lights of the church, have shamelessly given the sanction of religion, and the bible, to the whole slave system.—They have taught that man may, properly, be a slave; that the relation of master and slave is ordained of God; that to send back an escaped bondman to his master is clearly the duty of all the followers of the Lord Jesus Christ; and this horrible blasphemy is palmed off upon the world for christianity.

For my part, I would say, welcome infidelity! welcome atheism! welcome anything! in preference to the gospel, *as preached by those Divines!* They convert the very name of religion into an engine of tyranny, and barbarous cruelty, and serve to confirm more infidels, in this age, than all the infidel writings of Thomas Paine, Voltaire, and Bolingbroke, put together, have done. These ministers make religion a cold and flinty-hearted thing, having neither principles of right action, nor bowels of compassion. They strip the love of God of its beauty, and leave the throne of religion a huge, horrible, repulsive form. It is a religion for oppressors, tyrants, manstealers, and *thugs*. It is not that *"pure and undefiled religion"* which is from above, and which is *"first pure, then peaceable, easy to be entreated,* full of mercy and good fruits, *without partiality, and without hypocrisy."* But a religion which favors the rich against the poor; which exalts the proud above the humble; which divides mankind into two classes, tyrants and slaves; which says to the man in chains, *stay there;* and to the oppressor, *oppress on;* it is a religion which may be professed and enjoyed by all the robbers and enslavers of mankind; it makes God a respecter of persons, denies his fatherhood of the race, and tramples in the dust the great truth of the brotherhood of man. All this we affirm to be true of the popular church, and the popular worship of our land and nation—a religion, a church and a worship which, on the authority of inspired wisdom, we pronounce to be an abomination in the sight of God. In the language of Isaiah, the American church might be well addressed, "Bring no more vain oblations; incense is an abomination unto me: the new moons and Sabbaths, the calling of assemblies, I cannot away with; it is iniquity, even the solemn meeting. Your new moons, and your appointed feasts my soul hateth. They are a trouble to me; I am weary to bear them; and when ye spread forth your hands I will hide mine eyes from you. Yea! when ye make many prayers, I will not hear. YOUR HANDS ARE FULL OF BLOOD; cease to do evil, learn to do well, seek judgment; relieve the oppressed; judge for the fatherless; plead for the widow."

The American church is guilty, when viewed in connection with what it is doing to uphold slavery; but it is superlatively guilty when viewed in connection with its ability to abolish slavery.

The sin of which it is guilty is one of omission as well as of commission. Albert Barnes but uttered what the common sense of every man at all observant of the actual state of the case will receive as truth, when he declared that "There is no power out of the church that could sustain slavery an hour, if it were not sustained in it."

Let the religious press, the pulpit, the sunday school, the conference meeting, the great ecclesiastical, missionary, bible and tract associations of the land array their immense powers against slavery, and slave-holding; and the whole system of crime and blood would be scattered to the winds, and that they do not do this involves them in the most awful responsibility of which the mind can conceive.

In prosecuting the anti-slavery enterprise, we have been asked to spare the church, to spare the ministry; but *how*, we ask, could such a thing be done? We are met on the threshold of our efforts for the redemption of the slave, by the church and ministry of the country, in battle arrayed against us; and we are compelled to fight or flee. From *what* quarter, I beg to know, has proceeded a fire so deadly upon our ranks, during the last two years, as from the Northern pulpit? As the champions of oppressors, the chosen men of American theology have appeared—men, honored for their so called piety, and their real learning. The LORDS of Buffalo, the SPRINGS of New York, the LATHROPS of Auburn, the COXES and SPENCERS of Brooklyn, the GANNETS and SHARPS of Boston, the DEWEYS of Washington, and other great religious lights of the land, have, in utter denial of the authority of *Him*, by whom they professed to be called to the ministry, deliberately taught us, against the example of the Hebrews, and against the remonstrance of the Apostles, they teach *that we ought to obey man's law before the law of God.*

My spirit wearies of such blasphemy; and how such men can be supported, as the "standing types and representative of Jesus Christ," is a mystery which I leave others to penetrate. In speaking of the American church, however, let it be distinctly understood that I mean the *great mass* of the religious organizations of our land. There are exceptions, and I thank God that there are. Noble men may be found, scattered all over these Northern States, of whom Henry Ward Beecher, of Brooklyn, Samuel J. May, of Syracuse, and my esteemed friend on the platform, are shining examples; and let me say further, that, upon these men lies the duty to inspire our ranks with high religious faith and zeal, and to cheer us on in the great mission of the slave's redemption from his chains.

One is struck with the difference between the attitude of the American church towards the anti-slavery movement, and that occupied by the churches in England towards a similar movement in that country. There, the church, true to its mission of ameliorating, elevating, and improving the condition of mankind, came forward promptly, bound up the wounds of the West Indian slave, and restored him to his liberty. There, the question of emancipation was a high religious question. It was demanded, in the name of humanity, and according to the law of the living God. The Sharps, the Clarksons, the Wilber-forces, the Buxtons, the Burchells, and the Knibbs, were alike famous for their piety, and for their philanthropy. The anti-slavery movement *there,* was not an anti-church movement, for the reason that the church took its full share in prosecuting that movement: and the anti-slavery movement in this country will cease to be an anti-church movement, when the church of this country shall assume a favorable, instead of a hostile position towards that movement.

Americans! your republican politics, not less than your republican religion, are flagrantly inconsistent. You boast of your love of liberty, your superior civilization, and your pure christianity, while the whole political power of the nation, (as embodied in the two great political parties,) is solemnly pledged to support and perpetuate the enslavement of three millions of your countrymen. You hurl your anathemas at the crowned headed tyrants of Russia and Austria, and pride yourselves on your Democratic institutions, while you yourselves consent to be the mere *tools* and *body-guards* of the tyrants of Virginia and Carolina. You invite to your shores fugitives of oppression from abroad, honor them with banquets, greet them with ovations, cheer them, toast them, salute them, protect them, and pour out your money to them like water; but the fugitives from your own land, you advertise, hunt, arrest, shoot and kill. You glory in your refinement, and your universal education; yet you maintain a system as barbarous and dreadful, as ever stained the character of a nation—a system begun in avarice, supported in pride, and perpetuated in cruelty. You shed tears over fallen Hungary, and make the sad story of her wrongs the theme of your poets, statesmen and orators, till your gallant sons are ready to fly to arms to vindicate her cause against her oppressors; but, in regard to the ten thousand wrongs of the American slave, you would enforce the strictest silence, and would hail him as an enemy of the nation who dares to make those wrongs the subject of public discourse! You are all on fire at the mention of liberty for France or for Ireland; but are as cold as an iceberg at the thought of liberty for the enslaved of America.— You discourse eloquently on the dignity of labor; yet, you sustain a system which, in its very essence, casts a stigma upon labor. You can bare your bosom to the storm of British artillery, to throw off a three-penny tax on tea; and yet wring the last hard earned farthing from the grasp of the black laborers of your country. You profess to believe "that, of one blood. God made all nations of men to dwell on the face of all the earth," and hath commanded all men, everywhere to love one another; yet you notoriously hate, (and glory in your hatred,) all men whose skins are not colored like your own. You declare, before the world, and are understood by the world to declare, that you *"hold these truths to be self evident, that all men are created equal; and are endowed by their Creator with certain inalienable rights; and that, among these are, life, liberty, and the pursuit of happiness;"* and yet, you hold securely, in a bondage, which according to your own Thomas Jefferson, *"is worse than ages of that which your fathers rose in rebellion to oppose," a seventh part* of the inhabitants of your country.

Fellow-citizens! I will not enlarge further on your national inconsistencies. The existence of slavery in this country brands your republicanism as a sham, your humanity as a base pretence, and your christianity as a lie. It destroys your moral power abroad; it corrupts your politicians at home. It saps the foundation of religion; it makes your name a hissing, and a bye-word to a mocking earth. It is the antagonistic force in your government, the only thing that seriously disturbs and endangers your *Union.* It fetters your progress; it is the enemy of improvement, the deadly foe of education; it fosters pride; it breeds insolence; it promotes vice; it shelters crime; it is a curse to the earth that supports it; and yet, you cling to it, as if it were the sheet anchor of all your hopes. Oh! be warned! be warned! a horrible reptile is coiled up in your nation's bosom; the venomous creature is nursing at the tender breast of your youthful republic; *for the love of God, tear away,* and fling from you the hideous monster, and *let the weight of twenty millions, crush and destroy it forever!*

But it is answered in reply to all this, that precisely what I have now denounced is, in fact, guaranteed and sanctioned by the Constitution of the United States; that, the right to hold, and to hunt slaves is a part of that Constitution framed by the illustrious Fathers of this Republic.

Then, I dare to affirm, notwithstanding all I have said before, your fathers stooped, basely stooped.

> To palter with us in a double sense:
> And keep the word of promise to the ear,
> But break it to the heart.

And instead of being the honest men I have before declared them to be, they were the veriest imposters that ever practised on mankind. *This* is the inevitable conclusion, and from it there is no escape; but I differ from those who charge this baseness on the framers of the Constitution of the United States. *It is a slander upon their memory,* at least, so I believe. There is not time now to argue the constitutional question at length; nor have I the ability to discuss it as it ought to be discussed. The subject has been handled with masterly power by Lysander Spooner, Esq., and last, though not least, by Gerritt Smith, Esq. These gentlemen have, as I think, fully and clearly vindicated the Constitution from any design to support slavery for an hour.

Fellow-citizens! there is no matter in respect to which, the people of the North have allowed themselves to be so ruinously imposed upon, as that of the pro-slavery character of the Constitution. In *that* instrument I hold there is neither warrant, license, nor sanction of the hateful thing; but interpreted, as it *ought* to be interpreted, the Constitution is a GLORIOUS LIBERTY DOCUMENT. Read its preamble, consider its purposes. Is slavery among them? Is it at the gateway? or is it in the temple? it is neither. While I do not intend to argue this question on the present occasion, let me ask, if it be not somewhat singular that, if the Constitution were intended to be, by its framers and adopters, a slaveholding instrument, why neither *slavery, slaveholding,* nor *slave* can anywhere be found in it. What would be thought of an instrument, drawn up, *legally* drawn up, for the purpose of entitling the city of Rochester to a track of land, in which no mention of land was made? Now, there are certain rules of interpretation, for the proper understanding of all legal instruments. These rules are well established. They are plain, common-sense rules, such as you and I, and all of us, can understand and apply, without having passed years in the study of law. I scout the idea that the question of the constitutionality, or unconstitutionality of slavery, is not a question for the people. I hold that every American citizen has a right to form an opinion of the constitution, and to propagate that opinion, and to use all honorable means to make his opinion the prevailing one. Without this right, the liberty of an American citizen would be as insecure as that of a Frenchman. Ex-Vice-President Dallas tells us that the constitution is an object to which no American mind can be too attentive, and no American heart too devoted. He further says, the constitution, in its words, is plain and intelligible, and is meant for the homebred, unsophisticated understandings of our fellow-citizens. Senator Berrien tells us that the Constitution is the fundamental law, that which controls all others. The charter of our liberties, which every citizen has a personal interest in understanding thoroughly. The testimony of Senator Breese, Lewis Cass, and many others that might be named, who are everywhere esteemed as sound lawyers, so regard the constitution. I take it, therefore, that it is not presumption in a private citizen to form an opinion of that instrument.

Now, take the constitution according to its plain reading, and I defy the presentation of a single pro-slavery clause in it. On the other hand it will be found to contain principles and purposes, entirely hostile to the existence of slavery.

I have detained my audience entirely too long already. At some future period I will gladly avail myself of an opportunity to give this subject a full and fair discussion.

Allow me to say, in conclusion, notwithstanding the dark picture I have this day presented, of the state of the nation, I do not despair of this country. There are forces in operation, which must inevitably, work the downfall of slavery. *"The arm of the Lord is not shortened,"* and the doom of slavery is certain. I, therefore, leave off where I began, with *hope*. While drawing encouragement from "the Declaration of Independence," the great principles it contains, and the genius of American Institutions, my spirit is also cheered by the obvious tendencies of the age. Nations do not now stand in the same relation to each other that they did ages ago. No nation can now shut itself up, from the surrounding world, and trot round in the same old path of its fathers without interference. The time *was* when such could be done. Long established customs of hurtful character could formerly fence themselves in, and do their evil work with social impunity. Knowledge was then confined and enjoyed by the privileged few, and the multitude walked on in mental darkness. But a change has now come over the affairs of mankind. Walled cities and empires have become unfashionable. The arm of commerce has borne away the gates of the strong city. Intelligence is penetrating the darkest corners of the globe. It makes its pathway over and under the sea, as well as on the earth. Wind, steam, and lightning are its chartered agents. Oceans no longer divide, but link nations together. From Boston to London is now a holiday excursion. Space is comparatively annihilated.—Thoughts expressed on one side of the Atlantic, are distinctly heard on the other.

The far off and almost fabulous Pacific rolls in grandeur at our feet. The Celestial Empire, the mystery of ages, is being solved. The fiat of the Almighty, *"Let there be Light,"* has not yet spent its force. No abuse, no outrage whether in taste, sport or avarice, can now hide itself from the all-pervading light. The iron shoe, and crippled foot of China must be seen, in contrast with nature. *Africa must rise and put on her yet unwoven garment. "Ethiopia shall stretch out her hand unto God."*

Questions and Activities

1. Douglass argues that slavery is inconsistent with other principles that the United States seems to hold dear. Do you think this is an effective strategy for argument? Identify a policy or practice that

you believe is inconsistent with the stated principles of the group that follows it. Write an argument in which you urge that the policy or practice be changed because of the inconsistency.

2. Many of Douglass' statements seem calculated to offend or anger his audience (which suggests that he may have been speaking to people who agreed with him). For the argument you wrote in question 1, write two separate introductions: one to an audience that already agrees with you, and another to an audience that is hostile to your position.

Ain't I a Woman?

SOJOURNER TRUTH

Born a slave in New York, Sojourner Truth gained her freedom in 1827 and became a frequent and powerful speaker at antislavery rallies. In her speeches she argued not only for the abolition of slavery, but also for equality for women.

Well, children, where there is so much racket there must be something out of kilter. I think that 'twixt the negroes of the South and the women at the North, all talking about rights, the white men will be in a fix pretty soon. But what's all this here talking about?

That man over there says that women need to be helped into carriages, and lifted over ditches, and to have the best place everywhere. Nobody ever helps me into carriages, or over mud-puddles, or gives me any best place! And ain't I a woman? Look at me! Look at my arm! I have ploughed and planted, and gathered into barns, and no man could head me! And ain't I a woman? I could work as much and eat as much as a man—when I could get it—and bear the lash as well! And ain't I a woman? I have borne thirteen children, and seen them most all sold off to slavery, and when I cried out with my mother's grief, none but Jesus heard me! And ain't I a woman?

Then they talk about this thing in the head; what's this they call it? [Intellect, someone whispers.] That's it, honey. What's that got to do with women's rights or negro's rights? If my cup won't hold but a pint, and yours holds a quart, wouldn't you be mean not to let me have my little half-measure full?

Then that little man in black there, he says women can't have as much rights as men 'cause Christ wasn't a woman! Where did your Christ come from? Where did your Christ come from? From God and a woman! Man had nothing to do with Him.

If the first woman God ever made was strong enough to turn the world upside down all alone, these women together ought to be able to turn it back, and get it right side up again! And now they is asking to do it, the men better let them.

Obliged to you for hearing me, and now old Sojourner ain't got nothing more to say.

Questions and Activities

1. Sojourner uses the phrase "And ain't I a woman" as a sort of refrain. What does it contribute to her argument?

2. Summarize Sojourner Truth's argument about the relationship of intellect to equality, and then expand her argument, offering additional support for her position.

From "The Subjection of Women"

JOHN STUART MILL

John Stuart Mill, an Englishman who lived from 1806 to 1873, is probably best known for his essay, On Liberty. Written in 1859, it is a justly famous defense of the rights of the minority in the face of the power of the majority. Mill wrote The Subjection of Women in 1869, and it has become a classic argument for women's rights.

The object of this Essay is to explain as clearly as I am able, the grounds of an opinion which I have held from the very earliest period when I had formed an opinion at all on social or political matters, and which, instead of being weakened or modified, has been constantly growing stronger by the progress of reflection and the experience of life: That the principle which regulates the existing social relations between the two sexes—the legal subordination of one sex to the other—is wrong in itself, and now one of the chief hindrances to human improvement; and that it ought to be replaced by a principle of perfect equality, admitting no power or privilege on the one side, nor disability on the other.

Some will object, that a comparison cannot fairly be made between the government of the male sex and the forms of unjust power which I have adduced in illustration of it, since these are arbitrary, and the effect of mere usurpation, while it on the contrary is natural. But was there ever any domination which did not appear natural to those who possessed it? There was a time when the division of mankind into two classes, a small one of masters and numerous one of slaves, appeared, even to the most cultivated minds, to be a natural, and the only natural, condition of the human race. No less an intellect, and one which contributed no less to the progress of human thought, than Aristotle, held this opinion without doubt or misgiving; and rested it on the same premises on which the same assertion in regard to the dominion of men over women is usually based, namely that there are different natures among mankind, free natures, and slave natures; that the Greeks were of a free nature, the barbarian races of Thracians and Asiatics of a slave nature. But why need I go back to Aristotle? Did not the slaveowners of the Southern United States maintain the same doctrine, with all the fanaticism with which men cling to the theories that justify their passions and legitimate their personal interests? Did they not call heaven and earth to witness that the dominion of the white man over the black is natural, that the black race is by nature incapable of freedom, and marked out for slavery? some even going as far as to say that the freedom of manual laborers is an unnatural order of things anywhere. Again, the theorists of absolute monarchy have always affirmed it to be the only natural form of government; issuing from the patriarchal, which was the primitive and spontaneous form of society, framed on the model of the paternal, which is anterior to society itself, and, as they contend, the most natural authority of all. . . . So true is it that unnatural generally means only uncustomary, and that everything which is usual appears natural. The subjection of women to men being a universal custom, any departure from it quite naturally appears unnatural. But how entirely, even in this case, the feeling is dependent on custom, appears by ample experience. Nothing so much astonishes the people of distant parts of the world, when they first learn anything about England, as to be told that it is under a queen: the thing seems to them so unnatural as to be almost incredible. To Englishmen this does not seem in the least degree unnatural, because they are used to it; but they do feel it unnatural that women should be soldiers or members of parliament. In the feudal ages, on the contrary, war and politics were not thought unnatural to women, because not unusual; it seemed natural that women of the privileged classes should be of manly character, inferior in nothing but bodily strength to their husbands and fathers. The independence of women seemed rather less unnatural to the Greeks than to other ancients, on account of the fabulous Amazons (whom they believed to be historical), and the partial example afforded by the Spartan women; who, though no less subordinate by law than in other Greek states, were more free in fact, and being trained to bodily exercises in the same manner with men, gave ample proof that they were not naturally disqualified for them. There can be little doubt that Spartan experience suggested to Plato, among many other of his doctrines, that of the social and political equality of two sexes.

But, it will be said, the rule of men over women differs from all these others in not being a rule of force: it is accepted voluntarily, women make no complaint, and are consenting parties to it. In the first place, a great number of women do not accept it. Ever since there have been women able to make their sentiments known by their writings (the only mode of publicity which society permits to them), an increasing number of them have recorded protests against their present social condition: and recently many thousands of them, headed by the most eminent women known to the public, have petitioned Parliament for their admission to the Parliamentary Suffrage. The claim of women to be educated as solidly, and in the same branches of knowledge, as men, is urged with growing intensity, and with a great prospect of success; while the demand for their admission into professions and occupations hitherto closed against them, becomes every year more urgent. Though there are not in this country, as there are in the United States, periodical Conventions and an organized party to agitate for the Rights of Women, there is a numerous and active Society organized and managed by women, for the more limited object of obtaining the political franchise. Nor is it only in our own country and in America that women are beginning to protest, more or less collectively, against the disabilities under which they labor. France, and Italy, and Switzerland, and Russia now afford examples of the same thing. How many more women there are who silently cherish similar aspirations, no one can possibly know; but there are abundant tokens how many *would* cherish them, were they not so strenuously taught to repress them as contrary to the proprities of their sex. . . .

All causes, social and natural, combine to make it unlikely that women should be collectively rebellious to the power of men. They are so far in a position different from all other subject classes, that their masters require something more from them than actual service. Men do not want solely the obedience of women, they want their sentiments. All men, except the most brutish, desire to have, in the woman most nearly connected with them, not a forced slave but a willing one, not a slave merely, but a favorite. They have therefore put everything in practice to enslave their minds. The masters of all other slaves rely, for maintaining obedience, on fear; either fear of themselves, or religious fears. The masters of women wanted more than simple obedience, and they turned the whole force of education to effect their purpose. All women are brought up from the very earliest years in the belief that their ideal of character is the very opposite to that of men; not self-will, and government by self-control, but submission, and yielding to the control of others. All the moralities tell them that it is the duty of women, and all the current sentimentalities that it is their nature, to live for others; to make complete abnegation of themselves, and to have no life but in their affections. And by their affections are meant the only ones they are allowed to have—those to the men with whom they are connected, or to the children who constitute an additional and indefeasible tie between them and a man. When we put together three things—first, the natural attraction between opposite sexes; secondly, the wife's entire dependence on the husband, every privilege or pleasure she has being either his gift, depending entirely on his will; and lastly, that the principal object of human pursuit, consideration, and all objects of social ambition, can in general be sought or obtained by her only through him, it should be a miracle if the object of being attractive to men had not become the polar star of feminine education and formation of character. And, this great means of influence over the minds of women having been acquired, an instinct of selfishness made men avail themselves of it to the utmost as a means of holding women in subjection, by representing to them meekness, submissiveness, and resignation of all individual will into the hands of a man, as an essential part of sexual attractiveness. Can it be doubted that any of the other yokes which mankind have succeeded in breaking, would have subsisted till now if the same means had existed, and had been as sedulously used, to bow down their minds to it? If it had been made the object of the life of every young plebeian to find personal favor in the eyes of some patrician, of every young serf with some seigneur; if domestication with him, and a share of his personal affections, had been held out as the prize which they all should look out for, the most gifted and aspiring being able to reckon on the most desirable prizes; and if, when this prize had been obtained, they had been shut out by a wall of brass from all interest not centering in him, all feelings and desires but those which he shared or inculcated; would not serfs and seigneurs, plebeians and patricians, have been as broadly distinguished at this day as men and women are? and would not all but a thinker here and there, have believed the distinction to be a fundamental and unalterable fact in human nature?

The preceding considerations are amply sufficient to show that custom, however universal it may be, affords in this case no presumption, and ought not to create any prejudice, in favor of the arrangements which place women in social and political subjection to men. But I may go farther, and maintain that the course of history, and the tendencies of progressive human society, afford not only no presumption in favor of this system of inequality of rights, but a strong one against it; and that, so far as the whole course of human improvement up to this time, the whole stream of modern tendencies, warrants any inference on the subject, it is, that this relic of the past is discordant with the future, and must necessarily disappear.

For, what is the peculiar character of the modern world—the difference which chiefly distinguishes modern institutions, modern social ideas, modern life itself, from those of times long past? It is, that human beings are no longer born to their place in life, and chained down by an inexorable bond to the place they are born to, but are free to employ their faculties, and such favorable chances as offer, to achieve the lot which may appear to them most desirable.

On the other point which is involved in the just equality of women, their admissibility to all the functions and occupations hitherto retained as the monopoly of the stronger sex, I should anticipate no difficulty in convincing anyone who has gone with me on the subject of the equality of women in the family. I believe that their disabilities elsewhere are only clung to in order to maintain their subordination in domestic life; because the generality of the male sex cannot yet tolerate the idea of living with an equal. Were it not for that, I think that almost everyone, in the existing state of opinion in politics and political economy, would admit the injustice of excluding half the human race from the greater number of lucrative occupations, and from almost all high social functions; ordaining from their birth either that they are not, and cannot by any possibility become, fit for employments which are legally open to the stupidest and basest of the other sex, or else that however fit they may be, those employments shall be interdicted to them, in order to be preserved for the exclusive benefit of males. In the last two centuries, when (which was seldom the case) any reason beyond the mere existence of the fact was thought to be required to justify the disabilities of women, people seldom assigned as a reason their inferior mental capacity; which, in times when there was a real trial of personal faculties (from which all women were not excluded) in the struggles of public life, no one really believed in. The reason given in those days was not women's unfitness, but the interest of society, by which was meant the interest of men: just as the *raison d'état,* meaning the convenience of the government, and the support of existing authority, was deemed a sufficient explanation and excuse for the most flagitious crimes. In the present day, power holds a smoother language, and whomsoever it oppresses, always pretends to do so for their own good: accordingly, when anything is forbidden to women, it is thought necessary to say, and desirable to believe, that they are incapable of doing it, and that they depart from their real path of success and happiness when they aspire to it. But to make this reason plausible (I do not say valid), those by whom it is urged must be prepared to carry it to a much greater length than anyone ventures to do in the face of present experience. It is not sufficient to maintain that women on the average are less gifted than men on the average, with certain of the higher mental faculties, or that a smaller number of women than of men are fit for occupations and functions of the highest intellectual character. It is necessary to maintain that no women at all are fit for them, and that the most eminent women are inferior in mental faculties to the most mediocre of the men on whom those functions at present devolve. For if the performance of the function is decided either by competition, or by any mode of choice which secures regard to the public interest, there needs to be no apprehension that any important employments will fall into the hands of women inferior to average men, or to the average of their male competitors. The only result would be that there would be fewer women than men in such employments; a result certain to happen in any case, if only from the preference always likely to be felt by the majority of women for the one vocation in which there is nobody to compete with them. Now, the most determined depreciator of women will not venture to deny, that when we add the experience of recent times to that of ages past, women, and not a few merely, but many women, have proved themselves capable of everything, perhaps without a single exception, which is done by men, and of doing it successfully and creditably. The utmost that can be said is, that there are many things which none of them have succeeded in doing as well as they have been done by some men—many in which they have not reached the very highest rank. But there are extremely few, dependent only on mental faculties, in which they have not attained the rank next to the highest. Is not this enough, and much more than enough, to make it a tyranny to them, and a detriment to society, that they should not be allowed to compete with men for the exercise of these functions? Is it not a mere truism to say, that such functions are often filled by men far less fit for them than numbers of women, and who would be beaten by women in any fair field of competition? What difference does it make that there may be men somewhere, fully employed about other things, who may be still better qualified for the things in question than these women? Does not this take place in all competitions? Is there so great a superfluity of men fit for high duties, that society can afford to reject the service of any competent person? Are we so certain of always finding a man made to our hands for any duty or function of social importance which falls vacant, that we lose nothing by putting a ban upon one-half of mankind, and refusing beforehand to make their faculties available, however distinguished they may be? And even if we could do without them, would it be consistent with justice to refuse to them their fair share of honor and distinction, or to deny to them the equal moral right of all human beings to choose their occupation (short of injury to others) according to their own preferences, at their own risk? Nor is the injustice confined to them: it is shared by those who are in a position to benefit by their services. To ordain that any kind of persons shall not be physicians, or shall not be advocates, or shall not be members of parliament, is to injure not them only, but all who employ physicians or advocates, or elect members of parliament, and who are deprived of the stimulating effect of greater competition on the exertions of the competitors, as well as restricted to a narrower range of individual choice. . . .

> There remains a question, not of less importance than those already discussed, and which will be asked the most importunately by those opponents whose conviction is somewhat shaken on the main point. What good are we to expect from the changes proposed in our customs and institutions? Would mankind be at all better off if women were free? If not, why disturb their minds, and attempt to make a social revolution in the name of an abstract right? . . .

To which let me first answer, the advantage of having the most universal and pervading of all human relations regulated by justice instead of injustice. The vast amount of this gain to human nature, it is hardly possible, by any explanation or illustration, to place in a stronger light than it is placed by the bare statement, to anyone who attaches a normal meaning to words. All the selfish propensities, the self-worship, the unjust self-preference, which exist among mankind, have their source and root in, and derive their principal nourishment from, the present constitution of the relation between men and women. Think what it is to a boy, to grow up to manhood in the belief that without any merit or any exertion of his own, though he may be the most frivolous and empty or the most ignorant and stolid of mankind, by the mere fact of being born a male he is by right the superior of all and every one of an entire half of the human race: including probably some whose real superiority to himself he has daily or hourly occasion to feel; but even if in his whole conduct he habitually follows a woman's guidance, still, if he is a fool, she thinks that of course she is not, and cannot be, equal in ability and judgment to himself; and if he is not a fool, he does worse—he sees that she is superior to him, and believes that, notwithstanding her superiority, he is entitled to command and she is bound to obey. What must be the effect on his character, of this lesson? And men of the cultivated classes are often not aware how deeply it sinks into the immense majority of male minds. For, among right-feeling and well-bred people, the inequality is kept as much as possible out of sight; above all, out of sight of the children. As much obedience is required from boys to their mother as to their father: they are not permitted to domineer over their sisters, nor are they accustomed to see these postponed to them, but the contrary; the compensations of the chivalrous feeling being made prominent, while the servitude which requires them is kept in the background. Well brought-up youths in the higher classes thus often escape the bad influences of the situation in their early years, and only experience them when, arrived at manhood, they fall under the dominion of facts as they really exist. Such people are little aware, when a boy is differently brought up, how early the notion of his inherent superiority to a girl arises in his mind; how it grows with his growth and strengthens with his strength; how it is inoculated by one schoolboy upon another; how early the youth thinks himself superior to his mother, owing her perhaps forbearance, but no real respect; and how sublime and sultan-like a sense of superiority he feels, above all, over the woman whom he honors by admitting her to a partnership of his life. Is it imagined that all this does not pervert the whole manner of existence of the man, both as an individual and as a social being? It is an exact parallel to the feeling of a hereditary king that he is excellent above others by being born a king, or a noble by being born a noble. The relation between husband and wife is very like that between lord and vassal, except that the wife is held to more unlimited obedience than the vassal was. However the vassal's character may have been affected, for better and for worse, by his subordination, who can help seeing that the lord's was affected greatly for the worse? whether he was led to believe that his vassals were really superior to himself, or to feel that he was placed in command over people as good as himself, for no merits of labors of his own, but merely for having, as Figaro says, taken the trouble to be born. The self-worship of the monarch, or of the feudal superior, is matched by the self-worship of the male. Human beings do not grow up from childhood in the possession of unearned distinctions, without pluming themselves upon them. Those whom privileges not acquired by their merit, and which they feel to be disproportioned to it, inspire with additional humility, are always the few, and the best few. The rest are only inspired with pride, and the worst sort of pride, that which values itself upon accidental advantages, not of its own achieving. Above all, when the feeling of being raised above the whole of the other sex is combined with personal authority over one individual among them; the situation, if a school of conscientious and affectionate forbearance to those whose strongest points of character are conscience and affection, is to men of another quality a regularly constituted Academy or Gymnasium for training them in arrogance and overbearingness; which vices, if curbed by the certainty of resistance in their intercourse with other men, their equals, break out towards all who are in a position to be obliged to tolerate them, and often revenge themselves upon the unfortunate wife for the involuntary restraint which they are obliged to submit to elsewhere.

The example afforded, and the education given to the sentiments, by laying the foundation of domestic existence upon a relation contradictory to the first principles of social justice, must, from the very nature of man, have a perverting influence of such magnitude, that it is hardly possible with our present experience to raise our imaginations to the conception of so great a change for the better as would be made by its removal. All that education and civilization are doing to efface the influences on character of the law of force, and replace them by those of justice, remains merely on the surface, as long as the citadel of the enemy is not attacked. The principle of the modern movement in morals and politics, is that conduct, and conduct alone, entitles to respect: that not what men are, but what they do, constitutes their claim to deference; that, above all, merit, and not birth, is the only rightful claim to power and authority. If no authority, not in its nature temporary, were allowed to one human being over another, society would not be employed in building up propensities with one hand which it has to curb with the other. The child would really, for the first time in man's existence on earth, be trained in the way he should go, and when he was old there would be a chance that he would not depart from it. But so long as the right of the strong to power over the weak rules in the very heart of society, the attempt to make the equal right of the weak the principle of its outward actions will always be an uphill struggle; for the law of justice, which is also that of

Christianity, will never get possession of men's inmost sentiments; they will be working against it, even when bending to it.

The second benefit to be expected from giving to women the free use of their faculties, by leaving them the free choice of their employments, and opening to them the same field of occupation and the same prizes and encouragements as to other human beings, would be that of doubling the mass of mental faculties available for the higher service of humanity. Where there is now one person qualified to benefit mankind and promote the general improvement, as a public teacher, or an administrator of some branch of public or social affairs, there would then be a chance of two. Mental superiority of any kind is at present everywhere so much below the demand; there is such a deficiency of persons competent to do excellently anything which it requires any considerable amount of ability to do; that the loss to the world, by refusing to make use of one-half of the whole quantity of talent it possesses, is extremely serious. It is true that this amount of mental power is not totally lost. Much of it is employed, and would in any case be employed, in domestic management, and in the few other occupations open to women and from the remainder indirect benefit is in many individual cases obtained, through the personal influence of individual women over individual men. But these benefits are partial; their range is extremely circumscribed; and if they must be admitted, on the one hand, as a deduction from the amount of fresh social power that would be acquired by giving freedom to one-half of the whole sum of human intellect, there must be added, on the other, the benefit of the stimulus that would be given to the intellect of men by the competition; or (to use a more true expression) by the necessity that would be imposed on them of deserving precedency before they could expect to obtain it. . . .

Questions and Activities

1. List the typical arguments that are used to justify denying equality to groups of people (African Americans, women, disabled persons, etc.). Choose one of these and argue that it should not be used to deny equality.

2. Using Mill's examples and reasoning as your primary source of information, argue that the situation of women (particularly in relation to their political and economic equality with men) has or has not changed since Mill wrote.

Roe vs. Wade

JUSTICE HARRY BLACKMUN

In October 1972, the U.S. Supreme Court issued its decision in the case of Roe vs. Wade, a challenge to a Texas state law that prohibited abortion. With its decision, the Supreme Court legalized abortion in the United States under certain circumstances. Supreme Court decisions usually have the effect of ending public debate about an issue. But this particular decision had the opposite effect: It began a period of intense national debate and action about legalized abortion in the United States. That debate continues today.

MR. JUSTICE BLACKMUN delivered the opinion of the Court. This Texas federal appeal and its Georgia companion, *Doe v. Bolton, post,* p. 179, present constitutional challenges to state criminal abortion legislation. The Texas statutes under attack here are typical of those that have been in effect in many States for approximately a century. The Georgia statutes, in contrast, have a modern cast and are a legislative product that, to an extent at least, obviously reflects the influences of recent attitudinal change, of advancing medical knowledge and techniques, and of new thinking about an old issue.

We forthwith acknowledge our awareness of the sensitive and emotional nature of the abortion controversy, of the vigourous opposing views, even among physicians, and of the deep and seemingly absolute convictions that the subject inspires. One's philosophy, one's experiences, one's exposure to the raw edges of human existence, one's religious training, one's attitudes toward life and family and their values, and the moral standards one establishes and seeks to observe, are all likely to influence and to color one's thinking and conclusions about abortion.

In addition, population growth, pollution, poverty, and racial overtones tend to complicate and not to simplify the problem.

Our task, of course, is to resolve the issue by constitutional measurement, free of emotion and of predilection. We seek earnestly

Alfred L. Scanlan, Martin J. Flynn, and *Robert M. Byrn* for the National Right to Life Committee; by *Helen L. Buttenwieser* for the American Ethical Union et al.; by *Norma G. Zarky* for the American Association of University Women et al.; by *Nancy Stearns* for New Women Lawyers et al.; by the California Committee to Legalize Abortion et al.; and by *Robert E. Dunne* for Robert L. Sassone.

to do this, and, because we do, we have inquired into, and in this opinion place some emphasis upon, medical and medical-legal history and what that history reveals about man's attitudes toward the abortion procedure over the centuries. We bear in mind, too, Mr. Justice Holmes' admonition in his now-vindicated dissent in *Lochner* v. *New York*, 198 U. S. 45, 76 (1905):

> [The Constitution] is made for people of fundamentally differing views, and the accident of our finding certain opinions natural and familiar or novel and even shocking ought not to conclude our judgment upon the question whether statutes embodying them conflict with the Constitution of the United States.

I

The Texas statutes that concern us here are Arts. 1191–1194 and 1196 of the State's Penal Code.[1] These make it a crime to "procure

---

[1] "Article 1191. Abortion

"If any person shall designedly administer to a pregnant woman or knowingly procure to be administered with her consent any drug or medicine, or shall use towards her any violence or means whatever externally or internally applied, and thereby procure an abortion, he shall be confined in the penitentiary not less than two nor more than five years; if it be done without her consent, the punishment shall be doubled. By 'abortion' is meant that the life of the fetus or embryo shall be destroyed in the woman's womb or that a premature birth thereof be caused.

"Art. 1192. Furnishing the means

"Whoever furnishes the means for procuring an abortion knowing the purpose intended is guilty as an accomplice.

"Art. 1193. Attempt at abortion

"If the means used shall fail to produce an abortion, the offender is nevertheless guilty of an attempt to produce abortion, provided it be shown that such means were calculated to produce that result, and shall be fined not less than one hundred nor more than one thousand dollars.

"Art. 1194. Murder in producing abortion

"If the death of the mother is occasioned by an abortion so produced or by an attempt to effect the same it is murder."

"Art. 1196. By medical advice

"Nothing in this chapter applies to an abortion procured or attempted by medical advice for the purpose of saving the life of the mother."

The foregoing Articles, together with Art. 1195, compose Chapter 9 of Title 15 of the Penal Code. Article 1195, not attacked here, reads:

"Art. 1195. Destroying unborn child

"Whoever shall during parturition of the mother destroy the vitality or life in a child in a state of being born and before actual birth, which child would otherwise have been born alive, shall be confined in the penitentiary for life or for not less than five years."

an abortion," as therein defined, or to attempt one, except with respect to "an abortion procured or attempted by medical advice for the purpose of saving the life of the mother." Similar statutes are in existence in a majority of the States.[2]

Texas first enacted a criminal abortion statute in 1854. Texas Laws 1854, c. 49, § 1, set forth in 3 H. Gammel, Laws of Texas 1502 (1898). This was soon modified into language that has remained substantially unchanged to the present time. See Texas Penal code of 1857, c. 7, Arts. 531–536; G. Paschal, Laws of Texas, Arts. 2192–2197 (1866); Texas Rev. Stat., c. 8, Arts. 536–541 (1879); Texas Rev. Crim. Stat., Arts. 1071–1076 (1911). The final article in each of these compilations provided the same exception, as does the present Article 1196, for an abortion by "medical advice for the purpose of saving the life of the mother."[3]

---

[2]Ariz. Rev. Stat. Ann. § 13–211 (1956); Conn. Pub. Act No. 1 (May 1972 special session) (in 4 Conn. Leg. Serv. 677 (1972)), and Conn. Gen. Stat. Rev. §§ 53–29, 53–30 (1968) (or unborn child); Idaho Code § 18–601 (1948); Ill. Rev. Stat., c. 38, § 23–1 (1971); Ind. Code § 35–1–58–1 (1971); Iowa Code § 701.1 (1971); Ky. Rev. Stat. § 436.020 (1962); La. Rev. Stat. § 37:1285 (6) (1964) (loss of medical license) (but see § 14:87 (Supp. 1972) containing no exception for the life of the mother under the criminal statute); Me. Rev. Stat. Ann., Tit. 17 § 51 (1974); Mass. Gen. Laws Ann., c. 272, § 19 (1970) (using the term "unlawfully," construed to exclude an abortion to save the mother's life, *Kudish* v. *Bd. of Registration*, 356 Mass. 98, 248 N. E. 2d 264 (1969)); Mich. Comp. Laws § 750.14 (1948); Minn. Stat. § 617.18 (1971); Mo. Rev. Stat. § 559.100 (1969); Mont. Rev. Codes Ann. § 94–401 (1969); Neb. Rev. Stat. § 28–405 (1964); Nev. Rev. Stat. § 200.220 (1967); N. H. Rev. Stat. § 585:13 (1955); N. J. Stat. Ann. § 2A:87–1 (1969) ("without lawful justification"); N. D. Cent. Code §§ 12–25–01, 12–25–02 (1960); Ohio Rev. Code Ann. § 2901.16 (1953); Okla. Stat. Ann., Tit. 21, § 861 (1972–1973 Supp.); Pa. Stat. Ann., Tit. 18, §§ 4718, 4719 (1963) ("unlawful"); R. I. Gen. Laws Ann. § 11–3–1 (1969); S. D. Comp. Laws Ann. § 22–17–1 (1967); Tenn. Code Ann. §§ 39–301, 39–302 (1956); Utah Code Ann. §§ 76–2–1, 76–2–2 (1953); Vt. Stat. Ann., Tit. 13 § 101 (1958); W. Va. Code Ann. §61–2–8 (1966); Wis. Stat. § 940.04 (1969); Wyo. Stat. Ann. §§ 6–77, 6–78 (1957).

[3]Long ago, a suggestion was made that the Texas statutes were unconstitutionally vague because of definitional deficiencies. The Texas Court of Criminal Appeals disposed of that suggestion peremptorily, saying only,

"It is also insisted in the motion in arrest of judgment that the statute is unconstitutional and void in that it does not sufficiently define or describe the offense of abortion. We do not concur in respect to this question." *Jackson* v. *State*, 55 Tex. Cr. R. 79, 89, 115 S. W. 262, 268 (1908).

The same court recently has held again that the State's abortion statutes are not unconstitutionally vague or overbroad. *Thompson* v. *State* (Ct. Crim. App. Tex. 1971), appeal docketed, No. 71-1200. The court held that "the State of Texas has a compelling interest to protect fetal life"; that Art. 1191 "is designed to protect fetal life"; that the Texas homicide statutes, particularly Art. 1205 of the Penal Code, are intended to protect a person "in existence by

II

Jane Roe,[4] a single woman who was residing in Dallas County, Texas, instituted this federal action in March 1970 against the District Attorney of the county. She sought a declaratory judgment that the Texas criminal abortion statutes were unconstitutional on their face, and an injunction restraining the defendant from enforcing the statutes.

Roe alleged that she was unmarried and pregnant; that she wished to terminate her pregnancy by an abortion "performed by a competent, licensed physician, under safe, clinical conditions"; that she was unable to get a "legal" abortion in Texas because her life did not appear to be threatened by the continuation of her pregnancy; and that she could not afford to travel to another jurisdiction in order to secure a legal abortion under safe conditions. She claimed that the Texas statutes were unconstitutionally vague and that they abridged her right of personal privacy, protected by the First, Fourth, Fifth, Ninth, and Fourteenth Amendment. By an amendment to her complaint Roe purported to sue "on behalf of herself and all other women" similarly situated.

James Hubert Hallford, a licensed physician, sought and was granted leave to intervene in Roe's action. In his complaint he alleged that he had been arrested previously for violations of the Texas abortion statutes and that two such prosecutions were pending against him. He described conditions of patients who came to him seeking abortions, and he claimed that for many cases he, as physician, was unable to determine whether they fell within or outside the exception recognized by Article 1196. He alleged that, as a consequence, the statutes were vague and uncertain, in violation of the Fourteenth Amendment, and that they violated his own and his patients' rights to privacy in the doctor-patient relationship and his own right to practice medicine, rights he claimed were

---

actual birth" and thereby implicitly recognize other human life that is not "in existence by actual birth"; that the definition of human life is for the legislature and not the courts; that Art. 1196 "is more definite than the District of Columbia statute upheld in [*United States* v.] *Vuitch*" (402 U. S. 62); and that the Texas statute "is not vague and indefinite or overbroad." A physician's abortion conviction was affirmed.

In *Thompson*, n. 2, the court observed that any issue as to the burden of proof under the exemption of Art. 1196 "is not before us." But see *Veevers* v. *State*, 172 Tex. Cr. R. 162, 168–169, 354 S. W. 2d 161, 166–167 (1962). Cf. *United States* v. *Vuitch*, 402 U. S. 62, 69–71 (1971).

[4]The name is a pseudonym.

guaranteed by the First, Fourth, Fifth, Ninth, and Fourteenth Amendments.

John and Mary Doe,[5] a married couple, filed a companion complaint to that of Roe. They also named the District Attorney as defendant, claimed like constitutional deprivations, and sought declaratory and injunctive relief. The Does alleged that they were a childless couple; that Mrs. Doe was suffering from a "neural-chemical" disorder; that her physician had "advised her to avoid pregnancy until such time as her condition has materially improved" (although a pregnancy at the present time would not present "a serious risk" to her life); that, pursuant to medical advice, she had discontinued use of birth control pills; and that if she should become pregnant, she would want to terminate the pregnancy by an abortion performed by a competent, licensed physician under safe, clinical conditions. By an amendment to their complaint, the Does purported to sue "on behalf of themselves and all couples similarly situated."

The two actions were consolidated and heard together by a duly convened three-judge district court. The suits thus presented the situations of the pregnant single woman, the childless couple, with the wife not pregnant, and the licensed practicing physician, all joining in the attack on the Texas criminal abortion statutes. Upon the filing of affidavits, motions were made for dismissal and for summary judgment. The court held that Roe and members of her class, and Dr. Hallford, had standing to sue and presented justiciable controversies, but that the Does had failed to allege facts sufficient to state a present controversy and did not have standing. It concluded that, with respect to the requests for a declaratory judgment, abstention was not warranted. On the merits, the District Court held that the "fundamental right of single women and married persons to choose whether to have children is protected by the Ninth Amendment, through the Fourteenth Amendment," and that the Texas criminal abortion statutes were void on their face because they were both unconstitutionally vague and constituted an overbroad infringement of the plaintiffs' Ninth Amendment rights. The court then held that abstention was warranted with respect to the requests for an injunction. It therefore dismissed the Doe's complaint, declared the abortion statutes void, and dismissed the application for injunctive relief. 314 F. Supp. 1217, 1225 (ND Tex. 1970).

The plaintiffs Roe and Doe and the intervenor Hallford, pursuant to 28 U. S. C. § 1253, have appealed to this Court from that part

---

[5]These names are pseudonyms.

of the District Court's judgment denying the injunction. The defendant District Attorney has purported to cross-appeal, pursuant to the same statute, from the court's grant of declaratory relief to Roe and Hallford. Both sides also have taken protective appeals to the United States Court of Appeals for the Fifth Circuit. That court ordered the appeals held in abeyance pending decision here. We postponed decision on jurisdiction to the hearing on the merits. 402 U. S. 941 (1971).

III

It might have been preferable if the defendant, pursuant to our Rule 20, had presented to us a petition for certiorari before judgment in the Court of Appeals with respect to the granting of the plaintiffs' prayer for declaratory relief. Our decisions in *Mitchell* v. *Donovan*, 398 U. S. 427 (1970), and *Gunn* v. *University Committee*, 399 U. S. 383 (1970), are to the effect that § 1253 does not authorize an appeal to this Court from the grant or denial of declaratory relief alone. We conclude, nevertheless, that those decisions do not foreclose our review of both the injunctive and the declaratory aspects of a case of this kind when it is properly here, as this one is, on appeal under § 1253 from specific denial of injunctive relief, and the arguments as to both aspects are necessarily indentical. See *Carter* v. *Jury Comm'n*, 396 U. S. 320 (1970); *Florida Lime Growers* v. *Jacobsen*, 362 U. S. 73, 80–81 (1960). It would be destructive of time and energy for all concerned were we to rule otherwise. Cf. *Doe* v. *Bolton, post*, p. 179.

IV

We are next confronted with issues of justiciability, standing, and abstention. Have Roe and the Does established that "personal stake in the outcome of the controversy," *Baker* v. *Carr*, 369 U. S. 186, 204 (1962), that insures that "the dispute sought to be adjudicated will be presented in an adversary context and in a form historically viewed as capable of judicial resolution," *Flast* v. *Cohen*, 392 U. S. 83, 101 (1968), and *Sierra Club* v. *Morton*, 405 U. S. 727, 732 (1972)? And what effect did the pendency of criminal abortion charges against Dr. Hallford in state court have upon the propriety of the federal court's granting relief to him as a plaintiff-intervenor?

A. *Jane Roe.* Despite the use of the pseudonym, no suggestion is made that Roe is a fictitious person. For purposes of her case, we accept as true, and as established, her existence; her pregnant state, as of the inception of her suit in March 1970 and as late as May 21 of that year when she filed an alias affidavit with the District Court; and her inability to obtain a legal abortion in Texas.

Viewing Roe's case as of the time of its filing and thereafter until as late as May, there can be little dispute that it then presented a case or controversy and that, wholly apart from the class aspects, she, as a pregnant single woman thwarted by the Texas criminal abortion laws, had standing to challenge those statutes. *Abele* v. *Markle,* 452 F. 2d 1121, 1125 (CA2 1971); *Crossen* v. *Breckenridge,* 446 F. 2d 833, 838–839 (CA6 1971); *Poe* v. *Menghini,* 339 F. Supp. 986, 990–991 (Kan. 1972). See *Truax* v. *Raich,* 239 U. S. 33 (1915). Indeed, we do not read the appellee's brief as really asserting anything to the contrary. The "logical nexus between the status asserted and the claim sought to be adjudicated," *Flast* v. *Cohen,* 392 U. S., at 102, and the necessary degree of contentiousness, *Golden* v. *Zwickler,* 394 U. S. 103 (1969), are both present.

The appellee notes, however, that the record does not disclose that Roe was pregnant at the time of the District Court hearing on May 22, 1970,[6] or on the following June 17 when the court's opinion and judgment were filed. And he suggests that Roe's case must now be moot because she and all other members of her class are no longer subject to any 1970 pregnancy.

The usual rule in federal cases is that an actual controversy must exist at stages of appellate or certiorari review, and not simply at the date the action is initiated. *United States* v. *Munsingwear, Inc.,* 340 U. S. 36 (1950); *Golden* v. *Zwickler, supra; SEC* v. *Medical Committee for Human Rights,* 404 U. S. 403 (1972).

But when, as here, pregnancy is a significant fact in the litigation, the normal 266-day human gestation period is so short that the pregnancy will come to term before the usual appellate process is complete. If that termination makes a case moot, pregnancy litigation seldom will survive much beyond the trial stage, and appellate review will be effectively denied. Our law should not be that rigid. Pregnancy often comes more than once to the same woman, and in the general population, if man is to survive, it will always be with us. Pregnancy provides a classic justification for a conclusion of nonmootness. It truly could be "capable of repetition, yet evading review." *Southern Pacific Terminal Co.* v. *ICC,* 219 U. S. 498, 515 (1911). See *Moore* v. *Ogilvie,* 394 U. S. 814, 816 (1969);

---

[6]The appellee twice states in his brief that the hearing before the District Court was held on July 22, 1970. Brief for Appellee 13. The docket entries, App. 2, and the transcript, App. 76, reveal this to be an error. The July date appears to be the time of the reporter's transcription. See App. 77.

Carroll v. *Princess Anne,* 393 U. S. 175, 178–179 (1968); *United States* v. *W. T. Grant Co.,* 345 U. S. 629, 632–633 (1953).

We, therefore, agree with the District Court that Jane Roe had standing to undertake this litigation, that she presented a justiciable controversy, and that the termination of her 1970 pregnancy has not rendered her case moot.

B. *Dr. Hallford.* The doctors position is different. He entered Roe's litigation as a plaintiff-intervenor, alleging in his complaint that he:

> "[I]n the past has been arrested for violating the Texas Abortion Laws and at the present time stands charged by indictment with violating said laws in the Criminal District Court of Dallas County, Texas to-wit: (1) The State of Texas vs. James H. Hallford, No. C–69–5307–IH, and (2) The State of Texas vs. James H. Hallford, No. C–69–2524–II. In both cases the defendant is charged with abortion . . . ."

In his application for leave to intervene, the doctor made like representations as to the abortion charges pending in the state court. These representations were also repeated in the affidavit he executed and filed in support of his motion for summary judgment.

Dr. Hallford is, therefore, in the position of seeking, in a federal court, declaratory and injunctive relief with respect to the same statutes under which he stands charged in criminal prosecutions simultaneously pending in state court. Although he stated that he has been arrested in the past for violating the State's abortion laws, he makes no allegation of any substantial and immediate threat to any federally protected right that cannot be asserted in his defense against the state prosecutions. Neither is there any allegation of harassment or bad-faith prosecution. In order to escape the rule articulated in the cases cited in the next paragraph of this opinion, that, absent harassment and bad faith, a defendant in a pending state criminal case cannot affirmatively challenge in federal court the statutes under which the State is prosecuting him, Dr. Hallford seeks to distinguish his status as a present state defendant from his status as a "potential future defendant" and to assert only the latter for standing purposes here.

We see no merit in that distinction. Our decision in *Samuels* v. *Mackell,* 401 U. S. 66 (1971), compels the conclusion that the District Court erred when it granted declaratory relief to Dr. Hallford instead of refraining from so doing. The court, of course, was correct in refusing to grant injunctive relief to the doctor. The reasons supportive of that action, however, are those expressed in *Samuels* v. *Mackell, supra,* and in *Younger* v. *Harris,* 401 U. S. 37 (1971); *Boyle* v. *Landry,* 401 U. S. 77 (1971); *Perez* v. *Ledesma,* 401 U. S. 82 (1971); and *Byrne* v. *Karalexis,* 401 U. S. 216 (1971). See also *Dombrowski* v. *Pfister,* 380 U. S. 479 (1965). We note, in passing, that *Younger* and its companion cases were decided after the three-judge District Court decision in this case.

Dr. Hallford's complaint in intervention, therefore, is to be dismissed.[7] He is remitted to his defenses in the state criminal proceedings against him. We reverse the judgement of the District Court insofar as it granted Dr. Hallford relief and failed to dismiss his complaint in intervention.

C. *The Does.* In view of our ruling as to Roe's standing in her case, the issue of the Does' standing in their case has little significance. The claims they assert are essentially the same as those of Roe, and they attack the same statutes. Nevertheless, we briefly note the Does' posture.

Their pleadings present them as a childless married couple, the woman not being pregnant, who have no desire to have children at this time because of their having received medical advice that Mrs. Doe should avoid pregnancy, and for "other highly personal reasons." But they "fear . . . they may face the prospect of becoming parents." And if pregnancy ensues, they "would want to terminate" it by an abortion. They assert an inability to obtain an abortion legally in Texas and, consequently, the prospect of obtaining an illegal abortion there or of going outside Texas to some place where the procedure could be obtained legally and competently.

We thus have as plaintiffs a married couple who have, as their asserted immediate and present injury, only an alleged "detrimental effect upon [their] marital happiness" because they are forced to "the choice of refraining from normal sexual relations or of endangering Mary Doe's health through a possible pregnancy." Their

---

[7]We need not consider what different result, if any, would follow if Dr. Hallford's intervention were on behalf of a class. His complaint in intervention does not purport to assert a class suit and makes no reference to any class apart from an allegation that he "and others similarly situated" must necessarily guess at the meaning of Art. 1196. His application for leave to intervene goes somewhat further, for it asserts that plaintiff Roe does not adequately protect the interest of the doctor "and the class of people who are physicians . . . [and] the class of people who are . . . patients . . . ." The leave application, however, is not the complaint. Despite the District Court's statement to the contrary, 314 F. Supp., at 1225, we fail to perceive the essentials of a class suit in the Hallford complaint.

claim is that sometime in the future Mrs. Doe might become pregnant because of possible failure of contraceptive measures, and at that time in the future she might want an abortion that might then be illegal under the Texas statutes.

This very phrasing of the Does' position reveals its speculative character. Their alleged injury rests on possible future contraceptive failure, possible future pregnancy, possible future unpreparedness for parenthood, and possible future impairment of health. Any one or more of these several possibilities may not take place and all may not combine. In the Does' estimation, these possibilities might have some real or imagined impact upon their marital happiness. But we are not prepared to say that the bare allegation of so indirect an injury is sufficient to present an actual case or controversy. *Younger* v. *Harris*, 401 U. S., at 41–42; *Golden* v. *Zwickler*, 394 U. S., at 109–110; *Abele* v. *Markle*, 452 F. 2d, at 1124–1125; *Crossen* v. *Breckenridge*, 446 F. 2d, at 839. The Does' claim falls far short of those resolved otherwise in the cases that the Does urge upon us, namely, *Investment Co. Institute* v. *Camp*, 401 U. S. 617 (1971); *Data Processing Service* v. *Camp*, 397 U. S. 159 (1970); and *Epperson* v. *Arkansas*, 393 U. S. 97 (1968). See also *Truax* v. *Raich*, 239 U. S. 33 (1915).

The Does therefore are not appropriate plaintiffs in this litigation. Their complaint was properly dismissed by the District Court, and we affirm that dismissal.

V

The principal thrust of appellant's attack on the Texas statutes is that they improperly invade a right, said to be possessed by the pregnant woman, to choose to terminate her pregnancy. Appellant would discover this right in the concept of personal "liberty" embodied in the Fourteenth Amendment's Due Process Clause; or in personal, marital, familial, and sexual privacy said to be protected by the Bill of Rights or its penumbras, see *Griswold* v. *Connecticut*, 381, U. S. 479 (1965); *Eisenstadt* v. *Baird*, 405 U. S. 438 (1972); *id.*, at 460 (WHITE, J., concurring in result); or among those rights reserved to the people by the Ninth Amendment, *Griswold* v. *Connecticut*, 381 U. S., at 486 (Goldberg, J., concurring). Before addressing this claim, we feel it desirable briefly to survey, in several aspects, the history of abortion, for such insight as that history may afford us, and then to examine the state purposes and interests behind the criminal abortion laws.

VI

It perhaps is not generally appreciated that the restrictive criminal abortion laws in effect in a majority of States today are of relatively recent vintage. Those laws, generally proscribing abortion or its attempt at any time during pregnancy except when necessary to preserve the pregnant woman's life, are not of ancient or even of common-law origin. Instead, they derive from statutory changes effected, for the most part, in the latter half of the 19th century.

1. *Ancient attitudes.* These are not capable of precise determination. We are told that at the time of the Persian Empire abortifacients were known and that criminal abortions were severely punished.[8] We are also told, however, that abortion was practiced in Greek times as well as in the Roman Era,[9] and that "it was resorted to without scruple."[10] The Ephesian, Soranos, often described as the greatest of the ancient gynecologists, appears to have been generally opposed to Rome's prevailing free-abortion practices. He found it necessary to think first of the life of the mother, and he resorted to abortion when, upon this standard, he felt the procedure advisable.[11] Greek and Roman law afforded little protection to the unborn. If abortion was prosecuted in some places, it seems to have been based on a concept of a violation of the father's right to his offspring. Ancient religion did not bar abortion.[12]

2. *The Hippocratic Oath.* What then of the famous Oath that has stood so long as the ethical guide of the medical profession and that bears the name of the great Greek (460(?)–377(?) B. C.), who has been described as the Father of Medicine, the "wisest and the greatest practitioner of his art," and the "most important and most complete medical personality of antiquity," who dominated the

---

[8]A. Castiglioni, A History of Medicine 84 (2d ed. 1947), E. Krumbhaar, translator and editor (hereinafter Castiglioni).

[9]J. Ricci, The Genealogy of Gynaecology 52, 84, 113, 149 (2d ed. 1950) (hereinafter Ricci); L. Lader, Abortion 75–77 (1966) (hereinafter Lader); K. Niswander, Medical Abortion Practices in the United States, in Abortion and the Law 37, 38–40 (D. Smith ed. 1967); G. Williams, The Sanctity of Life and the Criminal Law 148 (1957) (hereinafter Williams); J. Noonan, An Almost Absolute Value in History, in The Morality of Abortion, 1, 3–7 (J. Noonan ed. 1970) (hereinafter Noonan); Quay, Justifiable Abortion—Medical and Legal Foundations (pt. 2), 49 Geo. L. J. 395, 406–422 (1961) (hereinafter Quay).

[10]L. Edelstein, The Hippocratic Oath 10 (1943) (hereinafter Edelstein). But see Castiglioni 227.

[11]Edelstein 12; Ricci 113–114, 118–119; Noonan 5.

[12]Edelstein 13–14.

medical schools of his time, and who typified the sum of the medical knowledge of the past?[13] The Oath varies somewhat according to the particular translation, but in any translation the content is clear: "I will give no deadly medicine to anyone if asked, nor suggest any such counsel; and in like manner I will not give a woman a pessary to produce abortion,"[14] or "I will neither give a deadly drug to anybody if asked for it, nor will I make a suggestion to this effect. Similarly, I will not give to a woman an abortive remedy."[15]

Although the Oath is not mentioned in any of the principal briefs in this case or in *Doe v. Bolton, post,* p. 179, it represents the apex of the development of strict ethical concepts in medicine, and its influence endures to this day. Why did not the authority of Hippocrates dissuade abortion practice in his time and that of Rome? The late Dr. Edelstein provides us with a theory: [16]The Oath was not uncontested even in Hippocrates' day; only the Pythagorean school of philosophers frowned upon the related act of suicide. Most Greek thinkers, on the other hand, commended abortion, at least prior to viability. See Plato, Republic, V, 461; Aristotle, Politics, VII, 1335b 25. For the Pythagoreans, however, it was a matter of dogma. For them the embryo was animate from the moment of conception, and abortion meant destruction of a living being. The abortion clause of the Oath, therefore, "echoes Pythagorean doctrines," and "[i]n no other stratum of Greek opinion were such views held or proposed in the same spirit of uncompromising austerity."[17]

Dr. Edelstein then concludes that the Oath originated in a group representing only a small segment of Greek opinion and that it certainly was not accepted by all ancient physicians. He points out that medical writings down to Galen (A. D. 130–200) "give evidence of the violation of almost every one of its injunctions."[18] But with the end of antiquity a decided change took place. Resistance against suicide and against abortion became common. The Oath came to be popular. The emerging teachings of Christianity were in agreement with the Pythagorean ethic. The Oath "became the nucleus of all medical ethics" and "was applauded as the embodiment of

---

[13]Castiglioni 148.

[14]*Id.,* at 154.

[15]Edelstein 3.

[16]*Id.,* at 12, 15–18.

[17]*Id.,* at 18; Lader 76.

[18]Edelstein 63.

truth." Thus, suggests Dr. Edelstein, it is "a Pythagorean manifesto and not the expression of an absolute standard of medical conduct."[19]

This, it seems to us, is a satisfactory and acceptable explanation of the Hippocratic Oath's apparent rigidity. It enables us to understand, in historical context, a long-accepted and revered statement of medical ethics.

3. *The common law.* It is undisputed that at common law, abortion performed *before* "quickening"—the first recognizable movement of the fetus *in utero,* appearing usually from the 16th to the 18th week of pregnancy[20]—was not an indictable offense.[21] The absence of a common-law crime for pre-quickening abortion appears to have developed from a confluence of earlier philosophical, theological, and civil and canon law concepts of when life begins. These disciplines variously approached the question in terms of the point at which the embryo or fetus became "formed" or recognizably human, or in terms of when a "person" came into being, that is, infused with a "soul" or "animated." A loose consensus evolved in early English law that these events occurred at some point between conception and live birth.[22] This was "mediate animation." Although Christian theology and the canon law came to fix

---

[19]*Id.,* at 64.

[20]Dorland's Illustrated Medical Dictionary 1261 (24th ed. 1965).

[21]E. Coke, Institutes III *50; 1 W. Hawkins, Pleas of the Crown, c. 31 § 16 (4th ed. 1762); 1 W. Blackstone, Commentaries *129–130; M. Hale, Pleas of the Crown 433 (1st Amer. ed. 1847). For discussions of the role of the quickening concept in English common law, see Lader 78; Noonan 223–226; Means, The Law of New York Concerning Abortion and the Status of the Foetus, 1664–1968: A Case of Cessation of Constitutionality (pt. 1), 14 N. Y. L. F. 411, 418–428 (1968) (hereinafter Means I); Stern, Abortion: Reform and the Law, 59 J. Crim. L. C. & P. S. 84 (1968) (hereinafter Stern); Quay 430–432; Williams 152.

[22]Early philosophers believed that the embryo or fetus did not become formed and begin to live until at least 40 days after conception for a male, and 80 to 90 days for a female. See, for example, Aristotle, Hist. Anim. 7.3.585b; Gen. Anim. 2.3.736, 2.5.741; Hippocrates, Lib. de Nat. Puer. No. 10. Artistotle's thinking derived from his three-stage theory of life: vegetable, animal, rational. The vegetable stage was reached at conception, the animal at "animation," and the rational soon after live birth. This theory, together with the 40/80 day view, came to be accepted by early Christian thinkers.

The theological debate was reflected in the writings of St. Augustine, who made a distinction between *embryo inanimatus,* not yet endowed with a soul, and *embryo animatus.* He may have drawn upon Exodus 21:22. At one point, however, he expressed the view that human powers cannot determine the point during fetal development at which the critical change occurs. See Augustine, De Origine Animae 4.4 (Pub. Law 44.527). See also W. Reany, The Creation of the Human Soul, c. 2 and 83–86 (1932); Huser, The Crime of Abortion in Canon

the point of animation at 40 days for a male and 80 days for a female, a view that persisted until the 19th century, there was otherwise little agreement about the precise time of formation or animation. There was agreement, however, that prior to this point the fetus was to be regarded as part of the mother, and its destruction, therefore, was not homicide. Due to continued uncertainty about the precise time when animation occurred, to the lack of any empirical basis for the 40–80-day view, and perhaps to Aquinas' definition of movement as one of the two first principles of life, Bracton focused upon quickening as the critical point. The significance of quickening was echoed by later common-law scholars and found its way into the received common law in this country.

Whether abortion of a *quick* fetus was a felony at common law, or even a lesser crime, is still disputed. Bracton, writing early in the 13th century, thought it homicide.[23] But the later and predominant view, following the great common-law scholars, has been that it was, at most, a lesser offense. In a frequently cited passage, Coke took the position that abortion of a woman "quick with childe" is "a great misprision, and no murder."[24] Blackstone followed, saying that while abortion after quickening had once been considered manslaughter (though not murder), "modern law" took a less severe view.[25] A recent review of the common-law precedents argues, however, that those precedents contradict Coke and that even post-quickening abortion was never established as a common-law crime.[26] This is of some importance because while most American

Law 15 (Catholic Univ. of America, Canon Law Studies No. 162, Washington, D. C., 1942).

Galen, in three treatises related to embryology, accepted the thinking of Aristotle and his followers. Quay 426–427. Later, Augustine on abortion was incorporated by Gratian into the Decretum, published about 1140. Decretum Magistri Gratiani 2.32.2.7 to 2.32.2.10, in 1 Corpus Juris Canonici 1122, 1123 (A. Friedburg, 2d ed. 1879). This Decretal and the Decretals that followed were recognized as the definitive body of canon law until the new code of 1917.

For discussions of the canon-law treatment, see Means I, pp. 411–412; Noonan 20–26; Quay 426–430; see also J. Noonan, Contraception: A History of Its Treatment by the Catholic Theologians and Canonists 18–29 (1965).

[23]Bracton took the position that abortion by blow or poison was homicide "if the foetus be already formed and animated, and particularly if it be animated," 2 H. Bracton, De Legibus et Consuetudinibus Angliae 279 (T. Twiss ed. 1879), or, as a later translation puts it, "if the foetus is already formed or quickened, especially if it is quickened," 2 H. Bracton, On the Laws and Customs of England 341 (S. Thorne ed. 1968). See Quay 431; see also 2 Fleta 60–61 (Book 1, c. 23) (Selden Society ed. 1955).

[24]E. Coke, Institutes III *50.

[25]1 W. Blackstone, Commentaries *129–130.

courts ruled, in holding or dictum, that abortion of an unquickened fetus was not criminal under their received common law,[27] others followed Coke in stating that abortion of a quick fetus was a "misprision," a term they translated to mean "misdemeanor."[28] That their reliance on Coke on this aspect of the law was uncritical and, apparently in all the reported cases, dictum (due probably to the paucity of common-law prosecutions for post-quickening abortion), makes it now appear doubtful that abortion was ever firmly established as a common-law crime even with respect to the destruction of a quick fetus.

4. *The English statutory law.* England's first criminal abortion statute, Lord Ellenborough's Act, 43 Geo. 3, c. 58, came in 1803. It made abortion of a quick fetus, § 1, a capital crime, but in § 2 it provided lesser penalties for the felony of abortion before quickening, and thus preserved the "quickening" distinction. This contrast was continued in the general revision of 1828, 9 Geo. 4, c. 31, § 13. It disappeared, however, together with the death penalty, in 1837, 7

---

[26]Means, The Phoenix of Abortional Freedom: Is a Penumbral or Ninth-Amendment Right About to Arise from the Nineteenth-Century Legislative Ashes of a Fourteenth-Century Common-Law Liberty?, 17 N. Y. L. F. 335 (1971) (hereinafter Means II). The author examines the two principal precedents cited marginally by Coke, both contrary to his dictum, and traces the treatment of these and other cases by earlier commentators. He concludes that Coke, who himself participated as an advocate in an abortion case in 1601, may have intentionally misstated the law. The author even suggests a reason: Coke's strong feelings against abortion, coupled with his determination to assert common-law (secular) jurisdiction to assess penalties for an offense that traditionally had been an exclusively ecclesiastical or canon-law crime. See also Lader 78–79, who notes that some scholars doubt that the common law ever was applied to abortion; that the English ecclesiastical courts seem to have lost interest in the problem after 1527; and that the preamble to the English legislation of 1803, 43 Geo. 3, c. 58, § 1, referred to in the text, *infra*, at 136, states that "no adequate means have been hitherto provided for the prevention and punishment of such offenses."

[27]*Commonwealth* v. *Bangs*, 9 Mass. 387, 388 (1812); *Commonwealth* v. *Parker*, 50 Mass. (9 Metc.) 263, 265–266 (1845); *State* v. *Cooper*, 22 N. J. L. 52, 58 (1849); *Abrams* v. *Foshee*, 3 Iowa 274, 278–280 (1856); *Smith* v. *Gaffard*, 31 Ala. 45, 51 (1857); *Mitchell* v. *Commonwealth*, 78 Ky. 204, 210 (1879); *Eggart* v. *State*, 40 Fla. 527, 532, 25 So. 144, 145 (1898); *State* v. *Alcorn*, 7 Idaho 599, 606, 64 P. 1014, 1016 (1901); *Edwards* v. *State*, 79 Neb. 251, 252, 112 N. W. 611, 612 (1907); *Gray* v. *State*, 77 Tex. Cr. R. 221, 224, 178 S. W. 337, 338 (1915); *Miller* v. *Bennett*, 190 Va. 162, 169, 56 S. E. 2d 217, 221 (1949). Contra, *Mills* v. *Commonwealth*, 13 Pa. 631, 633 (1850); *State* v. *Slagle*, 83 N. C. 630, 632 (1880).

[28]See *Smith* v. *State*, 33 Me. 48, 55 (1851); *Evans* v. *People*, 49 N. Y. 86, 88 (1872); *Lamb* v. *State*, 67 Md. 524, 533, 10 A. 208 (1887).

Will. 4 & 1 Vict., c. 85, § 6, and did not reappear in the Offenses Against the Person Act of 1861, 24 & 25 Vict., c. 100, § 59, that formed the core of English anti-abortion law until the liberalizing reforms of 1967. In 1929, the Infant Life (Preservation) Act, 19 & 20 Geo. 5, c. 34, came into being. Its emphasis was upon the destruction of "the life of a child capable of being born alive." It made a wilful act performed with the necessary intent a felony. It contained a proviso that one was not to be found guilty of the offense "unless it is proved that the act which caused the death of the child was not done in good faith for the purpose only of preserving the life of the mother."

A seemingly notable development in the English law was the case of *Rex* v. *Bourne,* [1939] 1 K. B. 687. This case apparently answered in the affirmative the question whether an abortion necessary to preserve the life of the pregnant woman was excepted from the criminal penalties of the 1861 Act. In his instructions to the jury, Judge Macnaghten referred to the 1929 Act, and observed that that Act related to "the case where a child is killed by a wilful act at the same time when it is being delivered in the ordinary course of nature." *Id.,* at 691. He concluded that the 1861 Act's use of the word "unlawfully," imported the same meaning expressed by the specific proviso in the 1929 Act, even though there was no mention of preserving the mother's life in the 1861 Act. He then construed the phrase "preserving the life of the mother" broadly, that is, "in a reasonable sense," to include a serious and permanent threat to the mother's *health,* and instructed the jury to acquit Dr. Bourne if it found he had acted in a good-faith belief that the abortion was necessary for this purpose. *Id.,* at 693–694. The jury did acquit.

Recently, Parliament enacted a new abortion law. This is the Abortion Act of 1967, 15 & 16 Eliz. 2, c. 87. The Act permits a licensed physician to perform an abortion where two other licensed physicians agree (a) "that the continuance of the pregnancy would involve risk to the life of the pregnant woman, or of injury to the physical or mental health of the pregnant woman or any existing children of her family, greater than if the pregnancy were terminated," or (b) "that there is a substantial risk that if the child were born it would suffer from such physical or mental abnormalities as to be seriously handicapped." The Act also provides that, in making this determination, "account may be taken of the pregnant woman's actual or reasonably foreseeable environment." It also permits a physician, without the concurrence of others, to terminate a pregnancy where he is of the good-faith opinion that the abortion "is immediately necessary to save the life or to prevent grave permanent injury to the physical or mental health of the pregnant woman."

5. *The American law.* In this country, the law in effect in all but a few States until mid-19th century was the pre-existing English common law. Connecticut, the first State to enact abortion legislation, adopted in 1821 that part of Lord Ellenborough's Act that related to a woman "quick with child."[29] The death penalty was not imposed. Abortion before quickening was made a crime in that state only in 1860.[30] In 1828, New York enacted legislation[31] that, in two respects, was to serve as a model for early anti-abortion statutes. First, while barring destruction of an unquickened fetus as well as a quick fetus, it made the former only a misdemeanor, but the latter second-degree manslaughter. Second, it incorporated a concept of therapeutic abortion by providing that an abortion was excused if it "shall have been necessary to preserve the life of such mother, or shall have been advised by two physicians to be necessary for such purpose." By 1840, when Texas had received the common law,[32] only eight American States had statutes dealing with abortion.[33] It was not until after the War Between the States that legislation began generally to replace the common law. Most of these initial statutes dealt severely with abortion after quickening but were lenient with it before quickening. Most punished attempts equally with completed abortions. While many statutes included the exception for an abortion thought by one or more physicians to be necessary to save the mother's life, that provision soon disappeared and the typical law required that the procedure actually be necessary for that purpose.

Gradually, in the middle and late 19th century the quickening distinction disappeared from the statutory law of most States and the degree of the offense and the penalties were increased. By the end of the 1950's, a large majority of the jurisdictions banned abortion, however and whenever performed, unless done to save or

---

[29]Conn. Stat., Tit. 20, § 14 (1821).

[30]Conn. Pub. Acts, c. 71, § 1 (1860).

[31]N. Y. Rev. Stat. pt. 4, c. 1, Tit. 2, Art. 1, § 9, p. 661, and Tit. 6, § 21, p. 694 (1829).

[32]Act of Jan. 20, 1840, § 1, set forth in 2 H. Gammel, Laws of Texas 177–178 (1898); see *Grigsby* v. *Reib*, 105 Tex. 597, 600 153 S. W. 1124, 1125 (1913).

[33]The early statutes are discussed in Quay 435–438. See also Lader 85–88; Stern 85–86; and Means II 375–376.

preserve the life of the mother.[34] The exceptions, Alabama and the District of Columbia, permitted abortion to preserve the mother's health.[35] Three States permitted abortions that were not "unlawfully" performed or that were not "without lawful justification," leaving interpretation of those standards to the courts.[36] In the past several years, however, a trend toward liberalization of abortion statutes has resulted in adoption, by about one-third of the States, of less stringent laws, most of them patterned after the ALI Model Penal Code, § 230.3,[37] set forth as Appendix B to the opinion in *Doe v. Bolton, post,* p. 205.

It is thus apparent that at common law, at the time of the adoption of our Constitution, and throughout the major portion of the 19th century, abortion was viewed with less disfavor than under most American statutes currently in effect. Phrasing it another way, a woman enjoyed a substantially broader right to terminate a pregnancy than she does in most States today. At least with respect to the early stage of pregnancy, and very possibly without such a limitation, the opportunity to make this choice was present in this country well into the 19th century. Even later, the law continued for some time to treat less punitively an abortion procured in early pregnancy.

6. *The position of the American Medical Association.* The anti-abortion mood prevalent in this country in the late 19th century was shared by the medical profession. Indeed, the attitude of the profession may have played a significant role in the enactment of stringent criminal abortion legislation during that period.

---

[34]Criminal abortion statutes in effect in the States as of 1961, together with historical statutory development and important judicial interpretations of the state statutes, are cited and quoted in Quay 447–520. See Comment, A Survey of the Present Statutory and Case Law on Abortion: The Contradictions and the Problems, 1972 U. Ill. L. F. 177, 179, classifying the abortion statues and listing 25 States as permitting abortion only if necessary to save or preserve the mother's life.

[35]Ala. Code, Tit. 14, § 9 (1958); D. C. Code Ann. § 22–201 (1967).

[36]Mass. Gen. Laws Ann., c. 272, § 19 (1970); N. J. Stat. Ann. § 2A:87–1 (1969); Pa. Stat. Ann., Tit. 18 §§ 4718, 4719 (1963).

[37]Fourteen States have adopted some form of the ALI statute. See Ark. Stat. Ann. §§ 41–303 to 41–310 (Supp. 1971); Calif. Health & Safety Code §§ 25950–25955.5 (Supp. 1972); Colo. Rev. Stat. Ann. §§ 40–2–50 to 40–2–53 (Cum. Supp. 1967); Del. Code Ann., Tit. 24, §§ 1790–1793 (Supp. 1972); Florida Law of Apr. 13, 1972, c. 72–196, 1972 Fla. Sess. Law Serv., pp. 380–382; Ga. Code §§26–1201 to 26–1203 (1972); Kan. Stat. Ann. § 21–3407 (Supp. 1971); Md. Ann. Code, Art. 43, §§ 137–139 (1971); Miss. Code Ann. § 2223 (Supp. 1972); N. M. Stat. Ann. §§ 40A–5–1 to 40A–5–3 (1972); N. C. Gen. Stat. § 14–45.1 (Supp. 1971); Ore.

An AMA Committee on Criminal Abortion was appointed in May 1857. It presented its report, 12 Trans. of the Am. Med. Assn. 73–78 (1859), to the Twelfth Annual Meeting. That report observed that the Committee had been appointed to investigate criminal abortion "with a view to its general suppression." It deplored abortion and its frequency and it listed three causes of "this general demoralization":

> "The first of these causes is a wide-spread popular ignorance of the true character of the crime—a belief, even among mothers themselves, that the foetus is not alive till after the period of quickening.
> "The second of the agents alluded to is the fact that the profession themselves are frequently supposed careless of foetal life . . . .
> "The third reason of the frightful extent of this crime is found in the grave defects of our laws, both common and statute, as regards the independent and actual existence of the child before birth, as a living being. These errors, which are sufficient in most instances to prevent conviction, are based, and only based, upon mistaken and exploded medical dogmas. With strange inconsistency, the law fully acknowledges the foetus in utero and its inherent rights, for civil purposes; while personally and as criminally affected, it fails to recognize it, and to its life as yet denies all protection." *Id.*, at 75–76.

The Committee then offered, and the Association adopted, resolutions protesting "against such unwarrantable destruction of human life," calling upon state legislatures to revise their abortion laws, and requesting the cooperation of state medical societies "in pressing the subject." *Id.*, at 28, 78.

In 1871 a long and vivid report was submitted by the Committee on Criminal Abortion. It ended with the observation, "We had

---

Rev. Stat. §§ 435.405 to 435.495 (1971); S. C. Code Ann. §§ 16–82 to 16–89 (1962 and Supp. 1971); Va. Code Ann. §§ 18.1–62 to 18.1–62.3 (Supp. 1972). Mr. Justice Clark described some of these States as having "led the way." Religion, Morality, and Abortion: A Constitutional Appraisal, 2 Loyola U. (L. A.) L. Rev. 1, 11 (1969).

By the end of 1970, four other States had repealed criminal penalties for abortions performed in early pregnancy by a licensed physician, subject to stated procedural and health requirements. Alaska Stat. § 11.15.060 (1970); Haw. Rev. Stat. § 453–16 (Supp. 1971); N. Y. Penal Code § 125.05 subd. 3 (Supp. 1972–1973); Wash. Rev. Code §§ 9.02.060 to 9.02.080 (Supp. 1972). The precise status of criminal abortion laws in some States is made unclear by recent decisions in state and federal courts striking down existing state laws, in whole or in part.

to deal with human life. In a matter of less importance we could entertain no compromise. An honest judge on the bench would call things by their proper names. We could do no less." 22 Trans. of the Am. Med. Assn. 258 (1871). It proffered resolutions, adopted by the Association, *id.*, at 38–39, recommending, among other things, that it "be unlawful and unprofessional for any physician to induce abortion or premature labor, without the concurrent opinion of at least one respectable consulting physician, and then always with a view to the safety of the child—if that be possible," and calling "the attention of the clergy of all denominations to the perverted views of morality entertained by a large class of females—aye, and men also, on this important question."

Except for periodic condemnation of the criminal abortionist, no further formal AMA action took place until 1967. In that year, the Committee on Human Reproduction urged the adoption of a stated policy of opposition to induced abortion, except when there is "documented medical evidence" of a threat to the health or life of the mother, or that the child "may be born with incapacitating physical deformity or mental deficiency," or that a pregnancy "resulting from legally established statutory or forcible rape or incest may constitute a threat to the mental or physical health of the patient," two other physicians "chosen because of their recognized professional competence have examined the patient and have concurred in writing," and the procedure "is performed in a hospital accredited by the Joint Commission on Accreditation of Hospitals." The providing of medical information by physicians to state legislatures in their consideration of legislation regarding therapeutic abortion was "to be considered consistent with the principles of ethics of the American Medical Association." This recommendation was adopted by the House of Delegates. Proceedings of the AMA House of Delegates 40–51 (June 1967).

In 1970, after the introduction of a variety of proposed resolutions, and of a report from its Board of Trustees, a reference committee noted "polarization of the medical profession on this controversial issue"; division among those who had testified; a difference of opinion among AMA councils and committees; "the remarkable shift in testimony" in six months, felt to be influenced "by the rapid changes in state laws and by the judicial decisions which tend to make abortion more freely available;" and a feeling "that this trend will continue." On June 25, 1970, the House of Delegates adopted preambles and most of the resolutions proposed by the reference committee. The preambles emphasized "the best interests of the patient," "sound clinical judgment," and "informed patient consent," in contrast to "mere acquiescence to the patient's demand." The resolutions asserted that abortion is a medical procedure that should be performed by a licensed physician in an accredited hospital only after consultation with two other physicians and in conformity with state law, and that no party to the procedure should be required to violate personally held moral principles.[38] Proceedings of the AMA House of Delegates 220 (June 1970). The AMA Judicial Council rendered a complementary opinion.[39]

7. *The position of the American Public Health Association.* In October 1970, the Executive Board of the APHA adopted Standards for Abortion Services. These were five in number:

> "a. Rapid and simple abortion referral must be readily available through state and local public health departments, medical societies, or other non-profit organizations.
>
> "b. An important function of counseling should be to simplify and expedite the provision of abortion services; it should not delay the obtaining of these services.
>
> "c. Psychiatric consultation should not be mandatory. As in the case of other specialized medical services, phychiatric consultation should be sought for definite indications and not on a routine basis.

---

[38]"Whereas, Abortion, like any other medical procedure, should not be performed when contrary to the best interests of the patient since good medical practice requires due consideration for the patient's welfare and not mere acquiescence to the patient's demand; and

"Whereas, The standards of sound clinical judgment, which, together with informed patient consent should be determinative according to the merits of each individual case; therefore be it

"*RESOLVED,* That abortion is a medical procedure and should be performed only by a duly licensed physician and surgeon in an accredited hospital acting only after consultation with two other physicians chosen because of their professional competency and in conformance with standards of good medical practice and the Medical Practice Act of his State; and be it further

"*RESOLVED,* That no physician or other professional personnel shall be compelled to perform any act which violates his good medical judgment. Neither physician, hospital, nor hospital personnel shall be required to perform any act violative of personally-held moral principles. In these circumstances good medical practice requires only that the physician or other professional personnel withdraw from the case so long as the withdrawal is consistent with good medical practice." Proceedings of the AMA House of Delegates 220 (June 1970).

[39]"The Principles of Medical Ethics of the AMA do not prohibit a physician from performing an abortion that is performed in accordance with good medical practice and under circumstances that do not violate the laws of the community in which he practices.

"In the matter of abortions, as of any other medical procedure, the Judicial Council becomes involved whenever there is alleged violation of the Principles of Medical Ethics as established by the House of Delegates."

"d. A wide range of individuals from appropriately trained, sympathetic volunteers to highly skilled physicians may qualify as abortion counselors.

"e. Contraception and/or sterilization should be discussed with each abortion patient." Recommended Standards for Abortion Services, 61 Am. J. Pub. Health 396 (1971).

Among factors pertinent to life and health risks associated with abortion were three that "are recognized as important":

"a. the skill of the physician,

"b. the environment in which the abortion is performed, and above all

"c. the duration of pregnancy, as determined by uterine size and confirmed by menstrual history." *Id.*, at 397.

It was said that "a well-equipped hospital" offers more protection "to cope with unforeseen difficulties than an office or clinic without such resources. . . . The factor of gestational age is of overriding importance." Thus, it was recommended that abortions in the second trimester and early abortions in the presence of existing medical complications be performed in hospitals as in-patient procedures. For pregnancies in the first trimester, abortion in the hospital with or without overnight stay "is probably the safest practice." An abortion in an extramural facility, however, is an acceptable alternative "provided arrangements exist in advance to admit patients promptly if unforeseen complications develop." Standards for an abortion facility were listed. It was said that at present abortions should be performed by physicians or osteopaths who are licensed to practice and who have "adequate training." *Id.*, at 398.

8. *The position of the American Bar Association.* At its meeting in February 1972 the ABA House of Delegates approved, with 17 opposing votes, the Uniform Abortion Act that had been drafted and approved the preceding August by the Conference of Commissioners on Uniform State Laws. 58 A. B. A. J. 380 (1972). We set forth the Act in full in the margin.[40] The Conference has appended an enlightening Prefatory Note.[41]

---

[40]   "UNIFORM ABORTION ACT

"SECTION 1. [*Abortion Defined; When Authorized.*]

"(a) 'Abortion' means the termination of human pregnancy with an intention other than to produce a live birth or to remove a dead fetus.

"(b) An abortion may be performed in this state only if it is performed:

"(1) by a physician licensed to practice medicine [or osteopathy] in this state or by a physician practicing medicine [or osteopathy] in the employ of the government of the United States or of this state, [and the abortion is performed [in the physician's office or in a medical clinic, or] in a hospital approved by the [Department of Health] or operated by the United States, this state, or any department, agency, or political subdivision of either;] or by a female upon herself upon the advice of the physician; and

"(2) within [20] weeks after the commencement of the pregnancy [or after [20] weeks only if the physician has reasonable cause to believe (i) there is a substantial risk that continuance of the pregnancy would endanger the life of the mother or would gravely impair the physical or mental health of the mother, (ii) that the child would be born with grave physical or mental defect, or (iii) that the pregnancy resulted from rape or incest, or illicit intercourse with a girl under the age of 16 years].

"SECTION 2. [*Penalty.*] Any person who performs or procures an abortion other than authorized by this Act is guilty of a [felony] and, upon conviction thereof, may be sentenced to pay a fine not exceeding [$1,000] or to imprisonment [in the state penitentiary] not exceeding [5 years], or both.

"SECTION 3. [*Uniformity of Interpretation.*] This Act shall be construed to effectuate its general purpose to make uniform the law with respect to the subject of this Act among those states which enact it.

"SECTION 4. [*Short Title.*] This Act may be cited as the Uniform Abortion Act.

"SECTION 5. [*Severability.*] If any provision of this Act or the application thereof to any person or circumstance is held invalid, the invalidity does not affect other provisions or applications of this Act which can be given effect without the invalid provision or application, and to this end the provisions of this Act are severable.

"SECTION 6. [*Repeal.*] The following acts and parts of acts are repealed:

"(1)

"(2)

"(3)

"SECTION 7. [*Time of Taking Effect.*] This Act shall take effect _____."

[41]"This Act is based largely upon the New York abortion act following a review of the more recent laws on abortion in several states and upon recognition of a more liberal trend in laws on this subject. Recognition was given also to the several decisions in state and federal courts which show a further trend toward liberalization of abortion laws, especially during the first trimester of pregnancy.

"Recognizing that a number of problems appeared in New York, a shorter time period for 'unlimited' abortions was advisable. The time period was bracketed to permit the various states to insert a figure more in keeping with the different conditions that might exist among the states. Likewise, the language limiting the place or places in which abortions may be performed was also bracketed to account for different conditions among the states. In addition, limitations on abortions after the initial 'unlimited' period were placed in brackets so that individual states may adopt all or any of these reasons, or place further restrictions upon abortions after the initial period.

"This Act does not contain any provision relating to medical review committees or prohibitions against sanctions imposed upon medical personnel refusing to participate in abortions because of religious or other similar reasons, or the like. Such provisions, while related, do not directly pertain to when, where, or by whom abortions may be performed; however, the Act is not drafted to exclude such a provision by a state wishing to enact the same."

VII

Three reasons have been advanced to explain historically the enactment of criminal abortion laws in the 19th century and to justify their continued existence.

It has been argued occasionally that these laws were the product of a Victorian social concern to discourage illicit sexual conduct. Texas, however, does not advance this justification in the present case, and it appears that no court or commentator has taken the argument seriously.[42] The appellants and *amici* contend, moreover, that this is not a proper state purpose at all and suggest that, if it were, the Texas statutes are overbroad in protecting it since the law fails to distinguish between married and unwed mothers.

A second reason is concerned with abortion as a medical procedure. When most criminal abortion laws were first enacted, the procedure was a hazardous one for the woman.[43] This was particularly true prior to the development of antisepsis. Antiseptic techniques, of course, were based on discoveries by Lister, Pasteur, and others first announced in 1867, but were not generally accepted and employed until about the turn of the century. Abortion mortality was high. Even after 1900, and perhaps until as late as the development of antibiotics in the 1940's, standard modern techniques such as dilation and curettage were not nearly so safe as they are today. Thus, it has been argued that a State's real concern in enacting a criminal abortion law was to protect the pregnant woman, that is, to restrain her from submitting to a procedure that placed her life in serious jeopardy.

Modern medical techniques have altered this situation. Appellants and various *amici* refer to the medical data indicating that abortion in early pregnancy, that is, prior to the end of the first trimester, although not without its risk, is now relatively safe. Mortality rates for women undergoing early abortions, where the procedure is legal, appear to be as low as or lower than the rates for normal childbirth.[44] Consequently, any interest of the State in protecting the woman from an inherently hazardous procedure, except

---

[42]See, for example, *YWCA* v. *Kugler,* 342 F. Supp. 1048, 1074 (N. J. 1972); *Abele* v. *Markle,* 342 F. Supp. 800, 805–806 (Conn. 1972) (Newman, J., concurring in result), appeal docketed, No. 72–56; *Walsingham* v. *State,* 250 So. 2d 857, 863 (Ervin, J., concurring) (Fla. 1971); *State* v. *Gedicke,* 43 N. J. L. 86, 90 (1881); Means II 381–382.

[43]See C. Haagensen & W. Lloyd, A Hundred Years of Medicine 19 (1943).

[44]Potts, Postconceptive Control of Fertility, 8 Int'l J. of G. & O. 957, 967 (1970) (England and Wales); Abortion Mortality, 20 Morbidity and Mortality 208, 209 (June 12, 1971) (U. S. Dept. of HEW, Public Health Service) (New York City); Tietze, United States: Therapeutic Abortions, 1963–1968; 59 Studies in Family

when it would be equally dangerous for her to forgo it, has largely disappeared. Of course, important state interests in the areas of health and medical standards do remain. The State has a legitimate interest in seeing to it that abortion, like any other medical procedure, is performed under circumstances that insure maximum safety for the patient. This interest obviously extends at least to the performing physician and his staff, to the facilities involved, to the availability of after-care, and to adequate provision for any complication or emergency that might arise. The prevalence of high mortality rates at illegal "abortion mills" strengthens, rather than weakens, the State's interest in regulating the conditions under which abortions are performed. Moreover, the risk to the woman increases as her pregnancy continues. Thus, the State retains a definite interest in protecting the woman's own health and safety when an abortion is proposed at a late stage of pregnancy.

The third reason is the State's interest—some phrase it in terms of duty—in protecting prenatal life. Some of the argument for this justification rests on the theory that a new human life is present from the moment of conception.[45] The State's interest and general obligation to protect life then extends, it is argued, to prenatal life. Only when the life of the pregnant mother herself is at stake, balanced against the life she carries within her, should the interest of the embryo or fetus not prevail. Logically, of course, a legitimate state interest in this area need not stand or fall on acceptance of the belief that life begins at conception or at some other point prior to live birth. In assessing the State's interest, recognition may be given to the less rigid claim that as long as at least *potential* life is involved, the State may assert interests beyond the protection of the pregnant woman alone.

Parties challenging state abortion laws have sharply disputed in some courts the contention that a purpose of these laws, when enacted, was to protect prenatal life.[46] Pointing to the absence of legislative history to support the contention, they claim that most state laws were designed solely to protect the woman. Because medical advances have lessened this concern, at least with respect

Planning 5, 7 (1970); Tietze, Mortality with Contraception and Induced Abortion, 45 Studies in Family Planning 6 (1969) (Japan, Czechoslovakia, Hungary); Tietze & Lehfeldt, Legal Abortion in Eastern Europe, 175 J. A. M. A. 1149, 1152 (April 1961). Other sources are discussed in Lader 17–23.

[45]See Brief of *Amicus* National Right to Life Committee; R. Drinan, The Inviolability of the Right to Be Born, in Abortion and the Law 107 (D. Smith ed. 1967); Louisell, Abortion, The Practice of Medicine and the Due Process of Law, 16 U. C. L. A. L. Rev. 233 (1969); Noonan 1.

[46]See, *e. g.*, *Abele* v. *Markle*, 342 F. Supp. 800 (Conn. 1972), appeal docketed, No. 72–56.

to abortion in early pregnancy, they argue that with respect to such abortions the laws can no longer be justified by any state interest. There is some scholarly support for this view of original purpose.[47] The few state courts called upon to interpret their laws in the late 19th and early 20th centuries did focus on the State's interest in protecting the woman's health rather than in preserving the embryo and fetus.[48] Proponents of this view point out that in many States, including Texas,[49] by statute or judicial interpretation, the pregnant woman herself could not be prosecuted for self-abortion or for cooperating in an abortion performed upon her by another.[50] They claim that the adoption of the "quickening" distinction through received common law and state statutes tacitly recognizes the greater health hazards inherent in late abortion and impliedly repudiates the theory that life begins at conception.

It is with these interests, and the weight to be attached to them, that this case is concerned.

VIII

The Constitution does not explicitly mention any right of privacy. In a line of decisions, however, going back perhaps as far as *Union Pacific R. Co.* v. *Botsford,* 141 U. S. 250, 251 (1891), the Court has recognized that a right of personal privacy, or a guarantee of certain areas or zones of privacy, does exist under the Constitution. In varying contexts, the Court or individual Justices have, indeed, found at least the roots of that right in the First Amendment, *Stanley* v. *Georgia,* 394 U. S. 557, 564 (1969); in the Fourth and Fifth Amendments, *Terry* v. *Ohio,* 392 U. S. 1, 8–9 (1968), *Katz* v. *United States,* 389 U. S. 347, 350 (1967), *Boyd* v. *United States,* 116 U. S. 616 (1886), see *Olmstead* v. *United States,* 277 U. S. 438, 478 (1928)

---

[47]See discussions in Means I and Means II.

[48]See, *e. g., State* v. *Murphy,* 27 N. J. L. 112, 114 (1858).

[49]*Watson* v. *State,* 9 Tex. App. 237, 244–245 (1880); *Moore* v. *State,* 37 Tex. Cr. R. 552, 561, 40 S. W. 287, 290 (1897); *Shaw* v. *State,* 73 Tex. Cr. R. 337, 339, 165 S. W. 930, 931 (1914); *Fondren* v. *State,* 74 Tex. Cr. R. 552, 557, 169 S. W. 411, 414 (1914); *Gray* v. *State,* 77 Tex. Cr. R. 221, 229, 178 S. W. 337, 341 (1915). There is no immunity in Texas for the father who is not married to the mother. *Hammet* v. *State,* 84 Tex. Cr. R. 635, 209 S. W. 661 (1919); *Thompson* v. *State* (Ct. Crim. App. Tex. 1971), appeal docketed, No. 71–1200.

[50]See *Smith* v. *State,* 33 Me., at 55; *In re Vince,* 2 N. J. 443, 450, 67 A. 2d 141, 144 (1949). A short discussion of the modern law on this issue is contained in the Comment to the ALI's Model Penal Code § 207.11, at 158 and nn. 35–37 (Tent. Draft No. 9, 1959).

(Brandeis, J., dissenting); in the penumbras of the Bill of Rights, *Griswold* v. *Connecticut*, 381 U. S., at 484–485; in the Ninth Amendment, *id.*, at 486 (Goldberg, J., concurring); or in the concept of liberty guaranteed by the first section of the Fourteenth Amendment, see *Meyer* v. *Nebraska*, 262 U. S. 390, 399 (1923). These decisions make it clear that only personal rights that can be deemed "fundamental" or "implicit in the concept of ordered liberty," *Palko* v. *Connecticut*, 302 U. S. 319, 325 (1937), are included in this guarantee of personal privacy. They also make it clear that the right has some extension to activities relating to marriage, *Loving* v. *Virginia*, 388 U. S. 1, 12 (1967); procreation, *Skinner* v. *Oklahoma*, 316 U. S. 535, 541–542 (1942); contraception, *Eisenstadt* v. *Baird*, 405 U. S., at 453–454; *id.*, at 460, 463–465 (WHITE, J., concurring in result); family relationships, *Prince* v. *Massachusetts*, 321 U. S. 158, 166 (1944); and child rearing and education, *Pierce* v. *Society of Sisters*, 268 U. S. 510, 535 (1925), *Meyer* v. *Nebraska, supra*.

This right of privacy, whether it be founded in the Fourteenth Amendment's concept of personal liberty and restrictions upon state action, as we feel it is, or, as the District Court determined, in the Ninth Amendment's reservation of rights to the people, is broad enough to encompass a woman's decision whether or not to terminate her pregnancy. The detriment that the State would impose upon the pregnant woman by denying this choice altogether is apparent. Specific and direct harm medically diagnosable even in early pregnancy may be involved. Maternity, or additional offspring, may force upon the woman a distressful life and future. Psychological harm may be imminent. Mental and physical health may be taxed by child care. There is also the distress, for all concerned, associated with the unwanted child, and there is the problem of bringing a child into a family already unable, psychologically and otherwise, to care for it. In other cases, as in this one, the additional difficulties and continuing stigma of unwed motherhood may be involved. All these are factors the woman and her responsible physician necessarily will consider in consultation.

On the basis of elements such as these, appellant and some *amici* argue that the woman's right is absolute and that she is entitled to terminate her pregnancy at whatever time, in whatever way, and for whatever reason she alone chooses. With this we do not agree. Appellant's arguments that Texas either has no valid interest at all in regulating the abortion decision, or no interest strong enough to support any limitation upon the woman's sole determination, are unpersuasive. The Court's decisions recognizing a right of privacy also acknowledge that some state regulation in areas protected by that right is appropriate. As noted above, a State may properly assert important interests in safe-guarding health, in maintaining medical standards, and in protecting potential life. At some point in pregnancy, these respective interests become sufficiently compelling to sustain regulation of the factors that govern the abortion decision. The privacy right involved, therefore, cannot be said to be absolute. In fact, it is not clear to us that the claim asserted by some *amici* that one has an unlimited right to do with one's body as one pleases bears a close relationship to the right to privacy previously articulated in the Court's decisions. The court has refused to recognize an unlimited right of this kind in the past. *Jacobson* v. *Massachusetts,* 197 U. S. 11 (1905) (vaccination); *Buck* v. *Bell,* 274 U. S. 200 (1927) (sterilization).

We, therefore, conclude that the right of personal privacy includes the abortion decision, but that this right is not unqualified and must be considered against important state interests in regulation.

We note that those federal and state courts that have recently considered abortion law challenges have reached the same conclusion. A majority, in addition to the District Court in the present case, have held state laws unconstitutional, at least in part, because of vagueness or because of overbreadth and abridgement of rights. *Abele* v. *Markle,* 342 F. Supp. 800 (Conn. 1972), appeal docketed, No. 72–56; *Abele* v. *Markle,* 351 F. Supp. 224 (Conn. 1972), appeal docketed, No. 72–730; *Doe* v. *Bolton,* 319 F. Supp. 1048 (ND Ga. 1970), appeal decided today, *post,* p. 179; *Doe* v. *Scott,* 321 F. Supp. 1385 (ND Ill. 1971), appeal docketed, No. 70–105; *Poe* v. *Menghini,* 339 F. Supp. 986 (Kan. 1972); *YWCA* v. *Kugler,* 342 F. Supp. 1048 (NJ 1972); *Babbitz* v. *McCann,* 310 F. Supp. 293 (ED Wis. 1970), appeal dismissed, 400 U. S. 1 (1970); *People* v. *Belous,* 71 Cal. 2d 954, 458 P. 2d 194 (1969), cert. denied, 397 U. S. 915 (1970); *State* v. *Barquet,* 262 So. 2d 431 (Fla. 1972).

Others have sustained state statutes. *Crossen* v. *Attorney General,* 344 F. Supp. 587 (ED Ky. 1972), appeal docketed, No. 72–256; *Rosen* v. *Louisiana State Board of Medical Examiners,* 318 F. Supp. 1217 (ED La. 1970), appeal docketed, No. 70–42; *Corkey* v. *Edwards,* 322 F. Supp. 1248 (WDNC 1971), appeal docketed, No. 71–92; *Steinberg* v. *Brown,* 321 F. Supp. 741 (ND Ohio 1970); *Doe* v. *Rampton* (Utah 1971), appeal docketed, No. 71–5666; *Cheaney* v. *State,*—Ind.—, 285 N. E. 2d 265 (1972); *Spears* v. *State,* 257 So. 2d 876 (Miss. 1972); *State* v. *Munson,* 86 S. D. 663, 201 N. W. 2d 123 (1972), appeal docketed, No. 72–631.

Although the results are divided, most of these courts have agreed that the right of privacy, however based, is broad enough to cover the abortion decision; that the right, nonetheless, is not absolute and is subject to some limitations; and that at some point the state interests as to protection of health, medical standards, and prenatal life, become dominant. We agree with this approach.

Where certain "fundamental rights" are involved, the Court has held that regulation limiting these rights may be justified only by a "compelling state interest," *Kramer* v. *Union Free School District, 395 U. S. 621, 627 (1969); Shapiro* v. *Thompson,* 394 U. S. 618, 634 (1969), *Sherbert* v. *Verner,* 374 U. S. 398, 406 (1963), and that legislative enactments must be narrowly drawn to express only the legitimate state interests at stake. *Griswold* v. *Connecticut,* 381 U. S., at 485; *Aptheker* v. *Secretary of State,* 378 U. S. 500, 508 (1964); *Cantwell* v. *Connecticut,* 310 U. S. 296, 307–308 (1940); see *Eisentstadt* v. *Baird,* 405 U. S., at 460, 463–464 (WHITE, J., concurring in result).

In the recent abortion cases, cited above, courts have recognized these principles. Those striking down state laws have generally scrutinized the State's interests in protecting health and potential life, and have concluded that neither interest justified broad limitations on the reasons for which a physician and his pregnant patient might decide that she should have an abortion in the early stages of pregnancy. Courts sustaining state laws have held that the State's determinations to protect health or prenatal life are dominant and constitutionally justifiable.

IX

The District Court held that the appellee failed to meet his burden of demonstrating that the Texas statute's infringement upon Roe's rights was necessary to support a compelling state interest, and that, although the appellee presented "several compelling justifications for state presence in the area of abortions," the statutes outstripped these justifications and swept "far beyond any areas of compelling state interest." 314 F. Supp., at 1222–1223. Appellant and appellee both contest that holding. Appellant, as has been indicated, claims an absolute right that bars any state imposition of criminal penalties in the area. Appellee argues that the State's determination to recognize and protect prenatal life from and after conception constitutes a compelling state interest. As noted above, we do not agree fully with either formulation.

A. The appellee and certain *amici* argue that the fetus is a "person" within the language and meaning of the Fourteenth Amendment. In support of this, they outline at length and in detail the well-known facts of fetal development. If this suggestion of personhood is established, the appellant's case, of course, collapses. . . .

All this, together with our observation, *supra*, that throughout the major portion of the 19th century prevailing legal abortion practices were far freer than they are today, persuades us that the word "person," as used in the Fourteenth Amendment, does not include the unborn.[51] This is in accord with the results reached in those few cases where the issue has been squarely presented. *McGarvey* v. *Magee-Women's Hospital*, 340 F. Supp. 751 (WD Pa. 1972); *Byrn* v. *New York City Health & Hospitals Corp.*, 31 N. Y. 2d 194, 286 N. E. 2d 887 (1972), appeal docketed, No. 72–434; *Abele* v. *Markle*, 351 F. Supp. 224 (Conn. 1972), appeal docketed, No. 72–730. Cf. *Cheaney* v. *State*,—Ind., at—, 285 N. E. 2d, at 270; *Montana* v. *Rogers*, 278 F. 2d 68, 72 (CA7 1960), aff'd *sub nom.* *Montana* v. *Kennedy*, 366 U. S. 308 (1961); *Keeler* v. *Superior Court*, 2 Cal. 3d 619, 470 P. 2d 617 (1970); *State* v. *Dickinson*, 28 Ohio St. 2d 65, 275 N. E. 2d 599 (1971). Indeed, our decision in *United States* v. *Vuitch*, 402 U. S. 62 (1971), inferentially is to the same effect, for we there would not have indulged in statutory interpretation favorable to abortion in specified circumstances if the necessary consequence was termination of life entitled to Fourteenth Amendment protection.

This conclusion, however, does not of itself fully answer the contentions raised by Texas, and we pass on to other considerations.

B. The pregnant woman cannot be isolated in her privacy. She carries an embryo and, later, a fetus, if one accepts the medical definitions of the developing young in the human uterus. See Dorland's Illustrated Medical Dictionary 478–479, 547 (24th ed. 1965). The situation therefore is inherently different from marital intimacy, or bedroom possession of obscene material, or marriage, or procreation, or education, with which *Eisenstadt* and *Griswold*, *Stanley, Loving, Skinner*, and *Pierce* and *Meyer* were respectively concerned. As we have intimated above, it is reasonable and appropriate for a State to decide that at some—point in time another interest, that of health of the mother or that of potential human life, becomes significantly involved. The woman's privacy is no longer

---

[51]Cf. the Wisconsin abortion statute, defining "unborn child" to mean "a human being from the time of conception until it is born alive," Wis. Stat. § 940.04 (6) (1969), and the new Connecticut statute, Pub. Act No. 1 (May 1972 special session), declaring it to be the public policy of the State and the legislative intent "to protect and preserve human life from the moment of conception."

sole and any right of privacy she possesses must be measured accordingly.

Texas urges that, apart from the Fourteenth Amendment, life begins at conception and is present throughout pregnancy, and that, therefore, the State has a compelling interest in protecting that life from and after conception. We need not resolve the difficult question of when life begins. When those trained in the respective disciplines of medicine, philosophy, and theology are unable to arrive at any consensus, the judiciary, at this point in the development of man's knowledge, is not in a position to speculate as to the answer.

It should be sufficient to note briefly the wide divergence of thinking on this most sensitive and difficult question. There has always been strong support for the view that life does not begin until live birth. This was the belief of the Stoics.[52] It appears to be the predominant, though not the unanimous, attitude of the Jewish faith.[53] It may be taken to represent also the position of a large segment of the Protestant community, insofar as that can be ascertained; organized groups that have taken a formal position on the abortion issue have generally regarded abortion as a matter for the conscience of the individual and her family.[54] As we have noted, the common law found greater significance in quickening. Physicians and their scientific colleagues have regarded that event with less interest and have tended to focus either upon conception, upon live birth, or upon the interim point at which the fetus becomes "viable," that is, potentially able to live outside the mother's womb, albeit with artificial aid.[55] Viability is usually placed at about seven months (28 weeks) but may occur earlier, even at 24 weeks.[56] The Aristotelian theory of "mediate animation," that held sway throughout the Middle Ages and the Renaissance in Europe, continued to be official Roman Catholic dogma until the 19th century, despite opposition to this "ensoulment" theory from those in the Church who would recognize the existence of life from the moment

---

[52]Edelstein 16.

[53]Lader 97–99; D. Feldman, Birth Control in Jewish Law 251–294 (1968). For a stricter view, see I. Jakobovits, Jewish Views on Abortion, in Abortion and the Law 124 (D. Smith ed. 1967).

[54]Amicus Brief for the American Ethical Union et al. For the position of the National Council of Churches and of other denominations, see Lader 99–101.

[55]L. Hellman & J. Pritchard, Williams Obstetrics 493 (14th ed. 1971); Dorland's Illustrated Medical Dictionary 1689 (24th ed 1965).

[56]Hellman & Pritchard, *supra*, n. 59, at 493.

of conception.[57] The latter is now, of course, the official belief of the Catholic Church. As one brief *amicus* discloses, this is a view strongly held by many non-Catholics as well, and by many physicians. Substantial problems for precise definition of this view are posed, however, by new embryological data that purport to indicate that conception is a "process" over time, rather than an event, and by new medical techniques such as menstrual extraction, the "morning-after" pill, implantation of embryos, artificial insemination, and even artificial wombs.[58]

In areas other than criminal abortion, the law has been reluctant to endorse any theory that life, as we recognize it, begins before live birth or to accord legal rights to the unborn except in narrowly defined situations and except when the rights are contingent upon live birth. For example, the traditional rule of tort law denied recovery for prenatal injuries even though the child was born alive.[59] That rule has been changed in almost every jurisdiction. In most States, recovery is said to be permitted only if the fetus was viable, or at least quick, when the injuries were sustained. . . .

With respect to the State's important and legitimate interest in the health of the mother, the "compelling" point, in the light of present medical knowledge, is at approximately the end of the first trimester. This is so because of the now-established medical fact, referred to above at 149, that until the end of the first trimester mortality in abortion may be less than mortality in normal childbirth. It follows that, from and after this point, a State may regulate the abortion procedure to the extent that the regulation reasonably relates to the preservation and protection of maternal health. Examples of permissible state regulations in this area are requirements as to the qualifications of the person who is to perform the abortion; as to the licensure of that person; as to the facility in which the

---

[57]For discussions of the development of the Roman Catholic position, see D. Callahan, Abortion: Law, Choice, and Morality 409–447 (1970); Noonan 1.

[58]See Brodie, The New Biology and the Prenatal Child, 9 J. Family L. 391, 397 (1970); Gorney, The New Biology and the Future of Man, 15 U. C. L. A. L. Rev. 273 (1968); Note, Criminal Law—Abortion—The "Morning-After Pill" and Other Pre-Implantation Birth-Control Methods and the Law, 46 Ore. L. Rev. 211 (1967); G. Taylor, The Biological Time Bomb 32 (1968); A. Rosenfeld, The Second Genesis 138–139 (1969); Smith, Through a Test Tube Darkly: Artificial Insemination and the Law, 67 Mich. L. Rev. 127 (1968); Note, Artificial Insemination and the Law, 1968 U. Ill. L. F. 203.

[59]W. Prosser, The Law of Torts 335–338 (4th ed. 1971); 2 F. Harper & F. James, The Law of Torts 1028–1031 (1956); Note, 63 Harv. L. Rev. 173 (1949).

procedure is to be performed, that is, whether it must be a hospital or may be a clinic or some other place of less-than-hospital status; as to the licensing of the facility; and the like.

This means, on the other hand, that, for the period of pregnancy prior to this "compelling" point, the attending physician, in consultation with his patient, is free to determine, without regulation by the State, that, in his medical judgment, the patient's pregnancy should be terminated. If that decision is reached, the judgment may be effectuated by an abortion free of interference by the State.

With respect to the State's important and legitimate interest in potential life, the "compelling" point is at viability. This is so because the fetus then presumably has the capability of meaningful life outside the mother's womb. State regulation protective of fetal life after viability thus has both logical and biological justifications. If the State is interested in protecting fetal life after viability, it may go so far as to proscribe abortion during that period, except when it is necessary to preserve the life or health of the mother.

Measured against these standards, Art. 1196 of the Texas Penal Code, in restricting legal abortions to those "procured or attempted by medical advice for the purpose of saving the life of the mother," sweeps too broadly. The statute makes no distinction between abortions performed early in pregnancy and those performed later, and it limits to a single reason, "saving" the mother's life, the legal justification for the procedure. The statute, therefore, cannot survive the constitutional attack made upon it here.

This conclusion makes it unnecessary for us to consider the additional challenge to the Texas statute asserted on grounds of vagueness. See *United States* v. *Vuitch*, 402 U. S., at 67–72.

XI

To summarize and to repeat:

1. A state criminal abortion statute of the current Texas type, that excepts from criminality only a *life-saving* procedure on behalf of the mother, without regard to pregnancy stage and without recognition of the other interests involved, is violative of the Due Process Clause of the Fourteenth Amendment.

(a) For the stage prior to approximately the end of the first trimester, the abortion decision and its effectuation must be left to the medical judgment of the pregnant woman's attending physician.

(b) For the stage subsequent to approximately the end of the first trimester, the State, in promoting its interest in the health of the mother, may, if it chooses, regulate the abortion procedure in ways that are reasonably related to maternal health.

(c) For the stage subsequent to viability, the State in promoting its interest in the potentiality of human life may, if it chooses, regulate, and even proscribe, abortion except where it is necessary, in appropriate medical judgment, for the preservation of the life or health of the mother.

2. The State may define the term "physician," as it has been employed in the preceding paragraphs of this Part XI of this opinion, to mean only a physician currently licensed by the State, and may proscribe any abortion by a person who is not a physician as so defined.

In *Doe* v. *Bolton, post,* p. 179, procedural requirements contained in one of the modern abortion statutes are considered. That opinion and this one, of course, are to be read together.[60]

This holding, we feel, is consistent with the relative weights of the respective interests involved, with the lessons and examples of medical and legal history, with the lenity of the common law, and with the demands of the profound problems of the present day. The decision leaves the State free to place increasing restrictions on abortion as the period of pregnancy lengthens, so long as those restrictions are tailored to the recognized state interests. The decision vindicates the right of the physician to administer medical treatment according to his professional judgment up to the points where important state interests provide compelling justifications for intervention. Up to those points, the abortion decision in all its aspects is inherently, and primarily, a medical decision, and basic responsibility for it must rest with the physician. If an individual practitioner abuses the privilege of exercising proper

---

[60]Neither in this opinion nor in *Doe* v. *Bolton, post,* p. 179, do we discuss the father's rights, if any exist in the constitutional context, in the abortion decision. No paternal right has been asserted in either of the cases, and the Texas and the Georgia statues on their face take no cognizance of the father. We are aware that some statutes recognize the father under certain circumstances. North Carolina, for example, N. C. Gen. Stat § 14–45.1 (Supp. 1971), requires written permission for the abortion from the husband when the woman is a married minor, that is, when she is less than 18 years of age, 41 N. C. A. G. 489 (1971); if the woman is an unmarried minor, written permission from the parents is required. We need not now decide whether provisions of this kind are constitutional.

medical judgment, the usual remedies, judicial and intra-professional, are available.

XII

Our conclusion that Art. 1196 is unconstitutional means, of course, that the Texas abortion statutes, as a unit, must fall. The exception of Art. 1196 cannot be struck down separately, for then the State would be left with a statute proscribing all abortion procedures no matter how medically urgent the case.

Although the District Court granted appellant Roe declaratory relief, it stopped short of issuing an injunction against enforcement of the Texas statutes. The Court has recognized that different considerations enter into a federal court's decision as to declaratory relief, on the one hand, and injunctive relief, on the other. *Zwickler* v. *Koota*, 389 U. S. 241, 252–255 (1967); *Dombrowski* v. *Pfister*, 380 U. S. 479 (1965). We are not dealing with a statue that, on its face, appears to abridge free expression, an area of particular concern under *Dombrowski* and refined in *Younger* v. *Harris*, 401 U. S., at 50.

We find it unnecessary to decide whether the District Court erred in withholding injunctive relief, for we assume the Texas prosecutorial authorities will give full credence to this decision that the present criminal abortion statutes of that State are unconstitutional.

The judgment of the District Court as to intervenor Hallford is reversed, and Dr. Hallford's complaint in intervention is dismissed. In all other respects, the judgment of the District Court is affirmed. Costs are allowed to the appellee.

It is so ordered.

Questions and Activities

1. How do Justice Blackmun's arguments resemble or differ from the popular arguments that are given for or against abortion? Choose a specific position that Blackmun takes, or a specific type of support that he offers, and compare it to the positions you are familiar with from the popular debate. Which do you find the more convincing, and why?

2. Identify and summarize what you believe to be Blackmun's central support for legalizing abortion. Then argue for or against Blackmun's position by concurring with and extending or attacking his support.

Crime and Criminals

CLARENCE DARROW

Clarence Darrow (1857–1938) was an American criminal defense attorney. He is perhaps best known for his defense of John Scopes in what has become known as the Monkey Trial in Dayton, Tennessee, in July 1925. Scopes was on trial for teaching the theory of evolution in a Tennessee high school, in violation of state law. Scopes was convicted, but the notoriety of the trial and Darrow's brilliant defense brought widespread fame. The trial is the subject of the book and film, Inherit the Wind. *Darrow presented the essay printed here as a speech to inmates in the Cook County Jail, Chicago, in 1932.*

If I looked at jails and crimes and prisoners in the way the ordinary person does, I should not speak on this subject to you. The reason I talk to you on the question of crime, its cause and cure, is because I really do not in the least believe in crime. There is no such thing as a crime as the word is generally understood. I do not believe there is any sort of distinction between the real moral condition of the people in and out of jail. One is just as good as the other. The people here can no more help being here than the people outside can avoid being outside. I do not believe that people are in jail because they deserve to be. They are in jail simply because they can not avoid it on account of circumstances which are entirely beyond their control and for which they are in no way responsible.

I suppose a great many people on the outside would say I was doing you harm if they should hear what I say to you this afternoon, but you can not be hurt a great deal anyway, so it will not matter. Good people outside would say that I was really teaching you things that were calculated to injure society, but it's worthwhile now and then to hear something different from what you ordinarily get from preachers and the like. These will tell you that you should be good and then you get rich and be happy. Of course we know that people do not get rich by being good, and that is the reason why so many of you people try to get rich some other way, only you do not understand how to do it quite as well as the fellow outside.

There are people who think that everything in this world is an accident. But really there is no such thing as an accident. A great many folk admit that many of the people in jail ought not to be there, and many who are outside ought to be in. I think none of them ought to be here. There ought to be no jails, and if it were not for the fact that the people on the outside are so grasping and heartless in their dealings with the people on the inside, there would be no such institution as jails.

I do not want you to believe that I think all you people here are angels. I do not think that. You are people of all kinds, all of you doing the best you can, and that is evidently not very well—you are people of all kinds and conditions and under all circumstances. In one sense everybody is equally good and equally bad. We all do the best we can under the circumstances. But as the exact things for which you are sent here, some of you are guilty and did the particular act because you needed the money. Some of you did it because you are in the habit of doing it, and some of you because you are born to it, and it comes as natural as it does, for instance, for me to be good.

Most of you probably have nothing against me, and most of you would treat me the same as any other person would; probably better than some of the people on the outside would treat me, because you think I believe in you and they know I do not believe in them. While you would not have the least thing against me in the world you might pick my pockets. I do not think all of you would, but I think some of you would. You would not have anything against me, but that's your profession, a few of you. Some of the rest of you, if my doors were unlocked, might come in if you saw anything you wanted—not out of any malice to me, but because that is your trade. There is no doubt there are quite a number of people in this jail who would pick my pockets. And still I know this, that when I get outside pretty nearly everybody picks my pocket. There may be some of you who would hold up a man on the street, if you did not happen to have something else to do, and needed the money; but when I want to light my house or my office the gas company holds me up. They charge me one dollar for something that is worth twenty-five cents, and still all these people are good people; they are pillars of society and support the churches, and they are respectable.

When I ride on the streetcars, I am held up—I pay five cents for a ride that is worth two-and-a-half cents, simply because a body of men have bribed the city council and legislature, so that all the rest of us have to pay tribute to them.

If I do not want to fall into the clutches of the gas trust and choose to burn oil instead of gas, then good Mr. Rockefeller holds me up, and he uses a certain portion of his money to build universities and support churches which are engaged in telling us how to be good.

Some of you are here for obtaining property under false pretenses—yet I pick up a great Sunday paper and read the advertisements of a merchant prince—"Shirtwaists for 39¢, marked down from $3."

When I read the advertisements in the paper I see they are all lies. When I want to get out and find a place to stand anywhere on the face of the earth, I find that it has all been taken up long ago before I came here, and before you came here, and somebody says, "Get off, swim into the lake, fly into the air; go anywhere, but get off." That is because people have the police and they have the jails and the judges and the lawyers and the soldiers and all the rest of them to take care of the earth and drive everybody off that comes their way.

A great many people will tell you that all this is true, but that it does not excuse you. These facts do not excuse some fellow who reaches into my pocket and takes out a five-dollar bill; the fact that the gas company bribes the members of the legislature from year to year, and fixes the law, so that all you people are compelled to be "fleeced" whenever you deal with them; the fact that the streetcar companies and the gas companies have control of the streets and the fact that the landlords own all the earth, they say, has nothing to do with you.

Let us see whether there is any connection between the crimes of the respectable class and your presence in jail. Many of you people are in jail because you have really committed burglary. Many of you, because you have stolen something: in the meaning of the law, you have taken some other person's property. Some of you have entered a store and carried off a pair of shoes because you did not have the price. Possibly some of you have committed murder. I can not tell what all of you did. There are a great many people here who have done some of these things who really do not know themselves why they did them. I think I know why you did them— every one of you; you did these things because you were bound to do them. It looked to you at the time as if you had a chance to do them or not, as you saw fit, but still after all you had no choice. There may be people here who had some money in their pockets and who still went out and got some more money in a way society forbids. Now you may not yourselves see exactly why it was you did this thing, but if you look at the question deeply enough and carefully enough you would see that there were circumstances that drove you to do exactly the thing which you did. You could not help it any more than we outside can help taking the positions that we take. The reformers who tell you to be good and you will be happy, and the people on the outside who have property to protect—they think that the only way to do it is by building jails and locking you up in cells on weekdays and praying for you Sundays.

I think that all of this has nothing whatever to do with right conduct. I think it is very easily seen what has to do with right conduct. Some so-called criminals—and I will use this word because it is handy, it means nothing to me—I speak of the criminals who get caught as distinguished from the criminals who catch them—some of these so-called criminals are in jail for first offenses, but nine-tenths of you are in jail because you did not have a good lawyer and of course you did not have a good lawyer because you did not have enough money to pay a good lawyer. There is no very great danger of a rich man going to jail.

Some of you may be here for the first time. If we would open the doors and let you out, and leave the laws as they are today, some of you would be back tomorrow. This is about as good a place as you can get anyway. There are many people here who are so in the habit of coming that they would not know where else to go. There are people who are born with the tendency to break into jail every chance they get, and they can not avoid it. You can not figure out your life and see why it was, but still there is a reason for it, and if we were all wise and knew all the facts we could figure it out.

In the first place, there are a good many more people who go to jail in the winter time than in the summer. Why is this? Is it because people are more wicked in winter? No, it is because the coal trust begins to get in its grip in the winter. A few gentlemen take possession of the coal, and unless the people will pay $7 or $8 a ton for something that is worth $3, they will have to freeze. Then there is nothing to do but to break into jail, and so there are many more in jail in the winter than in summer. It costs more for gas in the winter because the nights are longer, and people go to jail to save gas bills. The jails are electric-lighted. You may not know it, but these economic laws are working all the time, whether we know it or do not know it.

There are more people who go to jail in hard times than in good times—few people comparatively go to jail except when they are hard up. They go to jail because they have no other place to go. They may no know why, but it is true all the same. People are not more wicked in hard times. That is not the reason. The fact is true all over the world that in hard times more people go to jail than in good times, and in winter more people go to jail than in summer. Of course it is pretty hard times for people who go to jail at any time. The people who go to jail are almost always poor people—people who have no other place to live first and last. When times are hard then you find large numbers of people who go to jail who would not otherwise be in jail.

Long ago, Mr. Buckle, who was a great philosopher and historian, collected facts and he showed that the number of people who are arrested increased just as the price of food increased. When they put up the price of gas ten cents a thousand I do not know who will go to jail, but I do know that a certain number of people will go. When the meat combine raises the price of beef I do not know who is going to jail, but I know that a large number of people are bound to go. Whenever the Standard Oil Company raises the price of oil, I know that a certain number of girls who are seamstresses, and who work night after night long hours for somebody else, will be compelled to go out on the streets and ply another trade, and I know that Mr. Rockefeller and his associates are responsible and not the poor girls in the jails.

First and last, people are sent to jail because they are poor. Sometimes, as I say, you may not need money at the particular time, but you wish to have thrifty forehanded habits, and do not always wait until you are in absolute want. Some of you people are perhaps plying the trade, the profession, which is called burglary. No man in his right senses will go into a strange house in the dead of night and prowl around with a dark lantern through unfamiliar rooms and take chances of his life if he has plenty of good things of the world in his own home. You would not take any such chances as that. If a man had clothes in his clothes-press and beefsteak in his pantry, and money in the bank, he would not navigate around nights in houses where he knows nothing about the premises whatever. It always requires experience and education for this profession, and people who fit themselves for it are no more to blame than I am for being a lawyer. A man would not hold up another man on the street if he had plenty of money in his own pocket. He might do it if he had one dollar or two dollars, but he wouldn't if he had as much money as Mr. Rockefeller has. Mr. Rockefeller has a great deal better holdup game that that.

The more that is taken from the poor by the rich, who have the chance to take it, the more poor people there are who are compelled to resort to these means for a livelihood. They may not understand it, they may not think so at once, but after all they are driven into that line of employment.

There is a bill before the Legislature of this State to punish kidnaping children with death. We have wise members of the Legislature. They know the gas trust when they see it and they always see it—they can furnish enough light to be seen, and this Legislature thinks it is going to stop kidnaping children by making a law punishing kidnapers of children with death. I don't believe in kidnaping children, but the Legislature is all wrong. Kidnaping children is not a crime, it is a profession. It has been developed with the times. It has been developed with our modern industrial conditions. There are many ways of making money—many new ways that our ancestors knew nothing about. Our ancestors knew nothing about a billion-dollar trust; and here comes some poor fellow who has no other trade and he discovers the profession of kidnaping children.

This crime is born, not because people are bad; people don't kidnap other people's children because they want children or because they are devilish, but because they see a chance to get some money out of it. You cannot cure this crime by passing a law punishing by death kidnapers of children. There is only one way to cure it. There is one way to cure all the offenses, and that is to give the people a chance to live. There is no other way, and there never was any other way since the world began, and the world is so blind and stupid that it will not see. If every man and woman and child in the world had a chance to make a decent, fair, honest living, there would be no jails, and no lawyers and no courts. There might be some persons here or there with some peculiar formation of their brain, like Rockefeller, who would do these things simply to be doing them; but they would be very, very few, and those should be sent to a hospital and treated, and not sent to jail; and they would entirely disappear in the second generation, or at least in the third generation.

I am not talking pure theory. I will just give you two or three illustrations.

The English people once punished criminals by sending them away. They would load them on a ship and export them to Australia. England was owned by lords and nobles and rich people. They owned the whole earth over there, and the other people had to stay in the streets. They could not get a decent living. They used to take their criminals and send them to Australia—I mean the class of criminals who got caught. When these criminals got over there, and nobody else had come, they had the whole continent to run over, and so they could raise sheep and furnish their own meat, which is easier than stealing it; these criminals then became decent, respectable people because they had a chance to live. They did not commit any crimes. They were just like the English people who sent them there, only better. And in the second generation the descendants of those criminals were as good and respectable a class of people as there were on the face of the earth, and then they began building churches and jails themselves.

A portion of this country was settled in the same way, landing prisoners down the southern coast; but when they got here and had a whole continent to run over and plenty of chances to make a living, they became respectable citizens, making their own living just like any other citizen in the world; but finally these descendants of the English aristocracy, who sent the people over to Australia, found out they were getting rich, and so they went over to get possession of the earth as they always do, and they organized land syndicates and got control of the land and ores, and then they had just as many criminals in Australia as they did in England. It was not because the world had grown bad; it was because the earth had been taken away from the people.

Some of you people have lived in the country. It's prettier than it is here. And if you have ever lived on a farm you understand that if you put a lot of cattle in a field, when the pasture is short they will jump over the fence; but put them in a good field where there is plenty of pasture, and they will be law-abiding cattle to the end of time. The human animal is just like the rest of the animals, only a little more so. The same thing that governs in the one governs in the other.

Everybody makes his living along the lines of least resistance. A wise man who comes into a country early sees a great undeveloped land. For instance, our rich men twenty-five years ago saw that Chicago was small and knew a lot of people would come here and settle, and they readily saw that if they had all the land around here it would be worth a great deal, so they grabbed the land. You cannot be a landlord because somebody has got it all. You must find some other calling. In England and Ireland and Scotland less than 5 percent own all the land there is, and people are bound to stay there on any kind of terms the landlords give. They must live the best they can, so they develop all these various professions—burglary, picking pockets and the like.

Again, people find all sorts of ways of getting rich. These are diseases like everything else. You look at people getting rich, organizing trusts, and making a million dollars, and somebody gets the disease and he starts out. He catches it just as a man catches the mumps or the measles; he is not to blame, it is in the air. You will find men speculating beyond their means, because the mania of money-getting is taking possession of them. It is simply a disease; nothing more, nothing less. You can not avoid catching it; but the fellows who have control of the earth have the advantage of you. See what the law is; when these men get control of things, they make the laws. They do not make the laws to protect anybody; courts are not instruments of justice; when your case gets into court it will make little difference whether you are guilty or innocent; but it's better if you have a smart lawyer. And you can not have a smart lawyer unless you have money. First and last it's a questions of money. Those men who own the earth make the laws to protect what they have. They fix up a sort of fence or pen around what they have, and they fix the law so the fellow on the outside can not get in. The laws are really organized for the protection of the men who rule the world. They were never organized or enforced to do justice. We have no system for doing justice, not the slightest in the world.

Let me illustrate: Take the poorest person in this room. If the community had provided a system of doing justice the poorest person in this room would have as good a lawyer as the richest, would he not? When you went into court you would have just as long a trial, and just as fair a trial as the richest person in Chicago. Your case would not be tried in fifteen or twenty minutes, whereas it would take fifteen days to get through the rich man's case.

Then if you were rich and were beaten, your case would be taken to the Appellate Court. A poor man can not take his case to the Appellate Court; he has not the price; and then to the Supreme Court, and if he were beaten there he might perhaps go the United States Supreme Court. And he might die of old age before he got into jail. If you are poor, it's a quick job. You are almost known to be guilty, else you would not be there. Why would any one be in the criminal court if he were not guilty? He would not be there if he could be anywhere else. The officials have no time to look after all these cases. The people who are on the outside, who are running banks and building churches and making jails, they have no time to examine six hundred or seven hundred prisoners each year to see whether they are guilty or innocent. If the courts were organized to promote justice the people would elect somebody to defend all these criminals, somebody as smart as the prosecutor—and give him as many detectives and as many assistants to help, and pay as much money to defend you as to prosecute you. We have a very able man for State's Attorney, and he has many assistants, detectives and policemen without end, and judges to hear the cases—everything handy.

Most of all our criminal code consists in offenses against property. People are sent to jail because they have committed a crime against property. It is of very little consequence whether one hundred people more or less go to jail who ought not to go—you must protect property, because in this world property is of more importance than anything else.

How is it done? These people who have property fix it so they can protect what they have. When somebody commits a crime it does not follow that he has done something that is morally wrong. The man on the outside who has committed no crime may have done something. For instance: to take all the coal in the United States and raise the price two dollars or three dollars when there is no need of it, and thus kill thousands of babies and send thousands of people to the poorhouse and tens of thousands to jail, as is done every year in the United States—this is a greater crime than all the people in our jails ever committed, but the law does not punish it. Why? Because the fellows who control the earth make the laws. If you and I had the making of the laws, the first thing we would do would be to punish the fellow who gets control of the earth. Nature put this coal in the ground for me as well as for them, and nature made the prairies up here to raise wheat for me as well as for them, and then the great railroad companies came along and fenced it up.

Most of all, the crimes for which we are punished are property crimes. There are a few personal crimes, like murder—but they are very few. The crimes committed are mostly those against property. If this punishment is right the criminals must have a lot of property. How much money is there in this crowd? And yet you are all here for crimes against property. The people up and down the Lake Shore have not committed crimes, still they have so much property they don't know what to do with it. It is perfectly plain why those people have not committed crimes against property; they make the laws and therefore do not need to break them. And in order for you to get some property you are obliged to break the rules of the game. I don't know but what some of you may have had a very nice chance to get rich by carrying the hod for one dollar a day, twelve hours. Instead of taking that nice, easy profession, you are a burglar. If you had been given a chance to be a banker you would rather follow that. Some of you may have had a chance to work as a switchman on a railroad where you know, according to statistics, that you can not live and keep all your limbs more than seven years, and you can get fifty dollars or seventy-five dollars a month for taking your lives in your hands, and instead of taking that lucrative position you choose to be a sneak thief, or something like that. Some of you made that sort of choice. I don't know which I would take if I was reduced to this choice. I have an easier choice.

I will guarantee to take from this jail, or any jail in the world, five hundred men who have been the worst criminals and lawbreakers who ever got into jail, and I will go down to our lowest streets and take five hundred of the most abandoned prostitutes, and go out somewhere where there is plenty of land, and will give them a chance to make a living, and they will be as good as the average in the community.

There is a remedy for the sort of condition we see here. The world never finds it out, or when it does find out it does not enforce it. You may pass a law punishing every person with death for burglary, and it will make no difference. Men will commit it just the same. In England there was a time when one hundred offenses were punishable with death, and it made no difference. The English people strangely found out that so fast as they repealed the severe penalties and so fast as they did away with punishing men by death, crime decreased instead of increased; that the smaller the penalty the fewer the crimes.

Hanging men in our county jails does not prevent murder. It makes murderers.

And this has been the history of the world. It's easy to see how to do away with what we call crime. It is not easy to do it. I will tell you how to do it. It can be done by giving the people a chance to live—by destroying special privileges. So long as big criminals can get the coal fields, so long as the big criminals have control of the city council and get the public streets for streetcars and gas rights, this is bound to send thousands of poor people to jail. So long as men are allowed to monopolize all the earth, and compel others to live on such terms as these men see fit to make, then you are bound to get into jail.

The only way in the world to abolish crime and criminals is to abolish the big ones and the little ones together. Make fair conditions of life. Give men a chance to live. Abolish the right of private ownership of land, abolish monopoly, make the world partners in production, partners in the good things of life. Nobody would steal if he could get something of his own some easier way. Nobody will commit burglary when has a house full. No girl will go out on the streets when she has a comfortable place at home. The man who owns a sweatshop or a department store may not be to blame himself for the conditions of his girls, but when he pays them five dollars, three dollars, and two dollars a week, I wonder where he thinks they will get the rest of their money to live. The only way to cure these conditions is by equality. There should be no jails. They do not accomplish what they pretend to accomplish. If you would wipe them out there would be no more criminals than now. They terrorize nobody. They are a blot upon any civilization, and a jail is an evidence of the lack of charity of the people on the outside who make the jails and fill them with the victims of their greed.

Questions and Answers

1. Summarize Darrow's version of society, as he represents it in this speech. Try to produce a summary that Darrow would accept as an accurate reflection of his views. Then, based on your own experience and knowledge, argue that Darrow's vision of society is accurate or inaccurate.

2. Write an accurate summary of Darrow's definition of crime, and then write an argument in which you agree or disagree with that definition. As part of your support, use your own knowledge and experience of conditions that exist in society, and of specific crimes and criminals you know about.

From The New Organon

FRANCIS BACON

*Francis Bacon (1561–1626) was an English philosopher, essayist, and
statesman. In* The New Organon, *from which the following excerpt
is taken, Bacon proposed that scientific knowledge should be based
on direct observation and experimentation, which we now call the
inductive method. At the time, this was a new and radical proposal. Since then, of course, it has become the foundation of the sciences. In the selection printed here, Bacon discusses the Idols (or
modes of thought) that he believes have limited humans in the
past, and from which he wishes to escape.*

XXXVII

The doctrine of those who have denied that certainty could be
attained at all has some agreement with my way of proceeding at
the first setting out; but they end in being infinitely separated and
opposed. For the holders of that doctrine assert simply that nothing
can be known. I also assert that not much can be known in nature
by the way which is now in use. But then they go on to destroy the
authority of the senses and understandings; whereas I proceed to
devise and supply helps for the same.

XXXVIII

The idols and false notions which are now in possession of the
human understanding, and have taken deep root therein, not only
so beset men's minds that truth can hardly find entrance, but even
after entrance is obtained, they will again in the very instauration
of the sciences meet and trouble us, unless men being forewarned
of the danger fortify themselves as far as may be against their
assaults.

XXXIX

There are four classes of Idols which beset men's minds. To these
for distinction's sake I have assigned names, calling the first class
Idols of the Tribe; the second, *Idols of the Cave;* the third, *Idols of
the Market Place;* the fourth, *Idols of the Theater.*

XL

The formation of ideas and axioms by true induction is no doubt the proper remedy to be applied for the keeping off and clearing away of idols. To point them out, however, is of great use; for the doctrine of Idols is to the interpretation of nature what the doctrine of the refutation of sophisms is to common logic.

XLI

The Idols of the Tribe have their foundation in human nature itself, and in the tribe or race of men. For it is a false assertion that the sense of man is the measure of things. On the contrary, all perceptions as well of the sense as of the mind are according to the measure of the individual and not according to the measure of the universe. And the human understanding is like a false mirror, which, receiving rays irregularly, distorts and discolors the nature of things by mingling its own nature with it.

XLII

The Idols of the Cave are the idols of the individual man. For everyone (besides the errors common to human nature in general) has a cave or den of his own, which refracts and discolors the light of nature, owing either to his own proper and peculiar nature; or to his education and conversation with others; or to the reading of books, and the authority of those whom he esteems and admires; or to the differences of impressions, accordingly as they take place in a mind preoccupied and predisposed or in a mind indifferent and settled; or the like. So that the spirit of man (according as it is meted out to different individuals) is in fact a thing variable and full of perturbation, and governed as it were by chance. Whence it was well observed by Heraclitus that men look for sciences in their own lesser worlds, and not in the greater or common world.

XLIII

There are also Idols formed by the intercourse and association of men with each other, which I call Idols of the Market Place, on account of the commerce and consort of men there. For it is by discourse that men associate, and words are imposed according to the apprehension of the vulgar. And therefore the ill and unfit choice of words wonderfully obstructs the understanding. Nor do the definitions or explanations wherewith in some things learned men are wont to guard and defend themselves, by any means set the matter right. But words plainly force and overrule the understanding, and throw all into confusion, and lead men away into numberless empty controversies and idle fancies.

XLIV

Lastly, there are Idols which have immigrated into men's minds from the various dogmas of philosophies, and also from wrong laws of demonstration. These I call Idols of the Theater, because in my judgment all the received systems are but so many stage plays, representing worlds of their own creation after an unreal and scenic fashion. Nor is it only of the systems now in vogue, or only of the ancient sects and philosophies, that I speak; for many more plays of the same kind may yet be composed and in like artificial manner set forth; seeing that errors the most widely different have nevertheless causes for the most part alike. Neither again do I mean this only of entire systems, but also of many principles and axioms in science, which by tradition, credulity, and negligence have come to be received.

But of these several kinds of Idols I must speak more largely and exactly, that the understanding may be duly cautioned.

XLV

The human understanding is of its own nature prone to suppose the existence of more order and regularity in the world than it finds. And though there be many things in nature which are singular and unmatched, yet it devises for them parallels and conjugates and relatives which do not exist. Hence the fiction that all celestial bodies move in perfect circles, spirals and dragons being (except in name) utterly rejected. Hence too the element of fire with its orb is brought in, to make up the square with the other three which the sense perceives. Hence also the ratio of density of the so-called elements is arbitrarily fixed at ten to one. And so on of other dreams. And these fancies affect not dogmas only, but simple notions also.

XLVI

The human understanding when it has once adopted an opinion (either as being the received opinion or as being agreeable to itself) draws all things else to support and agree with it. And though there be a greater number and weight of instances to be found on the other side, yet these it either neglects and despises, or else by some distinction sets aside and rejects, in order that by this great and pernicious predetermination the authority of its former conclusions may remain inviolate. And therefore it was a good answer that was made by one who, when they showed him hanging in a temple a picture of those who had paid their vows as having escaped shipwreck, and would have him say whether he did not now acknowledge the power of the gods—"Aye," asked he again, "but where are they painted that were drowned after their vows?" And such is the way of all superstition, whether in astrology, dreams, omens, divine judgments, or the like; wherein men, having a delight in such vanities, mark the events where they are fulfilled, but where they fail, though this happen much oftener, neglect and pass them by. But with far more subtlety does this mischief insinuate itself into philosophy and the sciences; in which the first conclusion colors and brings into conformity with itself all that come after, though far sounder and better. Besides, independently of that delight and vanity which I have described, it is the peculiar and perpetual error of the human intellect to be more moved and excited by affirmatives than by negatives; whereas it ought properly to hold itself indifferently disposed toward both alike. Indeed, in the establishment of any true axiom, the negative instance is the more forcible of the two.

XLVII

The human understanding is moved by those things most which strike and enter the mind simultaneously and suddenly, and so fill the imagination; and then it feigns and supposes all other things to be somehow, though it cannot see how, similar to those few things by which it is surrounded. But for that going to and fro to remote and heterogeneous instances by which axioms are tried as in the fire, the intellect is altogether slow and unfit, unless it be forced thereto by severe laws and overruling authority.

XLVIII

The human understanding is unquiet; it cannot stop or rest, and still presses onward, but in vain. Therefore it is that we cannot conceive of any end or limit to the world, but always as of necessity it occurs to us that there is something beyond. Neither, again, can it be conceived how eternity has flowed down to the present day, for that distinction which is commonly received of infinity in time past and in time to come can by no means hold; for it would thence follow that one infinity is greater than another, and that infinity is wasting away and tending to become finite. The like subtlety arises touching the infinite divisibility of lines, from the same inability of thought to stop. But this inability interferes more mischievously in the discovery of causes; for although the most general principles in nature ought to be held merely positive, as they are discovered, and cannot with truth be referred to a cause, nevertheless the human understanding being unable to rest still seeks something prior in the order of nature. And then it is that in struggling toward that which is further off it falls back upon that which is nearer at hand, namely, on final causes, which have relation clearly to the nature of man rather than to the nature of the universe; and from this source have strangely defiled philosophy. But he is no less an unskilled and shallow philosopher who seeks causes of that which is most general, than he who in things subordinate and subaltern omits to do so.

XLIX

The human understanding is no dry light, but receives an infusion from the will and affections; whence proceed sciences which may be called "sciences as one would." For what a man had rather were true he more readily believes. Therefore he rejects difficult things from impatience of research; sober things, because they narrow hope; the deeper things of nature, from superstition; the light of experience, from arrogance and pride, lest his mind should seem to be occupied with things mean and transitory; things not commonly believed, out of deference to the opinion of the vulgar. Numberless, in short, are the ways, and sometimes imperceptible, in which the affections color and infect the understanding.

L

But by far the greatest hindrance and aberration of the human understanding proceeds from the dullness, incompetency, and deceptions of the senses; in that things which strike the sense outweigh things which do not immediately strike it, though they be more important. Hence it is that speculation commonly ceases where sight ceases; insomuch that of things invisible there is little or no observation. Hence all the working of the spirits enclosed in tangible bodies lies hid and unobserved of men. So also all the more subtle changes of form in the parts of coarser substances (which they commonly call alteration, though it is in truth local motion through exceedingly small spaces) is in like manner unobserved. And yet unless two things just mentioned be searched out and brought to light, nothing great can be achieved in nature, as far as the production of works is concerned. So again the essential nature of our common air, and of all bodies less dense than air (which are many), is almost unknown. For the sense by itself is a thing infirm and erring; neither can instruments for enlarging or sharpening the senses do much; but all the truer kind of interpretation of nature is effected by instances and experiments fit and apposite; wherein the sense decides touching the experiment only, and the experiment touching the point in nature and the thing itself.

LI

The human understanding is of its own nature prone to abstractions and gives a substance and reality to things which are fleeting. But to resolve nature into abstractions is less to our purpose than to dissect her into parts; as did the school of Democritus, which went further into nature than the rest. Matter rather than forms should be the object of our attention, its configurations and changes of configuration, and simple action, and law of action or motion; for forms are figments of the human mind, unless you will call those laws of action forms.

LII

Such then are the idols which I call *Idols of the Tribe,* and which take their rise either from the homogeneity of the substance of the human spirit, or from its preoccupation, or from its narrowness, or from its restless motion, or from an infusion of the affections, or from the incompetency of the senses, or from the mode of impression.

LIII

The *Idols of the Cave* take their rise in the peculiar constitution, mental or bodily, of each individual; and also in education, habit, and accident. Of this kind there is a great number and variety. But I will instance those the pointing out of which contains the most important caution, and which have most effect in disturbing the clearness of the understanding.

LIV

Men become attached to certain particular sciences and speculations, either because they fancy themselves the authors and inventors thereof, or because they have bestowed the greatest pains upon them and become most habituated to them. But men of this kind, if they betake themselves to philosophy and contemplation of a general character, distort and color them in obedience to their former fancies; a thing especially to be noticed in Aristotle, who made his natural philosophy a mere bond servant to his logic, thereby rendering it contentious and well-nigh useless. The race of chemists, again out of a few experiments of the furnace, have built up a fantastic philosophy, framed with reference to a few things; and Gilbert also, after he had employed himself most laboriously in the study and observation of the loadstone, proceeded at once to construct an entire system in accordance with his favorite subject.

LV

There is one principal and as it were radical distinction between different minds, in respect of philosophy and the sciences, which is this: that some minds are stronger and apter to mark the differences of things, others to mark their resemblances. The steady and acute mind can fix its contemplations and dwell and fasten on the subtlest distinctions; the lofty and discursive mind recognizes and puts together the finest and most general resemblances. Both kinds, however, easily err in excess, by catching the one at gradations, the other at shadows.

LVI

There are found some minds given to an extreme admiration of antiquity, others to an extreme love and appetite for novelty; but few so duly tempered that they can hold the mean, neither carping at what has been well laid down by the ancients, nor despising what is well introduced by the moderns. This, however, turns to the great injury of the sciences and philosophy, since these affectations of antiquity and novelty are the humors of partisans rather than judgments; and truth is to be sought for not in the felicity of any age, which is an unstable thing, but in the light of nature and experience, which is eternal. These factions therefore must be abjured, and care must be taken that the intellect be not hurried by them into assent.

LVII

Comtemplations of nature and of bodies in their simple form break up and distract the understanding, while contemplations of nature and bodies in their composition and configuration overpower and dissolve the understanding, a distinction well seen in the school of Leucippus and Democritus as compared with the other philosophies. For that school is so busied with the particles that it hardly attends to the structure, while the others are so lost in admiration of the structure that they do not penetrate to the simplicity of nature. These kinds of contemplation should therefore be alternated and taken by turns, so that the understanding may be rendered at once penetrating and comprehensive, and the inconveniences above mentioned, with the idols which proceed from them, may be avoided.

LVIII

Let such then be our provision and contemplative prudence for keeping off and dislodging the *Idols of the Cave,* which grow for the most part either out of the predominance of a favorite subject, or out of an excessive tendency to compare or to distinguish, or out of partiality for particular ages, or out of the largeness or minuteness of the objects contemplated. And generally let every student of nature take this as a rule: that whatever his mind seizes and dwells upon with peculiar satisfaction is to be held in suspicion, and that so much the more care is to be taken in dealing with such questions to keep the understanding even and clear.

LIX

But the *Idols of the Market Place* are the most troublesome of all—idols which have crept into the understanding through the alliances of words and names. For men believe that their reason governs words; but it is also true that words react on the understanding; and this it is that has rendered philosophy and the sciences sophistical and inactive. Now words, being commonly framed and applied according to the capacity of the vulgar, follow those lines of division which are most obvious to the vulgar understanding. And whenever an understanding of greater acuteness or a more diligent observation would alter those lines to suit the true divisions of nature, words stand in the way and resist the change. Whence it comes to pass that the high and formal discussions of learned men end oftentimes in disputes about words and names; with which (according to the use and wisdom of the mathematicians) it would be more prudent to begin, and so by means of definitions reduce them to order. Yet even definitions cannot cure this evil in dealing with natural and material things, since the definitions themselves consist of words, and those words beget others. So that it is necessary to recur to individual instances, and those in due series and order, as I shall say presently when I come to the method and scheme for the formation of notions and axioms.

LX

The idols imposed by words on the understanding are of two kinds. They are either names of things which do not exist (for as there are things left unnamed through lack of observation, so likewise are there names which result from fantastic suppositions and to which nothing in reality corresponds), or they are names of things which exist, but yet confused and ill-defined, and hastily and irregulary derived from realities. Of the former kind are Fortune, the Prime Mover, Planetary Orbits, Element of Fire, and like fictions which owe their origin to false and idle theories. And this class of idols is more easily expelled, because to get rid of them it is only necessary that all theories should be steadily rejected and dismissed as obsolete.

But the other class, which springs out of a faulty and unskillful abstraction, is intricate and deeply rooted. Let us take for example such a word as *humid* and see how far the several things which the word is used to signify agree with each other, and we shall find the word *humid* to be nothing else than a mark loosely and confusedly applied to denote a variety of actions which will not bear to be reduced to any constant meaning. For it both signifies that which easily spreads itself round any other body; and that which in itself is indeterminate and cannot solidize; and that which readily yields in every direction; and that which easily divides and scatters itself; and that which easily unites and collects itself; and that which readily flows and is put in motion; and that which readily clings to another body and wets it; and that which is easily reduced to a liquid, or being solid easily melts. Accordingly, when you come to apply the word, if you take it in one sense, flame is humid; if in another, air is not humid; if in another, fine dust is humid; if in another, glass is humid. So that it is easy to see that the notion is taken by abstraction only from water and common ordinary liquids, without any due verification.

There are, however, in words certain degrees of distortion and error. One of the least faulty kinds is that of names of substances, especially of lowest species and well-deduced (for the notion of *chalk* and of *mud* is good, of *earth* bad); a more faulty kind is that of actions, as to *generate, to corrupt, to alter;* the most faulty is of qualities (except such as are the immediate objects of the sense) as *heavy, light, rare, dense,* and the like. Yet in all these cases some notions are of necessity a little better than others, in proportion to the greater variety of subjects that fall within the range of the human sense.

LXI

But the *Idols of Theater* are not innate, nor do they steal into the understanding secretly, but are plainly impressed and received into the mind from the playbooks of philosophical systems and the perverted rules of demonstration. To attempt refutations in this case would be merely inconsistent with what I have already said, for since we agree neither upon principles nor upon demonstrations there is no place for argument. And this is so far well, inasmuch as it leaves the honor of the ancients untouched. For they are no wise disparaged—the question between them and me being only as to the way. For as the saying is, the lame man who keeps the right road outstrips the runner who takes a wrong one. Nay, it is obvious that when a man runs the wrong way, the more active and swift he is, the further he will go astray.

But the course I propose for the discovery of sciences is such as leaves but little to the acuteness and strength of wits, but places all wits and understandings nearly on a level. For as in the drawing of a straight line or a perfect circle, much depends on the steadiness and practice of the hand, if it be done by aim of hand only, but if with the aid of rule or compass, little or nothing; so it is exactly with my plan. But though particular confutations would be of no avail, yet touching the sects and general divisions of such systems I must say something; something also touching the external signs which show that they are unsound; and finally something touching the causes of such great infelicity and of such lasting and general agreement in error; that so the access to truth may be made less difficult, and the human understanding may the more willingly submit to its purgation and dismiss its idols.

Questions and Answers

1. Summarize Bacon's discussion of one of the four idols, and then write an argument in which you use Bacon's scheme as a framework for an argument that applies this idol to contemporary life.

2. Use a concrete event in your own experience to contrast knowledge you have gained from direct observation with knowledge that you have received from others. Then write an argument in which you evaluate the relative value of these types of knowledge.

The Morals of a Prince

NICCOLO MACHIAVELLI

Niccolo Machiavelli was a Florentine novelist, essayist, and historian. He lived from 1469 to 1527, and was closely associated with the Medici family, which he served in a variety of jobs. He is probably best known for The Prince, *a treatise about the art of governing, from which the following excerpt is taken. As a result of the pragmatic advice Machiavelli gives in* The Prince, *"machiavellian" has become a term of censure used to describe those with evil or cynical motives.*

Concerning Things for Which Men, and Especially Princes, Are Praised or Blamed

It remains now to see what ought to be the rules of conduct for a prince towards subject and friends. And as I know that many have written on this point, I expect I shall be considered presumptuous in mentioning it again, especially as in discussing it I shall depart from the methods of other people. But, it being my intention to write a thing which shall be useful to him who apprehends it, it appears to me more appropriate to follow up the real truth of a matter than the imagination of it; for many have pictured republics and principalities which in fact have never been known or seen, because how one lives is so far distant from how one ought to live, that he who neglects what is done for what ought to be done, sooner effects his ruin than his preservation; for a man who wishes to act entirely up to his professions of virtue soon meets with what destroys him among so much that is evil.

Hence it is necessary for a prince wishing to hold his own to know how to do wrong, and to make use of it or not according to necessity. Therefore, putting on one side imaginary things concerning a prince, and discussing those which are real, I say that all men when they are spoken of, and chiefly princes for being more highly placed, are remarkable for some of those qualities which bring them either blame or praise; and thus it is that one is reputed liberal, another miserly . . . ; one is reputed generous, one rapacious; one cruel, one compassionate; one faithless, another faithful; one effeminate and cowardly, another bold and brave; one affable, another haughty; one lascivious, another chaste; one sincere, another cunning; one hard, another easy; one grave, another frivolous; one religious, another unbelieving, and the like. And I know that every one will confess that it would be most praiseworthy in a prince to exhibit all the above qualities that are considered good; but because they can neither be entirely possessed nor observed, for human conditions do not permit it, it is necessary for him to be sufficiently prudent that he may know how to avoid the reproach of those vices which would lose him his state; and also to keep himself, if it be possible, from those which would not lose him it; but this not being possible, he may with less hesitation abandon himself to them. And again, he need not make himself uneasy at incurring a reproach for those vices without which the state can only be saved with difficulty, for if everything is considered carefully, it will be found that something which looks like virtue, if followed, would be his ruin; whilst something else, which looks like vice, yet followed brings him security and prosperity.

Concerning Liberality and Meanness

Commencing then with the first of the above-named characteristics, I say that it would be well to be reputed liberal. Nevertheless, liberality exercised in a way that does not bring you the reputation for it, injures you; for if one exercises it honestly and as it should be exercised, it may not become known, and you will not avoid the reproach of its opposite. Therefore, anyone wishing to maintain among men the name of liberal is obliged to avoid no attribute of magnificence; so that a prince thus inclined will consume in such acts all his property, and will be compelled in the end, if he wish to maintain the name of liberal, to unduly weigh down his people, and tax them, and do everything he can to get money.

This will soon make him odious to his subjects, and becoming poor he will be little valued by anyone; thus, with his liberality, having offended many and rewarded few, he is affected by the very first trouble and imperilled by whatever may be the first danger; recognizing this himself, and wishing to draw back from it, he runs at once into the reproach of being miserly.

Therefore, a prince, not being able to exercise this virtue of liberality in such a way that it is recognised, except to his cost, if he is wise he ought not to fear the reputation of being mean, for in time he will come to be more considered than if liberal, seeing that with his economy his revenues are enough, that he can defend himself against all attacks, and is able to engage in enterprises without burdening his people; thus it comes to pass that he exercises liberality towards all from whom he does not take, who are numberless, and meanness towards those to whom he does not give, who are few.

We have not seen great things done in our time except by those who have been considered mean; the rest have failed. Pope Julius the Second was assisted in reaching the papacy by a reputation for liberality, yet he did not strive afterwards to keep it up, when he made war on the King of France; and he made many wars without imposing any extraordinary tax on his subjects, for he supplied his additional expenses out of his long thriftiness. The present King of Spain would not have undertaken or conquered in so many enterprises if he had been reputed liberal. A prince, therefore, provided that he has not to rob his subjects, that he can defend himself, that he does not become poor and abject, that he is not forced to become rapacious, ought to hold of little account a reputation for being mean, for it is one of those vices which will enable him to govern.

And if anyone should say: Caesar obtained empire by liberality, and many others have reached the highest positions by having been liberal, and by being considered so, I answer: Either you are a prince in fact, or in a way to become one. In the first case this liberality is dangerous, in the second it is very necessary to be considered liberal; and Caesar was one of those who wished to become pre-eminent in Rome; but if he had survived after becoming so, and had not moderated his expenses, he would have destroyed his government. And if anyone should reply: Many have been princes, and have done great things with armies, who have been considered very liberal, I reply: Either a prince spends that which is his own or his subjects' or else that of others. In the first case he ought to be sparing, in the second he ought not to neglect any opportunity for liberality. And to the prince who goes forth with his army, supporting it by pillage, sack, and extortion, handling that which belongs to others, this liberality is necessary, otherwise he would not be followed by soldiers. And of that which is neither yours nor your subjects' you can be a ready giver, as were Cyrus, Caesar, and Alexander; because it does not take away your reputation if you squander that of others, but adds to it; it is only squandering your own that injures you.

And there is nothing wastes so rapidly as liberality, for even whilst you exercise it you lost the power to do so, and so become either poor or despised, or else, in avoiding poverty, rapacious and hated. And a prince should guard himself, above all things, against being despised and hated; and liberality leads you to both. Therefore it is wiser to have a reputation for meanness which brings reproach without hatred, than to be compelled through seeking a reputation for liberality to incur a name for rapacity which begets reproach with hatred.

Concerning Cruelty and Clemency, and Whether It Is Better to Be Loved Than Feared

Coming now to the other qualities mentioned above, I say that every prince ought to desire to be considered clement and not cruel. Nevertheless he ought to take care not to misuse this clemency. Cesare Borgia was considered cruel; notwithstanding, his cruelty reconciled the Romagna, unified it, and restored it to peace and loyalty. And if this be rightly considered, he will be seen to have been much more merciful than the Florentine people, who, to avoid a reputation for cruelty, permitted Pistoia to be destroyed. Therefore a prince, so long as he keeps his subjects united and loyal, ought not to mind the reproach of cruelty; because with a few examples he will be more merciful than those who, through too much mercy, allow disorders to arise, from which follow murder or robbery; for these are wont to injure the whole people, whilst those executions which originate with a prince offend the individual only.

And of all princes, it is impossible for the new prince to avoid the imputation of cruelty, owing to new states being full of dangers. Hence Virgil, through the mouth of Dido, excuses the inhumanity of her reign owing to its being new, saying:

> Res dura, et regni novitas me talia cogunt
> Moliri, et late fines custode tueri.*

Nevertheless he ought to be slow to believe and to act, nor should he himself show fear, but proceed in a temperate manner with prudence and humanity, so that too much confidence may not make him incautious and too much distrust render him intolerable.

---

*Translation: "Hard times and the newness of my realm oblige me to do these things and to look to the keeping of my borders."

Upon this a question arises: whether it be better to be loved than feared or feared than loved? It may be answered that one should wish to be both, but, because it is difficult to unite them in one person, it is much safer to be feared than loved, when, of the two, either must be dispensed with. Because this is to be asserted in general of men, that they are ungrateful, fickle, false, cowards, covetous, and as long as you succeed they are yours entirely; they will offer you their blood, property, life, and children, as is said above, when the need is far distant; but when it approaches they turn against you. And that prince who, relying entirely on their promises, has neglected other precautions, is ruined; because friendships that are obtained by payments, and not by greatness or nobility of mind, may indeed be earned, but they are not secured, and in time of need cannot be relied upon; and men have less scruple in offending one who is beloved than one who is feared, for love is preserved by the link of obligation which, owing to the baseness of men, is broken at every opportunity for their advantage; but fear preserves you by a dread of punishment which never fails.

Nevertheless a prince ought to inspire fear in such a way that, if he does not win love, he avoids hatred; because he can endure very well being feared whilst he is not hated, which will always be as long as he abstains from the property of his citizens and subjects and from their women. But when it is necessary for him to proceed against the life of someone, he must do it on proper justification and for manifest cause, but above all things he must keep his hands off the property of others, because men more quickly forget the death of their father than the loss of their patrimony. Besides, pretexts for taking away the property are never wanting; for he who has once begun to live by robbery will always find pretexts for seizing what belongs to others; but reasons for taking life, on the contrary, are more difficult to find and sooner lapse. But when a prince is with his army, and has under control a multitude of soldiers, then it is quite necessary for him to disregard the reputation of cruelty, for without it he would never hold his army united or disposed to its duties.

Among the wonderful deeds of Hannibal this one is enumerated: that having led an enormous army, composed of many various races to men, to fight in foreign lands, no dissensions arose either among them or against the prince, whether in his bad or in his good fortune. This arose from nothing else than his inhuman cruelty, which, with his boundless valour, made him revered and terrible in the sight of his soldiers, but without that cruelty, his other virtues were not sufficient to produce this effect. And short-sighted writers admire his deeds from one point of view and from another condemn the principal cause of them. That it is true his other virtues would not have been sufficient for him may be proved by the case of Scipio, that most excellent man, not only of his own times but within the memory of man, against whom, nevertheless, his army rebelled in Spain; this arose from nothing but his too great forbearance, which gave his soldiers more licence than is consistent with military discipline. For this he was upbraided in the Senate by Fabius Maximus, and called the corruptor of the Roman soldiery. The Locrians were laid waste by a legate of Scipio, yet they were not avenged by him, nor was the insolence of the legate punished, owing entirely to his easy nature. Insomuch that some one in the Senate, wishing to excuse him, said there were many men who knew much better how not to err than to correct the errors of others. This disposition, if he had been continued in the command, would have destroyed in time the fame and glory of Scipio; but, he being under the control of the Senate, this injurious characteristic not only concealed itself, but contributed to his glory.

Returning to the question of being feared or loved, I come to the conclusion that, men loving according to their own will and fearing according to that of the prince, a wise prince should establish himself on that which is in his own control and not in that of others; he must endeavour only to avoid hatred, as is noted.

Concerning the Way in Which Princes Should Keep Faith

Everyone admits how praiseworthy it is in a prince to keep faith, and to live with integrity and not with craft. Nevertheless our experience has been that those princes who have done great things have held good faith of little account, and have known how to circumvent the intellect of men by craft, and in the end have overcome those who have relied on their word. You must know there are two ways of contesting, the one by the law, the other by force; the first method is proper to men, the second to beasts; but because the first is frequently not sufficient, it is necessary to have recourse to the second. Therefore it is necessary for a prince to understand how to avail himself of the beast and the man. This has been figuratively taught to princes by ancient writers, who describe how Achilles and many other princes of old were given to the Centaur Chiron to nurse, who brought them up in his discipline; which means solely that, as they had for a teacher one who was half beast and half man, so it is necessary for a prince to know how to make use of both natures, and that one without the other is not durable. A prince, therefore, being compelled knowingly to adopt the beast, ought to choose the fox and the lion; because the lion cannot defend himself against snares and the fox cannot defend himself against wolves. Therefore, it is necessary to be a fox to discover the snares and a lion to terrify the wolves. Those who rely simply on the lion do not understand what they are about. Therefore a wise lord cannot, nor ought he to, keep faith when such observance may be turned against him, and when the reasons that caused him to pledge it exist no longer. If men were entirely good this precept would not hold, but because they are bad, and will not keep faith with you, you too are not bound to observe it with them. Nor will there ever be wanting to a prince legitimate reasons to excuse this non-observance. Of this endless modern examples could be given, showing how many treaties and engagements have been made void and of no effect through the faithlessness of princes; and he who has known best how to employ the fox has succeeded best.

But it is necessary to know well how to disguise this characteristic, and to be a great pretender and dissembler; and men are so simple, and so subject to present necessities, that he who seeks to deceive will always find some one who will allow himself to be deceived. One recent example I cannot pass over in silence. Alexander the Sixth did nothing else but deceive men, nor ever thought of doing otherwise, and he always found victims; for there never was a man who had greater power in asserting, or who with greater oaths would affirm a thing, yet would observe it less; nevertheless his deceits always succeeded according to his wishes, because he well understood this side of mankind.

Therefore it is unnecessary for a prince to have all the good qualities I have enumerated, but it is very necessary to appear to have them. And I shall dare to say this also, that to have them and always to observe them is injurious, and that to appear to have them is useful; to appear merciful, faithful, humane, religious, upright, and to be so, but with a mind so framed that should you require not to be so, you may be able to know how to change to the opposite.

And you have to understand this, that a prince, especially a new one, cannot observe all those things for which men are esteemed, being often forced, in order to maintain the state, to act contrary to fidelity, friendship, humanity, and religion. Therefore it is necessary for him to have a mind ready to turn itself accordingly as the winds and variations of fortune force it, yet, as I have said above, not to diverge form the good if he can avoid doing so, but, if compelled, then to know how to set about it.

For this reason a prince ought to take care that he never lets anything slip from his lips that he is not to replete with the above-named five qualities, that he may appear to him who sees and hears him altogether merciful, faithful, humane, upright, and religious. There is nothing more necessary to appear to have than this last quality, inasmuch as men judge generally more by the eye than by the hand, because it belongs to everybody to see you, to few to come in touch with you. Every one sees what you appear to be, few really know what you are, and those few dare not oppose themselves to the opinion of the many, who have the majesty of the state to defend them; and in the actions of all men, and especially of princes, which it is not prudent to challenge, one judges by the result.

For that reason, let a prince have the credit of conquering and holding his state, the means will always be considered honest, and he will be praised by everybody; because the vulgar are always taken by what a thing seems to be and by what comes of it; and in the world there are only the vulgar, for the few find a place there only when the many have no ground to rest on.

One prince of the present time, whom it is not well to name, never preaches anything else but peace and good faith, and to both he is most hostile, and either, if he had kept it, would have deprived him of reputation and kingdom many a time.

Questions and Answers

1. Choose one of the qualities Machiavelli names, such as liberality (generosity), cruelty, or integrity. Write an argument in which you state and support a position different from Machiavelli's on this quality of a ruler. As part of your argument, be sure you provide an accurate summary of Machiavelli's position and the support he provides for it.

2. Write an argument in which your position is that Machiavelli's reputation for cynicism and evil is undeserved. Instead, based on the selection printed here, argue that he was simply giving pragmatic advice that contributes to survival and good government.

From Leviathan

THOMAS HOBBES

Thomas Hobbes (1588–1679) was an English political philosopher. He is best known for Leviathani *(1651), from which the following excerpt is taken. In this treatise Hobbes argued that people should give absolute obedience to the state—the "Leviathan" of his title. The state, he argued, is all that preserves order among people, who are naturally selfish and aggressive. In exchange for granting absolute power to the state, citizens receive its protection from each other. Hobbes is often thought pessimistic and cynical for his description of life as "solitary, poor, nasty, brutish, and short."*

Of the Natural Condition of Mankind as concerning their Felicity and Misery

Men by nature equal. Nature hath made men so equal, in the faculties of the body, and mind; as that though there be found one man sometimes manifestly stronger in body, or of quicker mind than another; yet when all is reckoned together, the difference between man, and man, is not so considerable, as that one man can thereupon claim to himself any benefit, to which another may not pretend, as well as he. For as to the strength of body, the weakest has strength enough to kill the strongest, either by secret machination, or by confederacy with others, that are in the same danger with himself.

And as to the faculties of the mind, setting aside the arts grounded upon words, and especially that skill of proceeding upon general, and infallible rules, called science; which very few have, and but in few things; as being not a native faculty, born with us; nor attained, as prudence, while we look after somewhat else, I find yet a greater equality amongst men, than that of strength. For prudence, is but experience; which equal time, equally bestows on all men, in those things they equally apply themselves unto. That which may perhaps make such equality incredible, is but a vain conceit of one's own wisdom, which almost all men think they have in a greater degree, than the vulgar; that is, than all men but themselves, and a few others, whom by fame, or for concurring with themselves, they approve. For such is the nature of men, that howsoever they may acknowledge many others to be more witty, or more eloquent, or more learned; yet they will hardly believe there by many so wise as themselves; for they see their own wit at hand, and other men's at a distance. But this proveth rather that men are in that point equal, than unequal. For there is not ordinarily a greater sign of equal distribution of any thing, than that every man is contented with his share.

Form equality proceeds diffidence. From this equality of ability, ariseth equality of hope in the attaining of our ends. And therefore if any two men desire the same thing, which nevertheless they cannot both enjoy, they become enemies; and in the way to their end, which is principally their own conservation, and sometimes their delectation only, endeavor to destroy, or subdue one another. And from hence it comes to pass, that where an invader hath no more to fear, than another man's single power; if one plant, sow, build, or possess a convenient seat, others may probably be expected to come prepared with forces united, to dispossess, and deprive him, not only of the fruit of his labour, but also of his life, or liberty. And the invader again is in the like danger of another.

From diffidence war. And from this diffidence of one another, there is no way for any man to secure himself, so reasonable, as anticipation; that is, by force, or wiles, to master the persons of all men he can, so long, till he see no other power great enough to endanger him: and this is no more than his own conservation requireth, and is generally allowed. Also because there be some, that taking pleasure in contemplating their own power in the acts of conquest, which they pursue farther than their security requires; if others, that otherwise would be glad to be at ease within modest bounds, should not by invasion increase their power, they would not be able, long time, by standing only on their defence, to subsist. And by consequence, such augmentation of dominion over men being necessary to a man's conservation, it ought to be allowed him.

Again, men have no pleasure, but on the contrary a great deal of grief, in keeping company, where there is no power able to over-awe them all. For every man looketh that his companion should value him, at the same rate he sets upon himself: and upon all signs of contempt, or undervaluing, naturally endeavours, as far as he dares, (which amongst them that have no common power to keep them in quiet, is far enough to make them destroy each other), to extort a greater value from his contemners, by damage; and from others, by example.

So that in the nature of man, we find three principal causes of quarrel. First, competition; secondly, diffidence; thirdly, glory.

The first, maketh men invade for gain; the second, for safety; and the third, for reputation. The first uses violence to make themselves masters of other men's persons, wives, children, and cattle; the second, to defend them; the third, for trifles, as a word, a smile, a different opinion, and any other sign of undervalue, either direct in their persons, or by reflection in their kindred, their friends, their nation, their profession, or their name.

Out of civil states, there is always war of every one against every one. Hereby it is manifest, that during the time men live without a common power to keep them all in awe, they are in that condition which is called war; and such a war, as is of every man, against every man. For WAR, consisteth not in battle only, or the act of fighting; but in a tract of time, wherein the will to contend by battle is sufficiently known: and therefore the notion of *time,* is to be considered in the nature of war; as it is in the nature of weather. For as the nature of foul weather, lieth not in a shower or two of rain; but in an inclination thereto of many days together: so the nature of war, consisteth not in actual fighting; but in the known disposition thereto, during all the time there is no assurance to the contrary. All other time is PEACE.

The incommodities of such a war. Whatsoever therefore is consequent to a time of war, where every man is enemy to every man; the same is consequent to the time, wherein men live without other security, than what their own strength, and their own invention shall furnish them withal. In such condition, there is no place for industry; because the fruit thereof is uncertain: and consequently no culture of the earth; no navigation, nor use of the commodities that may be imported by sea; no commodious building; no instruments of moving, and removing, such things as require much force; no knowledge of the face of the earth; no account of time, no arts; no letters, no society; and which is worst of all, continual fear, and danger of violent death; and the life of man, solitary, poor, nasty, brutish, and short.

It may seem strange to some man, that has not well weighted these things; that nature should thus dissociate, and render men apt to invade, and destroy one another: and he may therefore, not trusting to this inference, made from the passions, desire perhaps to have the same confirmed by experience. Let him therefore consider with himself, when taking a journey, he arms himself, and seeks to go well accompanied; when going to sleep, he locks his doors; when even in his house he locks his chests; and this when he knows there be laws, and public officers, armed, to revenge all injuries shall be done him; what opinion he has of his fellow subjects, when he rides armed; of his fellow citizens, when he locks his doors; and of his children, and servants, when he locks his chests. Does he not there as much accuse mankind by his actions, as I do by my words? But neither of as accuse man's nature in it. The desires, and other passions of man, are in themselves no sin. No more are the actions, that proceed from those passions, till they know a law forbids them: which till laws be made they cannot know: nor can any law be made, till they have agreed upon the person that shall make it.

It may peradventure be thought, there was never such a time, nor condition of war as this; and I believe it was never generally so, over all the world: but there are many places, where they live so now. For the savage people in many places of America, except the government of small families, the concord whereof dependeth on natural lust, have no government at all; and live at this day in that brutish manner of life there would be, where there were no common power to fear, by the manner of life, which men that have formerly lived under a peaceful government, use to degenerate into, in a civil war.

But though there had never been any time, wherein particular men were in a condition of war one against another; yet in all times, kings, and persons of sovereign authority, because of their independency, are in continual jealousies, and in the state and posture of gladiators; having their weapons pointing, and their eyes fixed on one another; that is, their forts, garrisons, and guns upon the frontiers of their kingdoms; and continual spies upon their neighbours; which is a posture of war. But because they uphold thereby, the industry of their subjects; there does not follow from it, that misery, which accompanies the liberty of particular men.

In such a war nothing is unjust. To this war of every man, against every man, this also is consequent; that nothing can be unjust. The notions of right and wrong, justice and injustice have there no place. Where there is no common power, there is no law: where no law, no injustice. Force, and fraud, are in war the two cardinal virtues. Justice, and injustice are none of the faculties neither of the body, nor mind. If they were, they might be in a man that were alone in the world, as well as his senses, and passions. They are qualities, that relate to men in society, not in solitude. It is consequent also to the same condition, that there be no property, no dominion, no *mine* and *thine* distinct; but only that to be every man's, that he can get: and for so long, as he can keep it. And thus much for the ill condition, which man by mere nature is actually placed in; though with a possibility to come out of it, consisting partly in the passions, partly in his reason.

The passions that incline men to peace. The passions that incline men to peace, are fear of death; desire of such things as are necessary to commodious living; and a hope by their industry to obtain them. And reason suggesteth convenient articles of peace, upon which men may be drawn to agreement. These articles, are they, which otherwise are called the Laws of Nature: whereof I shall speak more particularly, in the two following chapters.

Of the First and Second Natural Laws, and of Contracts

Right of nature what. THE RIGHT OF NATURE, which writers commonly call *jus naturale,* is the liberty each man hath, to use his own power, as he will himself, for the preservation of his own nature; that is to say, of his own life, and consequently, of doing any one thing, which in his own judgment, and reason, he shall conceive to be the aptest means thereunto.

Liberty what. By LIBERTY, is understood, according to the proper signification of the word, the absence of external impediments: which impediments, may oft take away part of a man's power to do what he would; but cannot hinder him from using the power left him, according as his judgment, and reason shall dictate to him.

A law of nature what. Difference of right and law. A LAW OF NATURE, *lex naturalis,* is a precept or general rule, found out by reason, by which a man is forbidden to do that, which is destructive of his life, or taketh away the means of preserving the same; and to omit that, by which he thinketh it may be best preserved. For though they that speak of this subject, use to confound *jus,* and *lex, right* and *law:* yet they ought to be distinguished; because RIGHT, consisteth in liberty to do, or to forbear: whereas LAW, determineth, and bindeth to one of them: so that law, and right, differ as much, as obligation, and liberty; which in one and the same matter are inconsistent.

Naturally every man has right to every thing. The fundamental law of nature. And because the condition of man, as hath been declared in the precedent chapter, is a condition of war of every one against every one; in which case every one is governed by his own reason; and there is nothing he can make use of, that may not be a help unto him, in preserving his life against his enemies; it followeth, that in such a condition, every man has a right to every thing; even to one another's body. And therefore, as long as this natural right of every man to every thing endureth, there can be no security to any man, how strong or wise soever he be, of living out the time, which nature ordinarily alloweth men to live. And consequently it is a precept, or general rule of reason, *that every man, ought to endeavour peace, as far as he has hope of obtaining it; and when he cannot obtain it, that he may seek, and use, all helps, and advantages of war.* The first branch of which rule, containeth the first, and fundamental law of nature; which is *to seek peace, and follow it.* The second, the sum of the right of nature; which is, *by all means we can, to defend ourselves.*

The second law of nature. From this fundamental law of nature, by which men are commanded to endeavour peace, is derived this second law; *that a man be willing, when others are so too, as far-forth, as for peace, and defence of himself he shall think it necessary, to lay down this right to all things; and be contented with so much liberty against other men, as he would allow other men against himself.* For as long as every man holdeth this right, of doing any thing he liketh; so long are all men in the condition of war. But if other men will not lay down their right, as well as he; then there is no reason for any one, to divest himself of his: for that were to expose himself to prey, which no man is bound to, rather than to dispose himself to peace. This is that law of the Gospel; *whatsoever you require that others should do to you, that do ye to them.* And that law of all men, *quod tibi fieri non vis, alteri ne feceris.*

What it is to lay down a right. To *lay down* a man's *right* to any thing, is to *divest* himself of the *liberty,* of hindering another of the benefit of his own right to the same. For he that renounceth, or passeth away his right, giveth not to any other man a right which he had not before; because there is nothing to which every man had not right by nature: but only standeth out of his way, that he may enjoy his own original right, without hindrance from him; not without hindrance from another. So that the effect which redoundeth to one man, by another man's defect of right, is but so much diminution of impediments to the use of his own right original.

Renouncing a right, what it is. Transferring right what. Obligation. Duty. Injustice. Right is laid aside, either by simply renouncing it; or by transferring it to another. By *simply* RENOUNCING; when he cares not to whom the benefit thereof redoundeth. By TRANSFERRING; when he intendeth the benefit thereof to some certain person, or persons. And when a man hath in either manner abandoned, or granted away his right; then he is said to be OBLIGED, or BOUND, not to hinder those, to whom such right is granted, or abandoned, from the benefit of it: and that he *ought,* and it is his DUTY, not to make the void that voluntary act of his own: and that such hindrance is INJUSTICE, and INJURY, as being *sine jure;* the right being before renounced, or transferred. So that *injury, or injustice,* in the controversies of the world, is somewhat like to that, which in the disputations of scholars is called *absurdity.* For as it is there called an absurdity, to contradict what one maintained in the beginning: so in the world, it is called injustice, and injury, voluntarily to undo that, which from the beginning he had voluntarily done. The way by which a man either simply renounceth, or transfereth his right, is a declaration, or signification, by some voluntary and sufficient sign, or signs, that he doth so renounce, or transfer; or that so renounced, or transferred the same, to him that accepteth it. And these signs are either words only, or actions only; or, as it happeneth most often, both words, and actions. And the same are the BONDS, by which men are bound, and obliged: bonds, that have their strength, not from their own nature, for nothing is more easily broken than a man's word, but from fear of some evil consequence upon the rupture.

Not all rights are alienable. Whensoever a man transferreth his right, or renounceth it; it is either in consideration of some right reciprocally transferred to himself; or for some other good he hopeth for thereby. For it is a voluntary act: and of the voluntary acts of every man, the object is some *good to himself.* And therefore there be some rights, which no man can be understood by any words, or other signs, to have abandoned, or transferred. As first a man cannot lay down the right of resisting them, that assault him by force, to take away his life; because he cannot be understood to aim thereby, at any good to himself. The same may be said of wounds, and chains, and imprisonment; both because there is no benefit consequent to such patience; as there is to the patience of suffering another to be wounded, or imprisoned: as also because a man cannot tell, when he seeth men proceed against him by violence, whether they intend his death or not. And lastly the motive, and end for which this renouncing, and transferring of right is introduced, is nothing else but the security of a man's person, in his life, and in the means of so preserving life, as not to be weary of it. And therefore if a man by words, or other signs, seem to despoil himself of the end, for which those signs were intended; he is not to be understood as if he meant it, or that it was his will; but that he was ignorant of how such words and actions were to be interpreted.

Contract what. The mutual transferring of right, is that which men call CONTRACT.

There is difference between transferring of right to the thing; and transferring, or tradition, that is delivery of the thing itself. For the thing may be delivered together with the translation of the fight; as in buying and selling with ready-money; or exchange of goods, or lands: and it may be delivered some time after.

Covenant what. Again, one of the contractors, may deliver the thing contracted for on his part, and leave the other to perform his part at some determinate time after, and in the mean time be trusted; and then the contract on his part, is called PACT, or COVE-NANT: or both parts may contract now, to perform hereafter: in which cases, he that is to perform in time to come, being trusted, his performance is called *keeping of promise,* or faith; and the failing of performance, if it be voluntary, *violation of faith.*

Free-gift. When the transferring of right, is not mutual: but one of the parties transferreth, in hope to gain thereby friendship, or service from another, or from his friends; or in hope to gain the reputation of charity, or magnanimity; or to deliver his mind from the pain of compassion; or in hope of reward in heaven; this is not contract, but GIFT, FREE-GIFT, GRACE: which words signify one and the same thing.

Signs of contract express. Promise. Signs of contract, are either *express,* or *by inference.* Express, are words spoken with understanding of what they signify: and such words are either of the time *present,* or *past;* as, *I give, I grant, I have given, I have granted, I will that this be yours:* or of the future; as *I will give, I will grant:* which words of the future are called PROMISE.

Signs of contract by inference. Signs by inference, are sometimes the consequence of words; sometimes the consequence of silence; sometimes the consequence of actions; sometimes the consequence of forbearing an action: and generally a sign by inference, of any contract, is whatsoever sufficiently argues the will of the contractor.

Free gift passeth by words of the present or past. Words alone, if they be of the time to come, and contain a bare promise, are an insufficient sign of a free-gift, and therefore not obligatory. For if they be of the time to come as *tomorrow I will give,* they are a sign I have not given yet, and consequently that my right is not transferred, but remaineth till I transfer it by some other act. But if the words be of the time present, or past, *I have given,* or, *do give to be delivered to-morrow,* then is my to-morrow's right given away to-day; and that by the virtue of the words, though there were no other argument of my will. And there is a great difference in the signification of these words, *volo hoc tuum esse cras,* and *cras dabo;* that is, between *I will that this be thine to-morrow,* and, *I will give it thee to-morrow:* for the word *I will,* in the former manner of speech, signifies an act of the will present; but in the latter, it signifies a promise of an act of the will to come: and therefore the former words, being of the present, transfer a future right; the latter, that be of the future, transfer nothing. But if there be other signs of the will to transfer a right, besides words; then though the gift be free, yet may the right be understood to pass by words of the future: as if a man propound a prize to him that comes first to the end of a race, the gift is free; and though the words be of the future, yet the right passeth: for if he would not have his words so be understood, he should not have let them run.

Signs of contract are words both of the past, present, and future. In contracts, the right passeth, not only where the words are of the time present, or past, but also where they are of the future: because all contract is mutual translation, or change of right; and therefore he that promiseth only, because he that already received the benefit for which he promiseth, is to be understood as if he intended the right should pass: for unless he had been content to have his words so understood, the other would not have performed his part first. And for that cause, in buying, and selling, and other acts of contract, a promise is equivalent to a covenant; and therefore obligatory.

Merit what. He that performeth first in the case of a contract, is said to MERIT that which he is to receive by the performance of the other; and he hath it as *due.* Also when a prize is propounded to many, which is to be given to him only that winneth, or money is thrown amongst many, to be enjoyed by them that catch it; though this be a free gift; yet so to win, or so to catch, is to *merit,* and to have it as DUE. For the right is transferred in the propounding of the prize, and in throwing down the money; though it be not determined to whom, but by the event of the contention. But there is between these two sorts of merit, this difference, that in contract, I merit by virtue of my own power, and the contractor's need; but in this case of free gift, I am enabled to merit only by the benignity of the giver: in contract, I merit at the contractor's hand that he should depart with his right; in this case of gift, I merit not that the giver should part with his right; but that when he has parted with it, it should be mine, rather than another's. And this I think to be the meaning of that distinction of the Schools, between *meritum congrui,* and *meritum condigni.* For God Almighty, having promised Paradise to those men, hoodwinked with carnal desires, that can walk through this world according to the precepts, and limits prescribed by him; they say, he that shall so walk, shall merit Paradise *ex congruo.* But because no man can demand a right to it, by his own righteousness, or any other power in himself, but by the free grace of God only; they say, no man can merit Paradise *ex condigno.* This I say, I think is the meaning of that distinction; but because disputers do not agree upon the signification of their own terms of art, longer than it serves their turn; I will not affirm any thing of their meaning: only this I say; when a gift is given indefinitely, as a prize to be contended for, he that winneth meriteth, and may claim the prize as due.

Covenants of mutual trust, when invalid. If a covenant be made, wherein neither of the parties perform presently, but trust one another; in the condition of mere nature, which is a condition of war of every man against every man, upon any reasonable suspicion, it is void: but if there be a common power set over them both, with right and force sufficient to compel performance, it is not void. For he that performeth first, has no assurance the other will perform after; because the bonds of words are too weak to bridle men's ambition, avarice, anger, and other passions, without the fear of some coercive power; which in the condition of mere nature, where all men are equal, the judges of the justness of their own fears, cannot possibly be supposed. And therefore he which performeth first, does but betray himself to his enemy; contrary to the right, he can never abandon, of defending his life, and means of living.

But in a civil estate, where there is a power set up to constrain those that would otherwise violate their faith, that fear is no more reasonable; and for that cause, he which by the covenant is to perform first, is obliged to do so.

The cause of fear, which maketh such a covenant invalid, must be always something arising after the covenant made; as some new fact, or other sign of the will not to perform: else it cannot make the covenant void. For that which could not hinder a man from promising, ought not to be admitted as a hindrance of performing.

Right to the end, containeth right to the means. He that transferreth any right, transferreth the means of enjoying it, as far as lieth in his power. As he that selleth land, is understood to transfer the herbage, and whatsoever grows upon it: nor can he that sells a mill turn away the stream that drives it. And they that give to man the right of government in sovereignty, are understood to give him the right of levying money to maintain soldiers; and of appointing magistrates for the administration of justice.

No covenant with beasts. To make covenants with brute beasts, is impossible; because not understanding our speech, they understand not, nor accept of any translation of right; nor can translate any right to another: and without mutual acceptation, there is no covenant.

Nor with God without special revelation. To make covenant with God, is impossible, but by mediation of such as God speaketh to, either by revelation supernatural, or by his lieutenants that govern under him, and in his name: for otherwise we know not whether our covenants be accepted, or not. And therefore they that vow anything contrary to any law of nature, vow in vain; as being a thing unjust to pay such vow. And if it be a thing commanded by the law of nature, it is not the vow, but the law that binds them.

No covenant, but of possible and future. The matter, or subject of a covenant, is always something that falleth under deliberation; for to covenant, is an act of the will; that is to say, and act, and the last act of deliberation; and is therefore always understood to be something to come; and which is judged possible for him that covenanteth, to perform.

And therefore, to promise that which is know to be impossible, is no covenant. But if that prove impossible afterwards, which before was thought possible, the covenant is valid, and bindeth, though not to the thing itself, yet to the value; or, if that also be impossible, to the unfeigned endeavour of performing as much as is possible: for to more no man can be obliged.

Covenants how made void. Men are freed of their covenants two ways; be performing; or by being forgiven. For performance, is the natural end of obligation; and forgiveness, the restitution of liberty; as being a retransferring of that right, in which the obligation consisted.

Covenants extorted by fear are valid. Covenants entered into by fear, in the condition of mere nature, are obligatory. For example, if I covenant to pay a ransom, or service for my life, to an enemy; I am bound by it: for it is a contract, wherein one receiveth the benefit of life; the other is to receive money, or service for it; and consequently, where no other law, as in the condition of mere nature, forbiddeth the performance, the covenant is valid. Therefore prisoners of war, if trusted with the payment of their ransom, are obliged to pay it: and if a weaker prince, make a disadvantageous peace with a stronger, for fear; he is bound to keep it; unless, as hath been said before, there ariseth some new, and just cause of fear, to renew the war. And even in commonwealths, if I be forced to redeem myself from a thief by promising him money, I am bound to pay it, till the civil law discharge me. For whatsoever I may lawfully do without obligation, the same I may lawfully covenant to do through fear: and what I lawfully covenant, I cannot lawfully break.

The former covenant to one, makes void the later to another. A former covenant, makes void a later. For a man that hath passed away his right to one man to-day, hath it not to pass to-morrow to another: and therefore the later promise passeth no right, but is null.

A man's covenant not to defend himself is void. A covenant not to defend myself from force, by force, is always void. For, as I have showed before, no man can transfer, or lay down his right to save himself from death, wounds, and imprisonment, the avoiding whereof is the only end of laying down any right; and therefore the promise of not resisting force, in no covenant transferreth any right; nor is obliging. For though a man may covenant thus, *unless I do so, or so, kill me;* he cannot covenant thus, *unless I do so, or so, I will not resist you, when you come to kill me.* For man by nature chooseth the lesser evil, which is danger of death in resisting; rather than the greater, which is certain and present death in not resisting. And this is granted to be true by all men, in that they lead criminals to execution, and prison, with armed men, notwithstanding that such criminals have consented to the law, by which they are condemned.

No man obliged to accuse himself. A covenant to accuse oneself, without assurance of pardon, is likewise invalid. For in the condition of nature, where every man is judge, there is no place for accusation: and in the civil state, the accusation is followed with punishment; which being force, a man is not obliged to resist. The same is also true, of the accusation of those, by whose condemnations a man falls into misery; as of a father, wife, or benefactor. For the testimony of such an accuser, if not be willingly given, is presumed to be corrupted by nature; and therefore not to be received: and where a man's testimony is not to be credited, he is not bound to give it. Also accusations upon torture, are not to be reputed as testimonies. For torture is to be used as means of conjecture, and light, in the further examination, and search of truth: and what is in that case confessed, tendeth to the ease of him that is tortured; not to the informing of the torturers: and therefore ought not to have the credit of a sufficient testimony: for whether he deliver himself by true, or false accusation, he does it by the right of preserving his own life.

Questions and Answers

1. Summarize briefly Hobbes's view of people and how they interact with each other, and then argue that his views are or are not as applicable to the twentieth century as to the seventeenth.

2. Which of your rights would you give up in exchange for peace and protection? Which rights would you never give up, under any circumstances? Describe the choice you would make in response to these questions, and then argue that others should make the same choices that you have made.

Federalist Paper No. 10

JAMES MADISON

In 1787 and 1788, delegates gathered in New York at a Constitutional Convention to write a constitution to replace the Articles of Confederation, which had governed relationships among the states since 1777. While the Constitutional Convention met, John Jay, Alexander Hamilton, and James Madison wrote a series of newspaper essays in which they urged that the new constitution be ratified by the states. These essays are now known as the Federalist Papers. *At the time, the author was identified only as Publius. "Federalist Paper No. 10" has been attributed to James Madison (1751–1836), who became President of the United States in 1809.*

Among the numerous advantages promised by a well-constructed Union, none deserves to be more accurately developed than its tendency to break and control the violence of faction. The friend of popular governments never finds himself so much alarmed for their character and fate as when he contemplates their propensity to this dangerous vice. He will not fail, therefore, to set a due value on any plan which, without violating the principles to which he is attached, provides a proper cure for it. The instability, injustice, and confusion introduced into the public councils have, in truth, been the mortal diseases under which popular governments have everywhere perished, as they continue to be the favorite and fruitful topics from which the adversaries to liberty derive their most specious declamations. The valuable improvements made by the American constitutions on the popular models, both ancient and modern, cannot certainly be too much admired; but it would be an unwarrantable partiality to contend that they have as effectually obviated the danger on this side, as was wished and expected. Complaints are everywhere heard from our most considerate and virtuous citizens, equally the friends of public and private faith and of public and personal liberty, that our governments are too unstable, that the public good is disregarded in the conflicts of rival parties, and that measures are too often decided, not according to the rules of justice and the rights of the minor party, but by the superior force of an interested and overbearing majority. However anxiously we may wish that these complaints had no foundation, the evidence of known facts will not permit us to deny that they are in some degree true. It will be found, indeed, on a candid review of our situation, that some of the distresses under which we labor have been erroneously charged on the operations of our governments; but it will be found, at the same time, that other causes will not alone account for many of our heaviest misfortunes; and, particularly, for that prevailing and increasing distrust of public engagements and alarm for private rights which are echoed from one end of the continent to the other. These must be chiefly, if not wholly, effects of the unsteadiness and injustice with which a factious spirit has tainted our public administration.

By a faction I understand a number of citizens, whether amounting to a majority or minority of the whole, who are united and actuated by some common impulse of passion, or of interest, adverse to the rights of other citizens, or to the permanent and aggregate interests of the community.

There are two methods of curing the mischiefs of faction: the one, by removing its causes; the other, by controlling its effects.

There are again two methods of removing the causes of faction: the one by destroying the liberty which is essential to its existence; the other, by giving to every citizen the same opinions, the same passions, and the same interests.

It could never be more truly said than of the first remedy that it was worse than the disease. Liberty is to faction what air is to fire, an ailment without which it instantly expires. But it could not be less folly to abolish liberty, which is essential to political life, because it nourishes faction than it would be to wish the annihilation of air, which is essential to animal life, because it imparts to fire its destructive agency.

The second expediant is as impracticable as the first would be unwise. As long as the reason of man continues fallible, and he is at liberty to exercise it, different opinions will be formed. As long as the connection subsists between his reason and his self-love, his opinions and his passions will have a reciprocal influence on each other; and the former will be objects to which the latter will attach themselves. The diversity in the faculties of men, from which the rights of property originate, is not less an insuperable obstacle to a uniformity of interests. The protection of these faculties is the first object of government. From the protection of different and unequal faculties of acquiring property, the possession of different degrees and kinds of property immediately results; and from the influence of these on the sentiments and views of the respective proprietors ensues a division of the society into different interests and parties.

The latent causes of faction are thus shown in the nature of man; and we see them everywhere brought into different degrees of activity, according to the different circumstances of civil society. A zeal for different opinions concerning religion, concerning government, and many other points, as well of speculation as of practice; and attachment to different leaders ambitiously contending for pre-eminence and power; or to persons of other descriptions whose fortunes have been interesting to the human passions, have, in turn, divided mankind into parties, inflamed them with mutual animosity, and rendered them much more disposed to vex and oppress each other than to co-operate for their common good. So strong is this propensity of mankind to fall into mutual animosities that where no substantial occasion presents itself the most frivolous and fanciful distinctions have been sufficient to kindle their unfriendly passions and excite their most violent conflicts. But the most common and durable source of factions has been the various and unequal distribution of property. Those who hold and those who are without property have ever formed distinct interests in society. Those who are creditors, and those who are debtors, fall under a like discrimination. A landed interest, a manufacturing interest, a mercantile interest, a moneyed interest, with many lesser interests, grow up of a necessity in civilized nations, and divide them into different classes, actuated by different sentiments and views. The regulation of these various and interfering interests forms the principal task of modern legislation and involves the spirit of party and faction in the necessary and ordinary operations of government.

No man is allowed to be judge in his own cause, because his interest would certainly bias his judgment, and, not improbably, corrupt his integrity. With equal, nay with greater reason, a body of men are unfit to be both judges and parties at the same time; yet what are many of the most important acts of legislation but so many judicial determinations, not indeed concerning the rights of single persons, but concerning the rights of large bodies of citizens? And what are the different classes of legislators but advocates and parties to the causes which they determine? Is a law proposed concerning private debts? It is a question to which the creditors are parties on one side and debtors on the other. Justice ought to hold the balance between them. Yet the parties are, and must be, themselves the judges; and the most numerous party, or in other words, the most powerful faction must be expected to prevail. Shall domestic manufacturers be encouraged, and in what degree, by restrictions on foreign manufacturers? are questions which would be differently decided by the landed and the manufacturing classes, and probably by neither with a sole regard to justice and the public good. The appointment of taxes on the various descriptions of property is an act which seems to require the most exact impartiality; yet there is, perhaps, no legislative act in which greater opportunity and temptation are given to a predominant party to trample on the rules of justice. Every shilling with which they overburden the inferior number is a shilling saved to their own pockets.

It is in vain to say that enlightened statesmen will be able to adjust these clashing interests and render them all subservient to the public good. Enlightened statesmen will not always be at the helm. Nor, in many cases, can such an adjustment be made at all without taking into view indirect and remote considerations, which will rarely prevail over the immediate interest which one party may find in disregarding the rights of another or the good of the whole.

The inference to which we are brought is that the *causes* of faction cannot be removed and that relief is only to be sought in the means of controlling its *effects*.

If a faction consists of less than a majority, relief is supplied by the republican principle, which enables the majority to defeat its sinister views by regular vote. It may clog the administration, it may convulse the society; but it will be unable to execute and mask its violence under the forms of the Constitution. When a majority is included in a faction, the form of popular government, on the other hand, enables it to sacrifice to its ruling passion or interest both the public good and and the rights of other citizens. To secure the public good and private rights against the danger of such a faction, and at the same time to preserve the spirit and the form of popular government, is then the great object to which our inquiries are directed. Let me add that it is the great desideratum by which alone this form of government can be rescued from the opprobrium under which it has so long labored and be recommended to the esteem and adoption of mankind.

By what means is this object attainable? Evidently by one of two only. Either the existence of the same passion or interest in a majority at the same time must be prevented, or the majority, having such a coexistent passion or interest, must be rendered, by their number and local situation, unable to concert and carry into effect schemes of oppression. If the impulse and the opportunity be suffered to coincide, we will know that neither moral nor religious motives can be relied on as an adequate control. They are not found to be such on the injustice and violence of individuals, and lose their efficacy in proportion to the number combined together, that is, in proportion as their efficacy becomes needful.

From this view of the subject it may be concluded that a pure democracy, by which I mean a society consisting of a small number of citizens, who assemble and administer the government in person, can admit of no cure for the mischiefs of faction. A common passion or interest will, in almost every case, be felt by a majority of the whole; a communication and concert results from the form of government itself; and there is nothing to check the inducements to sacrifice the weaker party or an obnoxious individual. Hence it is that such democracies have ever been spectacles of turbulence and contention; have ever been found incompatible with personal security or the rights of property; and have in general been as short in their lives as they have been violent in their deaths. Theoretic politicians, who have patronized this species of government, have erroneously supposed that by reducing mankind to a perfect equality in their political rights, they would at the same time be perfectly equalized and assimilated in their possessions, their opinions, and their passions.

A republic, by which I mean a government in which the scheme of representation takes place, opens a different prospect and promises the cure for which we are seeking. Let us examine the points in which it varies from pure democracy, and we shall comprehend both the nature of the cure and the efficacy which it must derive from the Union.

The two great points of difference between a democracy and a republic are: first, the delegation of the government, in the latter, to small number of citizens elected by the rest; secondly, the greater number of citizens and greater sphere of country over which the latter may be extended.

The effect of the first difference is, on the one hand, to refine and enlarge the public views by passing them through the medium of a chosen body of citizens, whose wisdom may best discern the true interest of their country and whose patriotism and love of justice will be least likely to sacrifice it to temporary or partial considerations. Under such a regulation it may well happen that the public voice, pronounced by the representatives of the people, will be more consonant to the public good than if pronounced by the people themselves, convened for the purpose. On the other hand, the effect may be inverted. Men of factious tempers, of local prejudices, or of sinsiter designs, may, by intrigue, by corruption, or by other means, first obtain the suffrages, and then betray the interests of the people. The question resulting is, whether small or extensive republics are most favorable to the election of proper guardians of the public weal; and it is clearly decided in favor of the latter by two obvious considerations.

In the first place it is to be remarked that however small the republic may be the representatives must be raised to a certain number in order to guard against the cabals of a few; and that however large it may be they must be limited to a certain number in order to guard against the confusion of a multitude. Hence, the number of representatives in the two cases not being in proportion to that of the constituents, and being proportionally greatest in the small republic, it follows that if the proportion of fit characters be not less in the large than in the small republic, the former will present a greater option, and consequently a greater probability of a fit choice.

In the next place, as each representative will be chosen by a greater number of citizens in the large than in the small republic, it will be more difficult for unworthy candidates to practise with success the vicious arts by which elections are too often carried; and the suffrages of the people being more free, will be more likely to center on men who possess the most attractive merit and the most diffusive and established characters.

It must be confessed that in this, as in most other cases, there is a mean, on both sides of which inconveniences will be found to lie. By enlarging too much the number of electors, you render the representative too little acquainted with all their local circumstances and lesser interests; as by reducing it too much, you render him unduly attached to these, and too little fit to comprehend and pursue great and natural objects. The federal Constitution forms a happy combination in this respect; the great and aggregate interests being referred to the national, the local and particular to the State legislatures.

The other point of difference is the greater number of citizens and extent of territory which may be brought within the compass of republican than of democratic government; and it is this circumstance principally which renders factious combinations less to be dreaded in the former than in the latter. The smaller the society, the fewer probably will be the distinct parties and interests composing it; the fewer the distinct parties and interests, the more frequently will a majority be found of the same party; and the smaller the number of individuals composing a majority, and the smaller the compass within which they are placed, the more easily will they concert and execute their plans of oppression. Extend the sphere and you take in a greater variety of parties and interests; you make it less probable that a majority of the whole will have a common motive to invade the rights of other citizens; or if such a common motive exists, it will be more difficult for all who feel it to discover their own strength and to act in unison with each other. Besides other impediments, it may be remarked that, where there is a consciousness of unjust or dishonorable purposes, communication is always checked by distrust in proportion to the number whose concurrence is necessary.

Hence, it clearly appears that the same advantage which a republic has over a democracy in controlling the effects of faction is enjoyed by a large over a small republic—is enjoyed by the Union over the States composing it. Does this advantage consist in the substitution of representatives whose enlightened views and virtuous sentiments render them superior to local prejudices and to schemes of injustice? It will not be denied that the representation of the Union will be most likely to possess these requisite endowments. Does it consist in the greater security afforded by a greater variety of parties, against the event of any one party being able to outnumber and oppress the rest? In an equal degree does the increased variety of parties comprised within the Union increase this security. Does it, in fine, consist in the greater obstacles opposed to the concert and accomplishment of the secret wishes of an unjust and interested majority? Here again the extent of the Union gives it the most palpable advantage.

The influence of factious leaders may kindle a flame within their particular States but will be unable to spread a general conflagration through the other States. A religious sect may degenerate into a political faction in a part of the Confederacy; but the variety of sects dispersed over the entire face of it must secure the national councils against any danger from the source. A rage for paper money, for an abolition of debts, for an equal division of property, or for any other improper or wicked project, will be less apt to pervade the whole body of the Union than a particular member of it, in the same proportion as such a malady is more likely to taint a particular county or district than an entire State.

In the extent and proper structure of the Union, therefore, we behold a republican remedy for the diseases most incident to republican government. And according to the degree of pleasure and pride we feel in being republicans ought to be our zeal in cherishing the spirit and supporting the character of federalists.

Questions and Answers

1. Madison asserts that the unequal distribution of property creates factions (which he claims are not always bad). Based on your own experience, describe the effects of the unequal distribution of property and argue either that the distribution should remain the same, or that it should be changed for the good of society as a whole.

2. Write an argument in which you state and support the position that minorities (of various kinds) need to be protected. As Madison says, the majority "must be rendered unable . . . to carry into effect schemes of oppression." In your argument, use examples from your personal experience.

An Argument against Payment of Salaries to Executive Officers of the Federal Government

BENJAMIN FRANKLIN

Benjamin Franklin (1706–1790) was an early American writer, printer, scientist, and public official. He is perhaps best known for his Autobiography, *for* Poor Richard's Almanac, *and for flying a kite in a thunderstorm. He signed the Declaration of Independence and was the first U.S. Ambassador to France. He made the following speech on June 2, 1787, at the Constitutional Convention that wrote the U.S. Constitution.*

Sir, it is with reluctance that I rise to express a disapprobation of any one article of the plan, for which we are so much obliged to the honorable gentleman who laid it before us. From its first reading, I have borne a good will to it, and, in general, wished it success. In this particular of salaries to the executive branch, I happen to differ; and, as my opinion may appear new and chimerical, it is only from a persuasion that it is right, and from a sense of duty, that I hazard it. The Committee will judge of my reasons when they have heard them, and their judgment may possibly change mine. I think I see inconveniences in the appointment of salaries; I see none in refusing them, but on the contrary great advantages.

Sir, there are two passions which have a powerful influence in the affairs of men. These are *ambition* and *avarice:* the love of power and the love of money. Separately, each of these has great force in prompting men to action; but when united in view of the same object, they have in many minds the most violent effects. Place before the eyes of such men a post of *honor,* that shall at the same time be a place of *profit,* and they will move heaven and earth to obtain it. The vast number of such places it is that renders the British government so tempestuous. The struggles for them are the true source of all those factions which are perpetually dividing the nation, distracting its councils, hurrying it sometimes into fruitless and mischievous wars, and often compelling a submission to dishonorable terms of peace.

And of what kind are the men that will strive for this profitable pre-eminence, through all the bustle of cabal, the heat of contention, the infinite mutual abuse of parties, tearing to pieces the best of characters? It will not be the wise and moderate, the lovers of peace and good order, the men fittest for the trust. It will be the bold and violent, the men of strong passions and indefatigable activity in their selfish pursuits. These will thrust themselves into your government, and be your rulers. And these, too, will be mistaken in the expected happiness of their situation; for their vanquished competitors, of the same spirit, and from the same motives, will perpetually be endeavouring to distress their administration, thwart their measures, and render them odious to the people.

Besides these evils, sir, though we may set out in the beginning with moderate salaries, we shall find that such will not be of long continuance. Reasons will never be wanting for proposed augmentations, and there will always be a party for giving more to the rulers, that the rulers may be able in return to give more to them. Hence, as all history informs us, there has been in every state and kingdom a constant kind of warfare between the governing and the governed; the one striving to obtain more for its support, and the other to pay less. And this alone has occasioned great convulsions, actual civil wars, ending either in dethroning of the princes or enslaving of the people.

Generally, indeed, the ruling power carries its point, and we see the revenues of princes constantly increasing, and we see that they are never satisfied, but always in want of more. The more the people are discontented with the oppression of taxes, the greater need the prince has of money to distribute among his partisans, and pay the troops that are to suppress all resistance and enable him to plunder at pleasure. There is scarce a king in a hundred, who would not, if he could, follow the example of Pharaoh—get first all the people's money, then all their lands, and then make them and their children servants forever.

It will be said that we do not propose to establish kings. I know it. But there is a natural inclination in mankind to kingly government. It sometimes relieves them from aristocratic domination. They had rather have one tyrant than five hundred. It gives more of the appearance of equality among citizens; and that they like. I am apprehensive, therefore—perhaps too apprehensive—that the government of these states may in future times end in a monarchy. But this catastrophe, I think, may be long delayed, if in our proposed system we do not sow the seeds of contention, faction, and tumult, by making our posts of honor places of profit. If we do, I fear that, though we employ at first a number and not a single person, the number will in time be set aside; it will only nourish the foetus of a king (as the honorable gentleman from Virginia aptly expressed it), and a king will the sooner be set over us.

It may be imagined by some that this is an utopian idea, and that we can never find men to serve us in the executive department, without paying them well for their services. I conceive this to be a mistake. Some existing facts present themselves to me, which incline me to a contrary opinion. The High Sheriff of a county in England is an honorable office, but it is not a profitable one. It is rather expensive, and therefore not sought for. But yet it is executed, and well executed, and usually by some of the principal gentlemen of the country. In France, the office of Counsellor, or member of their judiciary parliaments, is more honorable. It is therefore purchased at a high price; there are indeed fees on the law proceedings, which are divided among them, but these fees do not amount to more than three per cent on the sum paid for the place. Therefore, as legal interest is there at five per cent, they in fact pay two per cent for being allowed to do the judiciary business of the nation, which is at the same time entirely exempt from the burden of paying them any salaries for their services. I do not, however, mean to recommend this as an eligible mode for our judiciary department. I only bring the instance to show that the pleasure of doing good and serving their country, and the respect such conduct entitles them to, are sufficient motives with some minds to give up a great portion of their time to the public, without the mean inducement of pecuniary satisfaction.

Another instance is that of a respectable society, who have made the experiment, and practiced it with success, now more than a hundred years. I mean the Quakers. It is an established rule with them that they are not to go to law, but in their controversies they must apply to their monthly, quarterly, and yearly meetings. Committees of these sit with patience to hear the parties, and spend much time in composing their differences. In doing this, they are supported by a sense of duty and the respect paid to usefulness. It is honorable to be so employed, but it was never made profitable by salaries, fees, or perquisites. And indeed, in all cases of public service, the less the profit the greater the honor.

To bring the matter nearer home, have we not seen the greatest and most important of our offices, that of General of our Armies, executed for eight years together, without the smallest salary, by a patriot whom I will not now offend by any other praise; and this, through fatigues and distresses, in common with the other brave men, his military friends and companions, and the constant anxieties peculiar to his station? And shall we doubt finding three or four men in all the United States, with public spirit enough to bear sitting in peaceful council, for perhaps an equal term, merely to preside over our civil concerns, and see that our laws are duly executed? Sir, I have a better opinion of our country. I think we shall never be without a sufficient number of wise and good men to undertake, and execute well and faithfully, the office in question.

Sir, the saving of the salaries, that may at first be proposed, is not an object with me. The subsequent mischiefs of proposing them are what I apprehend. And therefore it is that I move the amendment. If it is not seconded or accepted, I must be contented with the satisfaction of having delivered my opinion frankly, and done my duty.

Questions and Answers

1. Franklin makes his argument from the perspective of society and government. In more recent times, many people have argued that salaries for public service should *increase* in order to be competitive with those of the private sector and attract the best qualified person for each position. Reverse this ground. Argue that people should be willing to work in government for no salary (they might receive legitimate expenses) for the privilege of serving the public welfare.

2. Take a position that opposes Franklin's. Argue that the top executive officials in the federal government should be well compensated (perhaps receiving salaries equivalent to those paid to corporate executives). Provide any support you believe is necessary.

From Crito

PLATO

Plato, who lived in Athens from c. 428 to 348 B.C., *is widely regarded as
one of the greatest Greek philosophers, and perhaps as one of the
greatest thinkers in the history of Western Civilization. He was a
student of Socrates, and many of his works are in the form of dialogues between Socrates and a student. As the excerpt printed here
begins, Socrates has been condemned for misleading the youth of
Athens, and Crito has encouraged him to escape the sentence
because it is unjust. Note that, while the dialogue is supposedly
between Socrates and Crito, Socrates actually conducts an extended
conversation between himself and the laws of Athens.*

SOCRATES: . . . Ought a man to do what he admits to be right,
or ought he to betray the right?

CRITO: He ought to do what he thinks right.

SOCRATES: But if this is true, what is the application? In leaving
the prison against the will of the Athenians, do I wrong any? Or
rather do I not wrong those whom I ought least to wrong? Do I not
desert the principles which are acknowledged by us to be just—
what do you say?

CRITO: I cannot tell, Socrates; for I do not know.

SOCRATES: Then consider the matter in this way:—Imagine that
I am about to play truant (you may call the proceeding by any name
which you like), and the laws of the government come and interro-
gate me: "Tell us, Socrates," they say: "what are you about? Are you
not going by an act of yours to overturn us—the laws, and the whole
state, as far as in you lies? Do you imagine that a state can subsist
and not be overthrown, in which the decisions of law have no
power, but are set aside and trampled upon by individuals?" What
will be our answer, Crito, to these and the like words? Any one, and
especially a rhetorician, will have a good deal to say on behalf of the
law which requires a sentence to be carried out. He will argue that
this law should not be set aside; and shall we reply, "Yes, but the
state has injured us and given an unjust sentence." Suppose I say
that?

CRITO: Very good, Socrates.

SOCRATES: "And was that our agreement with you?" the law
would answer; "or were you to abide by the sentence of the state?"

Translated by Benjamin Jowett (3rd edition, 1982).

And if I were to express my astonishment at their words, the law would probably add: "Answer, Socrates, instead of opening your eyes—you are in the habit of asking and answering questions. Tell us,—What complaint have you to make against us which justifies you in attempting to destroy us and the state? In the first place did we not bring you into existence? Your father married your mother by our aid and begat you. Say whether you have any objection to urge against those of us who regulate marriage?" None, I should reply. "Or against those of us who after birth regulate the nurture and education of children, in which you were also trained? Were not the laws, which have the charge of education, right in commanding your father to train you in music and gymnastics?" Right, I should reply. "Well then, since you were brought into the world and nurtured and educated by us, can you deny in the first place that you are our child and slave, as your fathers were before you? And if this is true you are not on equal terms with us; nor can you think that you have a right to strike or revile or do any other evil to your father or your master, if you had one, because you have been struck and reviled by him, or received some other evil at his hands?—you would not say this? And because we think right to destroy you, do you think that you have any right to destroy us in return, and your country as far as in your lies? Will you, O professor of true virtue, pretend that you are justified in this? Has a philosopher like you failed to discover that our country is more to be valued and higher and holier far than mother or father or any ancestor, and more to be regarded in the eyes of the gods and of men of understanding? Also to be soothed, and gently and reverently entreated when angry, even more than a father, and either to be persuaded, or if not persuaded, to be obeyed? And when we are punished by her, whether with imprisonment or stripes, the punishment is to be endured in silence, and if she leads us to wounds or death in battle, thither we follow as is right; neither may any one yield or retreat or leave his rank, but whether in battle or in a court of law, or in any other place, he must do what his city and his country order him; or he must change their view of what is just: and if he may do no violence to his father or mother, much less may he do violence to his country." What answer shall we make to this, Crito? Do the laws speak truly, or do they not?

CRITO: I think that they do.

SOCRATES: Then the laws will say, "Consider, Socrates, if we are speaking truly that in your present attempt you are going to do us an injury. For, having brought you into the world, and nurtured and educated you, and given you and every other citizen a share in every good which we had to give, we further proclaim to any

Athenian by the liberty which we allow him, that if he does not like us when he has become of age and has seen the ways of the city, and made our acquaintance, he may go where he pleases and take his goods with him. None of us laws will forbid him or interfere with him. Any one who does not like us and the city, and who wants to emigrate to a colony or to any other city, may go where he likes, retaining his property. But he who has experience of the manner in which we order justice and administer the state, and still remains, has entered into an implied contract that he will do as we command him. And he who disobeys us is, as we maintain, thrice wrong; first, because in disobeying us he is disobeying his parents; secondly, because we are the authors of his education; thirdly, because he has made an agreement with us that he will duly obey our commands; and he neither obeys them nor convinces us that our commands are unjust; and we do not rudely impose them, but give him the alternative of obeying or convincing us;—that is what we offer, and he does neither.

"These are the sort of accusations to which, as we were saying, you, Socrates, will be exposed if you accomplish your intentions; you, above all other Athenians." Suppose now I ask, why I rather than anybody else? They will justly retort upon me that I above all other men have acknowledged the agreement. "There is clear proof," they will say, "Socrates, that we and the city were not displeasing to you. Of all Athenians you have been the most constant resident in the city, which, as you never leave, you may be supposed to love. For you never went out of the city either to see the games, except once when you went to the Isthmus, or to any other place unless when you were on military service; nor did you travel as other men do. Nor had you any curiosity to know other states or their laws: your affections did not go beyond us and our state; we were your special favourites, and you acquiesced in our government of you; and here in this city you begat your children, which is a proof of your satisfaction. Moreover, you might in the course of the trial, if you had liked, have fixed the penalty at banishment; the state which refuses to let you go now would have let you go then. But you pretended that you preferred death to exile, and that you were not unwilling to die. And now you have forgotten these fine sentiments, and pay no respect to us the laws, of whom you are the destroyer; and are doing only what a miserable slave would do, running away and turning your back upon the compacts and agreements which you made as a citizen. And first of all answer this very question: Are we right in saying that you agreed to be governed according to us in deed, and not in word only? Is that true or not?" How shall we answer, Crito? Must we not assent?

CRITO: We cannot help it, Socrates.

SOCRATES: Then will they not say: "You, Socrates, are breaking the covenants and agreements which you made with us at your leisure, not in any haste or under any compulsion or deception, but after you have had seventy years to think of them, during which time you were at liberty to leave the city, if we were not to your mind, or if our covenants appeared to you to be unfair. You had your choice, and might have gone either to Lacedaemon or Crete, both which states are often praised by you for their good government, or to some other Hellenic or foreign state. Whereas you, above all other Athenians, seemed to be so fond of the state, or, in other words, of us her laws (and who would care about a state which has no laws?), that you never stirred out of her; the halt, the blind, the maimed were not more stationary in her than you were. And now you run away and forsake your agreements. Not so, Socrates, if you will take our advice; do not make yourself ridiculous by escaping out of the city.

"For just consider, if you transgress and err in this sort of way, what good will you do either to yourself or to your friends? That your friends will be driven into exile and deprived of citizenship, or will lose their property, is tolerably certain; and you yourself, if you fly to one of the neighboring cities, as, for example, Thebes or Megara, both of which are well governed, will come to them as an enemy, Socrates, and their government will be against you, and all patriotic citizens will cast an evil eye upon you as a subverter of the laws, and you will confirm in the minds of the judges the justice of their own condemnation of you. For he who is a corrupter of the laws is more than likely to be a corrupter of the young and foolish portion of mankind. Will you then flee from well-ordered citizens and virtuous men? and is existence worth having on these terms? Or will you go to them without shame, and talk to them, Socrates? And what will you say to them? What you say here about virtue and justice and institutions and laws being the best things among men? Would that be decent of you? Surely not. But if you go away from well-governed states to Crito's friends in Thessaly, where there is great disorder and licence, they will be charmed to hear the tale of your escape from prison, set off with ludicrous particulars of the manner in which you were wrapped in a goatskin or some other disguise, and metamorphosed as the manner is of runaways; but will there be no one to remind you that in your old age you were not ashamed to violate the most sacred laws from a miserable desire of a little more life? Perhaps not, if you keep them in a good temper; but if they are out of temper you will hear many degrading things; you will live, but how?—as the flatterer of all men, and the servant of all men; and doing what?—eating and drinking in Thessaly, having gone abroad in order that you may get a dinner. And where will be your fine sentiments about justice and virtue? Say that you wish to live for the sake of your children—you want to bring them up and educate them—will you take them into Thessaly and deprive them of Athenian citizenship? Is this the benefit which you will confer upon them? Or are you under the impression that they will be better cared for and educated here if you are still alive, although absent from them; for your friends will take care of them? Do you fancy that if you are an inhabitant of Thessaly they will take care of them, and if you are an inhabitant of the other world that they will not take of them? Nay: but if they who call themselves friends are good for anything, they will—to be sure they will.

"Listen, then, Socrates, to us who have brought you up. Think not of life and children first, and of justice afterwards, but of justice first, that you may be justified before the princes of the world below. For neither will you nor any that belong to you be happier or holier or juster in this life, or happier in another, if you do as Crito bids. Now you depart in innocence, a sufferer and not a doer of evil; a victim, not of the laws of men. But if you go forth, returning evil for evil, and injury for injury, breaking the covenants and agreements which you have made with us, and wronging those whom you ought least of all to wrong, that is to say, yourself, your friends, your country, and us, we shall be angry with you while you live, and our brethren, the laws in the world below, will receive you as an enemy; for they will know that you have done your best to destroy us. Listen, then, to us and not to Crito."

This, dear Crito, is the voice which I seem to hear murmuring in my ears, like the sound of the flute in the ears of the mystic; that voice, I say, is humming in my ears, and prevents me from hearing any other. And I know that anything more which you may say will be vain. Yet speak, if you have anything to say.

CRITO: I have nothing to say, Socrates.

SOCRATES: Leave me then, Crito, to fulfill the will of God, and to follow whither he leads.

Questions and Answers

1. Socrates argues for obedience to the law, regardless of whether the sentence passed on him is just or unjust. This contrasts with the modern concept of civil disobedience, which is often used to justify disobeying laws that are thought to be unjust. Write an argument in which you respond to Socrates' arguments here and urge him to disobey an unjust law or sentence.

2. Envision a modern situation in which you might believe that obedience and allegiance to the state are more important than doing justice to an individual member of society. Describe the situation fully and then support your argument that the welfare of society at large is more important than doing justice to an individual. (If you wish, of course, you can argue the opposite.)

A Defense of the French Monarchy and Aristocracy

EDMUND BURKE

Edmund Burke (1729–1797) was an Irish politician, writer, and political philosopher who spent almost all of his entire adult life working in England. He worked as a private secretary to several politicians and aristocrats and was a member of Parliament for nearly thirty years. He became an advocate of freedom of speech and also an energetic defender of the traditional order against forces in the eighteenth-century Enlightenment that were undermining established religions and governments. He defended the American Revolution, believing that the colonists were attempting to preserve English values and liberties. He is best known for Reflections on the Revolution in France, *in which he condemns the French Revolution, primarily because he saw the principles of that revolution as a threat to English society.*

But admitting democracy not to have that inevitable tendency to party tyranny, which I suppose it to have, and admitting it to possess as much good in it when unmixed as I am sure it possesses when compounded with other forms, does monarchy, on its part, contain nothing at all to recommend it? I do not often quote Bolingbroke, nor have his works in general left any permanent impression on my mind. He is a presumptuous and artificial writer. But he has one observation which, in my opinion, is not without depth and solidity. He says that he prefers a monarchy to other governments because you can better ingraft any description of republic on a monarchy than anything of monarchy upon the republican forms. I think him perfectly in the right. The fact is so historically, and it agrees well with the speculation.

I know how easy a topic it is to dwell on the faults of departed greatness. By a revolution in the state, the fawning sycophant of yesterday is converted into the austere critic of the present hour. But steady, independent minds, when they have an object of so serious a concern to mankind as government under their contemplation, will disdain to assume the part of satirists and declaimers. They will judge of human institutions as they do of human characters. They will sort out the good from the evil, which is mixed in mortal institutions, as it is in mortal men.

Your government in France, though usually, and I think justly, reputed the best of the unqualified or ill-qualified monarchies, was still full of abuses. These abuses accumulated in a length of time, as they must accumulate in every monarchy not under the constant inspection of a popular representative. I am no stranger to the faults and defects of the subverted government of France, and I think I am not inclined by nature or policy to make a panegyric upon anything which is a just and natural object of censure. But the question is not now of the vices of that monarchy, but of its existence. It is, then, true that the French government was such as to be incapable or undeserving of reform, so that it was of absolute necessity that the whole fabric should be at once pulled down and the area cleared for the erection of a theoretic, experimental edifice in its place? All France was of a different opinion in the beginning of the year 1789. The instructions to the representatives to the States-General, from every district in that kingdom, were filled with projects for the reformation of that government without the remotest suggestion of a design to destroy it. Had such a design been ever insinuated, I believe there would have been but one voice, and that voice for rejecting it with scorn and horror. Men have been sometimes led by degrees, sometimes hurried, into things of which, if they could have seen the whole together, they never would have permitted the most remote approach. When those instructions were given, there was no question but that abuses existed, and that they demanded a reform; nor is there now. In the interval between the instructions and the Revolution things changed their shape; and in consequence of that change, the true question at present is, Whether those who would have reformed or those who have destroyed are in the right?

To hear some men speak of the late monarchy of France, you would imagine that they were talking of Persia bleeding under the ferocious sword of Tahmas Kouli Khân, or at least describing the barbarous anarchic despotism of Turkey, where the finest countries in the most genial climates in the world are wasted by peace more than any countries have been worried by war, where arts are unknown, where manufactures languish, where science is extinguished, where agriculture decays, where the human race itself melts away and perishes under the eye of the observer. Was this the case of France? I have no way of determining the question but by reference to facts. Facts do not support this resemblance. Along with much evil there is some good in monarchy itself, and some correction to its evil from religion, from laws, from manners, from opinions the French monarchy must have received, which rendered it (though by no means a free, and therefore by no means a good, constitution) a despotism rather in appearance than in reality.

Among the standards upon which the effects of government on any country are to be estimated, I must consider the state of its population as not the least certain. No country in which population flourishes and is in progressive improvement can be under a *very* mischievous government. About sixty years ago, the Intendants of the generalities of France made, with other matters, a report of the population of their several districts. I have not the books, which are very voluminous, by me, nor do I know where to procure them (I am obliged to speak by memory, and therefore the less positively), but I think the population of France was by them, even at that period, estimated at twenty-two millions of souls. At the end of the last century it had been generally calculated at eighteen. On either of these estimations, France was not ill peopled. M. Necker, who is an authority for his own time, at least equal to the Intendants for theirs, reckons, and upon apparently sure principles, the people of France in the year 1780 at twenty-four millions six hundred and seventy thousand. But was this the probable ultimate term under the old establishment? Dr. Price is of opinion that the growth of population in France was by no means at its *acmé* in that year. I certainly defer to Dr. Price's authority a good deal more in these speculations than I do in his general politics. This gentleman, taking ground on M. Necker's data, is very confident that since the period of that minister's calculation the French population has increased rapidly—so rapidly that in the year 1789 he will not consent to rate the people of that kingdom at a lower number than thirty millions. After abating much (and much I think ought to be abated) from the sanguine calculation of Dr. Price, I have no doubt that the population of France did increase considerably during this later period; but supposing that it increased to nothing more than will be sufficient to complete the twenty-four millions six hundred and seventy thousand to twenty-five millions, still a population of twenty-five millions, and that in an increasing progress, on a space of about twenty-seven thousand square leagues is immense. It is, for instance, a good deal more than the proportionable population of this island, or even than that of England, the best peopled part of the United Kingdom.

It is not universally true that France is a fertile country. Considerable tracts of it are barren and labor under other natural disadvantages. In the portions of that territory where things are more favorable, as far as I am able to discover, the numbers of the people correspond to the indulgence of nature. The Generality of Lisle (this I admit is the strongest example) upon an extent of four hundred and four leagues and a half, about ten years ago, contained seven hundred and thirty-four thousand six hundred souls, which is one thousand seven hundred and seventy-two inhabitants to each square league. The middle term for the rest of France is about nine hundred inhabitants to the same admeasurement.

I do not attribute this population to the deposed government, because I do not like to compliment the contrivances of men with what is due in a great degree to the bounty of Providence. But that decried government could not have obstructed, most probably it favored, the operation of those causes (whatever they were), whether of nature in the soil or habits of industry among the people, which has produced so large a number of the species throughout that whole kingdom and exhibited in some particular places such prodigies of population. I never will suppose that fabric of a state to be the worst of all political institutions which, by experience, is found to contain a principle favorable (however latent it may be) to the increase of mankind.

The wealth of a country is another, and no contemptible, standard by which we may judge whether, on the whole, a government be protecting or destructive. France far exceeds England in the multitude of her people, but I apprehend that her comparative wealth is much inferior to ours, that it is not so equal in the distribution, nor so ready in the circulation. I believe the difference in the form of the two governments to be amongst the causes of this advantage on the side of England. I speak of England, not of the whole British dominions, which, if compared with those of France, will, in some degree, weaken the comparative rate of wealth upon our side. But that wealth, which will not endure a comparison with the riches of England, may constitute a very respectable degree of opulence. M. Necker's book, published in 1785, contains an accurate and interesting collection of facts relative to public economy and to political arithmetic; and his speculations on the subject are in general wise and liberal. In that work he gives an idea of the state of France very remote from the portrait of a country whose government was a perfect grievance, an absolute evil, admitting no cure but through the violent and uncertain remedy of a total revolution. He affirms that from the year 1726 to the year 1784 there was coined at the mint of France, in the species of gold and silver, to the amount of about one hundred millions of pounds sterling.

It is impossible that M. Necker should be mistaken in the amount of the bullion which has been coined in the mint. It is a matter of official record. The reasonings of this able financier, concerning the quantity of gold and silver which remained for circulation, when he wrote in 1785, that is, about four years before the deposition and imprisonment of the French king, are not of equal certainty, but they are laid on grounds so apparently solid that it is not easy to refuse a considerable degree of assent to his calculation. He calculates the *numeraire,* or what we call "specie," then actually existing in France at about eighty-eight millions of the same English money. A great accumulation of wealth for one country, large as that country is! M. Necker was so far from considering this influx of wealth as likely to cease, when he wrote in 1785, that he presumes upon a future annual increase of two per cent upon the money brought into France during the periods from which he computed.

Some adequate cause must have originally introduced all the money coined at its mint into that kingdom, and some cause as operative must have kept at home, or returned into its bosom, such a vast flood of treasure as M. Necker calculates to remain for domestic circulation. Suppose any reasonable deductions from M. Necker's computation, the remainder must still amount to an immense sum. Causes thus powerful to acquire, and to retain, cannot be found in discouraged industry, insecure property, and a positively destructive government. Indeed, when I consider the face of the kingdom of France, the multitude and opulence of her cities, the useful magnificence of her spacious high roads and bridges, the opportunity of her artificial canals and navigations opening the conveniences of maritime communication through a solid continent of so immense an extent; when I turn my eyes to the stupendous works of her ports and harbors, and to her whole naval apparatus, whether for war or trade; when I bring before my view the number of her fortifications, constructed with so bold and masterly a skill and made and maintained at so prodigious a charge, presenting an armed front and impenetrable barrier to her enemies upon every side; when I recollect how very small a part of that extensive region is without cultivation, and to what complete perfection the culture of many of the best productions of the earth have been brought in France; when I reflect on the excellence of her manufactures and fabrics, second to none but ours, and in some particulars not second; when I contemplate the grand foundations of charity, public and private; when I survey the state of all the arts that beautify and polish life; when I reckon the men she has bred for extending her fame in war, her able statesmen, the multitude of her profound lawyers and theologians, her philosophers, her critics, her historians and antiquaries, her poets and her orators, sacred and profane—I behold in all this something which awes and commands the imagination, which checks the mind on the brink of precipitate and indiscriminate censure, and which demands that we should very seriously examine what and how great are the latent vices that could authorize us at once to level so spacious a fabric with the ground. I do not recognize in this view of things the despotism of Turkey. Nor do I discern the character of a government that has been, on the whole, so oppressive or so corrupt or so negligent as to be utterly unfit *for all reformation.* I must think such a government well deserved to have its excellences heightened, its faults corrected, and its capacities improved into a British constitution.

Whoever has examined into the proceedings of that deposed government for several years back cannot fail to have observed, amidst the inconstancy and fluctuation natural to courts, an earnest endeavor toward the prosperity and improvement of the country; he must admit that it had long been employed, in some instances wholly to remove, in many considerably to correct, the abusive practices and usages that had prevailed in the state, and that even the unlimited power of the sovereign over the persons of his subjects, inconsistent, as undoubtedly it was, with law and liberty, had yet been every day growing more mitigated in the exercise. So far from refusing itself to reformation, that government was open, with a censurable degree of facility, to all sorts of projects and projectors on the subject. Rather too much countenance was given to the spirit of innovation, which soon was turned against those who fostered it, and ended in their ruin. It is but cold, and no very flattering, justice to that fallen monarchy to say that, for many years, it trespassed more by levity and want of judgment in several of its schemes than from any defect in diligence or in public spirit. To compare the government of France for the last fifteen or sixteen years with wise and well-constituted establishments during that, or during any period, is not to act with fairness. But if in point of prodigality in the expenditure of money, or in point of rigor in the exercise of power, it be compared with any of the former reigns, I believe candid judges will give little credit to the good intentions of those who dwell perpetually on the donations to favorites, or on the expenses of the court, or on the horrors of the Bastille in the reign of Louis the Sixteenth.

Questions and Answers

1. Burke appears to argue that the quality of a country's government can be measured by the size of its population, its national wealth, and the improvement of its culture. Apply Burke's criteria to a twentieth-century country or government in order to support or oppose his conclusions. (For example, you might argue that Nazi Germany met Burke's criteria, or that Mussolini's government must have been a good one because the trains ran on time.)

2. What are reasonable criteria for establishing whether a government is a good one? Devise criteria that you think will measure the quality of governance. Then write an argument in which you apply your criteria to an organization to which you belong, or to a government you are familiar with.

Areopagitica

JOHN MILTON

John Milton (1608–1674) was an English poet and scholar. He is best known for his long, epic poem Paradise Lost, *in which he portrays mankind's fall from grace in the Garden of Eden. In addition to his substantial body of poetry, Milton wrote political and religious tracts about such subjects as divorce and freedom of the press. In "Areopagitica" he argues that books should be permitted to be published without a special license from Parliament.*

They who to states and governors of the Commonwealth direct their speech, High Court of Parliament, or, wanting such access in a private condition, write that which they foresee may advance the public good; I suppose them, as at the beginning of no mean endeavor, not a little altered and moved inwardly in their minds: some with doubt of what will be the success, others with fear of what will be the censure; some with hope, others with confidence of what they have to speak. And me perhaps each of these dispositions, as the subject was whereon I entered, may have at other times variously affected; and likely might in these foremost expressions now also disclose which of them swayed most, but that the very attempt of this address thus made, and the thought of whom it hath recourse to, hath got the power within me to a passion, far more welcome than incidental to a preface.

Which though I stay not to confess ere any ask, I shall be blameless, if it be no other than the joy and gratulation which it brings to all who wish and promote their country's liberty; whereof this whole discourse proposed will be a certain testimony, if not a trophy. For this is not the liberty which we can hope, that no grievance ever should arise in the Commonwealth—that let no man in this world expect; but when complaints are freely heard, deeply considered, and speedily reformed, then is the utmost bound of civil liberty attained that wise men look for. To which, if I now manifest by the very sound of this which I shall utter, that we are already in good part arrived, and yet from such a steep disadvantage of tyranny and superstition grounded into our principles as was beyond the manhood of a Roman recovery; it will be attributed first, as is most due, to the strong assistance of God our deliverer, next, to your faithful guidance and undaunted wisdom, Lords and Commons of England.

Neither is it in God's esteem the diminution of his glory, when honorable things are spoken of good men and worthy magistrates; which if I now first should begin to do, after so fair a progress of your laudable deeds and such a long obligement upon the whole realm to your indefatigable virtues, I might by justly reckoned among the tardiest and the unwillingest of them that praise ye.

Nevertheless, there being three principal things without which all praising is but courtship and flattery: first, when that only is praised which is solidly worth praise; next, when greatest likelihoods are brought that such things are truly and really in those persons to whom they are ascribed; the other, when he who praises, by showing that such his actual persuasion is of whom he writes, can demonstrate that he flatters not; the former two of these I have heretofore endeavored, rescuing the employment from him who went about to impair your merits with a trivial and malignant encomium; the latter, as belonging chiefly to mine own acquittal, that whom I so extolled I did not flatter, hath been reserved opportunely to this occasion. For he who freely magnifies what hath been nobly done and fears not to declare as freely what might be done better, gives ye the best covenant of his fidelity; and that his loyalest affection and his hope waits on your proceedings. His highest praising is not flattery, and his plainest advice is a kind of praising; for though I should affirm and hold by argument that it would fare better with truth, with learning, and the Commonwealth, if one of your published orders, which I should name, were called in; yet at the same time it could not but much redound to the luster of your mild and equal government, whenas private persons are hereby animated to think ye better pleased with public advice than other statists have been delighted heretofore with public flattery. And men will then see what difference there is between the magnanimity of a triennial parliament and that jealous haughtiness of prelates and cabin counsellors that usurped of late, whenas they shall observe ye in the midst of your victories and successes more gently brooking written exceptions against a voted order than other courts, which had produced nothing worth memory but the weak ostentation of wealth, would have endured the least signified dislike at any sudden proclamation.

If I should thus far presume upon the meek demeanor of your civil and gentle greatness, Lords and Commons, as what your published order hath directly said, that to gainsay, I might defend myself with ease, if any should accuse me of being new or insolent, did they but know how much better I find ye esteem it to imitate the old and elegant humanity of Greece than the barbaric pride of a Hunnish and Norwegian stateliness. And out of those ages, to whose polite wisdom and letters we owe that we are not yet Goths and Jutlanders, I could name him who from his private house wrote that discourse to the parliament of Athens that persuades them to change the form of democracy which was then established. Such honor was done in those days to men who professed the study of wisdom and eloquence, not only in their own country, but in other lands, that cities and seignories heard them gladly and with great respect, if they had aught in public to admonish the state. Thus did Dion Prusaeus, a stranger and a private orator, counsel the Rhodians against a former edict; and I abound with other like examples, which to set here would be superfluous. But if from the industry of a life wholly dedicated to studious labors and those natural endowments haply not the worst for two and fifty degrees of northern latitude, so much must be derogated as to count me not equal to any of those who had this privilege, I would obtain to be thought not so inferior as yourselves are superior to the most of them who received their counsel; and how far you excel them, be assured, Lords and Commons, there can no greater testimony appear than when your prudent spirit acknowledges and obeys the voice of reason from what quarter soever it be heard speaking; and renders ye as willing to repeal any act of your own setting forth, as any set forth by your predecessors.

If ye be thus resolved, as it were injury to think ye were not, I know not what should withhold me from presenting ye with a fit instance wherein to show both that love of truth which ye eminently profess, and that uprightness of your judgment which is not wont to be partial to yourselves; by judging over again that Order which ye have ordained *to regulate Printing: that no book, pamphlet, or paper shall be henceforth printed, unless the same be first approved and licensed by such*, or at least one of such as shall be thereto appointed. For that part which preserves justly every man's copy to himself, or provides for the poor, I touch not, only wish they be not made pretenses to abuse and persecute honest and painful men, who offend not in either of these particulars. But that other cause of licensing books, which we thought had died with his brother *quadragesimal* and *matrimonial* when the prelates expired, I shall now attend with such a homily as shall lay before ye, first, the inventors of it to be those whom ye will be loth to own; next, what is to be thought in general of reading, whatever sort the books be; and that this Order avails nothing to the suppressing of scandalous, seditious, and libellous books, which were mainly intended to be suppressed. Last, that it will be primely to the discouragement of all learning and the stop of truth, not only by disexercising and blunting our abilities in what we know already, but by hindering and cropping the discovery that might be yet further made both in religious and civil wisdom.

I deny not but that it is of greatest concernment in the church and commonwealth to have a vigilant eye how books demean themselves as well as men; and thereafter to confine, imprison, and do sharpest justice on them as malefactors. For books are not absolutely dead things, but do contain a potency of life in them to be as active as that soul was whose progeny they are; nay, they do preserve as in a vial the purest efficacy and extraction of that living intellect that bred them. I know they are as lively and as vigorously productive as those fabulous dragon's teeth; and being sown up and down, may chance to spring up armed men. And yet, on the other hand, unless wariness be used, as good almost kill a man as kill a good book; who kills a man kills a reasonable creature, God's image; but he who destroys a good book, kills reason itself, kills the image of God, as it were, in the eye. Many a man lives a burden to the earth; but a good book is the precious lifeblood of a master spirit, embalmed and treasured up on purpose to a life beyond life. 'Tis true, no age can restore a life, whereof perhaps there is no great loss; and revolutions of ages do not oft recover the loss of a rejected truth, for the want of which whole nations fare the worse. We should be wary, therefore, what persecution we raise against the living labors of public men, how we spill that seasoned life of man preserved and stored up in books; since we see a kind of homicide may be thus committed, sometimes a martyrdom; and if it extend to the whole impression, a kind of massacre, whereof the execution ends not in the slaying of an elemental life, but strikes at that ethereal and fifth essence, the breath of reason itself, slays an immortality rather than a life. But lest I should be condemned of introducing license, while I oppose licensing, I refuse not the pains to be so much historical as will serve to show what hath been done by ancient and famous commonwealths against this disorder, till the very time that this project of licensing crept out of the Inquisition, was caught up by our prelates, and hath caught some of our presbyters.

In Athens, where books and wits were ever busier than in any other part of Greece, I find but only two sorts of writings which the magistrate cared to take notice of; those either blasphemous and atheistical, or libellous. Thus the books of Protagoras were by the judges of Areopagus commanded to be burnt, and himself banished the territory for a discourse begun with his confessing not to know whether there were gods or whether not. And against defaming, it was decreed that none should be traduced by name, as was the manner of Vetus Comoedia, whereby we may guess how they censured libelling; and this course was quick enough, as Cicero writes, to quell both the desperate wits of other atheists and the open way of defaming, as the event showed. Of other sects and opinions, though tending to voluptuousness and the denying of divine providence, they took no heed. Therefore we do not read that either Epicurus, or that libertine school of Cyrene, or what the Cynic impudence uttered, was ever questioned by the laws. Neither is it recorded that the writings of those old comedians were suppressed, though the acting of them were forbid; and that Plato commended the reading of Aristophanes, the loosest of them all, to his royal scholar Dionysius, is commonly known and may be excused, if holy Chrysostom, as is reported, nightly studied the same author and had the art to cleanse a scurrilous vehemence into the style of a rousing sermon.

That other leading city of Greece, Lacedaemon, considering that Lycurgus their lawgiver was so addicted to elegant learning as to have been the first that brought out of Ionia the scattered works of Homer, and sent the poet Thales from Crete to prepare and mollify the Spartan surliness with his smooth songs and odes, the better to plant among them law and civility, it is to be wondered how museless and unbookish they were, minding nought but the feats of war. There needed no licensing of books among them, for they disliked all but their own laconic apothegms and took a slight occasion to chase Archilochus out of their city, perhaps for composing in a higher strain than their own soldierly ballads and roundels could reach to; or if it were for his broad verses, they were not therein so cautious, but they were as dissolute in their promiscuous conversing; whence Euripides affirms in *Andromache* that their women were all unchaste. Thus much may give us light after what sort books were prohibited among the Greeks.

The Romans also, for many ages trained up only to a military roughness, resembling most the Lacedaemonian guise, knew of learning little but what their twelve tables and the Pontific College with their augers and flamens taught them in religion and law, so unacquainted with other learning that when Carneades and Critolaus, with the Stoic Diogenes coming ambassadors to Rome, took thereby occasion to give the city a taste of their philosophy, they were suspected for seducers by no less a man than Cato the Censor, who moved it in the senate to dismiss them speedily, and to banish all such Attic babblers out of Italy. But Scipio and others of the noblest senators withstood him and his old Sabine austerity; honored and admired the men; and the censor himself at last, in his old age, fell to the study of that whereof before he was so scrupulous. And yet at the same time, Naevius and Plautus, the first Latin comedians, had filled the city with all the borrowed scenes of Menander and Philemon.

Then began to be considered there also what was to be done to libellous books and authors; for Naevius was quickly cast into prison for his unbridled pen and released by the tribunes upon his recantation; we read also that libels were burnt, and the makers punished by Augustus. The like severity, no doubt, was used, if aught were impiously written against their esteemed gods. Except in these two points, how the world went in books, the magistrate kept no reckoning. And therefore Lucretius without impeachment versifies his Epicurism to Memmius, and had the honor to be set forth the second time by Cicero, so great a father of the commonwealth; although himself disputes against that opinion in his own writings. Nor was the satirical sharpness or naked plainness of Lucilius, or Catullus, or Flaccus, by any order prohibited.

And for matters of state, the story of Titus Livius, though it extolled that part which Pompey held, was not therefore suppressed by Octavius Caesar of the other faction. But that Naso was by him banished in his old age for the wanton poems of his youth, was but a mere covert of state over some secret cause: and besides, the books were neither banished nor called in. From hence we shall meet with little else but tyranny in the Roman empire, that we may not marvel, if not so often bad as good books were silenced. I shall therefore deem to have been large enough in producing what among the ancients was punishable to write, save only which, all other arguments were free to treat on.

By this time the emperors were become Christians, whose discipline in this point I do not find to have been more severe than what was formerly in practice. The books of those whom they took to be grand heretics were examined, refuted, and condemned in the general councils; and not till then were prohibited, or burnt, by authority of the emperor. As for the writings of heathen authors, unless they were plain invectives against Christianity, as those of Porphyrius and Proclus, they met with no interdict that can be cited till about the year 400 in a Carthaginian Council wherein bishops themselves were forbid to read the books of Gentiles, but heresies they might read: while others long before them, on the contrary, scrupled more the books of heretics than of Gentiles. And that the primitive councils and bishops were wont only to declare what books were not commendable, passing no further, but leaving it to each one's conscience to read or to lay by, till after the year 800, is observed already by Padre Paolo, the great unmasker of the Trentine Council. After which time the Popes of Rome, engrossing what they pleased of political rule into their own hands, extended their dominion over men's eyes as they had before over their judgments, burning and prohibiting to be read what they fancied not; yet sparing in their censures, and the books not many which they so dealt with; till Martin V, by his bull, not only prohibited, but was the first that excommunicated the reading of heretical books; for about that time Wycliffe and Huss growing terrible, were they who first drove the papal court to a stricter policy of prohibiting. Which course Leo X and his successors followed, until the Council of Trent and the Spanish Inquisition, engendering together, brought forth, or perfected those catalogs and expurging indexes that rake through the entrails of many an old good author with a violation worse than any could be offered to his tomb.

Nor did they stay in matters heretical but any subject that was not to their palate they either condemned in a prohibition, or had it strait into the new purgatory of an Index. To fill up the measure of encroachment, their last invention was to ordain that no book, pamphlet, or paper should be printed (as if St. Peter had bequeathed them the keys of the press also out of paradise) unless it were approved and licensed under the hands of two or three glutton friars. For example:

> Let the Chancellor Cini be pleased to see if in this present work be contained aught that may withstand the printing.
> Vincent Rabbatta, Vicar of Florence.
>
> I have seen this present work, and find nothing athwart the Catholic faith and good manners: in witness whereof I have given, &c.
> Nicolo Cini, Chancellor of Florence.
>
> Attending the present relation, it is allowed that this present work of Davanzati may be printed.
> Vincent Rabatta, &c.

It may be printed, July 15.
Friar Simon Mompei d'Amelia,
Chancellor of the holy office of Florence.

Sure they have a conceit, if he of the bottomless pit had not long since broke prison, that this quadruple exorcism would bar him down. I fear their next design will be to get into their custody the licensing of that which they say Claudius intended but went not through with. Vouchsafe to see another of their forms, the Roman stamp:

Imprimatur, If it seem good to the reverend Master of the holy Palace,
Belcastro, Vicegerent.
Imprimatur,
Friar Nicolo Rodolphi, Master of the holy Palace.

Sometimes five Imprimaturs are seen together, dialoguewise, in the piazza of one titlepage, complimenting and ducking each to other with their shaven references, whether the author, who stands by in perplexity at the foot of his epistle, shall to the press or to the sponge. These are the pretty responsories, these are the dear antiphonies that so bewitched of late our prelates and their chaplains with the goodly echo they made; and besotted us to the gay imitation of a lordly Imprimatur, one from Lambeth House, another from the west end of Paul's, so apishly Romanizing that the word of command still was set down in Latin; as if the learned grammatical pen that wrote it would cast no ink without Latin; or perhaps, as they thought, because no vulgar tongue was worthy to express the pure conceit of an Imprimatur; but rather, as I hope, for that our English, the language of men ever famous and foremost in the achievements of liberty, will not easily find servile letters enough to spell such a dictatory presumption English.

And thus ye have the inventors and the original of book-licensing ripped up and drawn as lineally as any pedigree. We have it not, that can be heard of, from any ancient state, or polity, or church, nor by any statute left us by our ancestors elder or later; nor from the modern custom of any reformed city or church abroad; but from the most antichristian council and the most tyrannous inquisition that ever inquired.

Till then books were ever as freely admitted into the world as any other birth; the issue of the brain was no more stifled than the issue of the womb; no envious Juno sat cross-legged over the nativity of any man's intellectual offspring; but if it proved a monster, who denies but that it was justly burnt, or sunk into the sea? But that a book, in worse condition than a peccant soul, should be to stand before a jury ere it be born to the world and undergo yet in darkness the judgment of Rhadamanth and his colleagues, ere it can pass the ferry backward into light, was never heard before, till that mysterious iniquity, provoked and troubled at the first entrance of reformation, sought out new limbos and new hells wherein they might include our books also within the number of their damned. And this was the rare morsel so officiously snatched up, and so ill-favoredly imitated by our inquisiturient bishops and the attendant minorites, their chaplains. That ye like not now these most certain authors of this licensing order, and that all sinister intention was far distant from your thoughts, when ye were importuned the passing it, all men who know the integrity of your actions, and how ye honor truth, will clear ye readily.

But some will say, what though the inventors were bad, the thing for all that may be good. It may so; yet if that thing be no such deep invention, but obvious and easy for any man to light on, and yet best and wisest commonwealths through all ages and occasions have forborne to use it, and falsest seducers and oppressors of men were the first who took it up, and to no other purpose but to obstruct and hinder the first approach of reformation; I am of those who believe it will be a harder alchemy than Lullius ever knew to sublimate any good use out of such an invention. Yet this only is what I request to gain from this reason, that it may be held a dangerous and suspicious fruit, as certainly it deserves, for the tree that bore it, until I can dissect one by one the properties it has. But I have first to finish, as was propounded, what is to be thought in general of reading books, whatever sort they may be, and whether be more the benefit or the harm that thence proceeds?

Not to insist upon the examples of Moses, Daniel, and Paul, who were skillful in all the learning of the Egyptians, Chaldeans, and Greeks, which could not probably be without reading their books of all sorts: in Paul especially, who thought it no defilement to insert into holy scripture the sentences of three Greek poets, and one of them a tragedian; the question was notwithstanding sometimes controverted among the primitive doctors, but with great odds on that side which affirmed it both lawful and profitable, as was then evidently perceived when Julian the Apostate and subtlest enemy to our faith, made a decree forbidding Christians the study of heathen learning; for, said he, they wound us with our own weapons, and with our own arts and sciences they overcome us. And indeed the Christians were put so to their shifts by this crafty means, and so much in danger to decline into all ignorance, that the two Apollinarii were fain, as a man may say, to coin all the seven liberal sciences out of the Bible, reducing it into divers forms of orations, poems, dialogues, even to the calculating of a new Christian grammar. But, saith the historian Socrates, the providence of God provided better than the industry of Apollinarius and his son, by taking away that illiterate law with the life of him who devised it.

So great an injury they then held it to be deprived of Hellenic learning; and thought it a persecution more undermining, and secretly decaying the Church, than the open cruelty of Decius or Diocletian. And perhaps it was the same politic drift that the devil whipped St. Jerome in a Lenten dream, for reading Cicero; or else it was a phantasm bred by the fever which had then seized him. For had an angel been his discipliner, unless it were for dwelling too much upon Ciceronianisms, and had chastised the reading, not the vanity, it had been plainly partial; first to correct him for grave Cicero, and not for scurril Plautus, whom he confesses to have been reading not long before; next to correct him only, and let so many more ancient fathers wax old in those pleasant and florid studies without the lash of such a tutoring apparition; insomuch that Basil teaches how some good use may be made of *Margites,* a sportful poem not now extant writ by Homer; and why not then of *Morgante,* an Italian romance much to the same purpose?

But if it be agreed we shall be tried by visions, there is a vision recorded by Eusebius, far ancienter than this tale of Jerome to the nun Eustochium, and, besides, has nothing of a fever in it. Dionysius Alexandrinus was, about the year 240, a person of great name in the church for piety and learning, who had wont to avail himself much against heretics by being conversant in their books; until a certain presbyter laid it scrupulously to his conscience, how he durst venture himself among those defiling volumes. The worthy man, loth to give offense, fell into a new debate with himself what was to be thought; when suddenly a vision sent from God (it is his own *Epistle* that so avers it) confirmed him in these words: "Read any books whatever come to thy hands, for thou art sufficient both to judge aright and to examine each matter." To this revelation he assented the sooner, as he confesses, because it was answerable to that of the apostle to the Thessalonians: "Prove all things, hold fast that which is good."

And he might have added another remarkable saying of the same author: "To the pure, all things are pure"; not only meats and drinks, but all kinds of knowledge whether of good or evil; the knowledge cannot defile, nor consequently the books, if the will and conscience be not defiled. For books are as meats and viands are—some of good, some of evil substance, and yet God in that unapocryphal vision said without exception, "Rise, Peter, kill and eat," leaving the choice to each man's discretion. Wholesome meats to a vitiated stomach differ little or nothing from unwholesome, and best books to a naughty mind are not unappliable to occasions of evil. Bad meats will scarce breed good nourishment in the healthiest concoction; but herein the difference is of bad books, that they to a discreet and judicious reader serve in many respects to discover, to confute, to forewarn, and to illustrate.

Whereof what better witness can ye expect I should produce than one of your own now sitting in parliament, the chief of learned men reputed in this land, Mr. Selden; whose volume of natural and national laws proves, not only by great authorities brought together, but by exquisite reasons and theorems almost mathematically demonstrative, that all opinions, yea errors, known, read, and collated, are of main service and assistance toward the speedy attainment of what is truest.

I conceive, therefore, that when God did enlarge the universal diet of man's body, saving ever the rules of temperance, he then also, as before, left arbitrary the dieting and repasting of our minds; as wherein every mature man might have to exercise his own leading capacity. How great a virtue is temperance, how much of moment through the whole life of man! Yet God commits the managing so great a trust, without particular law or prescription, wholly to the demeanor of every grown man. And therefore, when he himself tabled the Jews from heaven, that omer which was every man's daily portion of manna, is computed to have been more than might have well sufficed for the heartiest feeder thrice as many meals. For those actions which enter into a man, rather than issue out of him, and therefore defile not, God uses not to captivate under a perpetual childhood of prescription, but trusts him with the gift of reason to be his own chooser; there were but little work left for preaching, if law and compulsion should grow so fast upon those things which heretofore were governed only by exhortation. Solomon informs us that much reading is a weariness to the flesh; but neither he nor other inspired author tells us that such or such reading is unlawful; yet certainly had God thought good to limit us herein, it had been much more expedient to have told us what was unlawful than what was wearisome.

As for the burning of those Ephesian books by St. Paul's converts; 'tis replied the books were magic, the Syriac so renders them. It was a private act, a voluntary act, and leaves us to a voluntary imitation: the men in remorse burnt those books which were their own; the magistrate by this example is not appointed; these men practised the books, another might perhaps have read them in some sort usefully.

Good and evil we know in the field of this world grow up together almost inseparably; and the knowledge of good is so involved and interwoven with the knowledge of evil, and in so many cunning resemblances hardly to be discerned, that those confused seeds which were imposed on Psyche as an incessant labor to cull out and sort asunder, were not more intermixed. It was from out the rind of one apple tasted, that the knowledge of good and evil, as two twins cleaving together, leaped forth into the world. And perhaps that is that doom which Adam fell into of knowing good and evil, that is to say, of knowing good by evil.

As therefore the state of man now is, what wisdom can there be to choose, what continence to forbear without the knowledge of evil? He that can apprehend and consider vice with all her baits and seeming pleasures, and yet abstain, and yet distinguish, and yet prefer that which is truly better, he is the true warfaring Christian. I cannot praise a fugitive and cloistered virtue, unexercised and unbreathed, that never sallies out and sees her adversary, but slinks out of the race where that immortal garland is to be run for, not without dust and heat. Assuredly we bring not innocence into the world, we bring impurity much rather: that which purifies us is trial, and trial is by what is contrary. That virtue therefore which is but a youngling in the contemplation of evil, and knows not the utmost that vice promises to her followers, and rejects it, is but a blank virtue, not a pure; her whiteness is but an excremental whiteness; which was the reason why our sage and serious poet Spenser, whom I dare be known to think a better teacher than Scotus or , Aquinas, describing true temperance under the person of Guyon, brings him in with her palmer through the cave of Mammon and the bower of earthly bliss, that he might see and know, and yet abstain.

Since therefore, the knowledge and survey of vice is in this world so necessary to the constituting of human virtue, and the scanning of error to the confirmation of truth, how can we more safely and with less danger scout into the regions of sin and falsity than by reading all manner of tractates and hearing all manner of reason? And this is the benefit which may be had of books promiscuously read.

But of the harm that may result hence, three kinds are usually reckoned. First is feared the infection that may spread; but then all human learning and controversy in religious points must remove out of the world, yea the Bible itself; for that ofttimes relates blasphemy not nicely, it describes the carnal sense of wicked men not unelegantly, it brings in holiest men passionately murmuring against providence through all the arguments of Epicurus; in other great disputes it answers dubiously and darkly to the common reader; and ask a Talmudist what ails the modesty of his marginal

Keri, that Moses and all the prophets cannot persuade him to pronounce the textual Chetiv. For these causes we all know the Bible itself put by the papist into the first rank of prohibited books. The ancienter fathers must be next removed, as Clement of Alexandria, and that Eusebian book of Evangelic preparation transmitting our ears through a hoard of heathenish obscenities to receive the Gospel. Who finds not that Irenaeus, Epiphanius, Jerome, and others discover more heresies than they will confute, and that oft for heresy which is the truer opinion?

Nor boots it to say for these and all the heathen writers of greatest infection, if it must be thought so, with whom is bound up the life of human learning, that they writ in an unknown tongue, so long as we are sure those languages are known as well to the worst of men, who are both most able and most diligent to instil the poison they suck, first into the courts of princes, acquainting them with the choicest delights and criticisms of sin. As perhaps did that Petronius whom Nero called his Arbiter, the master of his revels; and that notorious ribald of Arezzo, dreaded, and yet dear to the Italian courtiers. I name not him for posterity's sake, whom Harry VIII named in merriment his Vicar of hell. By which compendious way all the contagion that foreign books can infuse, will find a passage to the people far easier and shorter than an Indian voyage, though it could be sailed either by the north of Cathay eastward, or of Canada westward, while our Spanish licensing gags the English press never so severely.

But, on the other side, that infection which is from books of controversy in religion, is more doubtful and dangerous to the learned than to the ignorant; and yet those books must be permitted untouched by the licenser. It will be hard to instance where any ignorant man hath been ever seduced by papistical book in English, unless it were commended and expounded to him by some of that clergy; and indeed all such tractates, whether false or true, are as the prophecy of Isaiah was to the eunuch, not to be "understood without a guide." But of our priests and doctors how many have been corrupted by studying the comments of Jesuits and Sorbonists, and how fast they could transfuse that corruption into that people, our experience is both late and sad. It is not forgot, since the acute and distinct Arminius was perverted merely by the perusing of a nameless discourse written at Delft, which at first he took in hand to confute.

Seeing, therefore, that those books, and those in great abundance which are likeliest to taint both life and doctrine, cannot be suppressed without the fall of learning, and of all ability in disputation; and that these books of either sort are most and soonest catching to the learned, from whom to the common people whatever is heretical or dissolute may quickly be conveyed; and that evil manners are as perfectly learned without books as a thousand other ways which cannot be stopped; and evil doctrine not with books can propagate, except a teacher guide, which he might also do without writing, and so beyond prohibiting: I am not able to unfold how this cautelous enterprise of licensing can be exempted from the number of vain and impossible attempts. And he who were pleasantly disposed, could not well avoid to liken it to the exploit of that gallant man who thought to pound up the crows by shutting his park gate.

Besides another inconvenience, if learned men be the first receivers out of books and dispreaders both of vice and error, how shall the licensers themselves be confided in, unless we can confer upon them, or they assume to themselves above all others in the land, the grace of infallibility and uncorruptedness? And again, if it be true that a wise man, like a good refiner, can gather gold out of the drossiest volume, and that a fool will be a fool with the best book, yea or without book, there is no reason that we should deprive a wise man of any advantage to his wisdom, while we seek to restrain from a fool that which being restrained will be no hindrance to his folly. For if there should be so much exactness always used to keep that from him which is unfit for his reading, we should, in the judgment of Aristotle not only, but of Solomon and of our Savior, not vouchsafe him good precepts, and by consequence not willingly admit him to good books; as being certain that a wise man will make better use of an idle pamphlet than a fool will do of sacred scripture.

'Tis next alleged we must not expose ourselves to temptations without necessity, and, next to that, not employ our time in vain things. To both these objections one answer will serve, out of the grounds already laid; that to all men such books are not temptations nor vanities, but useful drugs and materials wherewith to temper and compose effective and strong medicines which man's life cannot want. The rest, as children and childish men, who have not the art to qualify and prepare these working minerals, well may be exhorted to forbear, but hindered forcibly they cannot be by all the licensing that sainted Inquisition could ever yet contrive. Which is what I promised to deliver next: that this order of licensing conduces nothing to the end for which it was framed; and hath almost prevented me by being clear already while thus much hath been explaining. See the ingenuity of Truth, who, when she gets a free and willing hand, opens herself faster than the pace of method and discourse can overtake her.

It was the task which I began with, to show that no nation, or well instituted state, if they valued books at all, did ever use this way of licensing; and it might be answered that this is a piece of prudence lately discovered. To which I return that as it was a thing slight and obvious to think on, so if it had been difficult to find out, there wanted not among them long since who suggested such a course; which they not following, leave us a pattern of their judgment that it was not the not knowing, but the not approving, which was the cause of their not using it.

Plato, a man of high authority indeed, but least of all for his commonwealth, in the book of his *Laws,* which no city ever yet received, fed his fancy with making many edicts to his airy burgomasters, which they who otherwise admire him, wish had been rather buried and excused in the genial cups of an Academic nightsitting. By which laws he seems to tolerate no kind of learning, but by unalterable decree, consisting most of practical traditions, to the attainment whereof a library of smaller bulk than his own dialogues would be abundant. And there also enacts that no poet should so much as read to any private man what he had written, until the judges and law-keepers had seen it and allowed it; but that Plato meant this law peculiarly to that commonwealth which he had imagined, and to no other, is evident. Why was he not else a law-giver to himself, but a transgressor, and to be expelled by his own magistrates; both for the wanton epigrams and dialogues which he made, and his perpetual reading of Sophron Mimus, and Aristophanes, books of grossest infamy; and also for commending the latter of them, though he were the malicious libeller of his chief friends, to be read by the tyrant Dionysius, who had little need of such trash to spend his time on? But that he knew this licensing of poems had reference and dependence to many other provisos there set down in his fancied republic, which in this world could have no place; and so neither he himself, nor any magistrate, or city ever imitated that course, which, taken apart from those other collateral injunctions, must needs be vain and fruitless.

For if they fell upon one kind of strictness, unless their care were equal to regulate all other things of like aptness to corrupt the mind, that single endeavor they knew would be but a fond labor; to shut and fortify one gate against corruption, and be necessitated to leave others round about wide open. If we think to regulate printing, thereby to rectify manners, we must regulate all recreations and pastimes, all that is delightful to man. No music must be heard, no song be set or sung, but what is grave and Doric. There must be licensing dancers, that no gesture, motion, or deportment be taught our youth, but what by their allowance shall be thought honest; for such Plato was provided of. It will ask more than the work of twenty licensers to examine all the lutes, the violins, and the guitars in every house; they must not be suffered to prattle as they do, but must be licensed what they may say. And who shall silence all the airs and madrigals that whisper softness in chambers? The windows also, and the balconies must be thought on; there are shrewd books, with dangerous frontispieces, set to sale; who shall prohibit them? Shall twenty licensers? The villages also must have their visitors to inquire what lectures the bagpipe and the rebeck reads even to the balladry and the gamut of every municipal fiddler, for these are the countryman's Arcadias, and his Monte Mayors.

Next, what more national corruption, for which England hears ill abroad, than household gluttony? Who shall be the rectors of our daily rioting? And what shall be done to inhibit the multitudes that frequent those houses where drunkenness is sold and harbored? Our garments also should be referred to the licensing of some more sober workmasters, to see them cut into a less wanton garb. Who shall regulate all the mixed conversation of our youth, male and female together, as is the fashion of this country? Who shall still appoint what shall be discoursed, what presumed, and no further? Lastly, who shall forbid and separate all idle resort, all evil company? These things will be and must be; but how they shall be least hurtful, how least enticing, herein consists the grave and governing wisdom of a state.

To sequester out of the world into Atlantic and Utopian polities, which never can be drawn into use, will not mend our condition; but to ordain wisely as in this world of evil, in the midst whereof God hath placed us unavoidably. Nor is it Plato's licensing of books will do this, which necessarily pulls along with it so many other kinds of licensing as will make us all both ridiculous and weary, and yet frustrate; but those unwritten, or at least unconstraining, laws of virtuous education, religious and civil nurture, which Plato there mentions as the bonds and ligaments of the commonwealth, the pillars and the sustainers of every written statute; these they be which will bear chief sway in such matters as these, when all licensing will be easily eluded. Impunity and remissness, for certain, are the bane of a commonwealth; but here the great art lies, to discern in what the law is to bid restraint and punishment, and in what things persuasion only is to work. If every action which is good or evil in man at ripe years, were to be under pittance and prescription and compulsion, what were virtue but a name, what praise could be then due to well-doing, what gramercy to be sober, just, or continent?

Many there be that complain of divine providence for suffering Adam to transgress. Foolish tongues! when God gave him reason, he gave him freedom to choose, for reason is but choosing; he had been else a mere artificial Adam, such an Adam as he is in the motions. We ourselves esteem not of that obedience, or love, or gift, which is of force. God therefore left him free, set before him a provoking object, ever almost in his eyes; herein consisted his merit, herein the right of his reward, the praise of his abstinence. Wherefore did he create passions within us, pleasures round about us, but that these rightly tempered are the very ingredients of virtue? They are not skilful considerers of human things who imagine to remove sin by removing the matter of sin. For, besides that it is a huge heap increasing under the very act of diminishing, though some part of it may for a time be withdrawn from some persons, it cannot from all, in such a universal thing as books are; and when this is done, yet the sin remains entire. Though ye take from a covetous man all his treasure, he has yet one jewel left—ye cannot bereave him of his covetousness. Banish all objects of lust, shut up all youth into the severest discipline that can be exercised in any hermitage, ye cannot make them chaste that came not thither so: such great care and wisdom is required to the right managing of this point.

Suppose we could expel sin by this means; look how much we thus expel of sin, so much we expel of virtue: for the matter of them both is the same; remove that, and ye remove them both alike. This justifies the high providence of God, who, though he command us temperance, justice, continence, yet pours out before us, even to a profuseness, all desirable things, and gives us minds that can wander beyond all limit and satiety. Why should we then affect a rigor contrary to the manner of God and of nature, by abridging or scanting those means which books freely permitted are, both to the trial of virtue and the exercise of truth?

It would be better done to learn that the law must needs be frivolous which goes to restrain things uncertainly and yet equally working to good and to evil. And were I the chooser, a dram of well-doing should be preferred before many times as much the forcible hindrance of evil-doing. For God sure esteems the growth and completing of one virtuous person more than the restraint of ten vicious. And albeit whatever thing we hear or see, sitting, walking, travelling, or conversing, may be fitly called our book, and is of the same effect that writings are; yet grant the thing to be prohibited were only books, it appears that this order hitherto is far insufficient to the end which it intends. Do we not see—not once or oftener, but weekly—that continued court-libel against the Parliament and City printed, as the wet sheets can witness, and dispersed among us, for all that licensing can do? Yet this is the prime service a man would think, wherein this Order should give proof of itself. If it were executed, you'll say. But certain, if execution be remiss or blindfold now, and in this particular, what will it be hereafter and in other books?

If then the Order shall not be vain and frustrate, behold a new labor, Lords and Commons. Ye must repeal and proscribe all scandalous and unlicensed books already printed and divulged (after ye have drawn them up into a list, that all may know which are condemned and which not) and ordain that no foreign books be delivered out of custody, till they have been read over. This office will require the whole time of not a few overseers, and those no vulgar men. There be also books which are partly useful and excellent, partly culpable and pernicious; this work will ask as many more officials, to make expurgations and expunctions, that the commonwealth of learning be not damnified. In fine, when the multitude of books increase upon their hands, ye must be fain to catalog all those printers who are found frequently offending, and forbid the importation of their whole suspected typography. In a word, that this your Order may be exact and not deficient; ye must reform it perfectly according to the model of Trent and Seville, which I know ye abhor to do.

Yet, though ye should condescend to do this, which God forbid, the Order still would be but fruitless and defective to that end whereto ye meant it. If to prevent sects and schisms, who is so unread or so uncatechized in story that hath not heard of many sects refusing books as a hindrance, and preserving their doctrine unmixed for many ages, only by unwritten traditions? The Christian faith, for what was once a schism, is not unknown to have spread all over Asia, ere any Gospel or Epistle was seen in writing. If the amendment of manners be aimed at, look into Italy and Spain, whether those places be one scruple the better, the honester, the wiser, the chaster, since all the inquisitional rigor that hath been executed upon the books.

Another reason whereby to make it plain that this Order will miss the end it seeks, consider by the quality which ought to be in every licenser. It cannot be denied but that he who is made judge to sit upon the birth or death of books, whether they may be wafted into this world or not, had need to be a man above the common measure, both studious, learned, and judicious. There may be else no mean mistakes in the censure of what is passable or not, which is also no mean injury. If he be of such worth as behoves him, there cannot be a more tedious and unpleasing journeywork, a greater loss of time levied upon his head, than to be made the perpetual reader of unchosen books and pamphlets, ofttimes huge volumes. There is no book that is acceptable unless at certain seasons; but to be enjoined the reading of that at all times, and in a hand scarce legible, whereof three pages would not down any time in the fairest print, is an imposition which I cannot believe how he that values time and his own studies, or is but of a sensible nostril, should be able to endure.

In this one thing I crave leave of the present licensers to be pardoned for so thinking; who doubtless took this office up, looking on it through their obedience to the parliament, whose command perhaps made all things seem easy and unlaborious to them; but that this short trial hath wearied them out already, their own expressions and excuses to them who make so many journeys to solicit their license, are testimony enough. Seeing, therefore, those who now possess the employment, by all evident signs wish themselves well rid of it, and that no man of worth, none that is not a plain unthrift of his own hours, is ever likely to succeed them, except he mean to put himself to the salary of a press corrector, we may easily foresee what kind of licensers we are to expect hereafter, either ignorant, imperious, and remiss, or basely pecuniary. This is what I had to show, wherein this Order cannot conduce to that end whereof it bears the intention.

I lastly proceed from the no good it can do, to the manifest hurt it causes in being first the greatest discouragement and affront that can be offered to learning and to learned men.

It was the complaint and lamentation of prelates, upon every last breath of a motion to remove pluralities and distribute more equally church revenues, that then all learning would be for ever dashed and discouraged. But as for that opinion, I never found cause to think that the tenth part of learning stood or fell with the clergy; nor could I ever but hold it for a sordid and unworthy speech of any churchman who had a competency left him. If, therefore, ye be loth to dishearten utterly and discontent, not the mercenary crew of false pretenders to learning, but the free and ingenuous sort of such as evidently were born to study and love learning for itself, not for lucre, or any other end but the service of God and of truth, and perhaps that lasting fame and perpetuity of praise which God and good men have consented shall be the reward of those whose published labors advance the good of mankind; then know, that so far to distrust the judgment and the honesty of one who hath but a common repute in learning, and never yet offended, as not to count him fit to print his mind without a tutor and examiner, lest he should drop a schism, or something of corruption, is the greatest displeasure and indignity to a free and knowing spirit that can be put upon him.

What advantage is it to be a man over it is to be a boy at school, if we have only scaped the ferula to come under the fescue of an Imprimatur; if serious and elaborate writings, as if they were no more than the theme of a grammmar-lad under his pedagogue, must not be uttered without the cursory eyes of a temporizing and extemporizing licenser? He who is not trusted with his own actions, his drift not being known to be evil, and standing to the hazard of law and penalty, has no great argument to think himself reputed, in the commonwealth wherein he was born, for other than a fool or a foreigner.

When a man writes to the world, he summons up all his reason and deliberation to assist him; he searches, meditates, is industrious, and likely consults and confers with his judicious friends, after all which done he takes himself to be informed in what he writes, as well as any that writ before him. If in this the most consummate act of his fidelity and ripeness, no years, no industry, no former proof of his abilities can bring him to that state of maturity as not to be still mistrusted and suspected (unless he carry all his considerate diligence, all his midnight watchings, and expense of Palladian oil, to the hasty view of an unleisured licenser, perhaps much his younger, perhaps far his inferior in judgment, perhaps one who never knew the labor of book-writing), and if he be not repulsed, or slighted, must appear in print like a puny with his guardian, and his censor's hand on the back of his title to be his bail and surety that he is no idiot or seducer; it cannot be but a dishonor and derogation to the author, to the book, to the privilege and dignity of learning.

And what if the author shall be one so copious of fancy as to have many things well worth the adding, come into his mind after licensing, while the book is yet under the press, which not seldom happens to the best and diligentest writers; and that perhaps a dozen times in one book. The printer dares not go beyond his licensed copy. So often then the author must trudge to his leave-giver, that those his new insertions may be viewed, and many a jaunt will be made, ere that licenser, for it must be the same man, can either be found, or found at leisure. Meanwhile, either the press must stand still, which is no small damage, or the author lose his accuratest thoughts and send the book forth worse than he had made it, which to a diligent writer is the greatest melancholy and vexation that can befall.

And how can a man teach with authority, which is the life of teaching, how can he be a doctor in his book as he ought to be, or else had better be silent, whenas all he teaches, all he delivers, is but under the tuition, under the patriarchal licenser to blot or alter what precisely accords not with the hidebound humor which he calls his judgment? When every acute reader upon the first sight of a pedantic license, will be ready with these like words to ding the book a quoit's distance from him: "I hate a pupil teacher, I endure not an instructor that comes to me under the wardship of an overseeing fist. I know nothing of the licenser, but that I have his own hand here for his arrogance; who shall warrant me his judgment?"

"The state, sir," replies the stationer, but has a quick return: "The state shall be my governors, but not my critics; they may be mistaken in the choice of a licenser as easily as this licenser may be mistaken in an author; this is some common stuff"; and he might add from Sir Francis Bacon, "That such authorized books are but the language of the times." For though a licenser should happen to be judicious more than ordinary, which will be a great jeopardy of the next succession, yet his very office and his commission enjoins him to let pass nothing but what is vulgarly received already.

Nay, which is more lamentable, if the work of any deceased author, though never so famous in his lifetime and even to this day, come to their hands for license to be printed, or reprinted; if there be found in his book one sentence of a venturous edge, uttered in the height of zeal, and who knows whether it might not be the dictate of a divine spirit, yet not suiting with every low, decrepit humor of their own, though it were Knox himself, the reformer of a kingdom, that spake it, they will not pardon him their dash; the sense of that great man shall to all posterity be lost, for the fearfulness, or the presumptuous rashness, of a perfunctory licenser. And to what an author this violence hath been lately done, and in what book of greatest consequence to be faithfully published, I could now instance, but shall forbear till a more convenient season.

Yet if these things be not resented seriously and timely by them who have the remedy in their power, but that such ironmolds as these shall have authority to gnaw out the choicest periods of exquisitest books, and to commit such a treacherous fraud against the orphan remainders of worthiest men after death, the more sorrow will belong to that hapless race of men whose misfortune it is to have understanding. Henceforth let no man care to learn, or care to be more than worldly wise; for certainly in higher matters to be ignorant and slothful, to be a common, steadfast dunce, will be the only pleasant life, and only in request.

And as it is a particular disesteem of every knowing person alive, and most injurious to the written labors and monuments of the dead, so to me it seems and undervaluing and vilifying of the whole nation. I cannot set so light by all the invention, the art, the wit, the grave and solid judgment which is in England, as that it can be comprehended in any twenty capacities how good soever; much less that it should not pass except their superintendence be over it, except it be sifted and strained with their strainers; that it should be uncurrent without their manual stamp. Truth and understanding are not such wares as to be monopolized and traded in by tickets and statutes and standards. We must not think to make a staple commodity of all the knowledge in the land, to mark and license it like our broadcloth and our woolpacks. What is it but a servitude like that imposed by the Philistines, not to be allowed the sharpening of our own axes and coulters, but we must repair from all quarters to twenty licensing forges.

Had anyone written and divulged erroneous things and scandalous to honest life, misusing and forfeiting the esteem had of his reason among men; if, after conviction, this only censure were adjudged him, that he should never henceforth write, but what were first examined by an appointed officer, whose hand should be annexed to pass his credit for him, that now he might be safely read; it could not be apprehended less than a disgraceful punishment.

Whence, to include the whole nation, and those that never yet thus offended, under such a diffident and suspectful prohibition, may plainly be understood what a disparagement it is. So much the more, whenas debtors and delinquents may walk abroad without a keeper, but unoffensive books must not stir forth without a visible jailor in their title. Nor is it to the common people less than a reproach; for if we be so jealous over them as that we dare not trust them with an English pamphlet, what do we but censure them for a giddy, vicious, and ungrounded people, in such a sick and weak estate of faith and discretion, as to be able to take nothing down but through the pipe of a licenser. That this is care or love of them, we cannot pretend, whenas in those popish places where the laity are most hated and despised, the same strictness is used over them. Wisdom we cannot call it, because it stops but one breach of license, nor that neither; whenas those corruptions which it seeks to prevent, break in faster at other doors which cannot be shut.

And in conclusion, it reflects to the disrepute of our ministers also, of whose labors we should hope better, and of the proficiency which their flock reaps by them, than that after all this light of the Gospel which is and is to be, and all this continual preaching, they should be still frequented with such an unprincipled, unedified, and laic rabble, as that the whiff of every new pamphlet should stagger them out of their catechism and Christian walking. This may have much reason to discourage the ministers, when such a low conceit is had of all their exhortations and the benefiting of their hearers, as that they are not thought fit to be turned loose to three sheets of paper without a licenser; that all the sermons, all the lectures preached, printed, vended in such numbers and such volumes as have now well nigh made all other books unsaleable, should not be armor enough against one single enchiridion, without the castle St. Angelo of an Imprimatur.

And lest some should persuade ye, Lords and Commons, that these arguments of learned men's discouragement at this your Order are mere flourishes, and not real, I could recount what I have seen and heard in other countries where this kind of inquisition tyrannizes; when I have sat among their learned men, for that honor I had, and been counted happy to be born in such a place of philosophic freedom as they supposed England was, while themselves did nothing but bemoan the servile condition into which learning amongst them was brought; that this was it which had damped the glory of Italian wits; that nothing had been written now these many years but flattery and fustian. There it was that I found and visited the famous Galileo, grown old, a prisoner to the Inquisition for thinking in astronomy otherwise than the Franciscan and Dominican licensers thought. And though I knew that England then was groaning loudest under the prelatical yoke, nevertheless I took it as a pledge of future happiness that other nations were so persuaded of her liberty.

Yet was it beyond my hope that those worthies were then breathing in her air, who should be her leaders to such a deliverance as shall never be forgotten by any revolution of time that this world hath to finish. When that was once begun, it was as little in my fear, that what words of complaint I heard among learned men of other parts uttered against the Inquisition, the same I should hear by as learned men at home uttered in time of Parliament against an order of licensing; and that so generally, that when I had disclosed myself a companion of their discontent, I might say, if without envy, that he whom an honest quaestorship had endeared to the Sicilians, was not more by them importuned against Verres, than the favorable opinion which I had among many who honor ye, and are known and respected by ye, loaded me with entreaties and persuasions that I would not despair to lay together that which just reason should bring into my mind toward the removal of an undeserved thraldom upon learning.

That this is not, therefore, the disburdening of a particular fancy, but the common grievance of all those who had prepared their minds and studies above the vulgar pitch to advance truth in others, and from others to entertain it, thus much may satisfy. And in their name I shall for neither friend nor foe conceal what the general murmur is; that if it come to inquisitioning again and licensing, and that we are so timorous of ourselves and so suspicious of all men as to fear each book and the shaking of every leaf, before we know what the contents are; if some who but of late were little better than silenced from preaching, shall come now to silence us from reading, except what they please, it cannot be guessed what is intended by some but a second tyranny over learning; and will soon put it out of controversy that bishops and presbyters are the same to us both name and thing.

That those evils of prelaty which before from five or six and twenty sees were distributively charged upon the whole people, will now light wholly upon learning, is not obscure to us; whenas now the pastor of a small unlearned parish on the sudden shall be exalted archbishop over a large diocese of books, and yet not remove, but keep his other cure too, a mystical pluralist. He who but of late cried down the sole ordination of every novice bachelor of art, and denied sole jurisdiction over the simplest parishioner, shall now at home in his private chair assume both these over worthiest and excellentest books and ablest authors that write them. This is not, ye covenants and protestations that we have made, this is not to put down prelaty; this is but to chop an episcopacy; this is but to translate the palace metropolitan from one kind of dominion into another; this is but an old canonical sleight of commuting our penance. To startle thus betimes at a mere unlicensed pamphlet will after a while be afraid of every conventicle, and a while after will make a conventicle of every Christian writing.

But I am certain that a state governed by the rules of justice and fortitude, or a church built and founded upon the rock of faith and true knowledge, cannot be so pusillanimous. While things are yet not constituted in religion, that freedom of writing should be restrained by a discipline imitated from the prelates, and learnt by them from the Inquisition, to shut us up all again into the breast of a licenser, must needs give cause of doubt and discouragement to all learned and religious men. Who cannot but discern the fineness of this politic drift, and who are the contrivers: that while bishops were to be baited down, then all presses might be open; it was the people's birthright and privilege in time of parliament, it was the breaking forth of light?

But now, the bishops abrogated and voided out of the church, as if our reformation sought no more but to make room for others into their seats under another name, the episcopal arts begin to bud again; the cruse of truth must run no more oil; liberty of printing must be enthralled again under a prelatical commission of twenty, the privilege of the people nullified; and, which is worse, the freedom of learning must groan again, and to her old fetters: all this the parliament yet sitting. Although their own late arguments and defenses against the prelates might remember them that this obstructing violence meets for the most part with an event utterly opposite to the end which it drives at; instead of suppressing sects and schisms, it raises them and invests them with a reputation: "The punishing of wits enhances their authority," said the Viscount St. Albans, "and a forbidden writing is thought to be a certain spark of truth that flies up in the faces of them who seek to tread it out."

This Order, therefore, may prove a nursing mother to sects, but I shall easily show how it will be a stepdame to Truth; and first by disenabling us to the maintenance of what is known already.

Well knows he who uses to consider, that our faith and knowledge thrives by exercise, as well as our limbs and complexion. Truth is compared in scripture to a streaming fountain; if her waters flow not in a perpetual progression, they sicken into a muddy pool of conformity and tradition. A man may be a heretic in the truth; and if he believe things only because his pastor says so, or the Assembly so determines, without knowing other reason, though his belief be true, yet the very truth he holds becomes his heresy. There is not any burden that some would gladlier post off to another than the charge and care of their religion. There be, who knows not that there be, of protestants and professors who live and die in as arrant an implicit faith, as any lay papist of Loreto.

A wealthy man addicted to his pleasure and to his profits, finds religion to be a traffic so entangled, and of so many piddling accounts, that of all mysteries he cannot skill to keep a stock going upon that trade. What should he do? Fain he would have the name to be religious, fain he would bear up with his neighbors in that. What does he, therefore, but resolves to give over toiling, and to find himself out some factor to whose care and credit he may commit the whole managing of his religious affairs; some Divine of note and estimation that must be. To him he adheres, resigns the whole warehouse of his religion with all the locks and keys into his custody; and indeed makes the very person of that man his religion; esteems his associating with him a sufficient evidence and commendatory of his own piety. So that a man may say his religion is now no more within himself, but is become a dividual movable, and goes and comes near him, according as that good man frequents the house. He entertains him, gives him gifts, feasts him, lodges him. His religion comes home at night, prays, is liberally supped, and sumptuously laid to sleep, rises, is saluted, and after the malmsey, or some well spiced brewage, and better breakfasted than he whose morning appetite would have gladly fed on green figs between Bethany and Jerusalem, his religion walks abroad at eight, and leaves his kind entertainer in the shop trading all day without his religion.

Another sort there be, when they hear that all things shall be ordered, all things regulated and settled, nothing written but what passes through the custom-house of certain publicans that have the tonnaging and the poundaging of all freespoken truth, will straight give themselves up into your hands, make 'em and cut 'em out what religion ye please. There be delights, there be recreations and jolly pastimes that will fetch the day about from sun to sun, and rock the tedious year as in a delightful dream. What need they torture their heads with that which others have taken so strictly and so unalterably into their own purveying? These are the fruits which a dull ease and cessation of our knowledge will bring forth among the people. How goodly, and how to be wished, were such an obedient unanimity as this, what a fine conformity would it starch us all into! Doubtless a staunch and solid piece of framework, as any January could freeze together.

Nor much better will be the consequence even among the clergy themselves. It is no new thing never heard of before, for a parochial minister, who has his reward, and is at his Hercules pillars in a warm benefice, to be easily inclinable, if he have nothing else that may rouse up his studies, to finish his circuit in an English concordance and a topic folio, the gatherings and savings of a sober graduateship, a harmony and a catena, treading the constant round of certain common doctrinal heads, attended with their uses, motives, marks, and means; out of which, as out of an alphabet of sol-fa, by forming and transforming, joining and disjoining variously a little bookcraft, and two hours' meditation, might furnish him unspeakably to the performance of more than a weekly charge of sermoning; not to reckon up the infinite helps of interlinearies, breviaries, synopses, and other loitering gear.

But as for the multitude of sermons ready printed and piled up on every text that is not difficult, our London trading St. Thomas in his vestry, and add to boot St. Martin and St. Hugh, have not within their hallowed limits more vendible ware of all sorts ready made; so that penury he never need fear of pulpit provision, having where so plenteously to refresh his magazine. But if his rear and flanks be not impaled, if his back door be not secured by the rigid licenser, but that a bold book may now and then issue forth and give the assault to some of his old collections in their trenches; it will concern him then to keep waking, to stand in watch, to set good guards and sentinels about his received opinions, to walk the round and counter-round with his fellow inspectors, fearing lest any of his flock be seduced, who also then would be better instructed, better exercised and disciplined. And God send that the fear of this diligence, which must then be used, do not make us affect the laziness of a licensing church.

For if we be sure we are in the right, and do not hold the truth guiltily, which becomes not, if we ourselves condemn not our own weak and frivolous teaching, and the people for an untaught and irreligious, gadding rout, what can be more fair than when a man judicious, learned, and of a conscience, for aught we know, as good as theirs that taught us what we know, shall not privily from house to house, which is more dangerous, but openly by writing, publish to the world what his opinion is, what his reasons, and wherefore that which is now thought cannot be sound? Christ urged it as wherewith to justify himself that he preached in public; yet writing is more public than preaching; and more easy to refutation, if need be, there being so many whose business and profession merely it is, to be the champions of the truth; which if they neglect, what can be imputed but their sloth or unability?

Thus much we are hindered and disinured by this course of licensing toward the true knowledge of what we seem to know. For how much it hurts and hinders the licensers themselves in the calling of their ministry, more than any secular employment, if they will discharge that office as they ought, so that of necessity they must neglect either the one duty or the other, I insist not, because it is a particular, but leave it to their own conscience, how they will decide it there.

There is yet behind of what I purposed to lay open, the incredible loss and detriment that this plot of licensing puts us to. More than if some enemy at sea should stop up all our havens and ports and creeks, it hinders and retards the importation of our richest merchandise, truth. Nay, it was first established and put in practice by Antichristian malice and mystery, on set purpose to extinguish, if it were possible, the light of reformation, and to settle falsehood; little differing from that policy wherewith the Turk upholds his Alcoran, by the prohibition of painting. 'Tis not denied, but gladly confessed, we are to send our thanks and vows to Heaven, louder than most of nations, for that great measure of truth which we enjoy, especially in those main points between us and the Pope, with his appurtenances the prelates; but he who thinks we are to pitch our tent here, and have attained the utmost prospect of reformation that the mortal glass wherein we contemplate can show us, till we come to beatific vision, that man by this very opinion declares that he is yet far short of truth.

Truth indeed came once into the world with her divine Master, and was a perfect shape most glorious to look on. But when he ascended, and his apostles after him were laid asleep, then straight arose a wicked race of deceivers, who, as that story goes of the Egyptian Typhon with his conspirators, how they dealt with the good Osiris, took the virgin Truth, hewed her lovely form into a thousand pieces, and scattered them to the four winds. From that time ever since, the sad friends of Truth, such as durst appear, imitating the careful search that Isis made for the mangled body of Osiris, went up and down gathering up limb by limb still as they could find them. We have not yet found them all, Lords and Commons, nor ever shall do, till her Master's second coming. He shall bring together every joint and member, and shall mold them into an immortal feature of loveliness and perfection. Suffer not these licensing prohibitions to stand at every place of opportunity, forbidding and disturbing them that continue seeking, that continue to do our obsequies to the torn body of our martyred saint.

We boast our light; but if we look not wisely on the sun itself, it smites us into darkness. Who can discern those planets that are oft combust, and those stars of brightest magnitude that rise and set with the sun, until the opposite motion of their orbs bring them to such a place in the firmament, where they may be seen evening or morning. The light which we have gained, was given us, not to be ever staring on, but by it to discover onward things more remote from our knowledge. It is not the unfrocking of a priest, the unmitering of a bishop, and the removing him from off the Presbyterian shoulders that will make us a happy nation; no, if other things as great in the church, and in the rule of life both economical and political, be not looked into and reformed, we have looked so long upon the blaze that Zwinglius and Calvin hath beaconed up to us, that we are stark blind.

There be who perpetually complain of schisms and sects, and make it such a calamity that any man dissents from their maxims. It is their own pride and ignorance which causes the disturbing, who neither will hear with meekness, nor can convince, yet all must be suppressed which is not found in their syntagma. They are the troublers, they are the dividers of unity, who neglect and permit not others to unite those dissevered pieces which are yet wanting to the body of Truth. To be still searching what we know not by what we know, still closing up truth to truth as we find it (for all her body is homogeneal and proportional), this is the golden rule in theology as well as in arithmetic, and makes up the best harmony in a church; not the forced and outward union of cold and neutral and inwardly divided minds.

Lords and Commons of England, consider what nation it is whereof ye are, and whereof ye are the governors; a nation not slow and dull, but of a quick, ingenious, and piercing spirit, acute to invent, subtle and sinewy to discourse, not beneath the reach of any point the highest that human capacity can soar to. Therefore the studies of learning in her deepest sciences have been so ancient and so eminent among us that writers of good antiquity and ablest judgment have been persuaded that even the school of Pythagoras and the Persian wisdom took beginning from the old philosophy of this island. And that wise and civil Roman, Julius Agricola, who governed once here for Caesar, preferred the natural wits of Britain before the labored studies of the French. Nor is it for nothing that the grave and frugal Transylvanian sends out yearly from as far as the mountainous borders of Russia and beyond the Hercynian wilderness, not their youth, but their staid men to learn our language and our theologic arts.

Yet that which is above all this, the favor and the love of Heaven, we have great argument to think in a peculiar manner propitious and propending towards us. Why else was this nation chosen before any other, that out of her as out of Sion should be proclaimed and sounded forth the first tidings and trumpet of reformation to all Europe? And had it not been the obstinate perverseness of our prelates against the divine and admirable spirit of Wycliffe to suppress him as a schismatic and innovator, perhaps neither the Bohemian Huss and Jerome, no, nor the name of Luther, or of Calvin, had been ever known; the glory of reforming all our neighbors had been completely ours. But now, as our obdurate clergy have with violence demeaned the matter, we are become hitherto the latest and the backwardest scholars of whom God offered to have made us the teachers.

Now once again by all concurrence of signs, and by the general instinct of holy and devout men, as they daily and solemnly express their thoughts, God is decreeing to begin some new and great period in his Church, even to the reforming of reformation itself. What does he then but reveal himself to his servants, and, as his manner is, first to his Englishmen? I say as his manner is, first to us, though we mark not the method of his counsels and are unworthy. Behold now this vast city, a city of refuge, the mansion house of liberty, encompassed and surrounded with his protection. The shop of war hath not there more anvils and hammers waking, to fashion out the plates and instruments of armed justice in defense of beleaguered Truth, than there be pens and heads there, sitting by their studious lamps, musing, searching, revolving new notions and ideas wherewith to present, as with their homage and their fealty, the approaching reformation; others as fast reading, trying all things, assenting to the force of reason and convincement.

What could a man require more from a nation so pliant and so prone to seek after knowledge? What wants there to such a towardly and pregnant soul but wise and faithful laborers to make a knowing people, a nation of prophets, of sages, and of worthies? We reckon more than five months yet to harvest; there need not be five weeks, had we but eyes to lift up; the fields are white already. Where there is much desire to learn, there of necessity will be much arguing, much writing, many opinions; for opinion in good men is but knowledge in the making. Under these fantastic terrors of sect and schism, we wrong the earnest and zealous thirst after knowledge and understanding which God hath stirred up in this city.

What some lament of, we rather should rejoice at, should rather praise this pious forwardness among men, to reassume the ill-deputed care of their religion into their own hands again. A little generous prudence, a little forbearance of one another, and some grain of charity might win all these diligences to join and unite into one general and brotherly search after truth; could we but forego this prelatical tradition of crowding free consciences and Christian liberties into canons and precepts of men. I doubt not, if some great and worthy stranger should come among us, wise to discern the mold and temper of a people, and how to govern it, observing the high hopes and aims, the diligent alacrity of our extended thoughts and reasonings in the pursuance of truth and freedom, but that he would cry out as Pyrrhus did, admiring the Roman docility and courage, "If such were my Epirots, I would not despair the greatest design that could be attempted to make a church or kingdom happy."

Yet these are the men cried out against for schismatics and sectaries; as if, while the temple of the Lord was building, some cutting, some squaring the marble, others hewing the cedars, there should be a sort of irrational men who could not consider there must be many schisms and many dissections made in the quarry and in the timber, ere the house of God can be built. And when every stone is laid artfully, together, it cannot be united into a continuity, it can but be contiguous in this world; neither can every piece of the building be of one form; nay rather the perfection consists in this, that out of many moderate varieties and brotherly dissimilitudes that are not vastly disproportional, arises the goodly and the graceful symmetry that commends the whole pile and structure.

Let us, therefore, be more considerate builders, more wise in spiritual architecture, when great reformation is expected. For now the time seems come, wherein Moses, the great prophet, may sit in heaven rejoicing to see that memorable and glorious wish of his fulfilled, when not only our seventy elders, but all the Lord's people, are become prophets. No marvel then though some men, and some good men too perhaps, but young in goodness, as Joshua then was, envy them. They fret and out of their own weakness are in agony, lest these divisions and subdivisions will undo us. The adversary again applauds and waits the hour. When they have branched themselves out, saith he, small enough into parties and partitions, then will be our time. Fool! he sees not the firm root, out of which we all grow, though into branches; nor will beware until he see our small divided maniples cutting through at every angle of his ill-united and unwieldy brigade. And that we are to hope better of all these supposed sects and schisms, and that we shall not need that solicitude, honest perhaps, though over-timorous, of them that vex in this behalf, but shall laugh in the end at those malicious applauders of our differences, I have these reasons to persuade me.

First, when a city shall be as it were besieged and blocked about, her navigable river infested, inroads and incursions round, defiance and battle oft rumored to be marching up even to her walls and suburb trenches; that then the people, or the greater part, more than at other times, wholly taken up with the study of highest and most important matters to be reformed, should be disputing, reasoning, reading, inventing, discoursing, even to a rarity and admiration, things not before discoursed or written of, argues first a singular goodwill, contentedness and confidence in your prudent foresight and safe government, Lords and Commons; and from thence derives itself to a gallant bravery and well grounded contempt of their enemies, as if there were not small number of as great spirits among us, as his was, who, when Rome was nigh besieged by Hannibal, being in the city, bought that piece of ground at no cheap rate whereon Hannibal himself encamped his own regiment.

Next, it is a lively and cheerful presage of our happy success and victory. For as in a body, when the blood is fresh, the spirits pure and vigorous not only to vital but to rational faculties, and those in the acutest and the pertest operations of wit and subtlety, it argues in what good plight and constitution the body is; so when the cheerfulness of the people is so sprightly up, as that it has not only wherewith to guard well its own freedom and safety, but to spare, and to bestow upon the solidest and sublimest points of controversy and new invention, it betokens us not degenerated nor drooping to a fatal decay, but casting off the old and wrinkled skin of corruption to outlive these pangs and wax young again, entering the glorious ways of truth and prosperous virtue, destined to become great and honorable in these latter ages.

Methinks I see in my mind a noble and puissant nation rousing herself like a strong man after sleep, and shaking her invincible locks. Methinks I see her as an eagle muing her mighty youth, and kindling her undazzled eyes at the full midday beam; purging and unscaling her long-abused sight at the fountain itself of heavenly radiance; while the whole noise of timorous and flocking birds, with those also that love the twilight, flutter about, amazed at what she means, and in their envious gabble would prognosticate a year of sects and schisms.

What should ye do then, should ye suppress all this flowery crop of knowledge and new light sprung up and yet springing daily in this city? Should ye set an oligarchy of twenty engrossers over it, to bring a famine upon our minds again, when we shall know nothing but what is measured to us by their bushel? Believe it, Lords and Commons, they who counsel ye to such a suppressing, do as good as bid ye suppress yourselves; and I will soon show how.

If it be desired to know the immediate cause of all this free writing and free speaking, there cannot be assigned a truer than your own mild and free and humane government. It is the liberty, Lords and Commons, which your own valorous and happy counsels have purchased us, liberty which is the nurse of all great wits. This is that which hath rarefied and enlightened our spirits like the influence of heaven; this is that which hath enfranchised, enlarged, and lifted up our apprehensions degrees above themselves. Ye cannot make us now less capable, less knowing, less eagerly pursuing of the truth, unless ye first make yourselves, that made us so, less the lovers, less the founders of our true liberty. We can grow ignorant again, brutish, formal, and slavish, as ye found us; but you then must first become that which ye cannot be, oppressive, arbitrary, and tyrannous, as they were from whom ye have freed us. That our hearts are now more capacious, our thoughts more erected to the search and expectation of greatest and exactest things, is the issue of your own virtue propagated in us. Ye cannot suppress that unless ye reinforce an abrogated and merciless law, that fathers may despatch at will their own children. And who shall then stick closest to ye, and excite others? no he who takes up arms for the coat and conduct, and his four nobles of Danegelt. Although I dispraise not the defense of just immunities, yet love my peace better, if that were all. Give me the liberty to know, to utter, and to argue freely according to conscience, above all liberties.

What would be best advised then, if it be found so hurtful and so unequal to suppress opinions for the newness, or the unsuitableness to a customary acceptance, will not be my task to say. I only shall repeat what I have learned from one of your own honorable number, a right noble and pious lord, who, had he not sacrificed his life and fortunes to the church and commonwealth, we had not now missed and bewailed a worthy and undoubted patron of this argument. Ye know him I am sure; yet I for honor's sake, and may it be eternal to him, shall name him, the Lord Brook. He, writing of episcopacy, and by the way treating of sects and schisms, left ye his vote, or rather now the last words of his dying charge (which I know will ever be of dear and honored regard with ye) so full of meekness and breathing charity that next to his last testament who bequeathed love and peace to his disciples, I cannot call to mind where I have read or heard words more mild and peaceful. He there exhorts us to hear with patience and humility those, however they be miscalled, that desire to live purely, in such a use of God's ordinances as the best guidance of their conscience gives them, and to tolerate them, though in some disconformity to ourselves. The book itself will tell us more at large, being published to the world and dedicated to the parliament by him who, both for his life and for his death, deserves that what advice he left be not laid by without perusal.

And now the time in special is, by privilege, to write and speak what may help to the further discussing of matters in agitation. The temple of Janus with his two controversial faces might now not unsignificantly be set open. And though all the winds of doctrine were let loose to play upon the earth, so Truth be in the field, we do injuriously by licensing and prohibiting to misdoubt her strength. Let her and Falsehood grapple; who ever knew Truth put to the worse, in a free and open encounter. Her confuting is the best and surest suppressing. He who hears what praying there is for light and clearer knowledge to be sent down among us, would think of other matters to be constituted beyond the discipline of Geneva, framed and fabriced already to our hands.

Yet when the new light which we beg for shines in upon us, there be who envy and oppose, if it come not first in at their casements. What a collusion is this, whenas we are exhorted by the wise man to use diligence, to seek for wisdom as for hidden treasures early and late, that another order shall enjoin us to know nothing but by statute. When a man hath been laboring the hardest labor in the deep mines of knowledge, hath furnished out his findings in all their equipage, drawn forth his reasons as it were a battle ranged, scattered and defeated all objections in his way, calls out his adversary into the plain, offers him the advantage of wind and sun, if he please, only that he may try the matter by dint of argument; for his opponents then to skulk, to lay ambushments, to keep a narrow bridge of licensing where the challenger should pass, though it be valor enough in soldiership, is but weakness and cowardice in the wars of Truth.

For who knows not that Truth is strong, next to the Almighty. She needs no policies, nor stratagems, nor licensings to make her victorious—those are the shifts and the defenses that error uses against her power. Give her but room, and do not bind her when she sleeps, for then she speaks not true, as the old Proteus did, who spake oracles only when he was caught and bound, but then rather she turns herself into all shapes except her own, and perhaps tunes her voice according to the time, as Micaiah did before Ahab, until she be adjured into her own likeness.

Yet is it not impossible that she may have more shapes than one. What else is all that rank of things indifferent, wherein Truth may be on this side, or on the other, without being unlike herself? What but a vain shadow else is the abolition of those ordinances, that handwriting nailed to the cross; what great purchase is this Christian liberty which Paul so often boasts of? His doctrine is, that he who eats, or eats not, regards a day, or regards it not, may do either to the Lord. How many other things might be tolerated in peace and left to conscience, had we but charity, and were it not the chief stronghold of our hypocrisy to be ever judging one another. I fear yet this iron yoke of outward conformity hath left a slavish print upon our necks; the ghost of a linen decency yet haunts us. We stumble and are impatient at the least dividing of one visible congregation from another, though it be not in fundamentals; and through our forwardness to suppress, and our backwardness to recover any enthralled piece of truth out of the gripe of custom, we care not to keep truth separated from truth, which is the fiercest rent and disunion of all. We do not see that while we still affect by all means a rigid external formality, we may as soon fall again into a gross conforming stupidity, a stark and dead congealment of "wood, and hay, and stubble" forced and frozen together, which is more to the sudden degenerating of a church than many subdichotomies of petty schisms.

Not that I can think well of every light separation, or that all in a church is to be expected "gold and silver and precious stones." It is not possible for man to sever the wheat from the tares, the good fish from the other fry; that must be the angels' ministry at the end of mortal things. Yet if all cannot be of one mind,—as who looks they should be?—this doubtless is more wholesome, more prudent, and more Christian, that many be tolerated, rather than all compelled. I mean not tolerated popery and open superstition, which, as it extirpates all religions and civil supremacies, so itself should be extirpate, provided first that all charitable and compassionate means be used to win and regain the weak and the misled; that also which is impious or evil absolutely, either against faith or manners, no law can possibly permit, that intends not to unlaw itself; but those neighboring differences, or rather indifferences, are what I speak of, whether in some point of doctrine or of discipline, which though they may be many, yet need not interrupt "the unity of spirit," if we could but find among us the "bond of peace."

In the meanwhile, if any one would write and bring his helpful hand to the slow-moving reformation which we labor under, if truth have spoken to him before others, or but seemed at least to speak, who hath so bejesuited us that we should trouble that man with asking license to do so worthy a deed? And not consider this, that if it come to prohibiting, there is not aught more likely to be prohibited than truth itself; whose first appearance to our eyes bleared and dimmed with prejudice and custom, is more unsightly and unplausible than many errors, even as the person is of many a great man slight and contemptible to see to. And what do they tell us vainly of new opinions, when this very opinion of theirs, that none must be heard but whom they like, is the worst and newest opinion of all others; and is the chief cause why sects and schisms do so much abound, and true knowledge is kept at distance from us; besides yet a greater danger which is in it. For when God shakes a kingdom with strong and healthful commotions to a general reforming, it is not untrue that many sectaries and false teachers are then busiest in seducing; but yet more than it is that God then raises to his own work men of rare abilities and more than common industry, not only to look back and revise what hath been taught heretofore, but to gain further and go on some new enlightened steps in the discovery of truth.

For such is the order of God's enlightening his church, to dispense and deal out by degrees his beam, so as our earthly eyes may best sustain it. Neither is God appointed and confined, where and out of what place these his chosen shall be first heard to speak: for he sees not as man sees, chooses not as man chooses, lest we should devote ourselves again to set places and assemblies and outward callings of men; planting our faith one while in the old Convocation house, and another while in the Chapel at Westminster; when all the faith and religion that shall be there canonized, is not sufficient without plain convincement and the charity of patient instruction, to supple the least bruise of conscience, to edify the meanest Christian who desires to walk in the Spirit and not in the letter of human trust, for all the number of voices that can be there made; no, though Harry VII himself there, with all his liege tombs about him, should lend them voices from the dead to swell their number.

And if the men be erroneous who appear to be the leading schismatics, what withholds us but our sloth, our self-will, and distrust in the right cause, that we do not give them gentle meetings and gentle dismissions, that we debate not and examine the matter thoroughly with liberal and frequent audience; if not for their sakes, yet for our own? Seeing no man who hath tasted learning but will confess the many ways of profiting by those who, not contented with stale receipts, are able to manage and set forth new positions in the world. And were they but as the dust and cinders of our feet, so long as in that notion they may yet serve to polish and brighten the armory of Truth, even for that respect they were not utterly to be cast away. But if they be of those whom God hath fitted for the special use of these times with eminent and ample gifts—and those perhaps neither among the priests, nor among the pharisees—and we in the haste of a precipitant zeal shall make no distinction, but resolve to stop their mouths because we fear they come with new and dangerous opinions (as we commonly forejudge them ere we understand them); no less than woe to us while, thinking thus to defend the Gospel, we are found the persecutors.

There have been not a few since the beginning of this Parliament, both of the presbytery and others, who by their unlicensed books, to the contempt of an Imprimatur, first broke that triple ice clung about our hearts, and taught the people to see day. I hope that none of those were the persuaders to renew upon us this bondage which they themselves have wrought so much good by contemning. But if neither the check that Moses gave to young Joshua, nor the countermand which our Savior gave to young John, who was so ready to prohibit those whom he thought unlicensed, be not enough to admonish our elders how unacceptable to God their testy mood of prohibiting is; if neither their own remembrance what evil hath abounded in the church by this let of licensing, and what good they themselves have begun by transgressing it, be not enough, but that they will persuade and execute the most Dominican part of the Inquisition over us, and are already with one foot in the stirrup so active at suppressing, it would be no unequal distribution, in the first place, to suppress the suppressors themselves; whom the change of their condition hath puffed up more than their late experience of harder times hath made wise.

And as for regulating the press, let no man think to have the honor of advising ye better than yourselves have done in that order published next before this, that no book be printed, unless the printer's and the author's name, or at least the printer's, be registered. Those which otherwise come forth, if they be found mischievous and libellous, the fire and the executioner will be the timeliest and the most effectual remedy that man's prevention can use. For this authentic Spanish policy of licensing books, if I have said aught, will prove the most unlicensed book itself within a short while; and was the immediate image of a Star Chamber decree to that purpose made in those very times when that Court did the rest of those her pious works, for which she is now fallen from the stars with Lucifer. Whereby ye may guess what kind of state prudence, what love of the people, what care of religion or good manners there was the contriving, although with singular hypocrisy it pretended to bind books to their good behavior. And how it got the upper hand of your precedent order so well constituted before, if we may believe those men whose profession gives them cause to inquire most, it may be doubted that there was in it the fraud of some old patentees and monopolizers in the trade of bookselling; who under pretense of the poor in their Company not to be defrauded, and the just retaining of each man his several copy (which God forbid should be gainsaid) brought divers glosing colors, and serving to the House, which were indeed but colors, and serving to no end except it be to exercise a superiority over their neighbors; men who do not, therefore, labor in an honest profession to which learning is indebted, that they should be made other men's vassals. Another end is thought was aimed at by some of them procuring by petition this Order, that having power in their hands, malignant books might have the easier scape abroad, as the event shows.

But of these sophisms and elenchs of merchandise I skill not. This I know, that errors in a good government and in a bad are equally almost incident; for what magistrate may not be misinformed and much the sooner, if liberty of printing be reduced into the power of a few; but to redress willingly and speedily what hath been erred, and in highest authority to esteem a plain advertisement more than others have done a sumptuous bribe, is a virtue, honored Lord and Commons, answerable to your highest actions, and whereof none can participate but greatest and wisest men.

Questions and Answers

1. Many people would like to control not only books, but also films, television, and even song lyrics. If you were establishing a policy that would regulate one or all of these media, what criteria would you use to decide what is approved and what is suppressed? Explain your criteria and then write an argument in which you support them as applicable to society at large.

2. Many people would ban speech (or books, films, etc.) that they find libelous or blasphemous. Write an argument in which you define one of these terms with some care, and then take and support the position that it should or should not be used as a criterion for judging whether speech is acceptable.

STUDENT ARGUMENTS

Best Friends Make Lousy Roommates

KRISTEN WOODALL

It may be an unwritten law that you should never move in with your best friend, but after the first few weeks of the Freshman year many believe it should be engraved in stone as the "Eleventh Commandment." As a senior in high school, I shared many great times with my two best friends. One of them chose to attend State also, so it only seemed logical to room together. Everyone, including our other best friend, warned us about the harsh realities of turning a best friend into a roommate. However, we chose not to hear this wise advice. Our friendship was too strong for trivial old wives' tales! Little did we know of the horror that would lurk behind the door of 600 Drummond. We may love each other as best friends, but as roommates each of us would gladly strangle the other as she sleeps.

Before agreeing to share a room with your best friend, there are some things you may want to consider. First of all, are your sleeping habits similar? For example, if you need lots of sleep in order to function but your roommate keeps the hours of a vampire, chances are there will be trouble. In my own experience, I have found that I need to go to bed before one o'clock in order to successfully reach my 8:30 classes. On the other hand, my roommate prefers to watch the sunrise and sleep until Tumbleweeds opens again. This is a sticky situation because I don't want to be disturbed after 12:30 and she wants it dark and quiet until noon.

The next thing to consider would be whether or not you and your roommate have mutual respect for each other and each other's personal belongings. Being the selfish, spoiled brat that I am, I do not like people to borrow my clothes. Despite much "discussion" on the issue, part of my roommate's daily ritual is to raid my closet and grab a couple of things for her friends. Another example of respect, or the lack of it, is that my roommate has her boyfriend in our room twenty-four hours a day, seven days a week. Not only does this make me totally uncomfortable, but it is also very inconvenient. For example, when I want to change clothes or take a shower, I have to gather all my stuff and hike down to the bathroom, which normally ends up to be a more lengthy process than the actual act of changing my clothes.

Another possible problem linked to respect is time limitations in regard to the phone, guests, or other noise. My roommate talks on the phone until 4:00 a.m. and has her boyfriend over until 2:00 a.m. I also love to talk on the phone and have guests, but there is a time to be reasonable and respectful. Not only do these actions curtail my privacy, but they also hinder my social life. I actually missed a date because my roommate was competing in the new olympic event, Phone Call Marathon. That was when I knew there was a problem!

In conclusion, probably the most important thing to take into consideration is that you may not truly know your best friend, and people do change. Some people just go absolutely wild when they leave the parental eye. Whether it is you, your roommate, or even both, the situation will not work and you won't be happy. Either set mutual ground rules when you agree to be roommates, or find another person to be your roommate. College is hard enough to adjust to, and if you lose your best friend on top of that, it would be unbearable. I've learned the hard way—keep your best friend.

Study What?

HEATHER MITCHA

What is irony? From what I have experienced, irony is most easily illustrated through the term, Study Hall. I find it quite amazing that the place where I have to go to "study" is actually called study hall. From beginning to end, there is not one moment when all thirty-seven girls are actively studying, which leads me to believe that study hall is most anything but studying.

I began my interesting observations on a Sunday night and compared my results to the study hall I observed on Wednesday night. Needless to say, I found myself laughing more than observing. One would never believe the type of activity that takes place during this supposed time of concentration. Study hall began at 7:00 and it took at least fifteen minutes for people to quiet down. Even then not everyone was quiet or silent. Giggles, whispers, and talking were amongst the many noises that interrupted my train of thought. As hard as I tried, I could not think over the many distractions that surrounded me. Girls constantly popped their knuckles and talked as if they had not seen each other in years. And of course, the giggling continued as did the rustling of papers and the sounds of chairs moving across the floor. What really grabbed my attention was the fascination with hair. When I looked around the room, half of the girls were playing with their hair or twisting it around their fingers. Then, of course, there are the girls that did nothing but stare into space. I referred to these girls as classic "space cadets." Finally breaktime came and the room cleared out as if there was an enormous fire. When it was time for the next hour to begin, the first pattern replicated. For the rest of the night, the behavior tended to be the same, with the exception of the sleepers. What else would top off this classic comedy but, sleepers? These girls were almost as fun to watch as the "space cadets." But have no fear, during the night I counted fourteen girls that attempted to study, which did not last. At one time or another, these girls joined in on the giggling and the whispering. In the beginning I thought that perhaps these behaviors were based on the day of the week. WRONG! These patterns only worsened on Wednesday (which I did not think was humanly possible). In my opinion, these girls find everything in the world to do, but study! If there was an award given for ways to slack off in study hall, every shelf in the house would be filled!! If only the members in the house would realize how ridiculous our study hall really is, then perhaps we might be able to have a real study hall. Then again, all members were pledges at one point in time, and I imagine that I am not the first to write a paper on this topic!

Roommates

KYDEN REEH

As I was driving home after a long, hot, exhausting day in biology lab, which was filled with the pungent aromas of formaldehyde and my fellow students' powerful body odor, the only thought on my mind was to kickback, relax, find space, and unwind. When I entered the apartment I noticed that both my roommates were home. Keith was in his bedroom trying to "read" his monthly Penthouse and Bill was in the living room listening to Guns 'N' Roses. Each thump of the music I could feel travel from my feet, up my legs, and disperse throughout my body.

I tossed my books and lab materials on the faded, dingy blue sofa and lumbered toward the kitchen to fix a bite to eat. The headache which was stabbing into the back of my eye called out for Excedrin. It was at that moment I realized my bone dry palate needed liquid refreshment, so I opened the refrigerator with only one thought—diet Coke. Without looking I just reached for the place I saw it last, but I only grasped at thin air. It was gone! Disappeared! My heart began to pound a little harder as desperation and anger began to fill my mind. My last thirst quenching diet Coke and someone, without any regard for my physical or mental state, stole it.

Reflecting on my college career I can honestly say that I had a string of horrible roommates. My first roommate, Jay, kept illegal drugs in the freezer. Jeff, my second roommate, thought everyday of the week was Friday and Saturday night. My third roommate, Todd, did not even use sheets on his bed. In my final roommate situation, both roommates, Keith and Bill, loved extremely loud music.

For the past two years I have lived alone. It was the most stress free two years of my life. I could go home and do whatever I wanted. The living arrangement was free from any kind of personality conflict. Compared with having roommates, living alone was the best living arrangement.

Living alone gives me the freedom to do whatever I want, whenever I want. If I want to be alone, I don't have to worry about a roommate entertaining company. When I want to have a party I don't have to ask for a roommate's permission or worry about bothering him. If I want to walk around in my boxer shorts, I do not have to worry if a roommate has anybody over. I'm free to act out a scene of *Hamlet* or sing the chorus of "We Are the World" whenever I please. Without roommates I get the whole refrigerator to myself. This, of course, creates ample room for my diet Coke.

Two things always seemed to happen when I had a roommate. First, they would always throw a party that made Mardi Gras look tame the night before the most crucial test of the semester. Second, the one morning I get to sleep late they test the Sony CD player's clarity at an unhealthy sound level.

Living alone, however, puts me in control of the apartment's atmosphere. When I studied, the apartment was perfectly quiet. When I slept late the loudest sound was. . . I'm not sure since I was still asleep. When I want to watch television I don't have to worry about disturbing a roommate. If I want to play Mozart's Fifth Symphony, I don't have to worry about offending anyone. If I want to burn sliced apple incense, I can. If I like the apartment cool at night during the winter, I simply turn down the thermostat. In my house I create the ambiance.

Keith refused to take out the garbage. He would let mold form before he even thought about cleaning the dishes. Jeff enjoyed seeing how many shades of brown the bottom of the shower could get.

When I live alone I clean the apartment how and when I see fit. When the garbage is full I empty it without having to feel like a maid. It means there is more work for myself but I do not mind because it is my mess that I'm cleaning. Cleaning for others is not my idea of fun.

Money is also a stress free subject when living alone. With roommates there is always conflict about money. Roommates do not care about credit ratings and always seem to cry broke at the end of the month. But, of course, they had enough money to get smashed on Coors the night before.

Living alone, without a doubt, is more expensive. But there is less stress when bills are due because you don't have to worry about when your roommate is going to pay. Also, there isn't any conflict about who made the long distance phone call to New York City. My philosophy is that you pay a little more, but you feel so much better.

Everybody has their own idiosyncrasies. It is rare that two people can live in harmony for long periods of time, but, of course, it is possible. In college, I am only concerned with getting good grades and receiving my degree. The last thing I want to worry about is a personality conflict with a roommate. I avoid stress by living by myself. After college I will worry about a roommate. The roommate, however, will be my roommate for life. Until then I will live alone in my stress free environment.

Acquaintance Rape: "No" Means No

HATCH SANDERS

I have had three intimate encounters with acquaintance rape, not as a rapist or a victim, but as close friends of the victim or the rapist. For two of the attacks, I was close friends with both the attacker and the victim. The depth and intensity of the emotional trauma experienced by the victims—my friends—I believe is unequaled in the remainder of the human experience. I believe acquaintance rape is the most personal and most violent crime that can be committed.

We all know a rape victim. One in three women will be raped in their lifetime, according to Robin Warshaw in *I Never Called It Rape*. Four out of five of these rapes will be acquaintance rape, making it the most common form of sexual assault in America (Warshaw 11). According to Lewis Irving, a sociology professor at the University of Central Oklahoma, "Acquaintance rape occurs when the victim and the rapist know each other. If the victim and the perpetrator have agreed to spend time together, the rape is called date rape. More than half of all reported rapes are date rapes, and at least 60 percent occur on American college campuses. Since acquaintance rape is the least frequently reported sexual assault, the actual frequency is likely much higher."

Though the prevalence of acquaintance rape is widely acknowledged today, fifteen years ago the idea was not well accepted. Before then, "rape" existed only when a stranger forced sexual intercourse in a dark alley; if a woman was forced to have sex on a date, she must have been "asking for it." Experts and most American citizens now agree that rape occurs when a person is forced to have sex without their consent, no matter who is doing the forcing—stranger, friend, acquaintance, sibling, or even spouse.

Date rape is the most psychologically damaging sexual assault (Warshaw 66). It is also the most difficult type of assault to prosecute, with less than 5 percent of perpetrators spending time in jail (Pritchard 114). Date rapes are particularly difficult to prosecute because of the very personal nature of the crime. It is much easier for a woman who has been attacked by a stranger in front of her home to report a rape and get a conviction, than it is for a woman who was attacked by a person with whom she had agreed to spend time. The old questions, "What did she expect to happen when she went to his room?", and "Why was she drinking alcohol with him in that deserted place?", will surely be asked. This line of questioning and its implications are known as victim prosecution, and serve to shift the blame from the attacker to the victim. Victim prosecution is more likely to occur in an acquaintance rape trial than in a stranger rape trial. This strategy often succeeds in placing enough doubt in the mind of the jury, about the intentions of the victim, to acquit the perpetrator (Warshaw 142).

Some date rapes are as unambiguous as stranger rapes. Most, however, occur in a gray area, often between sexually inexperienced and unsophisticated men and women who have been drinking or using drugs. Inexperience and substance abuse are two primary factors that are known to increase the likelihood of date rape. The reason drinking alcohol increases the chance of rape is obvious;

drinking alcohol results in a loss of inhibition for both partners. The perpetrator is likely to be more forceful and the victim is likely to offer less, if any, resistance to his attack. Seventy-five percent of the women and 55 percent of the men who responded to the *Ms.* magazine study were drinking before the attack.

The accepted definition of sexually inexperienced partners by sociologists is different for men and women. For a woman, it is one who is not confident enough to express herself clearly. For a man, it is one who is not sensitive enough to care about what the woman is feeling. In the heat of passion, men do not always hear what is being said, and women—especially those who are naive, are inexperienced, or are uncomfortable talking about sex—do not always express themselves as forcefully as they should (Eric Pooley). This inexperience factor is one of the main reasons most date rapes occur on college campuses. Men and women learn how to express themselves better as they gain experience; however, some become victims before this knowledge is acquired. In the *Ms.* study of acquaintance rape, 46 percent of female respondents said they were virgins when they were raped. Similarly, 48 percent of perpetrators responding to the same study said they had no previous sexual relations (118).

Date rape cannot be "prevented" by anyone but the potential rapists. But experts say there are things a woman can do to reduce the risk. Most of these things are old-fashioned advice that daughters have heard for generations. Ask mutual friends about a man before you go out with him. If he had a bad history, or seems too possessive, stay away. Double-date if you are not sure about the guy. Do not drink to excess. Do not allow yourself to be alone with him in a secluded place. Meet in public places—malls, theaters, restaurants—and keep to them.

Many will argue that this type of list removes much of the romance and spontaneity from dating. The real problem with it, however, is that it puts the burden of safety solely on the woman. This is unfortunate, because what is really needed is a change in most men's attitudes. Men must learn to view sex as communication, instead of conquest, to ask instead of demand. Lewis said, "These lessons are best learned in the family, because rape is a learned behavior. If a father is abusive to women, his son is likely to become abusive as well. If a father respects women, the son learns respect. I know this sounds like a simple solution, and it can be."

According to Debbie Smith, a social worker and family therapist who councils college students on date rape, "Men and women communicate differently. Women need to know how to say no very clearly and unambiguously. We always hear the women's side, but often the man accused of date rape is just as sincere in saying, 'I was

602   *Student Arguments*

led on' or 'she never said stop.' Women share a responsibility to communicate. They need to send clear signals." Though some women say no explicitly, and the men just ignore them, many do not, and the men assume that silence means okay.

Women, it is very important to use the word rape when trying to discourage your attacker in an acquaintance rape. For example, tell your attacker, "I have told you I do not want to have sex with you. If you force me, you are raping me!" The reason this often works in acquaintance rapes is because most acquaintance rapists do not believe they are rapists. For that matter, most do not even believe they are doing anything wrong. When they hear the word rape, and realize that you know it is rape, they will often cease the attack. Bear in mind, however, that this strategy is specific to acquaintance rapes and usually will prove ineffective in stranger rapes because the perpetrator is well aware of what he is doing, and that it is wrong.

Clearly, the most important things to decrease date rape are: first, to teach men and women, especially the young, to communicate effectively with their partners; and second, to increase awareness of acquaintance rape. Women must not assume that their partner will be attentive enough to correctly know what they want. They must say yes, or they must say no. The law in most states does not require that the woman say no during an attack; all she has to do is not say yes, or be incapacitated by drugs or alcohol to the extent that it prevents her from making a reasonable judgment. Men should take note of this law, because it is the law, and because it makes sense and should be common courtesy. Men must realize that maybe means no. A drunken yes means no. Silence means no. And no always means no.

Works Cited

Warshaw, Robin. *I Never Called It Rape.* Harper and Row, Publishers, 1988. (This is also referred to as the *Ms.* magazine study, and *The Ms. Report on Recognizing, Fighting, and Surviving Date and Acquaintance Rape.*)

Pritchard, Carol. *Avoiding Rape On and Off Campus.* State College Publishing, 1985.

Pooley, Eric. "Date Rape: When Intimacy Turns Into Violence." *Cosmopolitan,* January 1992: 114.

Irving, Lewis. Interview. 18 October, 1988.

Smith, Debra. "Date Rape on the College Campus." *Journal of Social Issues,* 38: 27.

Why I Believe the Japanese Are a Superpower

MIRANDA STERMER

Many Americans believe that Japanese equals genius. They see Japanese industries outselling American industries, Japanese students excelling over American students, and Japanese buying enormous amounts of American land and corporations. It's really no wonder so many Americans feel they are losing out to the Japanese. Some Americans believe the Japanese are born with a special gene that makes them excel. However, I feel this is purely a myth. I believe the Japanese have evolved into a superpower because of the high value they place on education, their willingness to study and derive from other cultures, their loyalty to their own ancient culture and customs.

You may be asking yourself, "Why should I listen to you?" or "What makes you such an authority on the Japanese and how Americans view them?" I believe myself to be somewhat of an expert on the subject because I, too, once was one of the foolish Americans believing that the Japanese surely were blessed with some sort of magical gene to make them excel. I believed that until the summer of 1989, when I observed first-hand what makes the Japanese tick from inside the home or a Buddhist priest in the large city of Fukuoka, Japan, located on the southernmost island of Kyushu. I observed the devotion children give to their education. I also saw many facets of other cultures, including our American culture, beside the ancient and sacred custom and culture of the Japanese. I left Fukuoka with a new-found respect and admiration for the Japanese.

The Japanese have developed a fine-tuned educational system that focuses around egalitarian education. Japanese schools refuse to recognize, or provide for, individual differences in ability. In Japan, achievement is all that counts. The Japanese maintain a remarkably uniform quality of education nationwide. This is accomplished through a system of allocation taxes that enable each local government, regardless of its financial capacity, to deliver a standard level of educational services. Japanese educators consider themselves responsible for their students' overall development both in and out of school, and maintain close ties to their students' families. For example, at the start of the school year, primary teachers visit each of their students' homes to meet their families and observe the circumstances under which they live and study. All these facets of the Japanese educational system provide children with a fair and equal opportunity to learn. Students in return show great respect for authority and devotion to their education.

While in Japan, I learned that the Japanese are very willing to study other cultures. When talking with Japanese students, many were eager to learn all they could about American culture. The Japanese I talked with were interested in everything from American music, food, and makeup to voting procedures, women in the labor force, and religion. Facets from a variety of cultures are seen all through Japan. I saw everything from a Japanese Dating Game to a Japanese dude ranch. The Japanese have adopted aspects from many cultures, incorporated them into their own, and thus become a more worldly and culturally aware people.

Even with all the industrial growth, the Japanese maintain a deep loyalty of their ancient culture and customs. The religions of Shintoism and Buddhism have long been part of the Japanese culture. Most homes still practice the custom of removing shoes before entering a house. Many of the older Japanese women continue to wear the customary kimono and gheta. Ancient Shinto shrines and Buddhist temples are in excellent condition and are visited by many. The Japanese also participate in many ancient festivals that their ancestors once joined in. The Japanese hold their ancient culture in high regard and strive to maintain ancient customs.

A few stubborn Japanese-bashing Americans continue to credit the Japanese rise to power to a miracle gene the Japanese people possess. Americans such as these usually believe that the United States is the perfect country and all others could never measure up. The fact is, there are good aspects to every country. However, I feel that the Japanese have made the most of their positive points and continually strive to diminish their negative ones.

I believe the Japanese have taken their highly valued educational system, their openness to other cultures, and their loyalty to their own ancient culture and customs and successfully combined them, along with a myriad of other positive aspects, to become the world power they are today. I don't believe the Japanese are born with a greater ability to learn and excel than Americans. But I do feel they use their assets to the full extent, something we Americans don't always do. My message is not that America must imitate Japan to be a more powerful country. However, I do feel we Americans should study the Japanese, as they have studied us, and seriously consider adopting some of their ideals into our culture.

Let's Ban Public Smoking

HATCH SANDERS

Last Saturday, Stephanie and I went to Red Lobster for dinner. We arrived about 7:30, went inside, and were greeted by a very friendly host. "How many?", she asked. I made the obvious reply that there were two in our party. She then asked, "Smoking, non, or first available?" "No smoke," I said. She took our name and informed us that there would be a short wait. If we would stand in the lobby, she would call us when our table was ready. About twenty minutes later she called, and we followed her to the "no smoking" section—right beside the smoking section.

We studied the menu for about five minutes and I have just about decided what I wanted, when a thin wisp of acrid tobacco smoke drifted across my face. I coughed, my eyes began to water, and my blood pressure began to rise, as Stephanie asked our waiter if we could relocate. The first two symptoms occurred as a direct result of the cigarette smoke. I am an asthmatic and I am allergic— very allergic—to tobacco smoke. I understand that tobacco smoke is just a nuisance for some people, but for over five million people in this country, myself included, it is a very immediate health threat (Cowley 59). After an hour in a smoke filled bar or restaurant, I will be ill for at least a couple of days.

My third symptom, rapidly rising blood pressure, is a direct result of the inadequacy of the smoking policy currently employed by restaurants in Oklahoma. The current plan of separating smokers and nonsmokers just does not work. Surely a smoker devised the current policy. This is true, I believe, because only a smoker could have thought that three or four feet of air—no walls—could prevent the inhalation of second-hand or side-stream smoke by nonsmoking patrons.

There are two types of environmental tobacco smoke, or ETS, exhaled main-stream smoke and side-stream smoke. Exhaled main-stream smoke is exhaled smoke that has been "filtered" by the filter on the cigarette and by the smoker's lungs. Side-stream smoke is the unfiltered smoke that continually rises from the tip of a lit cigarette. On average, a smoker will release ten puffs per cigarette of main-stream smoke, which accounts for only 15 percent of the toxic agents that are produced by that cigarette (Reuben 120). The remaining 85 percent are in the side-stream smoke, considered by scientists to be much more dangerous. That 85 percent is left for you and me to inhale.

Side-stream smoke is what drifted by me at Red Lobster. Besides being the more dangerous, it is the denser of the two types of ETS. Side-stream smoke lasts for hours in enclosed buildings and easily crosses the invisible "no-smoking" barriers that are so prevalent in our restaurants.

Usually, there are no physical barriers between smoking and nonsmoking sections, but even if there are, the two areas are connected by one central heat and air unit. Ventilation systems in restaurants carry hazardous smoke particles from their source and circulate them throughout the building. An analysis of airliner passenger cabins proved this. Nicotine levels in some parts of the nonsmoking areas were actually higher than those in the smoking section (Reuben 121). Obviously separating smokers from nonsmokers sharing the same building is ineffective at protecting the nonsmoker from ETS. Sharing the same recirculated air in that building nullifies any good that was done by physically separating the areas.

If you are not asthmatic or allergic to tobacco smoke, as I am, there is still great cause for you to be alarmed about ETS. According to doctor David Ruben, "Tobacco smoke is actually an aerosol, like bug spray or room deodorizer, composed of invisible particles dispersed in a gas. The deadly mixture contains at least four thousand chemical compounds, of which 43 are known carcinogens (120)". The tobacco industry has always maintained that these chemicals do not enter the bodies of nonsmokers in sufficient quantity to pose a threat. However, recent scientific evidence has shown otherwise. "Nonsmokers exposed to ETS convert the nicotine they breathe into cotinine, a chemical easily measured in blood or urine. Such measurements show that almost all of us are breathing tobacco smoke whether we realize it or not. One study of 663 nonsmokers in Buffalo, New York, for example, revealed that 91 percent had cotinine in their urine" (Reuben 121).

In 1990, the EPA declared airborne tobacco smoke itself a class-A carcinogen—a substance known to cause cancer in humans (Cowley). In fact, a recent study by Harvard physicist James Repace concluded that ". . . a nonsmoker is more likely to get cancer from environmental tobacco smoke than from all the hazardous outdoor air pollutants regulated by the EPA—including asbestos, arsenic, and radioactivity—combined."

A 1990 study by San Francisco heart researcher Stanton Glantz suggests that lung cancer is only the beginning of the problem. He calculates that passive smoking causes ten times as much heart disease as lung disease, making it the third leading cause of preventable death. Glantz and his partner, Dr. William Parmley, gathered and analyzed the results of 11 recent studies and concluded that roughly 50,000 deaths each year are attributable to passive smoking. This amounts to one nonsmoker killed by ETS for every eight smokers that die from smoking (Cowley 59).

Clearly, ETS is a very serious health problem in this country. Each day in the United States, 50 million smokers will subject over 100 million "involuntary smokers" to their smoke. We know that the current smoking policy does not protect nonsmokers. Other solutions have been proposed, such as better air filtering and self-restraint by the smoker. The first is not workable, because although the technology exists, the cost is too high. The second has proven its ineffectiveness for the last 100 years. Self-restraint has always been the tobacco industry's favorite method of controlling ETS, and they are still preaching it today. However, you and I still breathe ETS everyday. Perhaps we should ban smoking in confined public spaces altogether. Every time this solution is presented someone cries, "But that violates the smoker's rights." Let us look at the "rights" issue.

The right of nonsmokers to breathe clean air has long been a foothold in the campaign to regulate cigarette smoking in confined public spaces, restaurants in particular. For almost as long, the tobacco industry, along with smokers, has asserted that they have an equal right to smoke. On the surface, it appears that both sides have an equally valid argument. Closer analysis of the argument, however, reveals a crucial difference.

Smokers maintain that the displeasure they will suffer due to not smoking is equal to the discomfort that nonsmokers will endure by letting them smoke. Robert Goodin, a well-known philosopher and ethicist, recently wrote, "Each interferes with the other, it is true. But the nonsmoker merely wishes to breathe unpolluted air and, in the pursuit thereof, and unlike the smoker, does not reduce the amenity of others" (599). In other words, the symmetry suggested in the 'right to smoke versus the right to clean air' fails to exist. The crucial asymmetry is that the smoker would be neither better nor worse off if the nonsmoker did not exist, whereas the nonsmoker would be better off if the smoker did not exist (Goodin 600). In other words, the nonsmoker does not affect the smoker's environment, but the smoker pollutes the nonsmoker's environment. The U.S. Surgeon General has rightly concluded, "the right of smokers to smoke ends where their behavior affects the health and well-being of others; . . . the choice to smoke cannot interfere with the nonsmokers right to breathe air free of tobacco smoke."

We have laws against spreading most poisons in the environment. In most communities, it is illegal to burn leaves or garbage. Yet it is still legal in those same communities for smokers to light up noxious cigarettes whenever and wherever they wish, including right beside me at Red Lobster. Everyone should be able to go to a public place and expect to breathe clean air. Last year at OSU, everyone was up in arms because there was asbestos in the basement of the library. Remember the men in the space suits who worked for days to save us from being contaminated with asbestos, a class-A carcinogen? We need the men in blue suits to save us from being contaminated with environmental tobacco smoke, also a class-A carcinogen. After looking at the case against ETS, the only reasonable thing to do is to ban cigarette smoking in enclosed public spaces.

Works Cited

Goodin, Robert E. "Ethics of Smoking." *Ethics* 99 April 1989: 574–624.

Reuben, David. "Mind If I Give You Cancer?" *Reader's Digest* May 1991: 119–122.

Cowley, Geoffrey. "Secondhand Smoke: Some Grim News." *Newsweek* June 11, 1990: 59.

Just Do It!

JIMMY MARSDEN

I have written several papers in my lifetime, and I've had some good ones, and I've had a couple you could probably find if you went scuba diving to the bottom of the Mississippi River. Or if you took a walk through the back lawn of Patti's Dog Kennel. Nevertheless, I've had my share of papers.

Also, writing these papers, I've come across a couple of obstacles putting a damper on the production of my works. For instance, starting it! In the time it takes me to start a paper, I could jog a mile, cook a grilled cheese sandwich, or even down a whole six-pack of beer. Just kidding! I could probably drink twelve.

My point being, I spend too much time trying to make it right and trying to write exactly what my teachers want to hear that by the time I'm finished with the opening paragraph, I have to hurry to finish the rest of the paper. Not good. Now, I've changed my ways. No longer will I meditate and hesitate, I'll just do it.

Just do it. We've all heard of this one. I'm sure that one time or another everyone had told this little bit of advice to others or to themselves. Using these three words will either allow you to accomplish something great, or they will send you up the creek without a paddle. I'm saying, use it whenever you have the chance! Whenever you are in doubt, just do it. Whenever you are afraid, just do it. Whenever your buddies tell you to go jump off a cliff, well, you might want to think that one over. But, there are so many times when we are worried about what the consequences may be. It is then when the consequences usually come out to be for the worse.

For instance, we all know about that one roller coaster we're afraid to stand in line for. "Well, who knows, it might fly off that one corner and we'll get smashed into oblivion!" Or, "What if it gets stuck at the top of that loop and they just leave us hanging there?" What a bunch of wimps! Take a chance. How many roller coaster fatalities do you know of? People aren't stepping off the ride laughing and saying, "Man, that was awesome," for nothing. Something must have taken a jab at their jollies!

Or, what about those family reunions with the all you can eat oysters, asparagus, snails, and spinach buffets? Of course, we hear, "Raw oysters? Raw snails? Disgusting! Where are the hamburgers?" Or, what about, "If I wanted something that looked like that spinach and that asparagus, I would go pull some weeds in my yard and chew on them for a little bit!" I haven't heard a child gripe more than these people. Go out on a limb and try something new. Who knows? You might like it.

If we were to say "no" to everything, nothing would ever get accomplished. There would be no achievements to be proud about. I would rather take a chance and fail, than never try.

Speaking of trying, have you ever wanted to try out for sports in high school and didn't because you were worried you wouldn't make the team? This is so typical of high school students. Maybe the coach could see a certain characteristic in you that he couldn't find in the other players. If you don't make the team, so what. At least you can say, "Hey, I gave it my best shot, and I'm proud of myself." Pain is temporary, pride is permanent.

And the all time favorite, "Well, what am I going to say when she answers the phone?" It's that gut-wrenching debate over whether or not to ask that certain someone out on a date. "She'll probably say no and then I'll feel like a complete idiot!" You're an idiot if you don't call her. Chances are, she isn't going to come to you for a date. So get some courage and ask her out. What do you have to lose? Everything, if you don't call her.

Stepping aside from these common cases, there are some situations when you should definitely not say, "Just do it." For example, if you and your friends, all of a sudden, decide to get a good laugh by running naked through a department store, I understand if you decide not to take part in such an event. Or, if someone agreed to pay you a great deal of money if you would walk a tight rope across the Grand Canyon, my advice would be to, "Just say no." As common as these situations are I would advise that you keep an eye out for them, and whenever you come across such opportunities, use your best judgment.

Too often we are scared. Scared of what the world may think of us if we try. We need not possess this fear inside. The next time you have the chance to ride that gigantic roller coaster, ride it and love it! The next time you have the chance to try new foods or try out for sports, do it! You may be surprised with the results. Take risks. Do something you have never done before. Because, if you think you can do it, the odds are you can! We only go around this square old merry-go-round once, so don't stop to smell the roses. Remember, you have nothing to lose and everything, everything, everything to gain!

INDEX